A History of Europe
in the
Twentieth Century

THE DORSEY SERIES IN EUROPEAN HISTORY

A History of Europe in the Twentieth Century

DAVID E. SUMLER
University of Illinois

1973
THE DORSEY PRESS *Homewood, Illinois 60430*
IRWIN-DORSEY LIMITED *Georgetown, Ontario*

First Printing, March 1973

ISBN 0-256-01421-3
Library of Congress Catalog Card No. 72–93553
Printed in the United States of America

To my parents,
Joseph
and
Theora

PREFACE

There are two great epochs in 20th century European history: the decline of European domestic stability, cultural leadership, and international diplomatic dominance from the turn of the century until 1945; and the emergence of a new social and political synthesis after 1945. Yet these two epochs are but aspects of the continuous process that was the transition from the "modern" industrial world of the 1890s to the "contemporary" postindustrial society of the latter half of this century. It is argued in this book that for the Europeans this transition, which took approximately 60 years, resulted in a totally new form of society, the contours of which we are just beginning to see.

The present text is distinguished first by its insistence on the similarities of the national developments of the European states and its attempt to analyze these "patterns" in a comparative framework; and, second, by its investigation of the domestic political roots of international relations. For instance, the social and cultural crises experienced by all the Great Powers from 1900 to 1914 are seen as indissolubly linked to the origins of World War I. The international revolutionary impulse that followed the Bolshevik Revolution in 1917 was an important factor in the composition of the Versailles Treaty just as it was a key influence on the nature of postwar governments in London, Berlin, Vienna, and Budapest. Fascism can be understood for the *revolutionary* (rather than conservative) movement that it was when submitted to a comparative analysis that takes into account the variations and mutations which existed in France and England, Rumania and Hungary, as well as in Italy and Germany. The domestic aspects of the wartime experience—government planning and controls in Great Britain, resistance movements in France and elsewhere, the final disillusionment with liberal economics throughout Europe—were as important in determining the future of Europe's new society as the holocaust of war was in destroying the old Europe. Domestic politics and diplomacy were again inextricably intertwined in the years of the Cold War, when international polarity was paralleled by domestic polarization, and the decline of international tension by the resurgence of the Left in Western Europe.

More than in other texts on this period, an attempt has been made herein to explain the intricacies as well as the grand sweep of European domestic politics. Diplomatic history has taken second or third rank behind political and social history. This is a long-overdue attempt to establish a new perspective in the history of contemporary Europe. Hopefully, it will provide the beginning student with an intellectual and factual context which other texts do not supply. In the chapters on recent events, the particular events have been used as a framework for investigating the nature of the new society of Western Europe especially, and to a lesser degree of Eastern Europe. The discussions of social stratifications in Chapter 19 and of the student revolts of 1968 in Chapter 22, for two examples, offer students analytical theories to be tested by professors and students alike against present realities.

This is, indeed, a highly interpretive text. I hope that I do not fit neatly into any "school," but I am greatly indebted to certain historians who have profoundly influenced my analysis. Chief among these are Geoffrey Barraclough, Arno J. Mayer, H. Stuart Hughes, Eugen Weber, Theodore von Laue, and William A. Williams. A glance at the footnotes in each chapter will uncover legions of other historians who have supplied the bricks and mortar for my interpretations. Among those who contributed to the writing of this book, the staff of the University of Illinois Library was marvelously cooperative in making available to me the resources of a magnificent collection. Ms. Martha Friedman, History Librarian, was particularly helpful and generous of her time. My wife Claudia aided me immeasurably by her patience and understanding. And, finally, I owe much to the many students at the University of Illinois who helped me clarify my ideas and make them more precise.

February 1973   DAVID E. SUMLER

CONTENTS

LIST OF MAPS

The European bourgeoisie were at the height of their worldwide influence when they celebrated the Paris Exposition in 1900. (Courtesy of Roger-Viollet)

PART I

European Society in Transition to Contemporary History

Chapter 1

DOMESTIC CRISES, 1900–14

Europe of the late twentieth century is different in almost all social, economic, intellectual and political respects from the world of the 1890s. The first fifty years of this century were "a watershed between two ages."[1] The decline and disintegration of the "modern" world of the late nineteenth century and the gradual emergence of a new social and political synthesis which is the "contemporary" world is the theme of this book. Viewed from this perspective, certain phenomena of the twentieth century take on added meaning. Fascism was not just an aberrant movement confined to Germany or Italy but was one expression of a struggle against the decline of a social system. The resistance movements of World War II were not just Frenchmen, Italians, and Yugoslavs revolting against foreign domination but were the creators of new political forces which would renovate European society in the two decades after World War II.

Since all of history is a continuation of what has gone before, it is, of course, true that the aspects of society that we associate with the contemporary world were developing before 1900. Perhaps the most fundamental change was the urbanization of Europe. In the last decades of the nineteenth century an ever greater proportion of the population had crowded into large cities. Great Britain was the most urbanized European nation in 1900, with less than 10 percent of its population engaged in agricultural activities. Germany, having undergone tumultuous industrial and urban expansion since 1870, was the second most urbanized state, with only 35 percent of its population still dependent on the land for a livelihood. France reached the 50 percent-urbanized mark only in the 1890s.[2] The slowly growing French economy as well as the static French

---

[1] Geoffrey Barraclough, *An Introduction to Contemporary History* (New York: Basic Books, Inc., 1964), p. 2.

[2] Kim Munholland, *Origins of Contemporary Europe, 1890–1914* (New York: Harcourt Brace and World, Inc., 1970), pp. 35–36.

MAP 1.   Europe in 1914 (with alliances)

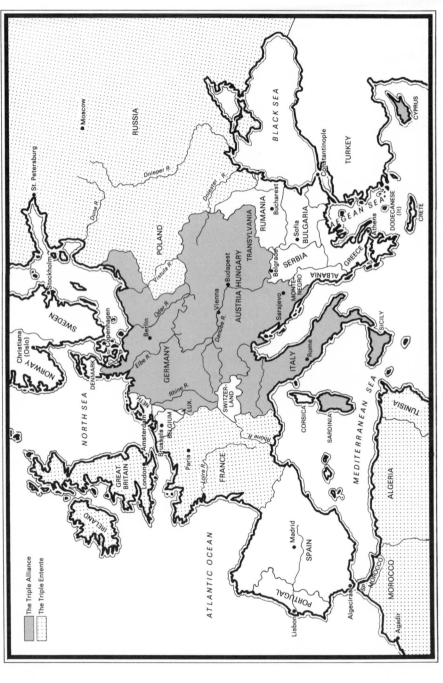

The Triple Alliance

The Triple Entente

SOURCE: Rene Albrecht-Carrie, *A Diplomatic History of Europe Since the Congress of Vienna* (New York: Harper & Bros., 1958), p. 322.

population were matters of some concern for French nationalists at the time. Eastern and southern Europe were far less urban and lacked major industrial centers except in a few cities such as Milan, Rome, Madrid, Vienna, Moscow, and St. Petersburg. It was, therefore, in northwestern Europe that the institutions and the problems of the twentieth century first took shape.

Almost synonymous with city life is mass society—that is, a social system in which institutions must meet the needs, not of individuals but of groups, of social classes, of depersonalized collectivities. Political parties in the 1880s and 1890s developed means of mobilizing hundreds of thousands of voters. A new form of journalism was invented to inform the public at a low price with short sentences, short words, and more sensationalism than factual reporting. Mass transportation—urban train systems, autobuses—and mass entertainment, especially the cinema houses, were important innovations of the period. At the same time, the concentration of economic power in a few hands through the development of trusts, cartels, monopolies, and restrictive trade agreements drove many individual entrepreneurs out of business and contributed to the growth of impersonal corporations and anonymous investment companies. This concentration of capital resulted in a greater concentration of labor in large factories and industrial complexes with the resultant growth of working-class neighborhoods that frequently degenerated into slums. New, militant labor unions were organized with national memberships drawn from many trades, able to act as counterweights to the cartels and trusts.

It was not easy for Europeans to adjust to these developments, especially since the pace of change accelerated greatly in the last decades of the nineteenth century. Social tensions, intellectual uncertainty, moral anguish, and recurrent economic crises were to be persistent features of European society for the first half of the twentieth century. It was a period of transition in which a system of values was being destroyed. World War I was followed by the Great Depression and the rise of fascism. Germans killed Frenchmen; Frenchmen killed Germans; Russians and Austrians murdered one another—all on a scale and in a manner possible only in a technologically advanced society. The greatest crime of man against man—the slaughter of the Jews during World War II—could have only been accomplished by an industrialized, modern state. Only after this fratricidal strife did the Europeans regain the stability they had enjoyed in 1900 and begin to rebuild.

Democracies in Crisis

The governments of the Great Powers of western Europe were dominated, in the decade prior to World War I, by politicians guided by the principles of liberalism. Liberalism as an ideology is a mixture of several currents of philosophical, political, and economic thought originating in the late eighteenth and early nineteenth centuries. Liberals believe that man is a rational creature, capable of judging his own best interest, and, therefore, governments should not interfere in his activities. Government should, on the other hand, remove any obstacles to the full development of the individual's capacities. The obstacles that liberals overcame during the nineteenth century included authoritarian monarchical governments, oppressive censorship, the legal privileges of aristocrats, the influence of established churches—the Anglican church in Great Britain and the Catholic church in France and Italy—and many others. By 1900 the liberal principles that had been the source of revolutionary struggles in 1789, 1830, and 1848—popular suffrage, freedom of the press, careers open to talent, freedom for economic competition—had been accepted in large part by the governing classes of western and central Europe; the leaders of Russia and Austria-Hungary were not so receptive.

These principles were embodied in certain political parties that drew their major support from the urban bourgeoisie—the industrial, financial, commercial, and professional communities—as well as certain sectors of the peasantry. Liberal voters, as most Europeans, assumed a continuation

TABLE 1.1. Party Strength in Prewar Elections

England: Election of December 1910		France: Election of June 1914	
Conservatives	272	Right	15
Liberals*	272	Catholic	23
Irish Nationalists	84	Independence	46
Labour	42	Republicans	89
		Democratic Left	34
Germany: Election of 1912		Radicals	99
Conservatives	43	Radical-Socialists*	172
Reichspartei	14	Republican Socialists	23
National Liberals	45	Socialists	103
Center*	91		
Progressives	42	Italy: Election of 1913	
Social Democrats	110	Nationalists	3
Polish party	18	Catholic	29
Guelphs	5	Constitutional Liberals*	318
Danish party	1	Republicans*	17
Alsace-Lorraine party	9	Radicals	70
Anti-Semites	3	Socialists	78
Other	16		

* Parties that advocated liberalism as their basic ideology.

of the "progress" of the nineteenth century in the form of economic prosperity, the expansion of the realm of individual freedoms, and the spread of parliamentary government. In the years just prior to World War I the liberals both achieved great legislative triumphs and were forced on the defensive by new political forces and intellectual currents. At the moment of liberalism's greatest successes in Great Britain, France and Italy, antiliberal pressures were building which would eventually destroy the liberal synthesis.

A period of Liberal party government began in Great Britain with the legislative election of 1906. In the following eight years, the Liberal party compiled a truly remarkable record for reform legislation. Under the leadership of two astute prime ministers—Henry Campbell-Bannermann (1906–08) and Herbert Asquith (1908–16)—and two ambitious and adventurous cabinet members—David Lloyd George and Winston Churchill—the Liberals tried to meet some of the demands of the British working class, and while doing so, laid the foundations for the welfare state. The length of the workday for miners was legally limited to eight hours, although in practice it remained half an hour longer. Old age pensions were established, and the first unemployment offices to be run by the government were organized. The Liberals achieved passage of the Insurance Act of 1911, which was England's first comprehensive social security measure, providing public insurance against sickness, disability, and unemployment.

As the Liberals enacted reform after reform which the Conservative party leaders considered socialist-inspired, the House of Lords, the hereditary upper house, began to use its veto power to overrule the popularly elected lower house. The showdown came in 1909 when Lloyd George, as chancellor of the exchequer, proposed a greatly increased budget to finance new social programs and an expansion of the British fleet. Because of the need for new funds, the budget included provisions for progressive taxation and sharp increases in inheritance taxes. The Lords refused to pass the budget, creating a constitutional crisis. Not since 1688 had the Lords tried to overthrow a government by denying it funds. The Liberal prime minister, Herbert Asquith, took the matter to the people in January 1910. His party won the election but only by a slim margin. After having passed Lloyd George's budget, the Liberals decided to consolidate their victory. In December 1910, Asquith called for another election. This time the issue was the Lords' power of veto, and the Liberals lost seats. They formed a cabinet, but they were dependent on the votes of the Irish Nationalist party and the Labour party. Still, the Conservatives refused to bow to democracy. Asquith threatened to have the King appoint 400 new peers who would vote for the Liberal bill abolishing the veto. Rather than allow the appointment of these *nouveaux riches,* the Lords passed the veto bill. This ended the Lords' right of veto and allowed the upper house only *to delay* the passage of a bill for two years, thus signaling the absolute victory of democratic political control.

After this victory, the Liberals were confronted with increasingly serious extraparliamentary crises. Many Britains felt that in the years 1910 to 1914 Great Britain was approaching domestic chaos, and civil war seemed possible. The suffragette movement, the labor movement, and the Ulstermen's revolt were the major sources of unrest. The suffragettes, with their long skirts, hair buns, and crusading songs, may seem like characters from a Gilbert and Sullivan operetta, but they were deadly serious. In 1910 they launched a campaign of window breaking in the shopping districts of London.   Emmeline Pankhurst claimed that the argument of broken glass is the most convincing argument. By 1912 the women had begun to burn buildings—empty houses, churches, a school, and a railroad station. Some of them glorified violence. One of the female revolutionaries said, "The militants will rejoice when victory comes, and yet, mixed with joy, will be the regret that . . . the militant fight [is] over—over, and so many have not yet known the exaltation, the rapture of battle. . . ."[3] The suffragettes did not win their struggle, of course, until 1918, after so many men had seen the "exaltation of battle," and women had begun to labor like men in the war factories.

The Liberal government was also challenged by a wave of strikes involving hundreds of thousands of laborers. This was a result of the same revolutionary syndicalism that gripped the French labor movement; only the British unions were far better organized, had larger strike funds, and could exert real pressure on the economy and the government. A miners' strike in 1912 forced Asquith's cabinet to pass a minimum wage law for miners, and membership in all trade unions increased from 2.3 million in 1910 to 4 million in 1914. In 1913 the three largest unions formed the triple alliance that included miners, railroaders, and transport workers—a total of 1.3 million union members. Together, they could cripple the nation. They threatened to do just that in the fall of 1914 if Parliament did not enact a minimum wage law for all workers. Only the outbreak of war prevented this strike.

Faced with this rapid growth of the Left, British Conservatives were willing to resort to extreme and even illegal action to prevent further reforms. The issue that precluded social reforms after 1911 and brought Great Britain to the brink of civil war was the question of Home Rule for Ireland. The Liberals had promised to push for Home Rule in return for the support of Irish Nationalist members of Parliament in the struggle against the Lords. A bill granting an independent parliament to Ireland was passed by Commons in 1912. The Lords refused to ratify. Therefore, the bill could not become law until 1914. During that two-year period, the Ulster Irish armed themselves to prevent Home Rule from being granted. The Ulstermen were Scot Presbyterians who lived in the north-

---

[3] Walter L. Arnstein, *Britain Yesterday and Today* (Boston: D. C. Heath and Co., 1966), p. 218.

eastern corner of the island. They despised the Catholic Irish as inferiors and feared the establishment of a semitheocratic Irish state. When the Ulstermen formed a volunteer army, the Catholics did the same. At this point, the new Conservative party leader, Bonar Law, decided to back the Ulstermen in the name of God, crown, and empire. Law declared, "There are things stronger than parliamentary majorities. I can imagine no length to which Ulster can go in which I should not be prepared to support them."[4] British army officers resigned their commissions rather than take up arms against the Ulstermen. In August 1914, an armed conflict appeared inevitable. Once again, the war intervened, sparing the British intense domestic strife.

The French counterpart of the Liberal party was the Radical party. The Radicals became dominant in the French Chamber of Deputies in the 1902 election and remained so until 1919. Their 1902 victory led to the disestablishment of the Catholic church in 1905, when the state ended all aid to the church and closed Catholic universities as well as elementary and secondary schools. On the basis of their anticlerical program, the Radicals won an even more complete victory in 1906, enabling them to carry out a program of reforms under the premiership of Georges Clemenceau. His ministry nationalized one branch of the national railroad network—one-seventh of all railroad mileage. Working conditions in most industries were brought under government regulations, and old age pensions and limited insurance against sickness, disability, and unemployment were voted. Furthermore, the Chamber of Deputies voted France's first income tax in 1909; but, because of the conservative nature of the French Senate, it did not become law until 1917.

The conservatives began to counterattack in 1909 under the lead of two right-wing liberals—Aristide Briand and Raymond Poincaré. Through parliamentary manipulation, Poincaré became premier in January 1912. During his year in that office, he encouraged nationalism and militarism among his countrymen.[5] Whenever the diplomatic situation arose, he used the strongest possible language in asserting French rights. He allowed the first military parades in Paris since 1899, when the Army had suffered political defeat in the Dreyfus Affair. In 1913, riding the crest of a sort of conservative backlash against Radical reforms, Poincaré was elected president of France, a mostly honorary position. He continued to influence public opinion, however, by making nationalistic speeches and embarking on ostentatious diplomatic voyages. Still, the conservatives were rejected in the 1914 parliamentary election. Poincaré refused to accept the verdict of the electorate. It was his duty to appoint the new premier, and he

---

[4] Ibid., p. 220.

[5] David E. Sumler, "Domestic Influences on the Nationalist Revival in France, 1909–1914," *French Historical Studies*, 6, no. 4 (1970): 517–37.

refused to appoint any leading leftist, forcing a conservative premier on the chamber. Thus, he made the French leadership more conservative, more nationalistic than the general public, just as the international situation was at its most dangerous.

Elections in Italy were always rigged in about one-third of the constituencies, and the man who rigged them most skillfully from 1903 to 1914 was Giovanni Giolitti, the leader of the Constitutional Liberal party. As premier in three different ministries, Giolitti was responsible for several significant reforms with which he hoped to win the Italian lower classes away from socialism. In defiance of tradition, he favored the establishment of trade unions for both workers and peasants, and he condemned the armed squads that landowners and industrialists had used to prevent such unions. He nationalized the most important branches of the railroad network and enacted a state monopoly of insurance. Most important of all his reforms was an extension of the very limited voting franchise that allowed workers and peasants to vote in 1912 for the first time. This increased the Italian electorate from three million to eight million voters and contributed to the rapid growth of the Italian Socialist party. Certainly, Giolitti did not succeed in winning the workers to liberalism. The Socialist party grew steadily, in spite of a curious mixture of reformists and revolutionaries, nationalists and antipatriots in its ranks. Of the seventy-eight Socialists elected in 1913, fifty-two had proclaimed in their electoral platforms that they would aid in destroying the parliamentary regime.

Nor was the labor movement quiescent. A sign of the strength of revolutionary syndicalism in Italy was the near revolution of June 1914, which became known as the Red Days. Simultaneous strikes were called by both agricultural and industrial unions. Strikers seized city halls and hoisted the red flag of revolution, and the army had to be used to restore order.

Italian conservatives were more successful than those of France and Great Britain. When Giolitti resigned in early 1914, he was replaced by a conservative, Antonio Salandra. Salandra sympathized with imperialist pressure groups and the army, and, of course, he opposed socialism. When war began in August 1914, Salandra was advised by the parliamentary majority (and by Giolitti) to remain neutral, and he did. Yet he used the war as an excuse to suspend all democratic institutions and to rule by decree. Consulting no one but his foreign minister, he negotiated with both the Central Powers and the Triple Entente in search of the higher bidder. An agreement was reached with Great Britain in early 1915 whereby Italy would obtain, if the Entente powers won, the South Tyrol, the ports of Trieste and Fiume, the Dodecanese littoral on the Turkish coast, and other territorial rewards. Promised these areas, Salandra committed Italy to enter the war on the side of the Entente without consulting Parliament.

The Constitutional Monarchies of Central Europe

The fact that at least the forms of constitutional monarchy had been accepted even by the conservative royal houses of Germany (in 1870), Austria-Hungary (in 1876), and Russia (in 1906) seemed irrefutable evidence to the liberals of western Europe that parliamentary government as practiced in the West was universal in its application. Such appearances were deceiving. Behind the parliamentary façade in each of the three empires real political power lay in the hands of the monarchy, the state bureaucracy, and various privileged elites. The fragmentation of political forces within these polities made it impossible for any government to gain majority support from a freely elected representative legislature or even to achieve a national consensus that could assure social and political stability. In the years after 1900, each state, therefore, underwent increasingly severe periods of instability.

Germany was governed through a complex constitutional framework that had been devised by Bismarck to guarantee the dominance of Prussia in the empire and the dominance of conservative classes within Prussia. The national legislature, the Reichstag, was elected by universal male suffrage and gave the appearance of a sovereign parliamentary body similar to the French Chamber of Deputies. But there were many safeguards against the Reichstag's influence. First, the chancellor was responsible not to the legislature but to the kaiser, as were all cabinet ministers as well. Therefore, only the kaiser could appoint or remove a government official. Second, an upper house, the Bundesrat, in which each state of the Empire was represented according to its population and size, could veto any act of the Reichstag. Furthermore, Prussia naturally dominated this upper house, since Prussia constituted approximately five-eighths of the territory of the empire and over one-half of its population. Representatives were elected to the Bundesrat by the legislatures of each state, and a three-class voting system in Prussia gave the very small class of Junker noble families, who were closely identified with agricultural interests and with the military, equal representation with the millions of salaried workers in Prussian cities. There was then Junker control of Prussia and Prussian control of the empire. The emperor was, of course, also the king of Prussia. The chancellor was also the Prussian head of government.

The result of this system was to allow the Reichstag to become ever more representative of demands for reform while the imperial government remained staunchly wedded to the status quo. An intelligent or innovative chancellor or emperor obviously could force the system to respond to changing conditions; but in the years between 1900 and 1914, the willingness of the men in these positions to let matters drift and to act only in a crisis situation led to a lack of governmental direction, with the representatives of various classes and interests—the agrarian interests,

This royal hunting party was also a family reunion, for the German and English nobility were closely related. England's King Edward is third from right, front row. Germany's Kaiser Wilhelm is third from right, second row. (Courtesy of Roger-Viollet)

heavy industry, the military leadership, the Catholic church, the labor unions—each trying to move the cumbersome governmental machine to favor its own clientele. This evil was compounded, perhaps, by the fact that the most influential interest groups were those that contributed to a bellicose foreign policy that repeatedly brought Germany into conflict with the other Great Powers. Around the turn of the century, the Naval League joined forces with the coal and steel industries to urge the construction of a fleet which would allow Germany to become a world-wide naval power. This was only fitting, they felt, for the foremost industrial power in Europe. The kaiser was easily persuaded.

Still, Germany was not simply a nation run by the wealthy for the wealthy. Rapid industrial expansion had raised the living standards of the lower classes as well, and strong unions had managed since 1890 to increase labor's share of the national prosperity. German workers also benefitted from the most advanced social welfare system in Europe. Government toleration of civil liberties was almost as great as in France or Great Britain and far-advanced over Austria-Hungary, not to mention repressive Russia. The political problem was that, regardless of their freedom to express their opinions, ordinary Germans could not effect government policy. This became increasingly clear as the majority in the Reichstag became more hostile to the established order and more insistent on the introduction of responsible government.

Two incidents illustrate this point. In 1908 Kaiser Wilhelm II, a very impetuous man, gave an interview to a British newspaper, the *Daily Telegraph,* in which he made outlandish claims of friendship to England during the Boer War of 1899–1902. All of Europe knew that the German government had encouraged England's opponents, and the German public was proud of the national policy. The kaiser's interview, then, raised a storm in the Reichstag, with demands made by all parties that limitations be set on the kaiser's ability to speak on foreign policy. Unfortunately for those Germans interested in constitutional reform, it was difficult to say who was really at fault in the matter. The chancellor, von Bulow, had perfunctorily approved the interview for publication but denied responsibility. When he offered a weak excuse to the Reichstag, in which he came close to admitting that the kaiser had acted unconstitutionally, and offered certain political favors to various legislators, the united front in favor of constitutional reform was broken, and the storm was over.

The 1912 Reichstag election returned a majority for political reforms. The Social Democrats had become the largest party in the Reichstag with 110 seats. They might have gained even more seats had it not been for an electoral alliance with the Progressive party, which had committed the SPD to support liberals in certain constituencies. With the remarkable victory by the SPD and the Progressives at the polls, it appeared that the passage of reform legislation might be possible. Yet, a major scandal in late 1913 concerning the army proved that the Reichstag was still impotent.

A German officer in the Alsatian town of Zabern arrested and mistreated several civilians. Although it was strictly illegal for the military to arrest civilians, the minister of war and the chancellor, now Theobald von Bethmann-Hollweg (1909–17), supported the officer in question, Colonel von Reuter. Once again a national storm of protest broke over the arbitrariness of the government. The chancellor's position suggested that the army was above the law. To prevent von Reuter from escaping completely unpunished, the Reichstag passed a resolution condemning his actions by 293 to 54. This had no effect whatsoever on the government. In a truly parliamentary system, Bethmann-Hollweg would have been required to resign; instead, in January 1914, a court-martial acquitted von Reuter, and the kaiser completed the insult to parliament by presenting the controversial officer with a medal.

Just how much longer the German government could continue to ignore the Reichstag became a live issue after the 1912 parliamentary election. The SPD was the largest and best organized Socialist party in Europe. If it continued the remarkable growth it had enjoyed since 1890, it would soon have a parliamentary majority, although this was unlikely due to the multiparty system. The German trade unions were growing just as rapidly, with the largest strike fund and largest membership in Europe and exerting the strictest discipline over their members. Yet, in spite of this strength, the German Left could not be called revolutionary. They had been granted social welfare by the kaiser and were not willing to gamble on a socialist regime. Still, as a parliamentary force, the SPD and the trade unions were a threat to the established order. Frustrated by the impotence of the Reichstag and by the aloof, arbitrary power of the Junker-dominated state bureaucracy and court, would such a powerful movement remain reformist? Or would it turn to revolution? No one could answer that question in 1914.

Politics in Austria-Hungary, a dual monarchy held together by allegiance to the Hapsburg emperor Franz-Joseph (1848–1916), were far more complex than those of other European states because of the many struggling nationalities of the empire. In 1866 defeat in war had forced the Austrian Germans to allow the Magyars of Hungary to govern the eastern half of the empire. Both states, Austria and Hungary, had a parliament and a cabinet of ministers; but they shared three imperial ministries—war, foreign affairs, and finance—as well as sharing their king. Both states were far from democracies, since heads of government were responsible to the emperor and not to parliamentary majorities. Elections were based on a restricted suffrage that guaranteed that the Germans would govern Austria and the Magyars would govern Hungary. The subject nationalities—Czechs, Ruthenes, Poles, Rumanians, Serbs, Croats, Slovenes, and Italians—were allowed minimal representation in the Austrian and Hungarian parliaments but were allowed to elect provincial assemblies (Landtage) to legislate on purely local matters. During the decade before 1914, the stresses on the political system of each state and on the empire as a whole were increasing so that many politicians throughout Europe were dubious about the continued existence of this ancient empire.

The major political conflict in Austria before 1907 was between the Germans and Czechs. The Czechs were the most highly educated of the minorities of Austria and demanded that their culture be respected and that they be given political autonomy within the empire. The emperor was willing to meet some of the Czech demands, but the German Liberals, the largest party in parliament at the turn of the century, were not. When in 1897 the Austrian government attempted to introduce the use of the Czech language into the administration of Bohemia, the Germans virtually rioted in parliament and made representative government impossible. For the next eight years Emperor Franz-Joseph ruled by decree.

At the end of this period, in an attempt to weaken both the German and Czech extremists, the emperor announced the establishment of universal suffrage in Austria. The first election held under the new electoral law, in 1907, only increased the difficulty of parliamentary government. There were more non-German than German deputies in the Reichsrat; so the Germans resorted to even more virulent obstructionism than before the reform. Also, the extension of the suffrage to the urban working class had resulted in adding social and economic divisions to the national divisions that already existed. To further complicate matters, the Austrian socialist movement was split into a Socialist party and a Christian Socialist party. The Socialists tried to include all nationalities in their party, while the Christian Socialists were German chauvinists and as anti-Semitic as they were anticapitalistic. With parliament so factionalized, it was impossible to form stable majorities.

The emperor was forced to take matters in his own hands once again in 1914. Czech nationalists had become insistent on reform under the influence of Neo-Slavism. This movement, originating in Russia, was unlike earlier Pan-Slavism in that it proposed a federation or association of autonomous Slavic states—to be carved out of Austria-Hungary—rather than the Russian-dominated Slavic union favored by the Panslavs. Czech agitation became so troublesome that, in 1913, the Czech Landtag was suspended and a Royal Administrative Commission was appointed to replace it. The Czechs reacted by completely destroying the orderly processes of the Austrian Reichsrat. Convinced that parliamentary government was once again impossible, Franz-Joseph dismissed the Reichsrat in March 1914, and ruled by decree. This was the situation when war began in the fall.

The Magyar rulers of Hungary maintained their position by a restricted suffrage which allowed only 6 percent of adult males to vote. And even within this small percentage, the Magyars were over-represented in parliament in relation to their numbers in the electorate. The power of this ruling nationality was based on the fact that its members owned huge estates while approximately ten million peasants were landless. This almost feudal aristocracy, therefore, controlled Hungary's economy as well as its politics, for Hungary was an agricultural state.

Hungarian parliamentary politics, as a result, were limited to struggles among different Magyar factions. The major schism was between the supporters of the Compromise of 1867 which had established the dual monarchy, on the one hand, and, on the other, the Independence party, a group of extreme nationalists who wanted greater autonomy from the Hapsburg crown, more control over imperial policies, and increased Magyarization of subject nationalities. The Independence party gained popularity in 1903 when it blocked increased military demands placed on Hungary by the imperial Ministry of War. The Magyar extremists encouraged a tax strike and resistance to military recruitment until certain concessions were made to allow Magyar control of the Hungarian contingents in the imperial army. Since the army was the physical expression of the unity of the empire, Franz-Joseph refused the demands. Instead, he threatened to introduce universal suffrage into Hungary as he did in Austria. This greatly frightened the Magyars; it would mean the end of their legal dominance of the state. Valuing Magyar dominance more than Hungarian independence, the Independence party forsook its demands on military issues rather than suffer an enfranchisement of the subject nationalities. Finally, the expansion of the army proposed in 1902 became law in 1912.

The attempts of the Magyars to force the national groups in Hungary to adopt Magyar culture caused or at least confronted increasingly militant autonomist or separatist movements. The Croats had been content to seek increased freedom within the Hapsburg empire until a series of repressive laws during the period 1905–10 caused them to despair of such a course. After 1907, talk of an independent Yugoslav (South Slav) state was heard at nationalist rallies in Croatia. The formation of such a state would be achieved by the union of the Croats and Slovenes of Austria with independent Serbia. Among other minorities, the Slovak National party and the Rumanian Cultural League grew rapidly. Magyar mistreatment of the Rumanians of Transylvania almost led to war between Hungary and Rumania. Therefore, the instability of Hungary was increasing as the second decade of the new century began.

This domestic instability could not be divorced from the international relations of Austria-Hungary. At least two nations—Russia and Serbia—consciously encouraged the disaffection of the national minorities. Russia's Neo-Slavists painted a rosy picture of a future of independent Slav states led by Mother Russia. Russian agents conducted active agitation among the Ruthenes of Hungary. A coup d'état in 1903 had put the Karageorgevich dynasty on the Serbian throne. The new king, Peter, was a captive of ultranationalist army officers who were intent upon expanding Serbia's borders to include as many of the South Slavs as possible. They organized secret societies to further these goals through agitation and, at times, assassination in Croatia and Bosnia. The attractiveness of Serbia and Russia was enhanced by the repressive policies of Hungary.

Obviously, the Germans and the Magyars would not passively watch the disintegration of the dual monarchy. Men who advocated taking forceful and aggressive action to stop the dissolution came to the fore. The chief of the general staff of the imperial army from 1906–11, Conrad von Hotzendorf, advocated a preventive war against Serbia. This view was widely held by the military and bureaucratic elite. Count Berchtold, foreign minister in 1914, felt that the dual monarchy had to protect itself by an aggressive foreign policy. Internal and international crises were one and the same to the Austrian and Hungarian leaders. They were aware that not only their political dominance but also society as they knew it were threatened by the many rebellious forces they had so long contained. The German ambassador to Vienna in 1912 summarized the anxiety of leaders of the Hapsburg empire in a letter to Kaiser Wilhelm:

They see with astonishment and anguish the sudden swelling of the Slav wave and on all lips is fluttering the anxious question, what will happen to Austria? The Germans are disheartened. One of their leaders told me recently in the

House of Lords: "That is the end of the Germans in Austria. They will lose all influence in the monarchy and I ask myself if they will not be compelled to secede. . . ."[6]

Russia: Toward Democracy or Revolution?

So much of the Russian czar's empire lay east of the Ural Mountains, the geographers' boundary for Europe, and was so economically undeveloped that a legitimate debate could develop as to whether Russia was a European or an Asian state. It was both. It had in 1900, despite a decade of rapid industrial growth, little industry outside a few centers such as St. Petersburg, Moscow, Warsaw, Odessa, and Kiev. The autocratic czarist regime perpetuated the court's dominance of politics, the Orthodox church's dominance of culture, and the landed gentry's dominance of society and the economy. The well-educated gentry class measured Russia against western Europe and found her wanting; therefore they requested the czar to modernize. Yet they hoped to preserve the distinctiveness of Russian culture, which would be inevitably imperiled if Russia followed the lead of Britain, France, and Germany. For Russian society continued to be based on the existence of a vast illiterate peasantry, bound legally to the land and to their communes. The very small middle class that did exist was not analogous to the striving, ambitious bourgeoisie that had accomplished the industrial revolution in western Europe; rather, it was composed of professionals—doctors, lawyers, academics, state bureaucrats—and a few wealthy peasants. Whatever private initiative that did exist in the industrial sector at the turn of the century was in danger of being choked by cartels and trusts that eliminated competition by controlling prices and production with government encouragement as in the metallurgical industries, in coal mining, in sugar processing, and in textiles.

It was to break out of this economic backwardness that Count Sergei Witte, as minister of finance, had been allowed by czars Alexander III (1881–94) and Nicholas (1894–1917) to introduce economic planning. Witte tried to obtain capital for a state-sponsored program of industrialization by selling as much of Russia's agricultural production, especially grain, on foreign markets as was possible without provoking famine in the empire. In fact, Witte pushed his program even during years of near-famine conditions. His success contributed to a rapid growth of cities and a spectacular increase in factory production of all kinds from the 1890s until 1914. Unavoidably, this industrialization and urbanization was accompanied by new social and political tensions which shook the foundations of the czarist system in 1905.

The Revolution of 1905 was occasioned by the stresses placed on Rus-

---

[6] Oscar Jaszi, *The Dissolution of the Hapsburg Monarchy* (Chicago: University of Chicago Press, Phoenix Books, 1961), p. 421.

sian society by an irresponsible war with Japan over the possession of Manchuria. The Russians were soundly defeated both on land and at sea. The economic hardships resultant from the war as well as the loss of governmental prestige that usually accompanies defeat in war led to strikes and demonstrations in the larger cities. When soldiers in St. Petersburg fired on a peaceful demonstration in January 1905, protests swept Russia. Incoherently, piecemeal, civil order disintegrated in the greater part of European Russia. Peasants began to seize and burn the gentrys' manors and to claim the land. The revolution entered its climactic stage when railroad workers went on strike throughout the Empire in June. Political parties that had existed underground began to surface and demand reforms. The Constitutional Democrats (Cadets) demanded a parliamentary system. The Socialist Revolutionaries and Socialist Democrats called for a redistribution of the land and the socialization of capitalist property. Czar Nicholas, who had dismissed Witte because of conservative resistance to Witte's reforms, once again called on the finance minister to take charge. Witte did so, but he gave the czar unwelcome advice. At least the semblance of a parliamentary regime had to be created, Witte argued. Reluctantly, Nicholas consented and promulgated the October Manifesto stating that, although the crown retained its prerogatives as an absolute monarch, a representative body would be elected to advise the government in legislative matters. The Duma, which would be elected indirectly to prevent democratic excesses, was to have very little power—it could neither originate legislation nor pass on the state budget; but many liberals—including the Cadets—considered this an excellent first step toward parliamentary government. Witte had split the revolutionary forces. An uprising in St. Petersburg in December was suppressed, and the Army began restoring order to the countryside.

The czar and his reactionary advisers had no intention of allowing representative institutions to gain a foothold in Russia. When the First Duma elected proved to be too reformist, it was dissolved within a matter of months. The Second Duma contained even more socialist deputies; therefore the election law was changed to give the majority of seats to the landed gentry and to deprive the peasantry and the urban workers of representation. Witte was ousted as soon as possible in early 1906 and replaced, after an interim, by Peter Stolypin, a man who could be trusted to oppose the demands of the Duma for a voice in government. The Third Duma, elected under the new electoral system, was as conservative as had been hoped by the court. It remained in session for its full term of five years.

Stolypin was not merely a reactionary. Although he used brutal methods to suppress dissent and was hated by the political representatives of the lower classes, he also achieved a notable agricultural reform intended to create a base for economic growth. The essence of his agricultural bill that passed the Duma in 1910 was its compulsory abolition of much communal property and the creation of private land holdings. In contrast to Witte, who drained agriculture to support industry, Stolypin hoped to create a prosperous peasantry as a basis for economic growth. The peasantry would supply a domestic market for Russian goods and free Russia from its dependence on foreign markets and foreign loans. There were also political reasons for the reform. Conservatives had thought before 1905 that the peasantry was a bulwark of tradition and that preservation of the village commune was necessary to the defence of the social status quo. They saw, however, that during the turbulence of 1905, the commune might become the basis of a society built on peasant socialism. Many influential aristocrats were, therefore, converted to the western concept of private property as a preventative of revolution. It was felt that if peasants owned land, the peasantry would have a stake in society and would not be attracted by collectivist doctrines. Another advantage of freeing the peasants from the communes would be to make available a labor force for new industry. It would become a simple matter for a young man to move to the city and thereby contribute to Russia's expanding economy.

The contradictions of Russian society were evident in the source of the resistance to Stolypin's reforms: the czar's court and certain elements of the gentry. The czar was encouraged by these elements in his belief that Stolypin was trying to usurp the prerogatives of the crown and become a prime minister on the British model. Furthermore, the reactionaries had such a commitment to the status quo that even a conservative such as Stolypin, who had ruthlessly executed hundreds of the czar's political opponents, was not trusted to make reforms. A strong coalition was forming against Stolypin when, in September 1911, he was assassinated, while attending a concert, by a man named Bogrov. The assassin had been an *agent provocateur* for the secret police and had been admitted to the theater by the police. Since Bogrov never came to trial the suspicion that he was employed by Stolypin's reactionary critics has never been confirmed nor disproved.

Stolypin's death came at the end of a period of relative social and political stability. Without his strong and moderating hand at the helm, increasingly reactionary elements influenced state policy. Among these and symbolic of them was the mystic Rasputin. A monk who had "cured" the czar's son of hemophilia, Rasputin captured the allegiance of the czarina, who in turn frequently dictated the actions of Czar Nicholas. Rasputin used his power over the Czarina Alexandra to assert the influence of the Orthodox church, to prevent any increase in political freedoms, and to gain official posts for his friends. Yet the reactionary forces should not be over-personalized. The gentry as a class was hostile to the reforms of 1905–07. The Union of Russian People was a propagandist organization supported by the landed gentry, the church, and nobles at court. It organized conservative elements of society to bring pressure on the Duma, the state council (the legislative upper house), and the czar personally. The union also made some attempt to divert demands for reform by encouraging anti-Semitism, and it supported and perhaps organized pogroms.

Faced with official reaction, the parliamentary moderates were becoming frustrated by their continued failure to gain more power for the Duma. The Fourth Duma elected in 1912 was not as conservative or passive as the Third Duma, but it was more helpless. This situation alienated many advocates of cautious reform and even forced left-wing Cadets and Octobrists into temporary coalitions with socialists in the Duma. This polarization between the state and the liberal bourgeoisie was paralleled by the increasing radicalism of the labor movement.[7] During 1912 and 1913 the Bolsheviks, the radical revolutionary wing of the Social Democratic party led by V. I. Lenin, gained majorities in the executive councils of several of the largest unions, including the Union of Metalworkers and the Printers Union. Yet even the Bolsheviks were not prepared for the storm of strikes and political demonstrations by workers that began in April, 1912.

The strike movement began as a protest against the Lena goldfields massacre. Striking miners had been shot by soldiers when they refused to return to work. Several days later 100,000 men struck in St. Petersburg in sympathy. Thus began the largest strike movement in Russian history except for the years of the 1905 revolution. In spite of government attempts to suppress the strike movement, it increased in scope and ferocity.

TABLE 1.2.   The Russian
Strike Movement

Year	Number of strikers
1909	64,166
1910	46,623
1911	105,110
1912	725,491
1913	887,096
January–June 1914	1,337,458

SOURCE: Leopold Haimson, "The Problem of Social Stability in Urban Russia, 1905–1917 (Part One)" *Slavic Review* 23, no. 4 (1964), p. 627.

During July 4–12, 1914, there was a massive strike in and around St. Petersburg, again involving approximately 100,000 workers. Only armed troops prevented the strikers from marching on the center of the city.

---

[7] Leopold Haimson, "The Problem of Social Stability in Urban Russia, 1905–1917 (Part One)," *Slavic Review* 23, no. 4 (1964), pp. 630–31.

As we have seen in other countries, the war began with internal divisions at the point of civil war.

Revolutionaries and Counterrevolutionaries

The domestic crises of the European states was strongly influenced by the parallel emergence of strong socialist parties on the left and of militant nationalist organizations on the right. Both extremes saw liberalism as their enemy. Conservatives felt that liberals were responsible for the growth of the revolutionary left and were not sufficiently concerned about the military and imperial prestige of the nation. Socialists regarded the liberals as representatives of the capitalist class and therefore enemies of the working class—even though temporary cooperation with the liberals for social reform might be acceptable. The growth of the extremes reduced the political maneuverability of centrist politicians and forced them to choose between these potential allies.

Socialist representation in European parliaments had increased rapidly since the 1880s, when they had first appeared as an organized force in France and Germany. (See Table 1.3.) At that time, throughout Europe,

TABLE 1.3.   The Progress of Socialism, 1890–1914

	Seats	Votes	Percentage of Total Vote
Great Britain:			
1895	..	...	..
1900	2	63,304	1.8
1906	30	329,748	5.9
Jan 1910	42	505,657	7.6
Dec 1910	40	371,772	7.1
France:			
1893	31	598,000	8.5
1898	55	888,000	11.3
1902	45	875,000	10.4
1906	53	877,000	10.0
1910	75	1,110,000	13.3
1914	103	1,408,000	16.9
Germany:			
1890	35	1,427,298	19.5
1893	44	1,786,738	23.2
1898	56	2,107,076	27.1
1903	81	3,010,771	31.7
1907	43	3,259,029	28.9
1912	110	4,250,401	34.8

SOURCES: *Great Britain:* David Butler and J. Freeman, *British Political Facts, 1900–1967* (London: Macmillan and Co., Ltd., 1968), p. 141; *France:* Peter Campbell, *French Electoral Systems and Elections Since 1789* (London: Faber and Faber Ltd., 1958), pp. 82–85; *Germany:* Koppel Pinson, *Modern Germany*, 2d ed (New York: The Macmillan Co., 1966), p. 602.

there were many socialist factions. Representatives of these groups met in Paris in 1889 to form the Second Socialist International. The strongest factions were the Marxists and the Anarchists. These two struggled for control of the International during the 1890s, and by 1896, the Marxists had emerged victorious. After this the battles would be among the followers of Karl Marx.

The first volume of Marx's major theoretical work, *Capital,* was published in 1867. It was a masterful attempt to understand the economic and social dynamics of the industrial revolution. It became the bible of international socialism. Marx argued that under the capitalist system laborers were robbed of a major portion of the value that labor gives to industrial products. Capitalist businessmen, he said, were expropriating this surplus value and using it to acquire more wealth. Several results would flow from this fundamental fact of exploitation. First, the size of the working class would grow as money and industrial production were concentrated into the hands of a few, sharpening a class division between the mass of workers and the few owners of property. Second, the concentration of wealth would lead to ever greater economic crises of inflation, under-consumption, and unemployment. Third, in these conditions the workers would become class-conscious, aware of their inevitable conflict with the capitalists. Finally, the combination of increasingly severe economic crises and increasingly class-conscious workers (the proletariat) would eventually and inevitably result in a socialist revolution in which the capitalists would be dispossessed and a socialist society established. Marx was certain that the revolution would occur as the inevitable result of economic forces.

If this were true, what was the role of socialist political parties? Should they refuse to cooperate with bourgeois governments or should they take part in parliamentary politics like any other party in hopes of improving the life of the workers? Marx was himself ambiguous on this point, which became a divisive factor in the Second International. Within each nation socialists took sides for or against cooperation with bourgeois regimes. The issue was brought to a head by a debate among French socialists as to whether or not a socialist should accept a ministry in a liberal cabinet. The issue was taken to the International Congress in 1904, and the International, dominated by the Germans, decided against cooperation.

The same battle was fought out within each national party along doctrinal lines. The "orthodox Marxists" argued that socialist participation in parliamentary coalitions would only confuse the workers and lessen class consciousness. Since the revolution is inevitable, it would be senseless to try to achieve minor reforms which might only perpetuate the capitalist system. The "revisionists" and reformers disagreed. Some—Edward Bernstein of Germany was one—maintained that, although Marx had correctly described the economy of the midnineteenth century, Marx's predictions

Jean Jaures, French Socialist leader, addressing a rally protesting a law lengthening the period of military service in 1913 (Courtesy of Roger-Viollet)

concerning the revolution were not valid. Instead of weakening, the capitalist system was becoming stronger. Workers were not becoming revolutionary, but they were instead enjoying higher salaries and better working conditions than ever. A socialist society, the revisionists argued, would have to be built block by block through a slow process of legislative reform.

Although the orthodoxists won the votes at national and international conferences, all European socialist parties but two followed revisionist policies until 1914. The day-to-day legislative process led them to make compromises, to trade votes, to make parliamentary alliances to pass or to block specific pieces of legislation. The two exceptions were the Italian Socialist party and the Social Democrats (Bolshevik faction) of Russia. The Italian Socialist party (PSI) was dominated by reformers until the 1912 party congress when a revolutionary wing won a majority. Benito Mussolini, a leading spokesman of the revolutionaries, became editor of the PSI newspaper, *Avanti,* and used it to denounce bourgeois parliamentary democracy.

V. I. Lenin had won a majority of the Social Democratic Congress of 1903 over to his revolutionary strategy. His followers were therefore known as the Bolsheviki or Majoritarians. Lenin insisted that, in a police state such as czarist Russia, a socialist party could not imitate the socialists of western Europe. Instead, he desired a tightlyknit, strictly disciplined core of dedicated agitators. These professional revolutionaries would work in secret, use aliases, change location frequently. They would be a revolutionary vanguard, ready to lead the proletariat when a revolutionary situation presented itself. Lenin's genius and, to a large extent, his most lasting theoretical contribution, was this revolutionary strategy. Later it was to be employed by revolutionaries throughout Asia, Africa, and Latin America.

Just as most socialist parties became increasingly reformist, they also became increasingly nationalistic. Theoretically all socialists were internationalists because they were the spokesmen for a social class, not for a nation. Imperialism and war were products of the capitalist system and of no interest to the workers. Yet, the socialists tended to find reasons for defending their homeland if the need arose. The French wanted to protect the Republic that guaranteed them freedom. The Germans feared subjugation to the czar and loss of the most advanced social welfare system in Europe. There were, however, a few socialists—such as Lenin and the Germans Rosa Luxemburg and Karl Liebknecht—who argued that, in case of war, socialists should try to achieve a revolution. Workers armed as soldiers should be encouraged to turn their guns on the capitalist class. Still, these were the exceptions. In spite of their nationalist sentiments, the socialists did attempt to provide an alternative to the international competition of the years 1900–14. As late as November 1912, 555 socialists from twenty-three different parties met in Basel to try to lessen the international tension caused by the Balkan wars.

The growth of the socialist left and of trade unions forced conservatives and the social classes they represented on the defensive. In parliamentary states, the right was losing strength at each election, while in authoritarian states, the ruling circles were threatened by a rising tide of popular support for democratic reforms (or, as in the case of Austria-Hungary, for the self-determination of national minorities). Unable to check the reformist forces by legislative politics, many conservatives turned to nonparliamentary extremist organizations. This was the origin of the radical right—conservatives willing to destroy traditional institutions in order to defeat socialism. These counterrevolutionaries shared with the revolutionary left a rejection of liberalism's emphasis on egoistic individualism and parliamentary government.

Radical right organizations began to appear in all countries around the turn of the century. Some were more extreme than others. All worked outside of the normal political system. The Primrose League, founded 1883, was concerned above all with the extension of the British Empire. *Action Francaise* advocated the violent overthrow of the French Republic and the restoration of the monarchy. The Pan-German League preached the superiority of the Germanic race, anti-Semitism, and the virtues of a German empire in Africa. The revival of the Italian nation through bloodshed and violence, preferably in a glorious war, was the goal of the Italian National party. The farcical occupation of Libya in 1911, during which the Italian army proved itself utterly incompetent although victorious, was heartily applauded by these rightwing extremists. The Pan-Slavs of Russia urged a war against Austria-Hungary in order to unify the Slavic peoples of eastern Europe with Mother Russia. All of these organizations were motivated by nationalism. They shared their assertions of national supremacy, their belief in the need for imperial expansion, their praise for the military, and their hatred of socialism.

If politically isolated, these extremists would have had no effect on their respective governments. Moderate conservatives, however, frightened by the specter of socialism, adopted the rhetoric of the nationalists. Poincaré, Millerand, and Briand did so in France. Bonar Law did so in Great Britain. This made rational foreign policy extremely difficult. In their desire to discredit their leftist opposition, moderates preached the gospel of nationalism and national pride so loudly that in July and August 1914, the voices of conciliation could no longer be heard.

Chapter 2

CULTURAL REVOLT AND
INTERNATIONAL TENSION

The domestic political crises of the various Great Powers were paralleled by an intellectual rebellion against established standards and by growing diplomatic tension brought about by rigid alliance systems, international naval competition, and old national animostites as well as new national ambitions. It is only by weaving together these various historical threads that we can comprehend the events of August 1914, when Europeans marched off to war.

The Destruction of Certainty

The fundamental assumptions concerning the nature of reality of European philosophers, artists and scientists were shaken during the period 1900 to 1914. Old certitudes and accepted codes of conduct were denounced, and certain thinkers substituted chiliastic creeds and calls to action for "rational" systems of thought. Each of the highly industrialized societies contributed to this cultural crisis; eastern Europe was less effected. The most important aspects of the crisis were the attack on positivism, the discovery of the subconscious, a glorification of the irrational, an attack on bourgeois values, and the growing popularity of antidemocratic and antiparliamentary philosophies. Before 1914 this crisis of the European spirit was limited to intellectuals; the shock of World War I made the general educated public susceptible to the same influences.

Innovative thinkers of the period 1890 to 1914 categorized everything they disliked—materialism, the glorification of machines, naturalism, scientism—as positivism. Self-confident and rational, the foundation of positivism was the faith that all things were knowable through the application of the scientific method to human affairs. The inherent confidence in progress—technological and mechanical as well as social progress—that the positivists espoused was peculiarly suited to the nineteenth-century march of western Europe from triumph to triumph in industrial expansion, improved living standards, population growth, imperial subjugation of Africa and Asia, and the spread of parliamentary forms across Europe even to Russia. Positivists assumed that man's behavior was understandable because it was rational and because men were guided by reason. While denying that established religions could offer absolute truth, positivists exalted a new religion: science. Extending from this scientific view of the world and rational view of man were certain artistic movements— especially naturalism—which asserted that the artist's whole task was to record accurately what he saw in the world, without distorting it by his own subjective reactions. At the turn of the century, these ideas were already under attack; and before 1914 the groundwork had been laid for a radically different conception of reality.

Foremost in laying the groundwork for a revolution in man's conception of his world were Sigmund Freud in psychology, Max Weber in sociology, and Albert Einstein in physics. Each of these men contributed to the destruction of positivism and of faith in progress by arguing that knowledge is relative, that there are no absolutes. Freud and the sociologists demonstrated that man did not control his environment but was in fact a product of it. While none of these men of science rejected the dominant values of their society as did most of the artists and philosophers we shall discuss—Nietzsche, Sorel, Marinetti, the fauvists—they perhaps did more to undermine the nineteenth-century world-view than did the cultural revolutionaries.

New perspectives were offered on virtually all scientific disciplines by the new physics. This is the term usually applied to the atomic physics developed around the turn of the century that destroyed basic concepts concerning the nature of matter, energy, and measurements. In the late nineteenth century, all matter was thought to be constructed of indestructible atoms—irreducible little billiard balls which might be rearranged but never destroyed. From 1895 to 1900 several scientists discovered that the atom was not solid at all, but was composed of positive and negative charges of electrical energy. In another field, Planck proved that light or radiant energy did not travel in a steady stream but in separate units or quanta—like raindrops. Other physicists, however, discovered that the quantum theory could not explain the results of their experiments. They continued to insist that light traveled in continuous waves. Even more disturbing was Albert Einstein's suggestion that both theories were equally true depending on what phenomenon was being explained. Some phenomena could only be explained, he said, by assuming that light and energy traveled in quantum jumps, while others could only be understood by assuming that radiant energy traveled in waves. While aiding scientists, this only increased uncertainty among the educated public. Evidently scientists did not know the truth about matter or energy or light—they could only offer workable theories. This came as a great shock to laymen steeped in positivism and its belief in the ever increasing certainty of scientific laws.

Einstein further increased the uncertainty by his theory of relativity. Simply put, he refuted the belief in universal scientific laws of weight, time, and measurement. Natural laws, he proved, are not absolute but are relative to the system (context) in which they are being applied. An example of relativity would be the relationships of two persons to a moving train: one being a passenger on the train, the other standing beside the track watching the train roar past. The passenger does not feel the train (his system) rushing through space because he is moving with it. The train and its passenger are a closed moving system. The man beside the track is in a stationary system. To him, the train is passing rapidly, creating a turbulent wind, and creating copious pollution. Einstein also proved that space, time, and mass are all relative to the system in which they exist. For instance, a clock runs slower as the velocity of its system increases. If a clock is on a train traveling at 60 mph, it will run slower than on a train moving 10 mph. Another finding was that mass gains in weight the faster it travels. Einstein's theory implied that the most elementary concepts of science—measurements—were not universally applicable. An inch is not always the same length; a pound does not always weigh the same. The security offered by the nineteenth-century faith in science had been shaken. Nothing was absolute. Everything had become relative.

Sigmund Freud published his most important theoretical works around 1900, but like Einstein, he was not noticed by the general public until after 1919. Freud's greatest contributions were his theories concerning the unconscious mind and the influence of sexuality on personality. Medically, his development of the techniques of clinical psychoanalysis was equally important. Freud demonstrated that much of the discussion about rationality and irrationality was meaningless, since the rational mind was controlled by the unconscious. By the end of the twenties his three-part division of the unconscious had become a usual conversation topic at cocktail parties: the *id* representing the animal desires; the *superego* being the inhibitions placed upon the id by society; and the *ego* acting as the mediator between the instinctual drives of the id and the paralyzing conformity to social morality dictated by the superego. In this three-way struggle to control man's behavior, Freud's sympathy lay with the ego, the expression of human rationality; but his research led him to the pessimistic conclusion that, in the conditions of modern society, the bestial instincts of the id were gaining the upper hand.

Of greater social importance than his theory of the unconscious was

Sigmund Freud
(Courtesy of UPI)

Freud's emphasis on sexuality as a basic element in character formation. He attacked Victorian society for having thwarted the sex drive, especially in women, and thereby having caused personal psychological suffering. He concluded that women of the Victorian age could never achieve true emotional satisfaction and that mature women in the 1890s had "only the choice between unappeased desire, infidelity, or neurosis."[1] Although a Puritan himself, he recommended more liberal attitudes toward premarital sex and homosexuality. In articles and books he condemned the prevalent attitudes toward sex. He charged that the systematic attempt by parents to keep their children in ignorance about sex had stultified the intellectual lives of those children when they became adults. He was not opposed to premarital sex relations—a scandalous point of view at the time.

Max Weber's productive years came between the turn of the century and the beginning of the war. Proceeding from his own historical studies, Weber argued that although the world was a rational one—that is, certain laws of cause and effect do exist—man usually is unaware of the forces that control his behavior. Therefore, men usually act irrationally, at the mercy of impersonal social forces. The best example of this was Weber's theory of the "charismatic leader." The charismatic leader is one who can demand devotion and loyalty from large masses of people merely by his presence, his speaking style, or his decisiveness.

Charismatic authority, hence, shall refer to a rule over men . . . to which the governed shall submit because of their belief in the extraordinary quality

---

[1] H. Stuart Hughes, *Consciousness and Society* (New York: Random House, Inc., 1958), p. 150.

of the specific *person*. The magical sorcerer, the prophet, the leader of the
hunting and booty expeditions, the warrior chieftain, the . . . "Caesarist"
ruler . . . are such types. . . . Charismatic rule is not managed according
to general norms, either traditional or rational, . . . and in this sense . . . is
"irrational."[2]

Interestingly, Weber did not disapprove of this irrational leadership. Like
Nietzsche before him, he thought that such a superman was needed. Weber
was discouraged by the increasing organization, the increasing bureau-
cratization of Western society that was reducing men to the level of robots.
He thought that perhaps a charismatic leader (or leaders) might appear
to protect individual freedom from the impersonal forces of a completely
bureaucratized society. One can find a foreshadowing of Nazism in this
concept, but it might equally apply to Franklin Roosevelt or John
Kennedy.

Weber's greatest contributions were in the field of sociological theory
and methodology. He suggested that society could best be analyzed by
the intellectual creation of "ideal types" for various phenomena. For instance, "monarchy" would be an ideal type for one form of governmental
organization. A theoretical definition of "capitalism" would be another
ideal type—this time of a form of economic organization. Since Weber
such theoretical constructs have been refined as "sociological models."
Weber argued that reality did not dictate the manner in which the sociologist constructed an ideal type; the limiting factor was the purpose and
the interest of the researcher. The ideal type was a working hypothesis
to be compared with reality, not to be determined by previous observa-
tions. This freed social scientists from the arid gathering of facts to which
the positivists had descended by the 1890s.

Emile Durkheim, another pioneer sociologist, began his career as a
positivist but became convinced of the relativity of human beliefs and
values during his study of the sociology of religion. He came to believe
that it was scientifically useless to concern oneself with the truth or falseness of religious dogma because the role of all religions was to fulfill
a social need.

In reality, then, there are no religions which are false. All are true in their
own fashion. . . . The reasons with which the faithful justify them may be,
and generally are, erroneous; but the true reasons do not cease to exist, and
it is the duty of science to discover them.

These were harsh words in an age in which religious piety was required
by social convention. Durkheim made great strides in establishing a
rigorous statistical methodology for social scientists, and he practiced his

---

[2] Max Weber, "The Social Psychology of World Religions," in [*Max Weber:
Essays in Sociology*, eds. and trans. H. H. Gerth and C. Wright Mills (New York:
Oxford University Press, 1946), pp. 295–96.

techniques in, among other studies, his remarkable book on suicide (1897).

A Time for Heroes

While the four men discussed to this point were developing theories with far-reaching implications, there were some thinkers who were more interested in action and in changing society. Bergson, Sorel, and Nietzsche had a much greater influence in the prewar decade than did Freud, Weber, or Einstein. Bergson's influence was indeed at its height in 1914, but he was all but forgotten after the war. Henri Bergson dominated French intellectual circles from the time he was appointed to the chair of philosophy at the College de France in 1900 until the Great War began. During that period he won almost every honor France could bestow on an intellectual (plus a Nobel prize). He completely rejected rationalism and argued that the only sure knowledge was gained through intuition. He postulated an all-pervading life-force, which he called *élan vital,* that was supposedly constantly gushing forth from individuals, through collectives such as nations, and through history.

All the living hold together, and all yield to the same tremendous push . . . the whole of humanity, in space and in time, is one immense army galloping beside and before and behind each of us in an overwhelming charge able to beat down every resistance and clear the most formidable obstacle. . . .[3]

As mystical as this may sound, it struck a chord among educated Frenchmen; perhaps it allowed them to believe that the alienation and loneliness of urban society did not really exist. This *élan vital* and Bergson's theory of intuition were actually very close to the religious concepts of an all-pervasive God who could only be known through faith. Bergson taught that one could only realize his potential by surrendering to the *élan vital* of a larger group. This, of course, was tailor-made for the nationalists of prewar France and probably explains much of Bergson's popularity. In essence, his philosophy was a glorification of the irrational forces within man that could be applied to any cause—religion, nationalism, an offensive-oriented army, or a militant labor movement. The imperative was for man to lose his individuality in a collective passion. Indeed, the French army seized on this idea and constructed an entire military strategy based on the offensive.

Georges Sorel used the same theory in a different form to justify a revolutionary doctrine for the rather weak French labor unions. Sorel, a thinker of much greater profundity than Bergson, also recognized the

---

[3] Bergson, *Creative Evolution* (1907) as quoted in Gerhard Masur, *Prophets of Yesterday: Studies of European Culture, 1890–1914* (New York: Harper and Row, Publishers, Colophon Books, 1966), p. 261.

importance of subconscious motivations. It is a startling comment of the prewar intellectual climate that Sorel, Bergson, and Freud arrived at similar conclusions independently. Sorel did owe a great deal to Bergson, but his thought was too original to classify him as a Bergsonian. He began his career as an engineer from 1870 to 1890. In 1889, at the age of forty-two he published his first book and moved to Paris to take up the life of a free intellect. His pessimism about bourgeois society resembled that of Nietzsche. He decided that man could only overcome this spiritual poverty by participating in a movement that promised both fervor and glory. On the contemporary scene, only the struggle of the proletariat offered such a promise. It was for this reason that Sorel became the leading theoretician of revolutionary syndicalism with the book *Reflections on Violence* (1908). In this book he argued that labor unions should reject parliamentary action and resort to ever larger and more violent strikes until a general strike of all workers could overthrow capitalist society. Sorel never expected such a general strike to occur but considered it a necessary "myth" needed to inspire the workers to continue their struggle. Yet his ideas had an even broader implication. He was convinced that proletarian violence could regenerate Western society, and, therefore, violence was desirable.

Proletarian violence not only makes the future revolution certain, but it seems also to be the only means by which the European nations—at present stupefied by humanitarianism—can recover their former energy.
Proletarian violence, carried on as a pure and simple manifestation of the sentiment of the class war, appears thus as a very fine and very heroic thing; it is at the service of the immemorial interests of civilization; it is not perhaps the most appropriate method of obtaining immediate material advantages, but it may save the world from barbarism.[4]

Sorel's entire emphasis was on action and the power of the subconscious to motivate men. He became more than a philosopher. Since his theories justified the militancy of the French labor movement, he became the storm-center of many semipolitical activities by leftist and rightist intellectuals.

Inherent in Sorel's work is a distaste for the society around him, a society of overfed businessmen competing for wealth and social position, of politicians without vision, of hypocritical religiosity and rampant public and private corruption. This vision—so different from the vision the European bourgeoisie had of themselves—was shared by many other intellectuals, who, like Sorel, dreamed of a new Europe. Their Europe would be one that would allow noble men to accomplish great deeds. They had a heroic vision which seduced the youth of the prewar years.

Friedrich Nietzsche was in the forefront of the assault on bourgeois

---

[4] Georges Sorel, *Reflections on Violence*, trans. T. E. Hulme and J. Roth (New York: Collier Books, 1961), pp. 92, 98. Reprinted with permission of The Macmillan Company. Copyright The Free Press, 1950.

values. Although he had developed and set forth his ideas between 1872 and 1889, it was only after 1900 that he reached his height of influence. His starting point was a revulsion at the mediocrity and hypocrisy of the German bourgeoisie. Germany and Europe as well had become decadent, over-civilized to the point that greatness, nobility, and grandeur were no longer possible. For Nietzsche, "traditional morality was merely the means by which the weak and powerless sought to hamper the natural energy of the strong, it was the expression of a slave mentality."[5] Society was inevitably divided between the weak and the strong, the leaders and the led, but it was not inevitable that the weak should dominate. It was Nietzsche's mission to point this out, to encourage the strong to exercise their will to power rather than submit to the hypocrisy of a desiccated Christianity that made men mask their ambition, their passion, and their brutality behind pious justifications. Nietzsche wanted men to free themselves from such shackles, to embrace all that was both good and evil in human nature, and to be proud to be men. If mankind would only be true to this vision, it might evolve into a higher and nobler race of supermen, as different from contemporary man as man is from the ape.

Nietzsche's most widely read and most influential book was *Thus Spake Zarathustra,* an extended philosophical allegory containing a critique of German society and offering a vision of the superman. Zarathustra was a hermit prophet who descended from the mountains to instruct the valley dwellers and to seek disciples. Zarathustra sought a small elite who might lead mankind out of its mediocrity. Failing this, the prophet decides that he must attempt the task alone, perhaps transforming himself into the superman. The loneliness of Zarathustra paralleled the life of Nietzsche, who withdrew from society to write and was so torn by his peculiar vision of the world that he went insane in 1889.

His sweeping indictment of bourgeois society was accepted by many intellectuals as essentially accurate. George Bernard Shaw wrote a play entitled *Man and Superman.* D'Annunzio, *the* Italian poet of the prewar period, fancied himself the superman who might revive Italian culture. Many others, as we shall see, accepted Nietzsche's glorification of virile action, of force, and of violence as ingredients of greatness.

But there were two sides to Nietzsche—a fact that his loudest disciples often overlooked. Alongside the praise of masculine, heroic, and elitist values, he also exhibited a poetic mysticism, an asceticism, and an aloofness from political and material interests exemplified by both his own and Zarathustra's withdrawal from society for the sake of the intellect. This conflict, this unflagging search for truth through introspection, was unfortunately lost amid his own cries for grandeur through action. He rejected democracy which limited the strong; he suggested that a society as decadent as Europe could be renewed only through a destructive war;

---

[5] Ronald Gray, *The German Tradition in Literature, 1871–1945* (Cambridge: Cambridge University Press, 1965), p. 23.

and he thereby invited the creation of a world in which prophets had no place.

During the 1890s and even more so after the turn of the century, a Nietzschean cult emerged among German and French youth. The most extreme proponent of Nietzsche's ideas was the great but perverse poet Stefan George. Elitism was at the center of George's thought.[6] He wanted to surround himself with beautiful and intelligent men in order to give birth to a new German cultural tradition. He despised democracy as much as he did naturalism in poetry. When he found his own personal superman in a teen-age poet named Maximilian Kronberger, George renamed him "Maximin," and heralded him as the hero for whom the world was waiting—a new Caesar. George became the dictatorial "Master" of a new religion devoted to Kronberger, and to elitism. Unfortunately, Kronberger died of meningitis at sixteen, adding to the legend. George's bizarre life did not detract from his greatness as a poet nor from his influence over Germany's university youth. In a periodical he edited, *Blatter fur Die Kunst (Writings on Art)*, George demanded art for art's sake and the philistine public be damned. He denounced whatever he considered commercial, vulgar, or mediocre. He exalted man far above woman, and German youths who did not know or did not care about the poet's homosexuality were greatly encouraged to pursue manly activities such as living out-of-doors and going into military service.

Gabriel D'Annunzio, Italy's most honored poet from 1900–14, was another disciple of Nietzsche. D'Annunzio was already an unbearable egotist before reading Nietzsche, but afterwards he began to see himself in the role of the superman who would restore Italy's greatness. A secondary poet in terms of content, D'Annunzio had impeccable style. His popularity could only be compared to that of an American movie star of the 1950s. In perhaps his greatest poem, *Child of Pleasure,* the hero excels at all things and dreams of his many conquests—financial, military, and sexual. Another of D'Annunzio's heroes, Cantelmo of *Maidens of the Rock,* believes he is "destined to sire the superman who will impose his greatness on Italy and restore the Latin race to purity."[7] This poem was consciously Nietzschean, as were D'Annunzio's campaign on behalf of Italy entering World War I in 1914 and his leadership of a military force to occupy Fiume in 1919 in defiance of the League of Nations and the state of Yugoslavia.

Probably the most Nietzschean phenomenon in Europe, although not inspired by Nietzsche alone, was the German Youth Movement. This back-to-nature movement was a genuine protest by young Germans against the falseness of their parents' lives. As one historian has described their

---

[6] Eric Bentley, *A Century of Hero-Worship,* 2d ed. (Boston: Beacon Press, 1957), pp. 198–202.

[7] Masur, *Prophets of Yesterday,* pp. 137–38.

motives: "They thought that parental religion was sham, economics un-
scrupulous, education stereotyped and lifeless, art trashy and sentimental."[8]
The movement was first organized by a university student in 1896. There
was no real program, only activities. The most common was a long hike
into a forest by a group of young men, who sang around campfires, practiced woodsman's skills, and discussed ways to change society. They gave
up tobacco and alcohol. They began wearing brown uniforms and inaugurated an official greeting, a raised right arm and the shout, "Heil!" The
only ideological basis of the Movement was a mixture of slogans from
Nietzsche, Fichte, Schopenhauer, and Henri Bergson. By 1914 this movement had mushroomed so that traditional institutions like the Socialist
party and the Catholic church had formed their own youth organizations.

Artists in Revolt

The intellectual revolt of the turn of the century was inevitably expressed by artists. This was most evident in painting. Between 1905 and
1912 the art world witnessed the birth of one radical movement after
another until the foundations for the twentieth century were finally laid
by Wassily Kandinsky, the prophet of nonobjective art. The movements
of this period—expressionism, cubism, futurism, abstract art, nonobjective
art—constitute an amazing break with painting of the past. The same
can be said for sculpture, music, and the novel; but the revolutions in
these arts were neither as rapid nor as complete as in painting.

The young artists of Paris showed the way. Influenced greatly since
1901 by retrospective exhibits of the postimpressionists—Gauguin, Van
Gogh, and above all, Cezanne, a group of young painters around Henry
Matisse shocked art critics with a 1905 exhibit of paintings that violated
all traditional standards. The Fauves (wild beasts), as an art critic labeled
them, appealed to the senses and not the intellect. Brilliant, intense colors
and designs created with harsh brush strokes replaced recognizable subjects. In Germany painters were experimenting with similar techniques
and calling themselves expressionists.

Fauvism was followed almost immediately by cubism. Georges Braque
and Pablo Picasso followed Cezanne's advice that nature is composed
of only "the cylinder, the sphere, and the cone" and destroyed the natural
appearance of their subjects and reconstructed them on canvas in a thousand spheres, cones, and cylinders. An intellectual relativism accompanied
this technique; the cubists argued that they were portraying all aspects
of an object simultaneously, not just that part that happened to appear
before their eye. Technique had triumphed over subject.

The most consciously revolutionary art movement was Italian futurism.

---

[8] Howard Becker, *German Youth* (London: K. Paul, Trench, Trubner and Co.,
Ltd., 1946), p. 51.

The futurists, led by Marinetti, were interested in politics, diplomacy, and technology, as well as in painting. They were distressed at the economic backwardness and political corruption of Italy and assumed the task of modernizing Italy and reinvigorating the national spirit. In painting this meant exaltation of power, force, and speed. Marinetti issued the *Futurist Manifesto* in February 1909. In it he announced that "velocity" was the essence of beauty. The subjects of paintings should be automobiles, trains, and airplanes. In practice this resulted in amazing paintings in which the speed of a racing car was transmitted to the highway, the countryside, the passengers until all were submerged in a frenetic sea of abstract movement. The futurists also worshiped power in politics. They were ultranationalist, antiparliamentary, and desirous of war. Marinetti campaigned for Italy to go to war over Libya, and when Italy was victorious, he made a speech that ominously foreshadowed fascism.

Having recently, and with much satisfaction, punched the faces of all those who tried with their frantic shrieks to prevent a declaration of war, we now proclaim against all pacifists the following principles:
1.   All liberties shall be granted except the right to be a coward.
2.   Let it be understood that the word *Italy* tops the word *Liberty*.
3.   The loathsome memory of Roman greatness must vanish in the splendor of infinitely greater Italian victories.[9]

Alongside Marinetti, Wassily Kandinsky seems tame indeed; but Kandinsky and *The Blue Rider* group of painters of Munich completed the break with nineteenth-century art. Kandinsky developed nonobjective art. The expressionists, futurists, and cubists all retained a subject in their paintings that they abstracted to create a design or mood that they desired. Kandinsky announced that design alone was enough. All that was necessary were straight lines, curves and angles given body, mood, and life by color. Technique had replaced subject.

Similarly profound initiatives were being launched in music. Arnold Schoenberg composed the first atonal work in 1908. In the novel, Marcel Proust and James Joyce had begun to create a new form based on the workings of the subconscious. Thomas Mann and John Galsworthy, in more conventional narratives, both took the decline of a bourgeois family as their theme and as a symbol of the decline of bourgeois European society. Indeed, among European intellectuals, the prewar status quo had few friends. The artists were in revolt against the past and the present. They looked forward to a heroic future built upon their innovations.

An End to Peace: International Relations

The Great Powers of Europe enjoyed forty-four years of peace from 1870 to 1914. After a Russo-Turkish clash in 1878, four minor wars

---

[9] Rosa Trillo Clough, *Futurism* (New York: Greenwood Press, 1969), p. 21. Used by permission of Philosophical Library, Inc.

in Europe's most unstable area, the Balkans, were settled by international conferences without the military involvement of the powers.* Since 1880 the powers had limited their military exploits to colonial areas. This long period of diplomatic stability originated not in a balance of power but from the clear dominance of one state on the continent. The German Empire had been created in a series of wars from 1863 to 1870 in which the Prussian army defeated successively the Danish, the Austrian, and the French military forces. Otto von Bismarck, the German chancellor who had masterminded the wars of unification, was determined to protect his accomplishments by preventing further boundary changes in central Europe and by isolating France, the one continental power which might be able to challenge German hegemony. In a series of treaties, he allied Germany with Austria and Italy, and managed to prevent Russia from looking for allies in France or England. As long as such clear German diplomatic superiority, buttressed by Germany's rapid industrial and demographic growth, was maintained, the European peace was secure, since no state would dare challenge the young Hohenzollern Empire.

The architect of this policy was ousted from office in 1890, and Germany's secure position was thereafter slowly eroded, largely as a result of Germany's own growing ambitions. Because Bismarck was not properly respectful to the energetic young monarch, Wilhelm II, who took the throne in 1888, the aging chancellor was forced to resign. Very soon, Wilhelm launched a new policy which became known as *Weltpolitik* ("global policy") intended to give Germany an international and imperial role equivalent to that of Great Britain and France. Entering the race for colonies late, Germany seemed extremely aggressive to the other imperial powers.

The competition for colonies had begun in earnest with the establishment of ground rules for the partitioning of Africa at the Berlin Congress of 1884–85. In the next fifteen years virtually all of Africa and southern and southeastern Asia came under European administration. (See Map 2.) Several times the competition for colonies seemed to lead the Great Powers to the brink of war. French and British troops met at Fashoda on the upper reaches of the Nile, and a conflict was avoided only by subtle and adroit diplomacy. The Germans sided with England's enemies during the Boer War in South Africa. The British and the Russians clashed in central Asia. The Middle East was divided into spheres of influence to prevent a confrontation there. With Africa and Asia divided among them, the Great Powers engaged in other forms of competition. The Germans announced in 1897 a navy bill that was intended to make the German navy strong enough to inflict unacceptable damage on even the world's mightiest fleet. That could only refer to the British fleet, and

---

* Serb-Bulgarian War (1885); Greek-Turkish War (1897); First Balkans War (October 1912–May 1913); Second Balkans War (June–August 1913).

MAP 2. African and Asian Empires of the Great Powers, 1914

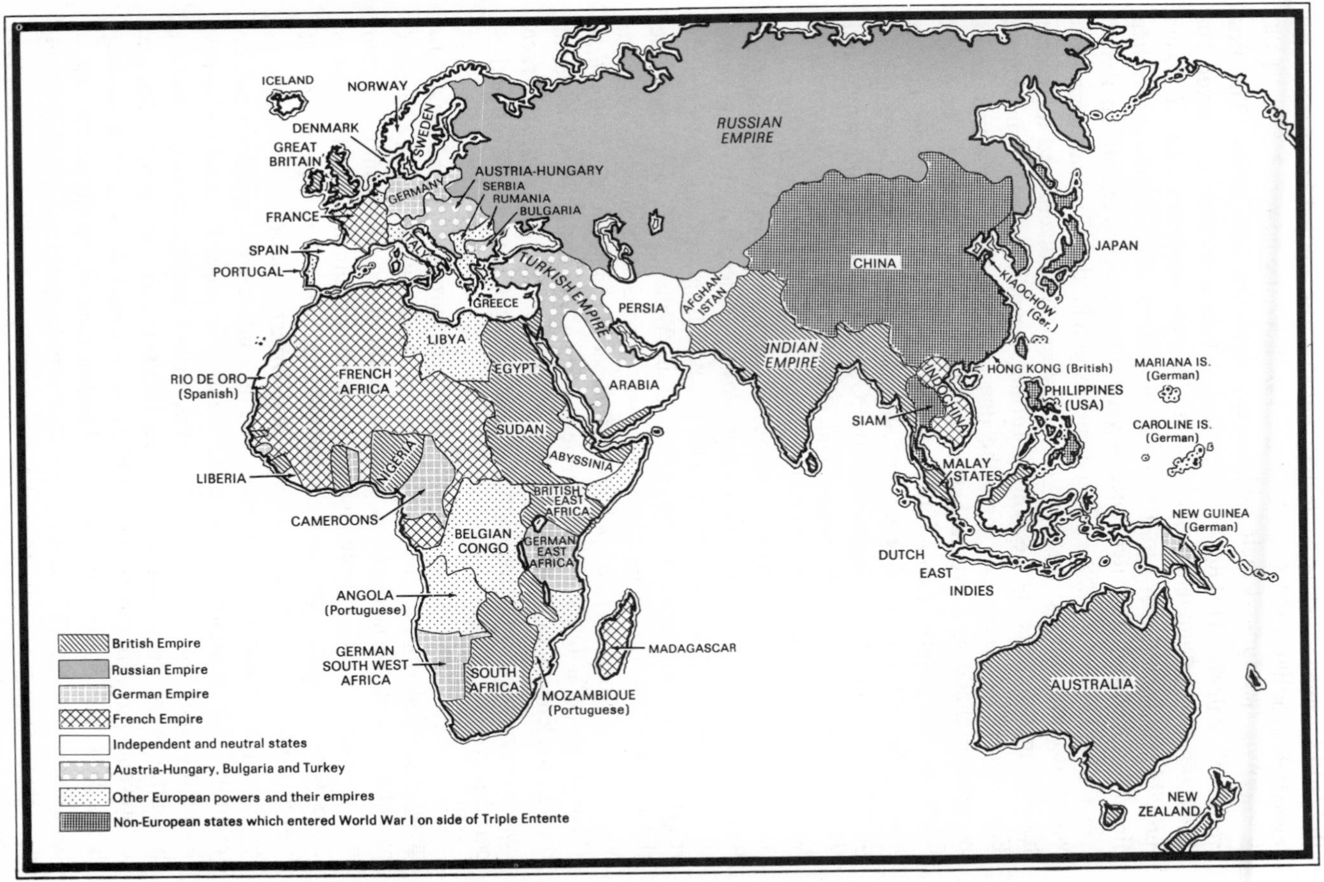

ICELAND
NORWAY
SWEDEN
DENMARK
GREAT BRITAIN
FRANCE
SPAIN
PORTUGAL
GERMANY
ITALY
GREECE
AUSTRIA-HUNGARY
SERBIA
RUMANIA
BULGARIA
TURKISH EMPIRE
RUSSIAN EMPIRE
PERSIA
AFGHANISTAN
ARABIA
INDIAN EMPIRE
CHINA
JAPAN
KIAOCHOW (Ger.)
HONG KONG (British)
PHILIPPINES (USA)
MARIANA IS. (German)
CAROLINE IS. (German)
NEW GUINEA (German)
INDO-CHINA
SIAM
MALAY STATES
DUTCH EAST INDIES
AUSTRALIA
NEW ZEALAND

RIO DE ORO (Spanish)
LIBERIA
LIBYA
EGYPT
FRENCH AFRICA
NIGERIA
CAMEROONS
SUDAN
ABYSSINIA
BELGIAN CONGO
BRITISH EAST AFRICA
GERMAN EAST AFRICA
ANGOLA (Portuguese)
GERMAN SOUTH WEST AFRICA
SOUTH AFRICA
MOZAMBIQUE (Portuguese)
MADAGASCAR

British Empire
Russian Empire
German Empire
French Empire
Independent and neutral states
Austria-Hungary, Bulgaria and Turkey
Other European powers and their empires
Non-European states which entered World War I on side of Triple Entente

Source: Adapted from Martin Gilbert, *Recent History Atlas* (London: Weidenfeld and Nicolson, 1966), map 23.

the British were not slow in developing a sort of paranoia that translated every German naval bill as an assault on British national security.

Yet, the naval race did not develop until the late 1890s. The first result of Wilhelm II's new course was to allow France to escape the isolation that Bismarck had so carefully perpetuated. Wilhelm II was a prey to many conflicting advisers and was never able to settle on a clear line of policy and stick to it. When a treaty with Russia came up for renewal, the kaiser followed advisers who recommended that it be allowed to lapse. The French had already begun courting the Russians with large loans and now pressed their advantage by offering a military pact. Isolated since 1871, France signed a mutual defense treaty with Russia in 1894. Another ally was thrust at France by Germany when Wilhelm II attempted to bully the English into an alliance on German terms at the end of the 1890s, while repulsing friendly compromises offered by Joseph Chamberlain, the British colonial secretary. France and Great Britain reached an Entente Cordial or "cordial understanding" on all major problems in 1904, and suddenly, France had two important allies. Germany scrupulously cultivated the friends she had left—Italy and Austria-Hungary, and the Triple Alliance, which had been renewed every five years since its initiation in 1882, was renewed again in 1902.

It took two rather severe international crises to convince England and Russia that they should end their perpetual colonial competition. In 1904 Russia became involved in an imperial war with Japan over Manchuria. The Russians suffered a humiliating defeat on both sea and land, and to add insult to injury, the lower classes at home attempted a revolution. After such a harrowing experience, the czar and his advisers felt receptive to a British friendship. The British were, on their part, becoming ever more suspicious of German ambitions. After all, the Germans had actually begun building a navy that might rival the British fleet. And, in Morocco in 1905, the Germans tried to use gunboat diplomacy to assert their importance as a naval power. The kaiser himself had landed at Tangiers to announce Germany's interest in the French-dominated Arab state. Evidently, Germany was testing the strength of the Anglo-French Entente. At the international conference called at Algeciras in 1906 to decide on the future of Morocco, the entente proved very strong indeed. In fact, Germany was isolated and outvoted on every issue. Even Italy deserted her ally. The British, however, realized that an armed conflict with Germany over Morocco or similar questions in the future was a possibility. Conversations between British and French military leaders were begun and continued until 1914. The British also admitted the logical extension of their alliance with France and began the talks which resulted in the Anglo-Russian Accord in 1907.

The alliance system completed in 1907 has often been cited as the "cause" of war in 1914. Certainly, it narrowed the alternatives of each nation. It also made it possible for one nation, such as Austria-Hungary, to drag its allies into a war against a member of the rival alliance. Any war between two Great Powers, therefore, might immediately become a general war including all states. Yet, the alliance system was not so rigid as to prevent Italy from changing partners in 1914. Nor was it so inhibiting as to prevent bilateral negotiations to settle major problems. A case in point was the second Moroccan crisis. Germany and France continued to compete over Morocco after Algeciras. In 1911, when it appeared that France was preparing to irrevocably capture Moroccan trade by conquering the country militarily, the Germans once again made a bold move. The German gunboat *Panther* steamed into the Moroccan port of Agadir in July 1911. This time the Germans seemed to be throwing down the gauntlet. The border garrisons of each country were mobilized. Actually, the Germans only wanted compensation for France's gains in Morocco. With a cool head, resisting the chauvinist press at home, the French premier Joseph Caillaux negotiated the two nations out of the confrontation situation created by the Germans. It could be done. Military conflict could be avoided, at least in 1911.

Morocco was not the only hotspot. The hottest was probably southeastern Europe, where the decaying Hapsburg Empire was separated from the decaying Turkish Empire by several very greedy young states—Serbia, Greece, Bulgaria, Rumania. The smaller states were willing to exploit any weakness of the empires or of one another to expand their national frontiers. The Hapsburgs, the German-Austrians, and the Magyars of Hungary felt they had to stop such expansion at any cost, or the Empire might fall apart as each national minority sought self-expression. (See above, pp. 16–19.) They were given such an opportunity during the Libyan War of 1911–12. The Italians had taken advantage of the diplomatic diversion created by the Agadir crisis to launch a colonial war that might have otherwise been opposed by the larger powers. Using trumped-up charges of mistreatment of Italians by Turk officials in Tripoli as an excuse, Italy declared war on the Ottoman Empire in October 1911. The war did not last long, and Italy, after some embarrassments, that revealed how utterly inefficient the Italian army was, annexed Tripoli, renaming it Libya. The war so weakened Turkey that it was a simple matter for the four Balkan states to drive her from Europe in the First Balkan War, producing spoils to be fought over in Macedonia and the Southern Dobrudja. Thus, the Second Balkan War soon began between the victors. This conflict ended in August 1913, and the area relapsed into a fitful peace.

Once again, a conflict had been limited and prevented from setting a flame that might consume Europe. The alliance system did not mean war. Russia had been at odds with Austria over the Balkans, but neither power had thought it worth a general European war to be able to determine the outcome of the Balkan conflict. Cool heads had prevailed. But compromise and concession were becoming more difficult. Anti-German feeling in Great Britain ran high, and Conservatives and Liberal imperialists demanded that Britain be ready to defend her Empire. The German military prepared to fight a two-front war, confident they could win. France's Poincaré had reinvigorated that nation's alliance with Russia, assuring the czar of French support in the Balkans. Italy was not sure what it might do if war began. In Vienna, serious consideration was being given to a preemptive war against Serbia to end the anti-Austrian agitation of that state, which aspired to become the homeland of all South Slavs, including those still in the Austro-Hungarian Empire.

It was, then, a Europe plagued by intense nationalism and divided by a rigid system of alliances that read, on the morning of June 29, 1914, of the assassination on the previous day of the heir to the Hapsburg Empire, Archduke Franz Ferdinand, and his wife by a Serbian nationalist. The Austrians were certain that the assassin was in the hire of the Serbian government, and most Europeans—even the leaders of Russia, France, and Great Britain—might have condoned some punitive action taken immediately against the Serbs. In fact, all diplomatic capitals were scandalized by the rejoicing in the Serbian press. The Austrian court realized the possibilities created by their tragedy, and General Conrad von Hotzendorf is reported to have said, "The hour has come for the Monarchy." The war party, which Conrad led, saw this as a time to settle once and for all with Serbia. Count Berchtold, the imperial foreign minister, agreed but wanted assurances of German support before entering on a venture that might lead to war with Russia.

On July 5–6 conversations were conducted between Austria-Hungary and Germany. Wilhelm II, grieved by the loss of a friend (he had visited with Franz Ferdinand only two weeks earlier), assured the Austrians that Germany would support any course of action the Hapsburg court felt necessary; only he urged that they act quickly and, in subsequent communications, he cautioned that they make Serbia and Russia appear to be the provokers of conflict. As events developed, the Austrians did neither.

With German support guaranteed, Berchtold was almost ready to act. A series of demands was drawn up which, if Serbia rejected them, could be the basis for a declaration of war. But the time was not right. Raymond Poincaré, now president of France, and the French premier, Réne Viviani, were to visit St. Petersburg on July 21 to 23; so it was decided in Vienna not to send the ultimatum to Serbia until the last evening of the visit. The Franco-Russian talks led to many pledges of mutual support, with the French being especially warm in their vows to stand by Russia in the present crisis. As the Frenchmen steamed away from Russia, however, they could not know how soon their loyalty was to be tested. At six

The assassination of Francis Ferdinand and his wife in Sarajevo touched off World War I. (Courtesy of Roger-Viollet)

o'clock on Thursday, July 23, the Austrian demands were handed to the Serbian government. The most important of the ten demands were that all propaganda against Austria stop immediately throughout Serbia, that Austro-Hungarian officials be able to enter Serbia and take part in the investigation of the conspiracy against the Archduke, and that Serbia give proof of its willingness to meet all Austrian demands unconditionally within forty-eight hours.

The ultimatum was a shock to all observers. No one had expected Austria to go quite so far—not even the Germans. The Russians began "measures preliminary to mobilization" of its army on July 25, the day the ultimatum expired. The Serbs were asked by virtually everyone to make concessions, and their reply to Austria appeared to be a surrender on all points but one; they refused to allow Austrian officials to enter Serbia. The Austrian ambassador had his instructions. When he saw that the Serbs had not accepted all ten points unconditionally, he broke off diplomatic relations and boarded a train for Budapest.

But Austria had lost the moral position it had in the days following the assassination. Serbia's skillful reply had weakened Austria's justification for resorting to military measures; even Germany's Bethmann-Hollweg thought war had been avoided when he read the Serb note. But the Germans felt they must support the Hapsburg Empire. The issues involved had expanded from a personal tragedy into matters of alliance solidarity and the balance of power. Germany, feeling encircled by the Triple Entente, was determined to guarantee the strength and prestige of her only true ally. France was just as determined to be a loyal ally of Russia, and Russia was bent upon retaining influence in the Balkans by supporting Serbia.

The tension of the weekend of July 25 and 26 and the days that followed was immense throughout Europe. Certainly some people—perhaps a majority of rural folk—relaxed, oblivious to the momentous decisions being made in Vienna, Belgrade, Berlin, and St. Petersburg. But the streets of major cities were filled with the curious and with newspaper hawkers. Special editions were printed; wall posters announced major events, such as the mobilization of the Serbian army on Saturday, July 25. Nationalists marched happily through the streets of Vienna when the Austro-Hungarian empire declared war on that international outlaw Serbia on Tuesday, July 28. Citizens of other nations applauded as their governments inexorably joined the parade. Russia, Germany, and France declared war on one another on August 1. Great Britain waited until Germany had violated Belgian neutrality on August 4. Italy alone stood aside. Italy bargained with both sides until 1915.

Chapter 3

WORLD WAR, 1914-19

Political Truce to Dictatorships, 1914–17

On warm August days in 1914 Europe marched to war. The citizens of the belligerent nations welcomed the news. French soldiers were showered with flowers, possibly picked from the fields where they would soon die. In a curious self-contradiction, H. G. Wells wrote in a left-wing English paper, "I find myself enthusiastic for this war against Prussian militarism. . . . Every sword that is drawn against Germany is a sword drawn for peace." Max Weber wrote to a friend, "This war, with all its ghastliness, is nevertheless grand and wonderful. It is worth experiencing." These were the sentiments of liberals, men of the center-left.

The war began with two lightning-fast offensives. In the west the Germans were threatening Paris three weeks after having declared war on France. This rapid advance promised to end the war within weeks. On September 2 the French government evacuated its capital. Due to a supreme effort organized by the French commander, General Joffre, the Germans were stopped only sixty miles from Paris. The Germans then extended their lines further west, trying to rush down the coastline to Paris. The British army had arrived and was able to prevent this. The Germans dug trenches to protect the ground already won. After futile assaults against these trenches, the British and French dug in to prevent German advances. By November 1914, an unbroken line of trenches stretched from the Belgian coast across the northeast of France to Switzerland. With minor changes, this front remained the same until June 1918, despite the sacrifice of millions of lives in attempts to change it.

The other offensive that opened the war was a Russian cavalry charge into East Prussia. The Russians held their positions for only a week before they were routed by the Germans at Tannenberg, where 120,000 Russian

MAP 3.   The Western Front, 1914

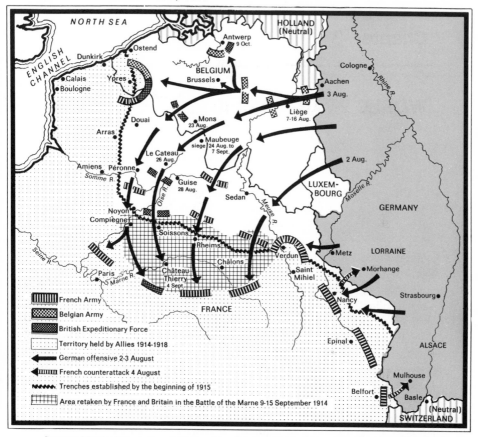

SOURCE: Martin Gilbert, *Recent History Atlas* (London: Weidenfeld and Nicolson, 1966), map 25.

soldiers surrendered. The German commanders at Tannenberg were Generals Hindenburg and Ludendorff, who were to play important political roles later in the war. After this battle the Germans pushed relentlessly toward Petrograd until the Russo-German Armistice of December 1917. Yet, the distances in eastern Europe are gargantuan, so that even the complete disintegration of the Russian army in 1917 did not allow the Germans to threaten the major Russian cities. Also in the east, the Austro-Hungarians, who had been first to declare war, were beaten soundly by the upstart Serbians in the fall of 1914. But in the following year the Germans aided the Austrians and Bulgarians in defeating all resistance to the central powers in the Balkans.

When the war began, politicians at home called for a political truce for the duration. This national solidarity was given special names in each country. It was the *Burgfrieden* in Germany, the National Union in Great Britain, and the *Union Sacrée* in France. In Britain and France the cabinets were reorganized so as to represent all parties. The French took the lead. On August 28 Premier Réné Viviani reshuffled his ministry to include a Catholic and two Socialists. Asquith followed suit in May 1915 by including Bonar Law, the Conservative party leader, and Arthur Henderson, the Labour party leader, in his cabinet. Henderson became the first Labourite to hold a ministerial post. In Germany no cabinet shake-up occurred, but Bethmann-Hollweg began to hold regular conferences with the SPD leaders.

The support of working class parties was essential to the war effort. The best way to assure the support of a populace for a war is to inspire them with war aims for which they are willing to die. As Arthur Rosenberg has written, "All the class differences known to modern Europe . . . came to life in the discussions over war aims. Thus the question of war aims became the great problem of German domestic politics throughout the war."[1] The same was true of France and Great Britain.[2] This question was so important because the various governments gambled their political existence on absolute victory and on the concrete territorial gains that they hoped to use as justification for the bloodletting. Conservative regimes that suffered defeat in the war were overthrown by revolutions. If those same regimes had won, they would have been strengthened as were the parties favoring the prewar status quo in France and Britain. The tenacity with which the upper classes in all countries held to the goal of absolute victory supports the theory that they felt a need for a military success to protect their positions in society.

If asked why he was fighting in 1914, the average Frenchman would have replied that he was fighting for *la Patrie* or against German militarism. Englishmen would have said the same, except "the Empire" might be substituted for *la Patrie*. Germans would have claimed to be resisting dictatorial Russia or to be breaking out of the encirclement of Germany by the Triple Entente. All of these were defensive goals, very vague and purely emotional and sincerely believed by the general public.

There were more concrete war aims, but the public did not know about these. When the war began, each government had expansionist war aims that were contained in secret treaties negotiated without the knowledge of the public and, in certain cases, without the knowledge of the national legislature. Great Britain and France were to have a free hand in redrawing Germany's western boundaries. Russia would have the same freedom in the east. France would regain Alsace-Lorraine (lost to Germany in 1870)

---

[1] *Imperial Germany, The Birth of the German Republic 1871–1918* (Boston: Beacon Press, 1964), p. 96.

[2] Arno J. Mayer, *Wilson vs. Lenin: The Political Origins of the New Diplomacy* (Cleveland, Ohio: World Publishing Co., 1964), pp. 33–44.

and could either occupy or annex the Ruhr, Germany's richest mining and industrial area that bordered on Alsace-Lorraine. Great Britain expected to obtain colonies in the Middle East, becoming the chief inheritor of the Ottoman Empire. Russian leaders had visions of extending the Romanov Empire westward from the Baltic to the Mediterranean, thus unifying the Slavic peoples and providing Russia with a buffer against invasion by Germany. Russia especially desired guarantees of Russian control over the straits leading from the Black Sea to the Mediterranean. Entering the war belatedly, Italy was able to bargain with each side. While still negotiating with Austria-Hungary, Salandra, the Italian premier, signed a treaty with England to enter the war against the Central Powers. Italy's booty was to be annexation of the South Tyrol, Trieste, and other areas along the east coast of the Aegean Sea. Italy also claimed a right to unspecified German colonies.

Only in Germany was there some awareness of the expansionist goals of the government. It was generally known that the kaiser was under the influence of the military and certain nationalist organizations that advocated expansion of the Reich. Even the German chancellor, Bethmann-Hollweg, who had a reputation for opposing extreme demands for annexations, was convinced that Germany had to annex certain areas so as to become completely dominant on the continent. Speaking in the Reichstag, he openly announced the German goals.

The greater the danger which we have to face from the ring of enemies round us . . . the more necessary is it for us to hold out until we have fought for and achieved all possible real guarantees and safeguards that none of our enemies will again dare appeal to arms, alone or in company.[3]

This implied a rejection of the balance of power in Europe in favor of German domination. Germany must control the iron and coal mines of Belgium, Luxembourg, and France, must control Poland and the Ukraine, and must gain new colonies.

Still, no publicity was given to specific territorial aspirations in Germany or elsewhere. Political leaders were aware that they could not ask the general public to fight for such goals. This concern for public opinion led to a strict censorship in all countries. Premier Viviani requested the French press not to discuss war aims since this could create "a very inconvenient state of opinion." Lloyd George made the same request when he became prime minister, and conservative newspapers like the *Times* of London denounced any demand for specific war aims or specific peace terms as injurious to the war effort.

The political truce could not survive a long war. It began to crack during the summer of 1916. General Joffre, leading the French and British

[3] Fritz Fischer, *Germany's Aims in the First World War* (London: Chatto and Windus Ltd., 1967), p. 195.

forces, thought he could gain a quick victory by a massive offensive that would break through the German trenches and force them into an unco-ordinated retreat. Joffre planned his assault along the Somme River, directly north of Paris, for July 1916. He was aware of German concentrations near the fortress of Verdun to his east, but he thought Verdun of little value. The German commander von Falkenhayn thought differently, as did the French government. They realized that Verdun was a symbol of the French will to fight, and von Falkenhayn wanted to take it at all costs. It was a sign of Joffre's independence that he refused requests from his premier to strengthen the Verdun garrison until it was almost too late. So, while Joffre prepared to attack on the Somme, von Falkenhayn began his assault on Verdun in late February 1916. The siege dragged on until July, when the Franco-British offensive was launched. The Somme battle was shorter but just as costly. Although thousands of men died each day, the battle lines were the same in December 1916 as they had been in January. All three countries lost so many young men that it became possible to speak of a "lost generation." German casualties were 350,000 at Verdun and 500,000 on the Somme. French casualties were 540,000 in both battles combined, and Great Britain lost 410,000 along the Somme. Such huge losses could no longer be hidden from the people at home. Joffre was replaced by General Nivelle, von Falkenhayn by Generals Hindenburg and Ludendorff.

The following winter was extremely severe, adding a shortage of food to the grief and suffering and overwork of the civilians. All countries suffered a shortage of consumer goods, but the food problem was most acute in Germany. Germans are famous for their ability to invent ways of cooking a potato. It was the staple of their diet. In 1916 an early frost spoiled the potato crop. Turnips and synthetic foods had to be substituted. The near-starvation of the Turnip Winter was more than the Germans could bear. The political truce ended in the spring in 1917. This was most clearly indicated by a strike by 200,000 Berlin workers on April 16, 1917, the first major wartime strike in the German capitol. The liberals and socialists in the Reichstag also revolted and passed a resolution in July requesting the government to seek a compromise peace. This peace resolution caused the fall of Bethmann-Hollweg, who was not succeeded by conciliatory men but by puppets of the German military. In France, 1917 was the year of mutiny. Early in the year new offensives ordered by Niville had resulted in immense losses without any advance. In May and June one company after another mutinied against its officers, refusing to go to the front lines, some deserting en masse. At the same time, strikes were occurring in Paris and other cities. Newspapers began to demand a compromise peace. In August, Socialists refused to sit in the cabinet. This was the formal end of the *Union sacrée*. The British crisis was not so grave as on the continent, but there was increasing sentiment among the workers for a compromise peace. Also in August, a specially called National Labour Conference endorsed sending representatives to an international socialist conference by a vote of three to one.[4] Of course, much of the labor agitation in western Europe was influenced by events in Russia, where a revolution swept away the czarist regime in March 1917.

The first result of this growing resistance to continued war was the establishment of dictatorships to prosecute the war more efficiently. In all of western Europe new leaders came to the fore who advocated "war to the end." In England the concentration of power in the hands of one man occurred on December 4, 1916, when, with Conservative support, David Lloyd George was able to oust Asquith and become prime minister. He established a War Cabinet of five men to make all crucial decisions. He rarely appeared in Parliament, nor did he feel it necessary for other members of the War Cabinet to do so. Being the dominant figure within the War Cabinet, Lloyd George enjoyed the most extensive powers any British executive had had for a century. The major restraint on his individual power was the continued criticism of the Labour party. During 1917 a revolt of organized labor seemed a possibility when Arthur Henderson resigned from the cabinet because of Lloyd George's refusal to sponsor a compromise peace.

No such obstacles stood in the way of one-man rule in France and Germany. The French legislature turned to Georges Clemenceau, a seventy-six-year-old Radical who stated clearly, "What is my domestic policy? I wage war. What is my foreign policy? I wage war." He never consulted the Chamber of Deputies except to allow them to endorse policies he had already adopted. Among his methods of waging war was to arrest those who publicly advocated a negotiated peace, especially if they were old political enemies. There can be no doubt that he did inspire the French nation to a renewed effort. In Germany, the dictator was a military man, General Ludendorff. After von Falkenhayn's disgrace in 1916, he was replaced as supreme commander by the Tannenberg team, Generals Hindenburg and Ludendorff. Actually, Hindenburg was the commander-in-chief; Ludendorff was supposedly only Hindenburg's quartermaster general. In reality, Ludendorff completely dominated Hindenburg who would not take any action without Ludendorff's approval. The public popularity and prestige of these two was so great that no chancellor dared offend them. If anyone, even the kaiser, tried to act counter to the advice of general headquarters, both heroes would threaten to resign. By 1918 Ludendorff controlled not only the army and the defense industries, but he also managed the national budget, directed the civilian police, and wrote laws.

---

[4] Mayer, *Wilson vs. Lenin*, p. 222.

During the last period of the war, government controls over the civilian population became extremely rigid. Rationing, direction of resources to key industries, and limitations of workers' freedom of movement were common. The British and French governments were burdened by laissez faire traditions and values. They met needs by frantic improvisations— creating new cabinet posts for new industries, creating regulatory agencies to meet each specific shortage of goods rather than dealing systematically with the entire economy. The Germans were, of course, more thorough. Ludendorff even imposed a system of forced labor on the entire population between sixteen and seventy years of age. According to the National Service Law of December 1916, often called the Hindenburg Program, every adult male not in military service was a member of the auxiliary services and could be shifted from industry to industry on orders from the minister of war. In the Second World War all nations adopted similar laws.

Wilson vs. Lenin, 1917–18

The establishment of dictatorships increased the efficiency with which each nation waged war, but it did not prevent the increasing opposition to the war. Socialists formed the core of the peace movements. The outbreak of war had split the socialists in all countries into three factions: social patriots, independent socialists, and maximalists. Obviously, these precise names were not employed everywhere, but the factions were clearly present. The term "social patriots" referred to the majority of socialists who supported their nation's war effort without wavering until 1917. Independent socialists were those who broke with the majority as early as 1915 and declared publicly that they would not support a war for territorial gains. They formed separate organizations in all countries during 1915 in order to propagandize for a compromise peace, for a return to the status quo ante, and for various guarantees against future wars. The third group, maximalists, demanded that the war be exploited to bring about a socialist revolution. Lenin was a leading spokesman of this faction—the only segment of the Second International to remain truly international. The maximalists were minuscule groups until 1917, but they did score propaganda successes with their conferences in Switzerland at Zimmerwald (1915) and Kienthal (1916).

The independents were the most important of these groups because they were the only dissenters from the political truce who offered a viable program of war aims. In England they had an already existing organization at their disposal, the Independent Labour party (ILP). The ILP had been a satellite of the national Labour party before the war but reclaimed its independence when the Labour party expressed support for the war. The ILP merged with some Liberals in 1915 to form the Union for Democratic Control (UDC), which had as its goal the popular control of foreign

policy. Woodrow Wilson was to get many of his ideas from the UDC.[5]
The comparable French organization was the *Comité pour la Reprise des Relations Internationales*. German dissidents worked within the regular SPD until December 1915, when, after refusing to vote for the military budget without an official statement of war aims, they broke away to form the Independent Socialist party (USPD).

All of the peace groups demanded that governments state their war aims publicly. Such demands were branded reckless agitation until December 1916. At that time the independent socialists gained an important ally who made their cause respectable—Woodrow Wilson. In the fall of 1916, Wilson was having a very difficult time with the British, who were violating United States' shipping rights. When Great Britain and France rejected a German proposal to begin talks concerning war aims, Wilson offered to mediate if the various governments would make "an avowal of their respective views as to the terms upon which the war might be concluded." None of the belligerents—not even Germany—welcomed this embarrassing initiative, but the UDC, the *Comité* in France, and even the French Socialist party sent Wilson letters of thanks for his proposal. Wilson encouraged the European left again on January 22, 1917, when he stated before the U.S. Senate that the only peace that the United States would be willing to help enforce would be a peace without victory, a peace among equals, without indemnities or annexations. He also said that a future peace could not be based on a "balance of power" but must be based on a "community of power," which suggested some form of international organization. Unfortunately, the German government's response was to begin unlimited submarine warfare on February 1, 1917. Within a short time, this brought the United States into the war on the side of the Entente powers.

Just as Wilson was strengthening the peace forces, they received another boost from the March Revolution in Russia. The czarist regime was replaced by a liberal-democratic provisional government composed of the leaders of the Duma. The provisional government immediately announced that it would continue the Russian war effort, but it had a competitor for power, the Petrograd Soviet, which demanded that Russia sign a separate peace. The Soviet was a spontaneous creation of a coalition of socialist and labor union forces that functioned as a rival government in the Petrograd area. As summer progressed, it established contacts with soviets (councils) in other cities and became the organizational expression of the extreme left of Russian politics. The Petrograd Soviet denounced the war as imperialist and expansionist and put pressure on the provisional government to announce its war aims. Under this pressure, the provisional government developed a brief explanation of its participation in the war which became known as the Petrograd Formula. It stated that "the purpose

---

[5] Ibid., pp. 334–39.

of free Russia was not the domination of other peoples . . . but the establishment of a permanent peace based on the self-determination of peoples."[6] Therefore, Russia became not only the first belligerent to repudiate territorial gains promised Russia by secret treaties but also the first to speak of the "self-determination" of peoples as a basis for peace. The independent socialists and maximalists throughout Europe responded to the Petrograd Formula by calling for similar statements from their governments.

The March Revolution had its greatest effect on the peace forces in Germany. Virtually overnight the social patriots had lost their excuse to support the war. Now Germany could be pointed to as the most reactionary regime in Europe, and the German liberals as well as the socialists realized the psychological advantage this gave Germany's enemies. This was a major reason for the passage of a peace resolution by the Reichstag in July 1917. Another reason was the obvious failure of submarine warfare, which, instead of ending the war in six months as the military had promised, had brought the United States into the war. The key phrases in the peace resolution were taken directly from the peace program of the USPD. It called for a "peace of understanding" based on no annexations, an end to tariff barriers, freedom of the seas, and the creation of an international organization for the legal settlement of disputes between nations. These terms differed from the Petrograd Formula most importantly in the absence of a plea for self-determination. With the Austro-Hungarian empire as Germany's only major ally, the Reichstag could not endorse the self-determination of the Slavic peoples. Still, the Reichstag majority had taken a momentous step. It had distinguished itself from the military dictatorship that insisted on a war of conquest. After July 1917, the forces desiring parliamentary democracy were identified with the demand for a compromise peace; the military and the monarchy were identified with the prolongation of the war and were blamed for the suffering the German nation had to endure in 1917 and 1918 as a result of the tightening British blockade.

The second Russian revolution, the Bolshevik Revolution in October, was another blow to the conservative leadership of Germany, France, and Great Britain. The first Bolshevik act was to issue two decrees. One called for the distribution of all land among the peasants. The other was a peace decree announcing the Bolsheviks' intention to seek an immediate and separate peace with Germany. The peace decree appealed to the citizens of the belligerent states to end the war and make a "just and democratic peace." This was only the opening shot of a propaganda offensive by the Soviets. They had no army with which to spread the revolution; so they used the idea of an immediate peace to encourage revolutionary forces in other countries. When the Germans accepted the Russian pro-

---

[6] Ibid., p. 75.

Successful
revolutionaries:
Lenin and Stalin
in 1922
(Courtesy of UPI)

posal for peace negotiations at Brest-Litovsk, they set the stage for a
carefully planned peace campaign. The Soviets insisted that the talks be
open to the press and thereby to the public. The Russian representative,
Adolf Joffe, presented six points to serve as the basis for an agreement.
In general these were the same as the UDC, the Committee, and the
USPD endorsed: no annexations, no indemnities, self-determination of
peoples of the Hapsburg Empire. But the Bolsheviks added a demand
for self-determination for colonial populations as well. While none of
the peace groups in the West had suggested this, Lenin made this championship of the colonial peoples a central theme in his public diplomacy.

The challenge of Brest-Litovsk had to be answered by the belligerents
if they hoped to retain the support of their workers and soldiers. The
German military rulers alone did not feel a need to compromise. The
Bolsheviks had refused to sign the treaty dictated to them by the Germans
at Brest-Litovsk. Therefore, General Hoffman, the military officer conducting the negotiations for Germany broke off the talks and resumed the
invasion of Russia. The Russians capitulated in March, and Germany
annexed vast expanses of territory. In direct response to this obvious
violation of the spirit of the peace resolution, the workers of Germany
rebelled in January 1918. The strikers numbered 400,000 in Berlin and
one million in all of Germany. They were demonstrating not only against
the expansionist policy that would prolong the war but also in sympathy
with the first socialist state—Soviet Russia. Ludendorff ordered the strike
movement crushed without mercy. More tinder was thrown on the revolutionary fire which was to consume Germany in November.

The Allies could not be so cavalier in their treatment of the peace movement. Lloyd George became concerned when the Labour party adopted the peace program of the UDC. Therefore, when he spoke to the Trades Union Congress on January 5, 1918, he accepted the principles espoused by the left. But, still, his speech was vague and noncommittal, carefully phrased to appease the left without surrendering to it. All that was clear was his acceptance of the basic principles of a peace program that he had been denouncing for two years.

Three days after Lloyd George's speech, Woodrow Wilson enunciated his Fourteen Points. In the introductory section of the speech, Wilson summarized the circumstances that led him to develop such a peace program. These remarks reveal that it was a practical reaction to the international situation intended to prevent the European left from turning to Russia. Wilson noted in his second sentence that "parleys have been in progress at Brest-Litovsk" and that these talks required all belligerents to define their war aims. Wilson stated that "the Russian representatives presented not only a perfectly definite statement of principles" but also a program of concrete applications.[7] Accordingly, Wilson had drawn up his program: "They call to us to say what it is that we desire; in what, if anything, our spirit differs from theirs; and I believe that the people of the United States would wish me to respond. . . ."

Wilson's principal points were precisely those of the Soviets at Brest-Litovsk, of the UDC, and of the German peace resolution. But Wilson went further than those in certain areas. Most Wilsonian were his emphasis on disarmament after the war and the establishment of a League of Nations. Most revolutionary, however, were his references to the class conflict within Germany. He said that as a preliminary to negotiations the Allies would have to know whether Germany's representatives spoke "for the Reichstag majority or the military party," clearly implying that the United States would not negotiate as long as "the military party" was dominant. Wilson was offering an alternative to the Bolsheviks. He was trying to retain the allegiance of the social patriots and gain the allegiance of the independent socialists by giving them war aims which they could support. He was also trying to strengthen the parliamentary democrats in Germany while weakening both the military and the socialist revolutionaries. In both of these attempts he was successful; but he was aided greatly by the policies of the German military leadership.

In the final Russo-German settlement, the Soviets were forced to surrender one-fourth of the territory of prewar Russia, 44 percent of its population, 27 percent of its revenue, 75 percent of its coal, and 73 percent of its iron. This was, however, a Pyrrhic victory for the German leaders. The Russian campaign occupied troops and arms in the east just when Ludendorff was launching his last major push in the west, a final attempt to break through the Franco-British front before the United

---

[7] Ibid., pp. 353–54.

States forces could be thrown into the battle. Although this was serious, the diplomatic and political effects were disastrous. The French and British determination to win was strengthened when they saw the manner in which Germany dealt with a defeated foe. Woodrow Wilson became convinced that the militarists were so powerful in Germany that the German army would have to be rendered helpless before peace could be discussed. This encouraged Wilson to throw all of his energy into the war effort instead of the campaign for a compromise peace. Perhaps worst of all from Ludendorff's viewpoint, the Russian campaign not only alienated the German working classes from the war effort but also from the prewar social hierarchy which had permitted the military such strength. After Brest-Litovsk a revolution was almost a foregone conclusion.

Ludendorff and Hindenburg launched their final series of offensives in March 1918. Five major offensives brought the German troops within thirty-seven miles of Paris. By July, however, the French general Foch, who was designated supreme Allied Commander, had large numbers of Americans and several hundred tanks at his disposal. The tanks made trench warfare obsolete, and the Americans' arrival gave the Allies a vast numeric superiority. After July 18 the Germans were retreating all along the front. Unable to establish a line of defense, Ludendorff, on September 28, literally ordered the establishment of a democratic government that could sue for peace on the basis of Wilson's Fourteen Points.

Within days Germany became a parliamentary democracy. The kaiser was reduced to the role of the British monarch. Prince Max of Baden, a nobleman known to politicians (but not to the public) as a liberal, became the first chancellor of the new regime and wrote Wilson asking for an armistice. Throughout October Wilson and Prince Max exchanged notes defining the terms of the armistice. Finally, all was arranged. On November 8, 1918, representatives of the German government met with General Foch in a railway car in the forest of Compiegn. After three days of negotiation, an armistice was signed and the fighting officially stopped.

While the armistice was being negotiated, there was a revolution in Germany. Strikes, demonstrations and riots throughout Germany forced the SPD leaders to declare Germany a republic to prevent the Spartacists—the revolutionary wing of the SPD—from declaring a soviet state. Out of these circumstances was to grow the nationalist lie that it was the republic that had surrendered, while Germany still had a strong army in the field.

The Fruits of War: Revolution in Russia and Germany

The consequences of defeat in World War I were institutional, economic, and social collapse. The monarchies of Germany, Russia, and

Austria-Hungary, discredited by the hardships of the war experience, were overthrown. If the conservative elements in these countries entered the war believing that a victorious military effort would strengthen their position in domestic politics, they discovered that defeat led to revolution. The three revolutions developed similarly. The initial challenge to the monarchy was made by liberals with the support of social democrats. The liberals established a provisional government which granted political freedoms and called for the election of a constituent assembly to decide on the final form of the new regime. Socialists then gained dominance in the provisional government and were forced by the leftward movement of political opinion to declare a republic. But, like the liberals, the social democrats continued to postpone any profound reforms until after a constituent assembly could meet. The final stage of the revolutionary process was a struggle for power between social democrats and revolutionary socialists. In Russia, the revolutionaries won; in Germany and Austria, the social democrats destroyed the revolutionaries with the cooperation of conservative elements of society.

The czarist regime was the first to fall. Instead of learning from the experience of 1905 and attempting either to avoid another war or to prepare the economy for war, the Russian autocracy had tried to suppress demands for change. Consequently, Russia entered World War I with all the inefficiencies that had been displayed in 1905. The army was still poorly trained, equipped, and led. The state's finances immediately collapsed. The economy was incapable of producing on the level necessary for modern warfare. Most ominous for the czarist government was the fact that, because the imperial bureaucracy was incapable of mobilizing the empire for war, democratic institutions gradually replaced it. Local elected councils formed regional federations to supply medical care for soldiers, aid refugees, and mobilize industry. The Duma established five committees to supervise various areas of the war effort. These committees slowly became real governmental ministries and bypassed the regular bureaucracy. The Duma also gained popular support by its outspoken criticism of Rasputin, a religious mystic who had a psychic hold on the czarina. Finally, the army's brutal tactics in dealing with domestic unrest arising from the war only intensified opposition to the regime.

These problems were accentuated by Rasputin's influence on the czarina, who in turn dominated Nicholas II. It was resentment of Rasputin, his intrigues, and his orgies that led to the first violent action against the regime. In December 1916, some liberal nobles assassinated the monk. On March 7, 1917, the grumbling dissatisfaction of women standing in a bread line in Petrograd burst into a demonstration against the government. The protest spread across the city and into the provinces in a matter of days. Soldiers refused to fire on the crowds. The czar abdicated on March 12. Liberals of the Duma quickly formed a provisional government, headed by Prince Lvov. They hoped to establish a constitutional monarchy but were forced by public opinion to accept the czar's abdication. Still, they refused to designate the regime a republic before a constituent assembly could be elected.

From the first the authority of the provisional government was challenged by the Petrograd Soviet. Both bodies had been organized on the same day, March 12,* but the czar, when he abdicated, recognized the provisional government as the legal authority. Russia's allies soon did the same. This government only existed, however, at the sufferance of the Petrograd Soviet. A spontaneous assemblage of "people's representatives," the Soviet at first contained more soldiers than workers or politicians. The Soviet's leaders, though, were socialist Duma members, returned political prisoners or exiles, and professional men. The Petrograd Soviet was the top of a national pyramid of soviets. At the end of August there were 600 local soviets throughout Russia. They constituted a separate and rival administration to the provisional government. Indeed, in some areas, the local soviet was the only governmental body. The power of the Soviet was demonstrated by the successful application of its famous Order No. 1, which required the election of army officers by the troops and announced that military orders of the provisional government should be obeyed only if they did not conflict with Soviet orders. The actual effect of this was to promote the disintegration of military discipline. Many officers who resisted were shot by their men. Order No. 1, more than any other act, illustrated the duality of power in Russia from the March Revolution to the November Revolution.

The conflict between government and Soviet was intensified by Lenin's arrival in Petrograd in April. For years a political exile, Lenin was the authoritarian leader of the most extreme faction of Russian socialism—the Bolsheviks. Shortly after he arrived, he announced the Bolshevik program in the April Theses. In essence, he argued that Russian soldiers had no responsibility to continue fighting, because Russia was still governed by a bourgeois regime. The revolution was not ended, he contended, but only in a period of transition. It would soon pass from the bourgeois democratic phase to the socialist stage, and all socialists should try to speed that transition. Finally, Lenin demanded all power be given to the soviets and all land to the peasants. The leaders of both the provisional government and the Petrograd Soviet dismissed Lenin's Theses as mere rhetoric, but huge crowds massed before the Bolshevik headquarters to hear Lenin constantly repeat, "All power to the soviets! All land to the peasants! End the war now!"

During the summer and fall the social structure of Russia was altered by the masses with very little political leadership. Soldiers' committees

---

* All dates are new style.

destroyed the military chain of command, and millions of soldiers deserted. Peasants distributed the land of large estates among themselves. This movement gained momentum as peasants discovered that there were no local authorities to hinder them. Workers' committees carried out a similar policy by seizing factories. State authority having disappeared, this revolution from below was inevitable. While the provisional government deplored it, Lenin and the Bolsheviks recognized its inevitability and encouraged it.

For this reason, the Bolsheviks were considered especially dangerous by the government. When a spontaneous uprising occurred in July, although the Bolsheviks first tried to stop it before joining it, the government used the opportunity to cripple them. The Bolsheviks had clearly not tried to seize power, only to cash in on a genuine demonstration of discontent on the part of a war-weary populace. The liberal government, however, issued warrants for the leading Bolsheviks. Most were arrested. Lenin fled to Finland. Others went underground in Petrograd.

The cause of the July Uprising had been a major, but futile, offensive by the army. Two individuals became prominent during the offensive: Alexander Kerensky and General Kornilov. Kerensky, as minister of war, toured the front to whip up enthusiasm for the war. After the offensive failed, General Kornilov was made commander-in-chief of the army. About the same time, Kerensky, a Social Revolutionary, became prime minister and until September lived with the twin threats of a revolution from the left led by the Petrograd Soviet and a counterrevolution from the right led by Kornilov. Finally, Kornilov marched on Petrograd, hoping to establish a military dictatorship. In desperation, Kerensky turned to the Soviet, arming the Soviet's supporters and freeing Bolshevik leaders to help rouse the people against Kornilov. An armed clash was avoided when the Soviet's agents convinced Kornilov's soldiers to refuse to support the counterrevolution and desert.

Kerensky emerged from this crisis apparently stronger than ever, but his strength was illusory. While the right was defeated, the Kornilov affair had greatly strengthened the left. Now the Soviet was armed, and the Bolsheviks were free to agitate. The Bolsheviks soon obtained a majority in the Petrograd and Moscow soviets. In October, Lenin returned secretly to Petrograd. In a meeting of the Bolshevik party's Central Committee which lasted ten hours, he demanded an immediate seizure of power. Leon Trotsky was chosen to head the Military Revolutionary Committee that would execute the coup d'état. On the night of November 7, troops loyal to the Bolsheviks seized the nerve centers of the capitol—railroad stations, bridges, the state bank, the central post office, the telephone exchange, and other public buildings. There was little opposition. The Winter Palace, where the provisional government was meeting, was taken after some farcical use of the artillery of the Peter and Paul Fortress across the river. Of the thirty to thirty-five shells fired, only two hit the Palace. The Women's Legion defending the Palace was easily overwhelmed; while Kerensky escaped in a car belonging to the American Embassy.

While the firing continued, Lenin issued two major decrees that rallied many Russians to the Bolshevik banner. A land decree abolished the private ownership of large estates and called for the administration of that land by local peasant soviets. This merely gave government sanction to a fait accompli in most areas. A peace decree called for an immediate and separate peace with Germany. There was no immediate attempt to establish a dictatorship, only to exercise the normal authority of a legal government. A fifteen-member Council of People's Commissars was established to act as a ministry. It was predominantly Bolshevik, but other parties were represented. Members of the Socialist Revolutionary party held seats until March 1918. Dissension among the members of this council was the rule rather than the exception. Indeed, how *do* doctrinaire revolutionaries—some of them having lived in exile for fifteen years—govern a country? No one was sure. Everyone improvised.

The revolution was completed in January 1918. After allowing a constituent assembly to be elected and to meet for one day, the Council dissolved it. Therefore the Council and, through it, the Bolshevik party, were the only authorities in the areas controlled by revolutionary forces.

Lenin believed the survival of the Revolution in Russia depended on the success of revolutions in western Europe which would remove the threat of a capitalist coalition against socialist Russia. Other revolutions did occur, but these were not the kind Lenin desired. In most cases, liberals or social democrats replaced the prewar monarchy and then crushed the communists who tried to establish a soviet state. Germany is the prime example.

When Prince Max of Baden formed a government based on the Reichstag majority, several leaders of the SPD were included in the Cabinet. With this democratic foundation, Prince Max opened negotiations with Wilson on the conditions of the armistice. At this time the American president made one of his gravest diplomatic blunders. He demanded that any armistice provide for the disarming of the German army. Max had to agree, but this would make it impossible for the Germans to negotiate, to bargain. They would be helpless before the western Allies. A dictated peace was the inevitable result. The demand also had a great impact on German domestic politics. The military high command refused to accept disarmament on October 24, and workers, soldiers, and sailors thought the generals were still in control. The September Revolution from above had been virtually invisible from below. Prince Max was, after all, a prince.

The November Revolution, then, was sparked by a fear that the military would continue the war. The revolt began in the Baltic fleet stationed at Kiel. The naval command decided to try a fairly safe raid on the British coast, but the sailors thought this was an attempt to prolong the war. A mutiny occurred on October 29 and 30. When officers tried to restore order by mass arrests, the result was more agitation. On November 4 the sailors seized the Kiel city hall and elected a sailor's soviet. The workers of Kiel joined the revolt and elected their own soviet. When the rebellion spread to army reservists stationed throughout Germany, it appeared that the Russian Revolution would be repeated. The aims of the revolutionary movement were not, however, primarily political or social. Rather, the revolt was a protest against the continuation of the war. Inevitably, it gradually broadened into an attack on the military and the monarchy. In Bavaria, soldiers ousted military authorities and established a socialist government. Everywhere the SPD emerged as the local leaders of the revolution. On November 9 the pace of events quickened. Massive strikes in Berlin against Prince Max led to the Social Democrats' withdrawal from his cabinet. Max then resigned, and Friedrich Ebert, SPD leader, became the acting head of government. Ebert was still willing to accept a parliamentary monarchy, but demonstrations in the streets forced him to announce a republic. The next day, November 10, the Berlin Workers' and Soldiers' Council approved his decision and elected Ebert chairman of the Council of the Representatives of the People, the name given the revolutionary government. Actually, the SPD had not acted too soon; for the Spartacists, soon to become the German Communist party, had planned to declare a soviet socialist state on November 11. Ebert's cabinet was dominated by the SPD and USPD, but deputies of the Center party and Progressive party were also included. Almost immediately, General Hindenburg swore his allegiance to the new government. He preferred a middle-class republic to the danger of a more radical revolution.

There was still a great deal of suffering in Germany after the armistice was signed. The Allies continued their blockade on food to Germany until March 1919. This made the social situation explosive during the 1918–19 winter. In his fear of a Bolshevik revolution, Ebert turned to the army and the Free Corps to maintain order. The Free Corps were bands of exsoldiers, equipped by the regular army, who sold their services to the state. These domestic mercenaries not only loved violence; they were antisocialist, antidemocratic, and reveled in the military life. Depending on such men was ruinous enough, but Ebert also made the mistake, suicidal for democracy in Germany, of appealing to the Officer Corps, the imperial administration, and the imperial judiciary to help him restore order. Of course, Ebert alone cannot be blamed for these errors of judgment. The majority of the SPD preferred a conservative restoration of order to a revolutionary transformation of society. As Kerensky had appealed to the left to protect him from the counterrevolution, Ebert appealed to the right to protect his government from the revolution.

The forces of revolution had not been satisfied by the establishment of the republic, and they were even more angered by Ebert's refusal to declare immediate and sweeping social reforms. The final clash came as a result of Ebert's attempt to replace the Berlin police chief, who was a USPD member and friendly with the Spartacists, with a man more inclined to support the SPD. This move on January 4, 1919, was met by a call to revolt by both Spartacists and the USPD. Workers, soldiers and sailors responded. The streets of Berlin were filled with demonstrations against the government. Ebert gave the antisocialist military free rein. Both regular army units and the vicious Free Corps were used. Artillery fired in the streets. The USPD and Spartacist supporters were shot summarily. On January 15, after the revolt had ended, Karl Liebknecht and Rosa Luxemburg, Spartacists and outstanding intellects of international socialism, were arrested and immediately murdered by cavalry officers. Sporadic uprisings continued through the spring. In March the SPD minister of war, Gustav Noske, ordered that anyone combating the government should be shot on the spot. About 1,200 individuals were killed in Berlin alone in fulfillment of these orders. By the end of spring 1919, Germany had been saved from bolshevism, but she had been saved by the same antidemocratic elements which fourteen years later would prefer nazism to democracy.

Revolution in Eastern Europe

The revolutions which shattered the Austro-Hungarian empire were of several types. The German model was repeated in Vienna, but there and in the successor states the dynamic force was nationalism and not socialism.[8] It must be remembered that the successor states still had agrarian, preindustrial economies. The vast majority of the population were peasants, and a few landed aristocrats formed the governing class. There was, of course, no urban working class to form the basis for socialist parties. There was no bourgeoisie to support liberalism except in German-Austria and among the Czechs of Bohemia. The middle class that did exist was different from the western European bourgeoisie in that they were not involved in commerce or industry, leaving these to the Jews. Moreover, they were not the product of upward mobility from the peasantry but were the unfortunate scions of aristocratic families who had been forced off the land by economic forces and compelled to enter

---

[8] Hugh Seton-Watson, *Eastern Europe Between the Wars,* 3d ed. (Hamden, Conn.: Archon Books, 1962).

the state bureaucracy or the professions. Therefore, they retained aristocratic values rather than adopting the liberal politics of the West.

The war had brought pressures to bear on the ancient Austro-Hungarian empire that were too heavy to be borne. As the war lengthened, representatives of the various national minorities of the empire—Czechs, Croates, Poles—set up governments-in-exile to plan for the day when the Hapsburgs would fall. When the Entente forces launched an offensive through Bulgaria in September 1918, even the imperial court admitted the inevitable. On October 18 Emperor Charles, hoping to save at least his throne, announced his willingness to recognize the freedom of the Czechs and to allow the formation of a Slavic state within the empire. The Entente troops ignored his statement and continued their advance. The German members of the Reichsrat, the Austrian legislature, decided to take control of events. They met on October 21 and declared themselves the provisional assembly of the state of "German-Austria." The form of the regime— monarchy or republic—was to be decided by a constituent assembly to be elected in February 1919. However, the November Revolution in Berlin forced the Austrians also to establish a republic. Emperor Charles abdicated on November 11, thus ending centuries of Hapsburg rule.

One of the first acts of the provisional assembly was to recognize the right of self-determination for the nationalities of the empire. In fact, the majority of the "revolutionists" hoped that they could safeguard their Germanic culture by eventually forming a union with Germany. This idea was firmly rejected by Clemenceau at Versailles. He even insisted that the name "German-Austria" be changed to "Austria."

The first year of Austria's politics was dominated by the struggle between the Social Democrats and the Austrian Communist party. On the very day a Social Democrat announced the republic, Communists tried to storm the parliament building. The Social Democrats, led by Karl Renner, as the SPD in Germany were more interested in political reform than in socialist revolution. Renner had two major weapons at his disposal: the soviets and the Volkswehr. The well-organized Social Democrats controlled Austria's labor unions, and through the unions, they obtained majorities in the soviets, which had appeared in the fall of 1918. The Volkswehr was a volunteer army very closely resembling the Free Corps of Germany. Professional soldiers, now unemployed, were hired to defend the middle-class republic against the communist onslaught.

The strength of these weapons was tested on April 17, 1919, when the Volkswehr was used to crush a Communist attack on the parliament building. Following this confrontation, the Communists tried to persuade the workers' soviets of Vienna to condemn the government's action. This move failed because of the Social Democratic majority in the soviets. The final battle occurred when the Allied leaders became convinced that Austria was in danger of "falling to communism" and encouraged Renner to use the Volkswehr to remove that danger. On the night of June 14–15, a total of 115 communist leaders were arrested. The Volkswehr occupied Vienna, and army units loyal to the Communists were confined to their barracks. This coup was the last battle; the revolution had been defeated.

The military defeats of 1918 had also led to a social democratic revolution in Hungary. Count Michael Karolyi organized a national council of liberals and socialists on October 24, 1918. When the Budapest garrison rallied to Karolyi, Emperor Charles recognized a fait accompli and named Karolyi prime minister. Karolyi immediately announced plans for a sweeping land reform and began by turning his own 50,000-acre estate over to the peasants who lived there. But Karolyi lost prestige and support because he was unable to prevent the secession of the several national minorities from Hungary. The Big Four at Versailles caused his final downfall by insisting that he agree to the territorial demands of Poland, Czechoslovakia, Rumania, and Serbia. The loss of large chunks of territory discredited the democratic regime in the eyes of the Hungarian nobility and bourgeoisie at the very time the threat of a Soviet revolution was increasing. Instead of agreeing to the Entente demand, Karolyi resigned on March 20, 1919, and welcomed the Communist government of Bela Kun.

Kun came to office as the symbol of national frustration. The army, the nobility, and the bourgeoisie were frustrated over the loss of territory. Workers and soldiers were desirous of social reforms. Peasants demanded land reform. All wanted the Allies' blockade on food to Hungary to be lifted. Unfortunately, largely because of international circumstances, Kun was unable to solve any of these problems. Twice, Rumanian armies, encouraged and aided by the Allies, invaded Hungary to topple the communist regime and to extirpate the revolution from central Europe. The first invasion was repulsed by a popular uprising. Peasants and workers rallied to their government. The military leadership, inspired by nationalism, remained loyal to Kun. The second invasion, however, was successful. Kun had alienated his supporters. He had failed to give land to the peasants but instead had tried to organize collective farms. The military had deserted him in favor of conservative politicians who were forming a government under the protection of the Rumanians. Therefore, when the Rumanians invaded again in August 1919, the communist regime had no defenders. Budapest was occupied; the Communists fled or were killed; and a conservative dictatorship was established by Admiral Horthy.

Horthy claimed to be acting as regent for Emperor Charles, but when Charles tried to claim his throne, Horthy refused to recognize his legitimacy. This made the dictator not only an admiral without a sea, but also a regent without a king. Horthy remained dictator of Hungary until World War II.

Throughout eastern Europe the Hungarian pattern was imitated by each of the new states. A nationalist revolution would lead to the establishment of a liberal democratic regime followed by a conservative dictatorship. In Poland, General Pilsudski carried out a military coup in 1925. King Alexander of Yugoslavia established a royal dictatorship in 1929 to prevent civil war between Serbs and Croats, and never rescinded it. Rumania's dictator was Carol II, who from 1930 fashioned his regime on that of Mussolini. In 1924 the Bulgarian army killed 20,000 peasants and workers who had supported the reformist government of Alexander Stamboliiski. King Boris then transformed Bulgaria's parliamentary monarchy into a military dictatorship. Only Czechoslovakia did not succumb to conservative reaction. This must be attributed to the large bourgeoisie of Bohemia and the high literacy rate among the Czechoslovak peasants and working classes. Where such social bases of democracy do not exist, there can be no democracy.

Versailles and Conservatism

While revolutions swept away the old order in central and eastern Europe, twenty-seven nations met at the Versailles Palace to write a peace settlement. The revolutions constantly impinged on negotiations among the Big Four—Wilson, Lloyd George, Clemenceau, and Orlando, the Italian premier. Not only did they have to decide what to do about the civil war in Russia, they were also faced with strong communist forces in Bavaria, Vienna, Hungary, northern Italy, and elsewhere. There was even a workers' revolt in Glasgow, Scotland, during which the red flag of revolution was briefly raised over the city hall and a soviet was organized. Several secondary figures at the peace conference noted in their diaries that everyone was aware of the race between peace and revolution.

Therefore, two political facts must be kept in mind when attempting to understand the Versailles negotiations. On the one hand, the specter of the Bolshevik Revolution floated over the *defeated* countries and created a sense of urgency among the participants of the conference which would not have otherwise existed. On the other hand, a conservative resurgence had occurred in all of the *victor* nations during the war, and the conservative legislatures of each country contributed as much to the final form of the treaty as did the negotiators. Throughout the conference, the legislators were demanding a peace of revenge and victory. For example, when Lloyd George and Clemenceau appeared to be conceding to Wilson on reparations, both received petitions from their conservative parliamentary supporters demanding that Germany pay the full costs of the war.

In Great Britain and the United States, national elections coincided with the end of fighting in Europe. Lloyd George, correctly guessing that the national coalition which had governed during the war would profit politically from Germany's defeat, called an election for December 1918. The Conservatives, led by Bonar Law, used the campaign to drown demands for social reforms with jingoist declarations that Germay should pay the full costs of the war to all the Entente powers. It was not Lloyd George but one of his overzealous Conservative supporters who promised "We'll squeeze the orange till the pips squeak!" Lloyd George actually began the campaign by taking a moderate stand on reparations, but being a total politician, he realized that the British public was reacting warmly to the demands that Germany pay. He soon joined the hue and cry, and his political instincts were proved accurate. The coalition of Conservatives and Lloyd George-Liberals won 500 of 707 seats in Commons. The Asquith-Liberals almost disappeared, while Labour made gains. The new Commons was filled with businessmen, and Lloyd George bitterly referred to his Conservative allies, who now controlled him, as the "Associated Chambers of Commerce."

Conservatives in the United States were not demanding concessions from Germany, but they did extend their opposition to Wilson's domestic reforms to include his idealistic peace program. They especially opposed his concept of a League of Nations which violated America's tradition of nonentanglement in European affairs. There was a congressional election in November 1918, which encouraged this criticism. Wilson made a disastrous mistake when he stated that the elections would be a test of his mandate from the people. When the Republicans swept the election, Wilson was placed in a very awkward diplomatic position. An indication of the sentiment which led to the Republican victory came from within Wilson's administration. In early 1919 Attorney General A. Mitchell Palmer ordered all aliens *with communist sympathies* be deported. Such a phrase could include many and did. Three thousand individuals were arrested in simultaneous raids throughout the country. There were thousands more on the attorney general's list. Although Wilson could disapprove of Palmer's activities, he could not ignore the sentiment that had condoned the Red Scare.

The leaders of the Latin nations had no preconference elections to contend with, but the political forces in France and Italy were similar to those among the Anglo-Saxons. Clemenceau was himself dedicated to a peace of revenge. He hoped to see Germany punished for 1870 and weakened so that it could not threaten France. Even Clemenceau was outdone, however, by Marshal Foch, commander-in-chief of the French army, who would have liked to split Germany into several small states. The Conservative legislature was also bent on revenge. The minister of finance even refused to submit a budget of taxes for 1919, arguing that he expected money collected from Germany to cover the government's expenditures. The Italian premier, Vittorio Orlando, was equally pressured. His cabinet depended on Conservative votes for its majority. Therefore, Orlando, a Liberal, was the captive of nationalist forces and especially of Sidney Sonnino, his foreign minister and the Conservative leader.

It was Sonnino, not Orlando, who drew up the Italian territorial claims presented at Versailles.

In opposing the advocates of a peace of conquest, Wilson had the support only of the Socialist parties and the labor unions of Europe. These leftists demonstrated en masse when Wilson visited France, Great Britain, and Italy before the conference opened. They realized that a peace of victory would increase the popularity of conservatives domestically; therefore, they tried to pressure their governments to accept Wilson's terms. But Wilson's supporters, no matter how numerous in the streets, did not have the votes in parliament, which was the real power to which the negotiators at Versailles had to respond.

So Wilson was almost alone at Versailles. Even some of his closest advisors—such as Colonel House—were willing to sacrifice Wilson's program in order to achieve a settlement. Still, Wilson was not without bargaining power. The United States alone had the economic power to feed and clothe a war-ravaged continent as well as to finance reconstruction in France, Belgium, Italy, and elsewhere. It was also to his advantage that he was the best informed man at Versailles on problems outside western Europe. This was largely due to the work of the Inquiry, a large staff of intellectuals that had been doing research on the problems of a peace settlement for months before the armistice. Finally, Wilson was the one man who comprehended the true significance of the Russian Revolution. The Inquiry had correctly informed him that it was an understandable rebellion against oppression and that more of the same type of revolutions could be expected in eastern Europe if the area were not stabilized quickly. Yet, Wilson's own perspective was even broader than this. He realized that the world was entering a new revolutionary period similar to that which followed the French Revolution.[9] He hoped to control these revolutions, so they might result in liberal democratic regimes—a policy still pursued by liberals in the United States. Therefore, Wilson, more than Lloyd George or Clemenceau, was able to view the peace settlement as a whole, rather than being limited by particular points of national interest. This was important; for while the Big Four debated, a civil war raged in Russia; Gandhi was beginning his campaign for Indian independence; the Japanese were establishing themselves as the dominant power in Northern China; and Kemal Ataturk was seizing power in Turkey. All were in flux. The international system had come unhinged, and four men were trying to put it together again.

The peace conference opened in Paris on January 18, 1919, and lasted six months. The first casualty was one of Wilson's most cherished ideals— open diplomacy. Only six times did all participating nations meet. The

---

[9] Arno J. Mayer, *Politics and Diplomacy of Peace-Making: Containment and Counterrevolution at Versailles 1918–1919* (New York: Alfred A. Knopf, 1967), pp. 4–5.

real business of the conference was conducted in closed sessions attended only by major powers. At first this included ten nations, but that number was soon reduced to the Big Four. On orders of these four men food was given to or withheld from starving people in Germany, Austria, Russia, Bulgaria, and elsewhere; the communist government of Hungary was overthrown by Rumanian troops; aid was given to the counterrevolutionary forces in Russia; and colonies were exchanged in Africa.

At Wilson's insistence the first topic on the agenda was the establishment of a League of Nations, "the one issue that took precedence over all the others in Wilson's plans and purposes."[10] But his concept of the League was in conflict with French ideas. The French desired a league of victors armed to maintain territorial boundaries and to prevent the rearming of Germany. This plan implied the presence of American troops in Europe. Wilson hoped for a league of equals including Germany, based on legal principles and the enlightened cooperation of all countries. Because of his firmness and his willingness to compromise on other issues, Wilson was able to gain adoption of his concept of the League.

Wilson and Clemenceau clashed again on the terms of the German treaty. Clemenceau was guided by the need for French security against another invasion. France had been invaded by Germans twice in thirty years, and Germany's population was 70 million compared to France's 40 million. At first Clemenceau suggested a plan urged upon him by Marshal Foch. Foch argued that the Rhineland should be separated from Germany and be an independent state permanently occupied by French troops. To this end, the French army organized a bogus "separationist movement." Wilson violently opposed any partition of Germany, warning that there was no better way to aid revolutionaries in central Europe. Clemenceau accused him of being pro-German. This led to one of the most acute crises of the conference. Wilson ordered that the *George Washington*, the presidential ship, be prepared to return to the United States. Faced with this threat, the French began to seek accommodations. It was agreed that the Allies would occupy the Rhineland for fifteen years and would then withdraw if Germany lived up to its commitments under other sections of the treaty. These commitments included limitations on the size of German military forces and on the production of military equipment.

The debate over the amount of reparations and indemnities Germany would be required to pay once again set the president against Clemenceau. On this topic Lloyd George supported the French. The European Allies insisted that Germany pay the full costs of the war to each country. Wilson just as adamantly argued that Germany should only be responsible for "civilian damages"—homes, farm houses, factories. He also hoped

---

[10] Arthur S. Link, *Wilson the Diplomatist* (Chicago: Quadrangle Books, Inc., 1965), p. 119.

Clemenceau, hat lifted, with Woodrow Wilson and Lloyd George, leaves a session at Versailles. (Courtesy of Roger-Viollet)

that a final sum could be set by the conference that was in accordance with Germany's ability to pay. On this issue Wilson suffered his worst and most obvious defeat. No sum was set, and the scope of "reparations" was extended far beyond what Wilson felt justified. One example was that Germany had to pay for the pensions of French and British soldiers. A reparations committee was established to collect yearly payments and to determine eventually the extent of German indebtedness. To guarantee payment, French troops were to be stationed in the Rhineland for twenty years. Justification of these reparations was contained in a so-called "War Guilt Clause," Article 231 of the treaty. It stated that Germany accepted full responsibility for all damages resulting from the war. It was this clause that created the strongest German resentment toward the treaty.

The Italian representatives did not play a major role in shaping the German Treaty, perhaps because they had their own claims to press and did not want to offend any of the other powers. Italian aspirations were embodied in the secret Treaty of London which had enticed Italy into the war in 1915. The most prized territories involved were granted to Italy, but Sonnino also demanded the Adriatic port Fiume, the only port of the new state of Yugoslavia. A variety of arguments were used to justify the annexation of Fiume, but Wilson insisted that this annexation would violate the principles of self-determination and of nationality. When Wilson could not sway Orlando and Sonnino, he tried to bypass them by appealing directly to the Italian people. He gave an interview to the Parisian press in which he outlined his stand and denounced Italy's claims as blatant violations of the Fourteen Points. This attempt to erode Orlando's political support at home infuriated the Italian premier, who immediately made a dramatic exit from the conference and returned to Rome. Wilson, however, could not be budged. Orlando later rejoined the conference and the Fiume question remained unresolved. Wilson had protected his principles.

As the controversy over Fiume had pointed out, questions of national boundaries presented great difficulties for the Big Four. This was especially true in eastern Europe, where several new states had emerged from the wreckage of the Austro-Hungarian, German, and Russian empires. These "successor states" included Finland, Poland, Czechoslovakia, Yugoslavia, and Albania. Older states—Germany, Austria, Hungary, Rumania, Bulgaria—had their boundaries redrawn at Versailles to accommodate the new nations. Supposedly, the principles of national homogeneity and self-determination of minorities were to be observed in drawing the new boundaries, but political arguments of strategic and economic necessity often outweighed these ideals. In many cases, homogeneous nations without sizable minorities could not be created without large-scale transfers of population. These conditions, combined with the super-heated nationalism generated by the war, created boundary disputes that lasted until 1939. For instance, the Ruthenians (or Ukranians) of prewar Hungary were divided between Poland and Czechoslovakia. Many Czechs lived in Teschen, which was presented to Poland. Rumania obtained Bessarabia, which historically and culturally had been a part of the Russian empire. Yugoslavia and Albania were constantly defending their Adriatic coasts from Italian annexations.

By far the most serious nationality problems were those involving German minorities. Just as Germany's wealthiest industrial region in the west was occupied by France, a major part of her richest industrial area in the east, Upper Silesia, was presented, after a delay of two years, to Poland. A plebiscite carried out in 1921, pursuant to a decision at Versailles, was indecisive. Approximately 60 percent of the votes favored union with Germany. An international commission of British, Italian, and French members could not agree. The British and Italians wanted to make the award as closely as possible along ethnic lines. The French, however, hoping to strengthen the fledgling Polish state, insisted that the bulk of Upper Silesia go to Poland. Finally, a decision was made by the Supreme Council of the League of Nations as a compromise between the French and British-Italian positions. As a result, many Germans were

MAP 4. The Europe Created at Versailles

SOURCE: Martin Gilbert, *Recent History Atlas* (London: Weidenfeld and Nicolson, 1966), map 43.

included in Poland. The Germans never accepted this award. Nor did they accept the separation of Danzig, a German city surrounded by Polish-inhabited countryside, from Germany. The Fourteen Points had promised the new Poland an opening to the sea. This was provided by giving the land corridor between Germany and Danzig to Poland by making Danzig an international free port with special relations with Poland. The Polish corridor to the sea prevented land contact between East Prussia and the rest of Germany. German minorities, therefore, were separated from their homeland in the Saar, in Poland, and in Czechoslovakia. These minorities remained a rallying point for German nationalists until Hitler's Nazi state rejoined them to the Fatherland.

If Wilson suffered defeat over application of the nationality principle in Europe, he was able to win a qualified victory on the question of German colonial possessions. Before the war, each imperial country was a law unto itself, and colonial peoples were often treated as less than human. Wilson refused to accept the parceling out of German colonies to new masters until a promise of eventual independence was extracted from Great Britain and France. This promise was embodied in the League of Nations mandate system. The League was even given power to investigate conditions in the mandated colonies and to publicize mistreatment of colonials. This was a giant step away from the brutal, lawless imperialism of the prewar period, since it established the principle that colonial empires were not to last forever. Although the preparation of Asians and Africans for independence was scoffed at by most Eruopeans, it inspired many nationalists among the subject people.

The felt need for a common Allied policy toward Soviet Russia once again found Wilson and Clemenceau opposed. Clemenceau and Marshal Foch were for armed intervention to crush bolshevism in Russia and anywhere else it appeared. Wilson constantly rejected any large scale venture although he did allow American troops to land in Russian ports. Wilson's position was that the Russians should be left alone to settle their own affairs. He made several attempts to get both sides together for negotiations—attempts which were sabotaged by the White Army generals who desired a return to monarchical government. Wilson opposed the spread of communism as strongly as Clemenceau. He was sure that bolshevism would lead to the utter collapse of any advanced state that was so unfortunate as to have a revolution. However, his preferred manner of fighting communism was to feed the hungry of central and eastern Europe, not to send armies into Russia. He realized the great economic strength of the United States and used it to promote liberal democratic governments and to weaken socialist movements. Actually, the outcome of this battle was Wilson's greatest success. Without a major armed effort such as Foch proposed, Wilson contained the Bolsheviks within Russia while preventing his allies from forcing a reactionary regime on the Russian people.

Therefore, it was not at Versailles that Wilson was defeated. He bargained masterfully and effectively to protect his ideals. The real determinants of international relations, however, were not to be found at Versailles, but in the social fabric of each European state. The prewar political polarization had been intensified by four years of suffering. The forces of both Left and Right were more militant in 1919 than in 1914. The liberals who had dominated prewar politics were forced to choose in 1919 between the revolution and the counterrevolution. Everywhere the majority of liberals sided with the counterrevolution. In each victor country the labor unions and the socialists were demanding sweeping social reform. To counter this, liberals joined conservatives in using nationalism and attacks on Germany to justify their attacks on the labor movement. Just as during the war the antiwar forces had been called "defeatists," during the Paris peace conference the Left was denounced as "appeasers" of the national enemy. French and British conservatives fought sorely needed tax reforms by shouting, "Germany will pay!" Woodrow Wilson's tragedy was that he was a man of the center. His liberal peace aims were not acceptable to the conservatives in power; his compromises were not acceptable to the leftists in the streets.

Chapter 4

IN SEARCH OF STABILITY, 1919–24

A major military conflict does not end with the signing of the armistice or with the signing of a peace treaty. On both the national and international plane, wars lead to political and social instability that continues after the combat stops. Certainly military clashes of a more limited nature continued after Versailles: the Russian Civil War, the Russo-Polish War, the Turkish War of Independence, the Irish War of Independence. In a more technical sense, the war did not end until the final peace treaty between Great Britain and Turkey—the Treaty of Sevres—was signed in 1924. Perhaps more important was the social instability throughout Europe and her colonies caused by the war. Germany was constantly on the verge of revolution or reaction until 1924. Great Britain suffered several major strikes and lost Ireland. The greatest imperial power was also faced with nationalist revolutions in the Middle East and India. French politicians feared revolution, while Italy discovered fascism. Socialist parties throughout the world were split into communists and social democrats. It was not until 1924 that European society seemed to recover its equilibrium and Germany and Russia reentered the family of nations.

Germany

Germany had experienced its revolution in November 1918. The extreme left-wing socialists had then attempted a revolt in January 1919, and had been suppressed unmercifully. Only days after, Germany began its return to normality with the election of a constituent assembly to govern the country, to make peace with the enemy, and to write a constitution. The assembly met in Weimar, a small town in central Germany southwest of Berlin. It was from this town that the new republic took its name.

The Social Democratic party had the most seats at Weimar with 165. The Catholic Center party was the second largest with 91, and the Democratic party followed with 75. These three republican parties formed a coalition that was to govern Germany until 1924.

Two socialists were chosen by the assembly to lead the nation. Friedrich Ebert was elected the first president of the republic, and he appointed Philip Scheidemann to be his chancellor. Scheidemann's first major task was to make peace with the Allied Powers at Versailles. His peace program was Wilsonian. He expected Germany to be treated as an equal and not to be saddled with onerous reparations payments. With such hopes, he and other German liberals were shocked when they learned the terms of the Versailles Treaty. Scheidemann called it a "document of hatred and delusion" and termed it absolutely unacceptable. The German nation agreed unanimously. Protest meetings were held throughout the country. Wilson was denounced—especially by those leftists who had put their trust in his promises of a peace of reconciliation. They felt they had been duped. Still, it was obvious to all but the most irresponsible that armed resistance was impossible and the treaty must be accepted. Leading members of the Center party urged acceptance on condition that the "Articles of Honour," which placed the responsibility for the war on Germany, be removed. The Allies refused even these concessions and issued an ultimatum—either sign by June 23 or prepare for an Allied invasion. Scheidemann resigned rather than accept the humiliating treaty, but another socialist chancellor, Gustav Bauer, sent a note of acceptance to Versailles only hours before the deadline.

While most Germans realized the necessity of this surrender, few accepted it as final. Vows not to forget came from all sides, not just the nationalists. A SPD spokesman said in a speech to the constituent assembly:

We vow, today, that we shall never abandon our compatriots who have been torn from us. . . . Unbreakable is the bond which ties us to the Germans in Bohemia, Moravia, and Silesia, in Tyrol, Carinthia, and Styria. In all of us lives the hope that all Germans . . . will soon be reunited. . . . We protest against the taking away of our colonies. . . . We shall not rest in our zealous task to create . . . the power . . . to renounce this treaty.[1]

All newspapers echoed these sentiments. It was from this atmosphere that the slogans later exploited by Hitler came: "November criminals," "Stab in the back," and "Diktat of Versailles."

The blow to the prestige of the new republic was immense. Instead of rewarding German democracy, the Allies had discredited it. They had also contributed to the revival of nationalism and militarism by demon-

---

[1] Koppel Pinson, *Modern Germany,* 2d ed. (New York: Macmillan Co., 1966), p. 399. Reprinted with permission of The Macmillan Company.

strating that the only law of international relations was military might. Any beneficial effects of Wilson's liberal diplomacy were completely blotted out by the harshness of the treaty and the way it was imposed upon Germany.

The second task of the Weimar assembly was to write a constitution. Several constitutional provisions later proved disastrous for the republic. Primary among these was the decentralization of authority. The new Germany was a federal state divided into *Laender*. Each *Land* had its own legislature and administration. Supposedly, these were subject to the federal government in Berlin, but in fact, their independence was so great that they were able to ignore laws passed in the Reichstag. Conservative, antidemocratic parties controlled several *Land* governments—notably Bavaria—and harbored right-wing enemies of the republic. Therefore, fascist groups flourished in provincial cities such as Munich. A second potential danger to democracy lurked in Article 48, whereby the president of the republic could assume dictatorial powers when he decided that a state of national emergency existed. Although this was intended as a tool to be used to defend the republic, it was eventually used by Hitler to establish a totalitarian state. A final weakness of the constitution was the virtual prohibition of any extensive social changes by a declaration that private property was sacred and inviolable. This ideological abdication by the SPD allowed the two strongest antidemocratic interest groups—the Junkers and the industrialists—to feel secure in attacking the republic.

With this shaky constitutional foundation, it was not surprising that in its first four years the republic faced two major crises that threatened its existence. The first was an attempted coup by certain military men and nationalist politicians, who had been intimidated into supporting the republican revolution until the threat of a Bolshevik revolution had subsided. In late 1919 they began planning for a restoration of the monarchy or a military dictatorship. The leaders of the conspiracy were General Luttwitz, the army commander of the Berlin area; Captain Ehrhardt, the commander of a Free Corps brigade near Berlin; and an arch-nationalist politician, Wolfgang Kapp. The immediate excuse for the putsch was the Allied demand that the German army be reduced to 200,000 men by April 1920. The government—headed by President Ebert and Chancellor Bauer—ordered Ehrhardt, famous for the bloody repression of the communists in Bavaria, to dissolve his Free Corps. Luttwitz told Ehrhardt to ignore the order, arguing that a strong army was still needed to combat bolshevism. This set the stage for the showdown between Luttwitz and the government. On March 13, 1920, the Ehrhardt brigade marched on Berlin, and Kapp was declared chancellor. Unsure of the army's attitude, the cabinet left Berlin for Dresden. The military, however, remained neutral. Most generals issued statements supporting one side or the other, but they did no more. The outcome of the putsch was decided by the action of the trade unions and the attitude of the state bureaucracy. Before leaving Berlin, the SPD government had called for a general strike so as to cripple the Kapp clique by halting the economy. Berlin and other cities were paralyzed. Also, key figures in the civil service remained loyal to the legal government and refused to cooperate with the coup. After five days in power, Kapp resigned and turned the problems of governing over to Luttwitz, who realized his adventure had failed; therefore, both of them fled, and the republican government reentered Berlin.

The defeat of Kapp had not been without its price. In order to insure the neutrality of the military and conservative parties, the Ebert-Bauer cabinet had to agree to hold new parliamentary elections at once and to allow popular election of the president of the republic. Conservatives felt certain that the political tide had turned in their favor since 1919, and they hoped not only to win a majority in the legislature but also to elect General Hindenburg president. In fact, they did gain legislative seats, and Hindenburg was elected in 1925. Another SPD concession was the appointment of General von Seeckt as head of the Reichswehr. Von Seeckt had remained neutral during the Kapp putsch, but he was known for his determination to rebuild the Army and the political influence of the Officer Corps.

The second great crisis of the Weimar Republic was a result of a French premier's attempt to weaken Germany through rigorous enforcement of the reparation clauses of the Versailles Treaty. In May 1921, the Allied Reparations Commission issued an ultimatum threatening to invade the Rhineland if payment on reparations did not begin in twelve days. The Germans agreed to pay, but in produce, not in money. Soon after the payments began the value of the mark plummeted. Although this runaway inflation had many causes, some originating in wartime financing, the Germans naturally blamed the inflation on reparations. Raymond Poincaré, the French premier, had no concern for Germany's problems and

TABLE 4.1. German Inflation, 1922–24
(marks needed to buy $1)

January 1922	162
September 1922	1,303
November 1922	7,000
August 1923	2,950,000

insisted the payments continue. The chief victims of this soaring inflation were the lower middle class and the workers. Most of the wealth of the lower middle class—shopkeepers, hotel owners, white-collar workers, artisans—was in savings. As inflation increased, these savings became worthless. Workers who lived on a fixed salary were in the same situation. Each week their paycheck would buy less. Workers were paid at the end of each day, so they could spend their money before it lost its value. The people who profited from the debacle were those who had wealth in real estate —Junkers who owned land and businessmen who owned industrial eqiupment.

Poincaré aggravated the situation gravely in January 1923 by using a brief delay in the delivery of some telephone poles as an excuse to declare Germany in default. Against British objections, he proceeded to occupy the coal-rich Ruhr mining and industrial area. The Ruhr was sealed off from the rest of Germany and treated as a part of France. Tariffs were imposed on goods from Germany into the occupied zone. The reaction of the German chancellor, Wilhelm Cuno, was to call for passive resistance by the workers in the Ruhr. This sit-down strike embarrassed the French for a time, but they were in a stronger position than the Germans, who were faced not only with economic collapse but also with a possible civil war. The rampaging inflation had polarized German politics—driving workers to the communists and the middle classes to the nascent fascist groups, such as Hitler's National Socialist party. The Communists (KPD) gained so much support (and the threat from the Right seemed so great) that the SPD governments of Saxony and Thuringia invited Communists to join their cabinets. Meanwhile, the KPD was preparing for civil war by organizing fighting units to face the Free Corps and the fascist squads, which were also growing rapidly. In Bavaria, the Right prepared to launch an attack on the republic. Gustav von Kahr, a monarchist, managed to have himself declared dictator of Bavaria by the legal Bavarian government. He then began to plan for the restoration of an independent Bavarian monarchy.

As the 1923 crisis worsened, the Reichstag majority looked for new leaders. Gustav Stresemann, a leader of the People's party, became chancellor in August 1923. The appointment of this moderate conservative marked a decisive turning point in the history of Weimar; for Stresemann was to dominate the republic until his death in 1929. He began by energetically attacking both domestic and foreign problems. He gained British and American support for a definite settlement of the reparations question and for large loans to Germany to help her rebuild her economy. He used Article 48 to declare a state of seige, enabling him to govern by decree. The contrast between his treatment of left-extremists and right-extremists was indicative of the politics of most Weimar cabinets. The army was used in Saxony and Thuringia to oust legally appointed Communists from office, and the Communist fighting units were forcibly disbanded. But Stresemann *negotiated* with the Bavarian separatist Kahr. Probably Stresemann felt that the army in Bavaria was more likely to support Kahr than Berlin. Kahr became convinced that the military stationed in the North would not allow an illegal coup d'état, so he agreed to withdraw from politics.

Still there was another man in Munich who hoped to take advantage of the chaotic times. Adolf Hitler, a minor politician, tried to win the support of Kahr for a march on Berlin. On November 8, 1923, when Kahr and others were gathered in a Munich beer hall, Hitler surrounded the hall with storm troopers. He then tried to convince Kahr to join him in his planned coup against Berlin. When General Ludendorff, the hero of World War I, endorsed Hitler's plan, Kahr appeared to be won over. However, Kahr slipped out and called the local army commander. The next morning, as Hitler, Ludendorff, and the the SA were marching triumphantly through Munich, they were blocked by the army. Thirteen storm troopers were killed, while Hitler fled. Ludendorff was arrested on the spot, Hitler later. The trial that followed was another example of the leniency the Weimar Republic extended to the right. Ludendorff was acquitted. Hitler was found guilty of high treason and given the extremely light sentence of five years in prison—he served only eight months.

With the crushing of the communists in Saxony and Thuringia and of the Kahr regime in Bavaria, the greatest threats to the republic were overcome. The economic genius of Hjalmar Schacht, aided greatly by loans from the United States and Great Britain, succeeded in reviving the economy by mid 1924. Germany was entering an era of economic prosperity that would last only until 1930. The architect of this remarkable recovery was Stresemann. Under his leadership—usually as foreign minister—the Weimar governments became increasingly conservative. The SPD had missed their chance for reforms in 1919. They would never regain that opportunity.

Italy

Italy emerged from World War I apparently as a victorious nation. Yet Italian domestic politics from 1919 to 1924 followed the eastern European pattern rather than that of France and Great Britain. There was the same widespread discontent, the same demands for land reform that was common to eastern Europe. A rapid expansion of the extreme Left was followed by a dictatorship. These similarities were a result of the economic backwardness of Italy. Like Poland and Hungary, Italy was predominantly an agricultural state with the majority of its land controlled by large landowners—aristocratic, Catholic, and nationalist. During the war, the peasant soldiers were promised a land reform—their own plot of land—as reward for their sacrifices. When the armistice was signed, all promises were forgotten, except by the peasants. During 1919 soldiers returning home began to seize the land.

The same process was occurring in the industrial centers of the north where the socialist labor unions were concentrated. The socialists, many now communists, encouraged the workers to seize factories. They preached the imminence of revolution. However, in contrast to the Bolsheviks of 1917, the Italian socialist leaders thought the revolution would simply occur when conditions were ripe and that they did not have to help it along. In 1919, when workers were seizing factories and city halls and hoisting the red flag over public buildings, this seemed to be true.

The election of November 1919 was held in this atmosphere of confusion. The dissatisfaction of the electorate with the wartime government was evident. In contrast to France, Great Britain, and the United States where conservative parties won postwar elections, the Italians voted heavily for the socialists. The Italian Socialist party (PSI) became the largest party in parliament with 175 seats. Giolittian Liberals won 129 seats. The Popolari party, created only in 1919, was third largest. This Catholic party appealed most to the deeply religious peasantry because it advocated land reform without espousing materialistic socialism. The Liberals and the Popolari formed the basis for the parliamentary majority because the PSI was isolated on the left.

The success of the PSI was made more striking by the failure of a group of antisocialist candidates who called themselves fascists and swore loyalty to Benito Mussolini. A leader of the revolutionary wing of the PSI before 1914, Mussolini had become an ardent nationalist during the war while retaining his socialist goals. His nationalist campaign for Italian entrance into the war had led to his expulsion from the PSI. He then began his own newspaper in Milan, the *Popolo d'Italia.* Advocating a nationalist socialism, he gained a large following during the last days of the war.

It was not until March 1919, just before the election, that Mussolini made an attempt to organize his supporters into a political party. The term "fascist" had no specific significance at the time. The word *fascio* was used for any political group, especially on the Right. The Fascist party adopted a program for the election which included many socialist-inspired reforms. It called for the nationalization of armaments factories, the control of industry and public services by proletarian organization (i.e., labor unions), the confiscation of all property belonging to religious organizations, and a steeply progressive tax on capital. The Fascists also advocated a national minimum wage and an eight-hour day for all workers. The only reference to foreign affairs was a call for "a foreign policy calculated to enable Italy to take her proper place in the peaceful competition among nations." Mussolini, however, compensated for this slight to nationalist sentiment in his speeches and editorials. He described Italy as a "proletarian" nation that was being exploited by the satisfied imperial powers. This analysis was convincing to those who felt Italy had been cheated at Versailles, especially in relation to Fiume. Still, the Fascists were not successful in the election. The temper of the country was revolutionary, and appealing to the same voters as the PSI, none of the twenty

Fascist candidates was elected. This defeat was a heavy blow to Mussolini, who talked about leaving politics. After this, he increasingly emphasized the nationalist elements of his program and eschewed social reform.

An unexpected event revived fascism and gave Mussolini new prestige. In September 1919, Gabriele D'Annunzio captured the city of Fiume at the head of a band of adventurers. D'Annunzio asked Mussolini to use *Popolo d'Italia* to win support for the annexation of Fiume to Italy. Before 1914 D'Annunzio, the most popular poet in Italy, had advocated the regeneration of Italy through glorious military action. During the war, this militaristic poet was allowed to serve in the army, navy, and air force and had won gold stars for bravery from all three services. He sometimes complained about the rule limiting to three the number of gold stars awarded to any one man, asserting that he deserved at least six. His "legions" were composed basically of exsoldiers, especially *arditi,* members of an elite army unit organized for dangerous and difficult missions. The *arditi* uniform consisted of a black shirt and hunting trousers with a black stripe down the side. This was the uniform Mussolini adopted for his fascist squads.

D'Annunzio ruled over Fiume for fifteen months. Mussolini visited there and acquired ideas which he later used during his own dictatorship. For D'Annunzio, the city was a stage. Frequent military parades were held; flags were draped everywhere; the *arditi* were encouraged to engage in manly activities—such as duels with hand grenades. D'Annunzio also tried to establish a corporate state. Although he did not succeed, the attempt impressed Mussolini. The end came for the ludicrous adventure when Italy and Yugoslavia agreed to make Fiume an international city. The Italian army ousted D'Annunzio's legions on Christmas Day, 1920. Oddly, but typically, Mussolini reversed his stand and approved the government action. This did not prevent the majority of D'Annunzio's followers from going to Milan and swearing allegiance to Mussolini.

During 1920 social turmoil increased. Waves of strikes broke out in the north, and peasants continued to seize land in the south. The premier, at this time was none other than the prewar Liberal leader Giolitti. Premier from June 1920 until July 1921, his policy was to have no policy. He hoped the discontent would run its course, and he feared that a policy of suppression would precipitate a revolution. Since the government would take no action, private citizens organized vigilante squads. Swearing allegiance to Mussolini, they put on the black shirts of the *arditi* and defended private property from striking workers and land hungry peasants. Italy was close to civil war. Virtually every city witnessed armed bands of Blackshirts doing battle with the usually unarmed socialists. The government was not neutral. It not only refused to disarm the Blackshirts; local police and military officials illegally supplied them with weapons, ammunition, and trucks in which to patrol the countryside. All of this was very similar to the relationship between the Free Corps and the government in Germany. Besides the support of the local police and the army, these fascist squads could count on the financial support of industrialists and large landholders.

The Fascist party gradually evolved out of this agitation. The local *fasci* were united in regional federations headed by a *ras*. The *ras*, autonomous regionally, were actually the real powers in the movement. They were held together by their allegiance to Mussolini as Il Duce, the leader. They needed Mussolini because of his charismatic influence over his followers, his newspaper, and his ability to give political direction to the movement. But it was Giolitti who actually transformed fascism into a national political force. In January 1921, he proposed that Fascist candidates run for parliament on the Giolittian ticket, virtually assuring their election. Nothing could have more graphically illustrated the lack of consistent principle of the Italian liberals. During the campaign Fascists continued their violent assaults on socialists. Between January and May 1921, (when the election was held), they destroyed 120 labor union headquarters and invaded 200 socialist offices, killing 243 and wounding 1,444.[2] Instead of denouncing these ruffians, the Liberals praised their active defense of the nation and of civilization against the socialist revolution.

The similarity between events in Italy and in other countries is significant; parallels can be found not only with Germany's Free Corps. In Austria the government used the Volkswehr to suppress communists. In Great Britain, unemployed soldiers and officers called Black and Tans (from their uniform) were pressed into action against the Irish nationalists. Giolitti was right when he told an English visitor inquiring about the fascists, "They are our Black and Tans." Throughout Europe conservatives, liberals, and even social democrats were turning to the ultranationalist unemployed soldiers for shock troops to suppress the revolution. In Italy, as later in Germany, the shock troops eventually captured the government.

The fascists won thirty-five seats in the 1921 election, and Mussolini became a parliamentary deputy. Electoral victory led to problems that Mussolini had not been forced to face before. He had to decide whether he was the leader of a parliamentary party or the Duce of a revolutionary movement. The resulting debate within the party reveals much about Mussolini's relationship to the movement and about his personality. Two factions struggled for control. Mussolini headed the faction that argued for the transformation of the movement into a parliamentary party. This implied the renunciation of violence, the formulation of a concrete program, and the willingness to enter parliamentary coalitions. Italo Balbo led the revolutionary wing. He argued that fascism was a revolutionary movement

---

[2] Ivone Kirkpatrick, *Mussolini: A Study in Power* (New York: Avon Books, 1968), p. 98.

dedicated to the seizure of power by force. Therefore, the Party could not forsake violence because of the danger that the squads might become weak through inactivity. Rather, the squads should be organized even more on military lines, so their fighting capability would be enhanced. Balbo represented the *ras*, who were not willing to surrender their local dictatorships simply because Mussolini wished to be a respectable politician. In August 1921, the *ras* of northern Italy were so strongly opposed to Mussolini's program that he resigned from the Fascist executive council. However, before the national congress of *fasci* met in November, Mussolini's importance to the movement as a symbol, as Il Duce, had become apparent. The national congress adopted the political program that he proposed.

The terms of this program indicated the extent of Mussolini's shift away from the 1919 program. It opposed any nationalization of property, stressing the importance of encouraging private initiative. There should be economy in government spending and decentralization of the administration. Strikes should be prohibited. The military should be made stronger and more efficient. The functions of the state should be purely political and juridical. Any other services or necessary functions of the government should be delegated to technically competent national councils elected by professional and economic corporations. This last proposal was the seed from which the fascist corporate state—a totalitarian state—was to grow.

Having brought the party under his control, Mussolini became very confident. He wrote an editorial criticizing the democratic regime and predicting that the people of Italy would soon turn for leadership to a dictatorship. But after the challenge to his leadership in 1921, he no longer tried to restrain the violence of the squads. Throughout 1922 they became ever bolder in their raids and the size of the forces used. Balbo was determined to show the "politicians" how powerful the Fascists had become. In May, he led 63,000 Blackshirts into Ferrara, a city near Venice, occupied the city and established his own administration. The pretext for this show of force was the government's refusal to begin certain public works projects to provide jobs for the unemployed in the region. This testified to the Fascists' ability to show concern for the workers while opposing socialism. After several days the government agreed to begin the projects, and Balbo withdrew his men. Encouraged by this success, Balbo carried out similar operations in Bologna, Ravenna, and Parma. The government was forced to negotiate with Balbo as with a foreign power. These raids embarrassed Mussolini, who was not willing to risk an armed confrontation with the army, but he was pleased by the additional prestige they conferred on him as the Duce.

The government was paralyzed. After Giolitti's cabinet fell in July 1921, several extremely weak premiers tried to form broad coalitions. Such coalitions could not agree on a firm policy toward either the socialists or the fascists. The majority of parliamentarians still feared a Bolshevik revolution, but they had no fear of a revolution from the right. As long as the fascists controlled the countryside, the liberals and conservatives were content to remain neutral. They judged Mussolini by traditional standards, believing that once in parliament, he would behave as any other politician.

The final crisis began on August 1, 1922, when Luigi Facta formed his second cabinet. Facta had made vague statements in favor of social reform; therefore he was greeted by a socialist sponsored general strike *in support of Facta.* It was a suicidal move. Facta needed a respite from disorder. Instead, the socialists gave the fascists their opportunity. The Fascist executive council issued an ultimatum: either the government must crush the strike or the Blackshirts would do so. Facta did nothing. As promised, the squads went into action. They captured several major northern cities—Milan, Bologna, Parma—and kept all public services and utilities operating. They cleared the streets of socialists and the factories of trade unionists. Weeks passed with no change in the situation. Finally, Mussolini met with Balbo and other Fascist leaders on October 16, and plans were made for a march on Rome to establish a Fascist government.

Facta had resigned, and no one could be found to replace him. All proposed coalitions were to include the Fascists, not to be against them; but Mussolini refused to join any cabinet except as premier. As the Fascist troops began to converge on Rome, Facta, still premier by default, finally found courage to declare a state of seige and to order the army to suppress the Blackshirts. Such action, however, had to have the king's signature, and King Victor Emmanual refused to sign. Instead, he recommended that a conservative ministry be formed with Mussolini as premier. Since the king's refusal to sign Facta's decree meant there would be no opposition to the fascists in any event, the parliamentary leaders asked Mussolini to accept the premiership. On October 30 Mussolini rendezvoused with a few thousand Blackshirts on the outskirts of Rome and walked into the city to become premier—hardly a case of storming the gates.

From this time until January 1925, Mussolini slowly constructed a dictatorship—sometimes by plan, sometimes by accident. From the first he ruled by decree. Opposition deputies who expressed disapproval were beaten both inside parliament and in the streets. In 1923 he bullied and persuaded the parliament into passing the Acerbo Electoral Law, which provided that the party receiving the largest popular vote would receive two-thirds of the seats in the legislature. The elections of April 1924, were so thoroughly controlled that there was no doubt of the outcome. The Fascists, who had only thirty-five seats before the election, had 403 of 558 seats in the new parliament.

Whether Mussolini would have proceeded to establish a totalitarian state if he had been able to choose his method of governing is an open

Mussolini's public
appearance emphasized
power and strength
of will.
(Courtesy of Roger-Viollet)

question. As it occurred the decision was taken out of his hands. When
the new parliament convened, a socialist deputy named Matteotti rose
to denounce the rigged elections. Shortly afterward Matteotti was murdered. Italy was shocked, and Mussolini conducted himself oddly. Immediately after the murder became known, he vowed that the state would
exert great efforts to find the murderers. In fact, he had not yet decided
to destroy all freedom and was embarrassed when certain newspapers
revealed the killers to be Fascists. For six months he wavered. This
angered the *ras*, who were now officers of a state-supported Fascist
militia—the Blackshirts in the pay of the state. Thirty of these officers
called on Mussolini at the end of December. They said that "they were
tired of clinging to the past," that "the prisons were now full of
fascists . . . while he, the Duce, refused to take responsibility for the
revolution."[3] This démarche, followed by a newspaper story accusing Mussolini of having ordered Matteotti's assassination, goaded him into action.

On January 3, 1925, he spoke to the Chamber of Deputies. He assumed
full responsibility for the murder and blamed the opposition for having
made parliamentary government impossible. Fascism was not dead, he
declared, and he warned that in the next twenty-four hours "the situation
will be cleared up." He was announcing the construction of the second
totalitarian state in Europe—Soviet Russia being the first. The day after
his speech all freedoms were ended, all newspapers were censored, all
opponents who spoke out were arrested.

This minor polemicist had become the head of a private army and
the dictator of Italy because the conservatives and liberals had refused

---

[3] Ibid., p. 231.

to recognize a counterrevolutionary movement as dangerous. They had welcomed any aid in fighting the socialist threat—no matter what the source. They failed to see that the Fascist movement was just as revolutionary as the Communist. This point is expressed in a comment taken from Italo Balbo's Diary.

> When I came back from the war, I, like so many others, hated politics and politicians, who it seemed to me had betrayed the hopes of the fighting men and had inflicted on Italy a shameful peace. . . . Many at that time, even the most generous souls, turned towards nihilist communism. . . . It is certain, I believe, that without Mussolini three-quarters of the Italian youth coming home from the trenches would have become Bolsheviks. They wanted a revolution at any cost.[4]

Great Britain and France

In contrast to Germany and Italy, Great Britain and France retained their governmental stability during the last phase of the war. The wartime coalitions remained in office until 1924. This did not, however, spare the victorious democracies from the domestic turmoil which swept all of Europe. In a perverse way, this turmoil had been produced by the governments in power as much as by economic conditions. Official propaganda had portrayed the world after the war as one from which the old politics of special interests and selfish class interests would be banned. It was assumed by many that the cooperation of government, business and labor necessitated by war would continue. This implied social reforms to raise the workers' standard of living as recognition of the workers' role in the victorious war effort. In kicking off the 1918 election campaign, Lloyd George had promised that Great Britain would become a "fit country for heroes to live in." These hopes for a new world were not fulfilled. It took only two or three years to disillusion even the most starry-eyed optimist. The result was extreme labor unrest, suppression by conservative governments, and parliamentary majorities for leftists in both countries by 1924.

The Conservative Party dominated the Government of National Union which took office after the British election of December 1918. But wartime conditions had not only strengthened the Conservatives, who were identified with victory. Indeed, the most significant result of the voting was the rise of the Labour party and the decline of the Liberals. Labour emerged as the largest party *outside* the national coalition with fifty-nine seats. Even this did not reflect the vast increase in Labour's popularity. The increase in votes was more striking: from 400,000 in 1910 to 2,374,000 in 1918. The Liberals lost 110 seats in 1918. The Lloyd

---

[4] Kirkpatrick, *Mussolini,* p. 112.

George-Liberals, who were partners in the National Government, and the Asquith-Liberals together won only 162 seats as compared with their 1910 total of 272. This election was the beginning of an irreversible decline for the Liberals, who were soon to be replaced by the Labour party as the only alternative to the Conservatives.

The growth of the Labour party was indicative of the growth of the labor movement as a whole. Union membership had doubled during the war from four million to eight million. In 1919 the unions felt they were strong enough to force social and economic reforms on the government, but Lloyd George, still prime minister but now a captive of the Conservative majority, proved to be too shrewd to be coerced. Labour's major demands were better working conditions, the continuation of wartime controls over industry, and the nationalization of inefficient industries. The Glasgow Uprising of January 1919 indicated the extremes to which some workers were willing to go. In defiance of union officials, workers demonstrating in favor of a forty-hour week seized the city hall and raised the red flag of revolution in a town square. After several days, Lloyd George dispatched the army to clear Glasgow's streets. A week of rioting and skirmishing ensued before the workers were subdued.

The Glasgow Uprising was only the first squall of a storm. In the next two years, Lloyd George had three major encounters with the workers, but he won each battle without granting any meaningful reforms. His major adversary was the Miner's Federation. In January 1919 the federation demanded the nationalization of the coal industry and the introduction of a six-hour day. This was not such a radical demand, since the state had been administering the mines as well as other industries during the war. Also, the inefficiency of the mines was notorious. Many of them were losing money; few had kept up with the technical advances employed in other countries. In brief, the miners seemed to have a good case for nationalization. Lloyd George, however, bought time by persuading the federation not to strike until a special commission composed of union officials, mine owners, and government experts could investigate the industry and make recommendations. The commission's report recommended nationalization. The mine owners retaliated by issuing a report recommending no government action, while an industrial engineer on the commission filed a separate, minority report advocating only government subsidies to the mines and mild government regulations. Lloyd George used the existence of the two unofficial reports to claim that there was no clear consensus, and therefore, he took no action at all. He had succeeded in his primary goal—to break the momentum of the strike.

He had only delayed the confrontation. The miners throughout Great Britain went on strike for a salary increase in October 1920, and this time they were joined by the railwaymen, who struck in sympathy. The transport workers, expected to follow suit, refused to come out. It was just as well, for Lloyd George used the railroad stoppage as his excuse for crushing the strike. He pushed through Commons the Emergency Powers Act which allowed him to govern by decree in such a crisis if he so chose. Rather than test the spunky Welshman, the railroaders backed down, forcing the miners to accept a negotiated settlement on the day after the Emergency Powers Act was passed. The prime minister had won round two.

The abortive general strike the following year was the last attempt by British Labour to force reforms on Parliament until 1926. The occasion for the strike was the government's decision to speed up the removal of controls over industry. Since 1914 the state had acquired vast powers of administration and regulation. It would have been easy to convert these powers into permanent legislation, as was requested by the trade unions. On the day controls ended, in March 1921, the mine owners reduced the wages of all their employees. The Miner's Federation again called for a nationwide strike, and the railwaymen and the transport workers again pledged their support. The miners struck on April 1. The other unions promised to come out on April 15 if the miners' wages were not restored to their previous level.

Lloyd George reacted in a most illiberal manner. He declared the Emergency Powers Act to be in effect and ordered the army to man the trains if necessary. He appealed for volunteers for a special Defence Force to be used as policemen and to man truck convoys of food. Seventy-five thousand young men volunteered in ten days. These were mostly middle-class and upper-class youths who detested the unions and socialism. All the ingredients for a civil war were present. Once more the miners' allies deserted them, and they had to accept the wage reduction dictated by their employers. Lloyd George, the hero of the left in 1911, had broken the power and prestige of the labor movement, which did not attempt to challenge the government again until 1926. Even then it failed and did not fully recover until after World War II.

At least the British working class did not suffer as greatly from the inevitable schism between communists and socialists as did the continental left. The Communist International (Comintern) was formed by socialists meeting in Moscow in March 1919. During the following two years the trade unionists and socialists of every European country were forced to choose between the Comintern's revolutionary doctrine and social democracy. In Great Britain only very small extremist groups were willing to join the Communist party and follow orders from Moscow. The Labour party and the groups affiliated with it were barely affected. Labourites sent to Russia as observers returned to report that the Soviet system was only a dictatorship under a different name. Therefore, when the newly formed British Communist party applied for affiliation with the Labour party, it was rejected. The unpopularity of communism can be traced partially to the strength of the parliamentary tradition in Great Britain, but the recent success of the Labour party in the 1918 election was probably just as important. As long as change appeared to be possible through constitutional means, British workers had little interest in revolution.

Although the coalition government resisted demands for sweeping reforms, it did pass some important if unspectacular pieces of social legislation. The House and Town Planning Act of 1919 provided for public housing built by municipalities but regulated and subsidized by the national government. The state accepted responsibility for aiding men involuntarily unemployed under the Unemployment Insurance Act (1920). This welfare responsibility was extended from the worker to his family by the Unemployed Workers' Dependents Act (1921), which provided a small payment for his wife and each child as long as he was out of work. These relief payments were derogatorily called "the dole" and were considered temporary measures; but since unemployment persisted throughout the interwar period, this step toward the welfare state became a permanent feature of British life.

Perhaps the most frustrating problem for Lloyd George was the revolt of the Irish Nationalists. During the war Irish nationalism had been rekindled by the Easter Rebellion of 1916. A handful of idealistic young Irishmen had challenged the British Empire, seized the public buildings in Dublin, and died as martyrs to the cause of Irish independence. In the 1918 elections an extremist group—the Sinn Fein—won seventy-three of the seventy-seven Irish seats in Parliament. The Sinn Feiners, having lost faith in the British Parliament, set up an Irish Parliament in Dublin. They declared Ireland independent of England in January 1919. They then transformed the Irish rebel bands into the Irish Republican Army (IRA). An entire governmental bureaucracy—including tax collectors and judges—was created. Any Irishman who cooperated with the British administration was considered a traitor and risked assassination at the hands of the IRA. This nationalist guerilla army relied on terrorism to control the countryside.

The coalition reacted by advertising for volunteers to go to Ireland to suppress the rebellion. Most of the volunteers were unemployed ex-soldiers desiring action. The Black and Tans, called so because of their uniforms, answered IRA terrorism with even more vicious reprisals against Irishmen. Many bands of the Black and Tans were no more than bandits who raided towns for beer and women rather than for political reasons. By mid 1921 the British press, scandalized by such barbarities, demanded an end to the bloodletting. Lloyd George finally reached a negotiated settlement with the Irish Parliament in December 1921. Ireland was to become an autonomous state within the Commonwealth. Ulster was separated from Southern Ireland and remained a part of the United Kingdom. Unfortunately, even though the British withdrew, the bloodshed did not end. The Irish began to fight among themselves. Extremists wanted "independence" from England, not "autonomy." Therefore, they tried to overthrow the "traitorous" government in Dublin. The years following independence were no less violent than the war between the IRA and the Black and Tans.

The event that brought about Lloyd George's fall from office was another imperial crisis—his failure to gain British dominance over Turkey. He had committed British prestige and armed forces to achieve this, but he was resisted by a nationalist movement led by a charismatic warrior, Kemal Ataturk. Ataturk rallied the Turish nation against the Europeans who hoped to divide the defunct Ottoman Empire among themselves. Lloyd George was forced to back down when it appeared a British force would be slaughtered at Chanak near the Dardanelles. This was a great humiliation for the empire, and the Conservative party could not forgive their Liberal prime minister. The Conservative Parliamentary party met at the Carleton Club, an exclusive social club in London, in October 1922, and voted to end the coalition.

No marked change in policy followed. Lloyd George was succeeded by Bonar Law, who governed for only a few months before losing his senses. When Law resigned, Stanley Baldwin became the Conservative leader and prime minister. He was prime minister more than any other man between the wars, and the period from 1923 to 1939 has been called the Baldwin Era. A very impressive looking individual, he oozed charm. Unfortunately, he was a weak man who devoted all of his energy—such as it was—to preventing change in Great Britain. In fact, he began his career as prime minister with a politically disastrous decision. He called an election in December 1923, on the issue of high protective tariffs. This was the one issue that could unite the Liberals and the Labourites, and the Conservatives suffered a crushing defeat. Even worse, Baldwin was not followed by a Liberal cabinet but by the first socialist cabinet in British history. The Labour government took office in January 1924, once again marking this year as a turning point in the twenties.

In France the wartime coalition also tried to perpetuate itself. It succeeded until 1924. The first postwar election was in November 1919. The elements of the wartime government, under the rubric "National Bloc," were similar to those of the coalition in Britain. The Radical party and the socialists, like the Asquith-Liberals and the Labour party, were unable to unite. The two major issues were bolshevism and patriotism. The Bloc insisted that a socialist was the same as a Bolshevik, and posters were distributed throughout France showing the face of a thin man with tousled hair and a knife in his teeth and labeled simply "bolshevism." Yet it was probably loyalty to the wartime leadership which decided the election. The conservatives had conducted a victorious war effort; the leftists had advocated a compromise peace short of victory. In the new

Chamber of Deputies the National Bloc had 406 seats out of 616. The new conservative majority was composed, as in Great Britain, of many amateur politicians. Because so many were war veterans, the legislature became known as the "horizon blue" legislature, from the color of the army dress uniform. The greatest passions of these conservative soldiers were hatred of Germany and hatred of socialism.

The election returns reflected only one aspect of the war's effect on French politics. The French labor movement, like the British, had grown rapidly. In 1913 there had been only 941,000 organized workers. There were 1,470,000 in 1919, and increased membership was matched by increased militancy. A wave of strikes swept through France in the two years following the armistice. As elsewhere, wartime governments had promised reforms and used force to prevent workers from obtaining those reforms when the war ended. For example, in early 1919 negotiations among unions, employers, and the government resulted in employer recognition of the right of collective bargaining and the limitation of the workday to eight hours. Unfortunately, the employers never respected either of these agreements, nor did the government ask them to do so. The unions called a massive demonstration on May 1, 1919, to protest the broken promises. Clemenceau, instead of persuading the employers to live up to their agreement, tried to prevent the demonstration, setting off a riot that raged through Paris. Although the army restored order, the newspapers discussed the possibility of a revolution.

The showdown between the National Bloc and the unions came one year later—May Day, 1920. Alexandre Millerand, an exsocialist, was the premier, having replaced Clemenceau after the November elections. The railroaders struck first, and other unions joined them, in order to force the government to nationalize the railroads. The General Confederation of Labour (CGT) had neither called nor encouraged this strike but decided to support it. The economy was paralyzed. Mines and steel plants were shut down; construction workers, electricians, and dock workers walked off their jobs. Millerand reacted with force—just as Lloyd George reacted to the general strike of 1921. Soldiers were used to man the railroads and electrical plants. Well-to-do students from the University of Paris and other volunteers were used to keep essential services in operation. But Millerand went further than his British counterpart dared to go. Union officials were arrested, and the CGT was declared illegal and ordered to dissolve. Over 20,000 railroaders were fired for having taken part in the strike. These tough measures had the desired effect. By the end of 1921 the membership in all unions had dropped to 500,000. This severely weakened the labor movement in France until the mid thirties.

The French working class was further weakened by a bitter conflict between communists and socialists. The Socialist Party Congress, meeting at Tours in December 1921, had to decide between joining the Comintern, which meant acceptance of the doctrine and tactics proposed by the Soviets, or remaining independent. In contrast to the British visitors to Moscow, the French observers of Soviet communism returned with glowing reports and recommended acceptance of the Twenty-One Conditions which the Soviets required all members of the Comintern to approve. Most of the older leaders at the Party Congress opposed joining the Comintern, but the vote was 3,200 to 1,938 in favor of the Twenty-One Conditions. One of the conditions was that all dissenters be expelled from the party, so the new French Communist party (PCF) ejected the very considerable minority. This minority, led by Leon Blum, contained fifty-five of the seventy-two socialist deputies and most of the local party leaders. Although crippled by the schism, the French Socialist party (SFIO) was quickly rebuilt by Blum and remained the chief parliamentary force on the Left.

The split in the socialist ranks was paralleled by a split in the trade union movement. The French trade unions had a tradition of avoiding political party ties. The Comintern, however, demanded that unions be subservient to the party. This was basic Leninism and led to the formation of a communist-dominated national federation of unions, the CGTU, in competition with the CGT. Ironically, the "U" stands for "United." To add to the confusion, a Catholic national labor organization, the CFTC, had been founded in 1919.

Of course, in France foreign affairs dominated public discussion. The major concern was with making Germany pay. Aristide Briand, premier during 1921, tried to find a compromise solution and was ousted by the nationalistic legislature. His successor, Raymond Poincaré, was never willing to compromise. It was his desire to cripple Germany and to extract the largest sum possible. Revenge was his policy and that of the conservative majority he represented. Using Germany's delinquency in delivering some telephone poles as an excuse, he occupied the Rhineland in January 1923. But this effort at military diplomacy had repercussions within France that Poincaré had not anticipated. In the first place, it raised the threat of an armed conflict, which the French people would not support, and this forced the public to face the implications of the National Bloc's demagogic claims that "Germany will pay!" Secondly, it strained the French treasury—which had suffered from a budgetary deficit since 1919—to its limits. France could not afford the military action. Finally, the military effort unleashed inflationary pressures which had been held in check. The public naturally blamed this on the occupation of the Rhineland. Certainly, this inflation was not as bad as that occurring in Germany at the same time; but it was still severe.

The dissatisfaction of the public caused by Poincaré's Rhineland policy made it possible for the Radical party and the socialists to unite against the National Bloc in the election of 1924. This coalition—the *Cartel des Gauches*—won the election and the years of Conservative domination

TABLE 4.2.   Course of French
Inflation, 1919–24
(francs needed to buy $1)

1919	11
1922	13
January 1924	20
March 1924	29

Adapted from data in Jacques
Chastenet, *Les Années d'Illusions,
1918–1931*, vol. V of *Histoire de la
Troisième République* (Paris: Librarie
Hachette, 1960), pp. 144–50.

were briefly interrupted. The Radicals were able to form a leftist government, not with socialist participation but with parliamentary support from
the socialists.

So by 1924 the Conservative coalitions that had gained control of power
during the war were replaced by leftist governments in both Great Britain
and France. The labor movements of both countries, however, had been
crippled, and this stripped the leftist governments of their extraparliamentary support. This was to make the conservative task of recapturing
power relatively easy.

Chapter 5

REVOLUTIONARY RUSSIA, 1917–33

Revolutionaries as Rulers

While western European states were trying to solve the problems of peacemaking and industrial democracy, the first communist state was emerging from the chaos of the Russian Civil War. Liberal historians have usually considered this development a deviation from the natural course of Russian history toward a liberal democratic society.[1] Industrialization, they argue, leads inevitably to democracy. They contend that Russians were learning to make parliamentary government work before World War I as the Duma members gained legislative experience and the Russian people became accustomed to the electoral process. Therefore, these historians see the Kerensky government of September and October 1917 as the true expression of the direction in which Russia was evolving. The Bolshevik Revolution was an aberration, and the Soviet dictatorship is an expression of an ideology, not of Russian society.

A more convincing case has been made by students of the process of modernization. They contend that the Bolshevik regime assumed a dictatorial form because of the strength of Russian traditions, the structure of Russian society, and the need for rapid modernization.[2] According to their analysis, Russia before 1914 was ruled by a small Westernized elite that had no contacts with the mass of Russians—the peasantry and the nascent proletariat. There was no significant bourgeoisie to achieve

---

[1] Hugh Seton-Watson, *The Decline of Imperial Russia* (New York: Frederick A. Praeger, Inc., 1961), pp. 377–78; Leopold Haimson, "The Problem of Social Stability in Urban Russia, 1905–1917 (Part One)," *Slavic Review,* 23, no. 4 (1964), pp. 621–23.

[2] Theodore H. Von Laue, *Why Lenin? Why Stalin?* (New York: J. B. Lippincott Co., 1964).

liberal reforms and to act as a buffer between the ruling elite and the masses. The economic backwardness of Russia required rapid industrialization if she were to remain a great power; but, lacking an entrepreneurial class, the state had to impose industrialization on an unwilling agricultural society. This led to increasing conflict between the elite and the masses and, even without the war, would probably have led to revolution or dictatorship. After the Bolsheviks consolidated their power, they found they were confronted with the same problem as the old Czarist elite: industrialization. The Communist rulers, however, were more thorough and more successful in coercing the peasantry into the modern world. That this required a dictatorial state, the "modernizers" contend, was evident in the structure of Russian society. This theory is more useful than that proposed by liberal historians. It allows the historian to escape the British model and to admit the possibility of alternative methods of modernization and to understand the full importance of the Bolshevik Revolution to undeveloped nations.

Although the Bolsheviks gained control of the governmental machinery in November 1917, they were by no means secure in their position. A popularly elected constituent assembly that met in January 1918 had an anti-Bolshevik majority. Therefore, the Bolsheviks forcibly dismissed it after it had met only once. But, if a dictatorship was established in the area under Bolshevik influence, it was not at first a one-party dictatorship. Whereas impersonal social forces may be the ultimate explanation for the Bolshevik suppression of all dissenters, accidents of personality and everyday events were the apparent and direct causes. Both the Social Revolutionary party and the Mensheviks were allowed to continue in existence until 1922. A left-wing faction of SRs shared power with the Bolsheviks on the Council of People's Commissars until March 1918 when they resigned in protest against the Treaty of Brest-Litovsk. They preferred a revolutionary war against the German imperialists. After that March, the Bolsheviks alone (now Communists) were responsible for governing that part of Russia under the control of revolutionary forces. Until the end of 1920 they had to defend their soviet state against one armed threat after another.

The term "civil war" is almost too refined to describe the chaos of those years. The Soviets' Red Army had to fight and defeat four organized White armies of the old Czarist military, innumerable peasant brigades, and nationalist armies of the subject peoples of the Romanov Empire. Their task was made no easier by the hostile intervention of Great Britain, France, the United States, and Japan; all maintained troops on Russian soil to aid the White armies from the fall of 1918 until December 1919. French and Japanese troops stayed longer.

That the revolutionary leaders of Soviet Russia maintained and even expanded the area under their control against such odds was remarkable.

MAP 5.   The Bolsheviks against the World: The Civil War, 1918

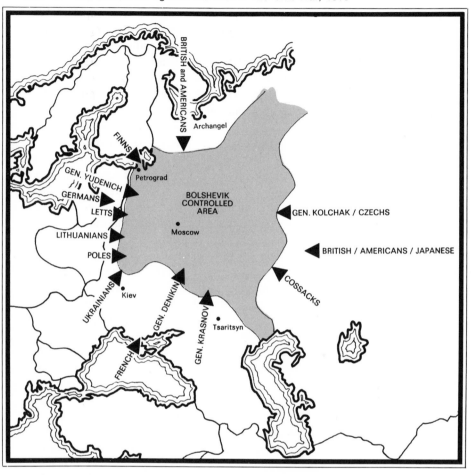

SOURCE: Adapted from *Atlas historique Stock* (Paris: Librairie Stock, 1968), p. 418, left panel.

Obviously, the explanation of their victory must be complex. In the first place, the Red Army had a strategic advantage since they were in the center of a circular battlefield and, therefore, had short and safe lines of communication. The White forces were not only divided into several armies scattered about the periphery of Russia; they were also divided by the personal ambitions of their commanding generals: Kolchak in Siberia, Denikin in the Ukraine, and others. The essential elements of the communist victory, however, were their leadership, their reorganization of the army at their disposal, and their ability to wage political warfare. Leon Trotsky was the commissar for war. His first act was to accept the services of Czarist officers. Most Communists objected to this. Next Trotsky reestablished military discipline. He replaced the soldiers' committees with political commissars. The commissars were said to represent the soldiers, but in practice, they helped the officers enforce discipline. In addition they made reports on the political reliability of officers and men—an adverse report could be a death warrant. On the other hand, Trotsky saw to it that his soldiers were well-fed and well-clothed. During the civil war the soldiers at the front ate better than urban workers. On the political level, it was no contest. The Whites had no chance of winning popular support. They offered peasants and workers nothing but a return to the old regime.

The civil war forced the Bolsheviks to begin the construction of a totalitarian state. Immediately after seizing power, they had to revitalize the army, mobilize the economy to supply that army, and suppress political opponents who might hinder or sabotage the war effort. The drastic measures resorted to are known collectively as "war communism." In order to obtain food for the army and cities, provision detachments of urban workers were formed to seize food from peasants who did not meet the production quota set by the local commissar of supplies. On the industrial front, control of the factories was wrested from the workers' committees, because, since the seizure of the factories by workers in 1917, production had declined drastically. In the first half of 1918, all factories were nationalized and put under the direction of the Supreme Council of National Economy. Trade unions were subordinated to the state bureaucracy, in spite of the friction this caused among the Communist leaders. The desperate need for manpower caused by the large army led to the formation of "labor armies." These were groups of men drafted by the government for civilian jobs such as collecting firewood, repairing railroads, building factories. This militarization of the civilian population was Trotsky's idea. Of course, the Communists quickly gained commanding majorities in all of the soviets of the areas they controlled. Therefore, the Communist party had established undisputed and dictatorial control over the army, the economy, and the political machinery of the state.

During the same period, the party itself underwent a transformation that further concentrated power into a few hands. Before the revolution, the party had been a loose confederation of cells (local committees) held together by their adherence to Lenin's interpretations of Marxism. With the responsibility of governing, the party had to define functions more clearly, had to divide responsibility for various tasks among specialized departments. In brief, it had to develop a bureaucracy. Ever greater centralization was the result. During 1917 and 1918 decisions were theoretically made by the Central Committee, a body of several hundred members elected by the annual party conference. Actually, decisions were made by Lenin and a small circle of party leaders. This was made official in March 1919, by the establishment of the Politburo (Political Bureau of the Central Committee of the Party). From 1919 to 1921 the Politburo was composed of Lenin, Trotsky, Josef Stalin, and two others. This small committee made policy, and the Central Committee was a rubber stamp. The Central Committee also created two other executive committees. The Organization Bureau or Orgburo was intended to oversee the implementation of Politburo decisions and to keep the party organization on the local level in working order. The Secretariat kept tabs on the members of the party: approved memberships, promotions, and changes of personnel, and handled the myriad petty problems of administration which were not important enough to be brought to the attention of the Politburo or Orgburo. At first there were three party secretaries with equal authority, but in 1922, their functions were combined in the office of general secretary. Stalin was given this post and made it his path to absolute power.

Stalin held another office that strengthened him personally. He was the head of Rabkrin, the Workers' and Peasants' Inspectorate. Rabkrin was charged with observing the state bureaucracy (as opposed to the party organization) and weeding out incompetence and corruption. Stalin used it as an excellent tool to spy on the political views of each state employee and to remove those individuals who were undesirable to Stalin personally. Of course, he would replace them with men loyal to himself. Therefore, combining Rabkrin and the Secretariat, Stalin was in a position to know and dictate the politics of every state employee and every party member.

If the war had brought the Communists almost absolute control of Russia, it had also created discontent among the peasants, who were angered by the provision detachments. By 1921 the peasants had stopped planting crops that they could not sell for money or which might be seized by the provision detachments. In addition, eight years of war (1914–21) had ruined the Russian economy. Production in most industries was one-fourth to one-third of 1913 levels. Lenin, therefore, was considering loosening controls on the economy and trying to placate the peasantry even before the Kronstadt Uprising forced him into action. Kronstadt was a naval fort near Petrograd. During January and February 1921, Mensheviks and SRs organized strikes and protests in Petrograd against the Communist dictatorship and war communism. Aroused by this agitation, the sailors at Kronstadt rebelled on March 1, arresting their commander and the ranking Party representative in the fortress. Lenin used the Red Army to quell the revolt, and many sailors were shot after the fortress was taken.

These conditions convinced Lenin and the Politburo that popular unrest was nearing the explosion level. At the Tenth Party Congress, only days after the Kronstadt Uprising, Lenin called for a complete economic about-face. He announced a New Economic Policy (NEP) that included a return to the free play of the market forces of supply and demand. Peasants were to be allowed to sell their crops at a profit, and instead of being required to pay taxes in produce, they were allowed to pay in currency. Small businesses were returned to private ownership. Heavy industry remained nationalized, as did railroads, communications and banks, but the market concept of competition among factories was accepted. Even finance capitalism was revived, as the Soviets actively sought loans in the capitalist countries—especially Great Britain and Germany. The NEP was successful. At the end of 1923 an approximation of normal economic conditions prevailed.

The other side of the NEP, however, was the further suppression of political discussion. The Tenth Congress also adopted a resolution on party unity making debate in the party virtually impossible. Any faction that advocated a program differing from the program of the Central Committee was made subject to expulsion from the party. Since the Central Committee was merely a rubber stamp for the Politburo, the decisions of the Politburo would be law. Any two people who disagreed with the Politburo could be declared a faction and expelled. This was the final capstone in consolidating the control of the Politburo over the party. What remained was for one man to gain control of the Politburo. During his years of leadership, Lenin listened to advice and was willing to keep men in the Politburo and Central Committee who disagreed with him. His successor was not so intellectually secure.

Obviously, Lenin had never been a democrat. He had set forth his ideas on the structure of the party in the pamphlet *What Is To Be Done?* published in 1902. He argued that a small, tightly knit band of revolutionaries must lead the proletariat. Within this group, freedom of expression would not contribute to rapid and reliable decisions but would cause vacillation and discord. He reasoned that

People who were really convinced of the fact that they had advanced knowledge would be demanding not freedom for the new views alongside of the old views, but the replacement of the latter by the former.

There can be no doubt that Lenin was always convinced that his understanding of Marxism had "advanced knowledge" and that his ideas should be dominant. As leader of Russia, however, this did not prevent him from seeking counsel.

Just after launching NEP, Lenin fell gravely ill. He was crippled by cerebral sclerosis, though only fifty-one. Until his death in January 1924, he was an invalid except for brief periods of convalescence. During 1923 he was replaced as a leader of the party by a Troika—Stalin, Zinoviev, and Kamenev. It might be said that Lenin had achieved his goal by 1924. The Bolshevik regime had been accepted by the Russian people, if not yet legitimate in their eyes. The success of NEP had restored trade relations to normal, and living standards were decidedly better than in the long period of tragedy, 1917–21. Few men have presided over such events.

The Communist International and European Socialism

Lenin was fully aware of the historic importance of the Russian Revolution. He and most Soviet leaders, however, wrongly interpreted conditions in the rest of Europe. At first, in 1917 and 1918, the Bolsheviks waited for news of Communist revolutions in Germany, France, Austria, Italy. The time seemed ripe for a project that Lenin had hoped to accomplish since at least 1914: the establishment of a third Socialist International, a truly revolutionary international. Encouraged by the fall of the German and Austrian monarchies in November 1918, the Soviets issued a call for all revolutionary working class parties to meet in Moscow in March 1919 to form a new International.

Simultaneously, the right wing of the European socialist movement was trying to revive the Second International. While the Soviets appealed to the maximalists in each country—those who had called for revolutionary resistance to the war, the right-wing Social Patriots of wartime wanted to specifically exclude these revolutionaries from their International. When the Social Patriots convened a conference in Berne in February 1919, they denounced authoritarian socialism as practiced by the Soviets and stated that true socialism could not exist "unless it rests upon triumphs of Democracy and is rooted in the principles of liberty."[3] Among the democratic forms that the Berne Conference insisted on were "freedom of speech and of the press, the right of assembly, universal suffrage, a government responsible to Parliament, . . . the right of association." It was obvious that none of these existed in Russia nor were the Soviets willing to institute them.

The Soviet answer came the following month, when the First Congress of the Communist International or Comintern met in Moscow. The Comintern congress adopted a resolution that denounced "false bourgeois democracy" as a dictatorship of the capitalist class and called for an immediate seizure of power by revolutionary means wherever this was possible and the establishment of a dictatorship of the proletariat. Only in this way, the Comintern argued, could socialism triumph. The congress further marked its revolutionary intent by writing a new Communist manifesto that concluded with a clarion call to revolt.

We appeal to the laboring men and women in all countries to join us under the Communist banner under which the first great victory has already been won. Proletarians in all lands! Unite to fight against imperialist barbarity, against monarchy, against the privileged classes, against the bourgeois state, and bourgeois property, against all kinds and forms of Social and National oppression. Join us—proletarians in every country—flock to the banner of

---

[3] Merle Fainsod, *International Socialism and the World War* (Garden City, N.Y.: Doubleday and Co., Inc., Anchor Books, 1969), p. 253.

the workmens councils, and fight the revolutionary fight for the power and the dictatorship of the proletariat.[4]

The battle lines were drawn between social democrats and social revolutionaries for control of the socialist movement. At its second congress, in 1920, the Comintern decided to force all socialists to choose between the two roads to socialism. The Comintern adopted twenty-one points that each member party must accept or be excluded. The essence of the twenty-one points was that each party must be organized along Leninist lines of discipline and centralized authority and that each party must be subordinate to the executive committee of the Comintern. This meant that, since the executive committee was controlled by a Soviet majority, all member parties would be pledged to follow the dictates of the Russians. The points also required that nonrevolutionary elements—i.e., the Social Patriots and pacifists of wartime—must be purged. Certain Italian and French moderates were mentioned by name.[5]

The challenge thrown down by Moscow split the socialist movement everywhere in the following months. The response varied, of course, from country to country. As we have seen, the British Labour party was almost unanimously antagonistic while a majority of the French socialists at the Tours Congress of December 1920 voted to join the Comintern. The major parliamentary leaders of French socialism, however, rebuilt the SFIO as a social democratic party. The German Communist party (KPD) had been formed in December 1918, by the Spartacus group. This was only a splinter group, however, and tried to win over other representatives of the labor movement. In October 1920, the Independent Socialist party (USPD) held a congress at Halle to decide on acceptance of the twenty-one points and merger with the KPD. A majority of the Congress voted for affiliation with the Comintern (236–156). A majority of USPD members, however, refused to follow the congress majority, but the KPD was able to claim a membership of 350,000 in 1921. Italy seemed to offer the most favorable conditions for the creation of a mass revolutionary party. A wave of violence in August and September 1919 had led to factory occupations and the formation of workers' councils in many north Italian cities. The Italian peasantry was also demanding land reform. Immediately after the first congress of the Comintern, the Italian Socialist party (PSI) had voted to affiliate with that body. But the Italian socialists wanted to maintain a broad party containing both moderates and revolutionaries. When Moscow demanded that certain moderates be ousted, the romance was ended. At a party conference at Leghorn in February 1921,

---

[4] Ibid., p. 271.

[5] Franz Borkenau, *World Communism* (Ann Arbor: University of Michigan Press, 1962), pp. 197–98.

the PSI rejected the twenty-one points and withdrew from the Comintern. An extreme leftist faction then consituted the Italian Communist party. The Soviets had lost the struggle for the control of the European socialist movement.

The Comintern remained intransigently revolutionary for only a very short time. When the Soviets were rethinking their domestic policy and adopting the New Economic Policy, they also initiated a new international communist policy of the "United Front." This policy, adopted in 1921 and followed until 1928, gave theoretical justification for Communist parties participating in parliamentary politics and trade union activity. It approved temporary alliances with other working class parties for the purpose of improving workers' living standards and working conditions. This reversal led to a purge of many leading Communists who refused to forsake their militancy. It was only the first of many purges the Comintern would carry out during the interwar period.

Russia and the World, 1919–24

Even if the Comintern failed in its attempt to gain leadership among Europe's socialists, the Russian Revolution was still an internationally important event because of the power of the example it set for revolutionaries elsewhere. For several years European diplomats were just as concerned with containing the revolution as the Russians were with spreading it. The anxiety was not only caused by the possibility of social upheavals at home but by the nationalist revolts occurring in the Middle East and Asia which threatened the European empires. Turkey and Afghanistan challenged the European powers and gained their national independence. In Egypt the British were forced to recognize the autonomy of the native ruler, and British rule in India was maintained only after the principle of eventual self-government was admitted and force had been used to prevent its occurrence. The anti-Western nationalists in China gained power and became pro-Western, but the Communist party of China was strictly anti-Western from its founding in May 1920. These revolutionary movements were supported or encouraged by Soviet Russia, thereby merging the socialist revolution with the cause of the colonial peoples. The cold war, then, began with the Russian Revolution if one sees that struggle not as a competition between two Great Powers but as a struggle between Western and non-Western peoples, between modernized and nonmodernized societies. The shape this struggle took after World War II as a competition between the United States and Russia only served to conceal its true nature. It was just that the nationalist and socialist revolutions which could be divided into two categories after World War I could no longer be separated after 1947.

The socialist revolution appeared to the Allies at Versailles to be the greatest international threat. The nationalist revolts in the colonies were considered only temporary disturbances. The official summary of the discussions of the Big Four for January 21, 1919, contains the following paraphrase of Clemenceau's argument for military encirclement of the Soviets.

Bolshevism was spreading. It had invaded the Baltic Provinces and Poland, and that very morning they had received bad news regarding its spread to Budapest and Vienna. Italy, also, was in danger. The danger was probably greater there than in France. If Bolshevism, after spreading in Germany, were to traverse Austria and Hungary and so reach Italy, Europe would be faced with a great danger. Therefore, something must be done against Bolshevism.[6]

There were various proposals for dealing with the Communists. At first, armed intervention was tried, with French troops in the Ukraine and United States and British troops both on the Baltic and in Siberia. Military supplies and food were shipped to the White armies. Wilson fought to keep this intervention as small as possible, but his misgivings were more tactical than strategic. He preferred to fight the Soviets not with guns but with political weapons (such as propaganda) and with economic weapons (such as free food or economic aid to the Whites).[7] By May 1919, it had become clear that the White armies were having little success in defeating the Soviets. There was increasing resentment in the United States and Great Britain to the maintaining of troops in Russia, and the French troops were on the verge of rebellion in Odessa. So gradually the Allies withdrew their troops, replacing them with money and equipment. The intervention had not been a small one. In mid 1919, of the non-Russian personnel aiding the Whites, there were 5,600 British, 760 French (mostly in the Ukraine), 2,000 Italians, 4,000 Serbs, 7,500 Americans, 10,000 Poles, 28,000 Japanese, and 55,000 Czechs. The total expense of the intervention to Great Britain was over $300 million and to France around $200 million.

The Allied policy of isolating the Soviets ended in March 1921, when the Anglo-Russian Trade Agreement was signed. Both countries had economic problems. Britain's industry was not recovering as rapidly as had been expected from the shift to peacetime production, and unemployment was high. Russia, of course, was devastated; any trade was welcome. The agreement was political as well as economic. Great Britain would end its blockade of Russia. In return the Russians would end their propaganda attacks on the British Empire. In addition, the two nations were to exchange trade missions with semidiplomatic standing. This was an

---

[6] Louis Fischer, *The Soviets in World Affairs* (New York: Vintage Books, 1951), p. 113.

[7] Arno J. Mayer, *Politics and Diplomacy of Peacemaking* (New York: Alfred A. Knopf, 1967), pp. 17–18, 21.

"armistice between two worlds."[8] The two systems—capitalist and communist—had tried to destroy each other for three years, but by 1921 both sides had tired of the battle. It should also be noted that the trade agreement was signed in the same month Lenin announced the New Economic Policy.

The Soviets made a further step back into the society of nations at Rapallo, Italy, in 1922. Lloyd George had called for an international conference at Genoa to discuss reparations and war debts. The Soviets sent Chicherin, their commissar of foreign affairs, who stopped at Berlin on the way. When the Russians found the Genoa negotiations unproductive, they met with the German delegation at the nearby town of Rapallo. The Rapallo Treaty was simple, but its implications were great. Each country renounced all claims of war damages against the other. They resumed normal relations, and the Germans promised to encourage private German investment in Russia. The treaty was most significant as a protest against Versailles. It was an act of friendship by revisionist powers in defiance of the victor nations. Rapallo also deprived the Allies of their most effective weapon against the Communist regime: their ability to isolate her economically and politically. In practical terms, Germany used its good relations with Russia to train an illegal army in the Ukraine and to experiment with new weapons—especially airplanes, which were forbidden to her by Versailles. The Soviets benefited from German aid in building the Red Army into one of the most modern in Europe, along German lines.

The Soviet Union was accepted as a legal regime by most European states in 1924. It was the Labour government of Great Britain that first extended legal recognition in February 1924. Other states quickly followed to profit from Russian trade and investment opportunities. The victory of the Cartel in France paved the way for French recognition in October 1924. So this year once again becomes a kind of a turning point. The dangerous revolutionaries of 1917 had become acceptable business clients. Time had proved the revolution could be contained. Yet, to most conservatives, the Soviet regime remained a cancer to be removed as soon as possible.

During its years of isolation, the Soviet regime had adopted the policy of supporting movements for national independence among colonial peoples. As Lenin saw the hopes of a revolution in central Europe die with the Bela Kun regime, he turned more and more to a revolution of the Asian peoples against the West as a possible source of allies for the new Russia. There was much ferment in Asia and the Middle East in the wake of the war, and it seemed that Lenin's hopes were not completely groundless. But the nationalist movements were not yet strong enough and the imperial powers not yet weak enough for the revolts to succeed.

---

[8] Fischer, *Soviets in World Affairs,* pp. 214–15.

One non-Western nation, however, was able to resist the Europeans with Soviet aid. This was Turkey. The Russians gave special attention to their neighbors on the south and east. In September 1920, they summoned a "congress of the peoples of the East" to meet in Baku—a city just north of Iran on the Caspian Sea. The Congress ended with Zinoviev, the president of the Comintern, shouting,

The Communist International turns today to the peoples of the East and says to them: "Brothers, we summon you to Holy War first of all against British Imperialism."[9]

These words were gratefully received by Turkish nationalists who were engaged in a war against the British.

The Ottoman Empire having collapsed in 1918, the Middle East became fair game for Great Britain, France, and Italy to divide among themselves. In secret treaties during the war they had even assigned parts of Turkey to Greece. In May 1919, the Greeks, ancient enemies of the Turks, landed at Smyrna to claim their territory. This invasion was met by a spontaneous nationalist uprising. A young Turk army officer, Mustafa Kemal, took the lead in the national resistance and vowed to drive all foreigners from Turkish soil. He also established a revolutionary government, accusing the regular government at Constantinople of subservience to England.

During 1920–21 Kemal spread his control over eastern Turkey and established good relations with Russia. A Russo-Turk Treaty declared the common interest of "the nationalist liberating movement of the peoples of the East and the struggle of the workers of Russia for a new social system."[10] In December 1921, the first Russian military aid arrived in the form of guns and ammunition and Red Army officers to advise Kemal's troops. Kemal soon launched his military campaign and had defeated all opposition by October 1922. He bottled up a British force at Chanak, near the Dardanelles, to be able to force the proud imperialists to negotiate or risk the loss of their troops. At Lausanne, Switzerland, Great Britain and her allies faced Turkey and Russia. The Soviets were Kemal's only support and helped him win meaningful concessions. The Treaty of Lausanne, signed in July 1924, recognized the new Turkey as a fully independent state.

Having gained independence, Kemal (now Kemal Ataturk) began a program of modernizing Turkey to give it an economic base strong enough to protect the nation's independence. For this purpose, Russian experts were called in, and the Soviet model of a state-directed economy was followed. Especially important was the construction and operation of heavy industries by the state. Farms were not collectivized, but peasant cooperatives were encouraged. Crash programs were begun for education, road

---

[9] Ibid., p. 205.

[10] Ibid., p. 288.

building, and agricultural machinery production. During the 1930s the Turks carried out two five-year plans in imitation of Russia.

The importance of the Turkish nationalist revolution, then, was not only that it was a successful armed rising against the West, but also that it identified communism with the anti-imperialist cause, thereby giving Russia great prestige among the undeveloped countries of the world. That prestige was already significant in the 1920s. A communist party was founded in Peking on May 4, 1920, by two college professors who felt communism was the most useful ideology with which to combat the West. Ho Chi Minh was trained in Moscow and then founded the Indochinese Communist party. Other nationalist revolutionaries looked to the Soviets for aid and guidance. Therefore, the Turkish rebellion is best seen as the first "war of liberation" supported by Russia.

Stalin's Revolution

Stalin had become the second most powerful man in the Communist party organization by 1922. Only Lenin was more powerful, but, in May 1922, Lenin had the first of three strokes that made him an invalid until his death in January 1924. Stalin's power was derived from his unique position as the only member of the Politburo, the party's executive, who also belonged to the General Secretariat, which controlled promotions in the party, the Central Control Commission, which checked on the political loyalty of all party members, and Rabkrin, which investigated the political opinions of civil servants. These four bureaucratic positions were key to the entire structure of Soviet government. The Soviet state was really governed by two parallel bureaucracies: the elected government and the Communist party. (See Map 5.) Stalin, in his roles as general secretary of the party and member of Rabkrin, was able to promote men in both the party and state bureaucracies who were his supporters. He could equally remove or discredit the supporters of any rival.

Although Stalin controlled the administration of the party machinery, he was not thought to be the leading candidate to follow Lenin as leader of the Soviet state. Most party leaders considered him a bureaucrat without imagination or ability as an ideologue. Instead, Leon Trotsky appeared the most likely to succeed Lenin. Trotsky was by far the most popular member of the Politburo, and as commissar of war, he controlled the Red Army, which he had created during the civil war. It was to prevent Trotsky from becoming dictator that Stalin, Kamenev, and Zinoviev formed the Troika within the Politburo. Gregory E. Zinoviev was the best known of the three both to the Russian people and to the international community as the head of the Comintern. His base of strength was the Petrograd party machine. Lev B. Kamenev controlled the Moscow party organization and was more moderate than Zenoviev in his calls for the

FIGURE 5.1.   Party and State in USSR, 1923–27

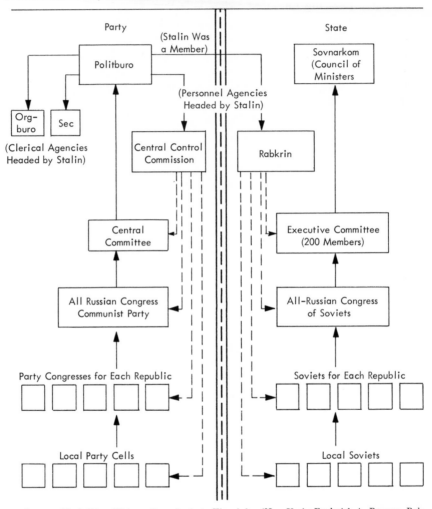

Source: Hugh Seton-Watson, *From Lenin to Khrushchev* (New York: Frederick A. Praeger, Publisher, 1960), pp. 79–83.

completion of the revolution at home and abroad. During Lenin's illness, the Politburo had only six members: Trotsky; the Troika; Mikhail P. Tomsky, a labor union leader who opposed Trotsky's proposals to regiment labor; and Nikolai I. Bukharin, an economist, who opposed Trotsky's desire to further socialize the economy.

The attack on Trotsky began in early 1923 when the Troika accused him of Bonapartism, of preparing the army for a coup, and they recommended "collective leadership" as a safeguard against Trotsky's ambitions. Stalin gradually replaced Trotsky's supporters with his own men. Trotsky did not try to organize an opposition. Instead, he criticized the economic policy that they were following—that is, the NEP—and urged the adoption of economic planning for rapid industrialization. He also demanded that free discussion be allowed within the party. In October 1923, forty-six leading party members issued a statement supporting him. Trotsky encouraged this revolt in a letter to *Pravda* entitled "The New Course." In the letter he condemned the bureaucratic control over the party exercised by "secretaries" such as Stalin. He warned that this bureaucratism would lead to an intellectual and political sterility. Therefore, he once again called for free debates within the party and, for the first time, for limitations on the power of bureaucrats.

Trotsky's letter brought the conflict into the open, but the Troika had the upper hand since Stalin was able to control the voting at all party conferences. At the Thirteenth Party Conference in January 1924, a resolution was passed condemning Trotsky and The Forty-Six for "deviation from Leninism" and for factionalism. Factions within the party had been outlawed in 1921 by the Tenth Party Congress. Although Zinoviev and Kamenev urged Trotsky's expulsion from the party, Stalin played the moderate and recommended leniency. The result was that Stalin appeared to be above the battle.

Lenin died two days after the party conference ended. This was a great stroke of luck for Stalin, since Lenin had become increasingly hostile to him. In early 1923, Lenin had intended to launch a campaign against Stalin's growing power and his brutal treatment of party members who had resisted his control. Since Lenin was disabled, he asked Trotsky to lead the attack, but Trotsky did not seize the opportunity. Lenin's support would have guaranteed victory. Instead, Trotsky accepted explanations of Stalin's behavior offered by Kamenev. In fact, Trotsky blundered away several such chances in 1923–24, as if he did not realize the finality of the struggle between Stalin and himself. One such occasion was the reading of Lenin's will to the Central Committee of the party in May 1924. The will was a direct attack on Stalin who was reported to have trembled as he listened to it being read. Once again, Kamenev and Zinoviev came to his defense, while Trotsky, for some unexplicable reason, remained silent. Stalin retained all his powers.

This was Trotsky's last real chance to stop Stalin. Still, the conflict continued on the ideological plane. During 1924 Stalin developed a theory concerning the possibility of "Socialism in One Country" to oppose to Trotsky's thesis of "Permanent Revolution." Trotsky had published a tract on the necessity of worldwide revolution in 1905. Until 1924 almost all Bolsheviks accepted his argument that the Socialist revolution could not survive in only one country because the capitalist powers would unite to destroy it. Especially would this be true in Russia because of the backwardness of the Russian economy. Either the revolution would be compromised so as to gain financial aid from the capitalists, or it would be corrupted from within because of the weakness of the proletariat. This analysis led Trotsky to recommend two policy goals: the immediate industrialization of Russia to increase the size of the proletariat and to strengthen Russia so she could resist the capitalist states; and Russian support for revolutions throughout the world so as to weaken the capitalist powers and to gain allies for the Soviets.

Stalin, on the other hand, argued that "Socialism in One Country" was possible. Instead of developing a theoretical argument. Stalin asserted that the facts spoke for themselves, that the Soviets had proved their ability to resist the capitalist powers and to begin building a socialist society. He went further to say that the best way to achieve a worldwide revolution was to plant socialism firmly in one country that might aid other revolutionaries. Stalin's argument had the most appeal to party members and to other Russians because it not only held out the hope of developing a true socialism without waiting for other revolutions, but it also flattered the Russians by picturing them as the vanguard of a new world order.

Stalin used this ideological debate as his lever to oust Trotsky. Finding himself isolated on the Politburo and the Central Committee, Trotsky offered his resignation as commissar of war in January 1925, thereby surrendering his last possible source of political influence. Yet he temporarily kept his party offices. Now he was entirely helpless to do anything but write and speak to party groups.

Soon, Trotsky discovered he had two unexpected fellow outcasts—Zinoviev and Kamenev. Stalin had cut his ties with these two left-wingers as soon as he had defeated Trotsky. Now he formed an alliance with the right wing of the party led by Bukharin, Tomsky, and A. I. Rykov (the latter having replaced Lenin on the Politburo). Stalin also had three of his closest supporters added to the Politburo—Molotov, Voroshilov, and Kalinin. The last three had no ideological convictions but were party bureaucrats who owed their careers to Stalin. From 1925 to 1927, Stalin leaned on the rightists, who felt the revolution had accomplished its major goals and should proceed slowly, to defeat the Left Opposition, who insisted on rapid industrialization and increased socialization of the economy. For the Left argued that the only way Russia could be industrialized was by heavy investment by the state in industries such as mining, steel, machinery, and electricity. The money had to come from Russia's major source of wealth—agriculture. Only by selling agricultural products abroad could the state get the needed money. Therefore, farmers had to produce more and eat less, so there would be more for export. Such rapid industrialization would also require the salaries of factory workers be cut and the prices of consumer goods raised, making more money available for reinvestment in the factories. Thus, the general standard of living might have to be lowered in order to achieve a modern economy.

At the 15th Party Congress in 1927, Stalin was consolidating his dominance over the Communist movement. Molotov sits on Stalin's left. (Courtesy of Roger-Viollet)

The Right objected to every point of this program. Bukharin was the chief spokesman for those who wanted to base economic growth on an alliance between the proletariat and independent farmers. To him this implied a continuation of NEP and less, not more, government control of the economy. He argued that industrialization could only be based on a wealthy peasantry who could buy the goods produced in factories. If their purchasing power were cut by high taxes, or worse yet, by collectivization of farms, there would be no market for manufactured goods. The Left accused Bukharin of applying capitalistic concepts to a socialist economy.

Stalin supported Bukharin and denounced the left opposition for forming a faction within the Party. In late 1927 Trotsky, Kamenev, and Zinoviev were expelled from the party. Actually, the Left had not tried to divide the Party. They sincerely believed that to do so would weaken it and might endanger the revolution. Consequently, they could not resist Stalin's skillful maneuvering. Zinoviev and Kamenev recanted after a year of political isolation and were readmitted to the party. Trotsky refused to recant and was exiled to Alma Ata, an isolated city in central Asia. From there he began his long odyssey that was to end when he was assassinated by one of Stalin's thugs in Mexico in 1940.

Stalin had rid himself of Trotsky and the Left Opposition, but events beyond his control soon forced or led him to adopt their economic policies in a more extreme form than they had been originally proposed. In hope of higher food prices, peasants had withheld food from the market after the harvest of 1925 and 1926. By 1927 the food shortage in urban centers was beginning to approach a condition of famine. Stalin reacted by ordering local party secretaries to take drastic measures, any measures necessary, to obtain the food quota from their districts. Obviously, this order was directly in conflict with Bukharin's concept of a prosperous peasantry forming the basis for industrialization. In early 1928 Stalin ousted all lower echelon party officials who might disapprove of his forceful handling of the food situation and replaced them with his own men. This was a very sizable change of personnel.

This new departure isolated and discredited Bukharin, Tomsky, and Rykov, who now were referred to as the "Right Opposition." Carrying his attack to its logical conclusion, Stalin even invited members of the Left Opposition to support his new policy. Some did. They publicly repented their crimes against the party and were permitted to resume work in the party and civil service. The parallel to the return of the Left was the purge of the Right. Tomsky lost his position as head of the trade unions. Bukharin was ousted from the Politburo and from his position as head of the Comintern. Rykov was also stripped of power. After January 1929 Stalin's personal dominance was absolute. He had skillfully defeated all rivals for leadership of the party. When he celebrated his fiftieth birthday in December 1929, Moscow was covered with his statues and portraits.

Stalin has reasons other than the need for food for his rapid reversal of policy in 1928. His theory of "Socialism in One Country" presupposed that Russia would industrialize rapidly. If the USSR were the only socialist country in the world, it had to be economically self-supporting and militarily strong enough to defend itself. Stalin expressed these ideas in a speech in 1931.

. . . Those who fall behind get beaten. . . . One feature of the history of Old Russia was the continual beating she suffered because of her backwardness. . . . She was beaten by the Polish and Lithuanian gentry. She was beaten by the Japanese barons. All beat her because of her backwardness, military backwardness, cultural backwardness. . . . It is the jungle law of capitalism. You are backward, you are weak—therefore you are wrong; hence, you can be beaten and enslaved. You are mighty—therefore you are right.

We are fifty or a hundred years behind the advanced countries. We must make good this distance in ten years. Either we do it, or we shall be crushed.[11]

Once again, Stalin was adopting Trotsky's policy and arguing that Russia had to modernize before it was too late.

[11] Basil Dmytryshyn, *USSR: A Concise History* (New York: Charles Scribner's Sons, 1965), p. 158.

The First Five-Year Plan was Stalin's means of coordinating his attack on the peasants and his industrialization program. The plan had been developed over a two-year period by the State Planning Commission or *Gosplan*. This was a corps of economists, statisticians, engineers, agriculturalists, and other technocrats who studied every aspect of Russian society and then recommended possible goals for economic growth. The plan was to run from August 1928 to August 1933. Its goals were staggering. They included a 250 percent increase in total industrial production, a 330 percent increase in heavy industry, a 150 percent rise in farm production, and the collectivization of 20 percent of all farms. It is interesting that these experts could develop this plan, which was clearly leftist and Trotskyite, just as Trotsky was being defeated. The technocrats obviously considered themselves outside ideological disputes and only concerned with what was efficient.

Stalin's ruthless implementation of the plan entailed a complete revolution in the social and economic structure of Russia. In agriculture the basic goal was to eliminate all small, uneconomical farms by consolidating them, to destroy any traces of agricultural capitalism, and to vastly increase the amount of food produced. It was felt these goals could best be achieved by "collective farms" or kolkhozes, huge cooperative farms on which peasants would split their work time between the collective and their private garden. The peasants were required to work a certain number of days per year for the kolkhoz and, in return, were supplied with machinery, clothing, seeds, and other necessities by the government. Every kolkhoz had a quota of produce that must be sold to the state. Any profit that might be made by selling excess produce would be split among all the farmers living on the collective. Each farmer also had his own private plot on which he could grow whatever he desired.

To get land, livestock and tools for the kolkhozes, Stalin tried to expropriate the wealthiest peasants—the kulaks—under the excuse that they were capitalists. The kulaks were the most successful farmers, usually employing several workers and enjoying some luxury. To attack them the government called on the aid of the muzhiks—the poorest peasants, who often owned no land and had to work for kulaks. The muzhiks were glad to have a chance to live on a kolkhoz. They had nothing to lose. However, these were not the only classes of peasants. Out of approximately 28 million peasants, only about 1.5 to 2 million were kulaks, and only 5 to 8 million were muzhiks. From 15 to 18 million were "middle peasants" who were not prosperous but owned some land and occasionally sold their surplus. When the government began attacking the kulaks, the middle peasants also fought back. Therefore, the army had to be used to carry out collectivization. Civil war raged in rural areas. Entire villages were surrounded and fired on by the army. The inhabitants might then be shipped together to Siberia or herded into forced labor brigades. Stalin later admitted to Winston Churchill that between five and ten million Russians had died during the First Five-Year Plan as a result of government policy, and most of these were peasants.

The peasants could not resist for long, but they could express their frustration by destroying their livestock, ruining their crops, and burning their homes and barns. The loss to the Soviet economy was great. Yet the collectivization was pushed through. By 1933, 65.6 percent of all peasants lived on collectives. In 1928 only 1.7 percent had lived on collectives.

TABLE 5.1.   Loss of Livestock in First Five-Year Plan

Stock	Total in 1929 (millions)	Total in 1933
Horses	36.1	15.4
Cattle	66.8	33.5
Sheep and goats	114.6	36.5

"The collectivisation of agriculture was accompanied by industrialization on a scale and at a pace never yet known in human history."[12] By superhuman effort and organizational genius as well as by the use of forced labor and the sacrifice of living standards, factories were built where forests had stood, mines were dug in areas in which there had previously been no roads, and electrical power was supplied to both. A major part of the plan was the construction of entire cities so that industrial complexes could be placed near the supply of raw materials or minerals. Cities such as Magnitogorsk in the Ural Mountains were built in a few years. The production of virtually every industry skyrocketed. The same growth, but slightly slower, was continued in the Second Five-Year Plan which ran from 1932 to 1937. A measure of the Russian economic achievement during these years can be reached by comparing the annual growth rate of economic production of Russia with that of other countries. The period of most rapid growth for American industry was 1900 to 1906. The growth rate of the American economy was 9 percent annually. Japan's greatest growth came in the period 1906 to 1913 with a rate of 11 percent. The Russian annual growth rate for 1929 to 1934 was 27 percent, and, for 1929 to 1939, it was 13 percent.[13]

One man must be recognized as the architect of this economic feat. Josef Stalin had absolute power after 1929, so he must be praised for

[12] Hugh Seton-Watson, *From Lenin to Khrushchev* (New York: Frederick A. Praeger, Inc., 1960), p. 159.

[13] W. Arthur Lewis, *Economic Survey, 1919–1939* (London: Unwin University Books, 1949), p. 125.

TABLE 5.2.   Production of Selected Goods in the USSR

Product and Unit	1921	1928	1933	1940
Industrial:				
Electric power, billion kwh	0.5	5.0	16.3	48.3
Crude oil, million tons	3.8	11.6	21.5	31.1
Coal, million tons	9.5	35.5	76.3	165.9
Steel, million tons	0.2	4.2	6.9	18.3
Machine tools, 1,000 units	0.8	2.0	21.0	58.4
Consumer:				
Automobiles, 1,000 units	....	0.1	10.3	5.5
Bicycles, 1,000 units	7.7	10.8	125.6	255.0
Radio sets, 1,000 units	....	....	29.0	160.5
Cotton fabrics, billion meters	1.5	2.7	2.7	3.9
Leather shoes, million pairs	28.0	58.0	90.3	211.0
Canned food, billion cans	0.1	0.1	0.7	1.1

SOURCE: Alfred R. Oxenfeldt, *Economic Systems in Action* (New York: Rinehart and Co., 1957), pp 104–08.

the progress as well as blamed for the suffering that occurred. At least one Western historian views Stalin as the most important national leader of the twentieth century. Francis B. Randall has written.

Stalin was probably the most important man who ever lived. . . . He constructed a system of government as absolute as any in history and far more total in its scope than any save that of his imitators. He transformed the USSR in one generation from a largely agrarian country into the largest industrial state in the Old World. This was probably his most important achievement, for industrialization is the most fundamental revolution in human affairs. . . . Stalin was the first to industrialize a country by that thoroughly statist means which he and most others called "socialism"—thereby setting a pattern for much of the world.[14]

To mention only Stalin's achievements and to overlook the horrible suffering caused by the First Five-Year Plan would be immoral as well as bad history, but to ignore the amazing accomplishments of this skillful politician makes it impossible for Westerners to understand the prestige his policies enjoy not only in Russia but also throughout the undeveloped world.

---

[14] Francis B. Randall, *Stalin's Russia: An Historical Reconsideration* (New York: Free Press, 1965), pp. 1–2. Reprinted with permission of The Macmillan Company.

PART II

Prosperity and Crisis

Chapter 6

THE UNCERTAIN TWENTIES

Intellectual Trends

It has become a cliché to speak of the cultural shock experienced in Europe during the last years of World War I. The cultural and intellectual trends of the twenties are attributed to the disillusionment caused by four years of death and deprivation. Yet, if ever Lenin's dictum, "War only accelerates history," was true, it is in reference to European culture from 1900 to 1930. All of the trends in art, literature, philosophy, and social thought that are generally associated with the "lost generation" of the twenties had appeared before 1914. The effect of the war was to spread these ideas to the general public. The war created the social discontent necessary for the new ideas to be accepted. The most notable trends were an increasing pessimism about the ability of western European society to meet the challenges of the twentieth century, an uncertainty about man's ability to comprehend his world, a rejection of Victorian morality, the application of psychoanalysis to the arts, and perhaps above all, the separation of elite culture from mass culture.

A book appeared in the summer of 1918 that seemed to summarize the feelings of many Europeans that were evident in other works but not clearly expressed. The book was *The Decline of the West* by Oswald Spengler. Spengler refuted the Darwinian belief that human society had been making progress since the beginning of history. Instead, he offered a cyclical theory of the rise and fall of civilizations. It is easy to gather from his title that Spengler felt western Europe had entered a period of decline. He argued that the era of individualism, humanitarianism, intellectual freedom, and religious skepticism was nearing its end, and a new era was beginning that would be characterized by "restrictions on individual freedoms, a revival of faith, and an increase in the use of force." This book had its greatest success in postwar Germany where it truly appeared that the nineteenth century had been destroyed by war and revolution.

During World War I Freud's probing into the irrational side of man had led him to equally pessimistic conclusions. In 1918 he wrote to. a friend, "I have not found much good in the average human being. Most of them are in my experience riff-raff." This might sound like antidemocratic prejudice, but it was based on Freud's objective clinical studies from which he concluded, ". . . the primitive, savage and evil impulses have not vanished from any individual, but continue their existence, although in a repressed state. . . ."[1] Latent in each individual, he decided, was a desire for aggression, to use one's fellow man, "to exploit his capacity for work without recompense . . . to seize his possessions, to cause him pain, to humiliate him, to torture and to kill him." These last lines were written in 1929, only four years before Hitler came to power. Freud's ideas should be considered both a symptom and a diagnosis of the cultural crisis that Europe was suffering in the first decades of this century. Old ethical standards were being rejected in favor of new relationships between individuals. The frustrations and psychic strains of industrial urban society were causing a general pessimism among sensitive men, who realized that the social values of the nineteenth century could not cope with social conditions of the twentieth.

Freud's pessimism eventually led him to an elitist view of society. There were three men who were best known for their elitist theories: Pareto, Mosca, and Michels. They had in common the fact that they all lived in Italy and their belief that rule by a small elite is inevitable. Gaetano Mosca developed his ideas by studying the Italian parliament in the 1880s. A legislative deputy himself, he concluded that even in a democracy the people do not govern, but pressure groups and adroit politicians manipulate elections by graft, influence, and vote rigging. Robert Michels extended this idea to mass organizations—especially to political parties and trade unions. In his classic book *Political Parties* (1915), he expounded an "iron law of oligarchy." This law holds that in any large organization power will inevitably be concentrated in the hands of a few men who will perpetuate their control over the organization. His famous example was the German Social Democratic party, whose leaders, he contended, had become a self-perpetuating oligarchy through the necessities of party discipline and administrative efficiency. This was not abstract theorizing. Michels had himself been expelled from Germany because of his socialist

---

[1] H. Stuart Hughes, *Consciousness and Society* (New York: Random House, Inc., 1958), p. 143.

political activity. His first-hand knowledge of the German and French socialists gave his ideas added influence.

Vilfredo Pareto was also concerned predominantly with politics, but he went further than Mosca and Michels by saying that not only was rule by an elite inevitable, but also that rule by an authoritarian elite was desirable. He reasoned that political movements could never be more than the work of active minorities and that the mass of mankind would always be passive instruments in the struggle among elites. People did, however, have a choice of the type of elite that might govern them. Pareto made a distinction between leaders who were "foxes" and those who were "lions." Democratic elites were foxes in that they lived by their wits, by graft, and by coalition governments. This allowed petty men to occupy the seats of power even though they had no program and never accomplished anything. The very weakness of such a regime would give rise to a lion who would establish an authoritarian regime and head a dynamic government. Of course, Pareto's lion was Mussolini, although Pareto developed his theory before and during World War I—before Mussolini had entered the political scene as a possible strong man. Here again was a thinker who was both diagnostician and symptom of the political situation. When Mussolini came to power he won the unqualified support of Pareto, the qualified support of Michels and the opposition of Mosca.

Radical departures were taken in the field of philosophy during the war years and immediately after. Two antagonistic developments—analytic positivism and existentialism—had in common their rejection of the Western philosophical tradition. The analytical positivists argued that the path to reliable knowledge was either through detailed scientific investigation using the principles of mathematics or through the painstaking analysis of the meaning of words. Determined to limit their studies to problems that could be treated in these ways, they insisted that philosophers should not concern themselves with metaphysics or ethics, the traditional subjects of philosophy. Existentialism, popular especially in Germany, was in direct contradiction to this ultrarationalism. Existentialists argued that knowledge could be gained not by observation or theorizing but only through experiencing life. Also denying any abstract moral code, they contended morality could not be reasoned but could only be practiced. Only by making moral decisions could one be moral. Both philosophical schools rejected the smugness of the Victorian age.

Toward the end of the twenties a reaction began against the trends in European thought since the 1890s. This reaction was limited, but it was a glimmer of a turnabout that would become dominant in the thirties. In 1927 Julian Benda, a Parisian intellectual, warned that abstract thinkers should begin to worry about the practical consequences of their ideas. Benda's *The Betrayal of the Intellectuals* warned that the basis of civilized values was being destroyed by the abstract glorification of irrationality and the rejection of liberal ideals. The "betrayal" of the intellectuals had been their

. . . desire to debase the values of knowledge before the values of action. . . . About 1890 the men of letters, especially in France and Italy, realized with astounding astuteness that the doctrines of arbitrary authority, discipline, . . . contempt for the spirit of liberty, . . . were haughty and rigid poses infinitely more likely to strike the imagination of simple souls than the sentimentalities of Liberalism and Humanitarianism.[2]

These intellectuals had exploited public preference for authority, for discipline, and for conformity instead of resisting it and had thereby intensified racial, class, and national passions. Far from condemning this irrationalism, the intellectuals had become its spokesmen. For this reason, Benda denounced the writings of Maurice Barrès, Charles Peguy, Henri Bergson, D'Annunzio, and Georges Sorel. He denounced them in the name of rationalism. Benda warned,

If humanity loses this jewel [of rationality], there is not much chance of finding it again. . . . People forget that Hellenic rationalism only really enlightened the world during seven hundred years, that it was then hidden . . . for twelve centuries, and has only begun to shine again for barely four centuries.[3]

Benda was fighting a losing battle. Rationalism as he knew it was on the defensive and was being defeated everywhere. The intellectuals did contribute to the rise of fascism; although the same men can hardly be blamed for the Soviet dictatorship. Yet the various trends in European thought after 1890 were not the result of particular ideas divorced from society. They reflected the impact of rapid social and economic change. The emphasis on irrational man, the cultural pessimism, the substitution of relativism for rigid moral codes, the refusal to believe in a Darwinian moral evolution were all responses to social conditions, not results of Freud's publication of *The Interpretation of Dreams*.

Art and Literature

The major innovations in twentieth century painting occurred before 1914—with the development of cubism, nonobjective art, and abstract art. However, there were two movements that grew directly out of the wartime experience: dadaism and surrealism. Both movements affected poetry and dramatics as well. Dadaism was the more ephemeral. A spontaneous artistic protest against the society that had allowed the war to occur, it contained all the intelligence of a scream. The dadaists wanted

---

[2] Ibid., p. 414.

[3] Ibid., p. 416.

to shock, to confuse, to insult the stupidity of Western society. They were anti-art as well as antiwar. Their art was intentionally nonsensical because to them the war made no sense. They denounced patriotism and technology in absurd sketchings or collages or paintings in which the colors were intentionally unpleasant. This outburst of indignation could not be long sustained, and it lasted only from 1916 to 1922.

Surrealism was also a protest, but it was much more intellectualized and had a more lasting effect. Andre Breton, usually considered its founder, gave the following definition of the movement in 1924:

Surrealism: Pure psychic automatism, by which it is intended to express verbally, in writing, or by other means, the real process of thought. Thought's dictation, in the absence of all control exercised by reason and outside all aesthetic or moral preoccupations. Surrealism rests upon the belief in the higher reality of specific forms of association . . . , in the omnipotence of dreams, and in the disinterested play of thinking.[4]

Breton is saying that anything that pops into the artist's mind should be recorded. True knowledge is obtained through free association and the study of dreams. Obviously, this was based on a distorted Freudian psychology. The painters most often associated with surrealism are Salvador Dali, Juan Miro, and Max Ernst.

Both dadaism and surrealism were attempts to rejuvenate European art and society by destroying old values and conventions. They succeeded in thoroughly scandalizing the art public—the middle-class gentlemen and ladies who liked to tour the galleries on a Sunday afternoon. If bourgeois values had been shaken by the horror of war, these outrageous painters shook them even more. To a man accustomed to photograph-like portrayals of pleasant scenes or to the gentle colors of the impressionists, the new trends must have seemed just as nonsensical and alien as the painters had hoped. So the poor average man was not only forced to face the loss of his son in the war, of his money to inflation, of his faith in scientists to explain his physical world, but now he must also face the loss of his pastime of gallery hopping since all of the young painters were either offensive or incomprehensible.

Worst yet, the same thing was happening in literature. In the last decades of the nineteenth century there had been a reaction against naturalism, against the realistic, scientific portrayal of everyday life. The revolt was led by Apollinaire, who developed a poetic style known as symbolism. The symbolists insisted there was more to life than the externals that the naturalists had been describing in such detail. Literature should be, they argued, more a matter of the emotions and the sensations

---

[4] Richard Ellman and Charles Feidelson, Jr., eds., *The Modern Tradition: Backgrounds of Modern Literature* (New York: Oxford University Press, 1965), p. 602.

of each artist. Only symbols, literary images, and not facts should be used in poetry; for it was felt that conventional language was inadequate to reflect personal feelings.

It was within this tradition that dada poets wrote. As cubist painters had tried to portray all aspects of an object simultaneously, the dada poets tried to portray all aspects of life simultaneously. At times this degenerated into nonsense—as when three or more poets tried to recite their poetry simultaneously. Blaise Cendrars's "Portrait," a description of a painter at work, is an example of how a surrealist poet employed the free association principle.

> He's asleep
> He's awake
> All at once he's painting
> He grabs a church and paints with
>   a church
> He grabs a cow and paints with a cow
> With a sardine
> With heads, with hands, with knives
> He paints with a beef tendon
> He paints with the dirty passions
>   of a little Jewish village
> He paints with his thighs
> His eyes are in his behind
> And all at once it's your portrait
> Reader it's you.[5]

The images evoked by this poem show the close connection between dada poetry and surrealist poetry.

Surrealism became the leading movement in French poetry just as in painting in the mid twenties. The same Freudian principles of free association and the re-creation of dreams that characterized surrealist canvases also were to be found in the poetry. The following segment of an Andre Breton poem could be describing a nightmare captured on a Salvador Dali canvas:

> My woman with wood-fire hair
> With thoughts of flashes of heat
> With an hourglass waist
> My woman with the waist of an otter
>   in a tiger's teeth
> My woman with mouth of cockade
>   and of bouquets of last magnitude
>   stars

---

[5] Blaise Cendrars, "Portrait," in *Surrealist Poetry in France: A Bilingual Anthology*, trans. Francis J. Carmody and Carlyle MacIntyre (Berkeley: California Book Co., 1953), p. 141. Reprinted with permission of Francis Carmody and Editions Denoël.

With the teeth of white mouse-tracks
          on white earth
With tongue of amber and glass
          rubbed together
My woman with the tongue of a host
          pierced by daggers
With the tongue of a doll that opens
          and closes its eyes
With tongue of unbelievable stone
My woman with lashes like children's
          writing strokes
With eyebrows of rims of swallows' nests.[6]

The surrealists were political as well as literary revolutionaries. In 1925 six leading poets announced their membership in the French Communist party. The association was not a happy one. Andre Breton, for example, was assigned to a cell composed of gas workers. He was soon asked to write a statistical history of Italian industry. That was too much. He ceased formal activity in the PCF but continued to consider himself a Communist, as did most of the other surrealists.

It was not only the rebellious young poets who rejected prewar values and literary standards. In a very different way two respected academic poets—T. S. Eliot and Paul Valery—rejected naturalism and the bourgeois society in which they lived. In two remarkable poems—*The Waste Land* (1922) and *The Hollow Men* (1924)—Eliot expressed his utter pessimism about the course of western society, a pessimism equaling that of Spengler. In *The Waste Land* Great Britain is a sterile land, incapable of growing crops or inspiring men. The terrible dreariness of modern cities has sapped men of feeling, and they live dull monotonous lives.

Unreal city,
Under the brown fog of a winter dawn,
A crowd flowed over London Bridge, so many,
I had not thought death had undone so many
Sighs, short and infrequent, were exhaled
And each man fixed his eyes before his feet.[7]

In contrast to the dadaists and the surrealists, Eliot's poetry was scholarly to a point that only other students of literature could understand his obscure literary allusions. The general public could only marvel at the complexity of his verse without comprehending its meaning. Therefore, Eliot initiated a movement toward elitist poetry, depending on literary reference to an unprecedented degree.

---

[6] Andre Breton, "My Woman," in Carmody and MacIntyre, *Surrealist Poetry,* pp. 23–25. Reprinted with permission of Francis Carmody and Librairie Gallimard.
    [7] Thomas Stearns Eliot, *Collected Poems 1909–1962* (New York: Harcourt, Brace and World, Inc., 1963, 1936), p. 55.

Eliot's French counterpart was Paul Valery. Valery took the French literary world by storm with the publication in 1917 of *La Jeune Parque*. This poem about a young man of Greek mythology was a masterpiece of intricate construction. Valery was consciously rebelling against what he considered the prostitution of the French language by such men as Anatole France who wrote for the general public. Like Eliot, Valery wrote only for the experts. This assertion of academism, which made Valery the most respected literary critic of France, once again signaled a clear break with prewar literature. In his own way, Valery was as difficult to understand as the youthful rebels.

The novel did not escape the radical transformations that were shaping the other art forms. Two novels were published in the early twenties that were milestones of literature. Both incorporated the concepts of Sigmund Freud, although the authors had not systematically studied Freud. Both Marcel Proust's *In Search of Times Past* and James Joyce's *Ulysses* dealt with the formation of the personality, the relativity of truth, the persistence of memory. Both also implicitly reject the values of Victorian society. Proust's narrator becomes increasingly disillusioned with society as he grows from boy to man. Joyce describes the inner thoughts of each character and shows social norms to be irrelevant.

If any generality can be made about the arts in the 1920s, it must be that there was abundant evidence that the values, forms, and standards of the 1890s had been rejected but had not yet been replaced by a new synthesis. Perhaps it is the intellectual crisis of the twentieth century that no new synthesis, no new consensus on standards can be achieved.

Popular Culture

During the war Europeans had learned to produce everything faster than ever before. Inevitably, this meant that more members of society would be able to share in the bounty of industrial production. And not only was more being produced, but the lower classes had more purchasing power. From 1914 to 1923 the real income of the average wage-earner in Great Britain increased by 20 to 30 percent. Increased earnings along with shorter working hours left the urban classes money to spend on leisure activities previously enjoyed only by the wealthy. The result was a qualitative change in popular culture. The entertainment industries, newspapers, and producers of consumer goods looked to the lower classes for their profits rather than to the rich and well-bred. This effected new departures in everything from the nature of advertising to the construction of apartment buildings, from the language used in newspapers to the marketing of food. Of course, aristocrats deplored this leveling of society, but there can be little question that it made the life of the "average man" easier to bear. Nor can there be any doubt that the tastes of the average man began to dominate Western culture in the 1920s and have done so since. The following discussion will be based primarily on the British experience because of the stability of British society when compared to the economic crises of Germany, Italy, and France.

The technological developments that ushered in mass culture were related to American techniques of mass production imported to Europe during the war. The assembly line or "chain belt" method of production, which required the standardization of parts and supplies, had been perfected by Henry Ford by 1909. The demands of war forced Europeans to adopt these techniques. Finally, the corollary to the standardization of parts was the standardization of the workers on the assembly line. The name of this science of human efficiency was Taylorism, developed around the turn of the century by another American, Frederick Winslow Taylor. Although the long-term result of Taylorism was to make workers dehumanized objects of social planning, the immediate results were nevertheless beneficial to them. For example, employers were shown "scientifically" that their practice of working men long hours and imposing strict factory discipline actually reduced individual productivity rather than increasing it. British industrialists, in spite of their continued opposition to unions, gradually adopted a policy of paternalism largely because Taylor had proved to them that this was profitable.

The social effects of mass production were immense. The gap between social classes was reduced by making the same consumer goods available to all at low prices. The most significant goods affected were clothing, household appliances, foods, and automobiles. The fact that blue-collar and white-collar workers could now afford suits and dresses that *looked* as good as those worn by the wealthy was a great step toward social democracy, because European social classes had always been distinguished by their style of dress. Before the twentieth century, working men rarely owned a suit. The manufacture of military uniforms, however, had revolutionized the garment industry, and after 1920, cheap copies of the best Paris styles for women or London styles for men were within the reach of most family budgets. This was also the decade during which long-term credit became generally available for the purchase of consumer goods. This form of credit was first introduced in England to aid workers purchasing public housing. It was soon extended to large appliances and cars. Of course, here again, the luxuries formerly reserved for the rich were made available to the general public.

The war had also advanced equality between the sexes. To fill the labor shortage resulting from the military call-up, women had taken jobs in industry by the millions. After the war, many of them kept these jobs and enjoyed an economic freedom never before thought possible. They also gained political power by the extension of the suffrage, in two stages, to include all women over twenty-one.

During the twenties several British governments subsidized public housing to replace the old slum tenements with homes the tenement dwellers could afford. Actually, the houses built were still too expensive for the poorer laborers, but many white-collar workers and well-paid blue-collar workers did move out of the slums. The flight to the suburbs had begun. These new homes were definitely a sign of upward social mobility and workers moving into them were likely to begin thinking conservatively. Of course, public housing developments had desirable and undesirable aspects. On the negative side, all the houses looked alike, with little shrubbery or landscaping. British literature is punctuated by disparaging comments about them. On the positive side, these houses had conveniences that had previously been reserved for the upper classes. They were new and clean. They had bathrooms, gas, and electricity. Such conditions were credited with the vast improvement of general health and the decrease in the infant mortality rate.

Closely related to the growth of the suburbs was the improvement in communications and transportation. Assembly line production brought the automobile within the price range of millions. And from 1920 to 1929 the two major British auto companies—Morris and Austin—actually cut their prices by two-thirds to meet American competition. The cheapest car sold by Austin in 1921 cost £325; in 1930, the new Morris Minor sold for £100. The availability of the car not only made commuting possible, it also allowed urbanites to escape into the countryside for a day and enjoy the fresh air that had been denied them since the early nineteenth century. New bus lines and the improvement of the train system further increased the mobility of the British populace.

The communications industry was most influenced by the commercial success of the radio. At first just a novelty, by 1922, the radio was so popular that the Government established the British Broadcasting Company as a publicly regulated private monopoly so as to control the growth of the industry. Light entertainment replaced the early broadcasts of classical music as the decade ended. Newspapers were frightened by this new competition for the reporting of news. The reaction was to accentuate the trend toward yellow journalism. Sensationalism was thought the key to circulation. One newspaper reported Einstein's complicated relativity theory with the headline: HUN PROFESSOR CATCHES LIGHT BENDING![8]

The Victorian moral code did not survive the war—at least, not for the young. The new morality was most evident in women's clothing and in attitudes toward sex. The length of the hemline was the symbol of the woman's liberation. The skirt had been shortened during the war

---

[8] Robert Graves and Alan Hodge, *The Long Week-End: A Social History of Great Britain 1918–1939* (New York: W. W. Norton and Co., Inc., 1963), p. 117.

to make it easier for women to work in factories. In 1922–23 it dropped back to just above the ankle. But the forces of enlightenment were not to be denied. By 1925 the hemline had risen to just below the knee. The following year the knee was seen in polite society for the first time in modern history, and the short skirt was accompanied by short hair (the Eton crop), another break with the past.

The new attitudes toward sex had several noted defenders. Bertrand Russell, the eminent philosopher, advocated free love in order to rid society of its frustrations and to allow individuals to develop healthy personalities. Dr. Marie Stopes waged a campaign for birth control—the first time such a topic had been debated publicly. After suffering much abuse and a few days in court, Dr. Stopes was victorious. By 1930 most British doctors gave birth control information.

The woman's lot was also made easier by the development of ready-to-serve canned foods (another product of the war), by cheap ready-to-wear clothes, and by the appearance of chain stores (Woolworth's) which contained many items and simplified the housewife's shopping.

With the increased income and increased leisure time, new forms of amusement became popular. One such was professional football. When soldiers returned to small towns they established local rugby and soccer teams. Soon there were community, industrial, and school leagues. National professional leagues followed. The working class nature of this phenomenon was evidenced by the fact that the "society press" refused to report game scores—even championship games with 100,000 spectators in attendance. Other sports also caught on—tennis and golf, especially, though these appealed more to the middle classes. Motoring or touring on a weekend became a national pastime. Popular literature had little in common with Joyce or Proust. It was dominated by harmless adventure stories by Edgar Wallace and Nat Gould.

The pop culture medium par excellence is the commercial cinema or, more simply, the movies. It was during the twenties that movies became really big business, that the star system was initiated by Charlie Chaplin, that the United States began to impose its culture on Europe via the silver screen. A nascent film industry had developed in all modern states before the war, but only that of the United States emerged from the war in competitive posture. American production and distribution methods destroyed the British and French companies in the immediate postwar years. Germany and Russia produced magnificent directors during the twenties, but Hollywood bought the Germans and Stalin handcuffed the Russians. As a result a pall of mediocrity fell over the cinema at the end of the decade. Still millions of Europeans flocked to the theaters as the least expensive form of evening entertainment available. No doubt many of their attitudes were shaped by what they saw.

The nightclub or cabaret was also an innovation of this hectic decade.

Charlie Chaplin's
popularity in Europe
symbolized the dominance
of American cinema
during the interwar period.
(Courtesy of
Columbia Pictures)

Restaurants had never put on professional floor shows—that had been left to large theater-restaurants such as the Moulin Rouge in Paris. Now many restaurants provided live entertainment—usually a jazz band. Jazz swept the Continent as well as staid old England. All new decorations and clothes were associated with it. The clientele of the cabarets were the first "jet set." The British called them "bright young things." These relatively wealthy young people were proud of their hedonism and violations of old standards. They in some ways set the tone for social life by their wild costume parties that the sensation-seeking press enjoyed publicizing. In their frenetic dash after happiness they also symbolized the rush of all western Europe through the prosperous years of 1925–29 into the apocalypse of the Great Depression, which wiped the smiles from all faces. A contemporary writer captured the carefree joy of the bright young things in a frivolous poem that seems an appropriate epitaph for the decade.

> Mother's advice, and Father's fears
> Alike are voted—just a bore.
> There's negro music in our ears,

The world is one huge dancing floor.
We mean to tread the Primrose Path
In spite of Mr. Joynson-Hicks.*
We're people of the Aftermath,
We're girls of 1926.

In greedy haste, on pleasure bent
We have no time to think, or feel,
What need is there for sentiment,
Now we've invented Sex-Appeal?
We've silken legs and scarlet lips,
We're young and hungry, wild and free,
Our waists are down about the hips,
Our skirts are well above the knee.

We've boyish breasts and Eton crops,
We quiver to the saxophone.
Come, dance before the music stops,
And who can bear to be alone?
Come drink your gin, or sniff your "snow,"
Since youth is brief, and Love has wings,
And time will tarnish, ere we know,
The brightness of the Bright Young Things.[9]

Politics: Great Britain and France, 1924–30

The last half of the 1920s was a period of domestic prosperity and international peace. Leftist governments came to power in both Great Britain and France in 1924, but neither lasted very long. The Labour cabinet of Ramsey MacDonald governed England only from January to November 1924. The *Cartel des Gauches* ministry of Edouard Herriot was in office from June 1924 until April 1925. During the brief time when they were both in office, they laid the foundations for the diplomacy of concord of the next five years. Yet in domestic politics neither MacDonald nor Herriot achieved anything significant. Both were succeeded by long-lived Conservative governments.

The reasons for MacDonald's failure were both in the situation and in MacDonald himself. The Labour party accepted power without a majority in the House of Commons. In the election of December 1923 they had won 191 seats; but the Liberals had captured 158; while the Conservatives controlled 258. Thus, the Liberal party had to choose between supporting the Conservatives or Labourites. Asquith, the Liberal leader, chose Labour. So the Labourites were dependent on Liberal votes to keep them

---

* Mr. Joynson-Hicks was home secretary in Stanley Baldwin's ministry, 1925–29.

[9] John Montgomery, *The Twenties, An Informal Social History* (New York: Macmillan Co., 1957), p. 171. Reprinted with permission of George Allen & Unwin, Ltd.

in office. MacDonald had a reputation as a fire-breathing socialist because of his courageous stand against British involvement in World War I. Actually, he had become quite bourgeois. He was an extremely handsome man and liked to dress very well. He spent his weekends on a country estate like any gentleman. He said, in 1924, that the most important thing for the Labour party to do was to make itself respectable. Certainly, he refused to push for legislation of a radical nature that might have alienated the "better people," the upper classes.

This hesitancy to attempt reforms also grew out of his weak parliamentary position. In fact, his cabinet was overthrown by its first real test: the Campbell case. Campbell was a Communist arrested for sedition and then released. The Liberals and Conservatives accused MacDonald of being "soft on communism," and voted "no confidence" in his government, 364–198. During the ensuing election, the Conservatives continued to red-bait. They even published a fake letter which called on the communists of Britain to vote Labour because a Labour victory would encourage the revolutionary forces. The letter was signed by "Zinoviev, President of the Third Communist International." Everyone believed in the authenticity of the letter except a few Labourites and the communists. The timing of its publication was perfect—on Saturday morning, four days before the election.

The Conservative victory was overwhelming. They won 415 seats. Labour, with 152 seats, had not lost so many seats, but the weakness of the Liberals was stunning. Down to only forty-two seats, they were hardly a major party any longer.

The Liberal ideology of no or very limited government interference in the economy was out-of-date. The choice after World War I was not a choice between socialism and capitalism but between alternative goals of government interference—to improve the lot of the lower classes or to protect the privileged position of the wealthy. The major issues were no longer "political" but were "social." Furthermore, the growth and the superior organization of the Labour party had robbed the Liberals of their traditional working class support. As late as 1918 the Liberals had received more working class votes than had the Labourites, but after Lloyd George had crushed the postwar strike movement workers turned more and more toward Labour.

The Conservatives, with Stanley Baldwin as prime minister, were in office from December 1924 until May 1929. They did not enact much notable legislation, the major event of these years being the General Strike of 1926. This strike, like the major strikes of the postwar period, began with the miners' union. The governments since 1919 had enacted none of the reforms recommended by the Sankey Commission, and in 1925, the mine owners were losing money and decided they must break their contract with the union and reduce wages. When the miners announced their determination to strike, the Trades' Union Congress said it would sponsor a general strike in all trades to support them. Baldwin stepped in and—like Lloyd George—appointed a commission to investigate. While the commission was preparing its report, Baldwin prepared to crush any eventual strike. The government organized regional and local committees to keep all public services and transportation facilities operating. Private citizens were encouraged by the government to form the Organization for the Maintenance of Supplies (OMS) to provide all areas with food and to replace strikers wherever the government felt it necessary. Small fascist groups appeared, and, when they offered their services as special deputies for the local police, several cities accepted the offer.

As could have been predicted, the commission's report was unsatisfactory for both sides, and the general strike began on May 3, 1926. It only lasted nine days, and there was very little violence, considering the fact that there were 2.5 million men on strike and others were idled. The potential for a civil war existed; yet, instead, strikers played soccer with the policemen. Finally, the TUC, outmaneuvered by Baldwin, called off the strike believing that he had persuaded the mine owners to renew negotiations. The owners refused to negotiate, but the spirit of the strike had been broken. Only the miners continued their work stoppage. When they finally surrendered, their wages were reduced and their workday was lengthened from the seven hours won in 1919 to eight hours.

Baldwin followed up this victory by enacting several anti-union laws in 1927. It was probably this class legislation, along with the memory of 1926, that resulted in the Socialist victory in the 1929 election. This time Labour emerged as the largest party, having won 287 seats. Once again the Labour party—as if breathing a death wish—chose Ramsey MacDonald to be their prime minister, and he led them into self-destruction during the Depression, which began as he took office.

Unlike the Labour government of 1924, the French *Cartel des Gauches** was not destroyed by attacks from its enemies but by its own inherent weaknesses. The major problem the coalition of socialists, radicals, and moderates had to confront was inflation. There was a general consensus that the inflation was caused by the perpetual deficit in the national budget, but there was no agreement on how to erase the deficit. The leftists in the coalition wished to increase government income by taxing the rich. They claimed that the income tax imposed during World War I was being evaded by the wealthy, while the state was taking taxes out of the pay envelope of every worker. A tax on capital—savings and investments—was also proposed. The right-wing radicals and moderates opposed this "soak the rich" solution and preferred the conservative policy of cutting expenditures. While willing to raise taxes, they wanted to in-

---

* Coalition of Leftist Groups.

crease indirect taxes or sales taxes on food, tobacco, and other goods required by all Frenchmen. Theoretically, this would share the tax burden equally among all Frenchmen. Actually, it would place the tax burden on the poor, since they would have to pay the same tax on a loaf of bread as the wealthy.

This internal debate over fiscal policy paralyzed the Cartel. In 1925 Herriot managed to gather enough votes to pass a modest tax on capital, but his bill was defeated by the Senate. Since either the Chamber or the Senate could topple a ministry, Herriot was forced to resign. In the next fourteen months, France had six different governments and seven different ministers of finance. The value of the franc was falling alarmingly. In March 1924, sixteen francs could buy one dollar. A dollar cost fifty francs in July 1926. It appeared the French middle class might suffer the fate of the Germans in 1923. It was at this point that Raymond Poincaré once again became premier. Even though the Cartel majority had been elected on a strictly anti-Poincaré program in 1924, the same deputies now made Poincaré premier. The absence of party discipline allowed right-wing radicals to split away from the leftist coalition. At any rate, Poincaré formed a conservative government of "national union" in July 1926, and immediately the franc began to regain its value.

The rapid recovery of the franc suggests that the French business community had prolonged the financial crisis to drive the Cartel out of office. Certainly, Poincaré did nothing to cause alarm among the wealthy. He raised indirect taxes, and he cut spending by reducing the size of the civil service—two measures equally popular with conservatives. Specific revenues were designated to pay off the national debt. Poincaré's greatest innovation was to allow the Bank of France to buy or sell francs on the international market as was necessary to maintain the franc's stability. These measures stabilized the franc at a value of twenty-five francs to the dollar or one-fifth of its 1913 value. It was not until after his supporters had won the election of 1928 that Poincaré returned to the gold standard. This assured the middle classes that the "good old days" of pre-1914 financial orthodoxy were back to stay.

Baldwin and Poincaré had given their countries prosperity that was mistaken for real stability. By crushing the general strike and by saving the franc, the two conservative leaders had prevented fundamental changes in the economies of their nations. Even if those changes had been made, however, they may not have lessened the impact of the Great Depression.

Politics: Germany, 1925–30

Germany shared in the general prosperity of the late twenties. Her recovery from the crisis of 1923 was so complete, in fact, that an eminent American political scientist commented in 1928:

Germany, after years of tribulation and suffering, [has] staged one of the most remarkable comebacks as well as conversions in history and taken her place among the truly democratic and liberal states of the world.[10]

Such a statement is understandable in light of the apparent solidity of German society. Social conflict had decreased greatly, and the demand for social reforms was hushed by relatively full employment and the stability of the mark. This increasing conservatism was most obvious in the presidential election of April 1925, made necessary by the death of the Socialist president Ebert. The outcome of the election was symbolic of the changed direction of Weimar politics. General von Hindenburg, military and nationalist hero, was elected on the second ballot largely because the Communist party voted for its own candidate rather than the republican coalition's candidate. Votes were also taken from the republican camp by the defection of the Bavarian branch of the Center party, which supported Hindenburg. Hindenburg's inauguration was the occasion for a celebration by ultranationalist paramilitary groups, who provided an honor guard for the new president. Hindenburg quieted many fears when, in his acceptance speech, he swore allegiance to the republic without any reservation, vowing to uphold its constitution. Indeed, he did prove to be a model president—above parties, the symbol of consensus—for several years.

The prosperity of 1925–28 had made many forget Versailles and turn their backs on the extreme nationalists as evidenced by the 1928 election in which both the Nazis and the Nationalist party lost votes. But the developments that were shaping the nation's future were not publicized. They were slow and imperceptible institutional changes. At the head of the state, General Hindenburg was deserting his neutrality and beginning to cooperate with the most conservative elements of society—the army and the Junkers. In 1927 he opposed a land reform that would have settled needy exsoldiers on farm land expropriated from Junker estates in East Prussia. The Junkers, feeling threatened, decried this as a step toward socialism. Hindenburg was persuaded. The following year he appointed General Wilhelm Groener, who was known to desire a revival of the Reichswehr, as minister of war.

Antidemocratic forces were gaining strength outside of government as well. The economy was being increasingly concentrated under the control of a few industrial giants such as I. G. Farben (the German dye trust) and the United Steel Works, which had been formed by a merger of the four largest German steel manufacturers. Unfortunately, the labor unions were, at the same time, losing their membership and their ability to bargain with these monopolies. This weakness was due above all to

---

[10] Raymond Leslie Buell, *Europe: A History of Ten Years* (New York: The Macmillan Co., 1928) as cited in S. William Halperin, *Germany Tried Democracy* (New York: W. W. Norton and Company, Inc., 1965), p. 362.

the division of the working class into socialist and communist unions. These unions competed against each other while management was becoming more consolidated.

Paramilitary rightist organizations formed in 1919 and 1920 continued to flourish with the aid of imperial bureaucrats still in office. Financed by wealthy Junkers and some businessmen, equipped by officers in the republic's army as well as police officials, protected by friendly judges, these private armies dedicated to overthrowing the republic grew until the regular police would have been useless against them. Only the army stood between the republic and the troops of the Steel Helmet and the Nazi S.A., both having over 200,000 armed men.

Still, in 1928, the republic was popular. After the elections, a leftist cabinet headed by Hermann Mueller, a Social Democrat, took office. This was to be the last democratic government of the Weimar Republic. Mueller had a great deal of difficulty maintaining the support of his own party, much less that of the grand coalition of the SPD, the Center party, and the People's party. The coalition split over two issues: military spending and means of combating unemployment. Mueller proposed, soon after taking office, that Germany construct four "pocket battleships." The Social Democrats argued the money could be better spent feeding undernourished children, of which Germany had many. The Center party and People's party demanded the battleships be built. After months of acrimony, Mueller postponed the vote on the proposal when the Social Democrats made it clear that it would vote against the cabinet.

Unemployment became a problem in late 1929 and early 1930 as the first effects of the Depression were reaching Germany. As the number of men on government relief increased, the national budget was forced into a deficit by decreased taxes. The Nationalist party and big-business wing of the People's party agitated for a reduction of unemployment payments as part of an austerity program. The Social Democrats, of course, strongly resisted this move. Therefore, Mueller, fighting conservative pressure, offered to raise the social security tax of each worker instead of reducing the payments to the unemployed. A Centrist deputy, Heinrich Bruening, suggested a compromise that would have made the social insurance system pay for itself—raising or lowering relief payments as needed to keep the system self-sufficient. But no compromise was possible. The issue divided the grand coalition along class lines, and Mueller was forced to resign on March 27, 1930.

He was succeeded by Bruening, who decided to govern without parliament. Bruening was not antidemocratic, but he felt or was convinced by the palace camarilla around President Hindenburg that it was impossible to obtain a stable legislative majority for the energetic measures needed to end the crisis. Therefore, President Hindenburg declared that a state of national crisis existed and gave Bruening the power to govern by decree under Article 48. The government was legal but was nonparliamentary; Bruening was responsible only to Hindenburg. Although he had made this move in order to save the Weimar Republic, Bruening had actually taken the first step toward the dictatorship that Hitler established in 1933.

Resurgence of Wilsonian Diplomacy

Diplomatic developments in the last half of the 1920s can be best understood as the complete triumph of Woodrow Wilson over Clemenceau. Until 1924 the old diplomacy dominated international relations just as the conservative coalitions dominated domestic politics. After 1924 all nations accepted the Wilsonian new diplomacy. Solutions based on international cooperation were sought for the central problems of French security and the war debts-reparations nexus.

Faced with a potentially overpowering Germany, France had sought security through the principles of balance-of-power diplomacy. Not only did the French try to perpetuate Germany's weakness, but they also tried to erect a network of alliances that would deny Germany military superiority if the Germans did rearm. Since France's traditional ally to the east, Russia, was isolated from Europe, French policy was based on alliances with the smaller East European states and Belgium. The Franco-Belgian Treaty of September 1920 was the first link in the chain which was to encircle Germany. A Franco-Polish alliance in 1921 was the second. The system was completed three years later when France pledged her support to the Little Entente, which included Czechoslovakia, Rumania, and Yugoslavia. The Little Entente had originally been founded—at French instigation—with the limited purpose of guaranteeing the boundaries of these states from Hungarian irredentism, but it soon became the cornerstone of French foreign policy. Of course, it was only as strong as France's will to help the smaller states if Germany or Hungary tried to reclaim the territory lost in 1918. Unfortunately for France, her new allies were not as strong as they appeared. Torn by domestic rivalries among various national groups, burdened with armies composed of illiterate peasants who could not use complicated weapons, having agricultural economies, the Eastern allies could never resist the army of a modern industrial state.

The missing link in France's encirclement policy was Italy. Even before Mussolini came to power there was evidence of Franco-Italian rivalry. All Italian nationalists, and especially Mussolini, resented French dominance of the Continent. With Germany's army destroyed, France was temporarily the greatest land power. Italian envy of France and disappointment at the treaty settlements of 1919 led to a desire to build a strong Italian army and to revive Germany to balance off against the French. The two Latin states clashed directly over Yugoslavia. One of Mussolini's fondest hopes was to annex Fiume, which would deprive Yugoslavia of her only seaport. French policy was predicated on a strong Yugoslavia—without a port it would be difficult for Yugoslavia to trade with or receive military aid from France. In defiance of the French, Mussolini resolved the issue by force. Italian troops first seized the Greek island of Corfu temporarily in August 1923. The following month Mussolini established a military protectorate over Fiume, which Yugoslavia accepted in a treaty in 1924. A third area of Franco-Italian dispute was North Africa. Mussolini claimed that France had not lived up to a wartime promise to cede part of Tunisia to Italy. This remained a source of tension into the 1930s when it was eclipsed by other, more grave problems.

The movement away from the old diplomacy and toward Wilsonian principles began with the French occupation of the Rhineland to collect reparations. When Stresemann decided Germany could no longer resist, Poincaré, faced with an economic crisis within France as well, accepted the Anglo-American idea of allowing a committee of experts to determine Germany's ability to pay. This committee of economic experts met in Paris from January to April 1924, under the chairmanship of an American, General Dawes. The Dawes Plan was formally accepted by Great Britain, France, the United States, *and Germany*. This was the first time since the war that Germany had been negotiated with as an equal. The plan provided that a large international loan would be floated to strengthen the German government and German industry. Furthermore, German payments were set at a specific scale ($350 million per annum) which would be easy for Germany to pay. Although no final sum was set, the figure of $33 billion was generally agreed upon. The handling of payments was taken away from the reparation commission set at Versailles and placed in the hands of an agent for reparations, who was to manage them like any commercial debt. Finally, the French agreed to remove their troops from the Ruhr within a year, although French troops would remain in other areas of the Rhineland.

With the reparations question out of the way, it was possible for Ramsay MacDonald and Edouard Herriot to seek a new basis for French security in the framework of the League of Nations. These two leaders of left-wing governments were, of course, more willing than conservatives to use the international organization. Therefore, when the fall session of the League opened in September 1924, MacDonald used the occasion to propose a treaty for the compulsory arbitration of international disputes. After Herriot endorsed the proposal, it was adopted by the League and became known as the Geneva Protocol. It provided for League arbitration in disputes between any members. Refusal to accept arbitration would be considered as admission of aggression. The League could then use force against the aggressor. France saw in this a way to gain British defense of French frontiers. Therefore, the French parliament ratified the protocol.

Briand (left) and Stresemann (right) dominated European diplomacy from the Locarno Conference depicted here until 1930. (Courtesy of Roger-Viollet)

MacDonald, however, was defeated by the Conservatives in the November 1924 elections, and Stanley Baldwin, once again prime minister, reflected the unwillingness of his party to be bound by the decisions of the League. Great Britain did not ratify.

Still the search for a mutual assurance treaty continued. A conference was called to discuss the idea at Locarno, a Swiss lakeside town, in September 1925. Many nations were represented, but three men dominated the conference: Austen Chamberlain for Great Britain, Gustav Stresemann for Germany, and Aristide Briand for France. Their success was such that two of them continued to conduct their nations' foreign policies until 1929 (Chamberlain and Stresemann) and the other until 1932. The results of Locarno were satisfactory to all—a rare thing in diplomacy. The main feature of the Locarno Pact was that the states involved guaranteed the sanctity of the Franco-German border and the Belgian-German border. England and Italy promised to fight either France or Germany, whoever violated the frontier; and France and Germany agreed to seek arbitration to settle their disputes. Finally, Germany was to become a member of the League of Nations.

The implications of this pact were perhaps more important than its written provisions. Primary was the admission that Germany had the right to negotiate as an equal. By allowing Germany to negotiate on the status of the frontiers, the Locarno Pact actually superseded the Versailles agreement and established the principle that a treaty signed by Germany voluntarily was more valid than one dictated to her. Second, the Locarno Pact did not specify Germany's eastern boundaries. In fact, Great Britain expressed the clear determination not to become involved in eastern Europe.

This had the effect of ranking Germany's frontiers into those guaranteed and those open to revision. Even when Germany later signed arbitration treaties with Poland and Czechoslovakia, Stresemann made it clear that Germany did not accept the eastern boundaries as final.

Briand continued to seek reconciliation with Germany during the following year. But there was an inevitable dilemma inherent in the negotiations. Briand wanted to achieve accommodations but from a position of strength. Stresemann was equally determined to wipe out the obstacles to German resurgence imposed at Versailles. The German statesman, pressured by nationalists, constantly upped the ante. Contrary to Briand's hopes, Stresemann was never satisfied. Concessions by France were not greeted with gratitude but with the contempt of a man who felt he was getting his rightful possessions back again. Stresemann demanded a quick evacuation of the southern half of the Rhineland, not due until 1930. The evacuation occurred in January 1926. Stresemann demanded abolition of the Inter-Allied Military Committee which observed German armaments industries. It was abolished in July 1926. Also in 1926, Germany was admitted as a full member of the Supreme Council of the League of Nations. This confirmed Germany's diplomatic recovery since 1919.

With Germany's entrance, the League of Nations—the most Wilsonian of the provisions of Versailles—reached the height of its prestige and influence. It was during 1925–27 that it· achieved its greatest successes in international arbitration. The disputes it settled, however, were always between minor states. The international body arbitrated boundary controversies between Turkey and Iraq, between Greece and Bulgaria, and between Poland and Lithuania. The prestige gained from these settlements was spurious—because no Great Power had yet directly challenged the League. The various members of the League also turned to it for leadership in disarmament negotiations, but several conferences resulted in no significant reduction in arms—although the limitation on naval forces agreed on at the Washington Conference of 1922 was extended with modifications in 1930.

Collective security was a la mode by the late twenties. The greatest purveyor of optimism was Aristide Briand, who continued his attempts to remove sources of conflict between France and Germany while trying to obtain international assurances of France's eastern frontier. He initiated the developments that led to the Kellogg-Briand Pact prohibiting war. In a warm message to the people of America on the tenth anniversary of the United States' entry into World War I he pledged France's eternal friendship. This greeting was soon followed by an offer of a treaty between the two countries renouncing the use of war against each other. Actually, this proposal was not as harmless as it appears; for Briand was hoping to gain American support to strengthen his bargaining power with other

European nations. Frank Kellogg, the American secretary of state, did not wish to be drawn into European problems and countered by appealing to all states to join in the nonaggression pact. This nullified any French claim to special American favor and made the whole affair a bit ridiculous, but Briand was too deeply involved to reject his own child.

Therefore, the representatives of fifteen states met in Paris on August 27, 1928, and signed a pact, the Kellogg-Briand Pact, outlawing war. In subsequent weeks fifty other governments—including the Soviet Union—adhered to the treaty. Although it had begun as a reasonable diplomatic ploy, the international reception of the pact indicated the degree to which the hope for a lasting peace had led politicians and the public to cling to the slender thread of a treaty that made war illegal. The aura surrounding the signing of the pact was amazing. Newspapers actually heralded the end of war for all time.

This atmosphere of optimism encouraged a new attempt to solve the war debts-reparations problem. Since the Dawes Plan had begun operation, a strange economic situation had developed that allowed Germany to rebuild her economy while paying reparations to France and others. Germans obtained their capital from loans floated in the United States. This freed German funds to be paid to France and Great Britain, and these two countries used the German money to pay their debts to the United States. Therefore, the United States was being paid with money it had loaned to Germany. The entire system depended on a healthy American economy. If the American cornucopia was suddenly emptied, the payments would have to stop, and the flourishing prosperity that was based on them would be jeopardized.

A new reparations committee was formed in 1929 with the orders to find a "complete and definite settlement" of the question of reparations. This committee met in Paris in February. Once again the chairman was an American, Owen Young, a financier. After several months the Young Plan was submitted to and accepted by the various governments. It was agreed that Germany's reparations would be paid in thirty-seven annual payments of $280 million. So the German reparations would be paid in full by 1966. Germany would then make twenty-two smaller payments to cover the war debts owed to the United States by France and Great Britain. Therefore, all payments would end in *1988!* Furthermore, all controls and inspections of the German economy would stop immediately. This meant that the German armaments industry would no longer be under foreign control and Germany could begin to rearm. Finally, all Allied troops were to be withdrawn from the Rhineland by January 30, 1930—five years ahead of the schedule set at Versailles.

Thus, in the halcyon years of peace and prosperity, 1925–30, Woodrow Wilson's ideas were revived and became the principles of international relations. Collective security had replaced the French alliance system as the guarantee of peace—at least in the minds of the public and, also, in the planning of some diplomats. By 1931 Briand was discussing plans for a United States of Europe. The reparations question had also been settled according to Wilsonian principles. The American president had argued at Versailles that a definite amount should be set to be paid in a definite length of time. Yet the Wilsonian international order survived for only a year. As the final arrangements were being made to put the Young Plan into operation, the Great Depression was destroying the social basis of the diplomacy of optimism.

Chapter 7

DEPRESSION AND RESPONSE

Origins of the Depression

The capitalist economy of western Europe had experienced alternating booms and slumps of varying magnitude throughout the nineteenth century. From 1929 to 1935 the nations of Europe suffered from a slump so severe that its effects were felt throughout the world. Indeed, it was a world economic crisis both in causes and effects and is usually called simply the Great Depression. World War I had caused a basic disequilibrium in the international market and in international financial relationships. The war debts-reparations cycle of United States' loans to Germany, German payments to France and Great Britain, and French and British payments to the United States had tied the economic fate of each nation to that of the others. The Great Depression has to be seen in this international context.

At the end of the war certain types of goods were being over-produced. This was especially true of agricultural production that had expanded throughout the world to feed the various armies. When the military demand for food ended, many farmers continued to produce at wartime levels. Such an over-supply drove prices down and drastically reduced the amount of cash farmers had available for consumer products. This in turn reduced the demand for manufactured goods, thereby causing a slowdown in industrial production. The effects of this shortage of purchasing power, however, were not evident at first because of savings the farmers had set aside during their better years. Another sector that was over-producing when peace broke out was the munitions industries. In most countries, the munitions manufacturers did not begin to produce consumer goods; instead they merely cut back their production of arms.

Not only did this result in a continuing over-supply of arms (ergo, lower profits), but also in unemployment for the men and women who had worked in the factories. Once again, the purchasing power of a large number of people had been severely curtailed.

The general result of the unemployment, lower prices, and reduced purchasing power was a decrease in world trade.[1] The sale of agricultural goods and raw materials depended on the ability of the urban populations to buy those goods. The production and sale of manufactured goods depended on the ability of agricultural populations around the world to buy them. It was a vicious circle. By the late twenties, economic indexes pointed to a general slowdown in business activity—especially in the industrialized areas, Europe and North America. Before the American Stock Exchange crisis of October 1929, there were signs that the American economy was moving toward a recession. There had been declines in capital construction, industrial production, and the prices of manufactured goods.

Yet, businessmen, investors, financiers refused to believe the indicators of bad fortune. Buoyed by the expansion of 1924–26, the bourgeoisie of the West were confident that the golden age of stability, peace, and permanent profits had arrived. In all countries there was over-speculation. Men invested more money than they had by obtaining credit from other men who had done the same. Companies sold stock worth far more than the company itself. And, especially in the United States, reckless investment in get-rich-quick schemes was rampant. Investment in the United States had doubled from September 1926 to September 1929, while business activity was slowing down. This was made more serious by the fact that the major European economies depended on the health of the American financial community. Since 1924 there had been a fantastic business boom in Germany, but this boom was financed almost entirely by American money. The American investments had encouraged British and French investors. So, by 1929, Germany was in debt to such an extent that her economy would crumble if the debts were ever called in. This is exactly what happened when the American stock market crashed in October 1929. Nearly $13 million of stock was sold on October 24. Business confidence was destroyed, and all loans were called in. Credit completely dried up. American banks very soon began to demand full payment on loans to European banks, spreading the crisis to the Continent.

The immediate result of the end of credit was the end of business expansion. This meant the building industry and others involved in expansion had to dismiss millions of workers. The demand for consumer goods dropped. Factory owners cut back production, lowered prices and reduced their work force. Once again purchasing power had been reduced. The

[1] W. Arthur Lewis, *Economic Survey, 1919–1939* (London: George Allen and Unwin Ltd., 1966), pp. 152–55.

economies of industrialized countries ground to a halt and the numbers of unemployed sky-rocketed.

The depression hit hardest in the United States and Germany. Unemployment was greatest in both countries in 1932 and 1933. During that period there were six million unemployed in Germany and fifteen million

TABLE 7.1.   Indexes of Industrial Production (1928 = 100)

Year	Germany	United States	France	Great Britain
1925	79.3	93.7	85.0	94.8 (1924)
1927	97.2	95.5	86.6	101.2
1929	101.4	107.2	109.4	106.0
1930	83.6	86.5	110.2	97.9
1931, August	71.9	74.8	99.2	84.6
1931, December	59.4	66.7	87.4	84.7
1932, January	55.2	64.9	82.7	90.1
1932, August	54.7	53.2	73.2	89.2

SOURCE: League of Nations, *Monthly Bulletin of Statistics*, vol. 13, no. 11 (1932), p. 490.

unemployed in the United States. In Great Britain about one-fifth of the work force, three million men and women, were without work. France had the lowest total unemployment, with only 800,000 in 1932. France, however, was to remain in the depression long after the other states had begun their recovery. Italy was scarcely affected by the international crisis, and this contributed to the popularity of fascism in other countries.

The final phase of the depression began in mid 1931. To alleviate the crisis, Germany and Austria had made plans in early 1931 for a tariff union to increase mutual trade. French leaders were afraid this was only the first step toward political union or *Anschluss*. Therefore, France threatened to use economic sanctions and military force if necessary to prevent the trade agreement. The French succeeded, but the failure of the tariff union precipitated a banking crisis that bankrupted hundreds of banks throughout Europe. With no confidence in Austrian banks, investors began to demand that Austrian banks pay all their debts. The largest Austrian bank—the Creditanstalt—declared itself insolvent in May 1931. German banks that had loaned large sums of money to Austrian banks had to close their doors. British and American banks, unable to collect from German banks, were the next to go. The complete collapse of Germany's industry and financial structure seemed imminent.

This likelihood prompted the first attempts to cope with the problem on an international level. President Herbert Hoover of the United States proposed a one-year moratorium on all war debts and reparations, but he expected all payments to resume at the end of the year. The moratorium ran until July 1932 and eased the crisis somewhat. As July approached, the Americans were alone in desiring a resumption of payments. The German Chancellor Bruening announced that a resumption was out of the question. It was not only impossible economically; it was also unacceptable to the German people. Bruening had good evidence for this last point. In the Reichstag election of September 1930, the Nazis had increased their representation in parliament from 12 to 107, on an anti-Versailles, antireparations program. France did not favor a cessation of payments, because France had been receiving more from Germany than it had been paying the United States. Therefore, the French insisted that, if Germany did not pay reparations, France would not pay its war debts. This later proved to be the case. Great Britain also resented the American demand for a return to the payment schedule. A conference was called at Lausanne in July 1932 to consider financial questions. Great Britain and France announced their willingness to cancel Germany's reparations payments if the United States would cancel their war debts. The American response was that there was no connection between the two questions, and it was made clear that all debtors were expected to pay their regular installments in December 1932. Great Britain paid, but France, Italy, and Yugoslavia defaulted. In France, Herriot, who was premier again, was overthrown when he suggested to the Chamber of Deputies that France should pay. No subsequent French cabinet felt bound by the American debt. England made two more token payments, and then she also stopped paying. The reparations question was settled in the same manner. When Hitler came to power in 1933, he refused to pay.

One last attempt to find an international solution to the economic crisis was made at the World Economic Conference of June 1933, meeting in London. This conference proved futile when the new Roosevelt administration rejected proposals for price and currency stability. Franklin Roosevelt, elected because he offered an alternative to the conservative economics of Hoover's administration, wanted to keep all options open. He had decided to raise American prices and revive American business through tariffs, subsidization of business, and the creation of demand through government spending. All of these programs required an isolated national economy, not international cooperation. This was the knock-out blow to the conference. After it failed, all European states turned inward in search of relief and recovery. Economic nationalism replaced the international cooperation of the twenties.

Responses: Great Britain and France

The manner in which each country solved the problems created by the depression was determined not by economists but by politics—by the balance of political power within each country and by the personalities of the individual politicians. The governments of each country were, however, reduced to choosing between the major alternatives of deflation or guided inflation. A deflationary policy entailed forcing prices down (or allowing them to fall) until consumption resumed. This came close to a laissez faire approach, since it was assumed that as soon as prices fell far enough the public would automatically begin purchasing goods again. Usually, advocates of a deflationary policy also favored government action to lower interest rates to encourage investment. An inflationary policy had the goal of putting money in the hands of the consumer instead of lowering prices. Prices would be maintained or even raised, but people would buy more with money supplied by the government. This would revive lagging industry and provide jobs. Incidentally, both policies implied a need for high tariffs, so the consumer would spend his money on domestic goods.

Of course, each of these policies had a political significance. Deflation, which emphasized a balanced budget because deficit spending encourages inflation, was the traditional method of responding to monetary crises and was favored by conservatives. Inflation, which depended on heavy government spending to stimulate the economy, was a leftist policy. It implied a certain redistribution of wealth since the purchasing power of the unemployed was to be supplied by taxes paid by the employed and the rich.

Of the major European states, only Hitler's Germany tried a thorough inflationary policy. Hitler increased industrial activity by government subsidies to the armaments industry and by the development of the steel industry to supply munitions makers. As Germany rearmed, unemployment was eliminated. The money earned by workers in military-related industries was pumped back into the economy and general prosperity was achieved. In economic terms, Germany's rearmament was equivalent to FDR's public works programs—although to equate weapons with the New Deal's schools or post offices would be morally blind. In Italy Mussolini also fought the depression by inflationary measures, with a combination of public works and arms spending.

Both France and Great Britain adopted deflationary policies. France was the last country hit by the depression and the last to recover. There were several reasons for France's apparent early immunity. France had a secure gold reserve that it had guarded jealously since 1918. This maintained business confidence, so investments and credit did not dry up as quickly in France as elsewhere. Moreover, the French work force contained many foreign workers—Spanish, Italian, Greek, and eastern European. The first unemployment hit these men who were forced to leave the country, while Frenchmen took the unskilled jobs the foreigners had vacated. The French government, then, was not faced with the problem of feeding a large number of unemployed. Finally, France was still an agricultural country when compared to Germany or Great Britain. Therefore, it was not necessary to import food, which was such a drain on the British economy. Also, workers who were idled by industrial cutbacks could return to small towns and farms instead of living on welfare in the cities.

It took a major political crisis before the Chamber of Deputies was willing to accept strong leadership. The depression had contributed to the growth of extremist political groups throughout Europe. France was no exception. On February 6, 1934, several thousand fascist and proto-fascist demonstrators tried to storm the French parliament building—the Palais Bourbon—and attack the deputies. They were repelled only by repeated cavalry charges of the Garde Mobile. This threat to democracy led to the formation of a so-called National Government under Gaston Doumergue, an old man with immense prestige (he had been president of the republic, 1924–31), but Doumergue lacked any comprehension of the situation. Given full powers by parliament, he governed by decree in an effort to balance the budget and restore business confidence. His only action with lasting effect was to fire many civil servants and to cut the salaries of those he did not fire.

Several rather meaningless governments followed with premiers either without a program or without parliamentary support. By early 1935, the depression had reached its lowest point in France. The Chamber of Deputies decided to turn to a most unlikely savior, Pierre Laval. Laval was premier from June 1935 to January 1936. He was a moderate conservative who had begun his career as a socialist. In 1914 he had been considered dangerous enough to be placed on a list of subversives who were to be arrested in case of war. During the twenties and thirties he became increasingly conservative until, after 1940, he became the chief collaborator with the Nazis.

When Laval came to power in 1935, there was a financial panic in course. France was finally losing gold and losing it rapidly. The fear of a devaluation led the Chamber to give Laval full powers. Authoritarian by temperament, Laval governed by decree for four months. During that time he issued five hundred emergency decrees, including the most deflationary measures yet. The national budget was cut by eleven billion francs, mostly by reducing aid to municipalities and railroads. The salaries of all state employees were cut by 10 percent, and the same 10 percent reduction was made in all pensions and in the interest paid by government bonds. Laval even authorized tenants to cut their own rent by 10 percent. Finally, he reduced the prices of electricity, gas, coal, and bread. These measures fit well into the conservative preference for deflation, but they made economic recovery almost impossible by reducing the amount of money in circulation, which had to furnish purchasing power, wages, and investments. Consequently, the economic slowdown continued until 1936 when the Socialist-dominated Popular Front inaugurated a French New Deal by resorting to inflationary policies.

Between Poincaré's last ministry in November 1929 and the Popular Front government of May 1936, France had nineteen different ministries with an average life of four months. This was the French response to the economic crisis—dynamic stagnation. Either a government could accomplish nothing because of parliamentary opposition or it was given complete power to rule by decree. It was the tragedy of French democracy that no middle ground, no balance between unproductive factionalism and authoritarian government could be found.

In contrast to the rapid turnover of governments in France, English cabinets during the 1930s were notable for their longevity. In 1931 the National Government was formed with representatives from all parties. Conservatives actually controlled the coalition and remained in power until 1940. Oddly enough, the man responsible for their ascendancy was the leader of the Labour party, Ramsey MacDonald.

Labour had won the 1929 election on a promise to decrease unemployment. This time Labour was the largest party.* Unfortunately, the depression hit Great Britain just as the new government was taking office. In 1930 alone unemployment rose from 1 million to 2.5 million. MacDonald's cabinet was divided as to how to stop this sky-rocketing unemployment and the banking crisis which accompanied it. The two most important members of the cabinet—MacDonald and Philip Snowden, his chancellor of the exchequer—favored a Conservative deflationary policy. In his desire for respectability, MacDonald was listening more and more to the advice of banking circles. On the other hand, the battle for an inflationary program of public works was waged by John Thomas, who had direct responsibility for ending unemployment, and one of Thomas's advisers, Oswald Mosley. The dispute came to an open quarrel in February 1930, when Mosley made public his personal program of government action. The famous Mosley Memorandum recommended the development of the home market in consumer goods instead of increasing exports as MacDonald planned. Mosley argued that if business were forced to pay high wages and if the state began large public works programs, the economy would be revived because the workers would be able to buy goods once again. Increased exports, he argued, only helped a few industrialists but did not increase national productivity. He further urged that a government board be created to regulate all prices. Snowden fought these proposals on "economic" grounds. Finally, the cabinet rejected Mosley's ideas, and Mosley resigned from the Labour party along with seventeen other Labour MPs. Later Mosley became the leader of the British Union of Fascists.

Despite this split in the cabinet, the Labour government was able to

---

* Labour won 287 seats; the Conservatives, 261; the Liberals, 59.

pass some significant legislation. For example, it enacted an Unemployment Insurance Act which abolished the requirement that a worker prove his inability to find work before receiving aid. It also extended aid to unemployed married women. Another act, the Coal Mines Bill, set quotas on coal production, so the price of coal could be maintained at a high level. These acts were steps toward the postwar welfare state in that they set precedents for government action.

The Labour party's fall and the formation of the National Government were brought on by the publication of the May Report. Sir George May, an insurance company executive, had been appointed to head a committee to study the economic situation and to recommend appropriate government action. Snowden must have known that the committee would propose strong deflationary measures, since it was composed of only two Labourites and five businessmen. The report was made public on July 31, 1931. It painted the situation in the darkest possible colors and urged the usual conservative antidote—less spending and higher taxes. Specifically, it suggested that unemployment insurance benefits be reduced. The banking community endorsed the report almost unanimously. During August 1931, MacDonald and Snowden tried to get the rest of the Labour cabinet to accept the report without success. The conflict climaxed when it became known that a large loan from New York bankers would not be given to the British until the cabinet had proved its seriousness about austerity by cutting unemployment payments. This split the cabinet—the majority opposing the American terms. MacDonald resigned.

The next day a National Government was formed with MacDonald as prime minister but dependent on Conservative and Liberal votes in the Commons. MacDonald had been approached by Conservatives about such a cabinet when the May Report appeared. They had asked him to head the coalition cabinet and to allow Baldwin, the Conservative leader, to share power with him under the title of Lord President. The two men governed jointly, with Baldwin increasingly making all important decisions. The government was composed of four Conservative ministers, two Labourites, and three Liberals. MacDonald was clearly a prisoner of his allies.

The result of his defection was to assure Conservative dominance until World War II. Labour was obviously split and discredited in the public's eye. The Liberals, who had been able to influence events as the center party before the National Government was formed, became mere "yes-men" to Baldwin. The Conservatives were *the* "National Party," and everyone knew it. In an attempt to save itself, Labour purged MacDonald, Snowden, and others who supported the coalition; but the party had lost its spirit, and it did not recover until 1945.

National Government policies were patterned on the May Report. Its

Ramsey MacDonald leaving
10 Downing Street in
1931 to resign as Prime
Minister and to form a
National Government
(Courtesy of UPI)

first act was to raise tariffs to protect British industry. This obviously raised prices. The salaries of all public officials and state employees were reduced. (This may have been where the French got the idea.) School teachers suffered the biggest cut—a 10 percent loss. The social insurance program was also cut. Benefits were reduced while the workers' contribution was increased. And workers were again required to pass a needs test to prove they deserved aid. Finally, the National Government went off the gold standard, which was equivalent to a devaluation of the pound. This was exactly what the Conservatives had insisted that Labour should not do. Going off gold made British goods sell more cheaply abroad and foreign goods more expensive in England.

After only two months in office, the Conservatives called for an election. It was a repetition of 1919, except that MacDonald was playing Lloyd George's role. The Conservative party emerged with an overwhelming majority.* The Conservative majority insisted so strongly on controlling policy that the coalition could not continue. When Baldwin insisted that high tariffs were a necessity, Liberals and Labourites like Snowden could no longer maintain the alliance. Accusing Baldwin of discouraging trade, they broke with him in September 1932. From this time the cabinet was supported solely by Conservatives, but Baldwin insisted in perpetuating the name "National Government." Probably the best assessment of the achievements of the period was given by Charles Mowat, who has written the best history of Britain between the wars: "The history of the National Government was one long diminuendo. From its triumph in 1931 it shambled its unimaginative way to its fall in 1940. . . ."[2]

But Great Britain *did* recover from the depression around 1935. How did this happen? The source of recovery was the development of the mass-consumption and service industries—that is, the home market—not an increase of exports as the Conservatives had planned.[3] Conservative policy had been based on the improvement of Britain's international trade position. Instead, the first sectors to recover included food distributors, auto manufacturers, radio and telephone companies, laundries, and dry cleaners as well as the entertainment and sports industries. "With all this, government policy had little to do."[4] Unintentionally, the Conservatives had stumbled into inflationary measures while trying to deflate the economy. They had planned balanced budgets for 1933 and 1934 but deficit budgets—that is, inflationary budgets—had resulted. When they finally had a budget surplus in 1934–35, they restored unemployment benefits and government salaries to their previous levels for political reasons. This made more consumption possible. Although the National Government rejected a public works program, it did provide sizable subsidies to private industry for the construction of commercial ships (the *Queen Mary* for one) and for the reconstruction of railroads. These subsidies resulted in increased employment and, again, increased consumption.

In summary then, both France and Great Britain responded to the depression by deflationary policies. In France, where the deflationary measures were successful, the depression was prolonged until 1936. The recovery of the British economy occurred because the results of government policy were the reverse of what had been intended. The differences do not stop there. While the economic crises resulted in great governmental instability in France, the Conservative majority remained in power in Britain from 1931 to 1940. Both countries, however, were able to survive

---

* The National Government coalition received 553 seats of which the Conservatives held 472. Independent Labourites numbered only forty-six.

[2] Charles Loch Mowat, *Britain Between the Wars 1918–1939* (Chicago: University of Chicago Press, 1955), p. 413.

[3] Ibid., pp. 415, 436–51, 455.

[4] Ibid., p. 455.

the crisis with their basic institutions intact. The same cannot be said for the other major democracy, Germany.

Germany's Response: Descent into Chaos

The Mueller cabinet had been destroyed by the depression. The new chancellor, Heinrich Bruening, governed not on the strength of a parliamentary majority but on the authority of the president's emergency powers embodied in Article 48 of the Weimar Constitution. He did not ignore the Reichstag but was willing to overrule its majority if necessary. He was forced to do this because his insistence on deflationary policies alienated the Social Democrats, the largest party in the Reichstag.

Outside of parliament, Bruening was faced with the rapid growth of antidemocratic forces. Both the Nationalist and Center parties chose new leaders at the end of 1928. Each came from the extreme right of his party. Alfred Hugenberg, the Nationalist leader, was outspoken about his desire to overthrow the republic. The Center party's leader, Monsignor Ludwig Kaas, supported the Weimar Constitution but was not a supporter of parliamentary democracy. As early as October 1929, he demanded that future governments be freed from dependency on the unpredictable parliamentary majority. At the same time, a group of men hostile to democracy were gaining decisive influence over President Hindenburg. The most important members of this palace camarilla were General Kurt von Schleicher, Hindenburg's military adviser; Oscar Hindenburg, the president's son who represented the Junkers' interests; and Otto Meissner, Hindenburg's private secretary. By far the most influential of these was Schleicher. He dreamed of creating a new conservative movement based on the best young men of all nonsocialist parties. In 1930 he hoped Bruening would lead this new coalition and urged his appointment to the position of chancellor.

Other more dynamic and potentially revolutionary forces were developing in German society. The Depression and the resultant unemployment had driven desperate men to nazism and communism. The KPD's growth was understandable. The communists were well-organized as well as being violently anticapitalist and, therefore, offered a perfect refuge for the newly destitute. The reasons for Nazi success were more complex. Superficially, it was the product of an attempt by ultranationalists and by industrialists to block the Young Plan in 1929. These groups felt they needed a propagandist to rouse Germans against this new humiliation, and they asked Adolf Hitler to play that role. He agreed eagerly, traveling throughout the state and becoming a nationally prominent politician overnight. He was given huge sums of money to finance his campaign, but he used much of it to strengthen the National Socialist party. The party's membership jumped from 120,000 in the summer of 1929, to 187,000 in December 1929, to 210,000 by March 1930.[5] With both Nazis and communists becoming more militant as well as more numerous, the two parties' followers often clashed in the streets of Berlin and other cities.

In the midst of this storm, Bruening fought to carry out a program of severe austerity for four months. The Reichstag became increasingly hostile. Hoping to strengthen his hand, Bruening dissolved the legislature and called for new elections in September 1930. This was a vast mistake. Not only did Bruening lose parliamentary support, but the Nazis and the KPD made gains. The growth of the Nazis shocked the political world. In 1928 they had won twelve seats with 810,000 votes, but this time they captured 107 seats with an amazing 6,409,000 votes to become the second largest party. The KPD increase was from fifty-four seats to seventy-seven. Bruening found that he had no choice but to rely completely on the dictatorial powers of Article 48. This meant that he was free of the Reichstag, but it meant that he held his power only as long as he retained President Hindenburg's confidence.

During the next two years Bruening fought the depression with a series of austerity measures which progressively alienated his supporters. When he decided the government could not afford to continue subsidies to the East Prussian landowners, the Junkers and Nationalists turned against him. His attempts to maintain unemployment payments by higher taxes antagonized industrialists. By late 1931 an antirepublican and anti-Bruening coalition was developing. The members of this coalition met in a small town named Harzburg in October 1931. Present were the leaders of the Nationalist party, the Junkers' Land League, the Steel Helmet (a paramilitary veterans' organization), and some representatives of big business. One of the featured speakers was Adolf Hitler. These groups—calling themselves the Harzburg Front—demanded the resignation of both Bruening and the Social Democratic government of Prussia.

Hitler was given an opportunity to gain more allies—this time among big business—when he was invited to speak to the Industry Club of the Rhineland in January 1932 at Dusseldorf. In his speech, Hitler tried to convince the industrialists that nazism would deliver them from the Weimar Republic and would be their shield with which to ward off a Bolshevik revolution. Although some contributions came to the Nazi party from big business after the Dusseldorf meeting, Hitler was never successful in allaying the industrialists' fears about the radicalism of the Nazi left-wingers. Therefore, Hitler received very little money from big business during the next critical months. He had more success with small and middle-sized businessmen threatened with bankruptcy by the depression.[6]

---

[5] Alan Bullock, *Hitler,* completely rev. ed. (New York: Harper and Row, Publishers, 1964), p. 150.

[6] Henry A. Turner, Jr., "Big Business and the Rise of Hitler," *American Historical Review,* vol. 75, no. 1 (1969), pp. 62, 69.

TABLE 7.2. German Elections, 1919–1933

	1919	1920	May 1924	December 1924	1928	1930	July 1932	November 1932	March 1933	November 1933
Reichstag Seats:										
National Socialists	...	...	32	14	12	107	230	196	288	661
Catholic Nationalist	...	...	...	...	10	19	1	...	...	...
Christian Socialist	...	...	...	...	...	14	3	5	4	...
Nationalists	44	71	95	103	73	41	37	52	52	...
People's Party	19	65	45	51	45	30	7	11	2	...
Democrats	75	39	28	32	25	20	4	2	5	...
Bavarian People's Party	...	21	16	19	16	19	22	20	18	...
Center	91	64	65	69	62	68	75	70	74	...
Social Democrats	165	102	100	131	153	143	133	121	120	...
Independent Socialists	22	84								
Communists	...	4	62	45	54	77	89	100	81	...
Total Seats	423	459	472	493	491	577	608	584	647	661
Percentages of Votes Cast:										
National Socialists	...	...	6.5	3.0	2.6	18.3	37.4	33.1	43.9	92.2
Nationalists	10.3	14.9	19.5	20.5	14.2	7.0	5.9	8.8	8.0	
Democrats	18.6	8.3	5.7	6.3	4.9	3.8	1.0	1.0	0.8	
Center	19.7	13.6	13.4	13.6	12.1	11.8	12.5	11.9	11.7	
Social Democrats	37.9	21.6	20.5	26.0	29.8	24.5	21.6	20.4	18.3	
Communists	...	2.1	12.6	9.0	10.6	13.1	14.6	16.9	12.3	

Source: Koppel Pinson, *Modern Germany* 2d ed. (New York: Macmillan Co., 1966), appendix B, pp. 603–4.

Having thus allied himself with the Nationalists at Harzburg, Hitler was prepared to challenge Hindenburg in the presidential election of 1932. Once again the Nazi vote increased. On the second ballot, Hindenburg received 19,360,000 votes to Hitler's 13,400,000. This was double the vote the Nazis had received in 1930. Yet, Bruening and Hindenburg used their electoral success to attack Hitler's party. Three days after the election Bruening ordered that the SA and SS dissolve, removing them from the streets briefly. This overdue measure did not help Bruening, however; for, when he was unable to gain an agreement from France on the cessation of reparations and on the rearming of Germany, Hindenburg, prompted by Schleicher, demanded Bruening's resignation.

Franz von Papen formed a ministry so conservative it became known as the "cabinet of barons." The ruling classes of pre-1914 were in power. Schleicher became the minister of war. The minister of the economy was connected with the German Dye Trust. The labor minister was a director of the Krupp Steel Works. A Junker who had been a Free Corps leader was appointed minister of interior. Within weeks a coup was undertaken by Papen to oust the SPD-dominated government of Prussia. Then Papen turned on the revolutionaries of the Right. He devised a policy of "attrition." He hoped to keep demanding legislative elections until the Nazis had no more funds. He was sure that Germany had begun her economic recovery and was confident that this would lead to a decline in Nazi popularity. So, in September, he dissolved the Reichstag and called for an election. He met with leading industrialists, and funds stopped flowing to the Nazis as if by magic.

The elections were to be on November 6. In the first days of the month an odd alliance was formed. On November 3 the Transport Workers of Berlin went on strike. Social Democrats denounced the strike, but communists and *the Nazi party* supported it. Hitler, competing with Papen for conservative votes, could not afford to risk the loss of working-class Nazis. The strike was still in progress on the day of the election. Papen's policy appeared successful. The Nazis lost thirty-four seats—their first setback since 1928. About one million voters had deserted the Nazi cause. To the distress of Papen, they had not switched to conservative parties. On the contrary, the KPD increased its Reichstag membership from eighty-nine to one hundred while the SPD and the Center party lost seats.

Frightened by a policy of attrition that led to communist gains, Schleicher began to plot against Papen. Soon Papen was bereft of support and had to resign in mid November. Papen advised Hindenburg to make Hitler chancellor so as to embarrass him by the obvious lack of parliamentary support for nazism. Hindenburg tried, but Hitler made such extravagant demands that Hindenburg withdrew the offer. Instead, he appointed Schleicher so as to end Schleicher's intrigues and make him responsible. When the scheming general became chancellor on December

3, 1932, not a single party in the country supported him. This was the logical consequence of the presidential dictatorship that Schleicher had done so much to create.

The lonely chancellor almost immediately offended his potential sources of support—the industrialists and the Junkers. He advocated more government aid to the poor, both urban unemployed and land-hungry peasants. Specifically, he suggested that certain large estates might be broken up and the land distributed among the unemployed. A cry of "Schleicher must go!" was heard before the general had been in office for one month. Various national groups began negotiating with Hitler on the formation of a government that would include all parties of the Right. Hitler would join such a cabinet *only as chancellor*. The Nationalists and President Hindenburg finally agreed to this. On January 30, 1933, Hitler was sworn in as chancellor of Germany. The German nation was to begin its most fantastic adventure.

Chapter 8

FASCISM IN GERMANY

The Nature of Fascism

The rise of fascism* in Europe during the interwar period has been one of the most important political phenomena of the twentieth century. The origins and the essence of fascism are still debated. Was Hitler's regime a product of German conditions alone? Was Italian fascism's success due to the presence of Mussolini? There are few who would question the assertion that, without the economic and social dislocation caused by the depression, Hitler would not have come to power. Yet, this is to say very little; for the United States also had an economic crisis, with an unemployment rate as high as Germany's. American demagogues appeared—most notably Huey P. Long, who formed his own storm troopers in 1934 to support his dictatorship over Louisiana; but such men never were close to gaining control of the national government. Also, the depression cannot be used to explain the emulation of Mussolini's Black Shirts by various political movements in France and Great Britain *before* 1929. Nor does it explain the similarity of the movements that sprang up during the thirties in Belgium, Finland, Hungary, Rumania, and again, in France and Great Britain.

An analysis of fascism reveals that it was not a conservative movement in any meaningful sense of the word. In Germany, for example, every traditional institution was destroyed, subverted, or subordinated to the Nazi party. Fascism, then, was a revolutionary movement. A "revolution" is the displacement of one political leadership by another when this in-

---

* In the following chapters "fascism" will be used to refer to the general political phenomenon; whereas the capitalized word "Fascism" will be reserved for reference to the Italian Fascist party.

volves or leads to a restructuring of social institutions. A *socialist* revolution aims at the replacement of the owners of property (the capitalists) by representatives of the proletariat. This means that the prerevolutionary elites are removed from positions of authority and social prestige. *Conservatives*—such as Franco of Spain, Admiral Horthy of Hungary, or Petain of Vichy France during World War II—desire the perpetuation of traditional elites and hope for an aristocratic resurgence to strengthen the social hierarchy while they try to slow the pace of modernization, which they blame for the leveling of society. *Fascists* displace the traditional elites from positions of power but do not destroy them. The new leaders of society are not recruited from the prerevolutionary elites but from within the mass movement, the fascist party itself. The party gains control of the economy, demands obedience of all citizens regardless of class, and rules by terror as well as by arousing devotion. Once again using Germany as the example, the Nazis tried to create a society in which all Germans *felt* themselves to be equal with all other Germans before the state and before the Fuehrer but a society in which social hierarchies would be preserved.

Fascism was a synthesis of militant nationalism and militant socialism in revolt against liberal democracy and laissez faire economics.[1] Nationalism had been exalted into the ultimate virtue for all men by the prowar propaganda of 1914–18. Socialism was also an ultimate ideal that had spread through society before the war and which gained new prestige after the Russian Revolution. In addition, national leaders had promised the millions of soldiers—mostly workers and peasants—a better world after the war, with an end of class privilege and exploitation. As Lloyd George put it, it would be a world "fit for heroes to live in." Unfortunately, in no country could the wartime promises be kept. In fact, the military was used everywhere to suppress revolutionaries and even to crush legitimate strikes.

After 1919 only the communists were willing to attempt a revolution for socialist ideals alone. Socialism was associated with internationalism; therefore, it conflicted with the supernationalism of the exsoldiers. These frustrated veterans began to look for other ways to change society. Fascism offered them change and the promise of social justice while permitting them to remain nationalistic. In fact, many fascist leaders came from socialist backgrounds. Italy's Mussolini is perhaps the most famous example. In France, Jacques Doriot was a communist before switching to fascism. Of course, Oswald Mosley was a member of the Labour party before he founded the British Union of Fascists. Leon Degrelle in Belgium had been a socialist. Most of these men brought their socialist doctrine and goals with them into fascism, but they adopted supernationalism,

---

[1] Eugen Weber, *Varieties of Fascism* (Princeton: D. Van Nostrand Co., Inc., 1964).

the use of violence, and the dictatorial party as necessities of the revolutionary struggle.

This is not to deny the strong middle-class support for fascism. The lower middle class (the *petite bourgeoisie*) was especially susceptible because it felt especially threatened. Normally meek and obsequious shopkeepers resorted to political extremism as a reaction to the increasing strength of big business and big labor. The following extract from the program of a German regionalist party which later supported the Nazis expressed the distress so deeply felt:

The craftsman has to be protected on the one hand against capitalism, which crushes him by means of its factories, and on the other hand against socialism, which aims at making him a proletarian wage-laborer. At the same time the merchant has to be protected against capitalism in the form of the great department stores, and the whole retail trade against the danger of socialism.[2]

Therefore, fascism was a product of the peculiar conditions existing in post-World War I Europe: a frustrated working class, a frightened lower middle class, and unstable economic conditions which in 1923 and 1929 intensified the passions of the two. Of course, political protest would not have taken the course it did if there had not been several decades of increasing attacks on liberalism by intellectuals of both left and right and the glorification of violence and "the will to power" which had figured so prominently in pre-World War I thought.

Volkish Ideology

Even though fascism was a European-wide movement, the form it took in each nation was dictated by the particular social conditions and national traditions of that country. Because Hitler's Nazi movement was similar to fascist parties in other countries, this does not mean that it was not also in many ways unique. In order to determine why German fascism assumed the monstrous and disastrous form it did, it is necessary to analyze German society, especially in the realm of intellectual history.

The German intellectual tradition is frequently cited as the determining factor which explains Germany's foreign policy as well as the extermination of the Jews. Authors like William Shirer trace the intellectual heritage of National Socialism back to Martin Luther or to Hegel.[3] But these attempts to prove Germany a nation of philosophers preoccupied with power and mysticism on the one hand and subservient soldiers on the other are based both on bad intellectual history and on a lack of knowledge

---

[2] Seymour Martin Lipset, *Political Man: The Social Basis of Politics* (Garden City, N.Y.: Doubleday and Co., Inc., 1963), p. 143.

[3] William Shirer, *The Rise and Fall of the Third Reich* (New York: Simon and Schuster, Inc., 1960); Klaus Epstein, "Shirer's History of Nazi Germany," *Review of Politics*, vol. 23, no. 2 (1961), pp. 230–45.

of German political history. To denounce these wrong-headed condemnations of German culture, however, is not to say that the ideas advocated by the Nazis were not widespread among Germans. But the ideas which laid the foundation for nazism were of a different kind than those of Hegel, Fichte, and Schopenhauer.

The direct source of Nazi doctrine was the Volkish ideology, a body of thought professing to explain German national character and the role of German culture in history.[4] The two men credited with having formulated the principles of the Volkish ideology in a systematic way were Paul de Lagarde and Julius Langbehn. Both were frustrated academics. Because of the seniority system in German universities, Lagarde had to teach secondary school until late in life. Langbehn never attained professorial rank. Still, their writings were influential enough to become the foundation for racist thought in Germany. The essence of the Volkish ideology was that each German lived in mystical union with the German Volk. The Volk was not just the other living Germans but was the spirit of the German nation which was eternal. It was a product of both the land on which Germanic tribes had lived since the days of the Roman Empire as well as the physical characteristics of the Germans. Yet the Volk was more than these. It was an ever-existent life force to which all Germans belonged.

This idea had developed during the struggle for national unity following the Napoleonic wars. Intellectuals felt that, if only the Germans could be united politically, then they would prove themselves the equals of any nation in cultural achievements and a utopian peacefulness would result. However, when national unification did occur in 1870, it was accompanied by the industrial revolution, which did not unite but divided Germany—into employer-employee, proletarian-capitalist, liberal-conservative. The nationalist intellectuals—like Lagarde and Langbehn—felt cheated, and they sought a spiritual unity for the nation that might succeed where the political union had failed. According to them, this unity could only be achieved by making all Germans aware of their national heritage and their national destiny. The values most praised were pastoral and primitive—the heroic, simple values of the Germanic tribes of ancient times. The ideal German was pictured as a warrior-peasant. The peasant and the countryside were so emphasized because Volkish thought was essentially antimodern. Lagarde, Langbehn, and their disciples blamed modernity for having disrupted German society and having weakened the true German values of loyalty, honesty, etc. Modernity in the form of large cities, the proletariat (especially labor unions), rationalism (especially liberalism), and technology were destroying the real Germany.

---

[4] Fritz Stern, *The Politics of Cultural Despair* (Garden City, N.Y.: Doubleday and Co., Inc., 1965); George L. Mosse, *The Crisis of German Ideology* (New York: Grosset and Dunlap, 1964).

Therefore, the Volkish thinkers advocated a Germanic revival that would reject the corrupting values of materialism and modernity in favor of a harmonious, creative society freed from modern complexities. From the first, the Jew was pointed to as the hated symbol of modernization. It was indeed true that the Jew functioned as the middle-man in many of Germany's agricultural regions, often being the only source of loans and the only source of capital for new economic ventures. Lagarde and Langbehn were not racist; they were exalting the German Volk and trying to explain German national frustrations. They both felt that a Jew could become a German by a religious conversion.

It was in 1894 that Houston Stewart Chamberlain pleased Volkish thinkers by popularizing racist concepts and giving them a pseudoscientific justification. The son of an English admiral, he adopted Germany as his home, became a German citizen, married Richard Wagner's daughter, and lived at Bayreuth in an atmosphere of extreme nationalism. In his last years he became a friend of Hitler, whom he admired greatly. Chamberlain's book, *Foundations of the Nineteenth Century* (1900), was a strange combination of mysticism, philology, and social Darwinism. He presented the history of Germany as a bitter struggle between the Germanic and Jewish races. These were, he contended, the only two pure races. The Germans were the carriers of all that was good while the Jews were evil. In opposition to Lagarde and Langbehn, he was not openly antimodern. He just blamed all the troubles caused by the industrial revolution on the Jewish race. The defeat of the Jews would automatically remove all obstacles to the unity of the German Volk which would then use technology for human benefit. But before this could happen there would have to be a "Germanic revolution" to make the Germans aware of their destiny. The revolution was to be spiritual, not political. It would facilitate the return of a harmonious society without class conflicts. Chamberlain's book quickly became the Bible of the Volkish movement.

Anti-Semitism was not just an intellectual phenomenon of late nineteenth-century Germany but also took political form there and in Austria. Certain politicians tried to counter the growth of materialist Marxian socialism during the 1870s and 1880s in Berlin and Vienna by appealing to a Christian socialism. The Lutheran pastor Adolf Stoecker founded his Christian Social Workers' party in Berlin in 1878. At first he emphasized the paternalistic role of the state and the need for social reform; but, when he discovered that his attacks on Jewish industrialists and financiers as the source of class conflict was more popular, he made anti-Semitism central to his "Berlin Movement." Stoecker's success as an agitator was imitated in the 1880s by even more extreme anti-Semites, and anti-Semitic parties flourished. The reception given these Christian, anti-socialist, prosocial reform groups, however, was partially a result of economic crises of the period, and the anti-Semitic parties in Germany largely disappeared after 1900. By that time, nationalist political parties and certain pressure groups—the Agrarian League, the Pan-German League—had absorbed anti-Semitism as an integral part of their programs.

On the other hand, organized anti-Semitism was so successful in Austria, where Adolf Hitler lived as a child, that it absorbed the traditional conservative parties. The Christian Social party of Vienna, organized in 1887, was the political machine of Karl Lueger. The Christian Socialists, like the German anti-Semites, demanded democratic reforms, an end to the abuses of capitalism, and anti-Semitic laws. One police official considered the Christian Socialists dangerous because "the Christian Social party also appeals, as does the Social Democratic party, to the coarse instincts of the lower orders and collaborates in a dangerous manner in the stirring up and incitation of the people."[5] By 1895 Lueger had become popular enough to be elected mayor of Vienna, the highest elective office in Austria since the prime minister was appointed by the emperor. Conservatives of the court, the church, and the state bureaucracy prevailed upon Emperor Franz Joseph not to confirm the election. Lueger had to be reelected three times before the emperor finally bowed to the electorate. It is obvious that Lueger's popularity rested on his social reform program as well as on his anti-Semitism, but it was the anti-Semitism that guaranteed him success instead of the Social Democrats. After conquering Vienna the Christian Social party proceeded to become the largest party in the Austrian Reichsrat in 1907 by absorbing the Conservative party. The rapid growth of the Social Democratic party was the major reason for the willingness of the Conservatives to merge with their former radical enemies.

Therefore, in the decades before World War I, the vast majority of Germans were exposed to Volkish and anti-Semitic thought. By 1900 it had been incorporated into textbooks and was praised by important university professors. An educational reform movement began in the 1890s with the avowed purpose of inculcating Volkish ideals among Germany's youth. The youth did not need much prompting; for the German youth movement was a direct application of the warrior-peasant values of Lagarde and Langbehn. The Pan-German League under Heinrich Class after 1908 advocated a series of anti-Semitic laws that would have virtually deprived Jews of their German citizenship. The Germans would have done well to heed the words of warning offered by a well-to-do Jew from Hesse in 1890:

Everywhere this anti-Semitic fury signifies nothing more and nothing less than the beginnings of the social revolution. Let it be clearly understood by all who support anti-Semitism openly or secretly, or who merely tolerate it; it is not a question of the Jews at all, it is a question of subverting the entire

---

[5] Peter G. J. Pulzer, *The Rise of Political Anti-Semitism in Germany* (New York: John Wiley and Sons, Inc., 1964), p. 181.

order of life, society and the state! Let no-one believe that one can throw the Jews as meat to the revolutionary beast and thus meanwhile salve oneself.[6]

Hitler and His Party, 1919–33

Adolf Hitler was born in Braunau, a small city on the Austrian side of the Bavarian frontier, in 1889. His father was an Austrian customs official, and young Adolf aspired to a career as an architect. His talents were not great enough to win him admittance to a Viennese school of architecture. When hostilities began in 1914, he volunteered his services to the German army. Gaining a respectable battlefield record, he achieved the rank of corporal and found the military life very much to his liking. During the chaotic and revolutionary months which followed the cease-fire, Hitler became a military instructor as part of the Reichswehr's program to indoctrinate soldiers as to the evils of socialism and revolution. His oratorical talents were considerable, and certain officers thought that he might be used to indoctrinate civilians as well.

In September 1919, Hitler was asked by his superiors in army intelligence to begin attending the meetings of a small political party, the German Worker's party. This party's program was a mixture of pan-German nationalism and Volkish theories. Hitler agreed with their ideas and was soon put in charge of the party's propaganda efforts. It proved to be the right move. Hitler's speeches began to draw large crowds; the party membership grew from the approximately fifty members of the party in 1919 to 2,500 in Munich alone by early 1921. Hilter had become indispensable. In 1921 Hitler threatened to resign if the party were not reorganized to give him dictatorial power as the Fuehrer. He was given the power. The party's name had already been changed to the National Socialist German Worker's party. The Nazi movement was begun.

The Nazi party grew slowly until the economic crisis of 1923–24, which aided all extremist groups. Hitler misinterpreted the degree of unrest, however, when he attempted a coup d'état that never made it past the Munich city limits. For his treasonous activity, he received the usual light sentence given to right-wing agitators by the Bavarian courts. He spent only eight months in a rather pleasant detention home fifty miles west of Munich. The word prison would be too severe. He was able to have guests, a private secretary, and to dress as he pleased. While there, he wrote *Mein Kampf,* which contained his political program.

While the Fuehrer was peacefully writing, the party was rent by internal feuds. Both the left wing of the party and the SA seemed on the verge of breaking with Hitler. The left wing was led by Gregor and Otto Strasser. They wanted to emphasize the "socialism" in the party name more than

---
[6] Ibid., p. 109.

the "nationalism." Gregor, sent to northern Germany to build the party organization there, had done so well that it appeared possible the Strassers would challenge Hitler's leadership. Gregor, especially, had concentrated on bringing workers into the party; so he was constantly trying to move the party to the left. His sharpest conflict with the Fuehrer occurred in 1925–26 over whether or not the state should expropriate the large estates of the former German royal family. Strasser favored the expropriation; Hitler opposed it. Through a skillful use of the party organization Hitler was able to force Strasser to back down, but the basic division in the party continued to exist.

The Storm Troopers also posed a problem for their Fuehrer. The leadership of the SA differed with Hitler on the relationship of this paramilitary force to the Nazi party. For Hitler, the SA, numbering 20,000 in 1925, had a political role, none other: it was to be an instrument of political intimidation and propaganda completely subordinate to the party. Ernst Roehm, commander of the SA, felt differently. He argued that the political and military movements were entirely independent of each other. He even appeared to exalt the SA leader to an equality with Hitler, the party leader. The SA leaders were also displeased with the parliamentary course Hitler chose to follow after 1924. They advocated a greater use of violence and preparation for another coup attempt. Hitler, however, was determined not to provoke the national government into using force against him again; therefore, he strongly opposed Roehm's ideas. The conflict became so bitter that in April 1925, Roehm resigned and left Germany for a brief career as a mercenary in Latin America.

It appeared that the party was indeed on the decline. Elections seemed to confirm this. In the Reichstag elections of May 1924, the Nazis had elected thirty-two deputies. This number shrank to fourteen in the December 1924, elections. Two more seats were lost in May 1928. This was an indication of the effects of national prosperity on the movement. Yet, this was a period of slow growth and development of the party machinery. Hitler, Gregor Strasser, Joseph Goebbels, and other party leaders traveled to the cities and towns of Germany to find new converts and to establish local party cells. The results of this work were revealed by the steady growth of the dues-paying membership.

The thousands of true believers who joined the Nazi party did so for various reasons, but there can be no doubt that between 1924–29 the party's appeal lay in its vague ideology. Later, during the economic and political crisis caused by the depression the ideology became less important and Hitler's charismatic personality was magnified until he and the ideology were indistinguishable. The official Nazi program, written as early as 1920, was known as the Twenty-five Points for obvious reasons. It had two basic sections that paralleled the conflict between "nationalist" end "socialist" wings of the party. The nationalist and racist goals of

TABLE 8.1.   Growth of Nazi Strength

Elections	Nazis Elected	Year	Party Membership
May 1924	32	1925	27,000
December 1924	14	1926	49,000
		1927	72,000
May 1928	12	1928	108,000
		1929	178,000
September 1930	107	1930	210,000

SOURCES: Alan Bullock, *Hitler, A Study in Tyranny*, rev. ed. (New York: Harper and Row, Publishers, 1964), pp. 141, 150; Koppel S. Pinson, *Modern Germany*, 2d ed. (New York: Macmillan Co., 1966), p. 602.

the party were as follows: All Germans were to be united in a greater Germany. The Treaty of Versailles was to be abrogated. The German army was to be revived. Jews were to be excluded from citizenship, and aliens who had entered Germany after 1914 were to be deported.

On the other hand, there were many anticapitalist proposals among the Twenty-five Points. All unearned income was to be abolished. All war profits were to be confiscated. The state should nationalize all trusts and share in the profits of large companies. Department stores should be nationalized and then occupied by small shops run by independent merchants. Government contracts should always go to small tradesmen. There were also drastic proposals for agrarian reform, such as the expropriation of land needed for national purposes, the abolition of rented farms, and the prohibition of land speculation. This platform represented a fierce anti-capitalism and a special solicitude for *petite bourgeoisie,* the small merchant.

Hitler never felt bound by the Twenty-five Points, although he insisted that they never change for public relations reasons. His own personal program was simpler. In foreign affairs, he emphasized that the German nation lacked power because of its democratic form of government and because of the limitations placed on Germany's military by Versailles. Therefore, Germany needed a strong, authoritarian government that would break through the chains of Versailles. In domestic affairs, all interests should be subservient to the state, and the state should be subservient to the Fuehrer who personified the Volk. When Hitler demanded that all interests be second to national interests, each frustrated German imagined that his personal enemy was the object of Hitler's scorn. The worker saw the capitalist humbled; the cobbler and tailor envisioned the department stores divided into small shops; the peasant saw the landlord removed; the employer knew the unions would be crushed; and the army saw itself as the prime national interest. Few imagined that Hitler meant that *all* should be subordinated to the Nazi party.

Hitler used other techniques that appealed to subconscious hatreds and anxieties. He never ceased repeating his hatred for Jews and his praise for Germans. This soothed the ego of a defeated nation and encouraged the myth that only Jewish businessmen were evil capitalists, while German businessmen were actually benevolent. The cultural anguish caused by modernization and expressed in Volkish anticapitalism was thus transferred to the Jews. To spread his ideas Hitler mastered the mechanics of propaganda. He developed the mass rally as a political event. No one else had used lights and loudspeakers as the Nazis did to stir a crowd, to create an atmosphere, to convey simple ideas of strength, power, dynamism. And the Nazis were all the more impressive since they were the first. Finally, Hitler recognized the propaganda effect of a show of force and violence. Not only did he use brutal words like "smash," "crush," and "ruthless," but he always had his brown-shirted bullies around. The disruption of opposition meetings, the marches through city streets, and the mass meetings were intended to give an impression of irresistible strength, of a movement destined to lead Germany.

In normal times, the Nazi program, propaganda, and racism probably would not have gained Hitler a large following—as shown by the decline in Nazi votes, 1924–28. Yet, thanks to the aid of traditional conservatives, Hitler became a nationally known politician on the eve of the depression, and the depression sent millions of voters in search of the Swastika. It was the debate over the referendum on the Young Plan that made Hitler famous. The campaign lasted from July 1929 to March 1930, during which Hitler traversed Germany with funds supplied by the Nationalist party. This new fame came at a propitious time for the Nazis. It was at this time that the depression idled millions of Germans. And there was a Reichstag election in September 1930. The Nazi party now became a *movement*.

Like men and women in a town stricken by an earthquake, millions of Germans saw the apparently solid framework of their existence crackling and crumbling. In such circumstances men are no longer amenable to the arguments of reason. In such circumstances men entertain fantastic fears, extravagant hatreds, and extravagant hopes. In such circumstances the extravagant demagogy of Hitler began to attract a mass following as it had never done before.[7]

The appeal of nazism was a shock to the German political system. (See Table 7.2.)

Once the Nazis were successful at the polls they began to obtain allies among traditional conservative groups that had previously ignored them. For instance, the army had disapproved of the violent tactics of Hitler's supporters. He had been warned in 1923 that the army would not permit

---

[7] Alan Bullock, *Hitler, A Study in Tyranny*, rev. ed. (New York: Harper and Row, Publishers, 1964), p. 153.

an armed insurrection. This did not imply a loyalty to the republic but a sense of duty to protect legal processes. Another point of conflict was the fear among soldiers that Roehm's SA was being prepared to replace the regular army. Hitler assured the friendly neutrality of the army during the crucial period 1930–33 by continually emphasizing his loyalty to legal means and his desire not only to retain the regular army but to expand it. He could count on the support of young officers because the limited size of the military since 1919 had made promotion slow and difficult to obtain. Hitler was also confident of army support because of General von Schleicher's sympathy for the Nazis and Schleicher's desire to build a conservative coalition including the Nazis.

After the Nationalists had sponsored Hitler's entrance to national politics in the Young Plan debate, German businessmen began to regard him in a new light. Yet his movement did not receive large contributions from the industrial community until the Dusseldorf speech. Speaking before the leading industrialists of the Rhineland, Hitler tried to explain away the anticapitalist parts of his party program. He assured the capitalists that they had nothing to fear from him. In fact, he insisted on his determination to crush bolshevism. He pressed upon them his belief in the need to extend the principle of inequality that prevailed in the economic realm, where the weak fail and the strong rule, to politics. Government, he said, should not be by the masses but by the talented few. The industrialists assumed that he was referring to them.

Although the conservatives were willing to cooperate with Hitler, there were still basic conflicts between the Nazis and the German aristocrats. Hitler spoke of a German revolution, and this worried conservatives. Hitler tried to calm them by saying he only wanted a spiritual revolution, not a social revolution. Secondly, there was opposition among left-wing Nazis to an alliance with the upper classes. Gregor Strasser denounced the Harzburg Front as cooperation with the "old gang" that the Nazis were supposed to be replacing. Strasser complained that, if Hitler were too closely identified with the Nationalist party or the industrialists, workers would desert to the communists. In fact, such a desertion took place in late 1932 and led to Strasser's resignation. Finally, Hitler, his closest associates, and his followers came from different social classes than did the conservatives. The middle-class, uncultured Nazi leader with a penchant for violence and a lack of scruples was repugnant to the highly principled Officer Corps, whose values were still those of the Junker nobility. It was not by chance that resistance to the Nazi revolution came from these groups; it was because the old elites realized that, far from honoring them, the Nazis hoped to replace them.

Still, in January 1933, the conservatives seemed to have no choice. Only two parties had the will to power, to govern Germany alone: the Nazis and the Communists. The democratic parties were not willing to assume the responsibilities of government and had abdicated before President Hindenburg's legal dictatorship. The Communists would accept office only alone. They refused a coalition with the SPD. This made a leftist cabinet impossible. The KPD even welcomed the prospect of a Nazi government, arguing that this was a sign of the collapse of capitalism and that a Nazi dictatorship would drive the masses into a communist revolution.

Still, the conservatives have to absorb the majority of the blame for Hitler's appointment to the chancellorship on January 30, 1933. Their hatred for democracy blinded them to the kindnesses the Weimar Republic had shown them. When Schleicher tried last-minute social reforms at the expense of the upper classes, they preferred Hitler rather than a loss of personal privilege. This was the thanks they gave the republic that had left the Junkers with their land, the army with its independence, the industrialists with their economic freedom. Hitler's regime was not to be so generous.

The Nazi Revolution

Hitler's first concern as chancellor was to consolidate his power, to establish an authoritarian regime. A necessary preliminary was the election of a Nazi parliamentary majority that would vote him full powers. This would maintain the façade of legality he felt was required by the army. Therefore, he forced the nation into another election by refusing to govern without a clear majority in the Reichstag. Having control of the national administration made it very simple for the Nazis to rig the election held in March 1933. Various excuses were used to limit the campaign activities of other parties. The most notorious of these was the Reichstag Fire incident. On February 27 the Reichstag building was consumed in flames. A Dutch communist named Van der Lubbe, a pitiful young man who was an admitted arsonist, was arrested at the scene. Hitler used this to implicate the entire KPD and to arrest its leaders. He went further, however, and suspended civil liberties for the duration of the election campaign. Effectively, only Nazi candidates were allowed to campaign.

Still, despite the harassment of democratic parties and despite the Nazi control of the police and administration, a majority of German voters refused to vote for the Nazi party. Even after he proscribed the KPD deputies as criminals, Hitler needed the support of the Center and Nationalists parties in order to pass the Enabling Law of March 23, 1933, which was the legal basis for the Third Reich. Here was the chance for the Center party and the Nationalists to protest the obvious crimes of the Nazis. They did not. The law, which passed the Reichstag by a vote of 441–94, gave Hitler the power to govern by decree without President Hindenburg's consent. Until this time, Hindenburg had been the only legal check on the chancellor; after this, there was no limit on Hilter's power.

With his personal position assured Hitler began a policy of *Gleichschaltung* (coordination) with the goal of subordinating every German institution to the Nazi party. Political parties were the first victims. The KPD and SPD were banned. The other parties voted themselves out of existence rather than face Nazi brutality. At the same time, Nazis were appointed to administrative positions throughout Germany. The continuity of administration was not broken as in most revolutions; the administrative personnel merely changed. The independence of the *Länder,* however, was abolished, and Germany became a fully unified state for the first time. Hitler then appointed Reich governors for each *land* directly responsible to him. Usually these governors were the local party leaders or *gauleiter.* On May 2, 1933, trade union headquarters were occupied by the SA and SS, and trade union officers were deported to concentration camps. The unions were then merged by government fiat into one national federation, the Labor Front. This was actually a ministry for the control and efficient mobilization of the labor force in accordance with the needs of the party. All other political or semipolitical organizations were either abolished or integrated into the state or party. By the end of July 1933, the Nazi party had absolute control of the German state. A mockery of an election was held in November 1933. All of the candidates were Nazis.

There was still a potential opposition, however, within the party: the SA. SA Commander Roehm wanted to replace the regular Reichswehr with his own revolutionary army. He even went so far as to threaten Hitler indirectly by complaining that the revolution had not gone far enough. The SA was, in fact, the direct descendant of the Free Corps of the early 1920s—rough, vicious, undisciplined, egalitarian, resentful of the prestige of the regular army. To counter these rowdies, who had been useful for street fighting but were not needed after nazism was in power, Hitler had developed the SS. Originally the elite personal guard of the Fuehrer, the SS had attracted the scions of aristocratic families who found promotion in the Reichswehr slow and difficult to gain. Much more conservative than the SA, the SS was more suited to governing. Therefore, Hitler listened to Heinrich Himmler, SS commander, and Hermann Goering, head of the new German air force, when they suggested that the SA be tamed. On June 30, 1934, after several months of relative calm in domestic affairs, the SS staged a night raid throughout Germany. The major victims were the leaders of the SA; but while they were about it, the SS also murdered many of Hitler's old political enemies, such as Schleicher and even Gustav von Kahr, who had been the Bavarian politician who suppressed the Munich beer hall putsch of 1923. This bloodletting, known as the "Night of the Long Knives," effectively ended all

The mass emotion of Nazi rallies was carefully orchestrated. (Courtesy of UPI)

open opposition to Hitler's regime, although various pockets of clandestine resistance gradually formed.

Having gained control of a nation of 65 million persons, Hitler felt no responsibility to any constituency or social class. He was guided only by the need to revive the economy and to make it strong enough to wage the war that he thought would be necessary to assert Germany's greatness. His policy consisted of gradually restructuring each sector of the economy until it was at the mercy of the Nazi party. The gradual exclusion of Jews from German society and their eventual extermination at concentration camps was the only Nazi policy that was clearly ideological rather than just a means of increasing Hitler's power.

The Labor Front, which was justified as a means of avoiding class conflict, was an example of the institutionalization of dictatorship. It regulated all aspects of labor conditions—wages, hours, factory safety, even entertainment and housing for workers. The results were not altogether adverse for the workers. They lost their freedom but gained full employment, a slightly higher standard of living, and vastly improved working conditions. The front worked through government-appointed Labor Trustees who had absolute control over individual enterprises. Not only could the trustees set wages arbitrarily, but they could also order an employer to build a cafeteria, a park, or low-cost housing for his employees. The result of such power was, indeed, an end to class conflict but not to the benefit of the worker or, in any exaggerated sense, of the employer. Only the state benefited.

The Labor Service was another aspect of labor policy. The term referred originally to a vast public works program that had been initiated by Bruening. The Nazi government greatly expanded the service and made it permanent in June 1935 by making registration in the service compulsory for all men. Work passes were introduced at the same time, so the government could know the exact employment of each German. Therefore, if a labor shortage existed in one industry, it could be filled by workers from an industry with a surplus of laborers. Of course, no one could change jobs without government approval. The state thus mobilized the labor force to further national policy goals. Obviously, the freedoms of workers were gradually eroded until their legal position was the equivalent of well-paid slaves.

Yet, even if this were objectively true, few German workers believed it. The majority of workers had material reasons to be satisfied with the Nazi system. For young workers, the unemployment of 1929–34, when they had entered the labor market, was fresh in their minds. By 1936 there was full employment, improved working conditions, opportunities for vacations at working class resorts, and even professional entertainment at special prices for the workers. More houses were available, as well as more food. Theoretically, management could no longer exploit labor because of the control over both enjoyed by the Labor Front. The eight-hour day became standard, and in all respects, the standard of living of Germany's working class improved.[8] To reinforce the impact of these economic changes, the Labor Front propaganda machine continuously repeated that Germany had become a national *socialist workers'* state.

The owners of heavy industry had far more reason to be satisfied with the Third Reich than did the workers. The government consistently courted them until 1936, when they also discovered that they had to bow to the Nazi party. One of Hitler's first decrees removed the legal limitations on cartels, which had been intended to protect small businessmen from unfair competition. For instance, this Decree on Cartels (July 1933) allowed a company with a monopoly to boycott retailers who did not belong to a national chain or to the company with the monopoly. For example, the German radio industry entered into a cartel agreement to supply only recognized wholesalers and retailers with radios. From 1933–35, radio wholesalers decreased from 1,500 to 750. In 1938 alone, radio retailers declined from 60,000 to 37,000.[9] The same process— greater concentration at the expense of small businesses—was occurring in other industries as well. Big business was also aided by financial support

---

[8] David Schoenbaum, *Hitler's Social Revolution: Class and Status in Nazi Germany 1933–1939* (Garden City, N.Y.: Doubleday and Company, Inc., 1966), chap. 3.

[9] Ibid., p. 133.

and by the policy of Aryanization. Government contracts always went to the largest, most efficient firms; and as Jews were forced to sell their businesses, the Aryans who bought them were great industrialists and financiers, not the *petite bourgeoisie* which had supported Hitler so fervently.

However, the Nazis were not helping big business because of an ideological commitment to capitalism. This is proved by two developments: the regime's struggle with the steel industry over military production and the construction of state-owned and party-owned enterprises. In October 1936. the government announced a Four-Year Plan of industrial expansion. The object was full military production in preparation for war. Dr. Hjalmar Schact, the financial wizard who had run the economy since 1933, resigned. He did not oppose rearmament, but he opposed the complete neglect of all economic principles that Hitler's Four-Year Plan implied. The steel industry also balked. It complained that it was absurd to build new armaments plants when the old plants were not working at full capacity. The industrialists likewise resented the price controls inherent in the plan. Therefore, Hitler decided to bypass the private sector in certain areas and force them to acquiesce in others. Hermann Goering, as plenipotentiary for the Four-Year Plan, was made the economic dictator of Germany, with powers to allocate or withhold raw materials, set prices, and direct state investments. The state built the Hermann Goering Steel Works, which became the largest producer of steel and steel products in the Reich. It expanded into many fields and destroyed lesser competitors from the private sector. The attitude of the steel industry was indicated by Fritz Thyssen's departure from Germany. Thyssen was one of Germany's wealthiest industrialists and had supported Hitler since the 1920s. He did not resent Nazi racism or police-state methods, but he could not support a regime that limited free enterprise. The Labor Front also developed an industrial empire; although it was not as directly a threat to private business as was the Goering Steel Works. The front built cars (the Volkswagen), ships, a chain of movie houses, and numerous other items. Nazi economic policy, therefore, was neither capitalist nor socialist. The Third Reich was pragmatic. It hungered after power—power for the German military, power for the Nazi party, power for Adolf Hitler. It destroyed or controlled businesses that did not cooperate, while businesses, such as those in the chemical industry, which cooperated with the Four-Year Plan prospered accordingly.

Of course, Hitler did not keep his promises to small businessmen or to farmers. As seen above, small businesses were forced to bow before the cartels. Agricultural laborers and small farmers fared no better. By freezing prices at the low level of 1933, the government made it impossible for farmers to make an economic recovery comparable to that of the urban population. The flight from the farm to the city continued. Perhaps this was Hitler's greatest deviation from the Volkish ideology, which glorified the rural life. In contrast, the Nazis in power emphasized big business and encouraged urbanization by that emphasis.

Hitler was faithful to one promise: the pledge to exclude Jews with German society. The attack on Jews began with a boycott of Jewish shops called by the Nazi party for April 1–3, 1933. In September 1935, the Nuremburg Laws took away the Jews' political and legal rights. The same laws prohibited marriages between Jews and Germans on racial grounds. (A Jew was defined as anyone having one Jewish grandparent.) Any other sexual relationship between Jews and other races—even casual friendships—were also forbidden. Of course, the courts gave the broadest possible interpretation of the Nuremburg Laws. Gradually, Jews were denied membership in one profession after another. Certainly, they could not practice law or medicine. In 1934 Jews were required to use only certain approved names for their children. Another law required them to carry special identification papers. Jewish property ownership became impossible after November 1938. In that month a German embassy official in Paris, General von Rath, was assassinated by a young Jew. Hitler used this as an excuse to extend the Aryanization of Jewish property that had already begun. Before this, Jews had been forced to sell their shares in a company or their partnership in a firm to Germans. They had also been required to register all of their property and wealth and had been forbidden to obtain new possessions. A week after von Rath's murder Jews were forbidden to carry on any trade whatsoever and were ordered not only to sell their property but also to deposit the proceeds (and all their wealth) in state banks. Of course, this meant the Jews would never see the money again.

The physical separation of Jews began with the prohibition of social contact between the races inherent in the Marriage Laws. Once again the von Rath assassination permitted more extreme measures. Jews were excluded from schools where they might mix with other Germans. They could shop only during certain hours, were barred from resorts and beaches, and had to be treated in separate hospitals. Certain apartment houses were designated as *Judenhauser*, and Jews could live nowhere else. These steps toward complete isolation were part of the transition from a policy of forcing Jews into exile to the final solution practiced in the death camps during World War II. The camps had begun as detention camps for communists and socialists in 1933. Only with the outbreak of war did they become death camps. Indeed, Hitler was keeping his campaign promises.

Not all Germans accepted Nazi crimes without complaint. There was a sizable, if divided and ineffectual, German resistance. Before World War II began, before Jews were systematically placed in concentration camps, there were already 200,000 enemies of the regime in German prisons. The opposition to Hitler was drawn from a broad political spectrum, including communists, socialists, christian democrats, and extreme-conservatives. It was not, however, equally broadly based. SPD opposition came from socialist party leaders, not from the rank-and-file party members or from trade unionists. The Communist effort was also carried out by party organizers at the higher levels. Conservative and Catholic resisters were disdainful of the public and had hated the Weimar Republic for the same reasons they opposed Hitler: fear of the destruction of German society as they knew it. The lower-middle class and the business community as well as the labor movement contributed almost nothing to the German resistance. As one German historian has written:

The social structure of the Opposition was comparatively homogeneous. Its members were predominately upper-class and regarded themselves . . . as personally qualified to assume a leading role.[10]

The first victims of the Nazis were the communists and socialists; they also supplied the first resisters. The KPD had taken the position, when Hitler came to power, that nazism should not be actively opposed. This attitude was based on the assumption that fascism was the last stage of capitalism and would force Germans to undertake a communist revolution. Instead, the KPD found itself under attack. Using the Reichstag fire incident as an excuse, the Nazis arrested many communist leaders in February and March 1933. The national party chairman was imprisoned while other party officials fled to Czechoslovakia and Russia. Every attempt to reorganize the national executive was crushed by the Gestapo, who seemed to have informers placed in the highest ranks of the party. Twice—in November 1933 and again in March 1935—the KPD established a national executive to work in secret within the Reich only to have all of its members arrested days after they first met. A more successful venture was the industrial sabotage and espionage ring known as the *Rote Kappele* (Red Chapel). Beginning in 1935, it collected and transmitted valuable information to Russia. This group was uncovered and destroyed in 1942.

The Social Democrats missed their opportunity for massive resistance to Hitler when in January 1933, the SPD leaders did not call upon the Reichsbanner, the fighting arm of the party, to challenge the Nazis to a test of strength. The Reichsbanner legions had even assembled throughout Germany to await the signal from their party officials—a signal that never came. In June 1933, Hitler proscribed the party and arrested its most important spokesmen. After this, two SPDs emerged. One was the party-in-exile that was headed by the Prague Executive. These socialists

---

[10] Hans Mommsen, "Social Views and Constitutional Plans of the Resistance," in *The German Resistance to Hitler* (Berkeley: University of California Press, 1970), p. 59.

managed to smuggle propaganda against the Nazis into Germany and to aid other anti-Nazis escape from the Reich. Inside Germany, the Berlin Regional Committee maintained contact with socialists throughout Germany by couriers. The Berlin group was discovered by the Gestapo, however, in 1935, and by the end of the following year the entire socialist underground had been disrupted. After this, there were individual socialist resisters but no socialist resistance movement.

There were many clergymen, both Catholic and Protestant, who openly denounced the Nazis from their pulpits. Two cardinal archbishops, Faulhaber of Bavaria and von Galen of Muenster, had their anti-Nazi sermons circulated to all churches under their authority and in other parts of Germany as well. Unfortunately, the defiance of these men and of the lesser Catholic clergy lost some of its effect because of the willingness of Pope Pius XI to coexist with the Nazi regime as long as the institutional Church was not too gravely threatened. Protestant resistance was led by Pastor Martin Niemoller. He directed the circulation of anti-Nazi petitions among clergymen, sent delegations to Berlin to protest Nazi barbarities, and organized mass demonstrations of pastors. One demonstration in Stuttgart in October 1934 drew 7,000 Germans, mostly pastors, who were willing to protest publicly. Of course, the great theologian Dietrich Bonhoffer died in prison for his part in the resistance.

The only resistance organizations to last until the end of World War II were the conservative groups. One, the Kreisau Circle, was intellectual; the other, the Beck Group of army officers, was activist and tried to assassinate Hitler. The Kreisau Circle began as a group of aristocratic landowners meeting to consider the future of Germany. It grew into several large conferences in 1942 and 1943 that included representatives of many political and social groups who held in common a reverence for Christian principles of individual worth. The members of the Circle supplied intellectual and moral leadership to the German resistance during the war years and elaborated plans for a cultural and social regeneration of Germany after Hitler. All that they did was guided by a Christian conservatism rather than by a desire for a democratic society. Their influence was wide because all the men who belonged to the Circle were members of Germany's pre-Nazi elite, and these men discussed ideas developed at Kreisau, the estate of Count Helmuth James von Moltke, with other members of the upper classes.

The opposition of the German Officer Corps to Hitler's military plans has been written of many times. Several times during the 1930s members of the Beck Group, named after General Ludwig Beck, tried to get guarantees from Great Britain and France that Hitler's adventures would be opposed with military force. Beck and his associates assured the British that the German army would not support a direct confrontation over the Rhineland, or later, over Czechoslovakia; and, if the British and

French would march against Hitler, the resistance movement in the Officer Corps would bring about a coup d'état to topple the dictator. Each time the generals were ignored completely. Some of the highest officers of the Reichswehr participated in the Beck conspiracy: Admiral Canaris, head of German counterintelligence; Franz Halder, chief of staff in 1934; and many other generals. Furthermore, Beck also had fellow conspirators in the diplomatic corps, another bastion of conservatism. These men tried several times to assassinate Adolf Hitler. Driven to desperation by the imminent defeat of Germany in 1944, they organized Operation Valkyrie. Hitler was to be assassinated, and government offices in Berlin were to be seized by troops loyal to the conspirators. On July 20, 1944, Colonel Claus von Stauffenberg placed a bomb in a conference room where Hitler was meeting with the military leaders of the Third Reich. By the purest accident, another officer kicked the bomb so as to put it on the opposite side of a table leg from Hitler. Hitler, therefore, survived the blast. In the meantime, the attempt to seize Berlin had begun but was crushed easily. In the following weeks, 7,000 alleged conspirators were arrested, and 5,000 were executed.

The ineffectiveness of the German resistance should not be difficult to understand. First, one must remember that the majority of their fellow citizens considered such resistance as illegal and perhaps treason. Second, there was a moral ambiguity about opposing one's national leadership (especially during a war). It took immense moral courage to revolt against one's basic loyalties. Third, the police-state techniques of the Gestapo made underground plotting extremely dangerous and had weakened any potential resistance by the mass arrests of anti-Nazis, particularly socialists and communists, in 1933 and 1934. An additional handicap was the lack of aid the German resisters received from British, French, and American sources. The Allied intelligence agencies refused to take the German resistance seriously. When Hitler was murdering the organizers of the July Conspiracy, Winston Churchill could only say, "The highest personalities in the German Reich are murdering one another, or trying to. . . ."[11] He had no praise nor sympathy for the conspirators.

---

[11] Gordon Wright, *The Ordeal of Total War* (New York: Harper and Row, Publishers, 1968), n. 5, p. 162.

Chapter 9

VARIETIES OF FASCISM

Interpretations of the orgins and nature of the Nazi regime have often been distorted by a narrow fascination with events in Germany. Without denying that the Nazi dictatorship was unique in certain ways, a general survey of European politics from 1919 to 1939 suggests that it was but one of many authoritarian regimes that replaced democratic governments in central and eastern Europe between the wars. The only states that were able to maintain democracies for the entire interwar period were those with stable democracies before World War I. The one striking exception to this was Czechoslovakia.

The English system of parliamentary democracy could not be imposed on nations with different political cultures.[1] Quite obviously, the political traditions of a people, based on their society's unique social structure, cannot be brushed aside merely by writing a constitution establishing a parliament. Parliamentary democracy developed out of the peculiarities of British history. A few continental countries—France, the Low Countries, Scandinavia—which had large middle classes and prosperous rural economies had made successful attempts to adapt it by 1914; and liberal democracy had flourished in certain off-shoots of Great Britain, such as Canada, Australia, and the United States. But there were very few countries in the world in 1919 that could adopt the British system. Germany was not one of them.[2] German liberals and socialists achieved a legal

---

[1] Barrington Moore, Jr., *Social Origins of Dictatorship and Democracy* (Boston: Beacon Press, 1966); C. E. Black, *The Dynamics of Modernization* (New York: Harper and Row, Publishers, 1966).

[2] Theodore Eschenburg and Ernst Fraenkel in *The Path to Dictatorship 1918–1933, Ten Essays by German Scholars,* trans. John Conway (Garden City, N.Y.: Doubleday and Co., Inc., 1966); Barrington Moore, *Social Origins,* chapters 7–9.

revolution that changed the monarchy into a republic, but they stopped short of the social revolution needed to change a hierarchical, authoritarian society into an open, pluralistic society. In 1929, as in 1914, German society was antidemocratic. The same was true of Italy and eastern Europe. The social revolution was prevented in Italy by the liberals' alliance with Mussolini. In eastern Europe, no real institutional change was attempted.

None of the dictatorships of eastern Europe was fascist. In the absence of industry and a strong bourgeoisie, dictators depended on the traditional conservative coalition of large landowners, the military, the church, and a few important financiers. Moreover, the conservative regimes of Hungary and Rumania were challenged in the 1930s by fascist revolutionaries who admired Mussolini and patterned their movements on his. Once again, Czechoslovakia was the exception due to the presence of a prosperous middle class and a well-educated peasantry that provided the basis for a parliamentary government.

The First Fascist State: Italy

Mussolini's regime, then, is important both as an international model and as the only fascist state that one can compare with Hitler's Germany. Before Hitler attained power, Mussolini was unique. He was admired greatly by conservatives in Italy and throughout Europe.

Above all, the [Italian] middle class and lower middle class were impressed by the steady rise in Italy's prestige abroad. In foreign newspapers, on sale everywhere, they read Mussolini's praises. *The New York Herald Tribune:* "Mussolini is the modern Caesar, the Napoleon of 1926." *Le Figaro* [Paris]: "Many people have got the habit, since three years ago, of taking one of those roads, all of which lead to Rome. The incredulous have finally realized how great is the interest aroused by Benito Mussolini and his works." London *Daily Mail:* "It becomes more and more evident that, in our time, we are witnessing another revolution of the world's ideas, a revolution started by the tireless and fertile genius of Mussolini."[3]

Although Mussolini had dictatorship virtually thrust upon him by the militants of the Fascist party, he was given credit for the form the regime took and was thought to be a man of iron will.

The legal basis for this much praised Fascist state was laid during 1925 and 1926. Several attempts to assassinate Il Duce were the pretext for ever greater limitations of freedom. The Socialist party and the Free Masons, associated with the Liberals, were banned. All other political and social organizations existed only at the sufferance of the government. Newspaper publishers rather than editors were made personally responsible

[3] John MacGregor-Hastie, *The Day of the Lion* (New York: Coward-McCann, Inc., 1964), p. 180.

The relationship between Hitler (left) and Mussolini was not always as genial as this. (Courtesy of UPI)

for the content and editorial policy of their papers. By 1930 only government approved news was printed. A special tribunal for the defense of the state was established to try those accused of treason. It was staffed by officers of the Fascist militia. A political police was created to search out opponents of the state. Its name was OVRA, but no one seemed to know exactly what that meant. Even the head of OVRA in the late thirties admitted that he did not know. Finally, Italy was declared a unitary state, and all local government was abolished. The central government appointed regional prefects, who in turn appointed mayors for the municipalities. Of course, only loyal members of the party were appointed. The last vestiges of parliamentary government were destroyed by the Law of Political Elections (March 1928), which provided that there would be only one list of candidates. The electorate must either accept or reject the entire list. Of course, all the candidates were fascists, and the public always accepted them. Not only political affairs but all social activities were brought under party control; so no independent organizations were possible. For example, the Italian National Olympic Committee was the only recognized sporting association in the nation. Likewise, the *Ballila*, a branch of the Fascist party, was the only legal youth organization. All social activities organized by students had to be approved by the *Ballila*.

While Mussolini could destroy all political opponents, there was one potential source of opposition with which he had to compromise—the Catholic church. Since the unification of Italy in 1870, popes had refused to accept the Italian state as legal. This put many Italians in an ambiguous position—torn between their religion and their nationalism. In 1925 Mussolini began secret negotiations with Pope Pius XI to achieve what the republican governments from 1870–1922 had been unable to achieve. After three years of quiet negotiations, Mussolini was able to announce a settlement in February 1929. Italy recognized the sovereignty of the Holy See over the Vatican City. The Pope recognized the legality of the Italian kingdom. Mussolini gained this concordat by conceding what Italian liberals would not surrender. The church was given a veto over the appointment of teachers and the selection of textbooks in the secondary schools. The state also recognized religious marriages as legal and admitted that only the church could approve a divorce. The agreement greatly antagonized anticlericals but was greeted with celebrations by the majority of Italians. This was probably the peak of Mussolini's popularity.

Under fascism, Italy supposedly became a corporate state. Corporatist theory held that class conflict and capitalist exploitation should be prevented by uniting employers and employees in national unions or corporations, one for each sector of the economy. In fulfillment of this ideal, a National Council of Corporations was established in 1926, headed by the minister of corporations, who was naturally appointed by Mussolini. The economy was divided into twenty-two sectors. For example, there was one corporation for the steel industry and another for the textile industry. The officers of each corporation were appointed by the minister of corporations. The corporation supposedly acted as the mediator between labor and management, but it had the power to regulate not only prices, wages, and profits, but also the allocation of raw materials and levels of production. Therefore, the corporate state brought the entire economy under the ultimate control of the Fascist party, just as the Labor Front in Germany served the political goals of the Nazi party.

The results of Mussolini's economic policies were similar to the economic trends in Germany. Big business prospered with higher profits and no labor conflict. The working classes did less well but still improved their position from 1928 to 1939. Wages rose by 10 percent from 1928 to 1935, and the length of the workday decreased for many workers. Mussolini's policies also helped ease the blow of the depression. Italy was the least effected of all the major powers. In 1932, when there were two million unemployed in Great Britain and three million in Germany, only 850,000 were unemployed in Italy.

The importance of agriculture in the Italian economy can partially explain this, but it was largely due to the grandiose public works program that Mussolini had initiated as early as 1927 for the modernization of the economy and for the regime's glory. Land reclamation was a major part of the program, and the draining of the Pontine Marshes made three million acres available for cultivation. Mussolini also undertook the reconstruction of Rome. With the taste of a politician for the large and grandiose, he destroyed many irreplaceable medieval buildings to construct pseudoclassic edifices. Aesthetically disappointing, these programs cushioned the shock of the depression by absorbing many unemployed. The land reclamation also made it possible to settle workers and bankrupt farmers on fertile land.

Perhaps the most publicized policies of the Fascist regime were the various "battles" that it waged. The Battle of Grain was an effort to make Italy self-sufficient in agricultural production. It was largely successful. There was also a Battle of the Lira, an attempt to increase exports. The Demographic Battle produced a few ludicrous developments.[4] Mussolini argued that Italy's population of 40 million condemned her to be a second-rate power. He hoped for 60 million in twenty years. Various incentives to population growth were employed. A tax was placed on bachelors that did not apply to married men. Prizes were given to especially prolific women. On December 23, 1933, Il Duce received the champion mothers from the provinces. These ninety-three women had given birth to over thirteen hundred children, or 13.9 children per woman. At the height of this heroic battle, a telegram was published in the press from a prefect who promised Mussolini "that he would make a personal contribution" in the interest of the nation.

After 1929, Mussolini's regime changed little. He had defeated his domestic enemies. He increasingly became an arbiter between his ministers rather than a decision-maker or an initiator of ideas. He did not deal with usual administrative problems or even with the condition of the party. His major ministers ran the nation and the party, while he lived increasingly alone except for his mistresses.* The only area of policy that interested him seemed to be foreign affairs, and it was to diplomacy that he turned, especially after 1934, for the further development of his "destiny."

As in Germany, there was a domestic resistance to the Fascist regime. There were, however, several differences between the two resistance movements. The Italian resistance began when Mussolini began severe suppression of his opponents in 1924. At first, it consisted of important Liberal politicians who ostentatiously withdrew from public life and urged their compatriots not to cooperate with the Fascists. This group was weak and never considered unconstitutional or violent action. With the increasing suppression of 1926–27 another resistance developed among emigres

---

[4] Ivone Kirkpatrick, *Mussolini* (New York: Avon Books, 1968), p. 268.

* Clara Petacci, the woman who died at Mussolini's side in 1944, became his mistress in 1937.

centered in Paris. These were mostly socialists and communists. Due to their party cell form of organization, the communists were able to do more inside Italy than the other groups. The Spanish Civil War became a focal point for this emigré resistance. They formed all-Italian battalions to fight against Hitler and Mussolini, who were aiding the Spanish conservatives. One emigré leader, Carlo Rosselli, was assassinated by Mussolini's agents in 1937 after he had advocated the use of the Italian volunteers in Spain in a guerrilla war against the Fascists inside Italy.

There was no effective domestic resistance to Mussolini after the late twenties until World War II, but there was a potential opposition among the king's retinue and the military leadership. It was this conservative group that finally overthrew Mussolini in 1943. The king disliked Il Duce personally and resented his usurpation of the prerogatives of the crown. The military resented the Fascist Militia, the fighting army of the party, just as the Wehrmacht resented the SA. They also felt Mussolini was not qualified to command them. These hostilities, however, did not result in action until after the tide of war had turned against Italy.

There were, then, many similarities between Fascist Italy and Nazi Germany. The party governed in each state, and institutions were changed radically. Yet there were dissimilarities as well. Mussolini gradually withdrew from the party, whereas Hitler maintained his personal control over it. In fact, certain branches of the Nazi party, such as the SS, became more important than the formal ministries. The dictatorship was never as harsh in Italy as in Germany. Terror was never so prevalent, and far fewer people were killed at Mussolini's orders than at Hitler's. Most importantly, racism did not play as great a role in Italy. Mussolini only became officially anti-Semitic in the thirties when it appeared that Hitler would be an inevitable ally. Finally, the strongest resistance to Mussolini came from the left and not the right as in Germany. This fact largely explains why the Italian Left was so powerful and so popular after 1945.

Eastern Europe

Admiral Horthy had gained power in Hungary in 1919 after having destroyed the communist government of Bela Kun. Although an avowed monarchist, Horthy refused to permit the Hapsburg heir to the throne to return and, instead, declared himself regent. He did not destroy parliamentary forms, but assured the conservative nature of the parliament by a very restricted franchise and by suppression of the freedoms of speech and press. Having emasculated the left, Horthy tried to keep the right divided. Pursuant to this policy, he encouraged the development of a radical Right, fashioned on the Italian fascists, to balance off the traditional conservatives. As long as this system worked, both factions looked to Horthy for favors.

Several national socialist parties arose during the 1920s and early 1930s. Two of these—the Hungarian National Socialist Workers party and the National Socialist Peasants and Workers party—gained some influence but neither won a mass following. Several such groups were united into a truly popular mass party in 1937 by Ference Szalasi. The new party was called the Arrow Cross, from its symbol.

Szalasi fits all the criteria of a fascist leader. He had been an outstanding young officer on the Hungarian army's general staff. His activities in politics led to his resignation from the army in 1935, when he founded his first party, the Party of National Will. He advocated a greater Hungary to include all of prewar Hungary—i.e., Czechoslovakia, Serbia, parts of Rumania, and more. The Magyars, the ethnic group that had governed before World War I, should once again be dominant. Anti-Semitism, corporatism, and anticommunism also figured in his program. He attacked communism as Jewish and offered instead National Socialism, which promised to raise the workers' living standards and distribute land among the peasants while guaranteeing the attainment of greater Hungary. Under the pressure of the Arrow Cross, conservative governments actually began a policy of land reform.

The Arrow Cross's popularity grew so rapidly in 1937–38 that rumors of a coup against Horthy were widespread. To prevent this possibility, Horthy had Szalasi arrested and sentenced to three years hard labor. In spite of this, Szalasi's party continued to grow. In the May 1939 elections, national socialist groups won fourty-eight seats out of 259. The Arrow Cross won thirty-one of these with 750,000 votes out of a total of two million. The war intervened, however, before the Arrow Cross could make its weight felt in parliament. Admiral Horthy stayed in power until 1944 by cooperating with Hitler. However, with the defeat of Germany imminent, Horthy tried to make a deal with Russia, Great Britain, and the United States. Hitler then ousted the Admiral and made Szalasi "the leader" of Hungary just before the Russian invasion.

Rumanian developments were very similar. King Carol had become dictator by a coup in 1930. The fascist movement which challenged him was led by Corneliu Codreanu. Codreanu began his political career in 1919, at the age of twenty, fighting against Bolshevik youths in the University of Iasi. However, he was not merely anticommunist. He also argued that the workers' rights must be defended against capitalist exploitation and that national workers' organizations should be formed to oppose politicians who did not consider the plight of the lower classes.

In 1922 he founded the Association of Christian Students based on the *fuehrer-prinzip*. This group soon merged with others to form the National Christian Anti-Semitic League, which adopted the swastika as its symbol because of the anti-Semitic connotations. Willing to use violence, Codreanu and some friends were arrested in 1923 for having planned the assassination of "pro-Jewish" politicians. He broke with the league in 1927 to form his own personal group, the Legion of Archangel Michael. The legion, he hoped, would rejuvenate Rumania by good works. It was composed mostly of idealistic university students who worked in the countryside to improve the life of the peasantry. Legionnaires established work camps and grew their own food for market, helped nearby villages build homes and public buildings, bridges and dykes, schools and roads, and studied the teachings of Codreanu.

The legion was transformed into a political party, the Iron Guard, in the early thirties. This party grew steadily during the thirties to become the third largest party in Rumania in the 1937 elections. In that election, Codreanu's supporters received 15.6 percent of the popular vote (478,000 votes) and won sixty-six of 390 seats. This success was too great a threat to King Carol's position. To this point Carol had been willing to use the Iron Guard to crush communists and other leftists, but now he banned the guard and all political parties. Trying to preempt the fascists, Carol established a one-party state and organized the economy along corporate lines. Codreanu did not try to resist; rather, he publicly dissolved the Iron Guard. Still, Carol had no mercy; Codreanu and his chief aides were arrested and murdered by their jailers.

Their leader's death only increased the militancy of the Iron Guard. Mass reprisals by both sides turned Rumanian politics into a sea of blood. The civil warfare continued during the first years of World War II, until Carol was discredited by Rumania's loss of territory to Russia and Hungary. The king was ousted, and a coalition government based on the Rumanian army and the Iron Guard replaced him. The army was uneasy with its uncertain ally, and in January 1941, with the aid of the German army, the Rumanian military suppressed the Iron Guard in one final bloodbath. Thus, ironically, the local fascists were destroyed by Germany.

The cases of Hungary and Rumania illustrate the inevitable conflict between fascists and traditional conservatives. This conflict was heightened by the fact that communists were officially banned, leaving workers and peasants no place to turn but to the fascists. This led, in eastern Europe, to a sort of class warfare between two wings of the Right, with the conservatives representing the landed aristocracy and the fascists representing the urban workers and land-hungry peasantry as well as parts of the lower middle class.

Great Britain and France

Fascist and other radical right-wing movements never became as powerful in Great Britain or France as they did in Hungary and Rumania. Both democracies had several small protofascist groups during the 1920s. These died out only to be replaced in the thirties by mass movements of a truly fascist nature. In neither country did these movements gain sufficient political backing to win significant parliamentary representation.

The grandfather of French fascism was Charles Maurras, a founder and authoritatian leader of *Action française,* an organization which was not itself fascist but was an ideological and organizational forerunner of fascism. The AF was founded in the heat of the Dreyfus affair. Maurras gradually became its authoritative spokesman, and from 1906, he remained its unquestioned leader until his trial for treason in 1945. In many ways, he foreshadowed later movements. Before World War I, Maurras was already a political anti-Semite; he already advocated a corporate state and argued that action was superior to wisdom. However, before and after the war Maurras differed from the fascists in his refusal to organize a mass party and enter the political arena, his desire for a return to monarchical government, and his praise of bourgeois values.

It was over this last point that George Valois broke with Maurras in 1924 and formed the first protofascist group in France, the *Faisçeau.* The economic crisis which followed the Rhineland Crisis of 1923 provided fertile ground for radical politics. Military veterans especially flocked to Valois' banner. His insistence on social reform as well as nationalism drew support from communist and socialist trade unions. Wearing blue shirts and marching in military order through Parisian streets, the *Faisçeau* were an exact copy of Mussolini's squads. But their numbers were small, and when Poincaré ended the inflation by stabilizing the franc in 1926, this and other similar groups withered away.

The depression gave rise to more small, fascist-inspired groups. One such was Marcel Bucard's *Françistes,* which emphasized its national *socialist* nature. Of its 30,000 members, 40 to 50 percent appear to have been members of trade unions or the Socialist party. The most successful group was the *Croix de feu,* which has often been mistakenly considered fascist. Organized in 1927, it was just another association of war veterans until Colonel Count de la Roque became its leader two years later. The *Croix de feu* or Fiery Cross was strictly a protest movement against industrialism and social welfare programs. There was nothing of socialism in de la Roque's program; even though he advocated a corporate society. His ideal had little in common with the industrial dynamoes that Hitler and Mussolini envisaged but was rather a yearning for a return to the early nineteenth century, when government was small and the artisan and farmer were not threatened by big business. At its height, the Fiery Cross had several hundred thousand members.

The only true French fascist movement was that of Jacques Doriot, a former leader of the French Communist party, who founded the *Parti Populaire Française* (PPF). Organized just after the elections of 1936 that brought the Popular Front to power, the PPF was never tested in an election but rather had the dubious distinction of becoming influential under the Vichy regime in collaboration with the Germans. Doriot had broken with the PCF because the French communists preferred parliamentary tactics to revolution. Therefore, he decided to align himself with the one revolutionary movement in Europe—fascism. He greatly admired the Nazis and became a member of the SS during World War II. Doriot attracted to himself men from both extremes of the French political spectrum, syndicalists as well as supporters of the *Croix de feu*. They had in common their desire to renovate France through revolutionary action.

In Great Britain Mussolini's success in 1922 led to a plethora of upper-class protofascist leagues. Their only program was a violent anti-Bolshevism. The names they adopted attest to the Italian influence: the British Fascists, the Fascist League, the British National Fascists, the Imperial Fascist League. But these groups were not fascist, despite their desire to be so, because they lacked a revolutionary program. Their social composition was entirely upper and middle class. In fact, the members of these groups usually remained members of the Conservative party. At no time were they willing to accept extensive social or institutional change. Everyone forgot about them in a short time as Great Britain basked in prosperity.

In 1930, however, Sir Oswald Mosley gave birth to British fascism by breaking with the Labour party over its economic policy and forming, first, the New party, which stood to the left of the Labour party, and then, after a visit to Italy to talk with Mussolini, the British Union of Fascists (BUF.) Mosley demanded that the BUF be completely subservient to himself and thereby alienated the best minds who had followed him in his revolt against the Labour party. Imitating Mussolini's Fascist militia as closely as possible, the BUF adopted the fascist salute and the black shirt as a uniform. Overdoing it a bit, perhaps, they had their headquarters in the Black House.

After Hitler came to power, the BUF began to model itself more on the Nazis than the fascists. Indicative of this were the mass meetings that the BUF staged in imitation, on a smaller scale, of Hitler's Nuremburg rallies. Mosley's increasing emphasis on anti-Semitism proved to be a very ill-advised tactic. Anti-Semitism had never been strong in England, and after 1936 Mosley had a sizable following only in the East End of London, where Jewish businesses were numerous. Finally, Mosley changed the name of his organization to the British Union of Fascists and National Socialists to formalize his orientation toward Berlin. This hurt the public image of the party and guaranteed its political isolation. At the outbreak of war, Mosley and most of his associates were arrested for the duration.

The BUF was never very strong. In 1933 it had 5,000 dues paying members. By 1938 this had fallen to 3,000 dues paying members and an estimated 15,000 inactive members. The leaders were drawn from the working class, largely from the Independent Labour party which was dissatisfied with the reformist policies of the regular Labour party.

Fascism had an audience in almost every country in the interwar period. No states were immune. Yet social and economic conditions as well as historical traditions determined that fascism should be stronger in Germany and Italy than in other countries. A product of a peculiar historical setting, it seems unlikely that fascism will be seen again in the same form. Yet, when intense nationalism and bitter frustration against social conditions combine, another breed of the same beast may reappear.

PART III

The Thirties: The Death of Liberalism

Chapter 10

TOTALITARIAN ALTERNATIVES

Years of Crisis: Involved Intellectuals

The depression and the growth of fascism radically changed the cultural atmosphere of Europe. The twenties had been a period of change and experimentation. Not only new art forms but also radically new clothes styles and new moral standards were tried. Particularly the end of the decade had been a time of optimism and self-indulgence. All of this disappeared as if overnight. The caesura was the financial crisis. When bread lines appeared in every large city, the fun went out of life. Hitler's rise to power also had a sobering effect. To see racists rule and all creativity destroyed in the land of Goethe, Kant, and Beethoven was a profound shock to European intellectuals. They suddenly became aware just how small the realm of freedom had become.

The parallel symbols of the thirties became the bread line and the emigré intellectual. Russia, Germany, and Italy forced their best thinkers into exile and suppressed their writings. The emigrés seemed to favor certain countries. The best German novelist and the most innovative German composer, Thomas Mann and Arnold Schonberg, fled to the United States. Thousands of lesser members of the German intelligentsia made the same journey. Not the least of these emigrés were thousands of Jewish families, generally from the better educated and wealthier strata of German society. Germany's cultural loss will be an enduring one. Italian emigrés usually settled in Paris because of the Latin atmosphere. Many of these returned to their homeland after the war, so Italy did not suffer as greatly as did Germany.

The Soviet dictatorship had welcomed innovative minds in the first years of the revolution. In fact, the experimentation in all areas of society had attracted writers, painters, and musicians rather than repulsing them. The movies of Eisenstein were magnificent examples. The cultural aspect of the First Five-Year Plan was a demand that all creativity be channeled into the service of the revolution—art became propaganda. The official art technique was "socialist realism." Socialist realism dictated that the artist portray the people—happy workers, happy farmers, idealistic party members—in traditional forms. It was assumed that abstract painting or experimental theater were elitist forms of art and, therefore, had no place in a socialist society. Russian art was murdered by the party. It is almost miraculous that certain free spirits continued to exist and work in secret, awaiting the thaw that came finally after the death of Stalin in 1953.

With the dictatorships suppressing creativity, it was in the democracies alone that significant intellectual trends developed. In both Great Britain and France there is a striking contrast between the art and literature of the 1920s and 1930s. Following World War I, authors had tried to escape from reality; after 1930 they became actively involved in reality—in political action and social reform. Before the depression, an aesthetic fascination with form and style had divorced artists from the general public; in the new decade they made a conscious effort to communicate a message—political or moral—to the public. Every author seemed to be a relativist in the twenties; by 1937 all were moralists and were seeking ways to apply their moral convictions to politics. Whereas interest in the individual had dominated the earlier decade, in the thirties authors felt a responsibility to portray social reality in hopes of initiating social reform.

The awakening of an interest in public affairs began with a spate of antiwar novels that appeared in 1928–29. The greatest of these was Erich Maria Remarque's *All Quiet on the Western Front*. From the German viewpoint, this described the horrors of trench warfare and the emptiness of the nationalist propaganda used to maintain support for the war on the home front. Almost simultaneously, similar books appeared in Great Britain, notably Richard Aldington's *Death of a Hero* and Robert Graves's *Good-bye to All That*, a recalling of the world destroyed by the war. But not too much emphasis should be placed on the antiwar novels. They represented more the frustrations that had been bottled up since 1918, as if the war had been too horrible to mention, rather than the trend of the coming decade. The new involvement was to be characterized by militancy and violence rather than by pacifism.

Authors distinctively of the thirties did not create great masterpieces of art. Perhaps partisan concerns limit the artist's ability to produce universally relevant works, but the involvement of these men was a moral burden that they would not trade for literary refinements. It was unemployment and the spread of fascism that required this involvement. The unemployment seemed to prove socialist indictments of capitalism, and the success of fascism in Germany and its appearance elsewhere created a situation in which the only alternatives seemed to be totalitarian alternatives: fascism or communism.[1] This choice became most apparent during the Spanish Civil War—when Russia aided the Spanish Republicans and Germany and Italy aided Franco, while the liberal democracies watched from the sidelines.

In England the new seriousness was reflected most strikingly in the poems of W. H. Auden, Stephen Spender, and Cecil Day Lewis. Their work was preoccupied with the German situation and the need for radical change, perhaps revolution, in Great Britain.[2] The three were first given publicity in 1932 in an anthology, *New Signatures*. Their anger was reflected in one of Spender's poems that appeared in 1933.

> They lounge at corners of the street
> And greet friends with a shrug of shoulder
> And turn their empty pockets out,
> The cynical gestures of the poor.
>
> Now they've no work, like better men
> Who sit at desks and take much pay
> They sleep long nights and rise at ten
> To watch the hours that drain away.
>
> I'm jealous of the weeping hours
> They stare through with such hungry eyes.
> I'm hounded by these images.
> I'm haunted by their emptiness.[3]

C. Day-Lewis summed up the frustrations of many of his contemporaries when he wrote:

> Revolution, Revolution
> is the one correct solution—
> We've found it and we know it's bound to win.[4]

This was a far cry from the academic abstractions and pessimism of Eliot's *The Waste Land*. These three poets were all attracted by communism. Spender even joined the party briefly.

British novelists felt the same pressure to analyze reality, to be involved. Christopher Isherwood wrote several novels describing the Berlin of 1931 and 1932 in which the German communists were treated sympathetically. The most famous of these was *The Last of Mr. Norris*. Graham Greene

---

[1] Richard Crossman, ed., *The God That Failed* (New York: Bantam Books, 1965), "Introduction."

[2] Neal Wood, *Communism and British Intellectuals* (New York: Columbia University Press, 1959), pp. 102–3.

[3] Spender, *Collected Poems, 1928–1953* (London: Faber and Faber, Ltd., 1955), p. 36.

[4] Day-Lewis, *A Time to Dance and Other Poems* (London: Hogarth Press, 1935), p. 62.

began writing his topical novels in the 1930s, always setting them in realistic political situations. Likewise George Orwell felt he could not remain in the ivory tower. He fought for the Republicans in Spain and became disillusioned with the communists there. *Homage to Catalonia* chronicles his experiences in the Spanish Civil War.

Of course, not all British literary figures turned to the left. T. S. Eliot offered a secular-Christian society based on pure racial strands as an answer to the social crisis. D. H. Lawrence presented an idealized dictatorship in *The Plumed Serpent*, a novel about Mexico.

Two trends were most apparent among French writers. First, a shift from the analysis of individual characters to an analysis of society, and, second, a turn away from introspective, contemplative studies to a glorification of concrete action. These changes can best be seen in the writings of Roger Martin du Gard and André Gide, whose careers had begun long before. Gide had first published in the 1890s. His work was popular and influential in the twenties because of a moral relativism that fit well with the public mood. Although he never joined the Communist party, Gide became one of its most prominent fellow-travelers during the period 1930–37. His writings of these years, mostly essays and reviews, reject relativism and praise the Soviet Union and communism as the hope of the world. In 1935 Gide was elected president of the Congress of Revolutionary Writers which met in Paris. However, a visit to Russia in the following year disillusioned him. In his public penance, *Return from the USSR*, Gide completely disowned communism. He said that social inequality was just as great in Russia as elsewhere, the bureaucrats were the new bourgeoisie, and the workers did not even have unions to defend their interests. Gide, then, became one of many intellectuals who made the journey to communism and back.

Martin du Gard had begun a multivolume novel in the twenties, *The Thibaults*, tracing the history of a bourgeoise family. The first volumes were contemplative, dealing with personality analysis of each character and containing introspective digressions. The style was highly polished. After a break of seven years, three more volumes were published in 1936 and a final one in 1940. The 1936 volumes, entitled collectively *l'Ete 1914 (Summer 1914)*, concentrated on political, social, and ideological controversies. Characters were almost lost among the long political debates. The responsibility for World War I was a main theme and led to the indictment of capitalism, nationalism, and impotent reformist socialism. The suggestion is obvious that a more revolutionary political course (communism?) was needed to change decadent liberal societies. This shift in Martin du Gard's interests is perhaps the most glaring individual example of the way the crises of the thirties forced authors out of their ivory towers.

Once again, not all French intellectuals turned to the left. Henry de

Montherlant and Pierre Drieu la Rochelle openly expressed praise for the heroism of the leagues, and Drieu la Rochelle went even further. Drieu la Rochelle became a theoretician of Jacques Doriot's fascist *Parti Populaire Francaise*. Essentially a moralist, Drieu la Rochelle believed political action a necessity. He resembled D. H. Lawrence in his rejection of the inhibitions of bourgeois society and his desire for a return to a simpler world in which men could have more freedom for self-fulfillment. In *Gilles*, an autobiographical novel, he described the attraction of fascism as being one of religious exaltation and of communion with other men through common action.

The rejection of moral relativity and the search for a new basis for morality was the essence of several Catholic writers, particularly Francois Mauriac, Georges Bernanos, and Jacques Maritain. Their concern was similar to the return to piety in England as seen in T. S. Eliot. This felt need for a new morality contributed to the popularity of existentialism in post-World War II France.

The glorification of action was a constant theme in French literature of the thirties. Andre Malraux and Antoine Saint-Exupery not only praised involvement in the revolutionary cause but also action for its own sake. They were sociological phenomena in French literary circles. Neither was a professional man of letters; rather both were men of action who wrote about the adventures they had lived. Malraux's *Man's Fate* is based on the Shanghai insurrection of 1927, a revolution which failed. *Man's Hope* is an account of the first year of the Spanish Civil War. In these novels, Malraux emphasizes the need for collective action against political evils. In *Man's Hope* he actually becomes a propagandist for the Republican cause. The Spanish Loyalists win all the battles and have the support of the people. One marvels that Franco defeated them.

Saint-Exupery, as Malraux, is one of the legendary figures of French literature: a novelist who looked more the hero of a novel than its author. He made his living as a commercial pilot over Africa and Latin America. Flying was still quite dangerous, and his novels contain accounts of the deaths of several fellow aviators. *Night Flight*, Saint-Exupery's first publicly acclaimed novel, and his later works—*Wind, Sand and Stars,* and *Flight to Arras*—were directly autobiographical. While being ultimately personal adventures, his books increasingly emphasized the communion of men through action. *Flight to Arras* is about a reconnaissance flight over France during the last days before France's defeat in 1940. As the pilot passes over the battlefield, he feels a unity with the soldiers below, indeed with the French nation. Saint-Exupery was himself shot down by the German air force during just such a flight in 1944.

Many European intellectuals were attracted by the ideals of the Communist International. The romance was short, and the heartbreak was great. It seems that these men turned to communism for negative rather than positive reasons. One such case was that of Arthur Koestler.[5] Koestler belonged to a Hungarian middle-class family that had lost its wealth in the inflation of the early twenties. Going to work as a free-lance reporter, he became, at the age of twenty-six, the editor of foreign affairs on a large German newspaper. In reaction to the Nazi electoral victories of 1930, he decided that he must choose between fascism and communism. He chose communism, joining the German Communist party in January 1932. At first he served the party by passing along useful information that came his way as a foreign affairs editor. However, he was soon found out and lost his job. From that time to 1937, he devoted himself to party propaganda—writing a book, then a travelogue praising the accomplishments of the Five-Year Plans and, later, writing articles in support of the Republican forces in Spain. It was over the Spanish war and Stalin's purges that Koestler broke with the communists. Writing free-lance articles for a British newspaper, he was ordered to denounce the Trotskyite socialists in Spain as tools of fascism. He refused and voluntarily resigned from the party in 1938. Still, he continued to consider the Soviet Union "our last and only hope on a planet in rapid decay" until August 1939 when the German-Soviet Pact was signed. This was the ultimate betrayal, and Koestler, like millions of other party members and fellow travelers, was able to cut the final strings.

The impact of the depression and of fascism on the literary world indicates the effect of these two events on the general intellectual climate. Increasingly, the most popular books were nonfiction. Everyone wanted to know why their society seemed to be falling apart. An aura of impending doom dominated. Some held tenaciously to their traditional values, as did the leadership of the Conservative party in Great Britain, while others were demanding an end to the liberal laissez faire policies which they blamed for all their problems. This general malaise and dissatisfaction with the status quo greatly contributed to the reorientation of European politics after 1945 and permitted the adventurous policies of the welfare state.

The Popular Fronts

The term Popular Front refers to two phenomena of the 1930s. One was the official Comintern policy adopted in 1935 that urged communist parties around the world to form alliances with other democratic parties in order to resist fascism. The second was the particular coalition of leftist parties in France. The French Popular Front is of special importance because its success led to the adoption of the policy by the Communist International.

Comintern policy during the twenties had been "united front from

---

[5] Crossman, *God That Failed,* pp. 11–68.

above." It permitted the leaders of communist parties to cooperate with the leaders of socialist parties on particular issues but prohibited rank and file party members from joining socialist organizations. All communist parties in Europe conformed to these tactics dictated from Moscow. Any party member who disagreed with Moscow was expelled. From 1929 to 1934 the Comintern urged tactics of "left extremism." During this period of social crisis, the social democratic parties were considered communism's worst enemies. This meant, at times, that communists should cooperate with fascists to destroy social democracy. The policy was summed up well by Ernst Thalmann, a German communist leader, in 1931.

Social Democracy, above all the "left-wing" SPD, is still *the main obstacle* [sic] in the German proletariat's revolutionary struggle for liberation. The Party and the working class cannot possibly be successful in the fight against fascism and against the capitalist system in general, without beating this main obstacle and destroying this most dangerous enemy in the camp of the working class.[6]

The communists were extremely slow in realizing that fascism might be more of a threat than socialism. As late as 1934 Stalin said,

Of course, we are far from being enthusiastic about the fascist regime in Germany. But fascism is not the issue here, if only for the reason that fascism in Italy, for instance, has not prevented the USSR from establishing the best relations with that country.[7]

It was during late 1934 and 1935, largely under the impact of events in France, that Stalin changed the Comintern's policy. His search for allies against Hitler had begun. He found that the eastern European countries that might be his allies were enmeshed in the French alliance system. He also discovered that France was eager to increase her own security by a mutual defense pact with Russia. Negotiations were begun. This change in Soviet foreign policy was accompanied by a complete reversal of Comintern strategy in July and August 1935. Stalin's spokesman at the Seventh Congress of the Comintern, Georgi Dimitrov, called for the establishment in each country of an antifascist popular front or people's front of all democratic forces.

The importance of the Popular Front policy cannot be overemphasized. Previously, communists had considered democracy as equally undesirable as fascism and, perhaps, even worse. Democratic institutions were said to hide the exploitation of the proletariat, whereas fascism revealed the true nature of capitalism and brought the revolution nearer. After 1935

---

[6] Babette Gross, "The German Communists' United-Front and Popular-Front Ventures," *The Comintern: Historical Highlights,* eds. Milorad M. Drackovitch and Branko Lazitch (New York: Frederick A. Praeger, Publishers, 1966), p. 115.

[7] Isaac Deutscher, *Stalin,* 2d ed. (New York: Oxford University Press, 1967), pp. 415–16.

communists recognized the benefits that they obtained from a liberal regime and vowed to protect political liberties from the fascist threat.

The French Popular Front, which was so influential on the Comintern, was created as a reaction to the attempt by right-wing, protofascist veterans' leagues to storm the Chamber of Deputies on February 6, 1934. Shocked by the strength of this antidemocratic demonstration, the Socialist Party and the *Parti Communiste Française* (PCF) began to draw together. They were able to form an electoral alliance for the local elections of August 1934, and their success was impressive. This success made the alliance more attractive and led to overtures from left-wing members of the Radical party, who usually avoided even socialist connections. The SFIO, led by Léon Blum, was skeptical about the sincerity of the Radicals, but the communist leader Maurice Thorez urged that the socialist-communist coalition be expanded further to the right.

The determining factor in the communist attitude was not the situation in France but the need to protect the Soviet Union. When a Franco-Russian pact was signed in May 1935, *Pravda* flashed the signal to the French communists: "Stalin fully understands and approves the policy of national defense followed by France in order to maintain her armed forces at a level necessary for her national security."[8] This was the first time the Soviet Union had approved armaments in a capitalist nation. The refusal of the PCF to vote for military spending had been a great obstacle to cooperation with nonsocialist parties; now that obstacle was removed. The PCF became the most aggressive champions of a broad popular front.

The official formation of the Popular Front was announced on July 14, 1935, a nationalist holiday usually dominated by the Right. Hundreds of thousands of demonstrators crossed Paris on foot led by Blum for the Socialists, Thorez for the PCF, and Edouard Daladier for the Radical party. Many other small leftist groups and trade unions also marched. At a sports stadium, the entire assemblage took an oath of loyalty to the Popular Front.

The spirit of cooperation was strong, but it still took six months to write a political program for the front. When the program was made public in January 1936, its main proposals dealt with the protection of democracy. This was to be obtained by the dissolution of the "fascist leagues" and by the enactment of a conflict of interest law for government officials to prevent the kind of scandal that had led to the February 6 demonstration. In foreign affairs the front advocated collective security, based on the League of Nations, and a general limitation of armaments. Economic and social policy was geared to putting the control of the economy in the hands of the government and to reviving the economy by increasing purchasing power as the New Deal was doing in the United

---

[8] Georges Lefranc, *Le Front Populaire* (Paris: Presses universitaires de France, 1965), p. 37.

Leon Blum was the scholarly leader of France's Popular Front government. (Courtesy of Roger-Viollet)

States. Many social welfare measures were included in the front's legislative package. This was the Popular Front's platform in the legislative election of April–May 1936. The overwhelming Popular Front victory had not been expected. The front had obviously profited from a severe polarization of the voters.

The second and last ballot took place on May 3, but the new Chamber of Deputies was not supposed to meet until June 5. In that interval, a wave of strikes broke across France bringing the economy to a standstill. These strikes were sit-down strikes, with workers occupying their plants. It was the first time the tactic had been used in France. The workers'

TABLE 10.1.   Results of the Popular Front Election, May 1936

Party	Seats Held Before	Seats After	Change
Communists	10	72	+62
SFIO	97	146	+49
Radicals	158	115	−43
Center-right parties	164	114	−40
Extreme-right	82	99	+17

militancy was the product of unrestrained enthusiasm sparked by the Popular Front victory. Workers felt that finally they could bargain without their employers' calling on the government to crush the strike action. Léon Blum, France's first Socialist premier, formed a ministry in the midst of the shut-down. Two days after taking office, he called representatives of labor unions and employers' associations to the Hotel Matignon. The

Matignon Accord was generally considered a complete defeat for the employers. They agreed to recognize the right to organize and not to penalize men who took part in a strike. They accepted the election of shopstewards to represent all the workers in bargaining and factory relations, and they bowed to a general application of the forty-hour week. Wages were to be increased for *all* workers. The increases would range from 7 percent for the best-paid to 15 percent for those with the lowest salaries.

The Matignon Accord was a resounding triumph for the Popular Front. Parliamentary victories followed. Almost all major items of the front's program became law in July and August 1936. The first bills passed provided for the workers' most urgent demands, giving the Matignon Accord a legal foundation. For instance, the forty-hour week was made a national legal standard. Blum then proceeded to make more profound reforms. Defense industries were nationalized. The Bank of France was brought under government control. A wheat office was established to regulate the price of agricultural products in a move to control inflation. Public works programs were initiated to provide jobs, and, of course, the radical right-wing groups such as the *Croix de feu* were declared illegal.

After this initial burst of energy, the Popular Front began to falter. No more significant reforms were enacted after August 1936. The reasons for this were both economic and political. The most intractable problems were unemployment and inflation. Even public works projects could not revive the economy quickly enough to absorb the unemployed. Furthermore, rising prices wiped out the wage increases the workers had won at Matignon. A continuing flight of gold from France—to some extent an intentional attack on the front by financiers—forced two devaluations of the franc. Each devaluation reduced the purchasing power of individuals living on fixed incomes such as factory workers and pensioners.

There were other problems that were strictly political. Blum broke with the communists over intervention in the Spanish Civil War. He refused both armed intervention and the public sale of arms to the Republicans, although he facilitated a black market in arms for the Republicans that operated in France. The Radical party withdrew their support because they felt Blum had become too socialistic. Finally, the employers associations recovered from Matignon and reorganized their political operations so as to obstruct Blum's proposals. They also began to violate the·Matignon Accord once they realized that the specter of revolution that had been raised by the sit-down strikes was not going to materialize.

These problems forced Blum to declare a "pause" to reform in February 1937. He remained in office until June but was able to accomplish little. His ministry finally fell because of Radical opposition in the Senate. Faced with a rapid decline in the value of the franc, caused by France's loss of gold, Blum requested power to govern by decree as Laval had in 1935; but, where Laval had been a safe conservative, Blum was a socialist.

Twice the Chamber of Deputies gave him a majority; twice the Senate denied him the power he requested. Blum was torn between opening a constitutional crisis by opposing the Senate—perhaps by calling for a general strike by the labor unions—or, his only alternative, resigning. He resigned on June 22, 1937. The cabinets that followed were based on the Popular Front majority until April 1938, but the period of the Popular Front can be considered ended with Blum's resignation. The impetus for reform had been lost.

Yet, the achievements had been great. The French communists had finally been brought into the political system as citizens having a voice in government. A path had been broken for social and economic reform that would have to be followed. Unfortunately, World War II prevented the nation from continuing Blum's work until 1945, but the postwar governments looked to the Popular Front for ideas and inspiration. As for the fascist threat, it was subdued. When France suffered defeat in 1940, the dictatorshhp which appeared was not fascist but a bumbling, inefficient expression of traditional French conservatism.

The Spanish Civil War

Russia's willingness to combat fascism—and the unwillingness of France and Great Britain to do so—was most clearly evident in the Spanish Civil War. Suddenly in 1936 governments and ordinary citizens had to choose between the legally elected Popular Front government or the conservative forces who wished to overthrow the Spanish republic. The war was pictured as either a war against international fascism or a struggle to save civilization from barbarian communism. Spain became the testing ground for new weapons and for ideologies. Many young idealists who fought in Spain resented the fact that France and Great Britain were not willing to fight for the survival of democracy.

A revolution had toppled the Spanish monarchy in 1931. A republic had been established, and parliamentary politics seemed to be accepted. However, the radical reforms enacted by the republicans aroused great hostility among large landowners, the Catholic hierarchy, and the army. When a Popular Front was formed in preparation for the 1936 legislative election, conservatives denounced it as a tool of Moscow and an agent of social revolution. The election was a clear victory for the Popular Front in terms of parliamentary seats, but the total vote was evenly divided between the front and its opponents. During the campaign political violence had reached a dangerous level. Street battles between fascists and communists were common. Churches were sacked and priests assaulted. Instead of ending the violence, the election results seemed to increase it. Intoxicated by the Popular Front victory, workers seized factories, and peasants executed landlords. Manual Azana became premier at the head of a Popular Front government, but he was unable to restore order. On July 12 the leader of the conservative coalition during the election, Calvo Sotelo, was assassinated. This was the spark that ignited the Spanish Civil War.

On July 17 the army rebelled against the Republic. The garrisons in Spain rose first; then General Francisco Franco, soon to be "leader" of the Nationalist forces, flew to Morocco and returned with the African army to join the attack Azana responded by arming the police, the civilian militia, the trade unions, and loyal citizens. A bloody and fierce civil war had begun.

When the Nationalists had decided to overthrow the republic, they had immediately called on Germany and Italy to aid them. Both responded favorably after some initial hesitation. Italian aid took the form of munitions, airplanes, and several divisions of Blackshirts, the elite of the Fascist militia. Mussolini's actions were consistent with his developing concept of Italy as the master of the Mediterranean and of himself as an international leader of fascism. A friendly Spain would give Italy control of the Straits of Gibraltar and, therefore, would greatly improve Italy's strategic position vis-a-vis Great Britain. Furthermore, Mussolini, who had been in contact with Spanish conservatives since 1931, was highly desirous of having a satellite government in Spain owing its existence to him.

Hitler was seeking prestige, but he also had strategic reasons for giving aid to Franco. The German air force, hidden until 1935, could use battlefield tests and experience. The young German officers created by the expansion of the Reichswehr could also profit from the experience. Technical developments in weapons needed to be checked. Spain, therefore, became Germany's military laboratory. Diplomatically, Hitler desired a friendly regime to the south of France, so France could not concentrate all her military forces on the German border in case of war.

The aid from both of these countries was substantial. It only began to decline at the end of 1937, when Germany's restlessness in central Europe distracted international attention from Spain. At that time, in addition to weapons and money, Italy had 40,000 troops invested in Spain. Germany had 10,000 men there.

Just as Franco turned to the fascist powers, Azana had turned to the Popular Front government in Paris. Léon Blum was inclined to give aid to the Republicans and ordered the sale of arms and planes to them. When news of the sale appeared in the press on July 23, French conservatives exploded in indignation. Even the Radical party, Blum's partner in the coalition, opposed any aid to the Spanish republic. Therefore, on July 25, the French cabinet voted to suspend the sale of war materials to Spain until the international situation could be studied. The Ministry of Foreign Affairs suggested a way out of the problem—an international nonintervention treaty. Blum accepted the idea gladly, as a way to keep the peace within his government while preventing aid to the rebellious army from other countries. He proceeded to propose such a treaty to all the countries involved—Germany, Italy, Russia, Great Britain, and Portugal.

Inside France public opinion was becoming increasingly polarized and inflamed. French conservatives began to chant the phrase, "Better Hitler than Blum!" Maurice Thorez, the PCF leader, conducted an equally virulent campaign for aid to the Spanish republic. He called mass meetings and demonstrations, during which clashes with right-wing groups were not unusual.

Blum persisted in his campaign for a nonintervention treaty. On August 8 he announced an embargo on all arms to Spain and attempted to have other states take similar action. The embargo's only effect was to allow Franco to obtain arms from Italy and Germany while denying arms to the Republicans. Eventually, however, the other powers agreed to the nonintervention scheme and, on September 9, an international nonintervention committee was established to investigate violations.

It was not necessary to investigate. By the end of October it was obvious that not only were Italy and Germany supplying weapons to Franco in large quantities but also that they were sending troops. Russia protested to the nonintervention committee, which took no action. Therefore, Russian aid began flowing to the Republicans. Blum could only watch helplessly as his policy failed. Finally, in March 1937, he decided not to enforce the embargo on arms to Spain; so, while not renouncing absolute neutrality, he allowed some arms to cross the French border. This was some comfort to the Republicans, but it was a matter of too little too late. After Blum fell in June 1937, his policy was not continued. The embargo was reimposed.

British policy toward Spain was set irrevocably at the beginning of the fighting: the conflict should be limited to Spain by international action and any means should be used to prevent a general European crisis. Therefore, Stanley Baldwin, the British prime minister, welcomed the French initiative toward nonintervention. Yet, while the cabinet was claiming neutrality, the London press insisted that neutrality was impossible. The *New Statesman* wrote of the danger of the "rolling ambitions of 'international Fascism' " and of the challenge to democracy posed by the Fascist powers. *The Observer,* on the other hand, praised the "historic crusade" that had opened in Spain against world communism, against the " 'one thick red thread' running through the web of international affairs." *The Observer* suggested that, if the Soviets continued their attempted subversion of Europe, England should assure itself "a lasting settlement and friendship with Germany," the "great anti-Communist dictatorship."[9] This attitude was shared by the

---

[9] Margaret George, *The Warped Vision, British Foreign Policy 1933–1939* (Pittsburgh, Pa.: University of Pittsburgh Press, 1965), p. 96.

Conservative party leadership. Baldwin confided to a friend, "I told Eden [his foreign secretary] yesterday that on no account, French or other, must he bring us in to fight on the side of Russia."[10]

When Russia denounced the intervention of the fascist powers in October, the British were forced to take a public position. Anthony Eden attacked the Russian charges as having been made prematurely, before sifting the evidence, and as having unnecessarily complicated matters. Eden was incensed, because Russia, in making the facts of fascist intervention public, had endangered the policy of nonintervention that was working well in the British government's view. In fact, the Conservative cabinet was not disturbed that Franco was making progress against the Republican forces. To protect British neutrality, Baldwin proposed, and the Commons enacted several laws forbidding British subjects to trade with Spain or to fight in Spain.

The Soviet Union, of course, did send aid to the Republicans. This was a logical extension of the Popular Front and collective security policies which the Russian government and the Comintern had adopted in 1935. Contrary to conservative opinion in France and Britain, Russia had not encouraged the revolutionary activities of the summer of 1936, nor had Stalin tried to take advantage of the situation to promote a revolution. When France proposed nonintervention, Russia accepted it without reservations, whereas Germany and Italy tried to qualify their agreement. It was not until after these two had poured men and equipment into Spain in September and October that large-scale Russian aid to the Republicans began. From the day of the Nationalists' rebellion, Italian planes had supported the Nationalist forces. By early November the German Condor Legion, numbering several thousand men, was already in battle. Soviet equipment did not arrive for the first time until November 7, but this was just a beginning. By the middle of 1937, all of the Republic's tanks were Russian; and 50 percent of the machine guns, 60 percent of the rifles, and 15 percent of the larger field pieces were Russian.

The Soviets also aided the Loyalists in other ways. Within three weeks after the fighting started, two million dollars had been raised in Russia through voluntary and forced contributions from Russian workers. The Comintern organized fund-raising groups in many countries. One example was the International Committee for Aid of the Spanish People based in Paris. Most of these groups were not known to be communist supported. The Soviet army sent technicians, pilots, and tank operators to instruct the Spanish in the use of modern weaponry. At first, the Russians themselves had to take the equipment into battle. The Republicans had a Russian air force just as the Nationalists had an Italo-German air force. As the war progressed, the Comintern sent many non-Russian communists to Spain.

---

[10] Ibid., p. 97.

MAP 6.   The Spanish Civil War

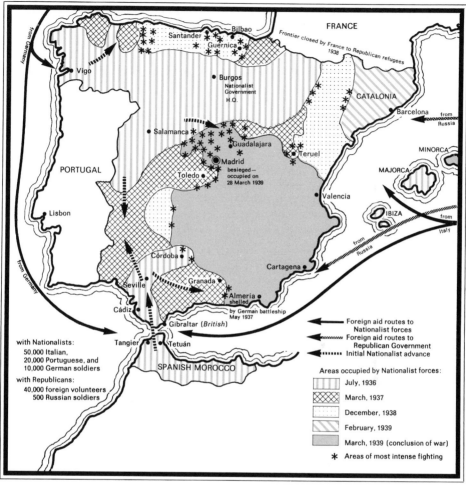

FRANCE

Santander   Bilbao
Guernica
Frontier closed by France to Republican refugees 1938

Vigo

Burgos
Nationalist
Government
H.Q.

CATALONIA

Barcelona   from Russia

Salamanca

Guadalajara

Teruel

MINORCA

PORTUGAL

MAJORCA

Toledo

Madrid
besieged —
occupied on
28 March 1939

Valencia

Lisbon

IBIZA   from Italy

Córdoba

Cartagena

from Russia

Granada

Seville

Almería
shelled
by German battleship
May 1937

Cádiz

Gibraltar (British)

with Nationalists:
   50,000 Italian,
   20,000 Portuguese, and
   10,000 German soldiers
with Republicans:
   40,000 foreign volunteers
   500 Russian soldiers

Tangier   Tetuán

SPANISH MOROCCO

— Foreign aid routes to
   Nationalist forces
— Foreign aid routes to
   Republican Government
····· Initial Nationalist advance

Areas occupied by Nationalist forces:

||||| July, 1936

XXXX March, 1937

       December, 1938

//// February, 1939

       March, 1939 (conclusion of war)

✻   Areas of most intense fighting

SOURCE: Martin Gilbert, *Recent History Atlas* (London: Wiedenfeld and Nicolson, 1966), map 55.

Usually political exiles from Germany, Italy, Poland, Hungary, or else-where, they sometimes fought in the ranks, but more often they were placed in key managerial positions to increase the efficiency of the Republican war effort. At the same time they increased the strength of the Spanish Communist party in relation to other political parties in the Republican camp. Finally, the Russians helped procure arms. Some arms were shipped directly from Russia, but, because of the fiction of nonintervention, this was made difficult by the need for secrecy. Large quantities of arms were obtained by agents of the Comintern in France, Great Britain, the United States, and even in Germany.

Russia did not send trained soldiers to Spain as Germany and Italy did, but the Comintern recruited volunteers from all countries. When they arrived in Spain, these men were organized into the International Brigades—fighting units composed of volunteers from all European countries and the Americas. Usually each country had its own brigade. For instance, the majority of United States citizens fought in the Abraham Lincoln Brigade. All the brigades were commanded and controlled by the Comintern. In fact, it was an ominous characteristic of Russian aid that it stayed completely under Russian or Comintern supervision. This eventually gave the Russians absolute control over the destinies of the Republican government.

In spite of Russia's aid, the Republican forces could not withstand the advances of the Spanish Nationalists and their German and Italian allies. By late 1936 Franco's forces controlled western and southwestern Spain, bordering on Portugal. The Republicans held the Atlantic coast in the north, Barcelona on the Mediterranean in the east, Madrid, and the rich agricultural area south and southeast of Madrid. Bilbao on the Atlantic fell to the rebels in the summer of 1937. Barcelona and all of Catalonia were separated from Madrid and the south in early 1938, and resistance there collapsed the following winter. Madrid, which had been under siege since November 1936, held out until March 1939 before bowing to the inevitable. When Franco entered Madrid, one more dictatorship had been established.

The Decline of Communist Prestige, Part 1: Spain

The Soviets intervened in Spain to save the republic, but, while trying to do so, they destroyed the noncommunist forces that originally composed the Republican coalition. Before Russian aid began, the Spanish communists were not an important political force. In fact, they were the weakest of the leftist parties. The Popular Front coalition included Republicans, socialists, anarchists, Trotskyists (POUM or Workers' Party of Marxist Unity), and the communists who were a minuscule group in 1936.[11] However, as Russian prestige and influence grew, the Spanish Communist party also grew. Actually, there was no separate communist organization after July 1936, when it merged with the Socialist party of Catalonia to form the United Catalan Socialist-Communist party (PSUC). However, the communists quickly gained control of PSUC and made it their instrument for controlling the Republican coalition.

From the first the PSUC was the least revolutionary member of the front. In fact, internecine conflict arose within the Republican forces pre-

---

[11] Hugh Thomas, *The Spanish Civil War* (New York: Harper and Row, Publishers, 1963).

cisely because the communists opposed revolutionary policies favored by the Anarchists and POUMists. Stalin's foreign policy dictated this conservatism.[12] The Russian dictator was trying to obtain anti-German alliances with Great Britain and France, and he wanted to appear as politically acceptable as possible. Certainly, he did not wish to give them an excuse to ally with Germany against Russia. Therefore, orders were given to communists in Spain to oppose any revolutionary activity on the part of the Republicans.

In fulfillment of this policy, the PSUC opposed the anarchist and socialist proposals that private property be expropriated and farms be collectivized. When POUM and the anarchists demanded that the Republican army become a citizens' militia with no permanent staff officers, the communists threatened to withdraw Russian aid if the traditional military hierarchy was eliminated. The positions were similar concerning the organization of the Barcelona police. The communists wanted a powerful police commander, because they knew they could appoint their own man. The anarchists and POUMists desired a collective command representing all parties. The communists had their way on all points during the winter of 1936–37. Each time the Socialist premier, Largo Caballero, objected to a communist policy, the PSUC would simply threaten to end Russian aid to the republic.

The communists were strong enough by the spring of 1937 to challenge their opponents for control of republican Spain. In May there was an armed clash in Barcelona between the anarchists and POUMists, on the one side, and the communists. Since the communists controlled the police and army, they won easily. They then arrested hundreds of their fellow Republicans, accusing them of being agents for Franco. Caballero was the next victim. He and certain Republican generals wanted to launch a military offensive in Estremadura. The Russian military advisers wished to attack at another point. The debate became a test of strength. The Russians refused to give any air support to the Republican army if it acted without their approval. Caballero had to admit defeat and could no longer stay in office.

The next premier, the right-wing Socialist Juan Negrin, remained in office until Franco's victory was obvious in 1939. Because of the lack of an alternative, he gave the communist political police (the NKVD), who were controlled from Moscow, a free hand in attacking their enemies.[13] Many stories of communist atrocities leaked out of Spain during this period. Actually, the prolongation of the war after mid 1937 was a tragedy. The Republicans had no real chance of surviving after Caballero was toppled, yet they continued to fight for their ideals. The communists wanted the war to continue for less noble reasons. They wanted to keep

---

[12] Franz Borkenau, *European Communism* (London: Faber and Faber, 1954).

[13] Thomas, *Spanish Civil War*, pp. 435–37.

the fascist powers occupied, so Germany would be less dangerous in eastern Europe. Once Hitler invaded Austria and began to threaten Czechoslovakia, Stalin had no thought of winning the Spanish war; he just wanted it to continue.

By late 1938 only two parties were left of the original five in the Republican coalition—the communists and the Republicans. The Republicans, realizing that further resistance to Franco was futile, demanded a compromise peace, but Premier Negrin and the communists insisted on fighting until the last moment. Finally, in March 1939, the Republican generals staged a coup, ousting Negrin and his communist advisers. While the latter fled to France, the generals tried to negotiate and insisted on an unconditional surrender. The three-year struggle had ended with the absolute defeat of the Spanish republic.

The Decline of Communist Prestige, Part II: The Purges

Many idealists turned away from communism and the Soviet Union because of the events in Spain. Simultaneously, a purge was taking place in Russia that alienated many more. The First Five-Year Plan had thrown the Soviet Union into turmoil. No one had foreseen the extent of the suffering, the coercion, the mobilization of manpower that the plan had required. In 1933 demands for a pause were being heard. Within the party itself, opinions were expressed in favor of a liberalization of the regime to allow more freedom of discussion, partially as a reward for the suffering endured in the previous years. The major spokesman for this tendency was S. M. Kirov, the party boss of Leningrad and the second most powerful man in Russia. On December 1, 1934, Kirov was murdered. Stalin rushed to Leningrad to mourn the death, to kiss the corpse.

Stalin blamed the murder on Trotsky, Kamenev, and Zenoviev—the old Left Opposition—and their followers. His retaliation for Kirov's death was the first step toward a mass purge. Trainloads of "Kirov's assassins" were shipped from Leningrad to Siberia. Thousands of party members were placed in concentration camps. Early in 1935 Kamenev and Zenoviev were tried secretly and given long prison terms. But Stalin did not want these men to be martyrs. He wanted them to make a public confession of their guilt in the murder of Kirov. To obtain this, he actually bargained with them. He would admit their innocence in the murder itself if they confessed that their ideas were responsible for such acts. Whether by persuasion or by torture, both men were convinced to make public confessions in the first show trial of August 1936. At this trial, which was given maximum publicity, the two old Bolsheviks "confessed" that they had formed a bloc with Trotskyites and had received orders from Trotsky. They "confessed" that they had arranged the murder of Kirov and had planned to overthrow the government and to murder Stalin.

Three more show trials followed in the next two years. After the trial of Kamenev and Zenoviev, there was a second trial of Left Oppositionists in January 1937, a trial of army generals in June 1937, and a trial of the Right Opposition in March 1938. All of these trials took the form of two men reciting a political catechism. The prosecutor would ask, "Did you scheme to kill Comrade Stalin and to overthrow the Soviet Socialist Republic?" The defendant would parrot him, "Yes, I schemed to kill Comrade Stalin and to overthrow the Soviet Socialist Republic." One defiant defendant showed his contempt for the trials by systematically changing one or two words in his reply. He greatly disconcerted the prosecutor.

The show trials were, however, only the tip of the iceberg. While the trials were being prepared and staged, millions of lesser party officials and citizens were arrested and shipped to Siberia or elsewhere to be used in forced labor. The party leadership was decimated; the army lost its top generals—even Marshal Tukhachevsky, the chief of the general staff. Seventy percent of the members of the Central Committee of the party were purged, along with 90 percent of the trade-union central committee. In addition to these high officials, many industrial managers, intellectuals, and ordinary bureaucrats of the party and the Comintern disappeared. Many of these were sent to work camps with their entire families, or their wives were forced to divorce them. It was a crime merely to be related to someone who had been arrested. It has been estimated that approximately eight million people were arrested from 1936 to 1938. Finally, the purges stopped when the head of the political police was himself purged.

The most plausible explanation for this incredible spectacle seems to be a combination of the interpretations offered by George Kennan and Isaac Deutscher.[14] Kennan points to the pathological side of Stalin's character, his inability to trust anyone, and, therefore, his fear at the possibility that anyone (such as Kirov or the old Bolsheviks) might publicly oppose him. Deutscher emphasizes the increasing international tension as well as Stalin's suspicious nature. He notes that Stalin was anticipating a war with Germany as early as 1934 and wanted to remove all rivals for power before a war began.

The motivations of the defendants who confessed are just as much an enigma. Their confessions seem to have been prompted by torture, brainwashing, and by a sense of duty to the Communist party. Arthur Koestler, an excommunist, gives greatest emphasis to the last—duty to the party—in his novel about the purges, *Darkness at Noon.*

The best of them kept silent in order to do a last service to the party. . . . They were too deeply entangled in their own past, caught in the web they had

---

[14] Kennan, *Russia and the West under Lenin and Stalin* (Boston: Little, Brown and Co., 1962), pp. 240–41; Deutscher, *Stalin*, pp. 376–78.

spun themselves, according to the laws of their own twisted ethics and twisted logic; they were all guilty, although not of those deeds of which they accused themselves.[15]

The ultimate result of the purges was to further concentrate power in Stalin's hands, eliminating any obstruction to his will. Stalin was a far more absolute ruler than any that had gone before—even more so than Hitler. He used this power to replace the purged leaders, mostly veterans of the revolutionary struggle of 1917–21, and to rebuild the party with bureaucrats. The new leaders in the party were to be Soviet men— men who had made a career in the party bureaucracy, who had matured since 1920. With these men, Stalin began to rebuild Russia in preparation for the war he expected to have to fight against Germany.

---

[15] Koestler, *Darkness at Noon* (New York: Macmillan Co., 1946), pp. 253–54. 1968), pp. 281–83.

Chapter 11

AGGRESSION AND APPEASEMENT

From the day Hitler became chancellor the initiative in foreign affairs rested with the two fascist powers. German rearmament, Italian imperialism, and German expansion went virtually unchallenged, the liberal democracies merely acquiesced in the faits accomplis. At no time before 1939 was a major obstacle put in the path of fascist foreign policy. Without doubt this contributed to the immense prestige Hitler and Mussolini enjoyed throughout the world as well as at home. After the Spanish Civil War the two dictators formed an alliance that seemed irresistible.

Diplomacy of the Dictators, 1933–36

It did not have to be that way. Mussolini was not necessarily pro-Nazi in 1933. He was flattered by what he considered to be Hitler's conscious imitation of Italian propaganda techniques, party organization, and economic policy. He also looked upon Hitler as a sort of protégé, but he did not anticipate an Italo-German alliance. In foreign affairs, however, Mussolini desired above all a revival of the Bismarckian system whereby the major powers would guarantee the peace of Europe through occasional international congresses. The idea was favored by Ramsey MacDonald, head of the National Government in Great Britain, and so it became the basis for a Four-Power Pact signed in June 1933. This was a fairly innocuous agreement on the part of Britain, Italy, France, and Germany to consult over any threat to the peace. Still, the pact caused a great deal of unrest in eastern Europe; for Poland, Czechoslovakia, Rumania, and Yugoslavia depended on French guarantees against attacks by Germany.

Hitler's first major move in the international arena was his reaction to the failure of the disarmament conference, meeting in Geneva for over a year, to reach an agreement on Germany's future military status. When it became obvious that the German inferiority in arms would be continued for another four years, Hitler bolted. First, he withdrew his representative from the conference, and, a week later, Germany withdrew from the League of Nations. The clear implication was that Germany would begin to rearm without international approval. German rearmament would violate the Versailles treaty, thus an intervention in Germany by Great Britain and France might have been legally defensible. In fact, the democracies reacted hardly at all. For his part, Hitler immediately assured all of Europe of his peaceful intent.

This series of events was to be characteristic of Hitler's foreign policy. First, he would make a claim for Germany that he knew his adversaries would not meet—in this instance, equality in arms. Then, arguing that Germany was being treated unfairly, he would achieve his goal through unilateral action. Finally, he would assure everyone that he was only interested in justice for Germany and that he would, in all future instances, employ only peaceful means. He always left the impression that each aggressive act was his last. For instance, in January 1934, he tried to prove his genuine desire for peace by signing a nonaggression pact with Poland. This raised a little opposition in Germany, but it served Hitler's purposes well as a source of favorable propaganda for international public opinion.

The two dictators had not yet met. By the spring of 1934, both men desired a meeting to discuss their common interests and their points of conflict. The greatest source of tension between them was Austria. Since 1925 Mussolini had said that he would not allow *Anschluss*, the unification of Austria with Germany. There had been vocal splinter groups in favor of the idea in both countries. After coming to power, Hitler encouraged this movement by financing the activities of the Austrian Nazi party. A negligible group of only 300 members when Hitler came to power, the Austrian Nazi party had grown to 40,000 members by the end of 1933.

Mussolini and Hitler met on June 14–16, 1934, at Venice. The conference was a comedy of errors.[1] Originally, Mussolini had insisted that the discussions take place in an old villa outside Venice. The villa, which had not been used for years, had no electricity and no kitchen equipment. Still, it was prepared. However, during the first day of talks, mosquitoes attacked in such force that the conference had to be moved to a golf club. Mussolini insisted on displaying his skill as a linguist and speaking to Hitler in German without a translator present. This proved catastrophic, for he could not comprehend Hitler's tirades nor could he express himself clearly. Worse than these minor flaws was Hitler's refusal to play the

---

[1] Ivone Kirkpatrick, *Mussolini: A Study in Power* (New York: Avon Books, 1968), pp. 281–83.

role of admiring disciple. Hitler even made slighting remarks about the superiority of the Nordic race and the negroid strain in the Mediterranean people. This was obviously not a compliment coming from Hitler. Hitler, for his part, was embarrassed by the fact that he had worn civilian clothes throughout the conference on the advice of his foreign minister von Neurath. Mussolini always wore striking military uniforms, and Hitler never forgave von Neurath. The failure of the encounter might be attributed partially to Hitler's preoccupation with the coming purge of the SA. When Mussolini heard of the "Night of the Long Knives," he denounced it as barbarian.

Relations between the two dictators reached their lowest point in July 1934, when the Austrian Nazis attempted a coup d'état in Vienna, killing the Austrian chancellor Dollfuss. Mussolini had repeatedly assured Dollfuss of Italy's determination to protect Austrian independence. The event was more odious to the Duce since Frau Dollfuss and her children were his guests, and he had to inform them of the assassination. He quickly concentrated troops and airplanes on the Austrian border. This show of force had its effect in Berlin where an initial celebration was transformed into a strict observance of international law and etiquette. In August Mussolini met with the Austrian foreign minister to once again guarantee Italy's continued protection of Austria. At that meeting he characterized Hitler as "a horrible sexual degenerate and a dangerous fool." But he also noted the lack of action during the crisis by Great Britain and France, adding, "I cannot always be the only one to march to the Brenner."

The Saar Plebiscite of January 1935 was an ominous portent of things to come. The plebiscite was to decide whether or not the Saar would rejoin Germany. Although they were aware of the crimes of the Nazis against political enemies and against the Jews, inhabitants of the Saar voted overwhelmingly for union with the Third Reich. This revealed the strength of nationalist passions and made the governments of Poland and Czechoslovakia—states that contained large German minorities—extremely uneasy.

Watching the German revival with apprehension, French leaders tried to secure allies to the east. During 1934 Louis Barthou, as minister of foreign affairs, had toured eastern European capitols and had even initiated negotiations with the Soviet Union. To encourage good relations, Barthou sponsored Russia's entrance to the League of Nations in September 1934. This careful cultivation resulted in the Franco-Russian Alliance of May 1935.

Hitler's next major move was to announce two more violations of the Versailles treaty: the existence of a German air force and a return to universal conscription as a means of expanding the German army. These moves did not deter the British from entering negotiations to settle all outstanding problems between the two countries as if nothing had hap-

MAP 7. German Expansion, 1935–July 1939

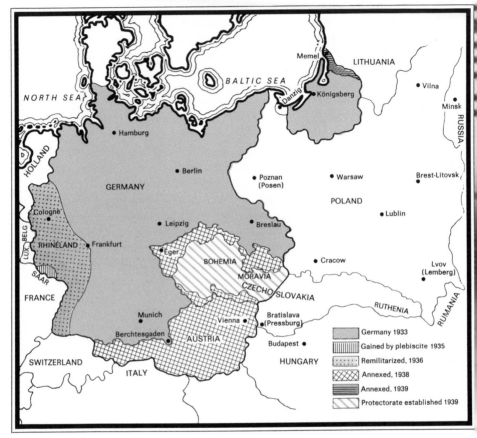

SOURCE: Martin Gilbert, *Recent History Atlas* (London: Weidenfeld and Nicolson, 1966), map 50.

pened. No doubt this greatly increased Hitler's contempt for the weak bourgeois diplomats of the democracies. Mussolini was not so weak. He called on the British and French to join him in a united front against Hitler. The three countries met at Stresa in April, but Mussolini could not obtain the strong commitments he wanted. Instead, Great Britain and France agreed to an innocuous condemnation of the German rearmament and a toothless pledge to cooperate in maintaining the peace of Europe.

The Stresa front was a ghost more than a living thing. The British desire to stay on good terms with Hitler was made only too clear when, without consulting France or Italy, England negotiated a naval agreement with Germany in July 1935. The Anglo-German Naval Agreement recognized the right of Germany to build a navy up to 35 percent the strength of the British fleet. This bit of double-dealing on Britain's allies was the first diplomatic act of Stanley Baldwin, again prime minister in his own right, and his foreign minister, Sir Samuel Hoare.

Mussolini was also willing to risk his good relations with the democracies. He had been considering a war to make Ethiopia, then called Abyssinia, an Italian colony. Naturally, he would have liked to have British and French neutrality if not approval. He thought he had received French approval in January 1935, when he met with Pierre Laval, the French minister of foreign affairs, in Rome. They apparently reached a verbal agreement. At the Stresa conference, Mussolini waited for the British to voice objections. They were aware of his preparations for war, for he had moved about one million soldiers through the British-operated Suez Canal in the months before the conference. Yet, the British did not mention Ethiopia, and Mussolini interpreted this as silent acquiescence. The occasion for the outbreak of hostilities was a minor clash between Italian troops and Ethiopian tribesmen at an oasis on the border between the small Italian colony of Eritrea and Ethiopia. Mussolini ordered his commanders to win a quick victory, so troops could be returned to Europe before Germany was fully rearmed. France remained silent about the conflict. The British reaction was slow and uncertain, but they eventually expressed disapproval. When the League of Nations convened in the fall, Samuel Hoare announced that Great Britain would cooperate in any measures of collective sanctions to which the League members agreed. The League reacted with enthusiasm to this rare resolute stand by speech after speech condemning Italy.

The Duce was not to be denied his imperial glory. On the day Italian and Ethiopian troops made first contact, October 2, he rallied the Italian people against the possibility of League sanctions. He referred to the proposed sanctions as "the blackest of all injustices" and an attempt "to rob [Italy] of a place in the sun." Five days later the League voted that Italy was guilty of aggression, and several forms of sanctions were adopted. An embargo was placed on arms shipments to Italy, while arms could still be sold to Ethiopia. Loans to the Italian government were prohibited. A trade embargo was placed on certain goods, although vital products—especially petroleum and other raw materials—were excluded. Compliance with the sanctions was half-hearted. Most importantly, the two industrial colossi—the United States and Germany—did not significantly limit their trade. Seeing that the sanctions were having little effect, the League recommended an embargo on oil, coal, pig iron, and steel. These products were crucial to the Italian war effort. Only ten members complied. Great Britain and France were not among them.

In early December 1935, Pierre Laval, now French premier, met secretly with Samuel Hoare and agreed on a compromise settlement that they would propose to Mussolini. Ethiopia would be divided. Italy would obtain the fertile plains, and the Ethiopian government would retain control over the mountainous inland areas. France and Britain would assure Ethiopian acceptance. The terms of the Hoare-Laval agreement foreshadow the Munich Agreement of 1938. There is the same acceptance of force, the same concealed surrender parading as a compromise, the same willingness of Britain and France to force a weak government to give in even while it was still fighting. The plan was never tried; for, the day after the secret agreement was reached, French newspapers carried its terms on the front page. British public opinion was so enraged that Hoare had to resign. Now there was no hope of British or French approval. Mussolini once again accelerated his offensive. In May 1936, Haile Selassie was forced into exile, and Ethiopia was annexed to Italy.

While the other states were preoccupied with events in Ethiopia and at home, Hitler occupied the demilitarized zone of the Rhineland in March 1936. It was a great gamble. The army's general staff had assured him that France could easily defeat the Germans if the French mobilized. To risk as few men as possible, Hitler sent only one division into the Rhineland, but he had little to fear. The French premier, Etienne Flandin, was in a difficult position. He headed a caretaker government to administer the country until the May legislative election. Flandin called in General Gamelin, the head of the army, to ask his opinion. Gamelin said that France could only hope to stop Germany if all French forces were mobilized and that, in the midst of an electoral campaign, this could not be considered. Also, Gamelin added, France must have assurance of British support. This statement of Gamelin's was intentionally pessimistic. As A. J. P. Taylor has commented, "Technical opinions reflect the political views of those who give them." Gamelin, in common with most of the French establishment, feared a revolution at home if a war began in the midst of the domestic turmoil caused by the Popular Front election.

The British also found reasons for not opposing the Rhineland occupation. Stanley Baldwin specifically refused to commit troops to the mainland when Flandin inquired. The traditional English sympathy for Germany was becoming distorted by conservative admiration for Hitler's anticommunism. Instead of seeing him as a threat, the English leaders were willing to accept Hitler's offer of negotiations for a comprehensive settlement of all problems. He had made the offer on the same day the German troops goose-stepped into the Rhineland. Of course, nothing came of this purely propagandistic proposal. Therefore, no action was taken against Hitler, and he became ever more confident of his ability to manipulate international affairs.

Aggression, Acquiescence, and the Munich Conference

The Ethiopian crisis and the Spanish Civil War served Hitler the signal service of driving a wedge between Italy and the democracies. Mussolini was envious of British naval strength and French international prestige and, for these reasons, desired their recognition of his imperial exploits and of his special interest in Mediterranean affairs. Instead, he found himself at odds with both countries over Spain and Ethiopia with no ally save Germany. Hitler tried to take advantage of this situation by drawing Italy into a formal alliance. Agreement was reached easily in October 1936. Count Ciano, Mussolini's foreign minister and son-in-law, called it the Rome-Berlin Axis, claiming that future European politics would turn on this alliance. The pact did not require specific commitments but contained a protocol in which the two fascist powers agreed to coordinate their foreign policy on all major questions.

In *Mein Kampf* Hitler had written of two desirable, if not necessary, alliances—one with Italy, the other with Great Britain. After his Italian success, he turned to Britain, requesting the formation of a common front against communism. Although this was not sufficient bait to draw England out of her isolation, it did attract an important ally. Japan considered herself an anticommunist power and was glad to have a European ally. Therefore, the Anti-Comintern Pact of November 1936 was signed. Ostensibly, Germany and Japan agreed to exchange information about the activities of the Comintern. The heart of the treaty, however, was aimed more at the Russian state than at the communist ideology. The new allies agreed not to aid Russia should either of them have a clash with the Soviets. Since Japan coveted China and Hitler hoped to expand eastward, such a clash was very probable. Italy subscribed to the Anti-Comintern Pact in the same month. The diplomatic world had been divided between the countries satisfied with the international status quo and the powers which desired territorial changes.

The following year was one of limited diplomatic activity. Hitler used this respite from international crises to consolidate his position at home and speed his armaments program. He instituted a four-year plan of military production, purged the military leadership, and removed his conservative foreign minister von Neurath, replacing him with the Nazi Ribbentrop. On the diplomatic front, also, Hitler prepared for the adventures of 1938. He already had Italy's approval for almost any action. He assured the Polish ambassador that Poland had nothing to fear. "Danzig," he said, "is bound up with Poland"; and Hermann Goering assured a Polish general, "We do not want the Corridor [which divided Danzig and East Prussia from the rest of Germany]. I say that sincerely and categorically; we do not need the Corridor." The Poles believed, because they wanted to believe, that, regardless of the fate of Austria, and perhaps Czechoslovakia, Poland had no cause for alarm. So, by the end of 1937, Hitler had neutralized all of the opponents of his policies who were susceptible to his influence.

The argument that Hitler was indeed making these preparatory moves with specific diplomatic and, if need arose, military actions in mind is supported by the Hossbach Minutes.[2] These are the minutes of a meeting Hitler held with the leaders of the army and the foreign service in November 1937 to give them a general view of his plans. He stated his determination to change the national frontiers of central Europe and emphasized that this would probably mean war. Germany would be best prepared for such a war around 1943, but his policy of expansion might begin as early as 1938, when he would like to reunite the Germans of Austria and the Sudetenland with the Reich. The men present who expressed doubts about such a program were purged in the next three months—Generals Blomberg and Fritsch and Foreign Minister von Neurath.

Hitler's foreign policy was to benefit also from events in Great Britain. Neville Chamberlain became prime minister in May 1937, and he had a well-thought-out plan for dealing with Nazi Germany. It was appeasement. To Chamberlain, appeasement implied the peaceful change of the status quo to accommodate the just grievances of Germany. He had no doubt that Germany had been unjustly treated at Versailles and that Hitler had every right to demand changes in central Europe. The new prime minister saw his mission in history as the mediator who would make changes possible without war. At first, his foreign secretary was Anthony Eden, who favored taking a hard line with Germany and Italy, but Chamberlain, aside from disagreeing with Eden, did not like to work through official channels. He preferred to send personal envoys to discuss problems face to face with other leaders. Consequently, he sent Lord Halifax, a secondary cabinet member but a trusted friend, to talk to Hitler in November 1937.

Halifax spoke to Hitler of possible "alterations of the European order which might be destined to come about with the passage of time." Halifax, not Hitler, mentioned as possible "alterations" the situations of Austria, Czechoslovakia, and Danzig. Halifax put only one limitation on Britain's willingness to accept these changes. They must be achieved peacefully. Alan Bullock has written of the Halifax mission, "However sincere Chamberlain's desire to reach a settlement with Germany, in practice it amounted to an invitation to diplomatic blackmail which Hitler was not slow to exploit."[3]

In early 1938 Hitler began the chain of events that finally triggered a world war. A police raid on the Austrian Nazi party's headquarters in Vienna disclosed plans for a rising against the government in the spring. This made the Austrian government uneasy, since it assumed the plans to have originated in Berlin. The Austrian chancellor Schuschnigg decided it was time to redefine Austro-German relations. On February 12 he met with Hitler in the Fuehrer's chalet at Berchtesgaden. After an angry and

---

[2] Alan Bullock, *Hitler,* rev. ed. (New York: Harper and Row, Publishers, 1964), pp. 369–71.

[3] Ibid., p. 367.

abusive tirade, Hitler demanded that Schuschnigg appoint Nazis to his cabinet and give the Austrian Nazis freedom of action in the streets. Schuschnigg had no choice but to accept. Among other appointments, Arthur Seyss-Inquart, a leading Nazi, became minister of interior, a position that gave him control of the police. However, the new arrangements were impossible to maintain. The Austrian Nazis became so violent and the new cabinet members were so independent that Schuschnigg decided to force a showdown. He called for a national referendum on Sunday March 13 by which the Austrian people would decide between independence and *Anschluss*.

This call for a referendum surprised and infuriated Hitler, who mobilized the border garrisons. Schuschnigg, rather than submit again, resigned. Seyss-Inquart, on orders from Berlin, used his position as minister of interior to invite German troops into Austria to prevent civil disorder. At dawn on March 12 German forces crossed the Austrian frontier. A military state was soon established. There were 75,000 arrests in Vienna alone. Germany's laws were applied, including the anti-Semitic laws. In a referendum conducted by the new regime, 99.75 percent of those voting endorsed complete union with the Third Reich. Hitler's first major territorial change had been accomplished.

The democracies did not react to the occupation of Austria. Chamberlain's comment to Commons was, "The hard fact is that nothing could have arrested what actually has happened—unless this country and other countries had been prepared to use force." Of course, neither Britain nor France was prepared for military action—not even for strong language.

The next crisis could have been predicted. Since 1935 Germany had been subsidizing a Sudeten German Nazi party in the predominantly German area of Czechoslovakia. After occupying Austria, Hitler ordered the Sudeten Nazis to agitate for such extreme demands that the Czech government could not possibly accommodate them. At the end of April a joint Anglo-French conference requested the Czechs to grant the utmost concessions to the Sudeten Germans. The Czechs refused, for they realized that their problem was in Germany and not the Sudetenland. Therefore, on May 20, when a rumor spread concerning German military movements, the Czechs mobilized their army to defend their frontier. Hitler, who was not ready for a military confrontation, embarrassedly assured the international community that he had no aggressive designs on Czechoslovakia.

Hitler, however, proceeded to prepare for the final denouement of the crisis. He neutralized Poland and Hungary by offering them chunks of the carcass of a defeated Czechoslovakia. He also assured himself Italian support, overcoming Mussolini's anxieties about Italy's preparedness for a major war. In retrospect, these precautions were unnecessary, since the British and French refused to discuss resistance to Hitler with the only Great Power in Eastern Europe, Russia.

Agitation in the Sudetenland became more violent, with the native Germans calling on Berlin to come to their aid. A German invasion seemed inevitable. If France then honored its alliance with Czechoslovakia, it meant a general war. At this point Neville Chamberlain decided, at the age of sixty-nine, to take his first plane trip. He flew to Berchtesgaden to discover Hitler's terms for not going to war with Czechoslovakia. Hitler made one condition that he was sure the Czechs would reject—self-determination by referendum of the Sudeten Germans. When Chamberlain persuaded the Czechs to accept this, Hitler was furious. He then escalated his demands. He wanted an immediate evacuation of the Sudetenland by the Czech military to be replaced by German troops, who would conduct the referendum. He also raised the claims of Hungary and Poland, demanding that they also be met. Finally, he set October 1 as the deadline for Czech acceptance of these terms.

By September 28 the Czechs still had not agreed to Hitler's terms. Once again a general war appeared probable. All of Europe was tense. In London civilians practiced air raid drills and bought gas masks. It was August 1914 all over again. At this juncture, Chamberlain made one more effort. He persuaded Mussolini to request Hitler to submit the question to an international conference. Hitler agreed, largely because he wanted to retain Italian support. The conference was held in Munich. Hitler and Mussolini met with Chamberlain and the French premier Edouard Daladier on September 29 to decide the fate of Czechoslovakia, the only democracy in eastern Europe. The Czechs were not allowed to participate.

The Munich Agreement, presented to the world as a compromise, was merely a surrender to Hitler's ultimatum. It was agreed that Britain and France would be responsible for obtaining Czech acquiescence. German troops were to enter the Sudetenland on Hitler's schedule. An international commission would redraw Czechoslovakia's frontiers so that all Germans who wished could become a part of the Third Reich. Czechoslovakia was forced to cede areas to Poland and Hungary. The Czech state was thereby reduced to an unviable rump. It lost five million citizens out of 15 million, its military fortifications in the west and south, and the Skoda Steel Works, one of the largest armaments factories in Europe. In the weeks that followed, Czechoslovakia, left at the mercy of Germany by the peacemakers of Munich, was even further truncated by Hitler's orders to make Slovakia and Ruthenia autonomous provinces within Czechoslovakia. Puppet governments loyal to Hitler were appointed for the two areas.

Yet peace had been maintained. On one day the specter of world war had hung over Europe. It had been dispelled by the action of the appeasers. Chamberlain and Daladier were greeted by wild ovations when they descended from their airplanes in London and Paris. Daladier had

Hitler welcoming Neville Chamberlain to Munich. Von Ribbentrop, Hitler's Foreign Minister, walks on Chamberlain's left. (Courtesy of Roger-Viollet)

the sense to be ashamed of his role at Munich; he thought at first that the crowd had come to the airport to lynch him. Chamberlain was proud. He waved a personal agreement between himself and Hitler at the cheering crowd and was pleased to report that he had not only brought them "peace with honor" but also "peace in our time."

The Roots of Appeasement

The policy of appeasement suffered great calumny after the beginning of World War II as a policy of cowardice unbefitting a great nation. Politicians since have usually rejected appeasement as a description for their compromises in diplomacy, considering it derogatory. Yet it was a perfectly respectable policy when followed by Aristide Briand in the 1920s as a means of easing international tension. Therefore, it is worth investigating the sources of French and British appeasement of Hitler, if only to correct the mistaken impression that it was a policy based on cowardice. The first step in such an analysis is to identify the appeasers. They were the leaders of conservative parties in France and Great Britain. More broadly, they were the parliamentary supporters of these men. During and after the Spanish Civil War, the political left in both countries was willing to risk war to stop Hitler, but they did not have the political power to force this policy upon their respective legislatures. Therefore, the following discussion will focus on the attitudes of conservatives in France and Britain toward the fascist governments of Germany and Italy.

French conservatives and nationalists had greeted Hitler's entrance to power with a mixture of horror, skepticism, and determination to enforce the Treaty of Versailles. For a brief while in 1933–34 all French parties were united in their desire to keep Germany weak and, if possible, to rid Germany of Adolf Hitler.

The first significant break in this united front resulted from the Italian invasion of Ethiopia. Conservatives opposed the sanctions voted by the League of Nations. They had never favored the League because it negated nationalism. On the other hand, they admired Mussolini's regime. A dilemma arose because Britain was determined to make a show of enforcing sanctions. The French right had to choose between British support on the Rhine and the friendship of fascist Italy. The majority preferred good relations with Italy, and their attitude was determined by ideological factors. The conservatives complained that the French left was for sanctions only because of its hatred for fascism. They saw a victory for Mussolini as a blow against the left, against communism.

Mussolini beaten, it is not England who would be victorious, but Moscow. Muscovite barbarianism sweeping over France first and next, without doubt, all over Europe, would find only Hitler in its path.[4]

A further polarization of French attitudes on foreign policy occurred in the spring of 1936 while a ratification of the Franco-Soviet Pact was being debated. The organization of the Popular Front had raised fears of a communist-dominated government, and conservatives feared an alliance with Russia might strengthen the domestic left. They opposed the treaty on the grounds that Stalin would be able to draw France into a war against the fascist countries in order to defend communism in Russia. The obvious result of such a war, they argued, would be a social revolution in France. They were rapidly developing an interpretation of international affairs that equated opposition to fascist aggression with aid

---

[4] Charles Micaud, *The French Right and Nazi Germany* (Durham, N.C.: Duke University Press, 1943), p. 64.

to the Comintern. This thinking was put into words by Charles Maurras in the reactionary newspaper *L'Action Française* when writing about Ethiopia and the German occupation of the Rhineland.

It is a question of intervening against friendly Italy in an affair that is none of our business. It is a question of satisfying the Masonic Lodges against the fascism they abhor, of serving the interests of England and obeying the Soviets who need this war in order to unleash the universal revolution.[5]

The Spanish Civil War completed the conversion of French nationalists into pacifists. With Léon Blum's Popular Front government in office, the conservatives felt themselves even closer to the revolution. From the day Franco attacked the legal Spanish government, conservatives denounced the Republicans as being "communist controlled" and argued that "to aid the government of Madrid is to furnish arms to communism, to permit it to establish itself firmly in Spain." As the Spanish war dragged on, the "Better Hitler than Blum!" mentality became very popular among opponents of Blum's reforms.

The Popular Front period was just whimpering to its end when Hitler invaded Austria in March 1938. Léon Blum, once again premier, called for a government of national unity, representing all parties, resolved to prevent further Nazi aggressions and to rearm the nation. The French nationalists, now convinced pacifists, greeted Blum's appeal, which implied communist participation in the cabinet, with scorn in the Chamber of Deputies.

Union with all French classes, yes! Union with chiefs taking their orders from Moscow? No! Neither in peace, nor in war, nor above all in government, the essential aim of which is to avoid war.[6]

During the Munich crisis several months later, the conservatives were just as adamantly against war. The nationalists of 1935 had, by 1938, begun to sound like the socialists of 1914. Pierre-Etienne Flandin, now the leader of the neopacifists, went so far as to advocate public opposition to mobilization.

I do not contest the legal right of the government to issue a decree for mobilization. I deny it the moral right, as long as France is not attacked, since mobilization is almost equal to a declaration of war. . . .[7]

After the Munich conference and the subsequent occupation of Czechoslovakia by Germany, the French right began to admit that Germany might be as great a threat as Russia. Still, however, they were not willing to have an alliance with Russia. Unfortunately, when they finally did decide

---

[5] Ibid., p. 90.

[6] Ibid., pp. 146–47.

[7] Ibid., p. 165.

that it was time to prepare for war, the war had already begun, and Germany was the inevitable victor.

This strange myopia of the French conservatives was symptomatic of the insecurity of the upper classes during the interwar period. The revolutions which had occurred at the end of World War I and the depression had shaken the foundations of the bourgeois world, based on laissez faire economics, that had seemed so permanent. Their ideals of economic freedom and private property were in grave danger of being discarded by the masses. The Popular Front election had confirmed the reality of the danger. Their fear and hatred of the extreme left, therefore, made the comfortable classes interpret all events in the context of the threat to their social position and their values, and it blinded them to the national enemy, Nazi Germany.

Contrary to the French, British Conservatives had welcomed Hitler. A great deal of British money was tied up in Germany, and a government which would restore order and financial stability was considered desirable. Moreover, in the early thirties, the Conservative leadership had become the most pacifist national leaders in Europe. Stanley Baldwin, never a man to lead when he could follow, was shocked in October 1933, when a Conservative MP was defeated in a by-election on a charge of war-mongering because he had called for rearmament. Baldwin and most political commentators concluded that the nation was deeply pacifist. Baldwin decided that the Conservative party should also be pacifist in the 1935 election. The international situation had no bearing on this decision; rather, Baldwin's foreign policy was adapted to what he thought was public sentiment.

Neville Chamberlain, as Baldwin's chancellor of the exchequer, cut the military budget drastically in an attempt to maintain a balanced budget. When questioned in Commons about Britain's defensive capabilities, Chamberlain argued that the manufacture of armaments would "inflict a certain injury on our trade from which it would take generations to recover." Baldwin, pursuing his newly found pacifism, did his best to convince the public that preparation for a war was futile because no one could be protected from bombs dropped from planes. He frequently concluded his speeches with "when the next war comes, and European civilization is wiped out, as it will be . . ." He also believed that "If London is bombed three nights running, nothing can avert a revolution." It is important that Baldwin made the connection between war and revolution, for it certainly contributed to the determination of Conservatives that there should not be a next war.

The use of League sanctions against Italy over Ethiopia was the biggest issue of the 1935 election. The Conservatives saw the dependence on League action as a way of preventing the need for a direct Anglo-Italian clash. They advocated sanctions while privately sympathizing with Mussolini. As staunch defenders of the British Empire, they really could not fault him for desiring an Italian empire. This sort of reasoning led to the ill-fated Hoare-Laval agreement recognizing Italy's dominance of Ethiopia. Most revealing is that, even though Sir Samuel Hoare was relieved of the foreign office, Baldwin's cabinet could not understand the moral indignation of the public and press over the agreement. Most cabinet members merely regretted that Hoare had handled the affair so clumsily.

When Hitler occupied the Rhineland, the British refused French requests for a show of force. Chamberlain, in a wild contradiction, told the French that such an action was dangerous since one could not be sure that "this mad dictator" would back down, and, instead, he suggested opening negotiations with the "mad dictator" for a general settlement of all problems.

The Spanish Civil War revealed the strong anticommunism that had been present but not blatant. The editor of *The Observer,* noted that a Bolshevik loss in Spain would end the threat of bolshevism in all western Europe, but, he continued, if Soviet subversion continued, it might lead to an attack on Russia by the "great anti-Communist dictatorship in Germany." To prepare for such an eventuality, he proposed a policy of "lasting settlement and friendship with Germany."

The most systematic and famous appeaser was Neville Chamberlain, who succeeded Baldwin as prime minister in May 1937. Chamberlain was a business executive above all else. Of the two sons of Joseph Chamberlain, Neville was the one least expected to succeed in politics. His distinctive traits were an ardent anticommunism, complete self-confidence, and a passion for a balanced budget. He approached foreign policy as he would a business deal. Assuming that all parties would be bound to any agreement as by a contract, he would always seek a bargain to end conflicts rather than resort to the political tools of trade discrimination, alliances, or military force. It was in this spirit that he dealt with Mussolini and Hitler. When Hitler invaded Austria, Chamberlain sought assurances that the aggression would not be repeated. When Hitler made demands on Czechoslovakia, Chamberlain refused to use threats against the Germans, but rather, he reached an agreement at Munich which was imposed on Czechoslovakia. Returning from Munich, Chamberlain probably believed, as he said, "the new Czechoslovakia will find a greater security than she has ever enjoyed in the past." After all, Hitler had signed a contract at Munich.

War Again

The next few months seemed quiet, but by March 1939, Czechoslovakia was again the center of attention. As in Austria, the Czech government decided it could not allow the process of disintegration to continue unchecked. The Czech president Hacha deposed the governments of Slovakia and Ruthenia. Hitler summoned Hacha to Berlin and bullied him into signing a request for German protection of the Czech state. Even before Hacha had arrived in Berlin, German troops had invaded Czechoslovakia.

This naked aggression was almost too much even for Chamberlain. Appeasement was apparently abandoned. Both Britain and France signed treaties of guarantee with the eastern European states. On March 31, Chamberlain, noting new German demands against Poland, stated in Commons,

. . . in the event of any action which clearly threatened Polish independence, and which the Polish government accordingly considered it vital to resist with their national forces, His Majesty's government would feel themselves bound to lend the Polish government all support in their power.[8]

This certainly sounded like a clear determination to resist further German expansion by force.

Yet Great Britain and France still were not willing to make the one alliance that could prevent German aggression in the East. During March, April, and June 1939, the Soviet Union pressed the democracies for a mutual defense pact. They responded by delaying their replies to urgent Russian inquiries and by sending second-rank officials, who had no authority to make decisions, to Moscow. Stalin became suspicious that perhaps the capitalist states would be pleased to see a war between Germany and Russia.

Hitler, meanwhile, was building pressure on Poland as he had done with Austria and Czechoslovakia. Nazis in Danzig, Poland's only major port and a free city, were agitating for unity with the Reich. Hitler secretly planned to invade Poland on September 1. A pretext would be provided by the Danzig Nazis. Having opened negotiations with the Russians in June, Hitler decided that his greatest coup and safest move would be to win Russia away from England and France. Just eleven days before his planned invasion was to begin, he sent a personal note to Stalin requesting a meeting between Ribbentrop and the Russian leader. The meeting was held on August 23 in the Kremlin. Agreement was reached that night. Eastern Europe was to be divided between Russia and Germany from the Baltic to Rumania. By this last-minute accord, Stalin protected the Soviet Union from a German invasion; Hitler saved Germany from a war on two fronts.

The Nazi-Soviet pact made the actual outbreak of war a mere formality. There was no other power in eastern Europe to resist Germany. If Great Britain was determined to limit German aggression, it could only attack in the west and on the sea. Chamberlain, realizing this, tried several last-

---
[8] Keith Eubank, *The Origins of World War II* (New York: Thomas Y. Crowell Co., 1969), p. 140.

minute gambits to preserve peace. Specifically, he proposed to the Poles that they might concede Danzig to Germany and allow the Corridor, Poland's only outlet to a sea, to become international territory. At the same time, the British ambassador to Berlin, Sir Neville Henderson, deplored the possibility of war over the "utterly foolish and unwise" Poles and assured Hitler that the hostility to Germany in England was merely "the work of Jews and enemies of the Nazis."

Chamberlain's willingness to surrender again was useless. Hitler would not be denied his war. At dawn, on September 1, certain SS units dressed in Polish uniforms staged incidents on the Polish border as the pretext for a German invasion. At 5:00 A.M. a German panzer division, led by the roar of motorcycles, trucks, and tanks rumbled across Poland's vast plains.

PART IV

War and the Division of Europe,
1939–48

Chapter 12

WORLD WAR II

The German attack on Poland, although expected for weeks, was a surprise when it came on the first day of September 1939. Hitler had not bothered to declare war on Poland before his troops began their offensive. German tanks, trucks, and motorcycles were virtually unopposed. Great Britain and France felt that now they had to resist. In 1935 they had watched as Germany had expanded her army in violation of the Versailles treaty. In 1936 they had not intervened when Hitler's troops marched into the Rhineland. Austria and Czechoslovakia had been deserted in the name of the preservation of international peace. Now Hitler had finally strained the appeasement policies of Neville Chamberlain, the British prime minister, and of Edouard Daladier, the French premier, once too often. Two days after the invasion of Poland began, at nine o'clock on a Sunday morning, Sir Nevile Henderson arrived at the German Ministry of Foreign Affairs to deliver a British ultimatum: unless Germany called off the attack within two hours, a state of war would exist between Britain and Germany. A French ultimatum soon followed. By the end of September 3, 1939, the second world-wide war in twenty-five years had begun. It was to be even more destructive, more debasing to the human spirit than the first.

The leaders of the European Great Powers did not realize that they were setting the stage for the destruction of European society as they had known it. Every European state would emerge from this war with a crippled economy and a disoriented society. Old political values that had served well for several generations would be destroyed—chief among them being faith in unfettered free enterprise and the limited role of the state in matters of social welfare. The colonial empires of France, Great Britain, Belgium, Holland, Portugal would be shaken by violent convulsions of nationalist revolt led by politicians of socialist persuasions. Europe would be divided shortly after this war into two ideological blocs—one dominated by communist Soviet Russia, the other by a capitalist and conservative United States. In short, the leaders of the Great Powers of Europe were, in 1939, completing the self-destruction of liberal European society that had been begun by the First World War and continued by the depression. World War II was the inferno in which a way of life was cremated.

Hitler Conquers Europe

The German victory over Poland was rapid and complete. By September 17 the Germans reached the outskirts of Warsaw. After ten days of seige the Polish capitol surrendered, and the Polish government went into exile—the first of many prewar governments to do so. The Russians, Germany's unlikely ally since the signing of the Nazi-Soviet Pact on August 23, had not expected war so soon nor so decisive. The speed of the Wehrmacht advance raised fears in Moscow lest the Germans continue their advance past the line agreed upon in August. The Red Army, therefore, marched into Poland from the east on September 17. Eleven days later the two totalitarian regimes officially divided Poland, roughly along the Curzon Line, a line determined in 1919 by an international commission to be an approximate demarcation between predominantly Polish areas and predominantly Russian and Ruthenian areas.

Hitler had achieved another easy victory and had increased his dominion in central Europe by 73,000 square miles and 22 million people. The rapid German victory was due to a new form of mechanized warfare—the Blitzkrieg or "lightning war." This was accompanied by a policy of *Schrecklichkeit*, a policy of terror intended to demoralize the civilian population. Both of these tactics were used throughout Europe by the Nazis. The Blitzkreig had four phases. First, an attack by the Luftwaffe would destroy the enemy's air force on the ground. Neither Poland nor any other nation had an early-warning system in 1939, making defensive measures almost impossible. During this first phase of the attack, the Luftwaffe would bomb means of communication and transportation, troop concentrations, and major cities as well, since the terrorizing of civilians was an integral part of German strategy. The Stuka dive-bombers contained sirens in their wings to increase the panic among their victims. After the enemy's forces were disrupted by air raids, motorized panzer divisions began the ground offensive. Light, fast vehicles led the way—motorcycles, light tanks, and some motordrawn light artillery. This steel spearhead made the breach in the enemy lines. Next, large formations of heavy tanks—a hundred or more in a group—would widen and secure the opening made by the lighter forces. Completely unprepared for such a mechanized steamroller, the Poles met the tanks with infantry and with cavalry on horseback—a futile and wasteful gesture. Finally, the tanks were followed by the regular infantry who sought out any remaining resistance and occupied the areas already won. This was a new form of warfare, a fully integrated use of machines and men.

The victory over Poland had been completed in twenty-seven days. The western democracies having declared war on Germany used their time for defensive, not offensive, measures. France had mobilized and done no more. Great Britain had sent several divisions of troops to the continent, where they were put under the command of the Allied commander-in-chief General Gamelin. Britain also announced a blockade of all goods being shipped to Germany. Still the British, under the faltering lead of Neville Chamberlain, did not take the necessary emergency measures to prepare their industry for full wartime production. Since Hitler did not choose to extend the war immediately, Europe settled into an anxious calm. The period of inactivity from September 1939 to April 1940 was called the "phoney war." It took its toll on the morals of the French and British soldiers, who had little enthusiasm for the war since their leaders had propagandized appeasement rather than preparedness. Sitting in trenches week after week, month after month, they began to question their reason for being there. Were they in a war with Germany, or just in a trench? The lack of action had the opposite effect on German military men, whose morale was high because of the easy victory over Poland.

The Russians, however, were not content with their territorial gains and invaded Finland while forcing the small Baltic states—Estonia, Latvia, and Lithuania—to accept Russian military bases on their soil, a prelude to the annexation of these countries. The Finns, better equipped and trained for a winter war and fighting for their homeland, gallantly fought against overwhelming odds, but warmer weather and superior weapons led inevitably to a Russian victory in March 1940. The Finns maintained nominal independence but lost 16,000 square miles of strategic territory on the Russian border. The Soviet victory worried Hitler who hoped to control the Baltic Sea. He feared that his chief source of iron ore, Sweden, would be threatened if Russia should decide to occupy Finland. Therefore, Hitler began to consider his own actions in Scandinavia.

Hitler was prepared as early as November 1939 to launch an invasion of Belgium, the Netherlands, and France. Twice during the winter his timetable had been set back because of bad weather. It became clear, however, in early 1940 that not only was his supply of iron ore endangered by the Russian victory in Finland but also by Franco-British plans to send an expeditionary force through Norway and Sweden under the pretext of aiding the Finns. Moreover, the British planned to lay mines in the Baltic Sea to obstruct German shipping. Hitler decided he should secure

Scandinavia before moving westward. A military force was transported to Norway's key ports in commercial vessels to guarantee surprise. On April 9, 1940, one day after the British had begun laying their minefield, Germans seized Norwegian ports, while German paratroopers dropped from the sky over Oslo and other interior cities. This brilliantly executed surprise invasion preempted any resistance by the Norwegians, and the few British troops sent to secure at least one Scandinavian port were withdrawn before they could be ousted by the Germans. Simultaneously, the Germans occupied Denmark. Hitler appointed a local Nazi sympathizer, Vidkun Quisling, to govern Norway. Quisling had the dubious honor of giving his name to all the regimes who supinely bowed to Hitler's wishes, and there were to be many "quisling" governments in Europe before 1945.

The failure of Great Britain to aid in the defense of Scandinavia, which was strategically far more important to the British Isles than was Poland, led to the fall of Neville Chamberlain. Winston Churchill became the leader of the British on May 10, 1940.

On that day the Wehrmacht unleased its long-awaited offensive in the west. The tactics of Blitzkrieg were repeated, with equal success, in Holland and Belgium. Luxembourg surrendered on the first day of the offensive, May 10. The Dutch capitulated five days later, and the Belgians could resist only until May 28. In order to speed the surrender of Holland, the Germans again resorted to terror. Bombers dived on Rotterdam. The raid lasted only seven and a half minutes, but 30,000 to 50,000 civilians were killed; two square miles in the center of the city was reduced to rubble.

France was the next victim. Throughout May, bombers had softened and distracted the French army, which had advanced into Belgium. The Allies expected the Germans to attack across the flat Flanders plain as they had in 1914. The only other likely route of attack, the Rhine valley and Alsace-Lorraine, was protected by the massive concrete bunkers of the Maginot Line, that monument to the defensive mentality of the French army. The area between the Maginot Line and Flanders was heavily wooded and mountainous and was considered by the French to be impenetrable. It was precisely there, through the Ardennes Forest, that the Germans struck in a daring thrust on June 5. The Allies had been convinced that tanks could not pierce the forest, and as the Germans swept south and then turned toward the English Channel north of Paris, the Anglo-French forces in Belgium were isolated from their main force and from supplies. There was no choice but to evacuate these forces to England or to lose them to the enemy. At the port of Dunkirk, all sorts of civilian crafts mobilized by the British government—fishing boats, yachts, tug boats—braved the bombs and strafing runs of the Luftwaffe in order to rescue 200,000 British and 140,000 French troops. French forces to the south of the offensive could offer little resistance and reeled backward. The progress of both armies was hampered by the hundreds of thousands of refugees fleeing southward. The German pilots took advantage of these open targets to sow more panic by bombing and machine-gunning the traffic jams which clogged the roads.

On June 10 the French government deserted Paris, and seven days later Marshal Philip Petain, the new premier of France, requested an armistice with the Germans. France was divided into two zones. A German zone in the north extended along the Atlantic coastline to Spain. Petain's government retained autonomy in southeastern France, including Marseilles and the Mediterranean coast. Even more importantly, the armistice divided the French people into the majority who accepted it and those few who were determined to continue resistance. Charles de Gaulle, one tank commander who had won a battle against the Germans, rallied this small resistance by flying to London and asking French patriots to join him there and to fight on in the name of Free France.

Hitler, now the supreme ruler of Europe from the Atlantic to Poland and from the Arctic Circle to the Austrian Alps, turned to the British with an olive branch, saying in a speech on July 19, 1940,

In this hour I feel it to be my duty before my own conscience to appeal once more to reason and common sense in Britain as much as elsewhere. . . . I can see no reason why this war should go on. I am grieved to think of the sacrifices it must claim.[1]

But Winston Churchill, not Neville Chamberlain, now led the British people. Chamberlain had been vacillating, ready to compromise, unwilling to make demands on the public. Thus, the British people had entered the war in a defeatist mood. Churchill was resolute, uncompromising, an aristocratic authoritarian, and an absolute political realist in foreign affairs. Unlike Chamberlain and other Conservatives, he had not allowed his hatred of the extreme left in domestic politics to cloud his assessment of Hitler's regime. Churchill had fallen from favor within his party during the thirties because of his unbending opposition to appeasement and his insistence that England rearm. As prime minister, his eloquent phrases were to inspire the British and to give them a sense of national destiny during the horrors of the Battle of Britain. In his first speech to the House of Commons as prime minister, he did not offer optimism, but, as he put it,

I have nothing to offer but blood, toil, tears and sweat.

We have before us an ordeal . . . many long months of struggle and of suffering.

You ask, what is our policy? I will say it is to wage war, by sea, land,

[1] Winston Churchill, *The Second World War,* vol. 2 (New York: Houghton Mifflin Co., Bantam, 1962), p. 222.

Rejected by his own
party during the 1930s,
Churchill was accepted
by all parties in 1940.
(Courtesy of UPI)

and air, with all our might and all the strength that God can give us; to
wage war against a monstrous tyranny, never surpassed in the dark, lamentable
catalogue of human crime. . . .

You ask, what is our aim? I can answer in only one word: It is victory,
victory at all costs, victory in spite of the terror; victory, however long and
hard the road may be; for without victory, there is no survival.[2]

Failing to come to an agreement with England, which he had evidently
sincerely desired, Hitler decided to bomb the island into submission in
preparation for an invasion. On August 6, 1940, a thousand planes of
the Luftwaffe attacked aircraft factories and air fields in southern England.
This was only the beginning of massive daily air raids on the British
Isles that lasted for two months. The German air force had almost twice as
many planes at its disposal than did the Royal Air Force, but the Germans
were never able to translate this numerical dominance into real air superiority. The telling factor was the ability of the British Spitfire and
Hurricane fighter planes (about 980 usually available for battle) to out-
maneuver the German fighters (1,200 available) flying escort for the
slow-moving German bombers (approximately 1,300 of all types). The
RAF planes were faster and more heavily armed, and in addition, were
aided by the newly developed radar that warned the British of approaching
planes. The Germans also aided the British resistance by continually shifting their bombing targets. For the first two weeks the Luftwaffe concentrated on British air defense installations in southern England. From August
24 to September 7, however, they tried to knock out the RAF fighter force
by bombing air fields, oil supplies, and planes on the ground. This tactic
was almost successful when it was abandoned. The British had lost 466

---

[2] Louis L. Snyder, *The War: A Concise History, 1939–1945* (New York: Dell
Publishing Co., Inc., 1960), p. 125.

planes and 231 pilots when the Germans switched their efforts to London as an act of revenge for British bombs dropped on Berlin. London was pounded for twenty-three consecutive days. Sections of the city were turned to rubble. But London was not a military target; and the German attempt to destroy the will of Britain was wasted effort. In the meanwhile the RAF was able to recover and began to inflict unacceptable losses on the German bomber fleets. The final blow was dealt to the German air campaign when the RAF downed fifty-six German planes on the night of September 15. Two days later Hitler abandoned plans for an invasion of the British Isles in the near future. Finally, on October 12, a brief directive to the Luftwaffe command stated that further bombing would only be for the purpose of maintaining pressure on British resources. Although sporadic raids continued in lesser intensity until June 1941, the Battle of Britain had been won by the RAF.

Thwarted by England, Hitler had already begun to look for new areas of expansion. His desire to gain control of the western Mediterranean from the British was disappointed by his allies. General Franco refused to allow German troops to pass through Spain and refused to join Germany in an assault on Gibraltar. Franco was protecting Spanish interests and was not willing to antagonize Britain, the dominant naval power in the Mediterranean. After a nine-hour interview with the stubborn Franco, Hitler remarked, "Rather than go through that again, I would prefer to have three or four teeth taken out." Marshal Petain was equally adamant. He refused to allow French ships, colonies, or ports to be used for German action in the Mediterranean.

The sharpest thorn in Hitler's side during the winter of 1940–41 may have been his inept ally, Mussolini. Italy waited until the French were defeated before declaring war on France in hopes of being able to share in the booty. Even then the Italian troops could only advance approximately one hundred yards into France before signing an armistice. Hitler had not informed Mussolini of the timing of his Scandinavian campaign nor of his western offensive. Il Duce, highly indignant, was resolved to repay Hitler in kind. Therefore, on October 28, 1940, without consulting Hitler, the Italians invaded Greece, having occupied Albania in 1939. Such independent action, never welcomed by Hitler, would have been acceptable had the Italians been successful, but by the end of the year, the Greeks had pushed the Italians out of Greece and were preparing to push them into the Adriatic Sea. The Greek offensive, combined with Yugoslav intransigence, threatened to disrupt Hitler's plans for an offensive against Russia in the spring of 1941.

The Russo-German alliance had functioned fairly smoothly since 1939. The Russians had scrupulously been good business partners of Germany, exchanging necessary war materiel with the Nazis. Stalin seemed willing to continue this arrangement indefinitely, but Hitler was not. As early as July 1940, Hitler had directed his generals to draw up plans for an invasion of the Soviet Union. After the failure of the Battle of Britain, these plans were accelerated. The reason for attacking Britain had been to avoid a two-front war; Hitler reassessed this possiblity in September and October 1940, and convinced himself that there was no real danger of Britain invading the Continent and decided he could turn his major infantry strength against Russia. The German offensive against Russia was to be launched on May 15, 1941. Hitler had assured the safety of his army's advance by establishing protectorates over Hungary and Rumania in the summer of 1940. Both states rightly feared that Russia had designs on their territory as was proved by the Soviet annexation by force of Rumania's Bessarabia and Northern Bukovina. Still not satisfied, Hitler required submission from Bulgaria, Yugoslavia, and Greece as well. Bulgaria caved in quickly, but the Yugoslavs refused to accept satellite status. The pro-German Prince Regent Paul was ousted by army officers, and an anti-Nazi regime under eighteen-year-old King Peter was instituted. Hitler reacted instinctively and unwisely. He ordered the attack on Russia delayed for four weeks while "operation punishment" could be carried out in Yugoslavia. Belgrade was bombed for three full days. Seventeen thousand people died. Hitler's troops occupied Yugoslavia, and at the same time, Germans marched into Greece. By April 27, 1941, Hitler controlled all of Eastern Europe from Poland to Greece. With no possibility of being attacked on its flank, the German army was now ready to invade Russia.

The diversion into the Balkans had cost the Germans precious time. Instead of beginning the Russian offensive in mid April, they began it in late June. Rushing panzer divisions lunged in three directions: toward Leningrad in the north, Moscow in the center, and Stalingrad in the south. The Russian army was completely unprepared for the Blitzkrieg, and Russian losses were gargantuan, large enough to cripple smaller nations. Near Minsk 300,000 Russian soldiers surrendered; 600,000 were captured at Kiev, and another 600,000 as German troops approached Moscow. Leningrad (old St. Petersburg) came under seige in September—the seige would not be lifted for three and a half years. By December German soldiers could see the towers of Moscow; Hitler announced in Berlin that the Russian army was no longer capable of fighting. But the Russians were prepared to fight in winter weather; the Germans were not. Evidence of Hitler's perverse sense of destiny was his insistence that the Russians would be defeated before cold weather and his refusal to provide his armies with winter clothing. Therefore, as the Germans neared Moscow, their guns were freezing, their tanks were freezing, and their hands and feet were freezing as well. The better prepared Russians could depend on short supply lines and even had reserve forces to support them. On December 6, 1941, Marshal Zhukov launched a Russian counteroffensive before Moscow. The Germans were helpless. In several weeks they were forced to retreat 200 miles. It was the first German retreat of the war.

When the German offensive had begun, Churchill immediately promised the Russians all the support Great Britain could supply. He also convinced Franklin Roosevelt that the United States had an interest in the survival of the Soviet Union, and United States aid began trickling to Russia by late December 1941. On the other side of the globe, the Japanese launched a surprise attack on a United States naval base at Pearl Harbor on the same December 7 the Russians drove the Germans back from Moscow. The conflict between the Japanese and Americans had been gestating for years, but the suddenness and ferocity of the destruction of Pearl Harbor compelled the United States into the war without the urging of FDR, who had been slowly involving his nation in the European hostilities. In accordance with its alliance with Japan, Germany declared war on the United States.

Churchill had been trying to commit Roosevelt to the British side from the time he became prime minister. In August 1941 the two had met in a bay off Newfoundland to draw up some very general war aims. The Atlantic Charter, in which they expressed their hopes for the postwar world, rejected the idea of territorial gains for the two countries should they emerge victors and expressed the desire that all peoples should choose the form of government under which they live. Another goal was an improvement in living standards for all. This was obviously meant to please the labor leaders in each country, as had been the promises of a world "fit for heroes" during World War I. In speaking of hopes for peace in the postwar period, the charter implied that one goal would be "the establishment of a wider and permanent system of general security." This Wilsonian statement implied that the United States and Great Britain had not deserted the concept of some form of international organization charged with keeping the peace.

After the United States was brought into the war by Pearl Harbor, Churchill was eager to begin close military cooperation. To decide on overall strategic objectives he met with FDR in Washington from December 22, 1941, to January 1, 1942. The goodwill, the friendship even, that developed between these two men was in great contrast to the suspicion and envy that marred the Hitler-Mussolini relationship; and this difference was no doubt an advantage to the Anglo-Americans, allowing them to coordinate their war efforts efficiently. At the Arcadia Conference, the British were determined to obtain an American commitment to consider Europe the primary theater instead of the Pacific. Although Roosevelt's military advisers were divided, the president was sympathetic to the British. Therefore, the general strategy agreed upon was the encirclement of Germany. The Axis Powers were to be gradually weakened by destroying their sources of raw materials, defeating their allies, and bombing their industrial cities. Then, when they had been so weakened that a direct invasion across the English Channel was assured of success, a frontal assault would be tried. The American military chiefs argued that the Allies should immediately strike a knock-out blow at the German heartland. Roosevelt preferred Churchill's more conservative course which was a logical extension of Britain's naval blockade of the Continent. Although the Arcadia decisions reflected the British view, the debates over a "knock-out blow" continued until 1944.

The USSR also opposed this policy of gradually "closing the ring." Since June 1941, Russia had borne the brunt of the war against Germany, trying unsuccessfully to resist the bulk of Germany's infantry forces. Battles in Russia dwarfed any others. In one maneuver in the Kiev region, the Germans took 600,000 prisoners. "Three months after the invasion began, the Soviet armies had lost some 2.5 million men (of a total of 4.5 million) killed, wounded, or captured, and had seen their tank force reduced from 15,000 to 700."[3] The Germans marched relentlessly toward Leningrad, Moscow, and through the agriculturally rich Ukraine. Stalin urgently requested his allies to launch an invasion of France as soon as possible to relieve the pressure on the crippled Russian army. The Soviet leader was extremely disappointed with the strategy chosen at Arcadia and suspected that perhaps his allies would not mind seeing the Soviet Union weakened even more.

The Allies Take the Offensive

Indeed, the spring and summer of 1942 were the most critical period of the war for the Allies. The German general Erwin Rommel, the Desert Fox, was advancing from the Italian colony of Libya across northern Africa toward the Suez Canal. Japan was tightening her control over Southeast Asia and the western Pacific and seemed to threaten India. In Russia the Germans were closing on Stalingrad—the last major city that could resist them in the Caucasus and the key to most of Russia's oil reserves.

Yet, by October and November of the same year, the entire European theater had changed. British general Bernard Montgomery attacked and defeated Rommel at El Alamein, stopping the Germans just sixty miles west of Alexandria. Rommel began a retreat that was to end in his expulsion from North Africa in May 1943. The victory was a needed boost to British morale, and it has become the turning point of the war in the English collective memory. Churchill later remarked, "Before Alamein we never had a victory. After Alamein we never had a defeat." Two

---

[3] Gordon Wright, *The Ordeal of Total War 1939–1945* (New York: Harper and Row, Publishers, 1968), p. 39.

weeks after Montgomery's victory a predominantly American force invaded the French North African colonies of Morocco and Algeria. After only brief but costly skirmishes, the French officials, until then loyal to Petain's Vichy Regime, called off armed resistance and agreed to cooperate with the Americans. The same November the scales of war also turned against the Germans on the eastern front. On November 19 the Russian army began a counteroffensive at Stalingrad.

Situated on the western bank of the Volga River between the Caspian Sea and Moscow, Stalingrad was of the highest strategic importance. Its capture would mean German control of the Caspian oil fields to the south, would deny the Russians many agricultural products, and would be a blow of immeasurable gravity to Russian morale. The city's symbolic importance was heightened by the fact that it was the scene of Stalin's greatest military victory as an officer in the Red Army during the civil war in 1918. The German general Friedrich Paulus attacked with the 330,000 men of the German Sixth Army on August 22, 1942. On the first day the German bombardment leveled three-quarters of Stalingrad. But the Russians were determined that the Germans should not gain control of the Volga. The rubble in the streets, the crumbling walls of bombed buildings became trenches and barricades. Block by block the Germans pushed the Red Army back toward the river bank until there was only six square miles of rubble in the city center between the Sixth Army and victory. Fighting became bestial. Hand-to-hand combat with any weapon available was the norm. Each building, each apartment, each block was taken, and then lost several times over. But the German losses were almost as heavy as the Russian, and while the Russians were massing men both north and south of the city, the Germans had no reserves.

On November 19 General Georgi Zhukov, the hero of Moscow, ordered a counterattack, encircling Paulus in a large pincer movement. Zhukov not only had fresh soldiers but also thousands of tanks. The arms of the pincer closed from the north and south, and the German Sixth Army was isolated from any German aid except by air. For the next two months the Russians tightened the ring, as winter set in, as German supplies ran out, as the proud German soldiers were reduced to eating their horses and dogs and rats. General Paulus asked Hitler for permission, first, to retreat and, later, to surrender. Both requests were refused. Hitler insanely required his soldiers to stand their ground when they could hardly stand at all. Paulus surrendered on February 2 with only 110,000 of his original 330,000.

This defeat spelled the end of Nazi hopes for victory over the Russians. The Germans had no fresh troops as the Russians did. The Russian tanks used at Stalingrad were an indication of the recovery of Russia's industry, much of which had been transported eastward when the Germans first attacked. At the time of Stalingrad Russia was producing 2,000 tanks per month while the Germans were producing only 350 per month.[4] Yet the Russians paid a heavy price for their victory. "They lost more men at Stalingrad than the United States lost in combat in all theatres of the entire war."[5] The price was militarily acceptable; for Russia began an advance after Stalingrad which, with only brief setbacks, ended in Berlin two years later.

Therefore, when the year 1943 began, Germany was on the defensive on both fronts. The concentration of Anglo-American forces in North Africa dictated that the next Allied action should be in the Mediterranean area. At the Casablanca conference in January 1943, Roosevelt and Churchill decided to invade Sicily and then Italy. Certain troops of the Free French, now headquartered in Algiers, could also be used. Of course, this implied that a cross-Channel invasion would have to be postponed for at least another year. This postponement led to charges by Stalin that the western Allies were hoping that Germany and Russia might destroy each other. Actually, the British were only continuing their policy of weakening the Axis Powers on the periphery before risking a direct confrontation with Germany. This strategy was forwarded by the invasion of Sicily in July and a beachhead landing in southern Italy in September.

Events within Italy made the implementation of the Allied strategy somewhat easier. In July a conservative coup ousted Mussolini, who was arrested and replaced as premier by Marshal Pietro Badoglio. On October 13, 1943, Italy declared war on Germany. Meanwhile, German military agents had whisked Mussolini away from his captors, and Hitler appointed him the leader of a puppet government in northern Italy. The Germans fought tenaciously to prevent the Allies from advancing north of Rome, and battles continued in the hilly and mountainous north until 1945.

By mid 1943 the Allies had also gained supremacy in the air and on the seas. Great Britain depended on shipping for its survival, and although the German surface fleet could not seriously challenge the British, the U-boats, or German submarines, threatened to successfully erect a blockade around the British Isles during 1942 and early 1943. One convoy attacked by U-boats lost twenty-two of thirty-three ships in the summer of 1942. But the U-boat campaign reached its height, on orders from Admiral Doenitz, in March 1943, when ninety-seven Allied ships were lost in twenty days. This was the last hurrah for the U-boat wolf packs, for the Anglo-American navies were just then perfecting weapons and techniques that soon drove the U-boats from the seas. The shortage of long-range aircraft had previously prevented bombing the German ships, but the first aircraft carriers went on duty in April and May 1943, carrying bombers equipped with microwave radar, which could not be detected

---

[4] Ibid., p. 188.

[5] Snyder, The War, p. 382.

by the submarines as could the older long-wave radar. Finally, Allied "support groups" of a dozen ships specializing in U-boat hunting were used as flying squadrons, always on call to aid a convoy under attack. With the introduction of these new elements into the fray, the U-boats were doomed. Forty-one U-boats were sunk in the first twenty-two days of May, and Admiral Doenitz called the rest back to port on May 23. The German submarines made occasional forays to sea after this, but they no longer were a grave threat to Allied shipping.

The Germans never used their air force effectively again after the Battle of Britain. In spite of the crushing raids on Rotterdam, Belgrade, and London early in the war, the Luftwaffe was trained essentially for the support of ground forces as in a Blitzkrieg. The sustained bombardment of military and industrial facilities and of civilian centers was a virtual monopoly of the Anglo-Americans because of Germany's lack of air power—especially of long-range bombers. The British debated heatedly among themselves about the merits of precision bombing of military and industrial targets versus "area bombing" of population centers. It was felt that area bombing would sow panic and demoralize the enemy. The decision to pursue area bombing was taken in March 1942, and adhered to for the remainder of the war. As proof that the policy could be effective Sir Arthur Harris, commander-in-chief of the RAF Bomber Command, ordered a raid against Cologne in May 1942, in which a thousand Lancasters unloaded their bombs in ninety minutes. Three days later the performance was repeated over Essen. When the Americans entered the air war in 1943, they insisted on precision bombing, so the two air forces achieved little coordination. They did cooperate, however, in the fire-bombing of Dresden.

Dresden was not the first or the only city to be fire-bombed. The technique was used first against the inhabitants of Hamburg in July and August of 1943. The idea was to drop a sufficient number of incendiary bombs to create a monstrous fire-storm that would consume a city and its inhabitants. Not only would those be killed who came into direct contact with the flames but also those in hiding in bomb shelters; for the fire-storm would devour all oxygen, suffocating any living thing nearby. Anyone approaching the fire-storm—such as rescue workers—would be scorched to death. These effects were similar to the effects of an atomic bomb. The case of Dresden was special because of the peculiar circumstances of the attack. It occurred in February 1945, when the German army was all but completely destroyed. Dresden had no industry to attack, and its population was greatly swollen by an influx of refugees fleeing the advance of the Red Army. These refugees were mostly women, children, and old men, as were the remaining inhabitants of the city, because virtually all able-bodied German men had been impressed into the army. Since the city had no military targets, it had been stripped of its anti-aircraft defenses, leaving it unprotected. The first armada of 250 bombers set the city ablaze on the night of February 13. The next wave of 597 planes increased the intensity of the inferno. Few escaped. The heat prevented rescue efforts in some areas for weeks afterward.

The air war remains perhaps the most controversial aspect of the Allied war effort. It did not break civilian morale. It did not disrupt German industrial production. In fact, German armaments production increased during 1943 and the first half of 1944. The bombing did slow down German production, however, and it did divert manpower and resources from the war effort to the task of reconstruction and repair. Still, it appears that Germany was ultimately weakened from a lack of resources rather than from bombardment.

As Germany weakened, the leaders of the Allied powers began to feel the necessity for a closer coordination of their future strategy. The time seemed right to strike at the German heartland. Therefore, the Big Three—Roosevelt, Churchill, and Stalin—met for the first time at Teheran, November 28 to December 1, 1943, and decided definitely that the time had come for the cross-Channel invasion. Operation Overload began on June 6, 1944, when 5,300 ships carried the invasion force and its equipment to Normandy's beaches. The operation was enormous: 18,300 paratroopers preceded the 165,000 infantry landed on *the first day*. In eleven days 587,000 British and American troops were ashore. In three weeks, over one million had been landed. The Germans, thrown back from the shore, were not able to stop the juggernaut that advanced across France. Paris was liberated by a French tank corps on August 25. On August 26, de Gaulle, having entered France immediately after the invasion against American and British wishes, led Free French troops and celebrating Parisians through the streets of Paris. Free French forces also landed on the Côte d'Azur and marched northward along the Rhone Valley to merge with the British and American armies in eastern France.

The Allied advance continued until October 1944, when it was halted short of the German frontier by the forest and the onset of winter. While General Eisenhower, the American Supreme Allied Commander, consolidated his gains and massed his troops for the final plunge into Germany, the Germans tried a last desperate offensive which created a pocket or "bulge" in the American lines forty-five miles wide and sixty-five miles deep. The Battle of the Bulge lasted from mid December until mid January 1945. The Germans were bested by American tanks and were already defeated when they were withdrawn from the west in order to block the Russian forces entering Germany from Poland. This opened roads for the final Anglo-American advance. The Germans would soon have to surrender; the time had come to discuss the terms of a peace settlement. Churchill, Roosevelt, and Stalin met at Yalta in February 1945 to do just that.

Hitler's Europe

By the time Allied troops reached the German frontiers, Hitler's Nazi regime had governed the European continent for four years. During that period, old political forces were destroyed and new ones were born. The postwar political configuration of every European state was determined by the wartime experience.

The Fuehrer had a vague idea of what he wanted to do with Europe after he conquered it. He wanted to create a New Order organized on racist principles and ignoring national boundaries. In the Tripartite Pact signed by Germany, Italy, and Japan on September 27, 1940, Japan recognized "the leadership of Germany and Italy of a new order in Europe," and the Axis powers recognized Japan's New Order in Asia. Evidently, the world was to be divided into several *Lebensraum* or "living spaces," each dominated by a certain race or culture. Each *Raum* would form an economic community that would assure prosperity.[6] The Germans and Italians would dominate the Euro-African *Raum*, with Germany supreme in northern and eastern Europe and Italy having preeminence in the Mediterranean area. Both would have African colonies. The less developed areas of each *Raum* would produce the raw materials for the industrial areas. Racial homogeneity would be achieved by population transfers from one "living space" to another.

This ideal situation seemed within Hitler's grasp in 1941. He ruled Europe and could do with its people as he pleased. Before 1944, however, it became clear that his concept of the New Order was constantly changing and that, in practice, it was more of a nightmare than a dream. Conquered areas were governed in one of three ways. If they were annexed directly to the Reich, they were merely given a German civilian bureaucracy. Areas that were considered not ready for direct annexation, but might be annexed in the future, were governed by a Reich governor or Reich commissioner who had dictatorial powers over the inhabitants. Poland and the Czech state were governed this way. Other areas were administered by native collaborators who did Hitler's bidding for various reasons—some were convinced Nazis, as were Quisling of Norway and Father Josef Tiso of Slovakia, and others were merely conservatives who felt they could gain concessions for their nation by cooperating with Hitler, as did Pierre Laval in France and King Boris of Bulgaria.

Whatever Hitler's designs for a New Order after the war, the German policy during the war was one of absolute exploitation of the areas under their control. This policy was most harshly carried out in the East—Poland, Bohemia-Moravia, and Russia. Poland was divided into

---

[6] Clifton J. Child, "The Concept of the New Order," in *Hitler's Europe*, eds. Arnold Toynbee and Veronica M. Toynbee (London: Oxford University Press, 1954), pp. 48 ff.

MAP 8. Hitler's Europe, 1942

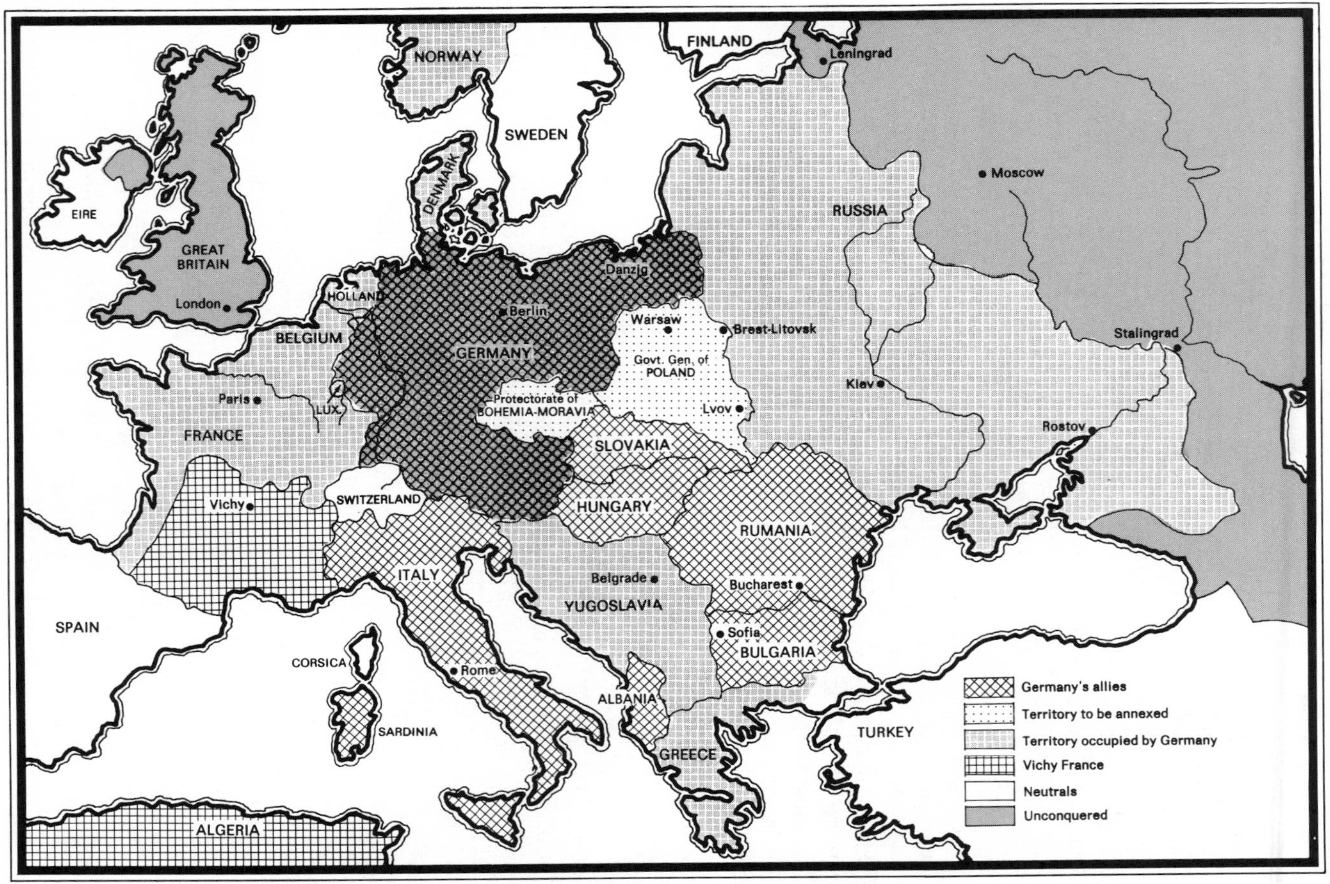

SOURCE: Original composite of two maps: Martin Gilbert, *Recent History Atlas*, basic format of map 72.

two governmental units—Danzig-West Prussia, which was annexed to the Reich, and the General Government, which was considered a colony of sorts. While industry in Danzig-West Prussia was expanded, the Government General, which included Warsaw, was stripped of raw materials, machinery, and even laborers. All three were shipped to Germany to produce for the war machine. The Ukraine was similarly stripped. In fact industry in the East was limited to preparing raw materials for shipment to Germany. Eastern European laborers were treated as slaves to be worked until they died. Heinrich Himmler, head of the SS, expressed the German attitude in 1943 while speaking to a meeting of SS officers:

What happens to a Russian, to a Czech does not interest me in the slightest. What the nations can offer in the way of good blood of our type, we will take, if necessary by kidnapping their children and raising them here with us. Whether nations live in prosperity or starve to death interests me only in so far as we need them as slaves for our Kultur. . . . Whether 10,000 Russian females fall down from exhaustion while digging an anti-tank ditch interests me only in so far as the anti-tank ditch for Germany is finished. We shall never be rough and heartless where it is not necessary, that is clear. . . . But it is a crime against our own blood to worry about them and give them ideals, thus causing our sons and daughters to have a more difficult time with them.[7]

Western European peoples were not treated so harshly because the Nazis felt a closer racial tie with the blonds of Scandinavia and the Dutch and Belgians, who were considered capable of being "Germanized." The eastern Europeans were, on the other hand, *Untermenschen* (subhumans). The industrial plants of the West were sacked at first, but it was more productive merely to divert French, Belgian, and Dutch industry into production needed by the Reich. Because of such exploitation of foreigners, the German civilian population did not feel the strain of a wartime economy until late 1942.

The European wide racial policy inherent in the Nazi New Order had three aspects: population transfers to create racially homogeneous areas; colonization by Germans to extend the Reich and to create an eastern frontier defense against the Slavs; and the extermination of all Jews. The first transfers began in October 1939. Non-Germans were moved out of the newly created Danzig-West Prussia into detention camps in the Government General. They were replaced by two types of German settlers—*Reichsdeutsche*, Germans living in the pre-1939 Reich who were encouraged to become settlers by the promise of free land, and *Volksdeutsche*, German-speaking people living in other countries before the war. For instance, *Volksdeutsche* from Estonia and Latvia were transported to

---

[7] Patricia Harvey, "Labour," ibid., p. 241.

Danzig-West Prussia. The non-Germans were simply deported, often to become forced laborers in a concentration camp or in Germany. Similar population transfers occurred in northeastern France, but the French were usually transported to southern France to live under the Vichy Regime. Vast utopian programs of colonization were conceived in 1941 and 1942, especially for Russia. Large areas of Russia were to be cleared of all their inhabitants, so German colonies could be established in the fertile Ukraine. Of course, the eastern resettlement program ended in 1943. After Stalingrad the Germans scrambled to remove the *Volksdeutsche* from areas threatened by the advancing Red Army. The result of resettlement, never a successful venture, was merely suffering and confusion for both the Germans and non-Germans involved.

The extermination of European Jewry was the logical result of Nazi ideology and propaganda, but before 1940, there is little evidence to suggest that even the Nazi leadership had considered actually attempting it. The anti-Semitic campaign had evolved through several phases before the "final solution" was decided upon. Jews had been first stripped of their citizenship and then denied any legal rights. Forbidden to mix socially with Germans, they were required to sell all of their property in November 1938 and place the money in state banks. These measures had the intended effect of forcing many Jews to leave Germany during the 1930s. The forced emigration was aided by the Nazis who made trains available to speed the Jews on their way.

The administration of Jewish affairs was left to Heinrich Himmler's SS and the Gestapo (state secret police), a subbranch of the SS. Hidden in the vast web of bureaucracy, in subsection B of the Gestapo, one man was given responsibility for the efficient handling of the Jewish problem: Adolf Eichmann, the perfect bureaucrat. The outbreak of war created immense problems for Eichmann and his immediate superior, Reinhard Heydrich. The policy of forced migration was, of course, no longer feasible. A stop-gap measure—isolating all Jews in ghettos—was tried. The largest of these was the Warsaw Ghetto with 470,000 Jews packed into 1.3 square miles and living with more than seven people in each room.[8] Yet, by 1941 it had become obvious that the Jewish question was too large to be solved even by the ghetto system. In July 1941, Heydrich was ordered to prepare a proposal for a "final solution." Heydrich presented his plan to representatives of all government ministries at the Wannsee Conference in January 1942. Most of those attending were Nazi party officials, but civilians who belonged to the pre-Nazi civil service were also present.[9] They offered their technical advice as to how Heydrich's final solution might be implemented. Eichmann later wrote that

---

[8] Raul Hilberg, *The Destruction of the European Jews* (Chicago: Quadrangle Books, 1967), pp. 152–53.

[9] Ibid., p. 264.

The final solution:
a German
concentration camp
(Courtesy of UPI)

until the Wannsee Conference he had harbored some doubts about "such a bloody solution through violence." At Wannsee, however, his doubts were dispelled. As he put it, "Here now, during this conference, the most prominent people had spoken, the Popes of the Third Reich. . . . At that moment, I sensed a kind of Pontius Pilate feeling, for I felt free of all guilt."[10]

Heydrich's final solution was the efficient, rapid, and unpublicized assembly-line murder by gas of all Jews in German controlled territories. The gassing was to take place at large concentration camps organized especially for that purpose in Germany and eastern Europe. Eichmann was given the job of devising the most efficient means of forcibly evacuating Jews from all over Europe to these death camps.

As early as 1933 the SS had used special buildings—warehouses, etc.— to isolate their political prisoners. By 1934 special detention camps had been built. It was only with the coming of the war that the camps grew into large self-sustaining torture chambers and death mills. By 1944 there were twenty major concentration camps, 165 smaller labor camps, and

---

[10] Hannah Arendt, *Eichmann in Jerusalem* (New York: The Viking Press, 1963), p. 114.

six killing centers that had been built in Poland. The largest of the killing centers were Auschwitz and Treblinka. The camps were manned by the SS death-head units, and they contained SS barracks, SS housing projects, factories where the prisoners were literally worked to death, the prisoners' barracks, and the death chambers.

TABLE 12.1.   The Jewish Dead by Territory

Reich-protectorate area	250,000
USSR	700,000
Baltic states	200,000
Poland	3,000,000
The Low Countries	130,000
France and Italy	70,000
Yugoslavia	60,000
Greece and Rhodes	60,000
Slovakia	60,000
Rumania	270,000
Hungary and Carpatho-Ukraine	300,000
Total	5,100,000

SOURCE: Raul Hilberg, *The Destruction of the European Jews* (Chicago: Quadrangle Books, 1967), p. 767.

Auschwitz was by far the largest of the death camps. It was not only a death camp but also an industrial complex run on slave labor. The camp commander was Rudolf Hoess, who perfected assembly-line murder by constructing air-tight gas chambers near incinerators where the dead bodies could be immediately burned. When he became commander of Auschwitz in 1941, it was still a sleepy town, but the camp's location at the junction of four rail lines made it the natural center for the destruction of Europe's Jews. In mid 1942, when the mass exterminations began, it was a "concentration city" guarded by 3,000 SS troops. After that a continuous stream of trains arrived with their human cargo. As the pace of exterminations increased, Hoess added new gas chambers and crematories. These new facilities were solemnly dedicated in the presence of important officials from Berlin. The maximum capacity of the camp was probably the 22,000 executions in twenty-four hours in June 1944, but the average was 12,000 to 15,000 deaths per day. Between one and two million people were killed at Auschwitz. The industrial activity of the camp included a Krupp armaments factory, an I. G. Farben chemical plant, and coal mines.

Administering Total War

A nation's form of government does not determine how efficiently it will prosecute a war. The quality of national leadership and the institutional provisions for the mobilization of each citizen's abilities are more important. Dictatorial Germany conducted its war effort in an inefficient, wasteful, and disorganized fashion, while dictatorial Russia was far more effective in utilizing its citizens and industrial capacity. Great Britain contributed an even greater amount of its national manpower, government funds, and industrial production to the war effort than did the two dictatorships. The United States war effort, while outside the scope of this book, was another example of how a democracy can mobilize for total war. Therefore, it would seem that the adage which holds that an authoritarian government is better able to wage war than a democratic regime has little substance.

Germany was by far the most militarized of the major powers in September 1939. Under the Four-Year Plan begun in 1936, Germany spent more on its military absolutely and in relationship to gross national product than did any other state. The façade was one of an economy dedicated to military production, prepared for total war. However, in the first years of the war, 1939–41, there was almost no increase in Germany's military production. Hitler believed that the war would be won by Blitzkrieg tactics and that these would not require a great expansion of Germany's industrial plant. He preferred to expand "in breadth"—that is, by producing more weapons in already existing factories. The Wehrmacht office of weapons and munitions as well as high-ranking civilian economists—such as Albert Speer—wanted to expand "in depth" by building new factories to insure greater production in the future.[11] Expansion in depth, however, would have meant forgoing the immediate production of weapons for several years, and Hitler could not wait.

He also rejected arguments in favor of a total war effort—severe rationing, limitation of consumer production, and militarization of the civilian labor force—until the defeats at Moscow, in Africa, and especially at Stalingrad forced him to face the prospect of an extended war that Germany might lose. In fact, until 1943 the German civilian population was spared the sacrifices that the British public had had to accept from 1940. Civilian consumption remained high, rationing was used only sparingly, and even then class distinctions were preserved. Although all Germans were registered with the Labor Front, there was no civilian conscription for the war effort. Until 1944 Germany's labor shortage was met not with Germans but with Poles, Danes, Frenchmen, and Russians.

Nor was there any unified direction of the German economy until 1943. The German regime was much like the court of an absolute monarch. Power and responsibility was bestowed on the Fuehrer's favorites, not on the most qualified. This led to petty wrangling among the branches of government for Hitler's approval, even when catering to his whims might be dangerous for the war effort. Hitler seemed to enjoy this game.

---

[11] Wright, *Ordeal of Total War*, pp. 45–46.

He remained relatively aloof from day to day administration, except to occasionally intervene to establish, for example, priorities for production (e.g., new airplanes instead of more rifles). And his interventions were so capricious as to make long-term planning impossible.[12] There were five organizations with independent power over German war production before Stalingrad: the Four-Year Plan headed by Goering, the Ministry of Economics, the Ministry of Labor, the army's war economy and armaments branch, and finally, the Ministry of Weapons and Munitions. Each sought to control military production.

Albert Speer was the man who finally mobilized the German nation for total war. He became minister for weapons and munitions in February 1942, and constantly argued for a more rational organization of the economy. Hitler only made small concessions to him before Stalingrad, but that battle convinced the Fuehrer that the Third Reich would have to use every national resource if it was to survive. Speer became the economic dictator of the nation in 1943, and his accomplishments reveal how little "militarized" the German economy had been. Total military production had barely increased from 1939 to February 1942, yet it increased rapidly after Speer took over. "Using February, 1942, as the base month, the overall index rose to 153 in July, 1942, to 229 in July, 1943, and to 322 a year later."[13] Production of every kind increased even in the face of Allied bombings. Germany produced only 2,316 planes in June 1943, but turned out 3,538 in September 1944. The number of tanks produced increased sixfold from 1942 to 1944.

On March 15, 1945, Speer wrote to Hitler, "Within 4–8 weeks one must . . . count on the final collapse of the German economy." This despair had been brought on not by the incessant bombing of German factories, means of transportation, and urban centers, but by the denial to Germany of raw materials from France, Belgium, Russia, and the Balkans. Each advance of the Allied armies decreased Germany's supplies of minerals, petroleum and agricultural products. Germany had to stop fighting because her sources of supply had been cut off.

Great Britain, in contrast to Germany, began the war on the assumption that the war would be won by a prolonged blockade. Therefore, instead of rushing into arms production the British government systematically organized for economic warfare. At first, under the vacillating leadership of Neville Chamberlain, the reorganization was slow and uncoordinated. Chamberlain's optimism that Britain's obvious superiority would be deterrent enough for Hitler lulled the nation into apathy until German troops began to move westward in the spring of 1940. When Norway and Denmark fell, Chamberlain's credibility was exhausted. Even though a majority

---

[12] Berenice A. Carroll, *Design for Total War* (Paris: Mouton and Co., 1968), chap. 11.

[13] Toynbee and Toynbee, *Hitler's Europe*, p. 193.

of the House of Commons (281–200) was still willing to follow him blindly, the desertion of one hundred Conservatives—forty voted against him and sixty abstained—revealed the deep opposition within his own party. Therefore, Chamberlain resigned on May 10, 1940, and the king asked Winston Churchill to form a cabinet.

Churchill's War Cabinet contained only five men: Chamberlain and Lord Halifax representing the Conservatives and Clement Attlee and Arthur Greenwood for the Labour party. When Chamberlain resigned because of health in October 1940, Ernest Bevin, another Labourite, was added to the War Cabinet as minister of Labour. Each man on the cabinet was given absolute power in one area, so that decisions could be made quickly, Bevin, for example, became a czar in matters of manpower. He required that working conditions be acceptable to the workers and maintained wages at their prewar level. He realized the importance of working class support for the war, and his socialist beliefs convinced him that the government should respond to workers' grievances. With these values and the determination to act on them, Bevin was in large part responsible for the high morale in Great Britain after 1940. Churchill was constantly occupied with military affairs and foreign policy. If the British chiefs of staff differed with him, they were expected to be able to justify their position to Churchill personally. The War Cabinet, then, acted jointly only on broad policy issues.

From the beginning of the war, British governments demanded more of ordinary citizens than German leaders did. Rationing was applied under Chamberlain and fell on all citizens equally, with no special privileges, as in Germany, for government officials or socially prominent people. In fact, many urban dwellers enjoyed a healthier diet on rationing than they had before the war. Taxes were steeply increased both to pay for the war and to prevent inflation by taking money out of consumers' pockets. Once again, the taxes were lightest on the lower classes, while they attained 97 percent of the income of the wealthiest tax category. An excess profits tax prevented war profiteering by taxing 100 percent of all profits above those of 1939. Rents were frozen at their 1939 level. The minister of labor was given control of all labor by the Emergency Powers Act of May 22, 1940, and was allowed to assign and attach workers to particular jobs by the Essential Work Order of March 1941. Speer did not acquire similar power in Germany until 1943. Bevin used these powers sparingly, and due to his solicitude of the workers' welfare, his actions were rarely resented. Every man between fourteen and sixty-four was at Bevin's mercy.

The war was a great leveler. With all Britishers making the same sacrifices, with steeply graduated taxes and food rationing forcing all to the same living standard, the majority of Britishers realized that the postwar world could not be the same as the prewar society. Social reforms were enacted during the war, but more were proposed for the postwar era of "reconstruction." Most influential of the official reports published during the war was the Beveridge Report on "social insurance and allied services" which advocated that every Britisher should be guaranteed an income at subsistence level. This idea of a guaranteed minimum income was immediately popular with the British press and public, and Churchill seemed a lonely figure when he announced that consideration of such reforms must wait until the war ended. He had his way, but he was defeated soundly in the first postwar election. Other official studies of social problems were contained in white papers that recommended such revolutionary ideas as a national health service, government guarantees of full employment, and secondary school education for all and university education for the talented at government expense.

Since the British anticipated a long war, their economic program had been a long-range program of expansion in depth, converting and building more factories to produce the basics of modern warfare—steel, copper, rubber, etc. This program came to full fruition in 1943 when the United Kingdom reached its peak of wartime production. In that year Great Britain was second only to Russia in the percentage of her national product and of her industrial manpower invested in war production. Great Britain could not bear this economic burden alone and became heavily indebted to the United States both financially and politically during the war. Still, in any quantitative measure, Britain had a more thoroughly militaristic economy after 1940 than Germany did.

Russia had not been prepared for full-scale war when the Germans launched the Barbarossa Offensive in June 1941. During the purges of the thirties more than half of the Soviet officer corps had been either executed or sent to prison. To compound the personnel problem, very few Russian soldiers of any rank had combat experience before 1939, and this was still true when the German invasion began. Furthermore, the training of specialists was hampered by a lack of material—tank drivers had never driven tanks before they entered battle, and pilots had few hours of flying time because of the shortage of planes. Psychologically, the Soviet government had used the wrong approach to the war. They had assured their soldiers and civilians that the Red Army was invincible. This made the shock of defeat greater and weakened the willingness of Russians to endure a long struggle. Economic preparation for war was based on the assumption of a brief conflict. The Second Five-Year Plan had provided 12.7 percent of the budget to be spent for defense. This was increased to 26 percent after 1939, but still, the Russian production of arms could not increase rapidly enough to meet the German challenge. Until the amazing Russian victory at Stalingrad, it was not at all evident that the Soviet regime would survive.

Of course, the Russians could not have won such a stunning and decisive victory without a remarkable recovery from the first shock of German attack. Nor could they have subsequently defeated the Germans without the mobilization of the entire strength of the nation. This mobilization was achieved in the post-Rostov period by sweeping changes in the Soviet regime. Some of these changes were for the duration of the war only; others were to shape Russian society and politics after the war. The first alteration of the regime was the formation of the state defense committee with five members—a body very similar to Churchill's War Cabinet. The members formed the postwar Soviet leadership. Stalin was, of course, responsible for the general direction of the war but did not make arbitrary decisions as Hitler did. Other members and their areas of competence were V. M. Molotov, foreign affairs; Lavrenti Beria, political police and internal security; Georgi Malenkov, party matters; and K. E. Voroshilov, military affairs. There is no doubt that Stalin made the significant decisions, but the several policy changes he made during the war indicate that he knew how to listen to advice.

Perhaps the most important of his policy decisions was the exaltation of Russian nationalism. On November 7, 1941, the anniversary of the Bolshevik Revolution, Stalin deemphasized Communist ideology and praised the Russian national heritage. He invoked the memory of the saints and military heroes of imperial Russia in order to inspire the soldiers. As the military defeats of 1942 depressed the national spirit, the Soviet leaders seemed to draw strength from recalling the great battles of the czarist regime. The Germans were depicted as "imperialists" and the Russians as nationalists fighting for their homeland. Patriotic books and plays replaced the socialist realism of the 1930s. Concert audiences would burst into tears when listening to Shostakovich's Leningrad Symphony.[14] Ilya Ehrenburg became the foremost national poet. Before the war he had been attacked by official critics for his bourgeois romantic nationalism; during the war, his nationalistic poems were printed daily in *Red Star*, the army's newspaper.

Stalin felt that to unify the nation, insistence on ideological purity had to be temporarily set aside. His use of nationalism is but one example of this. Other instances were his restoration of the army and his increased toleration, not to say encouragement, of the Russian Orthodox church. Following the revolution the army had been democratized. Outward insignias of rank, except the most minimal, were abolished, and discipline was greatly weakened. Military commanders had been subordinated to the party by the appointment of political commissars to each unit to assure the political allegiance of both officers and men. Actually, these commissars could overrule the officers, causing great confusion during the first months of World War II. After the fall of Rostov, the last obstacle

---

[14] Alexander Werth, *Russia at War, 1941–1945* (New York: Avon Books, 1964), p. 385.

to the German army's advance before Stalingrad, Stalin completely reversed this trend by returning to the traditions of the czarist army. The slightest disobedience or show of weakness by a soldier was to be punished by execution. Officers could even execute a soldier without a court martial. During Stalingrad the political commissars were abolished, and new officers' uniforms were instituted with red or gold epaulets. Such epaulets had been torn from officers' uniforms by revolutionary soldiers in 1917. Finally, Stalin identified himself with the army by assuming the rank of marshal and appearing in a military uniform at all times. Of course, such a propaganda tactic had its dangers. After the war the Red Army was a formidable political force that sometimes clashed with the party leadership.

Realizing that most of his peasant soldiers were extremely religious, Stalin reversed another long-standing policy and rehabilitated the Russian Orthodox church. This was begun by an exchange of friendly notes between Stalin and the metropolitan of Moscow, Father Sergei. In September 1943, a church council was summoned, and Sergei was elected partiarch of the church and allowed to reestablish a formal church government, the Holy Synod. Furthermore, the Soviet government began restoring old churches and ceased its antireligious propaganda. There was no longer pressure on the general populace not to attend church—such pressure being limited to party members and the Komsomol. Stalin benefited greatly from his new relations with the church. Not only did he receive the church's support for his policies, but he had also improved his relations with Great Britain and the United States. After 1945 the new arrangement was continued, with Stalin making diplomatic use of the Russian patriarch as the international head of the Orthodox church, especially in his relations with the Balkan peoples.

While the appeals to nationalism, military pride, and religious sentiment unified the Russian people, it was Russia's industrial might that overwhelmed the Germans. Key to this economic achievement was an almost miraculous evacuation of Russia's factories from west of Moscow to east of the Urals. About 1,500 factories and industrial enterprises were disassembled brick by brick in 1941, transported thousands of miles to the east, and reassembled for immediate use. Of course, workers moved with the factories, resulting in a massive shift in population. The transferral reduced Russian industrial capacity in 1941 and 1942 to a critical point, but it made possible an industrial resurgence that later outproduced Germany in all areas of armaments. The bulk of Russian heavy industry had been permanently shifted to the east. The Battle of Stalingrad, fought before large amounts of aid arrived from the United States, was the first indication that the relocation of Russian industry had been a success. The vast majority of weapons used by the Red Army at Stalingrad had been manufactured in Russia. This meant that the Russian forces could meet the German military with equal material even if the Anglo-American supply lines were cut.

Resistance Movements: Two Examples

Opposition to Nazi rule took the form of organized resistance movements throughout Europe. Probably the most important of these movements, because of their influence on postwar developments, were those of Yugoslavia and France, but their evolution was very similar to the evolution of resistance movements in other countries. The period of greatest resistance activity began in early 1943, after the Battle of Stalingrad had forced the Nazi regime to make greater demands on the peoples under its control. These demands were usually economic—severe rationing of goods and, most importantly, the drafting of forced labor to be used in Germany. Many young men preferred to join the resistance rather than be shipped to Germany. All of the movements were split into traditionalists and social reformers. The traditionalists had as a goal the reestablishment of the pre-Nazi or prewar governmental and social system, but these were a small minority of the resisters. The social reformers wanted to build a new society after the war based on social democracy or communism. What Allen Dulles has written about the German resistance can be applied to the resistance movements in general: ". . . It was their inability to agree whether to look eastward toward communism or westward toward democracy which was the most serious threat to their unity."[15]

The Yugoslavian resistance was a clear example of this conflict. After Yugoslavia had been occupied in May 1941, the anti-German king and his government fled, and a Nazi puppet government was installed, led by the quisling Nedič. The first resistance to this regime came from peasant bands in the mountains of central Serbia. These Chetniks, as they were called, were led by a conservative military man loyal to the king, General Draza Mihailovič. The Chetniks were actually the prewar home guard and were imbued with nationalism, conservatism, royalism, and anticommunism. In a very short time they gained control of rural Yugoslavia, while Nedič's regime controlled only the major cities and roads.

The Yugoslav Communist party had an extensive underground organization that was mobilized to oppose the Nazis after Hitler invaded Russia. A Yugoslav who had spent many years in Moscow assumed leadership of the communist resistance. Joseph Broz, who took the fighting name of Tito, had become the general secretary of the Yugoslav Communist party in 1937 when all other ranking members of that party were purged on Stalin's orders. Even Tito's wife had been a victim of the

---

[15] Allen Dulles, *Germany's Underground* (New York: Macmillan Co., 1947), p. 165.

purge, which he helped direct. He was not an intellectual, being more of a gangland character than a politician. Fortunately for his nation he gained stature with responsibility. Also fortunate was his Croat origin and the multinational membership of the Communist party. Prewar Yugoslavia had been dominated by the Serbian nationality—the king was a Serb, and the military and bureaucracy were controlled by Serbs. The Croatians, as the second largest nationality group, would probably not participate in a postwar state in which the Serbs appeared once again to be dominant. The Communist party was perhaps the only political faction in prewar Yugoslavia that was not identified with a nationality group. It was a perfect instrument for the expression of a Yugoslav interest rather than Serbian, Croatian, Macedonian, or Bosnian interests. Tito, then, was able to overcome the bloody conflicts among Yugoslavia's nationalities as perhaps no other political leader could.

A civil war between the Chetniks and the communists was inevitable. A personal meeting between Tito and Mihailovič in October 1941 only confirmed their opposition. The meeting was, however, a diplomatic success for Tito. A British intelligence officer present was impressed and recommended that England back the communist and not the royalist. This change in British policy, however, did not occur immediately; so it appeared, during the winter of 1941–42, that Mihailovič had all the cards. He was backed by the Yugoslav government-in-exile, by Great Britain, and even by Stalin, who did not want to offend the British or Americans. Stalin requested several times that Tito reach a reconciliation with the Chetniks. But Tito was not willing to heed such advice. He was building a base of power as quickly as possible. As early as November 1941 he had proclaimed a people's republic in western Serbia and had established soviets on the Russian model in the areas he occupied. His growing strength drove Mihailovič into the arms of Nedič and the Italians. This thoroughly discredited Mihailovič among Yugoslav nationalists who turned to Tito as the true expression of national aspirations. By the fall of 1942 Tito had begun to construct a state administration, a police force, and a regular army. His provisional government—AVNOJ (from Anti-Fascist Soviet of the People's Liberation of Yugoslavia)—was soon accepted by Britain and Russia as the only viable resistance organization. In the following spring Churchill decided that all British aid should go to Tito, basically because Tito was able to kill more Germans than was Mihailovič.

This British decision virtually assured the existence of a communist government after the war. Tito, in fact, emerged from the war as the strongest military and political power in Yugoslavia. The progressively weaker position of the German troops in 1944 permitted AVNOJ troops to liberate virtually all of their nation before Russian troops arrived on the scene. Tito could therefore be dictator in his own right, not a puppet of Russia.

The largest armed resistance movement in western Europe was in France. As long as Vichy France remained unoccupied (from 1940 to November 1942), the resistance was territorially as well as ideologically divided. The resistance in the north, due to the presence of German troops and the Gestapo, was forced into greater secrecy than was necessary in the south. Therefore, the southern groups tended to have more adherents but to be less violent. Resistance in both sectors began almost as soon as the armistice with Germany was signed. At first this resistance took the form of propaganda against the Germans and noncooperation with the Vichy regime. As the occupation dragged on, sabotage became common, and after 1943, armed bands were formed throughout France.

The most characteristic feature of the French resistance was its fragmentation into many small groups along the lines of the political parties of the left under the Third Republic. One new element was added—an aggressively reformist Christian Democrat movement dominated by a resistance group in the South known as Combat. The communists had the best national organization, since their party cells transformed easily into clandestine cadres, and their strict party discipline prevented factionalism. The third major force in the resistance was a loose coalition of socialists, independents, radicals, and trade unionists that fought under different titles in different areas of France.

In 1942–43 General de Gaulle tried to unify all of these movements under the leadership of the Free French in order to have a stronger bargaining position vis-à-vis the United States and Great Britain. It was toward this end that de Gaulle sent Jean Moulin to France as a personal representative in January 1942. The unification was difficult to achieve. De Gaulle was distrusted by many leftists as a reactionary, and therefore, Moulin had to convince them that de Gaulle was not wedded to a restoration of the social status quo ante. This done, political rivalries among the various resistance groups was still a major problem. The Communist party, especially its organization in the occupied northern sector, was the most recalcitrant, probably because it had its own plans for postwar France.

Still, by May 1943, Moulin had succeeded in unifying the three major factions. In that month the first meeting of the National Council of Resistance (CNR) was held. Because of the demands for autonomy of certain groups, the CNR was never more than a symbolic body, meant to coordinate the general goals of the resistance. Its main accomplishment was to draw up the CNR charter, a statement of the new political regime that the resistance groups hoped to establish. The charter was socialist in tone and content, aiming at no less than an economic and social revolution by legal means. It was the blueprint for the French welfare state and planned economy that emerged after the war.

When the Germans began in 1943 to demand compulsory labor service from the majority of healthy Frenchmen—usually entailing deportation to Germany—a new phase of armed guerilla warfare began. As young men fled to rural, usually mountainous areas to escape deportation, they formed bands of resistance fighters and attacked the Germans wherever they could. The bands were given the name *maquis*—from the French term meaning "bushlands" or "badlands." Their bands varied in size from 15 to 500 men. The largest bands lived in the mountains of central France and in the Alpine valleys of the Swiss and Italian frontiers. The Allied invasion of France made it possible for the *maquis* to emerge and fight as a regular army. It was soon obvious that a very strong underground movement had developed, since the *maquis* army numbered from eight to ten thousand armed men. As France was gradually liberated from German control, the CNR quickly appointed liberation committees for each town and region. This assured them that political power would be in friendly hands when the time came to establish a new government.

The French resistance, as the resistance forces of other countries, has been greatly romanticized by overenthusiastic partisans, largely in an attempt to wash out the stains of Vichyite collaboration. For the French nation, however, the resistance was the affirmation that the humanitarian ideals and the reckless courage of the French Revolution still existed; and, if the French exaggerate a little as to the number of patriots who supported the resistance, who can blame them.

De Gaulle, Churchill, and Roosevelt

While the French resistance was struggling against Nazism in their homeland, a singular leader was organizing the Free French across the English Channel. General Charles de Gaulle learned of the decision of his government to request an armistice with the invading Germans on June 17, 1940 in Bordeaux. An undersecretary of war until Petain became premier, de Gaulle had argued for continuing the fight from North Africa. When he was convinced that defeatists had gained control of the French cabinet, he made the most momentous decision in his life. He flew to London on a British plane in order to continue the fight.

Raised in a Catholic aristocratic family and given a military education, de Gaulle was a conservative nationalist. In fact, his nationalism was so intense as to be an obsession and was only matched by his belief in his own destiny. In several books written during the interwar period, he characterized the great military leader as a man prepared in time of crisis to disobey his superiors and follow his own judgment. In retrospect, it is obvious that he was predicting that someday he would be called upon to disobey an order to save France. This was what he did in 1940, and Marshal Petain immediately labeled him a traitor.

On the night of June 18, the day the Franco-German armistice was signed, de Gaulle made his first broadcast over the British Broadcasting Corporation with Churchill's blessing:

Has the last word been said? Must hope disappear? Is the defeat permanent? No.

For France is not alone. She is not alone. . . . She has a vast empire behind her. She can unite with the British Empire, which controls the seas. . . . She can, like England, make unlimited use of the immense industry of the United States.

. . .

I, General de Gaulle, now in London, invite French officers and soldiers who are on or can reach British territory, with or without their arms—I invite engineers and specialized workers of the armaments industry who are on or can reach British territory, to put themselves in contact with me.

Whatever happens, the flame of French resistance must not and will not go out.[16]

The Free French movement had been born. De Gaulle's actions were favored by Winston Churchill who, resenting the French armistice that had left Britain to face Germany alone, had broken relations with the Petain regime.

The attitude of the United States State Department was not so friendly. The Americans saw no reason to break relations with the Vichyites. Instead, Cordell Hull, secretary of state, made it a firm policy to court them. Hull felt that American friendship might help maintain Petain's independence from Germany and, thereby, assure the neutrality of the French fleet, provide a base for U.S. intelligence activities on the continent, and preserve the neutrality of French North Africa. With these goals in mind, the United States sent food to Vichy, oil to Algeria, and appointed an ambassador to Vichy who was very sympathetic to Petain's government.

Of course, the American position did not please de Gaulle, but in 1940–41, he was occupied by trying to gain control and/or the allegiance of the former French colonies, since they were potential sources of a considerable force of colonial troops. He met with success first in the colonies of French Equatorial Africa. The black African and Franco-African administrators did not wish to be subjected to Hitler's New Order based on race; so in September and October 1940 the colonies of Chad, Cameroon, and the French Congo swore allegiance to the Free French committee.

It was his attempt to win over French colonies that brought de Gaulle into sharp conflict with his host, Churchill, and his greatest potential ally, Franklin Roosevelt. The first significant conflict arose over an abortive attempt to seize the important West African port of Dakar by combined British and Free French forces. The attempt failed and recriminations

[16] Milton Viorst, *Hostile Allies: FDR and Charles de Gaulle* (New York: Macmillan Co., 1965), p. 27.

ensued. De Gaulle resented the Royal Navy's rejection of his plan for a land operation in favor of a purely naval action—an attempt to bombard the port into submission. Churchill shrugged off the mission as a bad gamble, but the American State Department accused the Free French of having leaked the plans to Vichy because of lax security precautions. Roosevelt resolved never again to inform de Gaulle of an important military mission in advance. The next crisis grew out of the Middle Eastern situation where Frenchmen fought Frenchmen for control of Syria and Lebanon. De Gaulle contended that this "fratricidal tragedy" could have been avoided had England committed troops to the area briefly to convince the Vichyites of the futility of resistance. De Gaulle's severest conflict with the United States before the North African landing occurred when he seized Saint Pierre and Miquelon, two islands off the Newfoundland coast of Canada. The Americans saw no reason why the Vichyites should be ousted by force and resented any military action in the western hemisphere without American approval. De Gaulle ignored Secretary Hull's protests. It was a matter of prestige for both sides and caused lasting bitterness toward de Gaulle among the professionals of the State Department.

The Allied invasion of North Africa in November 1942 marked the beginning of the most bitter conflict between de Gaulle and his reluctant Anglo-Saxon allies. The operation was planned without consulting the Free French because of FDR's hostility toward the French general. When the invasion took place, the Americans tried to find their own French leaders, who would be more cooperative than de Gaulle. First they tried Admiral Darlan, an expremier of Vichy France. He was assassinated within a few days. Another Vichy figure, General Giraud, was annointed governor-general of Algeria and continued to use the personnel and techniques of the Vichy police state. These machinations inspired a howl of criticism from both the American and British press, that could not understand why de Gaulle was being passed over and deals being made with Vichyites.

Churchill was advising FDR that de Gaulle should be brought to Algeria, and Roosevelt finally consented in May 1943. A French Committee for National Liberation was established with de Gaulle and Giraud as cochairmen. De Gaulle was to handle political questions, and Giraud military affairs. De Gaulle, however, had no intention of sharing power and slowly eased Giraud out of the picture. By September 1943, Giraud was ousted from the committee, and de Gaulle proceeded to transform the committee into a government-in-exile in preparation for the liberation of France.

The United States did all in its power to prevent de Gaulle from imposing his government on liberated France—even stooping to negotiate with Pierre Laval for a reconvening of the prewar French parliament. But de Gaulle organized his administration before D-Day, and with the aid of the British and the French resistance movement, he was able to install his own administration in the liberated areas and in Paris as soon as it was taken by the Allies. Faced with a fait accompli, Roosevelt recognized the Committee of National Liberation as the de facto government of France on July 9, 1944, a month after the Normandy invasion had begun. De Gaulle entered Paris on August 25 and established his government in the state offices. The next day he walked slowly, regally down the boulevards of Paris at the head of a cheering, laughing procession.

Chapter 13

THE SEARCH FOR A PEACE SETTLEMENT

The military cooperation of Great Britain, the United States, and the Soviet Union from 1941 to 1944 was an amazing feat not only of logistical coordination and strategic planning but also of diplomatic skill and imagination. Each nation had been willing to subordinate its individual independence to the collective goal of defeating Germany. The Big Three leaders were unlikely allies. Winston Churchill was a staunch Conservative and anticommunist. Franklin Delano Roosevelt was a dedicated democratic reformer, wedded to liberal democratic principles and the free enterprise system. Joseph Stalin was a communist dictator, who had for years heaped scorn on the capitalist leaders of western Europe and America. Still they managed to hold together a world-wide coalition through four years of war that strained each nation's economy and social system to the breaking point. The approach of victory, however, weakened the alliance as the need to plan for the postwar world became as urgent as the need to cooperate militarily.

Suspicious Allies and the Liberation of Europe

The western Allies had followed their victory in North Africa by invading Sicily on July 10, 1943. For some time the Italian military and royal court had realized that Mussolini had chosen the losing side. It came as no surprise to Allied intelligence, then, when the Fascist Grand Council—monarchists and Fascists led by Marshal Pietro Badoglio—deposed and arrested Mussolini two weeks after the Sicily invasion. The Badoglio government immediately began negotiations with the Allies over a satisfactory peace. The talks achieved little until the Allied invasion of the mainland in early September forced the issue, and Badoglio then declared war on Germany.

During 1944 two rivals to the former Fascists appeared in the CLN (Committee for National Liberation), in the liberated south, and the CLNAI (Committee for National Liberation of the North), in the Nazi-held area north of Rome. Both organizations initially refused to cooperate with Badoglio's regime which included fascist generals and the discredited King Victor Emmanuel. Churchill favored Badoglio because he felt the Committee for National Liberation was subservient to the United States, which was only partially true. Both the American State Department and the British could agree that the CLNAI should not be allowed to gain power because of the revolutionary social program it favored, and because of the overwhelming influence of communists among the armed resistance to the Germans. The Russians, contrary to the beliefs of the British and Americans, were not encouraging a revolutionary course in Italy. In fact, while the United States and Britain debated the fate of their fascist allies in Badoglio's clique, Moscow formally recognized Badoglio and Victor Emmanuel as representing the legal Italian government. In return, Palmiro Togliatti, Stalin's hand-picked leader of Italian communism, who had been forced into exile by Mussolini, was allowed to return to Italy in March 1944. Togliatti urged a nonrevolutionary course for Italian communism and advocated the unity of all nonfascist parties until the end of the war. Togliatti's support for Badoglio was disconcerting to the western Allies. It made the Communist party an even more formidable political force than it would have been had it recklessly tried to confront the occupying powers in a show of force. "No longer intransigent and sectarian, its very reasonableness made it the most important political factor in Italy, for it could attract more conservative leftists as well as radicals still unwilling to go elsewhere."[1]

The United States and Great Britain governed liberated Italy through the Allied Control Commission and AMGOT (Allied Military Government for Italy). Repeated Russian requests for an influential role on the control commission were rebuffed with the reasoning that Italy was still a battle area. While certain that the democracies intended to crush any strong leftist movement in Italy, the Russians did not insist on equal rights, bowing to the laws of occupation by military force. Stalin, however, made careful note of the Italian precedent and later demanded that the United States and Great Britain give him the same latitude in eastern Europe that he had given them in Italy.

While the Russians were piqued over the Italian situation, the western Allies were highly suspicious of Russian plans for postwar Poland. From his first contact with the British, Stalin requested a treaty recognizing Soviet conquests in Poland and the Baltic area. The British were unwilling to admit the full extent of 1939 Russian gains but were amenable

---

[1] Gabriel Kolko, *The Politics of War: The World and United States Foreign Policy, 1943–1945* (New York: Random House, 1968), pp. 54–55.

to moving the Russian border westward to the Curzon Line. Roosevelt and the State Department refused to make any binding commitments before the end of fighting, and Churchill willingly accepted the American view. Throughout the war Stalin returned to this question of boundaries and was always met by the American refusal to negotiate while the fighting continued.

Intimately related to the question of the Russian frontier was the problem of relations between Moscow and the Polish government-in-exile in London. Stalin insisted on two prerequisites to his recognition of any postwar Polish government: recognition of Russian conquests in eastern Poland (especially, the acceptance of the Curzon Line as the western Russian frontier), and a promise to follow foreign policies "friendly" to Russia. The London Poles, however, were a group of conservative, anti-communist ultranationalists who would consent to neither of these conditions. Instead, they hoped to enlist Anglo-American support to maintain Poland's 1939 eastern border while expanding westward at the expense of a defeated Germany. Still, a breakdown of relations between Stalin and the Poles did not occur until the summer of 1943 when the Katyn Forest Massacre came to light. In April the German radio announced that the German army had discovered a mass grave in which 15,000 Polish officers and soldiers were buried. The Germans, never so vocal about Auschwitz or Dachau, publicized the grave, because they knew that only the Russians could have killed these men, prisoners of war taken in 1939. The London Poles requested an international investigation. Stalin used this request as an excuse to break relations with them and began to look for a more amenable group of Poles with whom to deal. He invited Polish communists exiled in Russia to form the Polish National Council, which he later imposed on Poland as a puppet government.

A final point of contention among the Allies was Stalin's request for and the Anglo-American postponement of a second front in Europe to relieve Russia of the burden of fighting the German army alone. Since 1941 Stalin had been virtually pleading with his Allies to invade France. The Big Three—Churchill, Stalin, Roosevelt—met to discuss the second front and other problems troubling their alliance at Teheran in November 1943. To this, their first meeting, each leader brought personal beliefs and considerations as well as a desire to protect his nation's interests. Churchill was a confirmed conservative and anticommunist. It was only because he was a supreme realist that he was willing to sit at the same table with Stalin, the embodiment of the Bolshevik revolution. During the war, however, Churchill saw Stalin as the heir of the Czars, seeking in eastern Europe the goals sought by Nicholas II during the First World War. Stalin, for his part, was extremely unsure of himself in international diplomacy. He had done all possible to persuade the western leaders to meet him in Moscow where he was more at ease. In his Kremlin he had been isolated from the world and had probably never thought, before 1940, of the eventuality of negotiating face to face with the heads of the two strongest capitalist states. He did not trust his allies and appeared to fear that they might even desert him and sign a separate peace with Hitler. This was a major reason for his insistence on a second front—to assure himself of their resolve to destroy the Third Reich. But a betrayal of Russia was far from Roosevelt's mind at Teheran. In fact, the American president proposed that after the war peace could best be served by the Big Four (FDR included China) acting as world policemen in their spheres of influence. In their negotiations, Roosevelt usually played the role of middle-man in the absence of a concrete program. American policy toward most major questions of peace was to postpone action until the cessation of combat.

At Teheran, it was decided that a second front would be opened by an Anglo-American invasion of France in May 1944. Churchill had tried to delay this by arguing for a Balkan invasion near the Dardanelles. His argument was based on the need to avoid a direct clash with Germany until the Reich's sources of raw materials had been exhausted. A side effect of a Balkan action would have been to place Anglo-American troops between Russia and south-central Europe, thereby making containment of Russia easier if the need arose. His idea was rejected by the Americans who were eager to strike the final blow at Germany. Concerning Poland, Great Britain and the United States tentatively recognized Russia's claim to the Curzon Line as the Russo-Polish frontier. No agreement could be reached as to the future government of Poland. Partially in return for the western concession over Poland, Stalin promised to enter the war against Japan as soon as Germany surrendered. The Teheran conference was the first halting step toward a final peace. Most problems of the future were discussed in general terms without any attempt at resolution. All three statesmen left with a feeling of accomplishment.

The following year was one of continuous military victories for the Russians. They marched across eastern Europe slowly and relentlessly, never overextending their forces, never pausing for long. By February 1945, when the next great inter-Allied conference was held at Yalta, they had occupied Hungary, Rumania, Bulgaria, part of Czechoslovakia, and had crossed Poland to the German border. One event in this succession of victories gave rise to scandal and horror in the Allied countries and increased the Western mistrust of their communist ally. On August 1, 1944, as the Soviet troops approached Warsaw, the Polish resistance exploded in an armed rebellion, hoping to liberate the city from the Germans. The resistance leaders were exmilitary officers loyal to the London government-in-exile and anticommunist. The Russian army stopped its forward advance outside the city and waited until the Germans had brutally crushed the revolt before overpowering them and entering the city. The Polish resistance (and, with it, any effective opposition to Stalin's hand-picked Polish government) was destroyed in the Warsaw uprising. In January 1945, the Russians resumed their methodical advance across Poland and into Germany. In their wake they left a puppet government at Lublin in southern Poland.

The Russian advance across eastern Europe had been general from Finland to Yugoslavia. Rumania was the first former ally of Germany to be occupied. The Rumanians had tried to arrange a separate surrender to Great Britain and the United States, but the western states—while worried about the form of government the Soviets might establish—quite correctly insisted on a simultaneous peace with all three powers. An Allied Control Commission was formed with Russia carefully adhering to the Italian precedent. This meant that, as Russia had been given no administrative power in Italy, the United States and Britain were denied any influence over Rumania's fate. As Russian political observers had been limited in their ability to travel in Italy, so Americans and Englishmen were restricted in Rumania. As the Anglo-American military had ultimate power over all events in Italy, the Russian commander in Rumania did not leave any doubt that he was the supreme authority. Still, the Russians did not use this dominance to impose a government. The prewar antifascist parties were allowed to form a liberal democratic government that included a minority of communists and procommunist politicians. The same policies were followed by Russia in Bulgaria and Hungary—except that in Bulgaria the native communists commanded the loyalty of a major portion, perhaps a majority of the population and dominated the coalition government. In none of these countries did the Soviets attempt a social revolution before Yalta. In fact, American observers on the scene reported that the Russians were a restraining influence on domestic revolutionary forces.[2]

Czechoslovakia, Yugoslavia, and Greece complete the mosaic of eastern European states being liberated from the Nazi empire. After 1939 the leading Czech statesman of the war years and after, Edward Beneš, had decided that the only hope for his nation's security lay in a close alliance with Russia. During the war he had cultivated Stalin's favor and promised that a liberated Czechoslovakia would follow a foreign policy friendly (but not subservient) to Russia. The American State Department considered such realism as evidence that Czechoslovakia would become a communist state and refused to approve the Russo-Czech treaty of friendship signed in Moscow on December 11, 1943. When Soviet troops occupied Beneš' homeland in late 1944, however, the Russians were scrupulous not to impinge on Czech domestic politics.

Yugoslavia had by 1944 come almost entirely under Tito's control. The British had the greatest influence there because of the aid they had provided the partisans. Churchill continued to try to arrange the return

---

[2] Ibid., pp. 156–61.

of King Peter II; but when he found Tito adamant against this, he settled for a coalition between Tito and elements of Peter's government-in-exile. As the Russians swept westward across southeastern Europe, Tito specifically requested that they not interfere in Yugoslav domestic affairs and received grudging agreement from an angry Stalin. Relations between the two men had been cool throughout the war, with Stalin constantly trying to order Tito to be less revolutionary, more conciliatory toward the conservative government-in-exile. This was in keeping with the communist united front policy being practiced everywhere. Tito refused to listen.

The Greek cauldron was also of special interest to the British. Prior to the war Greece had been ruled by an extreme right-wing dictatorship that had the blessing of King George II. It was this government, exiled in Cairo since 1941, that Churchill hoped to reimpose on Greece in 1944. But an extremely strong resistance movement had developed that desired a republican government. The National Liberation Front (EAM) was composed mostly of western-style liberal democrats with only a small faction of communists. Churchill chose to label EAM's supporters Trotskyite communists and anarchists and to crush them if possible. When British troops escorted the monarchical government to liberated Athens in November 1944, they demanded that EAM lay down its arms and submit to the conservative regime. The resistance quite predictably refused, and a civil war ensued. The fighting ended temporarily in February 1945, with the disarming of the resistance, but this was actually only an interlude in a Greek tragedy that was to continue into 1950. Stalin was overzealous in his aloofness from these events. When Russia did intervene, it was to instruct the local communists to reach an agreement with Britain on British terms.

Perhaps Stalin's attitude toward Greece was shaped by an understanding he had reached with Churchill in October 1944 on future spheres of influence in eastern Europe. In his memoirs Churchill dramatically recounts how he and Stalin divided the liberated East during a personal meeting in the Kremlin.

The moment was apt for business, so I said, "Let us settle our affairs in the Balkans." . . . I wrote out on a half-sheet of paper:

Rumania		
Russia	90%	
The others	10%	
Greece		
Great Britain		90%
(in accord with USA)		
Russia		10%
Yugoslavia		50–50%
Hungary		50–50%
Bulgaria		
Russia		75%
The others		25%

I pushed this across to Stalin, who had by then heard the translation. There was a slight pause. Then he took his blue pencil and made a large tick upon it, and passed it back to us.[3]

As colorful as this is, one should not give too much weight to it as a determinant of future policy on Stalin's part. He never tried to claim his "50 percent" of Yugoslavia, nor did he allow Great Britain and the United States "50 percent" influence over developments in Hungary. It appears that Stalin was motivated more by a desire to maintain good relations with the West without sacrificing his nation's security. Obviously he felt he must have "friendly" governments on Russia's western border and did not at first insist that these be communist governments. No where did he favor or support social revolution that might have alienated his allies.

The Americans and the British, however, chose to misread Russian policy, even when their own observers in Rumania and Greece reported the communists' conservative behavior. Churchill had constantly opposed communism (or even socialism) as a threat to western civilization. He simply feared the spread of the socialist revolution, much as Clemenceau had feared it at the end of the First World War. American policy, as shaped by Secretary of State Cordell Hull and his advisers, was not only negative in being anticommunist but was also positive in seeking a perpetual expansion of the Open Door policy. The goal was equality of trading rights for the United States with all other nations in all areas of the world. The goal of expanded trade and investment opportunities was the sine qua non on which all else depended. While Woodrow Wilson had seen the causes of World War I in the Old Diplomacy, Cordell Hull was certain that World War II was a result of economic competition caused by high tariffs and closed markets. He and his advisers were equally convinced that free trade was the only sure guarantor of political freedoms. Any limitations on the right of American businessmen to invest wherever they pleased was considered not only a blow to the American economy but also an attack on political freedoms, free enterprise, and world peace. A State Department special committee reported as much in December 1943.

A great expansion in the volume of international trade after the war will be essential to the attainment of full and effective employment in the United States and elsewhere, to the preservation of private enterprise, and the success of an international security system to prevent future wars.[4]

---

[3] Winston Churchill, *The Second World War,* vol. 6, *Triumph and Tragedy* (New York: Bantam Books, Inc., 1962), pp. 196–97.

[4] "Special Committee on the Relaxation of Trade Barriers," Kolko, *Politics of War,* p. 252.

Basing its foreign policy on these principles, the American government could not accept a Russian hegemony over eastern Europe that might lead to the exclusion of American investments.

Therefore, the growing Russian presence in eastern Europe had begun to worry the State Department by the fall of 1944. This concern prompted Secretary Hull to request his embassy in Moscow to supply an interpretation of Soviet policy. The ambassador, Averill Harriman, and the counsellor of the embassy, George Kennan, filed separate reports. Both reports stated that the credibility of Russian pledges was dictated by the military situation. They warned that there was no doubt that Stalin intended to establish a Russian sphere of influence in eastern Europe, and that the Soviet leader would never allow an international organization—such as the proposed United Nations—to interfere in Russia's relations with its neighbors. Harriman and Kennan had sent similar messages to Washington in the past, which had been consistently ignored. These were read closely and became a basic tenet of State Department policy.

Yalta

It was thus in an atmosphere of distrust that the Big Three—Churchill, Stalin, and Roosevelt—plus their advisors met at Yalta on the Black Sea in February 1945. Military affairs were uppermost in all minds, even though this conference was to be the first step toward a final peace settlement for liberated Europe. Both the Russians and the Anglo-American negotiators felt that Germany would mount a prolonged and bitter struggle, but her defeat was clearly in sight. With the other war—the Pacific war against Japan, predictions were more dour. The Americans expected the Japanese to continue resistance for perhaps eighteen months after Germany fell. For this reason, Roosevelt made his primary goal at Yalta a reaffirmation of the Russian pledge to participate in the war against Japan as soon as the Germans surrendered. Stalin desired certain preconditions be granted before he would make such a pledge. In order to gain Russian dominance in North China, he requested American support for a reactivation of the Russian lease on the Manchurian railroad. This would give Russia an excuse for stationing troops in Manchuria. To guarantee access to the Pacific, Stalin also desired leases to the termini of the Manchurian railroad at Dairen and Port Arthur, both vitally important ports. Finally, he hoped to regain for Russia the southern half of Sakhalin Island and the Kurile Islands, former czarist possessions north of Japan off Russia's Pacific coast. These demands, which promised to greatly increase Russian power in the Far East, were made for the most part in bilateral discussions between Stalin and Roosevelt. The Americans did obtain certain modifications. It was agreed that Russia would share its control of the railroad with Chiang Kai-shek's regime and would lease

They were optimistic at Yalta, the last meeting of the Big Three—
Churchill, Roosevelt, and Stalin. (Courtesy of UPI)

only Port Arthur from China, with Dairen becoming a free port open
to all nations. A separate agreement stipulated that there should be a
joint Russo-American occupation of liberated Korea for an indefinite time
after hostilities ended. Churchill, barely consulted on these negotiations,
gave his approval.

Agreement on the treatment of a defeated Germany was not so easily
achieved—in fact, was never achieved. The only concrete program adopted
had been drawn up before the conference convened by the European
Advisory Commission, a body established by the Allied foreign ministers
in 1943 to propose the terms of surrender and technical means of handling

occupation immediately thereafter. The EAC suggested the division of Germany into British, Russian, and American zones of occupation. An Allied Control Commission, located in Berlin, would attempt to coordinate occupation policies. Berlin, in the Soviet zone, would similarly be divided into three zones with all Allies having equal access to the city. The plan was adopted easily, but the Americans and British at Yalta, requested that a French zone also be created and that France be seated on the Allied Control Commission. Stalin, who had posed as France's best friend for de Gaulle's benefit, resisted French participation in the occupation until near the end of the conference. He argued that it would merely mean another nation on the ACC and that Yugoslavia was more deserving of such a position than France. He finally gave in when Roosevelt and Churchill assured him the French zone would be carved out of their zones. Churchill was relieved, for he was certain that the United States would withdraw from Germany as soon as possible (Roosevelt predicted within two years); and then Great Britain would have to bargain with Russia alone.

There was much sentiment at Yalta—as there had been at Versailles 26 years earlier—that Germany should pay for her sins by being crippled economically, partitioned into several small states, and forced to pay for the destruction wrought by her armies. At the Second Quebec Conference, September 1944, Roosevelt and Churchill had adopted a proposal—the Morganthau Plan, named after its initiator, FDR's secretary of the treasury—which called for the reversion of Germany to a pastoral economy. They had abandoned this extreme position by February 1945. The British were now opposed to drastic measures, finding it difficult to conceive of a revived European economy without a revived Germany. Economic penalties would, of course, be necessary, but these could take the form of reparations. Only the Russians had definite demands on the amount of reparations. They proposed that Germany pay $20 billion to the Allies in the form of finished products, industrial equipment, and "labor services." Half of the total should go to Russia, the other half to the other allies. Churchill claimed that this was grossly excessive: the Germans would starve, and the western states would have to feed them and pay their reparations. Stalin conceded that the $20 billion was merely a basis for discussion, and Roosevelt could accept that. Unable to agree on anything more specific, the Big Three referred the matter—like so many others—to the Council of Foreign Ministers which was to meet after the conference ended. One aspect of the Russian proposal suggested a particularly ghastly precedent: the use of forced labor as a form of reparations. Molotov, Stalin's foreign minister, explained this would entail the deportation of two to three million Germans for reconstruction work in the Soviet Union for ten years. The workers were to be recruited from among lesser war criminals, active members of the Nazi party, and the unemployed. Neither the United States nor Great Britain raised objections to such a callous use of humans.

Discussions of Poland's future consumed more time at the conference than any other issue. Russian troops had already occupied Poland, and Russia had recognized the communist Lublin Committee as the de facto government of Poland. Furthermore, British and American observers were denied freedom of movement in Poland. The issues at Yalta were familiar: Poland's postwar boundaries and government. Since Churchill's October visit to Moscow, Stalin had enlarged his boundary claims for the new Poland he hoped to control. The Allies had tentatively agreed on a western boundary along the Oder River and the eastern branch of the Neisse River. At Yalta Stalin demanded that the Polish-German frontier run along the Oder and western Neisse, an alteration that would add another 8,100 square miles to Poland, an area with a prewar German population of six million. Having accepted the Curzon Line in the east, the Anglo-Americans opposed the western Neisse frontier, refusing to make an official commitment except to admit that Poland should be compensated in the west for area lost to Russia in the east. The "who shall govern" problem was just as intractable. The western powers adamantly refused to recognize the Lublin regime as the provisional government, insisting that a new coalition be formed of the communists, the noncommunists within Poland and the London Poles. Stalin insisted that the question of the nature of the provisional government was not vital, since it would last only a month or two, until elections could be held to determine the preferences of the Polish people. Somewhat relieved at this prospect, Roosevelt and Churchill were willing to accept a minor reorganization of the Lublin cabinet so as to include representatives of democratic elements from within Poland and from Poles abroad. The communists were still clearly the dominant element, but the Big Three also agreed that the reorganized provisional government "shall be pledged to the holding of free and unfettered elections as soon as possible on the basis of universal suffrage and a secret ballot." No international inspection was provided for this election, but the diplomatic representatives of the three powers in Warsaw were to serve as observers.

Both Roosevelt and Churchill desired influence in the administration of the other liberated areas of eastern Europe. In the absence of a clearly defined policy, the State Department proposed a joint Declaration on Liberated Europe that was intended to limit Russia's freedom of action. The proposed declaration stated that the Big Three would help the former Axis satellites to establish conditions of internal peace, to carry out emergency measures for relief of distressed peoples, and most importantly, "to form interim governmental authorities broadly representative of all the democratic elements in the population and pledged to the earliest possible establishment through free elections of governments responsive to the will of the people." The declaration was adopted, but each ally interpreted it differently. Roosevelt felt it was an alternative to the spheres of influence approach of Churchill and Stalin. The Declaration presupposed tripartite responsibility and action in all areas of Europe. Churchill envisioned a lever with which he might later pressure Russia over Poland. To Stalin, the declaration was apparently considered a piece of propaganda rhetoric and an expression of general goals without being a mandate for joint action.[5] In fact, the declaration guaranteed that no state would be censured by the other two by requiring unanimity to precede action.

When, in the opinion of the three governments, conditions in any European liberated state or any former Axis satellite state in Europe make such action necessary, *they will immediately consult on the measures necessary to discharge the joint responsibilities set forth in this declaration* [italics added].[6]

It should also be noted that Russia defined "democratic elements" differently than the Western Allies.

A final major question at Yalta was the organization of the United Nations. The establishment of an international organization symbolized the American determination to continue the wartime coalition of nations as a permanent peace-keeping force. Of course, the fact that the United States, with the votes of its client states in Latin America, was certain to dominate the United Nations also served American national interests. It was this probable American dominance that caused Stalin to demand safeguards for Russia—a veto on actions by the Security Council and membership in the General Assembly for White Russia, the Ukraine, and possibly Lithuania. The same probability encouraged the State Department to try to expand the powers of the proposed organization as greatly as possible by limiting the veto power of the members of the Security Council—i.e., the Great Powers. The British shared American hopes for an effective United Nations, but Churchill preferred to protect British interests by the more traditional combination of military strength and diplomatic accommodation. Therefore, the British were not as intensely interested in the structural questions as the Americans and Russians.

The general structure of the United Nations had been agreed on at the Dumbarton Oaks Conference of October and November 1944. There would be a General Assembly consisting of all members, each having one vote. A Security Council would contain the Great Powers—Great Britain, Russia, United States, France, China—as permanent members. Both of these bodies could initiate actions, with decisions on sanctions against violators of international law being reserved for the Security Council except in certain special circumstances. A Secretariat would supply

---

[5] William Hardy McNeill, *America, Britain and Russia, 1941–1946* (London: Oxford University Press, 1953), p. 551.

[6] William L. Neumann, *After Victory: Churchill, Roosevelt and Stalin and the Making of the Peace* (New York: Harper and Row, Publishers, 1967), p. 151.

a permanent corps of international civil servants to keep the UN operating and to administer its decisions for action. Finally, international disputes could be adjudicated by the International Court of Justice. Little in this structure was new, but the relationships among the various bodies differed from the League of Nations.

Membership in the UN was to be limited to those nations which had fought against Germany and Japan. The United States thus urged all the Latin American nations to declare war on Germany before the war ended. Great Britain insisted that the members of the Commonwealth—Canada, New Zealand, South Africa, even India—be granted separate seats. Faced with these two large blocs of Western capitalist states, the Soviets would be outvoted consistently. This was the fear that prompted Soviet requests for a Security Council veto and for multiple membership. At Dumbarton Oaks Russia proposed membership for all sixteen Soviet republics. At Yalta the number was reduced to three. Roosevelt tried to persuade Stalin to forego the extra votes by warning that American public opinion might require membership for each state of the Union if the Russian request were granted. Stalin would not be wavered and volunteered to support an American request for additional seats. Unable to deter the Soviets, Roosevelt agreed that the United States would support extra seats for Russia at the organizational meeting of the UN to be held in San Francisco in April 1945.

The veto question was worked out in an equally indecisive compromise. Whereas Russia wanted the Great Powers, as permanent members of the Security Council, to have a veto on all matters that came before that body, the United States proposed that the veto only apply to questions concerning positive action and that questions of procedure—such as whether or not a matter should be discussed—be exempted from the veto. After being convinced that this would still allow the Soviet Union enough latitude to protect itself from the American-dominated Security Council and General Assembly, Stalin agreed to this proposal.

The adjournment of the conference and the publication of declarations on Germany, Poland, and liberated Europe were greeted with praise and even joyous optimism in all allied countries. The Soviet press lavished fulsome praise on the agreements. *Pravda,* in a special edition, noted that "the alliance of the three big Powers possesses not only a historic yesterday and victorious today, but also a great tomorrow."[7] Optimism was just as evident in the West. Despite its several problems, the wartime alliance did indeed seem capable of enduring the tests of peace.

On to Potsdam: Conflict Outweighs Compromise

The goodwill engendered by Yalta and by victory on the battlefield was dissipated by events of the following months. In March and April

[7] McNeill, *America, Britain and Russia,* p. 563.

1945, as the Red Army swept across eastern Europe, the West became increasingly anxious over the spread of communism. A crisis developed in Rumania only two weeks after the Yalta Conference adjourned. A pro-Nazi dictator had been replaced in the fall of 1944 by a "Popular Front" government containing representatives of all Rumanian parties, including both communists and former German sympathizers. The premier who headed this strange coalition was General Nicolae Radescu. His cabinet was very slow in initiating social reforms—such as a redistribution of the land—and in purging profascists from the civil bureaucracy and courts. The Rumanian communists used the lack of reforms as a propaganda weapon to gain supporters, and they held violent demonstrations in Bucharest with the blessing of the Russian military. Radescu denounced these demonstrations on February 24, 1945, in a nationwide radio broadcast. He charged that a handful of communists were trying to subdue the nation by terror. The Soviet chairman of the Allied Control Commission reprimanded Radescu, and the communist press charged him with allowing the police to slaughter the demonstrators. Finally, communist cabinet members demanded that King Michael, whom the Russians had left on his throne, dismiss Radescu and replace him with someone more representative of the "democratic"—i.e., the communist—forces in the country. This obvious attempt by Russia to dictate the appointment of a premier led to strong protests from both the United States and Great Britain but to no avail. Stalin merely pointed to the Italian precedent where Moscow had been denied any voice in occupation policies.

Ignoring the West's protests, therefore, the Russians began a series of events that, with slight variations, was to be repeated many times in eastern Europe.[8] On February 27, A. Y. Vishinsky, a Soviet deputy foreign minister, arrived unannounced in Bucharest by plane from Moscow. He ordered King Michael to oust Radescu and find a premier acceptable to the Rumanian Communist party. King Michael searched for two days for a noncommunist premier, but no one he suggested satisfied the Communists. Finally, Vishinsky put forward his own candidate, Petro Groza, who, although not a communist himself, was known to favor much of the communist program. For this reason, moderates and conservatives refused to cooperate with him. Consequently, when Groza formed his government, thirteen of the seventeen ministries were headed by communists or communist supporters. Communist control of Rumania was guaranteed, even though other parties were still allowed to exist, and the myth of a Popular Front coalition was maintained.

Throughout this episode the United States and Great Britain protested Russia's unilateral actions. The protests were simply ignored until Groza had formed his government. Then the West was informed that the question was closed since a "democratic" government had been established in

---

[8] Hugh Seton-Watson, *The East European Revolution,* 3d ed. (New York: Frederick A. Praeger, Inc., 1966), pp. 206–07.

Rumania. The State Department formally replied that it did not consider the Groza regime a "representative" government as had been provided for at Yalta. The American complaint obviously had no effect.

In Bulgaria and Hungary the West also had reason to look suspiciously at their eastern Ally, although the Russians were not quite as high-handed in dealing with these countries. The advancing Red Army had encouraged and aided a revolutionary coup in Bulgaria in the fall of 1944. The following spring a communist minister of interior carried out a police purge of not only pro-Nazis but also of anitcommunist moderates. With the police in communist hands, there was little protection for opposition politicians, but a form of Popular Front coalition developed nevertheless. This meant that there could be free debate within the governing coalition but that such freedom did not extend to opponents of the coalition. Events in Hungary were remarkably similar, except that the noncommunist socialists were stronger in Hungary than in the Bulgarian coalition.

Poland, however, was the country most closely watched in the West. It was considered the ultimate test of Russian intentions.[9] The Yalta Conference had provided for the expansion of the Lublin government to make it "representative" of all democratic parties in Poland, which meant to the West the inclusion of the London government-in-exile's supporters. Yet, in the weeks after Yalta, Russia refused to allow any well-known, prestigous noncommunists to join the provisional government. Even more galling, in keeping with the Italian precedent, the Russians refused to allow American or British observers (officials or journalists) to travel freely in Poland. On March 13 Churchill wrote to FDR that, in Poland, they were witnessing an utter collapse of the Yalta agreement. Roosevelt still did not wish to become too deeply involved in the Polish question, but he found that the whole range of East-West conflicts was forcing him to support Churchill. At the end of March the two sent a joint protest to Stalin, saying that the Polish situation had become "entirely unacceptable." Stalin replied with an equally pessimistic defense of his policy. His note began, "Matters on the Polish question have really reached a dead end." He proposed a new start based on what had become known as the "Yugoslav Formula." In Yugoslavia Tito had formed a coalition government with a three-to-one communist majority, and Stalin suggested this be applied to Poland.

At this critical moment Franklin Roosevelt died. Harry Truman became the American president on April 12, 1945, and one of his first acts was to approve the British rejection of the "Yugoslav Formula." Stalin then recognized the Lublin government as the legal government of Poland. There is scant reason to believe that Roosevelt would have eventually acted differently than Truman. In fact, Truman kept Roosevelt's top

---

[9] Kolko, *Politics of War*, pp. 392–93.

foreign policy advisers and leaned heavily on them. Edward Stettinius, Truman's secretary of state, shared Cordell Hull's belief in the need for an ever-expanding market if the American way of life were to be preserved. Many of the high ranking State Department officials were more militant than Stettinius about the need to roll back the growing Soviet dominance of eastern Europe. The influence of these men on the' new president, who was reviewing all aspects of foreign policy, was great. They recommended that he have an "immediate showdown" with the Russians. Particularly significant were the dispatches of Averill Harriman from Moscow. Harriman bombarded the State Department with communiques in early April. Perhaps the most influential Harriman note arrived on April 6. The ambassador analyzed Russian policy in terms of three faces. One face radiated cooperation with the United States on such international projects as the United Nations. Behind the second face the Russians provided for their own security by securing control of states on their borders. The third face was that of the international communist conspiracy that sought to subvert other countries by using local democratic parties to take advantage of the democratic process and the dislocation caused by the war. Harriman concluded that there was much evidence that Roosevelt's attempts to work with the Soviets had been interpreted as a sign of weakness in Moscow.[10] This final argument was to be used by all future cold warriors who opposed conciliation and detente with the Soviet Union.

Truman then was faced with the choice of continuing Roosevelt's policy of obtaining American goals by negotiation with Stalin or of taking a hard line by basing future policy on considerations of power alone. Truman finally opted for the hard line, for a confrontation when the time was right, but, while changing tactics, his goals remained those of Roosevelt—expansion of the Open Door, preventing socialists from coming to power wherever possible, and resisting the extension of Russia's influence. The first occasion to test the hard line came soon. On April 23 Truman had an interview with the Russian foreign minister, Molotov, who was visiting the United States for the opening of the United Nations at San Francisco. Truman was extremely blunt. He repeatedly told Molotov that an agreement had been made on Poland, and the United States expected Russia to honor that agreement. Molotov commented, "I have never been talked to like that in my life." Truman replied, "Carry out your agreements and you won't get talked to like that."[11] When Stalin heard of the interview, he sent a note to Washington saying that the United States and Great Britain had not considered Russian interests in Belgium and Greece, and Russia had not interfered in those countries. Therefore, Russia did

---

[10] Gar Alperovitz, *Atomic Diplomacy: Hiroshima and Potsdam* (New York: Vintage Books, 1965), pp. 22–24.

[11] Ibid., p. 33.

not expect the United States or Great Britain to interfere in questions vital to Russian national security.

The already strained Soviet-American relations became even tenser when Truman abruptly ended lend-lease aid to Russia on May 8, the day the Germans formally surrendered. The Soviets felt betrayed. They had made economic plans on the assumption that the American aid would continue. Now they concluded that the Americans were trying to slow Russia's economic recovery from the war. Obviously, the Americans had decided that the possibility of economic aid was a better diplomatic tool than the existence of economic aid. A breakdown of Soviet-American relations seemed possible in the summer of 1945. It was avoided by continued cooperation on purely military matters—especially by the United States' decision to allow Russia to occupy Berlin and Prague. The decision on Berlin was made on strictly military grounds. Churchill and the British argued that Russian actions in eastern Europe showed that the western Allies should gain every advantage in central Europe by occupying major cities first. Truman consulted the Joint Chiefs of Staff, and they advised that political considerations should not overrule the "paramount military considerations." Truman heeded his military chiefs, not his ally; and the Russians entered Berlin on May 2, 1945. The same scenario occurred in relation to Prague. While Churchill urged Truman to push American troops deep into Czechoslovakia, Commanding General Eisenhower rejected the idea. The Red Army occupied Prague.

There seems to have been a contradiction between Truman's decision to follow a hard line and his willingness to see Russia ensconced in European capitols. In this regard the advice of Truman's secretary of war, Henry Stimson, was important, and American research on the atomic bomb was decisive. Stimson favored continued cooperation with the Soviet Union because it was the only way a new stability in Europe could be achieved. On the other hand, he also felt an understanding with Russia should be negotiated only when the United States could demonstrate its superior economic and military strength. Therefore, Stimson argued the United States should *postpone* a showdown with Russia until the atomic bomb had been tested. After that the United States would be able to force Stalin to listen to American advice about eastern Europe and the Far East. Truman adopted this policy of a "delayed showdown" which implied avoiding diplomatic crises until the bomb was ready.

Therefore, ignoring Churchill's continued pleas for a confrontation in central Europe, Truman sent a personal representative, Harry Hopkins, to Moscow at the end of May. Hopkins's mission was an overwhelming success. Almost all major questions between the United States and Russia were discussed, and a few were resolved. The key to the entire trip was that both sides were willing to compromise on Poland. Hopkins agreed to the Yugoslav Formula Truman had rejected only a month before. The

Polish government was to be reorganized with twenty cabinet members—four of them from the London group. Stalin agreed to allow some of the prominent exiled leaders to take these positions. Even Stanislaw Mikolajczyk, the obstinate former leader of the London Poles, was accepted. All other questions seemed suddenly capable of resolution. Agreements were soon reached on the occupations of Germany and Austria, and the new Polish government was appointed one week after Hopkins left Moscow.

Hopkins had prepared the way for the meeting of the Big Three that took place at Potsdam from July 17 to August 2. The American delegation arrived in an ambiguous position. The success of the Hopkins mission had led to the Big Three conference before the atomic bomb had been demonstrated publicly or even tested; therefore, Truman and his advisers decided to be firm at Potsdam but not to allow any final decisions. This strategy was followed with the result that the tension and distrust between East and West was exacerbated. On the first day of the conference, Truman bluntly charged that Russia had violated the Yalta Agreement on liberated Europe; and he suggested, to erase this breach of faith, the immediate reorganization of the Rumanian and Bulgarian governments and immediate consultations among the "democratic" factions in the various countries to plan free and unfettered elections. Stalin replied that these were domestic affairs and not the concern of the conference.

This bitter sparring continued for three days, until Truman received the report of the first successful test of the atomic bomb on July 21. With this knowledge, Truman lost all interest in bargaining. He was confident that once the bomb had been used on Japan the United States would be able to influence events in Europe by its obvious military superiority. After this, as Secretary Stimson has written, Truman "was frank about his desire to close the Conference and get away."[12] Churchill agreed with Truman about the importance of the bomb. He had been trying to convince the American president to lead Stalin into compromises, but the news of the bomb brought Churchill around to the policy of delay. The British leader later wrote, "From that moment our outlook on the future was transformed. We were in the presence of a new factor in human affairs, and possessed of powers which were irresistible."

This attitude of confidence and intransigence led to an impossible situation. Truman would make the most extreme American demands on each question and refuse to make concessions; this would be followed by a statement expressing willingness to postpone the question until a later date- –usually the Council of Foreign Ministers meetings to be held in the fall. By that time the bomb's power would have been demonstrated against Japan. As a result virtually all issues were passed along to the

---

[12] Ibid., p. 152.

Foreign Ministers Council. One clear position, however, was taken at Potsdam. The United States stated categorically that it would not officially recognize the communist-dominated governments until free elections were held.

The net result of the Potsdam Conference was to confirm the deepening rift between East and West, between Moscow and Washington. Atomic bombs were dropped on Hiroshima and Nagasaki only days after the conference adjourned—August 7 and 10, 1945. With the devastating power of the bomb clearly demonstrated, the United States tried once again to persuade Russia to change its policy of creating friendly communist governments. Once again, in spite of the bomb, the Russians refused. This confrontation occurred at the London Conference of Foreign Ministers in September 1945. It was the first major conference after Hiroshima, and the Americans learned their first lesson about the bomb. It was so powerful that it could rarely, perhaps never, be used again. Therefore, it had very limited value as a bargaining point. The political conferences had failed. It was left for the Americans and Russians to work out a peace based not on negotiations but on the balance of power.

Chapter 14

A NEW STABILITY ACHIEVED, 1945–48

During the period between the Potsdam Conference and the coup d'état that destroyed democracy in Czechoslovakia in January 1948, the European nations were divided into two military and ideological blocs. The Soviet Union and the United States usurped the leadership of these blocs and controlled the foreign and domestic policies of their allies to as great an extent as possible. For Russia's allies, this meant complete control. The United States' allies, being politically and economically stronger than the eastern European states, managed to preserve some independence. The Europeans, who had dominated world politics for so long, were reduced to a secondary role on the world stage, while the superpowers struggled like two Gullivers in Lilliputia. Neither Russia nor the United States desired this situation, although both societies were based on ideologies that pretended to world-wide applicability. The leaders of each state interpreted the world situation in such a way as to blind them to alternatives to global competition. The crucial matter is to understand the reasons for their failure to see alternatives.

Stalin's motives and the motives of his foreign policy advisers cannot be analyzed as can those of the Western leaders. Yet, enough evidence is available to reject the idea—once taken for granted by Western politicians—that Stalin wished to achieve a communist world and the communization of eastern Europe was only the first step. At the end of World War II, Stalin acted in accordance with a principle of "socialism in one zone"; just as in the 1920s he had adopted "socialism in one country."[1] There is no evidence of universal ambitions on the part of the Soviet leadership. Rather, there is abundant evidence that they desired increased

---

[1] Isaac Deutscher, *Stalin* (New York: Oxford University Press, 1967), pp. 552–53.

security for the Russian state and for the revolution in the form of friendly buffer states along Russia's European border. This was considered an essential minimum, a deserved reward for Russia's vast sacrifices. Stalin had demanded such a buffer zone from Hitler and, later, from Churchill in return for his participation in the war. All of the prewar eastern European governments, except Czechoslovakia, had been anticommunist dictatorships and Stalin was determined to prevent the emergence of such hostile neighbors again. Therefore, Soviet control over eastern Europe was little different than American control of Latin America. Russian demands for trade preference and suppression of anticommunists was little different from United States control of Latin American economies and the suppression of leftist governments that threatened American economic interests.

In the immediate postwar years Great Britain, Italy, and France were totally occupied with domestic reconstruction, radical departures in social welfare and economic planning, and crumbling empires. The United States had the only healthy economy among the liberal democratic states. The American leaders, therefore, looked to their economy as the hope of mankind in a world threatened by poverty and revolution. If that economy were to remain healthy, they felt, eastern European markets must remain open for American trade. They were also motivated by the more general fear of and contempt for the socialist threat to free enterprise. Therefore, their kindest interpretation of Russian policy was that it was an attempt to construct a Soviet empire. Their most severe interpretation (and the one most widely held) was that control of the eastern European economies was merely a prelude to an attempt to communize all of Europe and to destroy the United States by gradually closing off markets to American trade and investments. Ultimately, it was not profits that the Americans wished to protect but "the American way of life," which they could not divorce from free enterprise. Free enterprise and free trade, they felt, were necessary prerequisites to political freedom and individual happiness.[2]

Diversity in Eastern Europe

It is ironic that the fear of communism was increasing in the West at a time when the Soviet Union was acting as a conservative force to restrain revolutionary movements throughout Europe. Communist parties in all countries had been reduced to subservience to Moscow during the 1920s and 1930s. During the war, Stalin had to cooperate with the capitalist countries and ordered all communists to follow a United Front policy

---

[2] Barton Bernstein, "American Foreign Policy and the Origins of the Cold War," ed. Barton Bernstein, *Politics and Policies of the Truman Administration* (Chicago: Quadrangle Books, 1970), p. 59.

MAP 9. Central and Eastern Europe, 1945–1948

SOURCE: Martin Gilbert, *Recent History Atlas* (London: Wiedenfeld and Nicolson, 1966), map 94.

by joining with all antifascist parties, even the most conservative, in order to defeat Germany. Pursuing this policy, communists became important elements of the resistance movements throughout the Nazi empire, and they emerged from World War II as the strongest parties in France and Italy and as important parties, though not the most popular, in all the eastern European states. Continuing the United Front policy, communists entered postwar coalition governments from France to Bulgaria with strict orders from Moscow not to gain power through revolutionary means lest they jeopardize Russia's relations with the United States and Great Britain. In both France and Italy, for instance, the communists were more conservative than the socialist parties. It was because Tito did not follow these instructions and immediately established a communist dictatorship that he first came into conflict with Stalin.

Stalin did not desire revolutions in late 1945 and early 1946 for several reasons. He still hoped for financial aid from the United States and for agreement with both Western Powers over German reparations. Also, he could not be sure that the capitalist states would not interfere in eastern Europe and hoped not to provoke them into intervention. Most importantly, perhaps, spontaneous revolutions in eastern or western Europe probably would not have been communist controlled but would have been led by social democrats in the West and by agrarian or peasant parties in the East. These leftist groups were the communists' worst enemies because they might achieve reforms that would diminish communist support. Furthermore, there were few "pro-Soviet" politicians in eastern Europe who, having gained power in a domestic revolution, would be willing to follow Russia's foreign policy closely enough to satisfy Moscow.

The eastern European states could be divided into three categories on the basis of their prewar social structure.[3] Poland and Hungary were dominated by large landowners, aristocrats who employed large numbers of landless agricultural laborers. At the end of the war these land-hungry workers, now unemployed, agitated for sweeping land reforms—especially the distribution of the large estates to the peasantry in the form of small farms. The second category included the several Balkan states—Rumania, Bulgaria, Yugoslavia—where the problem was overcrowding of the land. The majority of farms in these countries were too small to support families or to supply produce to be sold commercially. The "underindustrialization" of the Balkans was largely responsible for this rural overcrowding and the poverty that accompanied it. There were no industrial cities to lure excess workers away from the farm. If urban centers could be developed, not only would the pressure on the land be eased but also a market would be created for commercial farming. The need, then, was evident for a Soviet-type rapid industrialization and a consolidation or collectiviza-

[3] Hugh Seton-Watson, *The East European Revolution,* 3d ed. (New York: Frederick A. Praeger, Publisher, 1956), pp. 6–22.

tion of farms into larger producing units. Czechoslovakia is the unique member of the third category—the only state to have a modern industrial plant and a large urban working class as well as a politically active bourgeoisie. It was also the only eastern European state with a democratic tradition. The Czech workers were predominantly Social Democrats, although the Communists had some support. In all of these countries, there were strong peasant parties before 1939 which had embodied the aspirations for justice of the rural populations. After the war, however, these parties had strong leaders only in Poland and Hungary.

TABLE 14.1. Percentage of Peasants in Total Population in 1939

Czechoslovakia	34
Hungary	55
Poland	63
Yugoslavia	75
Rumania	78
Bulgaria	80

SOURCE: Hugh Seton-Watson, *The East European Revolution*, 3d ed. (New York, Frederick A. Praeger, Publisher, 1956), p. 13.

Poland was the nation watched most closely by the West in an attempt to ascertain Russian intentions. Following the Hopkins mission, a coalition government had been formed consisting of sixteen communists and four representatives of other groups. Most importantly, Mikolajczyk became vice premier and minister of agriculture as a representative of the People's party, a peasant group. The Communists, however, controlled the key ministries of interior (the police), war (the military), and public information (the propaganda machinery). Moreover, when Mikolajczyk tried to reorganize his party, several of his leading supporters were assassinated. Still, he managed to rebuild the People's party sufficiently to call a national party congress in January 1946. The Communists had promised elections within a year after the coalition was formed but repeatedly postponed them, trying to pressure Mikolajczyk to merge his party into the government bloc, consisting of the Communist party and three subservient parties. Mikolajczyk refused, determined to make the elections a test of Communist popularity.

The Communists were not to allow that. Of the 2,000 delegates traveling to a People's party congress in March 1946, only 800 arrived—the others having been arrested. The Communist-controlled press denounced Mikolajczyk as a "British agent." Yet, in spite of this harassment, Mikolajczyk managed to present an opposition list of candidates in the parliamentary election of January 1947. It was to no avail. The government bloc won 394 seats; the People's party captured only twenty-eight seats; and other minor parties obtained twenty-two seats. Less than a month later the new Polish legislature adopted a constitution based on the USSR constitution of 1936. The persecution of Mikolajczyk's supporters was intensified, and, in October 1947, Mikolajczyk left Poland. The one-party state was confirmed by the merger of all parties into the Polish Workers' party in December 1948. After this, opposition to the government was illegal.

Besides physical intimidation and arbitrary, brutal police procedures, the Polish communists had also carried out positive reforms that won them popular support, and similar tactics were employed generally by communists in eastern Europe. Large landed estates were initially distributed among the peasants in small private plots. (Collectivization came later.) At first, land was taken only from "fascists" or "collaborators," but these definitions could be stretched to include all large landholders. Second, the communist government was able to expand the national boundaries with Soviet aid. For Poland, this entailed the annexation of East Prussia, the expulsion of Germans living there, and the distribution of the land to Poles. The distribution of such newly acquired land was skillfully handled so as to gain new supporters for the communists. Finally, major industries were nationalized in the name of penalizing Nazi collaborators. Actually, there was very little industry to be nationalized in most of eastern Europe, so this was merely a symbolic act that few opposed but many welcomed.

The Polish pattern of reform and the repression of opponents was followed, with local variations, in Bulgaria, Rumania, and Hungary—the states most clearly controlled from Moscow. Significantly, in each of these states as in Poland, an opposition was allowed to exist outside of the governing coalition until 1947. It was only after the Truman Doctrine had been enunciated and the Marshall Plan proposed that these states were Stalinized. This is a crucial fact to be considered when trying to judge Russian intentions in eastern Europe after Yalta. It does not appear that, before 1947, Stalin had decided to impose Soviet-type regimes on these countries. He hoped that communist-dominated coalitions would be sufficient to guarantee friendly neighbors for Russia. Of course, the internal logic of authoritarianism would probably have converted all of the satellites into one-party regimes eventually; but the conversion occurred when it did because of the increasingly bellicose position taken by the United States on the Greek question.

Two eastern European states did not follow the general pattern: Czechoslovakia and Yugoslavia. Czechoslovakia's social democratic leaders adopted a neutral position between East and West even before World War II ended and hoped to act as a bridge between the two ideological camps. According to an agreement between Stalin and the Czechoslovak government-in-exile, upon liberation local government was to be in the hands of "people's committees" until a legitimate national government could be established. Created in the wake of the advancing Red Army, the committees were usually dominated by communists. Therefore, a communist government could have been easily created in 1945 with little resistance from other parties, but the Soviets chose not to establish such a regime. Instead, the Russians remained true to the United Front policy, and a coalition was formed among communists, social democrats and the Peasant party. A parliamentary election was held in May 1946. This was an honest election, with the Communists doing well but falling short of a majority. They received 38 percent of the vote cast, the Socialists 18 percent, and the Peasant party 16 percent, with minor parties sharing the remainder. The Communist party leader, Klement Gottwald, as head of the largest party in the legislature, became premier and continued the United Front by bringing non-Communists into his cabinet.

Despite continual friction, this coalition functioned until the summer of 1947. By that time, abuses of power were diminishing, the rule of law was almost completely reestablished, and debates in parliament were free and open. Noncommunist politicians and newspaper editors spoke out against the Communist premier, and Gottwald had responded by observing legality, not by suppression. On July 7, 1947, however, the Czech government accepted an invitation to a preliminary conference on the Marshall Plan. An ultimatum from Stalin arrived the following day. The Czechs were to reject the invitation immediately or consider their friendly relations with the Soviet Union terminated. The Czechs, of course, rejected the invitation.

The rejection of the Marshall Plan by Czechoslovakia and other East European states marked the end of the United Front policy. The Czech Communists now assumed complete control of the nation. They accused the leaders of other political parties of treason, or of disrupting the national economic plan, or of other crimes. The Communist minister of interior Nosek packed the police with his supporters in preparation for the parliamentary elections the following spring. In February 1948 the crisis burst into the public. A majority of the cabinet—representatives of democratic parties—resigned in protest against the actions of Nosek. This was an ill-considered move. They had hoped to force Gottwald to resign. Instead, Gottwald armed communist trade unionists and allowed them to occupy the offices of the absent cabinet officers. Gottwald then formed a government controlled completely by the Communists. Any opposition to the government was considered treason. The one-party state was confirmed in the summer of 1948 by the fusion of all parties with the Communist party. An election in May returned a 90 percent vote for the government's candidates.

The one exception to Stalin's United Front policy was Tito's regime in Yugoslavia. Tito had achieved a 96 percent electoral victory as early as November 1945, because he had allowed only one list of candidates. Yugoslavia seemed to fit the Western stereotype of an orthodox Soviet state, and Tito often made much of his "orthodoxy." Yet, there was more conflict between Stalin and Tito than between Stalin and Gottwald, the leader of a very nonaggressive communist party. Tito's greatest crime was that he was too revolutionary; he had formed an orthodox one-party state while Moscow was endorsing United Front coalitions. This independent line might endanger Stalin's broader policy goal, which was continued cooperation with Great Britain and the United States.

Tito's habit of considering himself supreme in Yugoslavia led to many petty disputes with Moscow. For instance, Milovan Djilas, Tito's leading ideologue, dared to say that Russian army officers had behaved more roughly toward Yugoslav civilians than had British officers. The Yugoslav secret police dared to keep Russians under surveillance as if they were citizens of a bourgeois state, while the Yugoslav government dared to object to Russian secret service activities in their country. Stalin's wounded vanity at such insulting independence seems to have played a large part in the Tito-Stalin feud.

In 1947 the conflict was intensified when Tito began negotiating with other Communist regimes—Bulgaria in particular—with the goal of forming a Balkan Union of People's Democracies. This, of course, would amount to the elevation of Belgrade to the position of a second Vatican of communism. The idea rapidly gained popularity, promising Bulgaria and Rumania the chance to play Belgrade against Moscow, and, thereby, gain some flexibility in foreign policy. It was to some extent to preempt Tito that Stalin organized the Conference for the Exchange of Information among Communist Parties (Cominform). It was an attempt to return to the days when Moscow dictated policy to all communist parties through the Communist International (Comintern). This act meant the end of diversity in eastern Europe and the beginning of *Stalinism*. Stalinism was the assertion by Moscow that all communist regimes be directly subordinate to Soviet directives. This implied a uniform institutional structure in all states—monolithic, one-party states with identical political, social, and economic policies. Before this attempt to endorse conformity, there had been no ideological problem of Titoism. After the founding of the Cominform, however, there was no room for diversity—not even for an overzealous imitation of Stalin's Russia.

Tito and the Yugoslav communist leadership were determined to maintain autonomy for their party and for their state. In April 1948 Tito defined the situation for the party Central Committee: "Comrades, remember, this is not a matter here of any theoretical discussion. . . . The point here, first and foremost, is the relations between one state and another." Because of Tito's refusal to subordinate himself and his party, the Yugoslav Communist party was expelled from the Cominform on June 28, 1948. The year 1948, then, was not only the year a monolithic Soviet bloc was completed; it was also the year in which Titoism or "national communism" was born, a deviation from Stalinism that would later lead to considerable disunity within the Soviet bloc.

The Division of Germany

If Soviet dominance in eastern Europe troubled Great Britain and the United States, the joint occupation of defeated Germany was to become the source of more clashes. The Russians were suspicious of Western motives in arguing for low reparations for Russia. They were also alarmed by the hasty manner in which the Anglo-Americans deserted the wartime appeals for a demilitarized, deindustrialized Germany to call, in 1946, for a revived German economy. The Soviets were determined that Germany should not be restored to the position of a military power—a view shared by the French. Therefore, Germany soon became another testing ground for East-West cooperation.

The task of German reconstruction that faced the Allies was immense. Governmental authority had broken down. Major cities were rubble heaps. In Cologne, for example, only 50,000 of the city's 750,000 prewar population were still living in the city in June 1945, the rest having fled to small towns to escape the bombings. In addition to 66 million Germans seeking food and shelter, the Allied administrators had to provide for eight million nationals of other countries liberated from concentration camps and labor camps. German refugees expelled from Poland, Czechoslovakia, Hungary, and elsewhere amounted to another ten million displaced persons.

Until Yalta and Potsdam, it had been assumed that, in the immediate postwar period, such problems would be handled by an Allied Control Commission acting as a temporary administrator for all of Germany. This was not to be. As each power established an administration within its own zone of occupation it became increasingly clear that each wanted to mold Germany in its own image or, at the least, to its own interests. The United States was the most anxious of the three Western states to reconstruct a political system. Four *Laender* were organized on the pattern of American states but without a central government to coordinate their actions. Local governmental bodies were appointed by mid 1945, and *Land* elections for constitutional conventions were held in June 1946. The resultant constitutions provided for extremely strong *Laender,* guaranteeing a federal structure for any future German state. The British and French *Land* governments were modeled on those of the American zone. Yet, the British, in contrast to the Americans, did not allow the *Laender* to exercise the powers traditionally reserved for a national authority. Both occupying powers, however, soon recognized the need for German zonal authorities to aid in reconstruction. By 1946 the *Laender* in each zone had been brought under the authority of such zonal commissions. This was the first tentative step toward a single central government. The French protested against these attempts at Germany's political revival. No German zonal agencies were allowed in the French sector and very little local government. The French were intent upon arousing a separatist movement in the coal-rich Saar and in exploiting their zone to obtain reparations.

The most rapid centralization of authority occurred in the Russian zone. By October 1945, the Russians had created twelve central administrations to deal with industry, trade and supply, labor and social affairs, education, justice, and all the other responsibilities of a national government. Obviously, these administrations could be easily converted into a "cabinet"—the structure for a national government had been built. The next Soviet step was to sponsor the merger of the SPD in their zone with the Communists (KPD) to form the Socialist Unity party (SED). This party became Russia's instrument in controlling East Germany's politics.

The greatest source of friction between East and West over Germany was the matter of reparations.[4] Although no absolute total for reparations could be agreed on, the Russians insisted that they had been promised at least ten billion dollars at Yalta and immediately began stripping their zone of its industrial equipment even before the Potsdam Conference convened. At Potsdam it was agreed that each Ally should take its reparations from its own zone; but, since the Anglo-American zones were predominately industrial, the agreement further stipulated that industrial products from the western zones would be exchanged for agricultural products from the Russian zone, thereby hopefully making both sectors self-sufficient. There remained the problem of determining the industrial capacity needed to support Germany's population. In March 1946, the Four Powers decided that Germany's heavy industry would be reduced to between 50 and 55 percent of its 1938 level.

Unfortunately, all such calculations were built of sand. In the first instance, the cooperation among zones was not given a chance to function due to the insistence of France and the Soviet Union to immediately rebuild their own economies with German materials. By early 1946, the Russians had stripped their zone of one half of all its industrial facilities. Second, it soon became obvious that the Allies had underestimated the cost of keeping the Germans alive. The United States and Great Britain were forced by spring 1946 to decrease drastically the reparations taken from their zone and even to import certain goods. Their difficulties were compounded in May when the Russians defaulted on the delivery of food

---

[4] Edgar McInnis, Richard Hiscocks, and Robert Spencer, *The Shaping of Postwar Germany* (London: J. M. Dent and Sons, Ltd., 1960), pp. 26–31.

from the agricultural east. In retaliation, the American occupation authorities suspended the shipment of industrial reparations to the Soviet zone, and the British followed suit.

Their inability to secure Russian cooperation on economic matters, the restrictions placed on all parties except the SED in the Soviet zone, and alarm at Russian policy elsewhere in eastern Europe led the Anglo-American leaders to conclude in the summer of 1946 that they must reverse their policy toward Germany. The American secretary of state James Byrnes announced this reversal in Stuttgart on September 6, 1946, when he called for a revival of the German economy. Secretary Byrnes, to make his message clear, also rejected the Oder-Neisse Line as Germany's eastern boundary, called for the establishment of a provisional central government of all of Germany, and stated that the American military presence would not be withdrawn from central Europe in the foreseeable future. The policy change announced in this speech was soon given form by the fusion of the American and British sectors into a new economic and administrative entity called Bizonia. The Russians had already created the framework for an independent government in eastern Germany. The final division of Germany had begun.

A Global Conflict

The cold war between Russia and the United States had its origins in the Bolshevik Revolution and the Western reaction to it. It did not assume its final form, however, until March 1947, when Truman placed Soviet-American relations in the context of a global ideological struggle between freedom and tyranny. Since Yalta there had been many points of conflict between the two powers—Poland, Turkey, Germany—but these had been treated as separate conflicts that could be negotiated or resolved by the traditional principles of power politics. Only in 1947 did the separate incidents merge into a life or death struggle between "democracy" and "communism." The merger was purely an intellectual one—no more real in 1947 than in 1945, but beliefs held strongly enough have a way of being self-fulfilling. The American belief in the universality of the "Communist threat" was strengthened by the fact that the Western liberal democracies were on the defensive everywhere during 1945–47. Not only were Great Britain and France wracked by the economic stresses of reconstruction, but revolution-minded nationalists were rapidly gaining popularity in French and British colonies. The revolutionaries were invariably socialists, more friendly to Russia than to the United States. In China a powerful communist army led by Mao Tse-tung was battling an American favorite, Chiang Kai-shek, for control of the world's most populous nation.

Two incidents that suggested to Americans that Russia wished to build an empire beyond eastern Europe concerned Iran and Turkey.[5] In each case Russian goals were both limited and nonideological. Iran had been occupied by Great Britain and Russia during the war to prevent the vast oil fields from falling into enemy hands. Both powers and the United States, which had become omnipresent in the oil-rich Middle East, had agreed to withdraw their troops within six months after the end of hostilities in Europe. The Russians, however, hoped to use their position to gain oil concessions similar to those already enjoyed by the two western states. To this end, the Soviets sponsored an uprising among tribesmen in northern Iran against the national government and, on the pretext of supporting this revolt, started moving more military forces toward the Iranian border in March 1946. Alarmed, Secretary of State Byrnes dispatched a warning to Moscow that the United States was gravely concerned over the Iranian situation. This warning was sufficient to lead to Russo-Iranian negotiations and the withdrawal of the Russian troops. The Iranian prime minister promised Russia an oil concession in the Azerbaijan region, but stipulated that the Iranian parliament would have to ratify the agreement. After the Russian troops had withdrawn, the parliament refused to ratify the concession.

A similar confrontation occurred when Russia attempted to obtain a base at the Dardanelles, to guarantee herself a voice in the governance of the straits that connected the Black Sea with the Mediterranean. This had been a goal of Russian policy for at least a century and in no way had ideological overtones. Yet, when the Kremlin tried to force a treaty on Turkey recognizing joint control of the Straits, President Truman remarked to a cabinet meeting, "We might as well find out whether the Russians [are] bent on world conquest now as in five or ten years,"[6] and ordered the United States' largest aircraft carrier, the *Franklin Roosevelt,* four cruisers, and a destroyer flotilla to Istanbul. Turkey, obviously strengthened, rejected the Russian proposal, and the Soviets meekly dropped the matter.

Therefore, as late as August 1946, the United States and Russia were still reacting to each crisis as it arose, but the idea of a global ideological conflict was gathering strength. In a public speech in February 1946, Stalin personally warned Russian citizens that the struggle between capitalism and communism had not ended. The comment was part of a broader exhortation to the Soviet people to accept sacrifices for economic growth. The same month the Soviets brought charges in the Security Council of the United Nations against the attempts of the British and Dutch to suppress revolutionaries in Greece and Indonesia. The western response to Stalin came from an unofficial but immensely prestigious figure, Winston

---

[5] André Fontaine, *History of the Cold War,* trans. D. D. Paige (New York: Pantheon Books, 1968), pp. 279–90.

[6] Walter LaFeber, *America, Russia and the Cold War* (New York: John Wiley and Sons, Inc., 1967), p. 29.

Churchill. Having been removed from office by the British electorate after campaigning on the sole issue of anticommunism, Churchill was visiting the United States in March 1946, just as the Iranian crisis was reaching a climax. Speaking at small Westminster College in Fulton, Missouri, with Truman at his side, Churchill noted that an "iron curtain" had divided Europe and proposed a joint American-British military establishment to resist the expansion of communism. He advocated "the fraternal association of the English-speaking peoples" to protect "the freedom and progress of all the homes and families of all the men and women in all lands. . . ." Mentioning the strength of communism in Italy and France, Churchill warned that "in a great many countries, far from the Russian frontiers and throughout the world, Communist fifth columns are established and work in complete unity and absolute obedience to the directions they receive from the Communist center." Everywhere save in the Anglo-Saxon nations, "the Communist parties or fifth columns constitute a growing challenge and peril to Christian civilization."[7] Despite Truman's presence on the platform, the United States government announced that it had not endorsed Churchill's speech and considered it merely the expression of a private opinion. *Pravda* attacked Churchill, noting he had chosen to speak in the United States rather than in Great Britain where his "red danger" campaign had been rejected by the voters. Stalin bitterly commented that Churchill had begun "the work of unleasing a new war with a race theory, asserting that only English-speaking nations are full fledged nations, who are called upon to decide the fortunes of the entire world."[8]

The Anglo-Russian debate moved increasingly to the center of international affairs toward the end of 1946. When the Big Four foreign ministers met in Paris in mid June, Ernest Bevin, representing Britain, answered the Soviet accusations at the UN by commenting that imperialism was dead in Britain but perhaps "our place has been taken by others." Molotov then gave a concise statement of the Soviet interpretation of world affairs:

Nineteenth century imperialism may be dead in England, but there are new twentieth century tendencies. When Mr. Churchill calls for a new war and makes militant speeches on two continents, he represents the worst of 20th century imperialism [sic] . . . Britain had troops in Greece, Palestine, Iraq, Indo-China and elsewhere. Russia has no troops outside of security zones and their lines of communication. This is different. We have troops only where provided by treaties. Thus we are in Poland, for example, as our Allies are in Belgium, France and Holland. I also recall that Egypt is a member of UNO [United Nations Organization]. She demands that British troops be withdrawn. Britain declines. . . . What shall we say of UNO when one member imposes its authority upon another? How long can such things go on?[9]

[7] *Vital Speeches of the Day*, 12 (March 15, 1946), pp. 329–32.
[8] D. F. Fleming, *The Cold War and Its Origins, 1917–1950,* vol. 1 (Garden City, New York: Doubleday and Company, Inc., 1961), p. 353.
[9] LaFeber, *America, Russia and the Cold War,* p. 29.

It was the inability of Great Britain to maintain its dominance in the Middle East that precipitated the final crystallization of the cold war in the form of the Truman Doctrine. Since 1945 the British had been propping up conservative regimes in Greece and Turkey which would have toppled without such support. Having aided the Greek monarch George II crush the republican forces of ELAS, the British organized elections in 1946 that returned a majority for the king's supporters. The republicans then resorted to guerilla tactics, which they had once used against the Nazis, in an attempt to oust the king. Great Britain, which had 40,000 troops in Greece, concluded that Moscow was trying to extend its East European empire. Nothing could have been more erroneous. Stalin had scrupulously avoided involvement in Greek affairs and had counseled all communist states bordering Greece—Yugoslavia, Bulgaria, Albania—to do the same. It was another sign of Tito's independence from Moscow that Yugoslavia was the chief source of aid for the Greek rebels.

Whatever the source of the rebellion's strength, the British decided in early 1947 that they could no longer afford the vast expenditures necessary to prop up the Monarchy. Although the Labour government, with Ernest Bevin making policy, was eager to resist the communist flood, the British economy prohibited their attempting this. In the fall and winter of 1946–47, industrial production in England had slowed to a halt. Government expenditures for reconstruction and social welfare guaranteed a budgetary deficit. Therefore, on February 21, 1947, the British ambassador in Washington informed the State Department that Great Britain could no longer subsidize the Greek and Turkish regimes. The obvious implication was that the United States should assume leadership in the battle against the revolutionary forces.

The British announcement came as no suprise to the American government, which had been preparing for such an eventuality for some time. As early as September 1946, the same month that Byrnes announced a continued American military presence in Germany, the Truman administration had prepared programs of military aid for Greece and Turkey. An economic mission had been sent to Greece in January 1947 to estimate the regime's needs. So, on March 12, only nineteen days after the British ambassador's statement, President Truman went to Congress with a complete program. In presenting his request for funds to Congress, Truman did not limit himself to the Greek political situation but developed a comprehensive ideological justification for future requests and future American interventions to resist revolution.

. . . Totalitarian regimes [he said] imposed on free peoples, by direct or indirect aggression, undermine the foundations of international peace and hence the security of the United States.

.   .   .

President Truman announcing the Truman Doctrine to a joint session of the United States Congress, March 12, 1947 (Courtesy of UPI)

At the present moment in world history nearly every nation must choose between alternative ways of life. The choice is too often not a free one.

· · ·

I believe that it must be the policy of the United States to support free peoples who are resisting attempted subjugation by armed minorities or by outside pressures.

I believe that we must assist free peoples to work out their own destinies in their own way.[10]

The President then asked Congress to appropriate $250 million for aid to Greece and another $150 million for Turkey. The Truman Doctrine was accepted.

Having taken the vital plunge in terms of long-range policy, Truman and his advisers next turned to what seemed to them the critical state of western Europe. Communists were participating in governments in France, Italy, Belgium, and elsewhere. The European economy was not recovering rapidly, so it appeared that the communist parties would gain

---

[10] Norman Graebner, *Cold War Diplomacy 1945–1960* (Princeton: Van Nostrand, Inc., 1962), p. 151.

more supporters from the ranks of the unemployed. A comprehensive plan for economic recovery was needed, and only the United States had the wealth to subsidize such a plan. The new secretary of state George C. Marshall announced his country's proposal in a momentous speech at Harvard University on June 5, 1947. Noting the state of European affairs, Marshall said that Europe "must have substantial additional help, or face economic, social and political deterioration of a very grave character." While stressing the United States' desire to furnish the economic assistance needed, he made the conditions that "the initiative . . . must come from Europe" and "The program should be a joint one, agreed to by a number, if not all, European nations." The Marshall Plan, later officially entitled the European Recovery Program, had been offered to Europe.

France and Great Britain were quick to respond. Since Marshall's speech had specifically avoided excluding the East European communist states, Bevin and Georges Bidault, the French minister of foreign affairs, invited Russia to send a representative to Paris to discuss Europe's response. Foreign Minister Molotov arrived with a large retinue of economic advisers on June 26, apparently willing to consider participation in the American program. The Russian concept of the program, however, could not be reconciled with Anglo-French proposals. Molotov desired bilateral aid from the United States to recipient nations without international coordination and without prior agreement on the expenditure of funds. Bevin and Bidault thought this unworkable and preferred a unified European approach, which presumed a cooperative determination of the needs and priorities of each nation as well as of Europe as a whole. Unable to change their minds, Molotov broke off discussions on July 2 and returned to Moscow. Undaunted, Bidault and Bevin invited all European states except Spain, which was still considered fascist, to send representatives to a conference on the Marshall Plan to meet in Paris on July 12. The following days were crucial for the future of Europe. By July 11 every eastern European state had rejected the invitation. The Czechoslovak refusal was the most revealing. Even though the Czech prime minister was a communist, Klement Gottwald, the Czech cabinet voted unanimously on July 4 to attend the Paris conference. A threat soon arrived from Moscow that Czechoslovakia's attendance would result in the end of the Soviet-Czech alliance. Bowing to Russia's will, Czechoslovakia, the most independent of the East European regimes except for Tito's Yugoslavia, announced that it would not be at Paris. The Conference was attended by only the West European states plus Greece and Turkey and eventually requested $22 billion in aid from the United States.

Both sides continued to refine the justifications for their policies. In July an article appeared in the semiofficial American journal *Foreign Affairs* entitled "The Sources of Soviet Conduct" which argued that permanent war against capitalist nations was inherent in the nature of the Soviet regime. The author, actually George Kennan, head of Truman's new policy planning staff, warned that the United States' only safe course was "a long-term, patient but firm and vigilant containment of Russian expansive tendencies." Later Kennan would argue that he intended this policy of "containment" to apply only to Europe and only to acts of armed Soviet aggression, but, in 1947, it was greeted by the American press and public as a call to a world-wide crusade against socialism and revolution wherever they appeared. Thus, the article completed the development of American policy signaled by the Truman Doctrine and the Marshall Plan.

The Russian answer was the formation of the Cominform. Ostensibly a mechanism for the various communist parties to exchange information and ideas, this organization, announced by Molotov on July 6, 1947, became the conduit for Stalin's orders to other communist leaders. The first meeting of the Cominform was held in Poland in October. Stalin's number-two-man and leading ideologue, Andrei Zhdanov, shaped the communique issued at the end of the meeting. It read, in part,

Two camps have been set up in the world: on the one side, the imperialist and anti-democratic camp whose essential purpose is to establish world domination by American imperialism and to smash democracy; on the other side, the anti-imperialist democratic camp, whose essential purpose is to undermine imperialism, to reinforce democracy, to liquidate the remnants of fascism.

The statement also denounced the socialists of Italy, France, Germany, and other nations, making continued participation of communists in cabinet coalitions with socialists impossible.

The ideological division of Europe was further rigidified by domestic political developments. Shortly after Truman's speech announcing America's policy toward Greece, communists had either withdrawn or been expelled from coalition governments in France and Italy. Similarly, all dissent to communist rule in eastern Europe was definitively suppressed by February 1948. The iron curtain Churchill had spoken of at Fulton had finally been built. It not only divided East from West, but it also separated communists from their fellow countrymen in western Europe. It would be over a decade before cracks would begin to appear in the wall that would allow Europeans to speak to one another as neighbors once more.

Chapter 15

CAUTIOUS REVOLUTIONS IN WESTERN EUROPE

While communist regimes were being imposed on eastern Europe, popularly elected socialist governments were legislating sweeping reforms in western Europe. Conservatives in all countries had been discredited by their inability to deal with the depression and their sympathy for or collaboration with fascism. On the Continent, communists, socialists, and liberal Catholics had dominated the resistance movements and were determined to build a new society. In Great Britain the Labour party had been responsible for domestic war policy, while Churchill concentrated on foreign affairs, and had experimented with a planned, controlled economy. Therefore, the postwar adoption of socialist policies had been well-prepared, and the establishment of the welfare state was a foredrawn conclusion by 1945.

Great Britain's Cautious Revolution

Winston Churchill's defeat in the general election of July 5, 1945, was the most striking symbol of the rejection of the prewar Right. In the midst of the Potsdam Conference, Churchill and Clement Attlee, the Labour party leader, had returned to London for the counting of the votes. Only Attlee flew back to Potsdam, for the British people had rejected Churchill's leadership at the moment of victory. Great Britain had a Labour government and would have one for the next five and a half years. This government enacted a revolution in British economy and society, making impossible a return to laissez faire economics or governmental aloofness from problems of social welfare.

The contrast between Conservative and Labour campaign strategies had been apparent to all. The Conservatives offered Churchill and a continuation of the wartime coalition. The Labourites, rejecting continued coalition government, offered a comprehensive program of social and economic reform. Churchill led the Conservative attack on this legal revolution by trying to raise the specter of a communist tyranny in the Misty Isle. In a radio broadcast, he warned his listeners against the siren song of socialism.

There can be no doubt that Socialism is inseparably interwoven with totalitarianism and the abject worship of the State. . . . Socialism is in its essence an attack not only upon every enterprise, but upon the right of an ordinary man or woman to breathe freely without having a harsh, clumsy, tyrannical hand clapped across their mouth and nostrils.[1]

Churchill ended the broadcast with a horrible prophecy that Britons would live under such a totalitarian state if Labour won the election. Attlee ridiculed this antiquated approach to social reform—as did the press in general. *The Manchester Guardian* had no patience with what it called this "moth-eaten debate on Socialism versus free enterprise."

The Labour party, on the other hand, presented a program of specific legislative goals designed to achieve a more efficient and more just economic and social order through economic planning and public control of industry. These were the issues about which the public was most concerned. A public opinion poll taken during the campaign showed that the three top issues in the "public's mind" were housing, full employment and social security, in that order. The percentage of voters switching parties since the last election (12 percent) was the largest switchover since 1906.

TABLE 15.1.   Results of British Elections

Party	1945		1950		1951	
	Seats	Votes, %	Seats	Votes, %	Seats	Votes, %
Labour	393	47.6	315	46.1	295	48.8
Liberal	12	9.0	9	9.1	6	2.5
Conservative	213	39.6	298	43.5	321	48.0
Other	22	2.8	3	1.3	. . .	0.7

SOURCE: T. O. Lloyd, *Empire to Welfare State* (New York: Oxford University Press, 1970), pp. 269, 308, 313.

The British electorate was ready to accept Labour's program for several reasons. First, they remembered the horrors of the 1930s. Conservatives had governed Great Britain almost without break from 1919–39, and the result had been unemployment, appeasement of Hitler, and World War II. And few could forget that, in the 1930s, the Conservative party leader-

---

[1] Alfred F. Havighurst, *Twentieth Century Britain*, 2d ed. (New York: Harper and Row, Publishers, 1962), p. 365.

ship had refused to allow Churchill any position of authority or to listen to his warnings about Hitler. The war years, the national suffering, the common effort had convinced many middle-class and upper-class Englishmen that the lower classes—the workers and soldiers of wartime—deserved to share more in the wealth of the nation they had helped save. Government control of the economy during the war had proved that government interference in business could be efficient and frugal. In fact, many Britishers ate better during the war than they had before because of rationing. Finally, the War Cabinet had promised and publicized postwar reforms in order to keep morale high. The wartime suffering was justified because it would lead to a better life after the fighting ended.

The instruments of this policy of promises were special reports and white papers on social problems and their solutions. The most important of these was the Beveridge report on social insurance. Sir William Beveridge, an eminent economist and chairman of the committee that wrote the report, presented it to the House of Commons on December 1, 1942, and summarized its contents in a national radio broadcast the following day. The key proposal of the report was a national minimum income for all. The national government should assume the responsibility, the report advised, for guaranteeing each British citizen an income at the subsistence level. Beyond this, the report recommended that the various social welfare services be reorganized into a unified system of compulsory social insurance against sickness, unemployment, and old age without consideration of need or wealth. Finally, a minister of social security should be appointed to administer such programs. The report was an immediate sensation with the press and public. It was heralded as marking a new era in class relations, a new proof of the benefits of the democratic system. However, the Conservative-dominated War Cabinet was less enthusiastic, and the report was shelved until the Labour party revived it in the postwar election campaign.

White papers were published on numerous aspects of social policy during the war. All of these suggested sweeping reforms—almost always requiring greater governmental intervention in and control of the economy for the general welfare. Reports were filed on industrial injuries—recommending that the state absorb the cost of these but tax business more heavily to offset the expense, on a national health service operated by the state, on the state's responsibility to provide full employment, and, of course, on a social insurance system, outlining the administration of the Beveridge plan. Churchill shelved each of these reports after the initial publicity died away, insisting that the war be won first.

One significant reform that was enacted before the war ended was the Education Act of 1944. The first major change in the national education system since 1902, this act provided for a minister of education at the cabinet level, raised the school-leaving age from 13 to 15 years, provided secondary education (previously reserved for the wealthy) to all without fees, and established programs of financial aid for the university educations of worthy students. These reforms were intended to democratize education and society by extending to intelligent students from the lower classes the educational advantages reserved to the upper classes before 1939.

The "cautious revolution"[2] carried out by the Attlee cabinet between 1945 and 1949 had two aspects: nationalization of industry and the establishment of the welfare state. The program of nationalization was limited to industrial monopolies and public utilities—the so-called commanding heights of the economy. Certain of these were already so thoroughly regulated by the government that the transfer of ownership was merely a formality, as with the Bank of England, the telephone and radio industries, and civil aviation. There was no controversy over these nationalizations. The Conservatives did mildly contest takeovers in other, more competitive industries, but the Labourite majority marched through its program, passing the Coal Nationalization Act (1946), the Electricity Act (1947), the Transport Act (1947), the Gas Act (1947), and the Iron and Steel Act (1949). The greatest controversy was over the nationalization of the iron and steel industry.

The ferrous industry was the most efficient and prosperous sector of the British economy. It had attained this efficiency, however, by rigid centralization. The industry was dominated by the Iron and Steel Federation which set wages and prices, decided on which companies should expand, and eliminated all traces of competition. Its monopolistic nature made the steel industry a symbol of irresponsible capitalism, and the Labour party was determined to bring this monopoly under the control of the people's elected representatives. Because the industry was prosperous, however, the Conservatives chose it as the issue on which to wage a last battle against nationalization. It was not until 1949 that Labour was able to achieve passage of the Iron and Steel Act. By then the five-year mandate of the Labour party had almost expired, so it was agreed the nationalization would not go into effect until after the imminent general election.

The administration of the nationalizations was simple. The government would purchase the stock of all enterprises in a certain industry at a price set by the government. Some businessmen, as in the mining industry, were able to profit greatly from these purchases, since their businesses were operating at a loss. A state corporation would then be established to manage that industry. There were, for example, an Iron and Steel Corporation, a British Transport Commission, and a Ministry of Fuel and Power. Frequently, these governmental corporations were managed

---

[2] Ernest Watkins, *The Cautious Revolution* (New York: Farrar, Straus and Co., 1950).

This conservative looking group is the Labour Ministry of Clement Attlee (speaking), who are seen here at a meeting celebrating the nationalization of the coal industry in 1947. (Courtesy of UPI)

by the same executives who had managed the largest enterprises in each industry before nationalization. Actually, little changed except that the government was the only stockholder, and it controlled prices and wages. In fact, those sectors of the economy that remained in private hands profited greatly from the government's policy of supplying cheap energy and fuel to the public. As the Labourites hoped, such services benefited the poor, but they also benefited businesses. So, in many ways public funds began to subsidize private enterprise. Nor did employer-employee relationships change greatly. In 1950 80 percent of Great Britain's labor force still worked in private enterprises.

The two pieces of legislation on which the welfare state was based were enacted in 1946: the National Insurance Act and the National Health Service Act. The National Insurance Act not only provided for a "social security" system but also nationalized medical insurance companies, so benefits for all health problems or injuries were paid by the state. This was the fulfillment of the Beveridge report. The essence of the act was the government's acceptance of the responsibility for securing the economic welfare of the *entire population* against unemployment, sickness, or old age. All citizens were compelled to contribute; all citizens were protected. There was little controversy over the National Insurance Act, and it was a Conservative member of Parliament who perhaps best voiced the hopes and the concensus embodied in the act.

We regard this plan as part of a mosaic or the pattern of a new society. . . . The whole philosophy behind these measures, in which, . . . we have played our part, is that the good things of life shall be more widely shared.[3]

---

[3] Havighurst, *Twentieth Century Britain,* p. 374.

Other legislation was passed to supplement the National Insurance Act, but it remained the essential cornerstone.

In contrast to the insurance measures, the National Health Service Act was hotly debated both in and out of Parliament. During the 1930s, there had been general agreement that the British medical profession was understaffed, underequipped, and overpriced. The main complaint was the lack of facilities and the resultant high cost of service. Even the British Medical Association (BMA) suggested, as early as 1930, that the professions could only be met through a "planned" national health program. In 1942 the BMA requested that the state provide a system of regional hospitals to provide more service. Toward the end of the war a government commission produced a white paper entitled simply, "A National Health Service." This paper proposed certain principles to guide national policy in establishing a health service: any legislation should include a comprehensive but noncompulsory medical service for all who wished to use it; the existing doctor-patient relationship should be preserved, with freedom of choice on both sides; and direction of the service by a government agency—such as a ministry—should be directly responsible to Parliament.

When the Labour government took office, Attlee appointed a minister of health to shepherd the health service bill through parliament. The man was Aneuran Bevan, not to be confused with Ernest Bevin, Attlee's foreign minister. At this time the BMA reversed its position. It had previously supported the general idea of the government supplying more facilities, but it feared that a Health Service would destroy private practice. The BMA expressed special concern about lay control of the profession, the fate of voluntary or private hospitals, the doctor-patient relationship, and the effect of a salaried medical profession on the quality of medical practice. Bevan took these anxieties into consideration but insisted that the bill must be passed quickly. When it went into effect in July 1948, all hospitals became state property, and all medical bills were paid by the state. With patients naturally turning to the state-run hospitals, virtually all doctors were forced to join the health service. The doctors were given a choice between a simple "capitation fee"—a payment for each patient treated—or a combination of a fixed salary and a capitation fee. Also, doctors were allowed to continue a private practice not financed by the Health Service for patients who wished to pay the price. Competition was thus preserved for those who wanted it.

At first the Health Service staggered under the burden of unforeseen problems caused by the massive number of people who flooded hospitals, doctors' and dentists' offices, having never before had any medical aid because of the expense. After several months of initial crisis, however, the service was accepted by the medical profession; methods for handling the increased number of patients were developed; and the Health Service had become a permanent feature of British life. By 1950, 95 percent of the population was enrolled on doctors' lists; approximately 88 percent of all doctors and 95 percent of all dentists were participating in the service. Politically, the issue of "socialized medicine" was dead. When the Conservatives returned to office, they did not attempt to dismantle the service.

Most of Labour's reforms were enacted by the end of 1946, although many did not go into effect until later. It had been a remarkable legislative feat. From the winter of 1946–47, however, the Labour cabinet was beset with economic crises that eroded its popular following and discredited some of their reforms. Great Britain's essential economic problems have been chronic since the 1920s but were made worse by World War II: outmoded industrial equipment; the need for large quantities of imported goods (especially agricultural goods) without sufficient exports to maintain a trade balance; and, in consequence, an increasingly weaker national currency in relation to other currencies. But the major cause of the 1947 crisis was a freak of nature—the coldest winter since 1880–81. The freeze completely disrupted transportation, shut down factories and mines, and forced Britain to import even greater quantities of goods in the face of an already unfavorable trade balance. Though special austerity measures enabled some recovery in late 1947 and 1948, the unfavorable trade balance (the excess of imports over exports) and the resultant pressure on the pound sterling could not be lightened. Finally, in September 1949, Attlee's cabinet was forced to devalue the pound from an international value of $4.03 to $2.80. This aided trade temporarily by reducing the price of British goods for foreigners and by making foreign goods more expensive to Englishmen. Still, this was just a stop-gap measure that made the luxuries of life more expensive for all. The Labour government's popularity decreased as prices increased.

Simultaneously, the party's public image was damaged by bitter intra-party debate over foreign policy. The split paralleled the age-old split between trade unionists and socialist intellectuals. The issue was Britain's role in the developing cold war. The trade unionists, the party's majority and electoral base, favored cooperation with the United States and opposition to communism. The socialists wanted England to remain independent of the two giants and play the role of conciliator. The left wing also hoped Britain would cooperate more closely with the continental countries as a "third force" in world affairs, instead of accepting the division of Europe into two blocs. The trade unionists eventually won the argument. Their views were reflected in the cabinet by Foreign Secretary Ernest Bevin, a staunchly anticommunist union man who led his nation into a close relationship with the United States. The debate had greatly weakened the Labour party on the eve of a general election.

The election of 1950 was a defeat for Labour even though they preserved their majority. (See Table 15.1.) The Labour majority was reduced to only six votes. Three percent of the electorate had left Labour for other parties. With this slim majority and dubious endorsement, Attlee was hesitant to attempt to pass any controversial legislation. He therefore called another election in October 1951, hoping to obtain a clear mandate.

In the brief period between the two elections the internal dissension within the Labour party had exploded in open revolt. The issue was foreign policy once again, but it was now in the context of a "guns or butter" choice between social welfare programs and armaments. With the Berlin blockade of 1948, Britain had begun to rearm. The crisis atmosphere surrounding the Korean War increased this expenditure. In the 1951 budget the cabinet concluded that it could only rearm at a sufficient rate if it reduced domestic programs. It was decided that citizens would be charged for certain medical services—most notably dental and optical services. This seemed like a betrayal to the leftwing Labourites. Aneurin Bevan, minister of health, resigned from the cabinet in April 1951, to be followed by lesser figures—among them Harold Wilson, later to become prime minister.

The Conservatives exploited the divisions within the Labour party during the election campaign of 1951. They warned that national disaster would ensue if men such as Aneurin Bevan should gain control of government. Yet the campaign stirred few emotions. There seemed to be little difference between the Conservative and Labour programs. Labour had enacted all the reforms it had advocated in 1945 and was left with no new issues. The Conservatives had accepted the nationalizations (except that of the Iron and Steel Act) and were resigned to the welfare state, saying only that they would administer the nation more efficiently. Only one percent of the electorate voted differently than they had in 1950, but that small shift was enough to give the Conservative party a majority in the new Parliament. The remarkable Labour experiment had come to an end.

The social changes resulting from nationalization had been minimal. Production proceeded at a pace that more private enterprise would probably not have altered. The industrial managers of private industry became the industrial managers of public industry. Employees obtained no control of management, and their standard of living did not improve markedly. The welfare state, on the other hand, contributed to a far more democratic society by providing educational opportunity for all, redistributing the national wealth, and guaranteeing a minimum living standard for all. The psychological relationships among British social classes had also been altered. In the years of cold war that followed 1951, Great Britain was spared the alienation of the workers that occurred on the continent, where, as in France and Italy, communism became the political religion of 20 to 25 percent of the electorate and effectively isolated a large part of the working class from the legislative process.

France: From Liberation to Cold War Politics

After the liberation of Paris in August 1944, de Gaulle established a provisional government, with himself as president, composed of the National Committee of Liberation of Algiers and representatives of the resistance within France. De Gaulle was determined to reduce the power of the resistance as rapidly as possible. He was able to do so only because he received the cooperation of the French Communist party (PCF), the strongest element in the resistance. Although a confirmed anticommunist, de Gaulle had done all he could to tame the communists with kindness. Throughout the war he had curried Stalin's favor and constantly referred to the communists as "patriots." He facilitated the return of Maurice Thorez, the PCF leader, from Moscow in November 1944, and visited Moscow himself in the following month. This policy paid off when Thorez endorsed de Gaulle's attacks on the resistance, especially de Gaulle's decision to disarm the "patriotic militia" which might have formed the basis of a revolutionary army.

De Gaulle was receptive to many of the ideas of the resistance. During the period of the provisional government—August 1944 to October 1945—when he had the powers of a dictator, de Gaulle enacted several of the most important reforms in the Resistance Charter. The charter had been written by resistance leaders as a blueprint for a new postwar society. It called for no less than a social and economic revolution.[4] The charter demanded the destruction of the influence of the feudal masters of industry and finance over the national economy; the nationalization of sources of energy (coal and electrical industries), insurance companies, and banks; and the formulation of a national economic plan to set social priorities above private interests. Workers should share in the management of business enterprises, and a comprehensive social security program should guarantee the welfare of all. Education should be freely available to all to create "a true elite, not of birth but of merit." The charter extended its reforms to colonial subjects and advocated that they be granted their full political liberties. De Gaulle realized the popularity of the charter's program and personally desired many reforms of French society. Therefore, he carried out the recommended nationalizations and created the administrative machinery to begin economic planning. Through these actions, de Gaulle, governing only on the mandate he had asserted himself and which had not been ratified by an election, completely changed the context of French economics and politics.

By the fall of 1945, de Gaulle had succeeded in establishing civil order, reducing the resistance to impotence, and preparing the way for the elec-

---

[4] Jacques Chapsal, *La Vie politique en France depuis 1940* (Paris: Presses universitaires de France, 1966), pp. 70–71.

tion of a constituent assembly to write a new constitution. The election was held in October 1945, and the results indicated that French politics had moved considerably to the left.

De Gaulle was asked to stay on as president of the assembly and premier, but it soon became clear that he could not cooperate with the emerging communist-socialist coalition. These two parties wanted a constitution which would provide for a sovereign parliament—the parliament

TABLE 15.2. French Elections, 1945–46

Party	October 21, 1945		June 6, 1946		November 10, 1946	
	Seats	Votes, %	Seats	Votes, %	Seats	Votes, %
Communist (PCF)	161	26.2	153	25.9	183	28.2
Socialist (SFIO)	150	23.4	126	21.1	105	17.8
Christian Democrat (MRP) ...	150	23.9	169	28.2	167	25.9
Radical	28	10.5	32	11.6	43	11.1
Conservative	64	15.7	67	12.9	71	16.7
Other	33		36		49	

SOURCES: Data on seats held are from Philip H. Williams, *Crisis and Compromise: Politics in the Fourth Republic* (Garden City, New York: Anchor Books, Doubleday and Co., Inc., 1966), p. 532. Data on percentage of votes are from Jacques Chapsal, *La Vie politique en France depuis 1940* (Paris: Presses universitaires de France, 1966), pp. 579–81.

would not only pass legislation but would also choose the premier and would have the power to oust him. This, of course, would resemble the British House of Commons and was felt to be the ultimate expression of democracy, since all power would rest with the elected representatives of the people. De Gaulle, on the other hand, blamed the weaknesses of the Third Republic, which had been plagued by governmental instability, on the excesses of the legislature. His remedy was a strong executive independent of the political intrigues of the popularly elected assembly. When it seemed that the communist-socialist coalition was going to succeed in writing a leftist constitution, de Gaulle resigned, on January 20, 1946, and temporarily retired from public life.

The new president-premier had to be a man the Communists and the Socialist party (SFIO could agree on, and the search for that man revealed much about Communist policy and the PCF's relations with other political parties. Since the liberation French communists had continued their policy of cooperation with other democratic parties. There is no doubt that this policy of a United Front was dictated from Moscow, since it was followed by communist parties throughout Europe. In fact, within the PCF, the strongest advocates of parliamentary action as opposed to revolution were the leaders closest to Moscow—Thorez, the party's general secretary, and Jacques Duclos, a leading ideologue. Thorez had spent the war in Russia, and his conservative policy was challenged by communists who had fought in the resistance and were impatient for reforms.

Under Thorez's firm leadership, the French Communist party was a staunch advocate of parliamentary politics, the reestablishment of order, and economic recovery. Controlling the nation's largest trade union federation, the General Confederation of Labor (CGT), the Communists used their influence to encourage workers to oppose strikes and to sacrifice wages for the sake of productivity. *L'Humanité,* the party's newspaper, announced in August 1944 that "the battle of the barricades is won, but the battle for economic renascence has begun." The PCF motto became, "Unite! Fight! Work!," and Thorez told coal miners that "it is impossible to approve the smallest strike."[5] All strikes that did occur were denounced as Trotskyite, anarchistic, or the work of reactionary employers. Extending this policy of order and restraint to the French empire, the PCF took a very ambiguous position on the nationalist revolts of colonial peoples. It refused to sanction such revolts, in spite of Russia's sympathy for them. Instead the French communists merely called for reforms in colonial administration.

Having decided on a parliamentary course, the PCF needed allies among the other parties. Naturally, they hoped for an alliance with the SFIO, led by Léon Blum, the grand old man of French socialism. Blum was approaching seventy when he returned from internment in Germany to a hero's welcome. He had been strongly anticommunist since the 1920s, when he had struggled with the communists for control of the French socialist movement. Therefore, following de Gaulle's resignation, when the PCF proposed a Communist-Socialist cabinet with Thorez as premier, the Socialists, fearing that they might become captives of their allies, refused to enter any government that did not have the support of the Christian Democratic MRP. The SFIO thereby gave the MRP and its most influential leader, Georges Bidault, a veto over the selection of a premier. A new element in French politics, the *Mouvemente républicaine populaire* was a liberal Catholic party, bent on radical reforms, which had grown out of the resistance. The Catholics were more anti-German than anticommunist in 1945–46 and eager for social reforms, but they preferred a strong executive, such as de Gaulle offered, to the democratic regime favored by the PCF and the SFIO. The MRP consented to cooperate with a government headed by a socialist, not a communist. The colorless Pierre Gouin was chosen as the new president-premier. His weakness guaranteed that real power would rest with Thorez, Blum, and Bidault.

Gouin's provisional government inaugurated "tripartism" or three-party rule, which was to characterize French politics for the next year and a half. Under his relaxed leadership the Communists and Socialists pro-

---

[5] Alfred J. Rieber, *Stalin and the French Communist Party 1941–47* (New York: Columbia University Press, 1962), pp. 163, 190, and 231.

ceeded to write a leftist constitution that was far more democratic than the MRP would have liked. Therefore, the MRP opposed the draft when it was presented to the public in a referendum in May 1946. The defeat of the constitution necessitated the election of a second constituent assembly, and this time the MRP emerged as the largest party in France. With Bidault as premier, the MRP was able to attract the support of enough socialists to write a document giving more power to the executive and creating a second, senior house (Senate) which could temper the actions of the lower house (the National Assembly). The new constitution was passed in a national referendum in October 1946, clearing the way for the election of the first legislature of the fourth French republic in November.

During Bidault's term in office—i.e., during the second constituent assembly—France's independent position in international affairs became more difficult to maintain. Most importantly, after Byrnes's Stuttgart speech on German policy, it appeared that France's desire to keep Germany weak would be totally disregarded by the Anglo-Saxons, and, sooner or later, France would have to decide whether she could live with a revived Germany. Bidault's government resented the Anglo-American refusal to consider France's opposition to German recovery, and the French came to depend more heavily on the possibility of Russian support for the separation of the Ruhr from Germany.

The first election of the Fourth Republic once again made the PCF France's largest party. The Communists felt that they deserved the premiership, as, indeed, the rules of the parliamentary game usually dictated. However, after some maneuvering, a Socialist, Paul Ramadier was accepted by the tripartite coalition. Evidence of distrust among the three partners was growing; and Ramadier had to face the twin problems of international cold war and domestic economic crisis. He came into office only two months before international tensions were dramatized by the Truman Doctrine. The meaning of the Truman Doctrine for France was easily perceived by political commentators. Raymond Aron, who wrote for the centrist newspaper *Combat,* analyzed the situation a week after Truman spoke to the American legislature.

The Truman statement is a factor in the political game inside every country in the world. We knew all along that the Americans saw a threat to their own interests, and an advantage to the Soviet Union, in the progress made by *any* Communist party in *any* country of the world; only people seldom dared to admit it openly.[6]

Pierre Mendès-France, later in 1947, made a comment that capsulized the thinking of many French politicians.

---

[6] Alexander Werth, *France, 1940–1955* (Boston: Beacon Press, 1966), p. 351.

The Communists are rendering us a great service. Because we have a "Communist danger," the Americans are making a tremendous effort to help us. We must keep up this indispensable Communist scare.[7]

This is not to say that the American hard line automatically led to the ouster of the PCF from the tripartite coalition in May 1947. A colonial crisis, a domestic crisis, and the deterioration of Franco-Soviet relations also played their parts. The colonial crisis came first. As late as the end of April 1947, the PCF had supported Ramadier's policy in Indochina. That policy consisted of trying to reestablish French military control over the rebellious French colony. Six days after Truman's speech, on March 18, Jacques Duclos announced that the PCF would no longer vote funds to support the French army in Indochina. Ramadier considered resigning in order to form a new government without the Communists but was dissuaded from doing so by other leaders of the SFIO. The PCF then resorted to a bit of parliamentary chicanery. When votes on Vietnam came to the floor, the Communist cabinet members would vote with the government, while the rest of the Communist legislators abstained.

The domestic crisis concerned the government's wages and prices policy. The Ramadier cabinet had been following a policy of high prices and low wages in order to prevent inflation and to encourage business recovery. Largely because of its support for this policy, the PCF had been declining in popularity during the spring of 1947. Party membership had dropped from one million in January 1945, to 900,000 in March 1946, to 800,000 in March 1947. Prior to April 1947, the communists had continued their opposition to strikes of all kinds. When pickets appeared in front of Renault automobile factories on April 25, 1947, and demanded higher wages, PCF officials denounced the strike as a "weapon of the trusts" and labeled the strike leaders as "gaullist-trotskyite-anarchists."[8] But as the spontaneous strike spread the PCF began to have second thoughts. By April 28, twenty thousand workers had joined the strike. On April 30, the political bureau of the party attacked Ramadier for "refusing to make an equitable readjustment of workers' salaries." That evening Ramadier called his cabinet together. The Renault factories had been nationalized in 1945 by de Gaulle's provisional government because of the Renault family's cooperation with the Germans; therefore, the Communist attitude toward the Renault strike was considered as a test of PCF policy on all nationalized industries. It was all the more significant, therefore, when, at the cabinet meeting on April 30, Thorez refused to support continued government limitations on salaries.

At that same meeting Georges Bidault, once again minister of foreign

---

[7] Ibid., p. 351.

[8] Georgette Elgey, *La République des Illusions, 1945–1951, ou la Vie secrète de la IVe République,* vol. 1 (Paris: Fayard, 1965), p. 280.

affairs, reported on a conference of the foreign ministers of the Big Four—United States, Russia, Great Britain, and France—which had just ended in Moscow. Bidault had gone to the conference hoping to obtain Russian support for separating the Ruhr from Germany but had been rudely rejected by both Molotov and Stalin. Personally insulted, he had changed partners. Meeting with the American and British representatives, Bidault had signed an agreement on the future of Germany that accepted the economic revival of the defeated state. Thereby, the French minister had consciously and definitively rejected his former policy of the "honest broker" between East and West. Reporting these developments to the cabinet, Bidault commented with bitterness of Stalin's rude rebuff of his proposals. Thorez stated baldly, "Stalin was right." This comment made it clear that the Communists had decided to break with Ramadier on foreign policy as well as economic policy.

The PCF, however, still refused to withdraw from the cabinet; so, on May 4, Ramadier forced a vote of confidence in the National Assembly on his economic policy and won 360–186 with the PCF voting against him. That evening he informed the Communist cabinet members that they were being replaced by men who would support the government. The Communists resigned quietly. Since that day, although the PCF has remained the largest party in France, no communist has held a cabinet post. Approximately five million voters remain faithful to the PCF through prosperity and crisis, but only rarely do these millions effect government policy.

The rupture of tripartism was basically a result of increasing international tensions. Ramadier had decided on the ouster of the communists before the Renault strike, and PCF spokesmen have noted the impossibility of continued cooperation in a cold war atmosphere.[9] Why then the confrontation over salaries? Because neither side wanted to break the coalition on an unpopular issue. The PCF thought they could gain support by fighting for higher wages, while the MRP and the SFIO were equally sure that their anti-inflationary policy was popular. Therefore, the three parties used this domestic issue to achieve the rupture that the cold war had made inevitable.

International tension was reflected in French politics not only by the isolation of the PCF on the left but also by the appearance of an extremist movement on the right—the Rally of the French People (RPF) led by de Gaulle. The general seemed to have thrown caution to the wind in an attempt to regain power. Having announced the formation of the RPF in April 1947, he toured France in a series of meetings that resembled Hitler's Nuremberg rallies. The orchestrated enthusiasm included flags, floodlights, and thousands of supporters cheering, "De Gaulle to power!"

---

[9] Elgey, *République des Illusions*, pp. 278–80; Rieber, *Stalin and the French Communist Party*, p. 350.

De Gaulle's constant theme was the necessity to save France from a communist revolution. His campaign was successful, and Gaullist candidates won 40 percent of the vote in nationwide municipal elections in October 1947. But at this point de Gaulle overplayed his hand. He issued an ultimatum to the cabinet that called for the legal government to hold a referendum on his own return to power. The cabinet ignored the demand, and many of de Gaulle's supporters were shocked by such a Bonapartist tactic, and de Gaulle's prestige plummeted rapidly.

De Gaulle had planned on American aid for his anticommunist movement, but the legal government had become, by the fall of 1947, sufficiently anticommunist to satisfy Washington. The premier during this critical period from November 1947 to July 1948 was Robert Schuman. Faced with a series of communist-led strikes and riots during the winter which appeared to be preparations for a coup d'état, Schuman used flying squads of heavily armed policemen to disperse communist demonstrators and legitimate strikers alike. By the spring of 1948 the crisis had passed. The Marshall Plan had begun, and French industry was beginning to recover.

Italy: From Tripartism to Polarization

After Mussolini's ouster in July 1943, King Victor Emmanuel II had appointed Marshal Pietro Badoglio to head the Italian state and make peace with the Allies. Forced to flee Rome almost immediately by advancing German troops, Badoglio controlled only southern Italy, while the German army fiercely defended Rome and the northern half of the peninsula. Badoglio was challenged for the leadership of the liberated south by a coalition of antifascist parties. This coalition, under the name of the Committee for National Liberation (CLN), was, however, based in Rome and was therefore unable to influence significantly events until the liberation of Rome in June 1944. As soon as Rome was liberated, the anti-Fascists forced the king to drop Badoglio, and a CLN leader, Ivanoe Bonomi, a reformist Socialist who had been premier in 1922 before Mussolini came to power, formed a government.

The major conflicts between Badoglio and the CLN were centered around the fate of the monarchy and the aggressiveness with which fascists were to be purged from public life. The six parties that formed the CLN—Communist party, Socialist party, Action party, Republican party, Christian Democrats, Liberal party—wanted a democratic republic; Badoglio and the king still clung to a desire for an authoritarian monarchy. Great Britain supported Badoglio, not desiring to see a monarchy fall. The king realized that he was personally repugnant to the anti-Fascists because of his cooperation with Mussolini, and to save the monarchy, he offered to go into exile if his son were allowed to reign until a referendum could test the public will. The republicans were not willing to accept this until the Communist party (PCI) forced them to by announcing in April 1944 its willingness to accept the king's proposal. This was, once again, an expression of Russia's United Front policy. With the powerful PCI accepting the compromise, the other parties were virtually compelled to concede, as they did. The question of the ultimate fate of the monarchy was thereby postponed until after the fighting ended.

The goal of the majority of the CLN, which drew its strength from conservative southern Italy, was a parliamentary regime similar to that of pre-Fascist Italy. Therefore, the Bonomi government concentrated on merely restoring order and did not attempt any significant changes in Italian political and social institutions. There was, however, a revolutionary movement developing in northern Italy in the form of an armed resistance to the Germans. The center of the Italian resistance was in Milan, where the Committee of National Liberation for Northern Italy (CLNAI), pretended to the role of legal government of the German-held areas. In fact, Bonomi recognized this group as his representative in the North. The resistance was dominated by the political left—by communists, socialists, and the Action party, a liberal democratic group; and it depended primarily on industrial workers for its support. The resistance leaders envisioned a postwar Italy transformed by socialist policies into an efficient, prosperous, and egalitarian society. By the end of 1944 the resistance contained at least 200,000 armed men and aided the Allies in liberating the North.

With the liberation completed by June 1945, the struggle for control of postwar Italy began. The CLNAI was strong enough to topple Bonomi and to have the Actionist leader Ferruccio Parri, a resistance hero, appointed premier by Lieutenant General Prince Umberto. But he came to power just as the foundations of CLNAI strength were being systematically destroyed by the British and American military. First, the Allied commanders required the resistance to surrender their arms, which was done peacefully. Then, workers' councils that had taken over management of factories were displaced, and the employers were encouraged to reassert their authority with the support of the Allied armies. Finally, the local committees of liberation—the only local governing authorities in many areas since 1943—were replaced by military government. Thus, by the end of July 1945, whatever chances had existed for the resistance to become the basis for a national revolutionary movement had been eliminated.[10] Parri tried to enact reforms in spite of his weakened position, but members of the new Christian Democratic party (DC) in his cabinet constantly undermined his initiatives. Finally, he resigned in despair in November

---

[10] H. Stuart Hughes, *The United States and Italy,* rev. ed. (New York: W. W. Norton and Company, Inc., 1968), pp. 137–39.

316 A History of Europe in the Twentieth Century

1945. His resignation marked, perhaps, the decisive defeat of the ideals of the resistance.[11]

The new ministry was headed by Alcide De Gasperi, a Christian Democrat, who was to govern Italy for the next seven years. A master politician and a pragmatic conservative, De Gasperi was convinced that broad reforms were needed but was equally convinced that socialism was a threat to the very essence of Western civilization and to the Catholic church. Therefore, he was willing to ally himself with conservatives to prevent a socialist solution to Italy's problems. His first ministry was occupied by the task of preparing the first postwar election in June 1946. The election would create a constituent assembly, and a referendum to be held at the same time would decide the fate of the monarchy. The results were reassuring for the centrist parties. The monarchy was clearly rejected, making Italy a republic; and the Christian Democrats emerged as the largest party in the constituent assembly.

There had finally been a test of popular strength, and the public will was obviously in favor of a leftist government led by the DC. De Gasperi formed a new cabinet based on the tripartite formula of Communists, Socialists, and Christian Democrats. (This was also the period of tripartism in France.) The impossibility of cooperation between the DC and PCI was soon evident. The Communists and Socialists desired the maximum possible state control of industry; De Gasperi preferred the minimum interference in private enterprise. While his partners hoped for neutrality in the developing cold war, De Gasperi wanted to align Italy with the United States. The DC leader was aided by a split within the Socialist party (PSI) between the advocates of cooperation with the PCI, led by Pietro Nenni, and those who distrusted the Communists, led by Giuseppi Saragat. This debate became so intense during the fall of 1946 that the right wing of the party bolted, and Saragat founded the Social Democratic party (PSDI), which included fifty of the 115 socialist deputies in the constituent assembly.

With the extreme left splitting into factions, De Gasperi was ready to risk a political gamble that would free him from his Social-Communist allies. He hoped to end the tripartite coalition and build a centrist, anticommunist majority. The chief political issues in Italy in early 1947, as in France, were economic policy and foreign policy. Inflation was at a critical level, and while the DC proposed to freeze salaries and reduce government spending, the PCI demanded more state control of large industries and a vast program of economic reconstruction financed by the state. Still, the PCI cooperated with De Gasperi on crucial votes—even to the point of voting protection for the privileges of the Catholic

---

[11] Giuseppi Mammarella, *Italy after Fascism: A Political History, 1943–1965*, rev. ed. (Notre Dame, Indiana: University of Notre Dame Press, 1966), pp. 102–5.

TABLE 15.3.　Italian Elections, 1946 and 1948

Party	For Constituent Assembly June 1946		Party	For National Assembly April 1948	
	Seats	Votes		Seats	Votes
Communists (PCI)	104	4,356,686	Social-Communists (PCI-PSI)	183	8,137,047
Socialists (PSI)	115	4,758,129			
Action Party	7	334,748	Social Democrats (PSDI)	8	1,858,346
Republicans (PRI)	23	1,003,007	Republicans	3	652,477
Christian Democrats	207	8,080,644	Christian Democrats	304	12,712,562
Liberals	41	1,560,638	Liberals and Conservatives	7	1,004,889
Freedom Bloc	16	637,328			
Conservatives and Neo-Fascists	30	1,211,956	Monarchists	3	729,174
Others	12	1,025,130	Neo-Fascists	6	526,670

SOURCE: Giuseppi Mammarella, *Italy After Fascism: A Political History 1943–1965*, rev. ed. (Notre Dame, Indiana: University of Notre Dame Press, 1966), pp. 117, 194.

church. De Gasperi made his move when the Communists attacked the Truman Doctrine and compared American intervention in Greece to German imperialism.[12] The premier, praising Truman's initiative, began denouncing his cabinet partners as obstructionists in parliament. On May 12 he resigned, freeing himself to form a new coalition. Attempts were made to find other premiers, but De Gasperi had become the indispensable man. His new cabinet contained only Christian Democrats but was supported by all parties to the right of the PSI. This *monocolore* ministry presided over the drafting of Italy's postwar constitution.

With the first regular parliamentary election scheduled for April 1948, De Gasperi gradually formed an electoral bloc with the Social Democrats and the Republicans against the Social-Communists (PSI-PCI). Yet the battle was not between two blocs, but between the Communists and the Christian Democrats. De Gasperi proclaimed his party to be the only safeguard against a communist dictatorship. His appeal was effective among the upper and middle classes who were regaining their confidence, now that the revolutionary threat had receded. The DC also found sympathy abroad. The United States took an active role in the elections.

On the diplomatic front it gave support to the Italian Trieste claims, returned the gold taken from Italy by the Nazis, . . . and, with Britain, renounced claims to Italian ship reparations. The State Department announced it would deny visas to any Italian known to have voted Communist, and the Italo-Americans conducted a campaign with form letters urging relatives in Italy to vote against the [Social-Communist] bloc. . . . On a more direct level, the United States warned that Italy would receive no further aid if the People's Bloc won. . . .[13]

The American role was concrete proof of the influence De Gasperi had with the western nations. The Christian Democrats also received aid from the Cahtolic church, whose priests asked their parishioners to defend the Church against the threat posed by communism.

This concerted anticommunist campaign was an overwhelming success. (See Table 15.3.) Moderates and conservatives turned to the DC, deserting the smaller noncommunist parties in favor of the only sure bulwark against revolution. The 304 votes De Gasperi's party commanded in the national assembly made a one-party government possible, but De Gasperi chose to include representatives of the PSDI, the Republican party, and the Liberal party in his ministry. This insured the isolation of the PCI on the left and the neo-Fascists and monarchists on the right. The Christian Democrats governed Italy, in coalition with several minor parties,

---

[12] Ibid., p. 145.

[13] Joyce and Gabriel Kolko, *The Limits of Power* (New York: Harper & Row, Publishers, 1972), pp. 438–39.

for the next sixteen years, nestling the Latin state solidly in the American camp in the cold war.

Germany: From Defeat to Partnership

Germans in 1945 were a defeated people living in an occupied land. They were at the mercy of the Allies. Administrative chaos was paralleled by a lack of German political organizations—the fall of the Third Reich having left a political vacuum. The Allies attempted to fill this vacuum by selecting anti-Nazi politicians of the Weimar period as mayors and as provisional administrators of each *Land* or state. Konrad Adenauer, at the age of sixty-nine, was asked by the occupying authorities to be mayor of Cologne, a position he had held in 1933 when the Nazi regime forced his resignation. Four years later he was to become the chancellor of an independent Germany closely allied with the Western powers. It was through men like him that Germany reclaimed her role as a Great Power so soon after defeat.

The first task undertaken by the Allies, apart from supplying the necessities of life for the Germans and the millions of refugees who were in Germany, was to attempt to punish those Germans responsible for the aggressions and the barbarities of the Nazi regime. The most spectacular instrument of this policy was the International Military Tribunal at Nuremburg. In session from Nobember 20, 1945, until October 1, 1946, the Nuremburg Tribunal tried twenty-one leading Nazis for conspiracy "to commit crimes against peace, war crimes, and crimes against humanity." An unprecedented method of treating a defeated nation, the trials were given wide circulation by the occupation governments in order to force Germans to face the horrors of the Nazi system. When the drama was completed, the Tribunal had sentenced twelve leading Nazis to death by hanging, others to prison terms, and acquitted three.

Simultaneously, the Allies were conducting a more or less systematic policy called "denazification." This purge was meant to cleanse Germany of all traces of National Socialism. The military commanders found that this was much more difficult than it appeared to the politicians in Washington, London, and Paris. It soon became clear that all positions of even minor importance had been occupied by Nazi party members or sympathizers. The Allies approached denazification differently. The British made little effort to discover Nazis, prosecuting only well-known high officials. The French, distrusting all Germans, regarded a purge as useless and concentrated on restructuring German education within their zone. The Americans pursued the purge with zeal by means of a detailed "questionnaire" that all Germans were required to complete. It soon became apparent that low-ranking, idealistic Nazis were admitting their faith in Hitler, while the sophisticated and more important Nazis were falsifying their answers and escaping the dragnet. The whole effort was abandoned in 1947 when it was decided in Washington that West Germany would be a valuable ally.

Far more meaningful were attempts by Germans to search their own consciences and to convince their fellow citizens that there must be a new German attitude toward politics and social justice.[14] The leaders were theologians and socialist journalists who emphasized Nazi crimes during the war, denounced laissez faire economics, and encouraged political and social democracy. Eminent in the campaign were Karl Jaspers, a philosopher; Eugen Kogon, a liberal Catholic journalist who wrote *The Theory and Practice of Hell* describing concentration camp life; Hermann Hesse, the novelist; and many more intellectuals. One theme they insisted on was that Germany's role as a great military power had ended. It was better, they said, that a pacifist Germany should cultivate a spiritualized socialism and should devote her energies to the development of her cultural heritage.

Politicians had other ideas, however; and as so often, the sword proved to have more political punch than the pen. By 1946 the United States and Great Britain were beginning to realize the usefulness of a strong West German state in their developing struggle with Russia. After Byrnes's Stuttgart speech of September 6, 1946, the American emphasis on denazification, reeducation and democratization began to give way to economic reconstruction, political revival, and eventually rearmament. The American and British authorities soon agreed on the merger of their zones into a semiautonomous Bizonia.

This new creation was not welcomed by the French or Russians, but for opposite reasons. The French desired a continued partition of Germany and distrusted any step toward a revived German state. The Russians, on the other hand, protested against the exclusion of the socialist-communist forces of the Russian zone and preferred a central government including representation from all four zones. The Soviets formally complained that the Western Allies were trying to partition Germany in violation of the Potsdam Agreement. As for the Germans, they welcomed the new bizonal administration that the Anglo-Americans established, which included representatives from all the *Laender* in the two zones. A bizonal executive committee, a *Laender* council consisting of representatives from each *Land* parliament, and a bizonal economic council were organized to relieve the Allies of some of their administrative burden and to prepare the way for German self-government.

As relations among the Big Four deteriorated, the Anglo-Americans became ever more anxious for a German government that could mobilize the resources of the German nation on behalf of the West. When the

[14] Koppel S. Pinson, *Modern Germany,* 2d ed. (New York: Macmillan Company, 1966), pp. 546–53.

French became convinced, at the Moscow Foreign Ministers Conference in May 1947 that Russian goals were incompatible with their own, the way was cleared for the establishment of a West German government. It still did not arrive overnight. It was necessary for the Germans to develop new parties, find new leaders, and reach a concensus on the form of a new regime. Two parties were to dominate these processes: the Christian Democratic Union (CDU) of Konrad Adenauer and the German Socialist party (SPD) of Kurt Schumacher. The SPD had been the dominant party during most of the years of the Weimar Republic, but many of its leaders had been killed or driven into exile by the Nazis. At the end of the war the SPD embodied the desire of many German intellectuals to build a new Germany from the wreckage of the old. They favored a social welfare state, some nationalizations, a state-directed economy, and "comanagement" or worker participation in the management of industry. Konrad Adenauer and the dominant wing of the CDU were strongly antisocialist and virulently anticommunist. While favoring parliamentary democracy, this organizational descendant of the old Center party grouped all the respectable forces of German conservatism. Adenauer, writing and traveling from his base in Cologne, became, during 1946–47, the most influential CDU leader, a fact not unwelcome to the Americans who admired his staunch antisocialism. His eminence was not so warmly greeted by the Labour government in London.[15]

Seeking to revive the German economy, the Western Allies enacted a monetary reform, basically a devaluation of the Deutschmark, in their zones on June 20, 1948. The Russians responded with a blockade of all ground routes—by auto or by train—to Berlin. The blockade was to last almost a year, with the Western sectors of Berlin supplied by a massive airlift conducted primarily by the United States. This new crisis persuaded the Western Allies to delay no longer in establishing a German regime. On July 1, 1948, the eleven *Laender* parliaments were ordered to prepare for a constituent assembly. The parliamentary council, which convened on September 1, 1948, to write a German constitution, elected Adenauer to be its chairman, and he deeply influenced the Basic Law.

The Basic Law was as much a political document as it was a legal one. Its content had been influenced greatly by the occupying powers, who insisted on a federal structure for the new Germany. Certain other features of the Basic Law were conscious attempts to avoid the weaknesses of the Weimar Republic. The presidency was merely ceremonial. While the president could nominate the chancellor, this nomination could be rejected by the Bundestag, the lower house of parliament. On the other hand, the Chancellor could dismiss individual ministers without endangering the entire cabinet. Another precaution against governmental instability

---

[15] Charles Wighton, *Adenauer, A Critical Biography* (New York: Coward-McCann Inc., 1964), pp. 81–92.

provided that a chancellor could not be ousted, even if he did not have a majority, until a majority in the Bundestag had agreed upon his successor. This was later to afford greater stability to the regime than anyone imagined in 1949. Konrad Adenauer used this provision to remain in power for thirteen years as Germany's first chancellor. Safeguards were also established against the growth of minor, extremist parties. The Basic Law gave the courts power to ban or dissolve all parties hostile to democracy. This was used to ban the Communist party in 1953. An electoral law, enacted later to support the Basic Law, required that a party receive 5 percent of the national vote before receiving representation in the Bundestag. With the aid of these two laws, minor parties were indeed discouraged during the 1950s. The three major parties—the CDU, SPD, and the Free Democratic party (FDP)—received only 72.1 percent of the total vote in 1949 but received 94.1 percent in 1961.

With the completion of the Basic Law and its acceptance by the occupying powers, the German Federal Republic (West Germany) officially came into existence on May 23, 1949. The Russians reacted by recognizing the sovereignty of the German Democratic Republic (East Germany) on October 7, 1949. By then the first parliamentary elections had been held in West Germany. Three major parties emerged, but, unlike France and Italy, the parliamentary majority was on the center right and not the center left. Since no party had a majority, a coalition government was necessary. A highly significant debate and political struggle developed between proponents of an ideological "small coalition" based on the CDU and FDP and those who desired a "great coalition" based on the CDU and the SPD. Adenauer favored a conservative coalition, and, therefore, Schumacher did all in his power to prevent Adenauer from becoming chancellor. Adenauer was elected chancellor by the narrowest of margins, 202–200. He formed a cabinet containing the CDU, FDP, and representatives of several minor conservative parties. Adenauer had decided that the Bonn Republic would be a conservative republic.

Adenauer has been accused of using his position and personal prestige to become a democratic dictator and of converting the federal republic

TABLE 15.4.   German Election, August 1949

Party	Seats	Votes, %
Christian Democrats	139	31.0
Social Democrats	131	29.2
Free Democrats	52	11.9
Communist Party	15	5.7
Others	65	22.2

Source: Alfred Grosser, *The Federal Republic of Germany: A Concise History* (New York: Frederick A. Praeger, Inc., 1964), p. 50.

into a chancellor-republic. It cannot be denied that he brought both assets and liabilities to his office. He was a man of great patience and infinite negotiating skill, and these were needed talents. His first task was to free Germany from the military occupation and to regain full German sovereignty. He was, of course, aided in his relations with the United States by his ardent anticommunism. He was also a "good European," favoring the economic and political integration of Europe. Although a conservative, he was not a nationalist in the sense that de Gaulle was. At a time when Germany needed to be trusted by its neighbors, the country was fortunate to be led by a "European." Adenauer's weaknesses were his love for intrigue and his authoritarian personality. While these two characteristics were the keys to his political success, they were harmful to German democracy in that they strengthened the German penchant for strong leaders and disdain for the squabbling of democratic politics. Yet, Germany was extremely fortunate to have a statesman such as Adenauer to lead the fledgling republic during its first formative years.

A Western Bloc?

The democratic governments of western Europe had all opted for conservative leadership by 1951. Such an eventuality would have appeared impossible in 1945, when socialist-dominated parliamentary majorities were enacting revolutionary legislation in Great Britain, France, and Italy. Once again, however, events had proved the inescapable nexus between domestic politics and international politics. The emergence of the conservative governments and the Truman Doctrine were merely two aspects of the reestablishment of European stability. The flux and uncertainty caused by the devastation of war was replaced during the period 1947–51 by a new European order.

PART V

European Influence at Low Ebb

Chapter 16

THE INTERNATIONAL CONTEXT OF WEST EUROPEAN POLITICS: THE COLD WAR AND EUROPEAN INTEGRATION

It is a paradox of human affairs that unfortunate and discouraging circumstances often give birth to desirable and beneficial developments. So it was that the frustrations and tensions of the postwar era gave impetus to European economic and political integration that resulted in amazing economic prosperity. Although the diplomatic events of the 1950s were anything but encouraging, and in retrospect, offer further proof of man's failure to comprehend his fellow man, it should not be forgotten that these same events submerged the conflict between France and Germany, elevated supranationalism and an improved living standard above narrow nationalisms, and began the evolution of western Europe toward political integration.

The Cold War and Western Europe, 1948–53

The first step in this evolution was the agreement of sixteen states to participate in the European Recovery Program, better known as the Marshall Plan, in July 1947. The first American funds were provided to the Europeans in April 1948—a sum of $5.3 billion. The Organization for European Economic Cooperation (OEEC) was established in Paris the same month to distribute the American loans and coordinate the money's use. By 1951, when the Marshall aid was ended, the OEEC had distributed $40 billion. After this, the OEEC continued to exist as a data gathering and consultative international organization. The purpose of Marshall aid was to create the social and economic basis for liberal democracy in Europe, to revive the European market for American goods, and to remove the economic causes of social discontent so as to deny communist parties popular support. Although the latter was a misreading of the reasons for communist strength (as was evidenced by the continued support for communism in France and Italy), the American policy did have the desired effect of stabilizing western European society. Not only was the western European economy booming by 1951, but Christian Democrats and socialists had isolated the communists and thereby denied them any influence.

Although ERP was intended as an alternative to a military solution to the expansion of communism, it was a logical and easy step from economic cooperation to military alliance. The growing tension over Germany and the supposed communist threat led to the first multilateral military pact of the postwar era in March 1948. The Brussels Treaty was a fifty-five-year mutual defense alliance signed by Great Britain, France, Belgium, Holland, and Luxembourg. The treaty had been prompted by the Russian coup d'état in Czechoslovakia. The Soviets appeared to be trying to extend their hegemony westward, and the governing parties of western Europe felt the need of joint action to stop the Russians. Of course, the Brussels Pact nations would have been too weak to resist Russia alone, and they assumed the support and protection of the United States. This was a safe assumption. The Truman administration gave its full diplomatic and economic support to the alliance, especially after the Berlin blockade began in June 1948.

A decision was taken by the Brussels Pact nations plus the United States, meeting in London in March and April 1948, to include the three west German zones in the reconstruction of the European economy. Pursuant to this decision, the Western Allies introduced a currency reform to stabilize the mark. When they tried to extend this reform to the western sectors of Berlin, the Russians, on June 24, sealed off Berlin from all overland contact with West Germany. The Truman administration interpreted this as a test of the United States' resolve and four days later began a massive airlift of fuel, food, and other supplies into West Berlin. The contest of wills lasted 324 days with the airlift delivering an average of 13,000 tons of goods per day. During the crisis, Truman ordered airplanes carrying atomic bombs flown to Britain. This nuclear strategy probably prevented the Russians from using their overwhelming manpower advantage in the Berlin area. At any rate, when the Russians called off their unsuccessful blockade in May 1949, the West had proved that Berlin could not be taken except by military action.

The tension generated by the Berlin blockade and the explosion of Russia's first atomic bomb in September 1949 increased willingness to look to military solutions such as the Brussels Pact. In fact, the Brussels nations had formed the Western European Union, a consultative body for coordinating military activities. The impetus for American association with this alliance came from Senator Arthur Vandenburg and other prominent legislators, who had become convinced that the United States should desert its traditional policy of nonentanglement in European affairs.[1] With this proof of congressional support, Truman began negotiating with the Brussels nations on the possible form of a mutual defense association. The North Atlantic Treaty Organization (NATO) was established by a treaty appropriately signed in Washington on April 4, 1949—one month before the Berlin blockade ended. The treaty provided "that an armed attack against one or more of [the signatories] in Europe or North America shall be considered an attack against them all . . ." The treaty did not provide for the establishment of an integrated NATO force, but merely for the strategic coordination of the military actions of members of the alliance. Only under the impact of the Korean War was a standing army created under NATO command.

Korea, as Germany, had been divided at Yalta. The Russians had established a communist regime in the northern half of the peninsula (above the thirty-eighth parallel); and a conservative regime led by Syngman Rhee, who had spent thirty-seven of his seventy years in the United States, had been established in the South by the United States. On June 25, 1950, the northern regime invaded South Korea, meeting little resistance. There is some doubt as to how involved Russia was in the initiation of this attack. In fact, much evidence points the other way.[2] Russia was even boycotting the United Nations Security Council when the United States appealed for a resolution to repel the aggressor by force and the resolution passed. Yet the analogy between Korea and Germany was too clear to ignore, and all of western Europe steeled itself for another crisis perhaps more severe than the Berlin blockade.

The NATO nations were forced to recognize their weakness. If Stalin ordered his troops into western Europe, who could oppose them? Great Britain had no sufficient standing army, and France had committed her troops to regaining the French empire in Indochina. The obvious military solutions were the presence of American military forces on the continent and the rearming of Germany. There was no difficulty in obtaining an American commitment; but there was a great deal of opposition to German rearmament not only in France, where it was strongest, and in other countries that had been recent victims of the Third Reich, but also in Germany. Many German youths adopted the slogan *Ohne mich!* (Without me!) to summarize their opinion of rearmament. The French had no intention of allowing an independent German military establishment to be reborn. It was for this reason that Réné Pleven, the French premier in late 1950, proposed a European Defense Community (EDC) to be composed of troops from all West European nations with an international

---

[1] Jacques Freymond, *Western Europe Since the War* (New York: Frederick A. Praeger, Publisher, 1964), p. 57.

[2] David Horowitz, *The Free World Colossus* (New York: Hill and Wang, 1965), pp. 121–22.

command. This would be a truly international army and would foreclose the possibility of a revived German general staff. The United States quickly adopted the idea and pushed for its fulfillment. Great Britain, however, refused to place troops permanently on the Continent. The French insisted on a British presence to balance the German influence that would inevitably develop. The Americans and British considered the French position merely obstructionist. Still, after much ill will was generated among the three nations, a treaty creating EDC was initialed by the foreign ministers of France, West Germany, Italy, and the Benelux countries on May 27, 1952. The British still held aloof. The incongruous climax of the affair was that, after stalling from January 1953 until August 1954, the French National Assembly refused to ratify the treaty; thereby the French killed the French proposal. EDC was dead, and the French had, intentionally or not, delayed the rearmament of Germany for four years.

The day was saved by the Anglo-Saxons. Sensing that without British participation there might not be a West European defense force and being under great pressure from the United States, Great Britain finally agreed to commit British troops to the Continent for as long as the NATO command deemed it necessary. This cleared the way for French acceptance of at least partial rearming of Germany, and in September 1954, West Germany was voted into NATO. This decision was formalized in the Paris Accords, signed the same month, which also officially ended the Allied occupation of West Germany. Konrad Adenauer, who had assumed the office of foreign minister as well as chancellor, had achieved the full independence of the new Germany by using the West's desire for German military power as his bargaining point.

New Faces, New Policies, Same Results: 1953–56

Both the United States and Russia changed national leaderships in the first half of 1953. President Dwight D. Eisenhower's administration took office in Washington in January, and Josef Stalin died on March 5 to be replaced by a collective leadership. Ostensibly, this was an excellent opportunity for an easing of international tensions. Under new leaders, both governments were free to launch new policies without losing face, and in fact, both nations did initiate changes, at least rhetorically. While the Soviet Union gave several clear indications of interest in some form of detente, the new American secretary of state John Foster Dulles announced his intention of reorienting American policy from the negative and defeatist policy of containment to the dynamic and positive policy of "liberation" of peoples under the yoke of communist tyranny.

The first indicators that suggested the new Soviet leaders might adopt a new foreign policy were the relaxation of censorship and oppression within Russia and an easing of the economic controls over and exploitation of the satellites. Winston Churchill, once again prime minister, sensed a "thaw" behind the iron curtain and called for a summit meeting to settle the problems capable of solution and to find a modus vivendi for the ones that remained. At least, he suggested, it appeared possible to talk again. The American reaction was cool, haughty, and ideological. Churchill was virtually accused of being senile, and John Foster Dulles expressed the opinion to the Congress that the Soviet-American rivalry was "an irreconcilable conflict." Dulles was progressing along the ideological course begun by Truman.

> What it amounted to was the adoption of anti-Communism for an official American ideology. . . . The struggle with Russia was a struggle not between nations and men but between good and evil. . . . Thus in place of a clearer national purpose this blanket ideology came to substitute the more traditional concepts of American patriotism.[3]

The idea of a summit meeting was dropped for some time.

Yet more evidence mounted of the new direction of Russian policy. Four months after Stalin died, an armistice was signed in Korea. In 1954 the Geneva Conference on Southeast Asia permitted an orderly French disengagement from Vietnam. Georgi Malenkov, temporarily dominant in the Russian Presidium immediately after Stalin's death, even offered to negotiate the future reunification of the two Germanies on the basis of a neutralized Central Europe. At home he spoke out for a lessening of international tensions before the Supreme Soviet. He may have been encouraged to be conciliatory by a new sense of security, since in the same speech, he announced Russia's first test of a hydrogen bomb. In any event, he cut the Russian defense budget for 1955 and put more state funds into the production of consumer goods, calling for "peaceful coexistence" with the West. It was his economic policy that led to his defeat in February 1955 by Nikita Khrushchev, who came to power as a spokesman for the military-industrial complex.

Once in power Khrushchev did not substantially change Malenkov's policy of detente and peaceful competition with the West, although he did take steps to strengthen Russia's diplomatic position and to extend Russian influence. In 1955 the Warsaw Pact, an East European version of NATO, was imposed on the satellite states. Visiting Mao Tse-tung and leaders of noncommunist states of Asia, Khrushchev emphasized the new look in Soviet policy by extending loans and technical aid to underdeveloped nations and by avoiding confrontations with American interests. Surprising everyone in the West, he journeyed to Yugoslavia, admitted the possibility of independent paths to communism, and blamed the past bad relations between the two regimes on Stalin. The most overwhelming evidence of Moscow's goodwill was Russian willingness to agree to an Austrian peace treaty. Austria, as Germany, had been divided into four

---

[3] John Lukacs, *A New History of the Cold War,* 3d ed. (Garden City, New York: Doubleday and Company, 1966), pp. 114–15.

These men formed the "collective leadership" which succeeded Stalin's dictatorship: front row, left to right, are Lazar Kaganovich, Bulganin, Krushschev, Georgi Malenkov, and Voroshilov. (Courtesy of UPI)

zones in 1945. In 1955 Russia agreed to take part in a mutual withdrawal from Austria if Austria agreed to become a neutral as Switzerland was. The removal of Western and Russian troops from Austria was seen at the time as auspicious. The superpowers had taken a first step toward disengagement.

The Eisenhower-Dulles administration was wary of Russia's conciliatory measures and made the military encirclement of Russia a prime diplomatic objective. A Middle East Treaty Organization, similar to NATO, included Great Britain, Turkey, Iran, Iraq, and Pakistan. When France finally ended its agony in Indochina by withdrawal, the United States immediately organized the Southeast Asia Treaty Organization (SEATO) along with France, Great Britain, Australia, New Zealand, Thailand, Pakistan (once again), and the Philippines. Cambodia, Laos, and South Vietnam were later associated to SEATO by a separate protocol. Both of these agreements stated that an attack against any member nation would be considered an attack against all, and each state was pledged to aid the other signatories. However, Dulles realized that the other states, especially France and Britain, were not as committed to the anticommunist crusade as the United States was.

"If we take a position against a Communist faction within a foreign country, we have to act alone," he lamented. "We are confronted by an unfortunate fact—most of the countries of the world do not share our view that Communist control on any government anywhere is in itself a danger and a threat."[4]

With a policy based upon the belief that communism was a danger anywhere and everywhere, it was difficult to accept the evidence that the Russians might desire a detente and that negotiation was actually possible.

By 1955 the pressure from America's European allies for some attempt at a relaxation of tension was becoming very strong. The Austrian State Treaty almost necessitated some further gesture. Therefore, a summit meeting was arranged at Geneva in July 1955 with Eisenhower; Nikolai Bulganin, the Russian premier; Anthony Eden, Churchill's successor as prime minister; and Edgar Faure, the French premier of the moment. It would be easy to say that the Geneva Summit was an exercise in futility, signifying nothing. Actually, it probably impressed both superpowers of the gap between them and the difficulty of finding common ground. The Russians wanted to discuss the fate of Germany, hoping to achieve a neutralized, if unified, Germany in the pattern of Austria. The Americans insisted on discussing all problems at once—from Germany to Southeast Asia. One specific proposal was an American desire for aerial inspection of the military installations of all countries. The Russians did not consider this a serious idea, preferring to stick to Germany. A demilitarized Central Europe, however, did not fit into American plans, which called for a strong Germany tied to the West as a bulwark against communism—the role assigned to Germany since 1918 by Western leaders. The conference ended in a show of goodwill, but diplomatic tensions had not been lessened, as the dramatic events of 1956 were to show.

Two international crises occurred almost simultaneously—the Suez Crisis and the Hungarian Revolt—which greatly clarified the power relations of the postwar world. The Suez Crisis began when the United States decided in July 1956 that it would not loan Egypt funds for the Aswan High Dam, a project that Egyptian leaders considered vital to the industrial and agricultural future of their nation. Until the spring of 1956, both the United States and Great Britain had pledged to finance the project. However, when Gamal Abdul Nasser, the charismatic nationalist leader of Egypt's revolutionary military government, purchased arms from Czechoslovakia, the United States labeled him "procommunist" and withdrew its promise of aid. Great Britain, never very fond of Nasser, also backed out.

Nasser struck back by announcing that he was going to nationalize the Suez Canal Company. The British government owned the majority of stock in the company, and a few British troops were stationed in the Canal Zone by treaty. The British reaction was hysterical and violent. Nasser was compared to Hitler, and any proposal to negotiate with him

---

[4] Walter Lafeber, *America, Russia and the Cold War* (New York: John Wiley and Sons, Inc., 1968), p. 167.

was termed "appeasement." There was also the feeling among the Conservative majority in Commons that the time had come to settle scores with the Egyptian nationalists. Therefore, many pretexts were developed for England's continued presence in the Canal Zone. The most insulting of these was the argument that the Egyptians were too backward as a people to run the canal efficiently. So Anthony Eden, the British prime minister, began to plan the use of force against Nasser. In searching for support of this course, Eden found allies in France and Israel. The French believed that all of their troubles in North Africa (in Algeria especially) were due to the subversive influence of Nasser. The Israelis were naturally concerned about Nasser's purchase of arms from Czechoslovakia and hoped to wage a preemptive war before Egypt could become fully armed.

So a plan was devised during a secret Anglo-French and Israeli meeting in the French countryside.[5] Israel would invade Egypt on some handy pretext. Then Great Britain and France would occupy the Canal Zone in order to keep it open to international commerce. In this way, Israel could destroy the Egyptian army and air force, while Nasser was being discredited for losing the Canal Zone. The plan was evolved in several secret meetings in France during September 1956. Throughout the planning stage, the United States refused to take a clear stand. Eden has maintained that at one point Dulles promised American support for the invasion. Dulles always denied this.

Israel attacked Egypt at 4:00 P.M. on October 29. The next morning France and Britain sent a joint ultimatum requiring both sides to withdraw ten miles from the canal or suffer an invasion. Of course, Egypt did not consent, and, on October 31, two hundred French and British aircraft began to bomb Egyptian airfields. Two days later the United Nations passed a cease-fire resolution supported by *both* the United States and the Soviet Union. Feeling betrayed, the British could not stop because their troops had not yet landed. On November 5, one thousand Franco-British paratroops landed near Port Said and occupied the zone. Having secured their position, the French and British agreed to a truce.

The truce lengthened into a permanent peace. The Europeans were soon forced to withdraw their troops because of American economic sanctions. The United States had begun to sell pounds sterling, driving the pound's value down on international markets. Facing a major economic crisis, Eden was forced to surrender meekly, withdraw his troops, and submit to the Egyptian nationalization. The Suez venture had been disastrous for Great Britain and for the West in terms of relations with the Third World. Not only had Great Britain and France discredited themselves in the Middle East, but they had also fanned the flames of hostility toward the West among the newly emerging nations of Africa and Asia.

One reason for American circumspection in the Suez Crisis was that

---

[5] Peter Calvocoressi, *Suez: Ten Years After* (New York: Pantheon Books, 1966), pp. 94–95.

the United States was denouncing Russian intervention into Hungary at the same time. Since the death of Stalin, the Soviet Union had been easing the controls over her satellites, and the ruling communist parties within each state had been easing the restrictions—economic and political—on their citizens. By lifting the lid slightly, East European leaders discovered they had uncovered a boiling cauldron. In Poland Wladislaw Gomulka became first secretary of the Polish Communist party, representing a faction that demanded independent economic policies, rejected agricultural collectivization, and desired a reconciliation with the Catholic church. The Poles stopped short of weakening the one-party system or of questioning the Warsaw Pact alliance system, and after initial bluster and threats, the Soviets accepted the fait accompli and made their peace with Gomulka. Events in Hungary went much further. Imre Nagy, as premier and first secretary of the CP, declared that Hungary would allow noncommunist political parties to form and would become a neutral in world affairs. Russian troops crushed Hungarian dreams and occupied Budapest. Nagy was arrested (and later shot), and Janos Kadar, a Soviet puppet, was placed at the head of the Hungarian party and state. (See Chapter 18.)

Washington's reaction to events in Hungary was based on a pragmatism that belied the rhetoric of "liberation" and may have been a foreshadowing of the years of negotiation and summit meetings that were to come. Embarrassed by their own allies' actions in the Middle East, the Americans limited themselves to attempting to rally world opinion against Russia's rude invasion of a neighboring state. Annually, until 1960, the United Nations, on American urging, passed a resolution condemning Russia as an aggressor. Actually, the United States' refusal to take other action was a realistic assessment of the situation. The United States could not, in 1956 any more than in 1945, change the boundaries of Soviet influence without a major war. It was apparent then at the end of 1956 that the division of Europe into East and West was more permanent than most statesmen had been willing to admit. The Russians could only welcome this realization with a sigh of relief.

In November 1956, for the first time, Khrushchev could tell himself and his colleagues that the United States was to be trusted at least to the extent of not interfering with the Russian Empire in Eastern Europe. . . . While in the United States indignation about Hungary's fate set back the thaw in the cold war for at least two years, from the Russian point of view the chances of Russian-American friendship . . . were getting better.[6]

Economic Unity: Origins of the Common Market

The concept of a united Europe had been discussed since the late nineteenth century, but there was no organized effort to propagate the

---

[6] Lukacs, *New History of the Cold War*, p. 154.

idea until after World War I. During the 1920s a nobleman of the Austro-Hungarian empire, Count Coudenhove-Kalergi, began a one-man propaganda campaign for a Pan-European Union. Count Coudenhove was the personal friend of many leading politicians—among them was Aristide Briand. As France's minister of foreign affairs from 1925–32, Briand was an advocate of European reconciliation and peace through international cooperation. In 1929 he presented Coudenhove's ideas to the League of Nations in a speech calling for a United States of Europe. Public opinion was obviously not ready for such ideas, and the onset of the depression destroyed any hopes of international cooperation.

With the outbreak of World War II, Coudenhove left continental Europe and carried his message to Great Britain and the United States. His most notable, perhaps his most important, convert during the war was Winston Churchill. When at the war's end, electoral defeat had freed Churchill from the every day affairs of government, he turned his attention to the construction of a united Europe. Speaking at a convocation at the University of Zurich in September 1946, Churchill put his immense prestige in the service of the movement for European unity which had developed since 1945. In one line of his speech, he said explicitly, "We must build a kind of United States of Europe. . . ." He expressed his concern for the future relations between France and Germany in particular, saying that a federation might prevent further conflict. Churchill's ideas and proposals were vague, but at that early stage in the movement, this was an advantage rather than a handicap. It is also important to note that his proposal was meant solely for Western Europe and was complementary to his iron curtain speech in Fulton, Missouri, the previous March. In May 1948, Churchill convoked a conference at the Hague with the purpose of unifying the several organizations advocating European unity in one body. The result was the founding of the European Movement, an organization dedicated to political unity and hoping to attain this through applying pressure on the various national parliaments through a general public relations campaign and through direct lobbying. The movement received encouragement and impetus from the tentative moves toward West European military and economic cooperation embodied in the Marshall Plan, the Brussels Pact, and NATO. Each of these diplomatic events served to give the Europeans a sense of their common problems and the usefulness of cooperation.

The movement's goal was the establishment of some form of European parliament or assembly. In October 1948, the Brussels Pact powers set up a committee to study the possible formation of a Council of Europe. At this time, however, when dreams were becoming realities, a sharp and fundamental difference emerged between Great Britain and continental advocates of unity over its nature and extent. The British wanted organizations that would perform certain limited and specific functions but would have no governmental powers. The continental advocates of unity, known as federalists, saw the ultimate goal as one of complete political integration, and they tended to regard any limited organization as only a first step.[7] The federalists further wanted each state to surrender its own power, its sovereignty to international agencies. In 1948 this basic difference emerged in a debate over the form of the Council of Europe. The federalists hoped it would be a sovereign assembly, with members selected or elected by the various national parliaments and with some power to effect broad economic policy binding on each nation. This assembly would act as any parliamentary body in that majority votes would be binding. The British, on the other hand, insisted on a council of foreign ministers or their representatives that could only take action by unanimous votes. By requiring unanimity, the national sovereignty of each state would be preserved. The outcome was a hybrid. The Council of Europe, as established in May 1949, consisted of both a Council of Ministers and a Consultative Assembly. Britain had won, for the Council of Ministers retained a veto over the recommendations of the assembly.

The British victory had been purchased at great expense. It cost Britain the goodwill of the leading advocates of integration on the continent—such men as Léon Blum; Robert Schuman, France's minister of foreign affairs; de Gasperi of Italy; and Paul-Henri Spaak, the Belgian foreign minister. These men reached the decision that a united Europe would have to be built without England. The first session of the Consultative Assembly confirmed this decision. The British constantly blocked moves to transform the council into a supranational political body. This forced the "good Europeans" to turn to new tactics. They adopted a variation of the functionalist theory termed the "sector approach." The strategy was to construct several international agencies dealing with specific problems or areas of the European-wide economy and to grant supranational powers to these agencies within one economic sector. Eventually these agencies would merge, and the basis for political as well as economic integration would have been achieved.

The Schuman plan for a Franco-German coal and steel authority, later expanded to include other states, was a product of the "sector approach." The actual formulator of the plan was not Robert Schuman but Jean Monnet, the technocrat-extraordinaire who headed the French national planning commission. Monnet developed the idea quietly within his staff and then sold it to Schuman, who announced on May 9, 1950, that the French government was prepared to place all of its production of coal and steel under a single international authority if other states would make a similar move. Not only Germany but also the Benelux countries and Italy expressed an interest. Negotiations began almost immediately among

[7] U. W. Kitzinger, *The Politics and Economics of European Integration,* rev. ed. (New York: Frederick A. Praeger, Inc., 1963), pp. 4–7.

the six nations. Attempts were made to bring in other states, especially Great Britain. Harold Macmillan, the leader of the Conservative opposition, summed up the British response, "Our people will not hand over to any supra-national authority the right to close down our pits or our steelworks." George Bidault, speaking in the Consultative Assembly, answered for France by stating that he and his colleagues "could not subordinate the creation of Europe to its acceptance by any one country, however great."

The French proposal was not entirely unselfish. Certainly France hoped that a coal and steel authority would contribute to general prosperity, and western Europe was only beginning to recover from the economic crisis of 1945–47. But there were other motives. France had exerted great effort to limit German industrial activity as an occupying power. However, the Americans had clearly decided against this policy, and the Schuman plan represented a logical about-face. In the framework of a coal and steel authority, France would be able not only to observe and perhaps influence German industrial development, but she would also win the praise and gratitude of the United States for having contributed to the reconstruction of western Europe. Moreover, a most important area of conflict between France and Germany—the Saar Basin—could be removed as a political problem and source of nationalist agitation by effectively internationalizing it. This might serve to make France and Germany partners rather than enemies. Finally, the French, who had hoped to include Great Britain in a united Europe to counterbalance Germany, had decided that Britain would never cooperate in European integration. The Germans were receptive to the French proposal because it implied readmittance for them into the family of nations as well as economic reconstruction.

The European Coal and Steel Community (ECSC)—including France, Germany, Italy, Belgium, Luxembourg, and the Netherlands—was created by treaty on March 19, 1951. It took another year to obtain ratification in each state's parliament. ECSC offices were set up in Luxembourg in August 1952, and began operations in 1953. The institutional structure of ECSC later became the foundation for other international agencies. Its executive was the High Authority, composed of nine members and independent of national governments. It was responsible to a European Parliamentary Assembly, similar to the Consultative Assembly of the Council of Europe. A Council of Ministers, containing the foreign ministers of the member states, appointed the High Authority but could not veto its decisions. Finally a Council of Justice was established to decide matters of legal question, especially when the ECSC becomes involved in disputes with member states. Time has proved the Parliamentary Assembly to be more prone to supranationalism than the other branches. Composed of parliamentarians of the Six, its members have become a pressure group within each country for further integration.

MAP 10.   European Economic Blocs, 1947–70

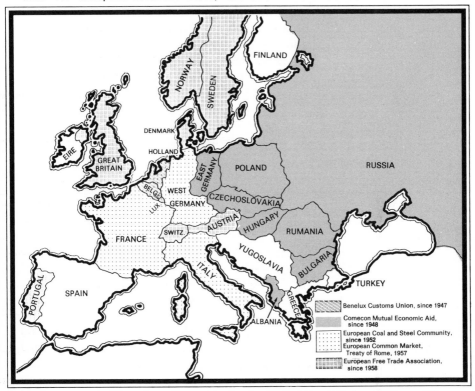

SOURCE: Martin Gilbert, *Recent History Atlas* (London: Weidenfeld and Nicolson, 1966), map 111.

The ECSC, with its sweeping powers over the economies of the Six, was the greatest victory for the "Europeans" to that date. It came just as they were suffering defeats in other areas, and it was itself responsible for a new division of western Europe. Many who favored unity had placed much hope in the passage of the EDC and an integrated military. Part of the EDC proposal had been a true European parliament to administer and coordinate both EDC and ECSC. When the EDC was defeated, the European parliament was also sacrificed.

This setback did not stop the movement toward integration; it merely forced it once again into the economic arena where it seemed most needed. The initiative this time came from the Benelux countries. In 1955 they proposed a fusion of national economies into a common market to be realized through the progressive reduction and then disappearance of import quotas and tariffs. Such a commitment would presuppose an adjustment of internal economic policy so there would be a truly free and competitive common market. This adjustment or "harmonizing of the economies" would be done gradually, over a period of years. The Benelux countries also proposed internationally coordinated programs in the areas of transportation, production of energy, and atomic research. The supranational aspects of the proposals were played down. It was to be a return to the sector-by-sector integration that had led to the ECSC.

A conference was held at Messina, Italy, in May and June 1955, to discuss the Benelux proposals. The six ECSC countries took part and endorsed the common market concept. Paul-Henri Spaak was requested to prepare a report on the steps necessary to bring about this goal. His report, presented one year later, called for a European Economic Community (EEC) and a European Atomic Energy Commission (Euratom) for the peaceful development of atomic energy. Spaak contended that the European states could not continue their economic progress as watertight compartments divided by tariffs because national markets and resources were too small to allow effective international competition with such giants as the United States. The following is extracted from the Spaak report.

There is not a single automotive enterprise in Europe large enough to use economically and feasibly the most powerful American machines. Not one of the nations on this continent is capable of constructing large transport planes without outside aid. In the field of atomic energy, the knowledge acquired at great expense in several nations of Europe amounts to only a fraction of the knowledge the United States now puts freely at the disposal of its industries and of other countries. It would take years to produce a few thousand kilos of enriched uranium, of which America has just announced it can put a surplus of forty tons at the disposal of its industry and of other countries.[8]

The reaction of the Six to Spaak's report was positive. Steps were taken to implement it.

Two treaties were signed in Rome on March 25, 1957, establishing EEC, better known as the Common Market, and Euratom. In contrast to ECSC, these two organizations were not independent of the Council of Ministers, which could veto their decisions. However, they had the same relationships to the European Parliamentary Assembly and the Court of Justice. Yet, even though legally decision-making power rested with the Council of Ministers, the power of the new commissions gradually increased due to their technical competence and the remarkable success of the Common Market.

Once again, however, the success of the Six had thickened the economic walls between them and the rest of western Europe. Great Britain, the Scandinavian states, Switzerland, Austria, and Spain watched the construction of the Common Market with foreboding and anxiety. If the Six developed a low-tariff or tariff-free market, the countries on the outside of

---

[8] Freymond, *Western Europe*, p. 132.

FIGURE 16.1.   Institutions of the Common Market in 1958

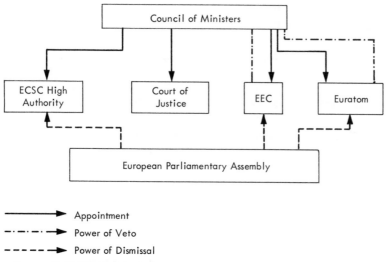

Appointment

Power of Veto

Power of Dismissal

Source: U. W. Kitzinger, *The Politics and Economics of European Integration* (New York: Frederick A. Praeger, Publisher, 1963), pp. 65–69.

the market's tariff barriers might lose their most important customers.

It was to prevent this possibility that Britain offered an alternative—a European-wide free trade area. In December 1956 the British proposed that all members of OEEC—all Marshall Aid countries—participate in this free trade arrangement. The British proposal suggested a reduction or disappearance of tariffs within the free trade area, but each state would be free to follow independent tariff policies toward other states. This was contrary to the EEC which was based on the concept of a common external tariff determined by a supranational commission. The British plan made any supranational political body superfluous. Once again the British had assumed the role of opponents of true European integration. For these reasons, the Six rejected Britain's wooing and proceeded to construct the Common Market.

Great Britain, therefore, looked to the remaining West European states for economic cooperation. In December 1959, seven nations formed the European Free Trade Association (EFTA)—Austria, Denmark, Norway, Portugal, Sweden, Switzerland and, of course, Great Britain. Finland associated itself with EFTA in 1961. Since both the EFTA and the EEC provided for a gradual reduction of tariffs until their disappearance in 1970, the economic integration of Europe, if not its political unity, had been prepared.

Chapter 17

THE INTERNATIONAL CONTEXT: REVOLT AGAINST THE WEST

Between 1945 and 1954 the European states lost their Asian empires. During the 1950s the Arab states of the Middle East and North Africa became aggressively independent of European influence. And by 1964 most of the sub-Saharan African colonies had emerged as independent nation states. The Second World War was the catalyst. Just as the First World War had weakened the European grasp on these countries, and just as the Russian Revolution had led to the first revolt of colonial peoples in the 1920s, World War II and the Japanese conquest of East Asia gave the final push to the decaying empires so they could but topple over after the war.

The nationalist movements in Asia and Africa occurred in three stages.[1] The first stage of indigenous reaction to European colonial rule was the formation of protonationalist movements, attempts by precolonial elites to save what could be salvaged of precolonial society. A second stage—that of bourgeois nationalism—paralleled the rise of a new native leadership, drawn from a modern bourgeoisie created by the industrial growth and bureaucratic administration that followed colonization. Desiring their nations to be free and independent parliamentary democracies on the European pattern, these leaders appealed only to the middle classes and were essentially conservative on social questions. During the final stage of the liberation struggle, the nationalist movements became mass movements by mobilizing peasants and workers behind a program of not only political independence but also social reform (especially land reform). The leaders in this third stage—Nehru of India, Mao of China, Nkrumah

---

[1] Geoffrey Barraclough, *An Introduction to Contemporary History* (Baltimore: Pelican Books, 1967), chap. 6.

of Ghana, Bourguiba of Tunisia—rejected a preservation of or a return to the precolonial society. They were modernizers as well as social revolutionaries. The length of time it took for the three stages to develop varied greatly from colony to colony. In the Asian countries and in the Arab states the process was slow, having begun in the nineteenth century. In sub-Sahara Africa the process was telescoped into ten or fifteen years, beginning during World War II and culminating in independence in the 1960s. It can be said that those nationalist leaders who mobilized the masses—the peasants and workers—succeeded; and those who held back and refused to employ mass agitation and social action did not. As Nkrumah said: "A middle-class elite, without the battering ram of the illiterate masses," could "never hope to smash the forces of colonialism."[2]

India and the British Withdrawal

The nationalist movement in India was fully developed by the 1920s. In the 1930s, the British began to make meaningful concessions to the Congress party's demands for self-government. The Government of India Act of 1935 provided for the election of provincial legislatures and the establishment of provincial cabinets responsible to the legislative majorities. Led by Gandhi, the Congress party won majorities in eight of the eleven provinces and was the largest single party in the other three. Just at this moment of success, a split between the Moslem and the Hindu leadership of Congress occurred. Mohammed Ali Jinnah, leader of the Moslem League, charged that Moslems were treated better under British rule than under the Congress-dominated provincial governments.

In 1939 the British requested Congress to give public support to the British war effort. Gandhi, Jawaharlal Nehru and other Indian leaders refused, and Congress representatives in provincial governments resigned, withdrawing their cooperation in hopes of forcing Great Britain to grant independence to India. Instead, the British viceroy jailed the nationalists. Three years later, however, the British had become more conciliatory under the pressure of a protracted war. And not only were the European and North African fronts discouraging, but also, in Asia, the Japanese were advancing through Indochina and Burma toward the frontiers of India. At this point the War Cabinet sent Sir Stafford Cripps to India to negotiate with Congress. Gandhi had just designated Nehru as his successor as leader of Congress, so Nehru played a major role in the negotiations. Cripps offered the Indians full dominion status within the British Commonwealth *after the war*. As soon as the war ended, he promised, a constituent assembly would be called to write a constitution for India as an independent dominion. The policy of postponement was all too familiar, and Congress leaders demanded some immediate sign of British

---

[2] Ibid., p. 190.

MAP 11. The End of Empire in Asia, 1945–65

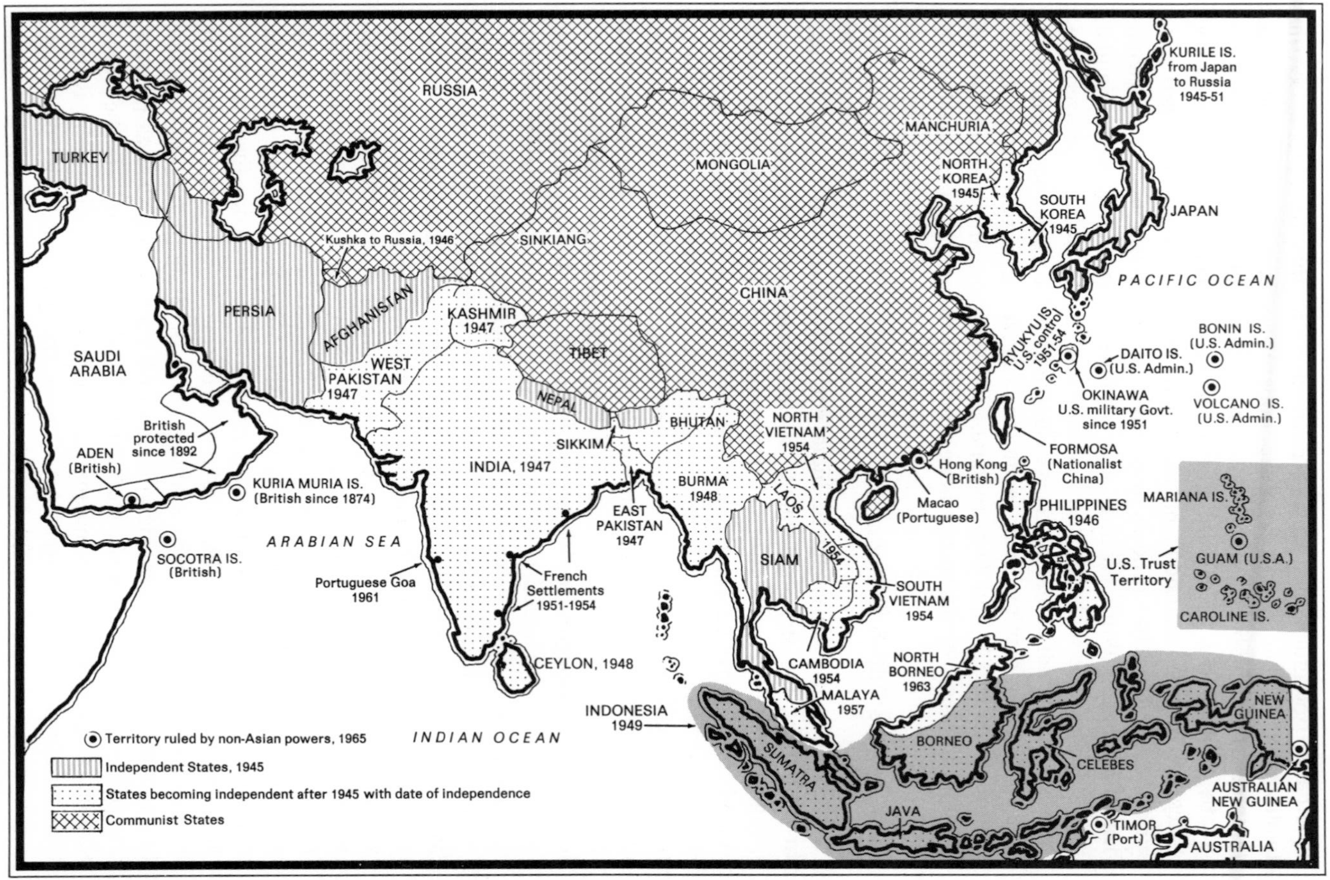

KURILE IS.
from Japan
to Russia
1945-51

JAPAN

PACIFIC OCEAN

BONIN IS.
(U.S. Admin.)

VOLCANO IS.
(U.S. Admin.)

GUAM (U.S.A.)

NEW
GUINEA

AUSTRALIAN
NEW GUINEA

AUSTRALIA

MARIANA IS.

CAROLINE IS.

U.S. Trust
Territory

DAITO IS.
(U.S. Admin.)

TIMOR
(Port.)

SOUTH
KOREA
1945

OKINAWA
U.S. military Govt.
since 1951

CELEBES

NORTH
KOREA
1945

RYUKYU IS.
U.S.
control
1951-54

FORMOSA
(Nationalist
China)

PHILIPPINES
1946

MANCHURIA

Hong Kong
(British)

Macao
(Portuguese)

SOUTH
VIETNAM
1954

NORTH
BORNEO
1963

BORNEO

MONGOLIA

CHINA

NORTH
VIETNAM
1954

LAOS
1954

CAMBODIA
1954

MALAYA
1957

1957

JAVA

SUMATRA

RUSSIA

SINKIANG

TIBET

BHUTAN

SIKKIM

SIAM

BURMA
1948

INDONESIA
1949

Kushka to Russia 1946

AFGHANISTAN

KASHMIR
1947

NEPAL

EAST
PAKISTAN
1947

French
Settlements
1951-1954

CEYLON, 1948

WEST
PAKISTAN
1947

INDIA, 1947

INDIAN OCEAN

PERSIA

KURIA MURIA IS.
(British since 1874)

Portuguese Goa
1961

ARABIAN SEA

TURKEY

British
protected
since 1892

SOCOTRA IS.
(British)

SAUDI
ARABIA

ADEN
(British)

⊙ Independent States, 1945

☷ States becoming independent after 1945 with date of independence

⊠ Communist States

⊙ Territory ruled by non-Asian powers, 1965

Source: Martin Gilbert, *Recent History Atlas* (London: Weidenfeld and Nicolson, 1966), map 9 5.

good faith. Nehru might have compromised at this point, but Gandhi would accept nothing short of independence. So the Cripps mission failed to reconcile the British administration and the Indian nationalists.

Angered by the British position, a Congress party conference passed the "Quit India Resolution" on August 8, 1942. This was a virtual ultimatum from Gandhi to the British Raj. It contained an offer and a challenge. In part, it promised that, if immediate independence were granted, "a Free India will become an ally of the United Nations . . . ," but, if it were not granted, Congress would sanction "a mass struggle on non-violent lines on the widest possible scale" with the goal of expelling the British from India. The day following the passage of the resolution all the members of the Congress executive were arrested, including Gandhi and Nehru, and they remained in prison until the end of the war. Their arrests ignited an explosion throughout India. Violence by Indians was met by repression by the British. Jinnah took advantage of the imprisonment of the Congress leaders to build the strength of the Moslem League at the expense of Congress. Before the war, Congress had contained many Moslems. When the war ended the vast majority of Moslems had joined the league and were demanding the establishment of a separate Moslem state.

The election of a Labour government in Britain in 1945 led to a complete change in the relations of Britain and India. Clement Attlee, the Labour prime minister, announced elections for a Central Legislative Assembly for December 1945. The assembly was dominated by the Congress party and the Moslem League. Nehru, chosen to head an interim government, tried to draw the Moslem League into the cabinet, but its leaders refused to collaborate with him. In the months that followed, the Hindu-Moslem conflict, intensified by a food shortage, led to violent clashes and thousands of deaths. After various unsuccessful attempts to mediate the dispute, the Labour government accepted the solution of creating two states instead of one—India and Pakistan. In February 1947, Attlee announced that by June 1948, all governmental power would be transferred to the interim government—Nehru's cabinet—and provision would be made for provinces that wished to remain outside the new Indian state (i.e., the predominately Moslem provinces).

Lord Louis Mountbatten was sent from London to arrange for the transfer of power. Mountbatten was an admiral and a polished diplomat. He became a close friend of both Nehru and Jinnah and convinced the Congress leadership that partition was inevitable. Finally, on August 15, 1947, several months ahead of schedule, India and Pakistan became fully independent, sovereign nations. This peaceful transfer of power was marred by horrible massacres of both Hindus and Moslems. In the brief period before the end of the year, 500,000 had died, and millions more had been forced to migrate to escape persecution. The withdrawal of the British had uncovered religious and cultural hatreds that their presence had suppressed.

Indochina and French Follies

With the outbreak of World War II, the various nationalist forces in Indochina, having been crippled by French repression in the early 1930s, saw a new opportunity for independence. The defeat of France by Germany in mid 1940 raised their hopes even higher. At this time, the Indochinese Communist party (PCI) and the VNQDD, the leading liberal democratic nationalist movement, formed a united front with other smaller groups to achieve the expulsion of the French. They took the name of League for Vietnamese Independence or Viet Minh. The Viet Minh, expecting aid from the Japanese, attempted to drive the French out by force in 1940. The Japanese gave no aid, however, and the French managed to crush the revolt, forcing the nationalists underground until 1945.

Since the Vichy government followed a policy of collaboration with the fascist powers, the Japanese allowed French officers to continue administering their colonies. Meanwhile, the Viet Minh built a parallel government in northern Vietnam, ready to replace the French administration whenever the opportunity arose. This underground government managed to organize and arm 10,000 men. When the Japanese position in Southeast Asia was threatened in 1945, the Japanese began to prepare for an Indochina dominated by Asians rather than by Europeans. The French administrators were arrested, and Japanese weapons were delivered to the Viet Minh. The retreating Japanese left the hereditary emperor Bao Dai on his throne when they evacuated, and Bao Dai declared Vietnam independent from France. The Viet Minh, however, did not desire a conservative regime, and Ho Chi Minh, the communist leader of the Viet Minh, declared the establishment of the Democratic Republic of Vietnam (DRV). Bao Dai, unable to gain popular support, abdicated and recognized the DRV as the only governmental authority in Vietnam. British troops were sent by the Allies to accept the Japanese surrender and to administer Indochina south of the sixteenth parallel. The Nationalist Chinese, followers of Chiang Kai-shek, were charged with administering the north. This was the first postwar division of Vietnam.

The British refused to recognize the legitimacy of the Viet Minh, and instead, they released the French from prison, rearmed the French military, and helped it restore French control over the Saigon area and other cities. The Chinese resisted the return of French personnel until American pressure and the communist threat within China required Chiang to withdraw his troops from Vietnam in March 1946.[3]

---

[3] Joseph Buttinger, *Vietnam: A Political History* (New York: Praeger Publishers, Inc., 1968), pp. 221–38.

In Paris, the three members of the tripartite coalition were in disagreement on the future of Indochina. A few Socialists anticipated an early independence. The majority of Socialists and the Communists desired independence for French colonies, but within some form of association with France that would maintain trade and cultural relations, similar perhaps, to the British Commonwealth. The MRP was for continued French control of Indochina and specifically opposed any solution that might allow the Viet Minh, which the MRP considered communist-dominated, to gain control of Vietnam. Under the influence of the Socialists and Communists and in keeping with the general reformist spirit of 1946, the French government opened negotiations with Ho Chi Minh in February 1946 in search of a peaceful solution. At the time, the Viet Minh slogan was "independence and Alliance." Ho preferred close cooperation with France to its alternative—domination of Vietnam by Chiang Kai-shek's conservative Nationalist Chinese military.

Negotiations conducted in France resulted in the Ho-Sainteny Agreement of March 6, 1946, which seemed to favor the Viet Minh position. France recognized Vietnam as a free state with its own parliament, army, and finances. The unification of the ancient kingdoms of Tonkin in the north and Annam in the center, both controlled by the Viet Minh, with Cochin China in the south was to be decided by a referendum. A later conference was to be held to determine the exact status of Vietnam as a member of an Indochinese federation of states the French intended to create from her former colonies. Finally, the French were allowed by the Viet Minh to land 15,000 men in Annam and Tonkin to restore order, but these were to be withdrawn at a rate of 3,000 per year. Ho Chi Minh received a great deal of criticism from his fellow nationalists for allowing the return of French troops, and the criticism was well founded.

The Ho-Sainteny Agreement was based on the assumption that the French government would be able to fulfill its part of the bargain. This it was unable to do. A third force existed, comprised of French *colons* in Vietnam—a coalition of military men, colonial administrators, and both French and Vietnamese businessmen—known as the Saigon Clique. Any French governmental policy had to be filtered through the Saigon Clique. The clique immediately sabotaged the Ho-Sainteny Agreement. The first step in this process was the establishment of a puppet regime in the south, at Saigon. Admiral Thierry d'Argenlieu, the military governor of Indochina, acting on his own authority, recognized this artificial creation as the free state of Cochin China. Ho Chi Minh was en route to Paris for further negotiations when this coup was carried out in Saigon. Negotiations were now impossible, but a good-faith cease-fire between the French and the Viet Minh was agreed on. Returning to Hanoi, Ho eliminated most of the moderates of the VNQDD from his government and formed a more leftist cabinet. By this time the Viet Minh had established a dictatorship over the North.

Open war was precipitated in December 1946 by two incidents. The first occurred at Haiphong, Tonkin's major port, when the French administration demanded the right to collect customs duties on incoming ships. Since this was a large portion of the DRV's revenue, the northern regime refused the demand. On November 21 the French issued an ultimatum requiring the evacuation of all Vietnamese military units from Haiphong and total freedom of movement for French troops. The ultimatum was issued without consulting the government in Paris, headed at that time by the SFIO leader Léon Blum. The Vietnamese predictably neither surrendered nor evacuated, and fighting began. The local French commander called on a French cruiser in the harbor to open fire on the Vietnamese quarter of the city, where Viet Minh troops were located. The dead totaled approximately 6,000, mostly civilians. This naval bombardment was the actual beginning of the Indochinese War, although the official declarations of war were not issued until after the so-called Hanoi Massacre a month later. According to reports in the French press, which were carefully orchestrated by the Saigon Clique, the Hanoi Massacre was an attempt by the Viet Minh to kill all the Europeans in Hanoi. The facts are that, after a night and a day of fighting in Hanoi on December 19 and 20, only forty Europeans had been killed, but 200 hostages had been taken. It seemed more an attempt to obtain human pawns for bargaining rather than mass murder. The French military reacted by occupying Hanoi, capturing the DRV offices, and driving the Viet Minh government and army into the mountains of western Tonkin, near Laos. Ho Chi Minh issued an appeal on December 21 for a general uprising. Within two days guerilla warfare had begun throughout the country.

The war evolved in two stages. From 1946 until 1949, it was primarily a guerilla war with no large battles. During 1949, fighting began on a larger scale until, by the time of the Geneva settlement of 1954, it had become a conventional war. The year 1949 constitutes a turning point for several reasons. It was during 1949 that the French established a rival national Vietnamese government under Emperor Bao Dai. This new government was heralded as the legal government of all of Vietnam, not only Cochin China. In an agreement with Bao Dai, the French once again recognized the independence of Vietnam. The emperor was not a servile lackey, and he even tried to include Ho Chi Minh in a coalition government until the French high commissioner pointedly told him that sovereignty would be transferred "only to a Government in which France has the fullest confidence." So Bao Dai gradually and against his wishes became a prisoner of French policy. This policy was to make the Bao Dai regime an anticommunist alternative to the DRV. At this time France recognized the theoretical independence of the State of Vietnam and granted real independence to both Cambodia and Laos. French troops were withdrawn from Cambodia and Laos, the leaders of which desired continued close economic ties with France, to fight in Vietnam.

The Chinese communist defeat of Chiang Kai-shek also occurred during 1949. In control of the China-Vietnam border, the Red Chinese were in a position to supply war materials to the Viet Minh. Not long after the Chinese began to do so, the United States extended aid to the French and the Bao Dai regime. Until 1948, the official American view of the Indochinese situation had been that France was trying to quell a nationalist revolt and regain control of her empire. During late 1948 and early 1949, faced with the collapse of Chiang, the Truman administration redefined the conflict as a struggle against communist subversion aided from Moscow and Red China. Shocked by the Korean War, the United States rapidly increased its economic aid to Bao Dai in mid 1950. The amount of aid continued to grow from $150 million in 1950 to $1.3 billion in 1954. By the date of the Geneva Conference, the United States was paying 80 percent of the war costs to the French, and a few military advisers had been sent to Saigon.[4]

Despite American aid, France had lost control over all but a minor portion of the country by the end of 1953, but that portion contained the major cities. Seeking to break the Viet Minh's hold on the countryside, the French established an isolated base deep in enemy territory near the Laotian border on November 20, 1953. This base, Dien Bien Phu was transformed into a formidable garrison from which the French general Navarre hoped his troops would be able to strike at the enemy's base camps and lines of communication. By February 1954, Dien Bien Phu was firmly encircled by Viet Minh forces. On March 16 the attack began. Viet Minh artillery denied the French garrison the air support it needed to survive. After fifty-six days the French surrendered. Over 16,000 prisoners were taken on May 7, 1954. On May 8 negotiations began in Geneva for settling the Vietnamese conflict.

The Geneva Conference had been planned before the siege of Dien Bien Phu began, but the fall of the French garrison placed the French negotiators in a very weak position. The French premier Joseph Laniel and his minister of foreign affairs Georges Bidault had one last hope— intervention by the United States. Throughout the siege, they had tried to persuade the Americans to send air support to Dien Bien Phu. Eisenhower had refused because of a desire to avoid another Asian war such as the Korean War. Yet, when Bidault went to Geneva, he still hoped to *save* Vietnam for France with American help.

The patience of the French public and parliament had, however, been

---

[4] George M. Kahin and John W. Lewis, *The United States in Vietnam* (New York: Delta Books, 1967), pp. 30–32.

exhausted. The MRP, which had occupied the two key ministries of foreign affairs and colonies almost without break since 1946, had clung to a disastrous policy too long. On June 9 the Laniel cabinet received its coup de grace from a speech in the National Assembly by Pierre Mendès-France, a Radical–Socialist. Mendès-France began by recalling that the MRP had delayed the end of the Indochinese War by labeling all who favored concessions as "Moscow agents."[5] He then attacked Laniel for having stalled through the negotiations at Geneva, and for requesting French draftees to be sent to Vietnam. To that point the war had been fought by the professional army, and it was the request for draftees that had turned many Frenchmen against the war. Mendès-France concluded his speech by warning, "It must be made obvious that what we want is not American intervention but an honourable ending to this horrible war." That night the Laniel government was toppled, and on June 17 Mendès-France was the premier.

On his first day in office, PMF, as the press labeled him, announced that if he had not achieved a satisfactory solution to the Vietnam problem within one month, by July 20, then he and his cabinet would resign. Astonishing everyone, he went to Geneva and reached an agreement with Ho Chi Minh, Red China, and Russia before the deadline. The United States, which was represented at the conference by John Foster Dulles, refused to be associated with the Geneva Accords and would not even make a verbal commitment to uphold them. The Geneva Accords provided that the Viet Minh would administer Vietnam north of the seventeenth parallel and the French would administer the southern half of the country. These were not to be two separate states, but only administrative zones pending the holding of a general election throughout both sectors in July 1956 to determine which government would have national authority—the DRV or the Bao Dai regime. Laos and Cambodia were to be neutral in this process (and in the cold war). An international control commission was created to observe the compliance with these provisions.

After nine years of attempting to reclaim a colony, France had escaped from Indochina. French military and administrative personnel were withdrawn as rapidly as possible. The United States quickly assumed the French role of protector of the southern regime, and the DRV obtained aid from China and Russia. Dictatorships were established in both North and South, and the elections of 1956 were never held.

The Middle East and European Influence

The Arabian states of the Middle East had been nominally independent since World War I, but in 1945 British troops were still stationed in

---

[5] Alexander Werth, *France, 1940–1955* (Boston: Beacon Press, 1966), p. 673.

the Suez Canal Zone and up the Nile Valley into the Sudan under a treaty that would not expire until 1968. British advisers influenced Egyptian economic policies, and British engineers operated the Suez Canal. Other Arab states felt the pressure of the British presence and were dependent on Europe and the United States as markets for their one significant product: oil. Aristocratic oligarchies dominated these states and resisted the modernization of their economies or the democratization of their political regimes.

In Egypt, as in all Arab states, a new elite developed during the 1920s and 1930s that had nothing but contempt for this corrupt aristocracy. These young men were sons of middle-class families and had received their educations in the ultranationalistic military academies. Some were educated in Europe. They had accepted the ideals of the American Revolution, the French Revolution, and the British parliamentary system. As one African nationalist leader said, "We took the French school books seriously." However, by the mid twentieth century, political liberties alone were not enough for this new elite. They had also read the classics of European socialism, learned the tenets of Marxism-Leninism, and observed the remarkable achievements of the Soviet economy. Finally, they had come to distrust the Europeans because each day they observed British violations of human rights in Egypt as well as the French denial of political liberties to the Syrians. Their discontent was intensified by the lack of careers open to talent in their own hierarchical, economically underdeveloped societies. The only career open to the university-educated young man was the military. So the army, with its camaraderie and cohesion, became the center of reformist movements.

Still, this new elite was not moved to challenge the position of the conservative oligarchs until a great tragedy and humiliation befell the Arab states and their armies—the Arab-Israeli War of 1948–49. In 1917 the British had encouraged the founding of a Jewish national home in Palestine, which had an almost purely Arab population. During the following decades Jews immigrated to Palestine by the thousands, with the tempo increasing as anti-Semitism became official policy in central Europe. During World War II the British tried to limit the number of Jews entering Palestine. Israelis, seeing in this policy an extension of Hitler's concentration camps, began to use terroristic tactics in protest. Arabs in neighboring states, seeing the Arab Palestinians gradually driven from their homeland, demanded that the British prohibit all immigration. It was this double-edged crisis that led the British Labour government to ask the United Nations to adjudicate the Palestinian problem in 1947. United Nations observers visited Palestine in mid 1947, and the UN eventually approved a plan for the three-way partition of Palestine into one Arab state, one Israeli state, and the Holy Places (Jerusalem and environs) which were to be international territory administered by the UN. Since the United

Nations offered them an honorable settlement, the British accepted it and withdrew their troops from Palestine in early 1948.

The withdrawal of the last British soldier on May 15, 1948, was the signal for the beginning of the first Arab-Israeli war. The Arabs were divided, poorly led, and poorly equipped. The Israelis, though greatly outnumbered, were militarily superior in every way. Interestingly enough in retrospect, the Israelis had bought their arms from communist Czechoslovakia with American money—funds channeled through the World Zionist Organization. The war ended in February 1949. The Israelis had not only successfully defended the territory assigned to them by the UN commission, but they had begun to expand the area under their control when armistice terms were agreed upon with the various Arab states. An Israeli state had been created with blood and iron, while 750,000 Arab refugees had fled from Palestine into permanent exile. These exiles had increased to two million by 1970. None of the Arab states would accept them because that would imply de facto recognition of the permanence of Israel.

The Arab military leaders were greatly humiliated by the war. Their initial outbursts of wrath against the Western powers, whom they blamed for the UN decision, soon gave way to a searching criticism of the weaknesses within the Arab world. The major weaknesses they found were the antimodern conservative ruling class and the lack of Arab unity. Effects of this self-criticism were felt first in Syria. In March 1949, the Syrian army, led by a young officer, Colonel Zaim, ousted the regular government. Arab reformers in other countries thought that perhaps this was the beginning of real change. Such hopes were dashed when Zaim was assassinated six months later, and Syria entered a period of instability—with conservatives being dominant—that lasted for five years. Similar events occurred in Jordan.

The signal for a profound and permanent revolution in Arab society and politics came from Egypt. During the winter of 1951–52, there were sporadic clashes between Egyptian nationalist guerilla fighters and British troops in the Canal Zone. On January 25, 1952, the British attacked an Egyptian police post and killed forty men. The following day is known as "Black Saturday." Cairo was the scene of mass rioting. The rioters directed their wrath carefully at symbols of British authority and at businesses of the conservative oligarchy that had run the country for so long. In retaliation, King Farouk tried to weaken the position of the young army officers whom he felt responsible for the agitation. After several months of struggle with the king, the army staged a coup d'état on July 23, 1952.

News of the Egyptian Revolution flashed across the Arab world. The coup's leader, General Naguib, denounced the corrupt and inefficient old elite and announced plans for the modernization of Egypt. The monarchy was abolished, and a republic was created by fiat. A prime task of the young officers was to obtain the full independence of Egypt by the withdrawal of the British troops from the Canal Zone. It was during negotiations on this subject, in 1953, that Gamal Abdul Nasser eclipsed Naguib as the spokesman for Egyptian and Arab aspirations. Nasser was more concerned with asserting Egypt internationally than Naguib had been, and he quickly became a popular hero. In July 1954, he reached agreement with the British for withdrawal of British troops within two years.

Nasser suddenly emerged as the leader of the twin movements for Arab unity and for Arab neutrality in the cold war. The United States tried to pressure the new regime into a Middle East Defense Organization similar to NATO, but Nasser refused. As an alternative, the United States sponsored a treaty between Iran and Turkey, already a member of NATO, which resulted in the Baghdad Pact, a mutual-defense treaty. Since the treaty was obviously aimed at Russia, it placed Iran squarely in the Western camp. Nasser launched his first major foreign policy campaign to denounce the Iranian move as a blow against Arab unity and neutrality. At about the same time, he was suppressing the Egyptian Communist party. Demonstrations in all Arab states supported Nasser, catapulting him into the leadership of the Arab world.

Events during 1955 propelled Nasser and Egypt further toward "positive neutralism." In February 1955 Israeli troops attacked the Gaza Strip—their first excursion into Egyptian territory—to retaliate against a guerilla raid. This only further unified the Egyptians behind Nasser, and it increased Nasser's distrust of the West, since he felt the Israelis were Western puppets. The following summer the Bandung conference met in Indonesia. A conference of Afro-Asian leaders desiring to remain neutral in the cold war, it was an historic assertion of the independence of the former colonial peoples. It was also a perfect stage for Nasser to expound his ideas on neutralism, and it reinforced his belief in the possibility of a strong neutralist bloc of "Third World" peoples. Finally, in September 1955, Nasser negotiated an Egyptian-Czech arms deal. Almost unanimously, politically conscious Arabs praised Egypt's arms deal with the Soviet bloc as a master stroke by which Nasser had broken the West's monopoly of arms in the Middle East. He had asserted Arab independence in the most concrete way possible.

Nasser was therefore at the crest of his popularity when he confronted Great Britain and France by nationalizing the Suez Canal in 1956. The two European nations and Israel invaded Egyptian territory to prevent the nationalization and to further their separate interests. Because of fortuitous international circumstances—including the confusion caused by the Soviet invasion of Hungary, Nasser was able to ride out the storm although clearly defeated militarily. He was able to complete the nationalization of the canal, and the British withdrew. This rid the Middle East of the last major vestige of European influence, even though Britain insisted on becoming involved in bloody and expensive wars over tiny sheikdoms in the 1960s.

Africa and One-Party Government

The colonial subjects of sub-Sahara Africa gained independence after 1957. The new states which they founded had special problems not shared by the Arab states of the Middle East or by French North Africa. The cultural tradition of Black Africa is tribal, fragmented, variegated, while that of the Arabs is uniform, transnational, and sometimes urban. Therefore, the nationalist governments which came to power in the sub-Saharan states had to construct unity from diversity, achieve prosperity without an industrial base, and mobilize a citizenry whose primary loyalties were local. Ghana, a British colony, was the first state of Black Africa to gain independence, doing so in March 1957; it stirred other colonial peoples by its example. Guinea became the first to gain independence from France in 1958. The years since 1960 have seen a veritable flood of newly independent states.

The case of Ghana offers a case study of the type of nationalist movement which was successful in the Black African colonies. British colonial policy after 1945 was based on the assumption that, sooner or later, colonies would become self-governing members of the Commonwealth; although the date for this devolution of sovereignty was seen far in the distant future. Therefore, the British, as in India, did attempt to train their colonial subjects in self-government, while always keeping ultimate power securely in British hands. The Gold Coast colony (later Ghana) was the pacesetter in Africa for this policy. Until 1946 the colony was governed by a British governor who had absolute power. He appointed an advisory council, which was dominated by Englishmen. This council was given legislative power and an African majority in 1946. Five years later a new constitution was proclaimed establishing an elected legislature. The British were greatly embarrassed when Kwame Nkrumah's Convention People's party (CPP) won the legislative elections, for Nkrumah was locked in a British prison.

When Nkrumah had returned to the Gold Coast in 1948 after ten years of study in the United States and England, his advocacy of full independence and liberal democracy was considered extremist. He soon began to transform the nationalist movement from a bourgeois party into a mass party on west European lines and, in its final form, into a tightly disciplined revolutionary party with socialist goals. This transformation, which had taken half a century in India and thirty years in Indochina, took only seven years in the Gold Coast. Nkrumah, from the first, was a disciple of Gandhi; and shortly after returning from abroad, he launched a "positive action" campaign to arouse the workers and peasants. This campaign resulted in strikes and boycotts and, eventually, in Nkrumah's imprisonment. After the CPP swept the 1951 legislative election, the British freed him to participate in parliamentary politics. He became prime minister of the Gold Coast and formed an all-African cabinet. After six years of peaceful political evolution, the Gold Coast became the independent state of Ghana in 1957.

Because Nkrumah was the head of the first Black African state to gain its independence, he rapidly attained great prestige and influence among other African nationalists. He became the leading spokesman for Pan-Africanism, the cooperation of all Africans to gain and maintain their independence from non-African powers and to develop the continent economically and culturally.

Nkrumah was plagued by the myriad problems shared by the newly independent sub-Saharan states. The ethnic diversity within these states deprived them of the internal cohesion of the European "nations." Their citizens do not share a common culture of a common language but are members of greatly different tribes or religious sects who coincidentally lived in an area coveted by Great Britain, France, Belgium, Germany or Portugal because of its economic benefits. The ethnic diversity and intertribal rivalries were not lessened by the period of colonial rule but only suppressed. Economic and social changes during the colonial period had, in fact, added new strains and stresses. A rapidly growing population was faced with a static food supply. Cities had been growing steadily before World War II, but increased economic activity during and after the war caused an urban explosion. Yet, the colonial rulers made no efforts to modernize agricultural production to feed the urban population. Such modernization was impossible partially because the Europeans had not trained the Africans in the technological skills necessary for modern production whether agricultural or industrial and partially because European agricultural techniques simply did not apply to certain African conditions. Finally, this hesitancy to educate the colonial peoples resulted in a vast shortage of technically competent professionals, engineers, and administrators when independence was achieved.

Nkrumah (as many other African leaders) met these problems by concentrating more and more power in his own hands; by attempting to create "national" unity around his political party, the CPP; and by creating a personality cult around his self. In 1960 the British constitution was replaced by a CPP-written constitution giving the Ghanaian president, Nkrumah, the power to rule without Parliament when he felt it necessary. Soon political parties other than the CPP were forbidden. A Preventive Detention Act was passed allowing Nkrumah to arrest his political enemies without making any legal charges against them, and this power was used to snuff out criticism of the regime. After several years of arbitrary rule,

MAP 12.   The End of Empire in Africa, 1956–65.

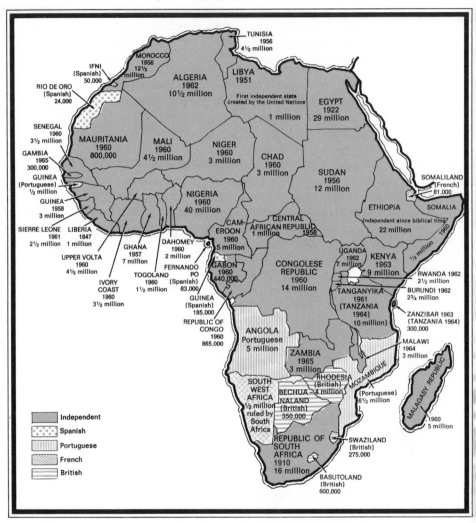

SOURCE: Martin Gilbert, *Recent History Atlas*. (London: Weidenfeld and Nicolson, 1966), map 68.

Nkrumah was himself ousted by the Ghanaian military. It was a pattern to be followed in many emerging nations.

Some Concluding Thoughts

No doubt the European imperial states could have resisted the revolt of the colonial peoples longer than they did if their citizens would have accepted the effort. After World War II there was no longer popular support for an imperial policy. Social welfare, reconstruction of domestic industry, and a surcease from warfare were the prime goals of Europeans. Although the colonial subjects were rebelling against European rule, their revolt did not really threaten the ruling nations. The revolutionary nationalist leaders were not essentially anti-Western, except in so much as they had to be to oust the British, the Dutch, and the French. In many states, however, the nationalists were forced to turn to the Soviet bloc for aid because of the lack of an alternative. This did not mean that the nationalists had become puppets of Moscow, but only that, like any politicians, they chose their friends from among those who were willing to help them.

PART VI

Emergence of a New Society

Chapter 18

RUSSIA AND THE SOCIALIST STATES, 1948-64

Russia had suffered greatly during World War II. Approximately twenty million Soviet citizens had died. This had inevitably been a shock for the Russian psyche as well as for the economy. There had been an equivalent shock to the Stalinist regime. Many Soviet citizens had lived in areas occupied by the Germans, who not only spread anticommunist literature but also dissolved the collective farms and began a redistribution of the land to the peasants. The Germans had also favored separatist movements among various national minorities—especially the Ukrainians. Soviet soldiers who had marched through eastern and central Europe were able to compare for the first time Soviet and non-Soviet living standards and political philosophies. Furthermore, Stalin had loosened the reins of cultural control during the war when authors, painters, and playwrights could be trusted to be patriotic. There existed in postwar Russia, therefore, many potential sources of opposition to a restored totalitarian regime.

Russian Recovery, Stalin's Death, and Khrushchev's Rise

In early 1946 Stalin launched a campaign to return Soviet society to its prewar state of terror-inspired conformity. The man charged with this task on the cultural level was Andrei Zhdanov, Stalin's heir apparent. His severe attack on free expression among intellectuals was known as the *Zhdanovshchina* (Zhdanov terror). First writers, then social scientists, and finally even natural scientists were forced to adhere narrowly to a "party line." Any variation from the official line in any area was considered treason. Any suggestion of Western influence was denounced as "cosmopolitanism." Neglect of ideology was charged of such prominent men as the composers Sergei Prokofiev and Dmitry Shostakovich and the film director Sergei Eisenstein. It was during the *Zhdanovshchina* that Trofin Lysenko's unscientific theories on genetics were endorsed by the Central Committee. Lysenko argued that the inheritance of acquired characteristics was possible. Therefore, good Bolsheviks could pass on their political views to their children. The scientist who dared suggest that perhaps the genetic experiments of Mendel were more valid was in danger of arrest and imprisonment. Fortunately, Zhdanov died under mysterious circumstances in August 1948. Yet, as if to complete the *Zhdanovshchina*, Stalin soon launched a purge of the party and of certain professional groups. This campaign was clearly anti-Semitic, and Jews were charged with an inherent tendency to worship the West and its culture. After 1948 the insistence on ideological conformity and the purges were extended to the Soviet satellites of eastern Europe.

With Zhdanov's death the second place in the Russian hierarchy was filled by Georgi Malenkov, head of Stalin's private secretariat. Malenkov, however, shared eminence with Lavrenty Beria, who had been chief of the secret police (the NKVD) since the end of the show trials in 1938. These two carefully removed Zhdanov's followers from the party leadership during 1949–50 and emerged as competitors for Stalin's favor.

Russia's economic system had suffered just as great a shock during the war as the political system. The Fourth Five-Year Plan was initiated in 1945. It provided for a massive program of economic reconstruction, concentrating primarily on rebuilding what the war had destroyed. The Fifth Five-Year Plan (1950–55) projected and achieved a great expansion of Soviet production. The achievements of these two plans was impressive. Almost all sectors of the economy were producing less in 1945 than in 1940—except for the war industries. Yet, steel production, which had been 18 million metric tons in 1940, had increased to 38 million tons by 1953. In the same period, annual coal production had risen from 166 million metric tons to 318 million tons and the production of electricity from 48 billion kilowatt hours to 133 billion kilowatt hours.

Such rapid growth and the urbanization and industrialization that accompanied it created new problems as Stalin pointed out in a speech convening the Nineteenth Party Congress in October 1952. This congress, the first since 1938, was most notable for an article published just before it met, setting its tone, entitled "Economic Problems of Socialism in the USSR," the article has become known as "Stalin's Testament." Stalin seemed to retreat from previous policy in two key areas: economic policy and foreign affairs. He wrote that objective economic laws could not be subordinated to the political needs of the state. This appeared to be a decision to slow the forced pace of economic growth in Russia since 1929. Concerning international relations, Stalin deemphasized the conflicts between the capitalist and communist camps. He implied that the revolutionary flood of the postwar years, which had led to the establishment of the satellites, would be followed by an ebbing of revolutionary forces. This was interpreted to mean that a detente with the West might be possible since Russia had secured its control of eastern Europe. At the Nineteenth Congress, Stalin launched a "peace offensive" by suggesting that negotiations with the West could be profitable. It seemed that Stalin was preparing for a reversal of policy in many areas.

His commitment to new policies was never tested; for, after the Congress, Stalin had but a few months to live, and those months were marred by the so-called Doctors' Plot, the culmination of his anti-Semitic campaign. In January 1953, *Pravda* denounced nine doctors, six of them Jewish, of having assassinated Zhdanov and other leading Soviet figures. It appeared that a major purge had begun. Of course, Stalin alone knew who would be the victims. The purge never was carried out because Stalin died of a brain hemorrhage and paralytic stroke on the evening of March 5. There were many rumors in the West that the dictator had been assassinated, but all evidence indicates that he indeed suffered a stroke while presiding over a meeting of the party Presidium (the old Politburo) on March 4 and never regained consciousness. At age seventy-three, the man who had built Russia into the world's second greatest power and had created a Soviet empire in eastern Europe had disappeared from the stage.

Stalin's death was followed, as Lenin's had been, by a momentous debate over the future of the communist state. This debate, as the earlier one, took the form of a struggle for power by rival individuals and factions in the party's Central Committee. The immediate emergence of Georgi Malenkov as the new general secretary of the party and also as chairman of the Council of Commissars (i.e., prime minister) misled many Western observers to think such a struggle would not take place. Malenkov's ascendancy was very shortlived. His name appeared alone in *Pravda* and other journals only from March 6 through 11. The new general secretary was a party official but one who had served in the state administration for so long he had begun to identify with it. In fact, he was considered a spokesman for the economists, engineers, and other technicians who had been chafing under the yoke of Stalinist dictatorship. Malenkov aligned himself with these technocrats even against the party organization. Whereas it had been party dogma and Soviet policy since 1929 that heavy industry should have first priority in economics, Malenkov and the technocrats advocated a "new course" that would emphasize light industry and consumer goods. Among Malenkov's first acts was the appointment of five economic experts to the party Presidium as advisers. Among these was Alexei Kosygin, who had formerly been the minister for light industry and consumer goods.

After March 11, Malenkov's name in newspapers was always accompanied by those of Beria and Molotov. Beria, commissar (or minister) of the interior, was feared because of his ability to use the NKVD as a private army. Vyacheslav Molotov, minister of foreign affairs, was respected more for his personal qualities and political acumen. These two began to share the public spotlight with Malenkov only weeks after Stalin's death. They were only the most powerful members of the fourteen-member Presidium, which actually ruled Russia collectively. After having been given new freedom by Stalin's death, neither the Central Committee nor the Presidium was willing to allow another man to gain the power of life or death over them. Other important members of the Presidium were Nikita Khrushchev, a deputy secretary of the party, and Nicolai Bulganin, minister of defense. Throughout the political maneuvering and policy changes of the period 1953–56, no one man acted independently of the Presidium majority. Each man's power rested on his ability to persuade a majority of the members of the Presidium and the Central Committee to follow his lead.

During the first months of "collective leadership" several steps were taken to end the worst abuses of the Stalin era. Beria announced a broad amnesty for short-term, nonpolitical prisoners. He also promised that the penal code would be examined with a view to making it less severe. The "cult of personality," the servile worship of the head of state, was denounced—without, however, any mention or direct criticism of Stalin. In fact, Stalin's name all but disappeared completely from newspapers and speeches by public and party officials. The Doctors' Plot was unmasked as a hoax, and the doctors who had been arrested were released and rehabilitated.

Simultaneously, censorship on literature was considerably relaxed. This released a current of free expression which, with only occasional setbacks, gained strength until the regime attempted to reimpose rigid censorship in the mid 1960s. During the summer of 1953 leading artists in various fields published articles in literary reviews and elsewhere demanding that Russian artists express themselves freely. Khachaturian, a noted composer, was allowed to write, "I believe the time has come to change the existing system of official supervision of composers. Creative problems cannot be solved by bureaucrats." Ilya Ehrenburg published an article advocating a true portrayal of the Russian people, without the glowing recitation of statistics that the bureaucracy had demanded. Ehrenburg also published a book, *The Thaw,* in mid 1954 that gave a name to this period of Russian cultural history. *The Thaw* contrasted the lives of two painters—one who adapted his work to the party line and one who tried to keep his creative independence in spite of the state's disapproval. Of course, Ehrenburg sympathized with the second artist. There were other novels, plays and poems that criticized the bureaucracy, the standard of living, or the suffering under Stalin. By late 1954 the government had become alarmed at the torrent it had loosed, and it once again began to insist on "socialist realism," works that glorified communist society. But it was too late to return to Stalinist conformity, and the new rulers did not wish to do so.

The thaw in Russia and the fact of Stalin's death had their repercussions in the satellites. Demonstrations occurred in scattered cities—especially in Poland and Czechoslovakia—demanding more freedoms. The greatest disturbance, which led to Beria's fall, was the East Berlin general strike of June 1953. An increase in production quotas for East German workers touched off a protest in Berlin that escalated into a riot against the communist regime. Russian troops and tanks were called in to crush the uprising. Several weeks later it was announced in Moscow that Beria had been arrested. It is now known that he was assassinated almost immediately, but his execution was not announced until the following December. Although the role played by one of Beria's deputies in East Berlin was used as an excuse for the arrest, and Beria's past abuses of his exalted position were cited against him, it was fear of the power of the NKVD that led to his execution. The Presidium members were not willing to allow this independent army to remain the private tool of one politician. There would still be a secret police, but it would be an instrument of the Presidium, not a threat to the collective leadership.

Yet there seems to be a necessity for one man to be first among equals in any political organization. Malenkov, therefore, had rivals for the role of Soviet leader. His most formidable foe was Nikita Khrushchev, an excellent party administrator and a technical expert on agricultural policy. Only ten days after Stalin's death, when collective leadership was being adopted, Malenkov had been required to surrender his title of general secretary of the party. Khrushchev was not officially given that title, but his name was always listed first among the five deputy secretaries. Khrushchev used his position to pack the various party organizations with his own men, while removing Malenkov's followers from key offices.

The struggle between Malenkov and Khrushchev, which was really a struggle between the state administration and the party organization, began to come into the open in the fall of 1953. On August 8 Malenkov publicly announced his new course in economic policy, which, besides emphasizing consumer goods, would entail a decentralization of the economy. One month later, on the day Khrushchev was finally installed as general secretary of the party, Khrushchev gave a major speech on the deplorable state of Russian agriculture and suggested that this was an area that should receive top priority. Four months later he outlined his own Virgin Lands Program for the development of seventy million acres of arid land in Asian Russia. This massive undertaking would require much manpower—to be supplied by volunteers from the party and the Communist Youth League (Komsomol)—and a great amount of new agricultural machinery, including 120,000 tractors and 10,000 harvest combines. The machinery necessary could be produced only by sacrificing Malenkov's new course.

The struggle raged during 1954 between the proponents of the two economic programs. Malenkov was no match for Khrushchev or the party machine, which stood to gain power and prestige by organizing the Virgin Lands manpower drive. Khrushchev toured the vast Soviet Union in the manner of a western politician, speaking to farmers and mobilizing support within the party, while Malenkov remained in Moscow. Two events indicate that Khrushchev had won by December 1954. One was the trial of a leading Malenkov supporter, Abakumov, for his role in various Stalinist purges. This condemned Malenkov by implication. The second indicator was an article in *Pravda,* signed by Khrushchev, stressing the priority of heavy industry. It was essentially a public announcement that the new course advocates had been defeated. Malenkov resigned as chairman of the Council of Commissars in February, 1955, and Khrushchev nominated Bulganin to replace him. Khrushchev was obviously the first among equals in the Presidium.

Eastern Europe under Stalinism

The formation of the Cominform in September 1947 had marked the gradual imposition of Stalinist uniformity on the East European regimes. The first indication of this was the adoption by all of the satellites of constitutions modeled on the Soviet constitution. The term "people's democracy," used to describe the satellite political systems, was redefined. Immediately after the war this term referred to rule by coalitions of democratic parties, with the communist party dominant. During 1948 it became the official line that "people's democracy" was one of the two historically established forms of the proletarian dictatorship, the other being the Soviet form.

In practice this redefinition signified the transformation of the east European states into carbon copies of the Russian model. The role of the party in the state became all-important. Communists occupied all top political and administrative posts. Party members were given special rights and privileges, and certain stores were reserved for the sale of luxury goods to party members only. The bureaucracy grew enormously and was reorganized on the Soviet model, with administrative agencies paralleling specialized economic sectors. The long-range economic plans adopted by all countries contributed to this bureaucratic sprawl, for the plans required researchers, planners, investigators, and regulators for each economic problem. The worst import from the Soviet Union was the increased use of terror as a government policy and the exaltation of the secret political police. Public show trials were conducted in each state to intimidate those who might be dissatisfied with the regime. Real or imagined enemies of the state were rounded up and detained in concentration camps or used in forced labor brigades. The number of *identified* camps alone suggests the scale of this coercion: 124 camps in Czechoslovakia, 199 in Hungary, 97 in Poland. Another aspect of the institution of police states was the requirement that each citizen carry an "internal passport," an identification booklet that he must produce on command.

The show trials were part of a much broader purge of party personnel that occurred during 1949–52. The purges were urged by the Soviet leadership of the Cominform, and the charges were mere mimicry of the charges being used to justify the simultaneous purge in Russia. Usually the accused party members were denounced as Titoists, although the charges of "cosmopolitanism" and "Zionism" were frequently employed against Jews. The purges were not limited to party leaders, but regular party members as well were purged in large numbers. Anyone who had not spent World War II in Russia was suspect of having absorbed western ideas and having become cosmopolitan. This included many who had fought in Spain against France and some who had fought in the French, Italian, and Greek resistance movements against the Nazis. Approximate figures indicate that about one in every four party members was purged.

Aside from the purges, the most spectacular evidence of the impact of Stalinization was the adoption of economic planning by the east European states during 1949 and 1950. Each state adopted a five-year plan—except Poland, which adopted a six-year plan. Of course, these were patterned on the Russian experience and were closely coordinated with the Soviet Five-Year Plan of 1950–55. The Soviet Union was able to influence directly the economic fate of the satellites as the result of certain jointly owned companies imposed by the Russians. Using tactics similar to western capitalists in underdeveloped areas of Asia, Africa, and Latin America, the Russians negotiated joint ownership of major industries in the satellites. For instance, the Russians merely replaced the Americans and British as owner and operator of the oil fields of eastern Europe. Virtually all prewar German property became postwar Russian property. Sixteen joint companies were created in Rumania, six in Hungary, and seven in Bulgaria. In this manner and by requiring the east Europeans to coordinate their economic planning with Russia's, the Soviets tied the satellites to the Socialist homeland with an ever tightening noose of economic dependency.

The east European five-year plans had two goals: the rapid collectivization of agriculture and the rapid expansion of heavy industry. In general these goals were accomplished. The pace and degree of collectivization varied from country to country, reflecting national differences in economic structure and the strength of the ruling communist parties. In industry the achievements were considerable. The underdeveloped nature of the economies of Hungary, Rumania, and Bulgaria required that they first

TABLE 18.1.   Trade with the USSR and Other People's Democracies
(imports and exports as percentage of total)

Country	1937	1948	1949	1950	1951
Bulgaria	12	74	82	88	92
Hungary	13	34	46	61	67
Poland	7	34	43	59	58
Rumania	18	71	82	83	79
Czechoslovakia	11	30	45	52	60

SOURCE: N. Ivanov, "The Foreign Trade of the European People's Democracies," *Vneshnaia Torgovlia*, no. 10 (1952), as cited in Zbigniew K. Brzezinski, *The Soviet Bloc* (New York: Frederick A. Praeger, Inc., Publishers, 1961), p. 127.

lay a basis for industrialization and urbanization. Poland and Czechoslovakia, being already industrialized, doubled their entire industrial
production from 1949 to 1953. By that date eastern Europe equaled
West Germany in steel production and coal extraction.

TABLE 18.2.   Percentage of Arable Land in Collective Farms

Country	1950	1953	1954	1956	1957
Poland	12	17	19	24	14
Rumania	12	21	26	35	50
Hungary	19	37	32	33	22
Czechoslovakia	25	48	44	45	70
Bulgaria	44	62	60	62	90
East Germany	...	8	30	33	40
Yugoslavia	18	24	...	9	...

SOURCE: Zbigniew K. Brzezinski, *The Soviet Bloc* (New York: Frederick A. Praeger, Inc., Publishers 1961), p. 99.

The price paid for such rapid growth was great, for the forced pace
soon began to create new problems as well as solve old ones. The growth
of industry drew hundreds of thousands of residents into urban centers,
but there were no houses or apartments for them to live in or transportation by which they could commute to work. Sewage and sanitation facilities
were inadequate. Agricultural production did not increase quickly enough
to meet increasing urban demands. The emphasis on heavy industry—especially on armaments industries during the Korean War—was nonproduc-
tive. The Soviets had insisted on the development of arms, but these
industries did not feed back into the economy as the production of agricultural machinery would have. East European leaders began to gripe
about Stalinization and the economic difficulties and imbalance it was
causing even before Stalin's death.

Stalinization also dictated the foreign policies of the satellites. Their international relations were limited to contacts with the Soviet Union. Diplomatic contact with the West all but ceased. Stalin or his agents approved each contact with a non-Soviet bloc nation. The guiding maxim was that what harmed the Soviet state harmed all socialist states and what aided Russia aided all socialist states. A natural adjunct of this veneration for Soviet interests was the extension of the Stalinist personality cult from Russia to the satellites. Stalin was hailed as infallible by the Soviet bloc leaders. A Czech radio station broadcast this paean of praise: "So calm, wise, human, sincere and illuminated by the stars . . . Behold! This is Stalin!" The worship of Stalin was part of the worshipful imitation of all things Russian. The school systems were patterned after the Russian; the Russian language became each superior student's second language; and Russian books, plays, and movies dominated cultural life. As the pressures of the cold war increased, this imitation was considered a form of security by Stalin and the East European leaders alike. Their alliance against capitalism was strengthened by it, just as anticommunism supplied cement for the NATO alliance.

During the years of Stalinism, Yugoslavia, led by Tito, was developing an alternative to the Soviet model of a communist society. Having been expelled from the Cominform and isolated by the Soviet bloc because he would not bow to Stalin, Tito turned to the West for aid. This allowed him to maintain a precarious independence from both camps. Milovan Djilas, Tito's foremost ideologue, produced an ex post facto theoretical basis for Titoism in 1950. This justification also included an indictment of the Russian CP for having become overbureaucratized and for not allowing the state to wither away as Marxist theory predicted. This debate, as most debates among Marxists in power, was basically a question of economic policy. The Yugoslavs insisted that the highly centralized Soviet economic structure was not suitable for Yugoslavia.

The alternative economic model offered by the Yugoslavs differed from Russian practices in three major ways. First, the Yugoslavian economy was declared to be a "socialist market economy."* Competition and the rules of supply and demand, not governmental agencies, were to dictate production quotas. The state, owner of all enterprises, would allow the management of each firm or factory a great deal of freedom in buying, selling, and negotiating contracts. Factories could even compete by cutting production costs or by public relations campaigns. Second, workers' councils were created to allow workers to participate in management. Workers would elect representatives to sit on the councils, which acted as managerial boards for individual enterprises. Various categories of

---

* To be distinguished from the "*social* market economy" of West Germany. See Chapter 19, p. 397.

"workers" always outnumber managerial and technical personnel on the councils. Workers, therefore, can and do overrule management on factory policy. The councils become, in essence, "socialist capitalists," deciding on wage scales, paying dividends to the firm's employees based on profits, and borrowing money from banks for plant expansion. Finally, the Yugoslavs rejected agricultural collectivization. Although some forced collectivization was attempted, the CP decided that improvement of methods of individual production and not collective farming was the best way to raise production. Much of the land already collectivized by 1950 was decollectivized, but a few large collectives were continued. These heretical economic policies marked Tito's state off from the other East European countries, and after Stalin's death, the Yugoslav model became increasingly attractive to the citizens of the satellites.

Khrushchev's Victory

Khrushchev's reorientation of Soviet domestic and foreign policy was debated by various party bodies during 1955. The changes in foreign affairs were especially striking. More emphasis was placed on peaceful competition with the West. Khrushchev and Bulganin made several flamboyant foreign tours, most notably to Asia and to Yugoslavia. Stalin had denounced the leaders of the new India as bourgeois nationalists; Khrushchev embraced them as fellow victims of the capitalist West. Stalin had heaped scorn on Tito and ordered a purge of Titoists; Khrushchev blamed all Russo-Yugoslav disagreements on Stalin and urged cooperation between the two socialist states. Before leaving Belgrade Khrushchev and Tito initialed a joint declaration stating that there were several paths to communism. Such policy reversals were not popular with many Russians who had made their career as faithful servants of Stalin.

It appeared that the Twentieth Party Congress, to be held in February 1956, would be a test of Khrushchev's strength and an indication of the future course of the Soviet Union. In preparation for the congress, Khrushchev replaced party officials of the Stalin period with younger men more in tune with the new policies. In Georgia alone, 2,589 party cell secretaries were changed. One of the most important changes was the appointment of Leonid Brezhnev to the post of first secretary of the republic of Kazakhstan. Other precautions were both petty and portentous. The secret police was purged of individuals who had conducted the show trials of 1936–38, and the victims of those trials were rehabilitated in school textbooks. Stalin's ornate architectural style was condemned and ridiculed; while a simpler, more economical and functional style was adopted. Party journals criticized dogmatism and the foolish memorization of clichés. Historians were encouraged to make more contacts with scholars of other countries and to avoid the narrow nationalism of the

Krushchev's travels abroad and his flamboyant manner contrasted with Stalin's seclusion. Here he and Soviet Deputy Premier Anastas Mikoyan accept a bouquet in East Berlin. (Courtesy of UPI)

Stalin years. An amnesty was even announced for Soviet citizens living abroad. It seemed that the thaw would touch all phases of Soviet life.

Still, no one but the top party officials expected the remarkable events of the Twentieth Party Congress. Khrushchev made two major speeches: one public, the other in closed session. In a public speech on foreign affairs, Khrushchev repeated and enlarged on the Belgrade declaration, emphasizing that there were different roads to socialism. He stated that war between capitalism and socialism was not inevitable. Since imperialism had ceased to be a world system, war might be avoided. Therefore, he advocated peaceful competition or "coexistence" with the West. This was mild compared to the subject of the secret speech. On February 24, 1956, Khrushchev denounced the crimes of Josef Stalin and condemned the Stalinist system of personal, arbitrary rule. The speech was extremely long—approximately 20,000 words, it was the length of a sixty- or seventy-page book. Those attending the secret session sat in amazement as Khrushchev enumerated the evils of Stalinist Russia. He attacked Stalin for the great purge of the 1930s, for his interference in the military conduct of World War II, for manufacturing the Doctors' Plot, for more general sins such as stifling initiative and creativity, and above all, for having created a "cult of personality"—that is, exalting himself as an individual above the party. Although the speech was given in secret session, it was circulated to all the party cells in the USSR within several weeks. The outside world learned of it through the United States State Department, which obtained a copy in eastern Europe and published it in June 1956.

This denunciation of Stalin by the general secretary of the CP of the Soviet Union and the official campaign of de-Stalinization that followed the close of the congress was a great shock to the Russian people and the east Europeans. In Georgia students rioted to protest the desecration of the greatest Georgian. Other Russians felt a moral vacuum had engulfed them. The national father since 1928 had been called a criminal by the highest party official. One journalist who was very familiar with Russian affairs and personalities has recorded the following encounter soon after the Twentieth Congress.

I remember asking a correct, well-groomed, and very young Soviet diplomat to tell me what [Khrushchev's denunciation of Stalin] meant to him personally. He had just poured me out a drink at one of those immense formal parties. He stared at me, and his eyes were suddenly stricken. "How can you ask me that!" he exclaimed. "How can you possibly ask me that?" Tears stood in his eyes, he swung away violently to hide them, tried to put his glass down on the table behind him but smashed it against another, and fled from the room.[1]

In eastern Europe the Twentieth Party Congress signified the end of Stalinization more so than had Stalin's death, and the Soviet leaders soon discovered they had lifted the lid on a boiling cauldron. As the word spread through the satellite states, workers began demonstrating against low wages, which they blamed on economic subservience to Moscow, and intellectuals began demanding that the thaw be extended to Poland, Hungary, Czechoslovakia. The cauldron first boiled over in Poland in June 1956, when a strike escalated into violence against the regime and a demand for liberal reforms. Within the Communist party, Wladislaw Gomulka led a faction—quickly becoming the majority—which sympathized with the workers. By October Gomulka's supporters were strong enough to make him first secretary of the party, and Poland was ready to challenge Russia's leadership. The same day Gomulka was elected, the Soviet leaders flew to Warsaw, and Soviet troops began threatening maneuvers in Poland. At first Khrushchev warned the Poles of dire consequences if they tried to follow an independent policy, but when he saw that Gomulka had firm party support, the Soviet leader mellowed and finally confirmed Poland's "national communism."

The victory of the Polish Communists sent a shudder of excitement through eastern Europe. Perhaps the Soviet yoke could be thrown off.

---

[1] Edward Crankshaw, *Khrushchev: A Career* (New York: Avon Books, 1967), p. 238.

This hope was put to the test by the Hungarians. Hungary, always strongly anti-Russian and poorly governed by Moscow's puppets, exploded into open revolt on October 23. With the Polish experience to inspire them and with American promises of "liberation" since 1953 to give them hope, the Hungarians turned to the nationalist wing of their Communist party and demanded that Imre Nagy be made premier. The Hungarian Central Committee chose Nagy as premier on the night of the 23rd as Russian troops entered Budapest to suppress the rioting. Once again a Soviet delegation appeared, and once again the popular revolt was ratified by the Russians. On October 28, already having shed Hungarian blood, the Russian troops began withdrawing toward the Soviet border.

But the scenario then took a sinister turn. A meeting of the Soviet Politburo decided that the Hungarian revolt could not be allowed to succeed. Nagy had already permitted the formation of several political parties and had announced that Hungary would be neutral in the East-West struggle. The same night that Franco-British airplanes were flying to bomb Egyptian bases, the Russian tanks reversed their direction, and the suppression of the Hungarian revolt had commenced. Pitched battles between unarmed citizens and Russian tanks began on November 4, and the Hungarian resistance lasted until the end of November. Nagy was eventually taken prisoner and shot. Janos Kadar was placed at the head of the Hungarian Communist party to reimpose Stalinist uniformity.

The shock waves of these events made all of eastern Europe tremble. The former slavish vassal states began to speak more and more as representatives of their own nations and less and less as instruments of Moscow. They realized that their loyalty to Moscow need not be taken for granted but could be sold for a price. The Soviet government, until 1956 obtaining all the benefits from the satellite system, was compelled after 1956 to grant concessions to its allies in order to get cooperation. The Poles demanded loans as compensation for past exploitation. The Hungarians demanded aid to prop up the Kadar regime which Moscow had imposed. So as not to appear to be rewarding the anti-Soviet revolts, the Russians had to be equally generous with the other satellites.

Thus, a completely unexpected result of the Twentieth Party Congress was a completely new relationship between the Soviet Union and eastern Europe. Many Soviet citizens began to think of eastern Europe more as burden than a benefit. Second, nationally oriented leaders replaced the uncompromising Stalinists in the satellites. And finally, the turmoil fatally weakened the Stalinist monolith and forced Russia to differentiate among the east European states, dealing with them on a country-by-country basis and, in effect, ending their dependence on the USSR while maintaining their political and diplomatic subservience.

Understandably the events of October 1956 weakened Khrushchev's grasp on party leadership. The next eight months witnessed another

Russian tanks occupied the streets of Budapest to crush the Hungarian Revolt of 1956. (Courtesy of UPI)

struggle for power similar to the one which had led to Malenkov's fall in 1955. The Central Committee was informed in December 1956 of a major financial crisis. It was announced at this secret meeting that the Sixth Five-Year Plan might have to be abandoned because of a shortage of capital for investment. In part, the shortage of funds was a result of the cost of the intervention in Hungary and the aid given to bolster the Kadar regime. The crisis was exploited by certain high state technocrats to attack Khrushchev, and they were joined by party men, like Bulganin, who wished to limit Khrushchev's power. Since none of the official statements which issued from the meeting contained Khrushchev's name, it appears that his opponents definitely had him on the defensive. To extricate the nation from the crisis, the State Economic Commission was strengthened and an economic czar, G. Pervukhin, was appointed to head it. This centralized control of the economy, strengthening the influence of the technocrats.

Khrushchev countered in February 1957 by charging that the reason for the economy's weakness could be found in the system of centralized agencies that directed it. He proposed a radical decentralization that would place real responsibility in regional economic commissions called *sovnarkhozy*. Once again a struggle for power was to be decided by a debate on economic policy. From March through May the pages of *Pravda* and other journals were filled with articles advocating either greater centralization under the State Economic Commission or decentralization.

Behind this debate was the realization that, contrary to what Malenkov had thought in 1953, centralized control would give power to the professional managers of the economy, the technocrats who had supported Malenkov, and that a system of *sovnarkhozy* would maintain party dominance, for on the regional level the economic administrators would have less influence than the party leaders. In the course of the debate, Khrushchev, a master politician, mobilized the party on his behalf and gained as an ally the military, in the person of Minister of Defense Marshal Zhukov, the hero of Stalingrad. In May the Central Committee supported Khrushchev and decentralization.

This was only the first round, however. When Khrushchev left for Finland on another of his goodwill tours in June, his opponents—later labeled the "antiparty group"—planned a coup. At a meeting of the Presidium shortly after his return, Khrushchev found himself outvoted on the Presidium, seven to four. One after another, his opponents—Malenkov, Molotov, Kaganovich, Bulganin—rose to attack him mercilessly for fouling the economy and for violating the principle of collective leadership. Still, Khrushchev refused to resign and demanded a full meeting of the Central Committee to decide on his leadership.

The meeting was held on June 22. Khrushchev used special planes to assure the attendance of his supporters. This appeal to party democracy was the first such since the 1920s. Khrushchev's opponents opened the meeting by repeating their attacks on him, but Marshal Zhukov launched a counterattack. The "antiparty group" was denounced and defeated. Outvoted in the Central Committee, they were helpless. Again a purge was carried out, but this time it was a peaceful, bloodless purge, setting a pattern for future party conflicts. Malenkov was sent to oversee a power station in Siberia. Molotov was given a post in Outer Mongolia, but he was later appointed to the meaningless but comfortable diplomatic position at the Hague. Bulganin was allowed to remain chairman of the council of ministers (prime minister) until March 1958, when Khrushchev assumed that post—finally reuniting party and state.

Into the vacancies created by the purge, Khrushchev appointed young party men. These men were loyal but not subservient to the new party boss. One such was Leonid Brezhnev, who entered the Presidium at this time. In October 1957, Khrushchev removed his last personal rival—Marshal Zhukov. Zhukov was accused of having fostered a "cult of personality" within the army and of trying to make the army independent of the party.

The Khrushchev Era, 1957–64

Although Khrushchev gained power through debates on domestic economic policy, or because of this, there were few major debates on domestic policy until 1963. Recurrent international crises required the new Soviet leader to occupy himself with diplomacy, while domestic peace gave him the freedom to do so. The Berlin Crisis of 1958–59, the U-2 spy plane affair, the Cuban Revolution, the construction of the Berlin Wall were related to the cold war and will be discussed in a later chapter. The worsening relations between Russia and China, however, had a lasting effect upon the Soviet bloc.

Each of Khrushchev's successes seemed destined to cause conflict with the Chinese communists. When Khrushchev denounced Stalinism, for example, Mao Tse-tung's regime was glorifying Stalinism. Mao's great failure—the proposed Great Leap Forward of 1957–58—was an attempt, very similar to Stalin's First Five-Year Plan, to rapidly collectivize and communize all aspects of Chinese society. It was both an economic and a social failure; and, thereby, it committed the Chinese even more strongly to Stalinist techniques of suppression and glorification of "the leader" as a symbol of national unity and purpose. Every Russian criticism of Stalin, therefore, became a criticism of Mao.

Ironically, the successes of Russian atomic and space research also led to Sino-Soviet tension. The Soviets had exploded an atomic bomb in 1949 and a hydrogen bomb in 1953. They were the first to launch a rocket into outer space and place man-made satellites into orbit with the successful launchings of *Sputnik I* and *Sputnik II* in October and November 1957. This appeared to indicate a Russian superiority over the United States in intercontinental ballistic missiles (ICBMs), even after the United States launched its first satellite in February 1958. The Chinese differed very strongly with the Russians concerning the implications of this tactical superiority. The Chinese argued that the socialist countries could use this advantage to expand the Soviet bloc. The Russians preferred to view these weapons as a protective shield behind which the USSR could feel secure to develop its domestic economy without constant fear of attack from the capitalist West. In fact, Khrushchev was confident of a nuclear stalemate between East and West and was ready to accept a detente with the United States, as evidenced by the summit conferences of 1959 (Camp David) and 1960 (Paris). The Chinese insisted that war between capitalism and socialism was inevitable. In September 1959, Khrushchev visited Eisenhower at Camp David, near Washington, where a very amicable, relaxed mood prevailed. The Chinese response was contained in a manifesto entitled "Long Live Leninism," published in April 1960, which denounced the Russian desertion of the revolutionary struggle. Khrushchev retaliated by withdrawing 3,000 Russian military and economic advisers from China and sharply reducing Soviet trade with China. This was an escalation of the conflict, since it struck a direct blow at China's economy, Khrushchev also revived his anti-Stalinist campaign. At the Twenty-Second Party Congress in October 1960, an elderly female party member claimed to have received a message from Lenin that he slept uncomfortably beside Stalin in the mausoleum on Red Square. Within days Stalin's body was removed, and placed in a much less distinguished spot. Before the coffin could be moved, however, Chou En-lai, Mao's foreign minister, placed a wreath on it to indicate continued Chinese adherence to Stalinist policies.

Interestingly enough, the more Khrushchev denounced Stalin, the more Khrushchev's Russia began to resemble Stalin's in the cultural area. The thaw of 1953–54 had regained some of its warmth by 1957, but a controversy arose that led to a new attempt at repression. Boris Pasternak's novel *Dr. Zhivago* had been published in Italy, after Soviet authorities had refused publication in Russia because the novel could be interpreted (and was in the West) as criticism of the regime. Pasternak's hero represents the civilized values of czarist Russia's cultivated society, values which could not be destroyed in the melee of the Russian Revolution, the civil war, or the imposition of a one-party dictatorship. Pasternak was awarded the Nobel prize for literature in 1958, but Khruschev compelled him to refuse it or be barred from Russia. The novelist chose to remain in his homeland. Pasternak died two years later. The *Dr. Zhivago* controversy inspired many young writers, poets, and artists to express their own impressions more truthfully. On the other hand, it also led to the organization by the state of the Union of Writers to suppress free expression. Any author who hoped to publish in Russia had to belong, and only those whose work was politically acceptable could belong. Khrushchev, after Pasternak, took a more personal interest in Soviet cultural trends and tried to impose his banal distaste for innovation in art on all Russian intellectuals. Still, his regime never lapsed into the severe censorship of the Stalin period.

Khrushchev's interest in agriculture and his desire to strengthen the party led to a notable change in administrative organization of the agricultural sector. Machine-tractor stations (MTS) had served since the collectivization of the 1930s as the agencies for party control of rural areas. These stations, staffed by the central government, were the only source of agricultural machinery and repairmen for the collectives. Party officials were stationed at each MTS. When Khrushchev began merging the existing collectives into ever-larger units in 1955, it became more efficient for each new *sovkhoz* (the larger farms) to own its own machinery. At the same time, the party official became the most important administrator of each farm. This gave the party direct control of the countryside, rather than the indirect control it had exercised through the MTS. Therefore, the creation of the *sovkhozy* complemented the administrative decentralization Khrushchev had achieved with the *sovnarkhozy,* and the Soviet state and economy were brought even further under the control of the party.[2]

It was then inevitable that Khrushchev, as party leader, should be

---

[2] Donald W. Treadgold, *Twentieth Century Russia,* 2d ed. (Chicago: Rand McNally and Company, 1964), p. 493.

blamed for the weakness of the Soviet economy that became increasingly apparent from 1960 to 1964. Industrial production had begun to slow down in 1959, and despite a 17 percent increase in land sown between 1960–63, grain production did not meet Russia's needs. Only massive wheat imports from Canada in September 1963 prevented a major famine, and a form of bread rationing had to be instituted in the winter of 1963–64. These problems, of course, decreased confidence in Khrushchev's leadership, since he had been the originator of the Virgin Lands Program.

Another factor in the decline of his popularity, especially among the party leadership, was his hectic style. His ebullient globe-trotting, off-the-cuff crudeness, and tendency to make contradictory public statements contrasted greatly with the cold severity and quiet cautiousness of most Soviet officials. Khrushchev also seemed to be developing a "personality cult" of his own. His travels, his public exhibitionism, the publicity given his family, and his manner of making major decisions on agricultural policy without consulting the Central Committee increased the opposition to him.

Khrushchev's strongest opposition ultimately came from the very groups of heavy industry advocates that had helped him defeat Malenkov. By September 1964, Khrushchev had decided to emphasize consumer goods at the expense of heavy industry. He had been moving in this direction for several years, probably as a result of the east European revolts. He seemed to take the demands of the German, Polish, and Hungarian workers to heart and hoped to prevent such discontent in Russia. A vast program of urban housing begun in 1960 was one indication of this policy. His program of consumer goods production was opposed by a military-industrial complex. The Soviet military had for some time been uneasy about Khrushchev's negotiations on the limitation of arms with the United States and his attempts at detente. Their anxiety was shared by the managers of heavy industry. Finally, most influential Russians were also concerned about the Sino-Soviet split. This had led to a decrease in Russian influence in eastern Europe and among the western European communist parties.

These issues came to the surface on October 13, 1964. As in 1957, Khrushchev's opponents took advantage of his absence from Moscow to prepare a coup. He was vacationing on the Black Sea when he was summoned back to Moscow for an urgent meeting of the Presidium. Again he was denounced, but this time he had no reserve of support with which to resist the attack. His control of the party organization had been undermined by Leonid Brezhnev, who replaced Khrushchev as general secretary of the party. Khrushchev demanded a hearing before the Central Committee for the next day, but when he tried to justify his conduct and policies, he was condemned for "phrase-mongering," for advocating "hair-brained schemes," and for developing a cult of personality. On that day Khrushchev was stripped of all his offices.

His successor as head of the party, Brezhnev, was the real power in the new regime, but Brezhnev shared the public stage with Alexei Kosygin, a strictly bureaucratic figure, who became chairman of the Council of Ministers. For a brief while, collective leadership was again the rule, and there was a precarious balance among the various factions within the Presidium. Khrushchev was treated rather kindly, being retired to a comfortable obscurity. The Soviets had achieved an orderly transfer of power and proved the stability of post-Stalin Russia.

The Soviet Bloc, 1957–64

The major problem facing the Soviet bloc after the 1956 revolts was the reconstruction of unity among the communist states. During the debate over how to best achieve unity, several major schools of Marxism-Leninism developed. The Yugoslavs were labeled "revisionists" because they sought to revise Lenin's teachings as interpreted by Moscow so as to justify their innovations in economic policy. Internationally, then, revisionism was dissent from the Moscow party line. The Chinese advocated "centralism" as an antedote. Centralism implied absolute subservience to Moscow internationally and to Stalinism domestically. This policy would place the Russians in the position of forcibly requiring absolute adherence to Soviet dictates and would make such experiments as those in Yugoslavia or in Poland impossible. The third alternative, "national communism," was most closely identified with Poland and Wladislaw Gomulka. He and his supporters argued that, while maintaining international solidarity in the cold war, each state should build a socialist society in accordance with prevailing national conditions. No two states could collectivize at the same rate or develop industry at the same rate. This implied that the local CPs must be given enough freedom by Moscow to make such adjustments to national conditions as might be necessary. Oddly, the Russians were never fully committed to any of these three. They rejected revisionism and based their policy on a mixture of centralism and national communism.

The Soviet solution to unity without resort to force was economic integration. The Council of Economic Mutual Assistance (Comecon) had been founded by Stalin but allowed to become moribund. Khrushchev reactivated it in a conference held at Moscow in January 1958. A plan was developed for the coordination of economic growth through cooperative economic planning. The coordination was as important politically as it was economically. Each nation was to specialize in certain products or industries and to depend on other members of the bloc for other goods. In general, raw materials would be supplied by Russia, Bulgaria, and Rumania to East Germany, Czechoslovakia, and Poland. The latter three industrialized states plus Russia would then sell finished goods to the lesser developed states. Only the Soviet Union would have a fairly self-supporting economy; the other states would be in economic bondage—especially Rumania and Bulgaria. At the Moscow conference, however, all the satellites agreed to this arrangement and provisions were made for an international economic plan extending from 1959–65. This agreement assured not only increasing interdependence but also Russian dominance.

While this apparent unity was being achieved the amicable relations between Russia and Yugoslavia, so carefully nurtured by Khrushchev, encountered their first test. In November 1957, at a conference honoring the fortieth anniversary of the Bolshevik Revolution, the Chinese demanded an endorsement of centralism by the conference, an act that would isolate the Yugoslavs. The Chinese were obviously not willing to bow to Moscow's leadership; rather, they were trying to commit Khrushchev to policies he had rejected. The Soviets were in a particularly difficult spot. Continued good relations with Yugoslavia depended on the Russians renouncing their own primacy over eastern Europe, which the Soviets would not do. Therefore, a resolution was passed supporting the Chinese position. Only the Yugoslav delegation refused to support it.

Instead of accepting the conference's decision, Tito and his ideologues developed a coherent theoretical rebuttal. In the Draft Program for the Yugoslav Party Congress of March 1958, the Yugoslavs claimed for the first time that they were the true Marxist-Leninists. Indeed, they contended, Lenin had been a revisionist of earlier socialist thought. The Draft Program went even further. It rejected the concept of a bipolar world and accused the Soviets as well as the capitalist bloc of perpetuating world tensions. Finally, it rejected the sacrosanct idea that Communist parties were the only agents of the construction of socialism. Rather, the Yugoslavs asserted that social and technological developments were pushing all states toward socialism. This was a clear and a friendly reference to the emergence of welfare states in western Europe.

The Draft Program caused strong reactions from other communist states. The USSR and China both announced that the 1948 isolation of Yugoslavia was again in force. Khrushchev quickly returned to the pre-1954 state of relations with the renegades. To further demonstrate that such revisionism would not be accepted in the bloc, Imre Nagy was executed in June 1958. Nagy, of course, had tried to lead Hungary on a neutralist course. A few days after Nagy's execution, Gomulka of Poland sided with the centralists in denouncing Tito and Nagy. Apparently, the unity of the bloc had been restored at the expense of renewed bad relations with Yugoslavia.

Perhaps Gomulka's actions were motivated by a desire to win more independence from Russia for his own "national communist" regime. Gomulka was perhaps the only man who could have succeeded. He was a convinced communist and believed that a monolithic party should dominate the state, using force against political opponents if necessary. Yet he also believed that communism could never win the allegiance of the Poles unless it was adapted to Polish society. This implied some freedom for the Catholic church, and Gomulka was able to achieve a modus vivendi with the church. The strength and political traditions of the Polish peasantry led Gomulka to decollectivize the majority of Polish farming. Workers were allowed to organize councils that were strangely similar to trade unions. And Gomulka even experimented with allowing political clubs to form where ideas could be exchanged freely.

The free expression of ideas and popular spontaneity are inimical to one-party government, however, and only a year after the 1956 revolution Gomulka began to withdraw the freedoms granted and to reestablish an orthodox regime. He purged various party leaders and intellectuals who would not fall into line and banned the political clubs. Gomulka, however, still offered innovative theories. He insisted that communism could not be forced on a people but that ruling communist parties should change the attitudes of their citizens gradually by employing education, culture, the press, and any other means. Even when one-party rule had been fully restored, therefore, the Poles enjoyed more freedoms than before 1956, and Polish independence from Russia in domestic policy was real.

Other eastern European leaders were overzealous in their return to Stalinism after 1956. In fact, these countries went so far that they appeared to be following the Chinese model rather than the Russian. This was true in Hungary, Bulgaria, Czechoslovakia, and East Germany. These states were also practicing a form of national communism, since they were being more Stalinist, more dictatorial, than the Russian government. The manner in which East Germany reformed its economy in 1958 was but one example. Claiming that their reform was similar to Khrushchev's, the East Germans actually centralized rather than decentralizing their economic administration.

This form of national communism or "domesticism" (having a different domestic policy than Russia) was carried to its extreme in Rumania, where it became the basis for economic and diplomatic independence from Russia. The Rumania bid for autonomy began in 1958, and its success was in large part a result of the Sino-Soviet schism which made Russian disciplinary actions against Rumania unlikely. By 1960 the USSR and China had reached the point of direct, overt, and explicit exchanges of abuse. Many issues which had formerly been hidden came to the fore. In late 1963 China laid claims to territories in Russian Siberia. Mao Tse-tung accused the Russians of imperalist expansion in 1945, pointing not only to Russian annexations of the Chinese territories of Sinkiang and Amur, but also to parts of Poland, Rumania, and Finland. The territorial dispute between the two communist giants only aggravated their ideological dispute. The Chinese even went so far as to say Russia's economic reforms were a return to capitalism. Rumania tried to step into this heated debate as a mediator, and by doing so, the Rumanian Communist party was elevating itself into a free and independent diplomatic equal of Russia and China, a captive of neither protagonist.

This assertion of independence was only a symbol of profound developments within Rumanian communism. Since the early 1950s there had been a struggle for control of Rumania between the Muscovites and the Partisans. The Muscovites are those communists who had spent the World War II years in Russia and were more amenable to Moscow's leadership. The Partisans, who remained in Rumania and participated in the underground resistance movement, were no less convinced communists than the Muscovites, but they were more nationalistic and less willing to bow before Russia's orders. Gheorgi Gheorghiu-Dej, leader of the Partisans, had become first secretary of the CP in 1952, but the Muscovites held important positions in the party and state administration until 1957, when they were purged. Gheorghiu-Dej then moved Rumania slowly and cautiously toward national autonomy. A trade delegation was sent on a tour of western Europe in 1959, and in the same year, Rumania adopted an economic plan in conflict with the five-year Comecon plan. The party rewrote Rumanian postwar history, denouncing the Muscovites for the suffering caused by collectivization. The role of the Russian army in the liberation of Rumania from the Nazis was minimized, while the Rumanian Partisans were given full credit for the liberation as well as the establishment of the communist state.

The party took additional steps to make communism Rumanian. Requirements for entrance to the party were greatly relaxed so that many Rumanians could join. This broadening of membership was matched by a deemphasis on the ideological purity of members. The traditional Western orientation of Rumanian culture was once again encouraged. The Russian language was no longer so central to the school curriculum, in which Western languages—French and English—were now offered as alternatives. Western literature was also allowed to reenter the country. The dark side of the Partisans nationalism was that they began to persecute the several national minorities—Hungarian, German, Jewish—found within Rumania.

Gheorghiu-Dej's refusal to participate in Comecon was Rumania's most significant challenge to bloc unity. In 1964 the Soviet Union proposed a single supranational planning body to coordinate (perhaps to direct) all of the socialist states' economies. The planning body would inevitably be dominated by the Russians. In response, Gheorghiu-Dej announced Rumania's impatience with the role of a supplier of raw materials and the lack of modernization that role implied. He stated that Rumania intended to become an industrialized nation as rapidly as possible, and to achieve that goal, the Rumanians were prepared to borrow ideas and techniques from all countries, regardless of their social systems. Since this remarkable declaration of independence in April 1964, the Rumanians have withheld their cooperation from certain Soviet bloc organizations, playing a role in eastern Europe very similar to the one de Gaulle's France played in western Europe during the 1960s.

Concluding Thoughts on the Independence of Satellites

An eastern European state that becomes independent of Russia is not necessarily more democratic than states that fail to gain autonomy. In fact, the reverse is usually the case. The three states that have successfully asserted some independence from the Soviet Union—Yugoslavia, Poland, Rumania—were more Stalinist, more authoritarian than Russia at the time they challenged Russian hegemony. This would have to be qualified only slightly for Poland, where, after the experimentation of 1956–57, the regime lapsed into the orthodox, authoritarian one-party system. Perhaps the Soviets have allowed ideologically safe regimes to exercise some independence because there is little danger of these governments permitting a multiparty system or free expression to exist within their borders. There is, therefore, some reason to doubt that an eastern European state can become democratic and independent from Russia at the same time. In such a case, the Soviet Union has in the past felt impelled to intervene to prevent excesses of anti-Soviet propaganda and to protect Soviet citizens from ideas inimical to the Russian regime.

Chapter 19

CONSERVATIVE DOMINANCE IN WESTERN EUROPE

The 1950s was a decade of retrenchment and consolidation by conservative legislatures throughout western Europe. Reeling under the impact of the cold war, leftists and reformers were on the defensive everywhere. The Conservative party in Great Britain and the Christian Democrats of Italy and Germany as well as the centrist parties of France governed during a decade of growing prosperity and international tensions. Nowhere did they try to destroy the institutions of the welfare state that had been built in the fervor of postwar demands for a new society. Everywhere, however, they prevented new adventures with social legislation while developing new concepts of the role of the state in the national economy which were to protect and perpetuate the fragile industrial recovery begun under the umbrella of the Marshall Plan.

Great Britain

Torn by debates on Britain's role in the cold war and at a loss for new issues once they had established the welfare state, the Labour party had little to offer the electorate in the 1951 general election. Conservatives, on the other hand, offered to "free the economy" of rationing and other restrictions, to build 300,000 new houses each year, and to make Winston Churchill prime minister once more. The voters liked this program well enough to give the Conservatives a seventeen-seat majority in the new House of Commons. Winston Churchill did indeed become prime minister, at the age of seventy-seven, and remained in that position until 1955. It was the afterglow of a brilliant career, and his presence reminded many Britons that, although the war and the domestic revolution that followed had changed much in England, traditions were still strong, and stability, normalcy were possible.

The Conservatives wanted stability and not a repeal of the postwar reforms. Churchill was concerned that the Conservatives be respectable, and therefore, his cabinet maintained the welfare state in all its aspects, except for imposing slight fees on several medical services. The nationalizations, too, were challenged only in specific and not highly controversial areas. The steel and iron industry was sold back to private companies; but when the government tried to sell transportation facilities, it discovered that the former owners were quite happy to be rid of financially weak enterprises; so only a few trucking firms reverted to private ownership, while railroads remained a nationalized industry. The other nationalized industries were not questioned.

One reason for the lack of domestic legislation during Churchill's last government was that Churchill devoted his time to international diplomacy and gave his ministers no clear lead in home affairs. The vacuum of leadership was filled by R. A. Butler, chancellor of the exchequer. Butler took it upon himself to fulfill the campaign pledge to free the economy and stimulate free enterprise. The Labour governments had imposed many restrictions on economic activity to permit state direction of economic growth. Butler reduced the number of types of construction that had to be licensed by the state, ended rationing of foods, reduced the income tax, removed restrictions on the right to strike and on the use of credit to purchase household appliances and other goods.[1] The Labourites had also "blocked" Britain's international debts so that a creditor nation that wished to collect would have to spend his funds in Great Britain. This, of course, gave the British government strict control over its gold reserves. Butler "unblocked" these funds, allowing creditors to spend their funds as they wished.

While the easing of restrictions appeared to be the product of economic theory and was meant to aid all classes of society, other aspects of Conservative policy were more political in intent. To assure the lower classes that Conservatives were just as concerned with their welfare as Labourites, the Churchill cabinet made good on its promise of 300,000 new homes per year after 1953. There had been little home construction since 1939, and the housing program was welcomed by the public. Harold Macmillan, later to be prime minister, made his name as minister of housing. The Conservatives reduced the income tax rate several times during this period. Accompanied as it was by the end of subsidies to keep food prices down, the income tax reduction had the effect of taking less money from the rich while requiring the poor to pay more for their food. Thus, the net effect was to reverse the policy of wealth redistribution followed since 1945.

A business boom began in 1954 that resulted in full employment and

---

[1] T. O. Lloyd, *Empire to Welfare State* (New York: Oxford University Press, 1970), p. 322.

increased prosperity for all Britishers. Seeing this as a propitious time to hand over the reigns to a younger man, Churchill retired in April 1955. The heir-apparent was Anthony Eden, whom Churchill had designated as his successor already during World War II. The business boom guaranteed both fond memories of the retiring hero and a Conservative victory at the polls if an election were called quickly. This was done, and Conservative chances were enhanced by the announcement of an income tax cut in the 1955 budget. The result was a stronger Conservative majority—one strong enough to give the government real freedom of action. Shortly

TABLE 19.1.   Results of British Elections

Party	1955		1959	
	Seats	Votes, %	Seats	Votes, %
Labour	277	46.4	258	43.8
Liberal	6	2.7	6	5.9
Conservative	344	49.7	365	49.4

SOURCE: T. O. Lloyd, *Empire to Welfare State* (New York: Oxford University Press, 1970), pp. 334, 357.

after the election a second budget was introduced that increased the sales tax on all items and imposed a sales tax on certain household goods that had previously been exempted. Once again, the effect of the two budgets was to shift the weight of taxation from the rich to the poor. As a result of this political trick and the slowing of the business boom, R. A. Butler fell into disfavor and was replaced at the exchequer by Harold Macmillan.

Eden was still prime minister but the character of the Conservative party majority had been changed slightly by the elections. The new MPs were more prone to desire a return to "before the war" policies. Many hoped for a reassertion of old values such as social hierarchy and British international influence. It was probably this yearning for past imperial greatness that led Eden into the folly of the Suez Canal occupation of 1956. When the adventure ended as a fiasco, the Conservatives did not blame Eden but the United States, which was pictured as unsophisticated in international affairs and unfaithful to friendly allies. Therefore, it really *was* Eden's health that forced him to resign at the beginning of 1957 and not a party rebellion, for he remained quite popular with the Conservative party organization.

Macmillan was chosen by the parliamentary Conservatives to be their next leader. He had been a staunch defender of Suez, and he kept Selwyn Lloyd, Eden's foreign secretary, at his post to indicate that he had no doubts that British policy had been correct. "Supermac," as he was dubbed

Harold Macmillan, British
Prime Minister 1957–63
(here with his wife),
symbolized the conservative
west European leadership
of the 1950s.
(Courtesy of UPI)

in the Labour press, concerned himself principally with military affairs and attempts to ease the tensions of the cold war. He made many official state visits to other capitols and earned his publicly acclaimed role of a statesman rather than a politician. Domestically, Macmillan's cabinet was strongly influenced by the traditionalist wing of their party. This influence was evident especially in the 1959 budget. The goal of the budget was price stability rather than economic growth. Investment was reduced in the nationalized industries to slow expansion and prevent inflation, and banks were discouraged from making loans. The Labour party complained that these intentional restraints would result in unemployment, but the cabinet was willing to accept the price to avoid inflation and the danger of a devalued pound. Macmillan also presided over the passage of the Rent Act of 1957 which repealed the wartime limitations on landlords. Some increase in rents occurred, but it was not painful because of general prosperity.

The prosperity of the 1950s was a major factor in the continued Conservative dominance, but the divisions within the Labour party prevented it from offering an attractive alternative. As material well-being increased, as each family obtained a refrigerator, a vacuum cleaner, an automobile, and a television, the British no longer cared for socialist slogans concerning nationalization. Nor could the Labourites develop a new program. Instead they engaged in suicidal in-fighting between the Bevanites and the followers of Attlee, and, after Attlee retired in 1955, of Hugh Gaitskell. Bevan had walked out of the Labour cabinet in 1951 because social services were reduced to pay for increased military spending. This remained the issue through the 1950s. The contending factions changed in 1957, however, when the issue arose as to whether Britain should develop a hydrogen bomb. Macmillan had decided to proceed with such a project, arguing that it would allow a reduction in conventional forces and in military expenditures. Pacifists expected Bevan to lead the opposition to the bomb, but instead, he defended it as a way for Britain to gain independence from the United States and to speak in international conferences as an equal of the superpowers.

The Labour left wing found its voice in an extraparliamentary organization: the Campaign for Nuclear Disarmament (CND), which was militantly pacifist. From 1958 to 1963 CND held annual mass demonstrations in London—usually at Trafalgar Square—with 60,000 to 100,000 in attendance. In 1960 the crowd was addressed by such eminent persons as Bertrand Russell, who participated in each protest march; Michael Foot, a Labour member of parliament; A. J. P. Taylor, the noted historian; and a bishop of the Anglican church. While including dissident Labourites, the CND extended outside of the usual political arena to involve the radical Left and the disaffected who desired peace above all. It was an awakening from the quietude of the 1950s and the revitalization of political debate.

Labour was also challenged to find new policies and a new philosophy by the New Left. This was an assortment of intellectuals who wrote for the *New Left Review*, published from 1959–63, and who emphasized the ethical and humanitarian aspects of socialism rather than class conflict and economic controls. Shocked by Russia's disregard for life and freedom in Hungary and Great Britain's disregard for self-determination in the Suez Crisis, the New Left hoped for a new society built on the free distribution of goods, without the need for wealth inherent in a consumer society. Raymond Williams, an intellectual from a working class background, proposed such a new world in his book *The Long Revolution* (1961). He and other members of the New Left became closely involved in the "Ban the Bomb!" movement, but they remained critical of the Labour party.

During 1958 the British economy entered another boom period similar to that of 1954–55. Macmillan, who had been busy in Moscow, Paris, Bonn, and Washington, called for an election in 1959 to capitalize on prosperity, his personal publicity, and the disarray of the Labour party. Labour finally began to readjust its program, deserting nationalization for more emphasis on providing full employment and an expanding economy through government action. Macmillan's popularity, however, was at its height, and the Conservative party gained an even larger majority. Although accumulated weaknesses in the British economy soon began to show, the Conservatives were able to remain in power for another four years, until 1964.

Immobilism in France

French and Italian politics continued to exhibit striking similarities after the expulsion of the communists in 1947. As the 1950s progressed these similarities gave way to profound differences. Whereas both countries were victims of extreme governmental instability until 1958, in that year France's legal government submitted to an authoritarian coup, whereas Italian problems were resolved, for a decade at least, by a regular legislative election.

The governing coalition which emerged in France in late 1947 was called "the Third Force" by journalists. It was considered a democratic, centrist alternative to the French Communist party (PCF) on the left and to Gaullist authoritarianism on the right. Parties participating in the coalition were the Socialists (SFIO), Radicals, Christian Democrats (MRP), and Moderates (actually a union of several small groups). All cabinets from 1948 to 1958 were based on this four-party formula. Quadripartism, however, was a fragile creation, and the defection of any one party (or faction of one party) could topple a cabinet. Henri Queuille, premier from September 1948 until October 1949, summed up the relations of these parties when he said, "You are condemned to live together." Queuille symbolized the real significance of quadripartism—a return to the Third Republic. He had often been a cabinet minister in the 1920s and 1930s. As a member of the ideologically bankrupt Radical party, Queuille represented the inability of the Third Force to move off dead center.

French politics was dominated by international affairs—the collapse of empire, the cold war, the rearming of Germany and European integration. The entire French empire was being shaken by the colonial revolt. The official response everywhere (except in Morocco) was repression. The natives of Madagascar, an island colony off the east coast of Africa, rebelled in 1947. The French authorities killed 80,000 natives in crushing the revolt. North Africa, the next rebellious area, could not be treated so brutally. Morocco and Tunisia were legally protectorates, not colonies. Each had a nominally independent government although financial and military power were in French hands. Pan-Arab nationalism as well as traditional nationalism stirred the intellectuals in these countries and in Algeria, which was a "French possession" governed directly by the Ministry of War and not by the Ministry of Colonies. During 1948 a Committee for the

Liberation of North Africa was formed in Cairo by Tunisians, Algerians, and Moroccans, and the demands of the committee were echoed by the Moroccan and Tunisian governments. The Third Force bought time, but solved no problems, by granting some freedom of action to the native governments; this only encouraged demands for full independence. In Algeria, a legislature was established that was intended to permit representation of the Algerians. The French *colons,* however, sabotaged the elections, arrested Algerian candidates, and drove the Algerian nationalists underground. The nationalists, frustrated in their attempts to win concessions, began the formation of a guerilla army.

One reason, a major one, why no French cabinet dealt successfully with the colonial revolt was that French domestic politics was little more than a struggle for power among various factions of the quadripartite coalition. The four parties did unify to pass a new electoral law meant to disenfranchise extremist parties just prior to the 1951 election. Election was based on proportional representation in the Fourth Republic, meaning each party received the same percentage of seats as its percentage of the total vote. The new law allowed several parties to pool their votes to obtain a greater representation than if each ran independently. This favored the centrist coalition to the detriment of the PCF on the left and Gaullist RPF on the right. The law acted as expected, but both extremes maintained enough strength to weaken the parliamentary system.

TABLE 19.2.   French Elections, 1951–58

Party	1951		1956		1958	
	Seats	Votes, %	Seats	Votes, %	Seats	Votes, %
Communist	101	26.9	150	25.9	10	19.2
Socialist	107	14.6	99	15.2	47	15.7
MRP	96	12.6	84	11.1	64	11.1
Radical	76	10.0	75			
Moderates	19		19	15.2	40	8.5
Conservatives ...	98	14.1	97	16.4	129	22.1
Gaullists	120	21.6	22	3.9	206	20.4
Others	10	...	50*	13.2*	81†	...†

* Poujadists.
† Algerians.
Sources: Data on seats held from Philip H. Williams, *Crisis and Compromise: Politics in the Fourth Republic* (Garden City, New York: Anchor Books, Doubleday and Co., Inc., 1966), p. 532. Data on percentage of vote from Jacques Chapsal, *La Vie politique en France depuis 1940* (Paris: Presses universitaires de France, 1966), pp. 579–81.

It took the new parliament five weeks to find a premier who could muster a majority, and his cabinet lasted only four months. The man was René Pleven, famous for having proposed the European Defense Community. There were deep and bitter differences within France over this scheme to allow Germany to rearm under the control of a European army. The centrist parties favored the idea, while the Communists and the Gaullists were united in opposition. But partisan political divisions were accompanied by a sort of "generation gap." Old leaders of the MRP were opposed to rearming Germany under any conditions; while young advocates of European unity supported the EDC.

This issue, as the many gnawing colonial problems, was not resolved until Pierre Mendès-France became premier in June 1954. The delicate balance of forces within quadripartism had condemned France to immobilism, to political paralysis. PMF refused to play the parliamentary game by the rules. He had been brought to power by the Vietnam crisis, and as we have seen, he demanded an end to that war and achieved this goal within one month at the Geneva Conference. He also took action on North Africa by initiating negotiations that led to the independence of Morocco and Tunisia in 1956. He personally visited Tunisia where he installed a resident whom he could trust to begin the process of granting independence. In domestic affairs, he shocked everyone by excluding the MRP from his cabinet that was composed of Radicals and Socialists. He solved the EDC question by merely not supporting the treaty when it came before the National Assembly. Finally, while his popularity was at its height, he attempted a reform of his own party, by discarding its outdated economic liberalism and moving toward the Socialist policy of economic planning. This attempt to renovate an old ship only caused it to fall apart, and several dissident groups withdrew from the Radical party in protest of such vigorous leadership. By early 1955 Mendès-France had antagonized too many parliamentarians to remain in power. The occasion for his fall was the appointment of Jacques Soustelle, an MRP conservative, to the post of governor-general of Algeria. This was indeed a bad appointment; for Soustelle soon was identified with the die-hard French *colons* who refused to accept Algerian independence. The PMF experiment ended, therefore, on February 5, 1955.

France sunk again into immobilism. The despair and disaffection of many Frenchmen took the form of the Poujadist movement. Poujadism was an emotional and incoherent protest against the modernization of France. Pierre Poujade, a smalltown shopkeeper, first gained notoriety in 1953 when he rallied a group of merchants in his town to resist the tax collectors who were trying to prevent tax evasion. He had soon organized a national Association for the Defense of Shopkeepers and Artisans to oppose the collection of taxes. The rapid growth of his organization encouraged Poujade to form a political party and enter the legislative election of 1956. His support came from *petite bourgeoisie* like himself—shopkeepers, artisans, small farmers, hotel owners—and all the "little people" whose economic existence was threatened by the rapid modernization of France. They appeared to be a new radical Right, but most were nonideological, merely protesting against their inevitable fate. As one commentator put it, the movement had "as much intellectual content as a scream."

The 1955 election was the first test of Poujadism's popularity. The voting returns revealed the fragmentation and the malaise of French politics. Four parties each received between 15 percent and 26 percent of the vote. Only the PCF was clearly strongest, receiving 25.9 percent; but it was hermetically sealed—prohibited from participation in cabinets by its own decisions and by the hostility of other parties. This extreme factionalism made a coherent majority capable of carrying out any consistent program impossible.

When the Algerian crisis evolved into a possible civil war among Frenchmen, the weaknesses of quadripartism became painfully clear. Algerian nationalists, demanding independence, began a campaign of terrorism in November 1954. The French *colons* charged that the nationalists had been encouraged by Mendès-France's Geneva agreement over Indochina and his concessions to Morocco and Tunisia. After the 1956 elections, the new premier Guy Mollet, a Socialist, visited Algiers. A hostile mob of Europeans greeted him with a shower of rotten fruit and invective. Whether it was this intensity of feeling or other factors that influenced Mollet, he reversed his policy into one of repression. French troops were flown into Algeria until there were approximately 450,000 present. Faced with overwhelming forces, the Algerians resorted to a terrorist campaign of indiscriminate assassination and fire-bombing both in Algeria and in France. Many Frenchmen soon became convinced that France could survive only by ridding herself of Algeria. French politics were becoming increasingly unstable. France was without a government for five weeks during the fall of 1957, and when the new cabinet fell in April 1958, it took a month to find a successor.

The desire to be rid of Algeria had reached such a pitch that the Army and the French *colons* felt certain they would be deserted by the home government. It took only the selection of a premier favorable to concessions to the Algerian nationalists to set off a revolt. When finally a premier was found, it was Pierre Pflimlin who was willing to negotiate with the Algerians. On the same day Pflimlin was to present his government to the Chamber of Deputies, there was a mass demonstration in Algiers. The *colons* invaded French administrative offices and established a committee of public safety in French revolutionary tradition. The Pflimlin government was intimidated and tried to open negotiations with the rebellious Frenchmen and the military which was supporting them. Ten days later a military force from Algiers seized the island of Corsica—legally a part of metropolitan France. Rumors of an impending invasion of Paris spread. Only one man appeared capable of commanding enough respect among the Army to prevent a coup d'état. On June 1, 1958, General de Gaulle was given full power for six months to settle the Algerian problem and to write a new constitution. The French had ended their governmental instability by acquiescing to an authoritarian regime.

Quadripartism in Italy

The quadripartite coalition in Italy also suffered from instability. Held together only by their opposition to communism, the four parties were divided over fundamentals of economic policy. The Social Democrats, led by Giuseppi Saragat, and the left wing of the Christian Democratic party (DC) wanted economic planning, the nationalization of major industries, and land reform. The Liberals, Republicans, and the more conservative DC members opposed governmental interference in the economy except to aid business (e.g., tariffs, tax concessions). Only the consummate skill of Alcide de Gasperi, who headed three different cabinets from 1948 to 1953, made effective government possible. He was able to achieve passage of two extremely important economic programs. First, the land reform of 1949 and 1950 enabled the state to expropriate large estates and redistribute the land to peasants. The rural South was most effected, because large estates there had been unproductive while an illiterate peasantry starved. The peasants were quite naturally grateful to the Christian Democrats and many shifted their allegiance from the PCI to de Gasperi's party.

Economic planning, of a sort, was the second major achievement of de Gasperi's administrations. Three state-owned industrial corporations were used to coordinate national investment and guide the economy's growth. The Institute for Industrial Reconstruction (IRI), a leftover from the Fascist regime, controlled all state shareholdings in industries, banks and financial societies and was therefore entitled to a representative on the directing boards of such enterprises. Through this leverage and through the IRI's control of banks, the state was able to direct investment into industries in accordance with national priorities rather than allowing private profitability dictate investment. The National Petrochemical Corporation gave the state a virtual monopoly over the production of oil and chemicals, and it gave the state a vehicle for research and development of new sources of energy. Finally, the *Cassa del Mezzogiorno* or "Fund for the South" was assigned the massive task of transforming the natural environment of the undeveloped areas of Italy to make modernization and industrialization easier. This entailed "regulating rivers, stopping erosion of the land, reclaiming swampy areas, constructing roads, aqueducts, agricultural villages, stables for cattle, industrial installations for the use of local agricultural products, etc."[2]

---

[2] Giuseppi Mammarella, *Italy after Fascism* (Notre Dame, Indiana: University of Notre Dame Press, 1966), p. 231.

De Gasperi was strongly pro-Western in foreign affairs. A champion of the NATO alliance, he was also a leader in the development of the Common Market along with Christian Democrats of France (Robert Schuman) and Germany (Konrad Adenauer). It was in fact, this foreign policy that held the four-party coalition together and isolated the political left. Pietro Nenni had led the Italian Socialist party (PSI) into a close alliance with the PCI rather than accept international alliance with the capitalist states against Russia. The Social Democratic party (PSDI) was just as adamant in its denunciation of Russia and its adherence to NATO. The PCI had little choice; for its stand on such matters before 1956 was dictated from Moscow.

Italian parliamentary government never seemed secure during the 1950s, in spite of de Gasperi's personal ascendancy. Not only was the PCI very strong, but several neofascist parties also challenged the repub-lic—the most important fascist group being the Italian Social Movement (MSI). To counter these threats from both extremes, the governing coali-tion followed the French lead in passing an electoral law favoring coali-tions. De Gasperi's law, passed just before the 1953 election, provided that 65 percent of the legislative seats would go to any joint list of parties receiving 50.1 percent of the popular vote. In the election, however, the quadripartite list failed to obtain 50 percent of the vote. Instead, both the PCI and the MSI registered strong gains. The PCI was the second largest party and controlled 143 seats in parliament.

TABLE 19.3.   Italian Elections

Party	Seats Won, 1953	Seats Won, 1958
PCI	143	140
PSI (Nenni)	75	84
PSDI (Saragat)	19	22
Republicans	5	6
DC	216	273
Liberals	14	17
PMP	...	14
PNM	40	11
MSI	29	24
Others	4	5

SOURCE: Giuseppi Mammarella, *Italy After Fascism* (Notre Dame, Indiana: Uni-versity of Notre Dame Press, 1966), pp. 254, 310.

The electoral setback to quadripartism prevented de Gasperi from form-ing a new cabinet because a secure majority could not be patched together. Pietro Nenni suggested that the PSI was willing to break with the Com-munist party if the Socialists were given an important place in de Gasperi's cabinet. The DC, however, refused PSI support and proceeded to form a weak government with a narrow majority—thereby making bold or significant legislation impossible. For the next five years, Italy also succumbed to immobilism. The defection of only ten votes could topple a cabinet. Consequently, all controversial legislation was either avoided or suffered defeat until the next legislative election in 1958. Fortunately, this was a period of decreasing international tensions and of rampant domestic prosperity. The parties of the Left were less militant as a result, while the neofascists were unable to find supporters.

Still, new leaders were emerging within the various parties who promised more dynamic leadership in the future. The DC party congress of 1954, meeting at Naples, chose Amintore Fanfani as its new secretary (or leader). Fanfani represented the left wing of the party, and he began to transform the DC into a party of the Left rather than, as under de Gasperi, a party of the center. Fanfani tried to convert the party to social reform and to safeguarding the rights of the working class. This implied a willingness to seek new allies on the Left—such as Nenni's PSI, and Fanfani spoke of "an opening to the left." Simultaneously, the Liberal party, on the far right of the quadripartite coalition, was becoming more conservative under new leaders. These developments, which effected parliamentary coalitions only slightly before 1958, were greatly accelerated by the 1958 election, in which the conservative parties lost seats and the PSI gained. This shifted the center of gravity of the new Chamber of Deputies to the left and made a PSI-DC alliance seem more realistic. The continued strength of the Communists, in spite of the embarrassment of Russia's repression in Hungary, also encouraged Fanfani to try to woo the PSI away from their traditional partners on the extreme left. Yet, the ideological chasm was so great between the Socialists and the Christian Democrats that the "opening to the left" was not achieved for three more years. In the meantime, the DC had strengthened its majority in the 1958 election and had been given a clear policy direction by Fanfani. Italy had emerged from immobilism, at least temporarily, without following the French example but by turning to the political center represented by Christian Democracy. This solution, however, was to give Italy only a brief respite from instability.

Chancellor Democracy and the German Miracle

Konrad Adenauer, at the age of seventy-three, found himself the chancellor of an occupied Germany. A communist regime governed East Germany, and Great Britain, the United States, and France occupied the Bonn Republic. Therefore, to obtain West Germany's independence was Adenauer's first priority. He was aided in this cause by the Korean War half-way around the globe. As the Korean conflict transformed the cold war into a hot war, Adenauer's ability to bargain was greatly increased.

Germany was the center of attention in Europe, since Germany was divided just as Korea had been before the conflict began. A war scare spread through western Europe, with a Russian advance westward predicted by some. The American response was to demand the rearming of Germany to aid in the defense of the "free world" as defined in Washington. The French EDC proposal, although attempting to subordinate a German army to a European command, accepted the concept of a revived German military.

It was highly contradictory of the Allies to continue to occupy Germany as a conquered state while discussing the German role in European defense. Adenauer realized this and exploited it to the fullest. In 1951 the Occupation Statute, which governed the Federal Republic's relations with the Allies, was revised to allow West Germany to establish a foreign office and a diplomatic corps. Adenauer promptly appointed himself foreign minister. Through patient negotiations he was able to tie the EDC treaty, signed by the Western Allies in May 1952, to a recognition of German sovereignty. This strategy failed however, when the French parliament rejected EDC. Immediately, diplomatic activity shifted to the NATO level. With a British commitment to keep troops on the Continent, the French agreed to the rearmament of Germany within NATO. These agreements were formalized in the Paris treaties signed in October 1954. The first of the four treaties recognized the sovereignty of the Federal Republic and announced the end of the Allied occupation (the following year) in return for a German pledge not to attempt the reunification of the two Germanies by force. The second and third treaties admitted West Germany into the Western European Union (the extended Brussels Pact alliance) and into NATO. A final treaty dealt with the Saar, which remained a source of conflict between France and West Germany despite the ECSC agreement. A referendum was to be held that would allow the Saarlanders to vote for or against independence from Germany. When the vote was taken, they rejected independence and became a German state. Therefore, on May 5, 1955, when the Paris treaties went into effect, the West Germans were a free people again.

The glory went to Adenauer who had conducted the negotiations. His foreign policy successes were rewarded in the election of 1953, when the CDU gained a clear majority in the Bundestag. Adenauer was not satisfied with just a majority, however; for the provisions of the Bonn Basic Law prohibited the establishment of a German military, and a two-thirds majority of the Bundestag was required to amend the Basic Law. The chancellor therefore formed a cabinet coalition of four parties— enough to insure him the votes needed to revise the Constitution as he saw fit. Indeed, he rearmed Germany *before* he changed the Basic Law. This was only one instance of Adenauer's abuse of his ascendancy over the parties of the Bundestag. From 1953 until 1959 he conducted what

TABLE 19.4. German Elections, 1953–61

Party	1953 Seats	1953 Votes, %	1957 Seats	1957 Votes, %	1961 Seats	1961 Votes, %
Social Democrat	151	28.8	169	31.8	190	36.2
Christian Democrat ...	243	45.2	270	50.2	242	45.4
Free Democrat	48	9.5	41	7.7	67	12.8
German party	15	3.2	17	3.4	...	2.8
Refugees	27	5.9	...	4.6	...	
Bavarian party	...	1.7	...	...	...	...
Extreme Right	...	1.1	...	1.0	...	0.8
Communist	...	2.2	...	...	...	...
Others	3	2.3	...	1.3	...	1.9
Total	487		497		499	

Source: Alfred Grosser, *The Federal Republic of Germany*, trans. Nelson Aldrich (New York Frederick A. Praeger, Publishers, 1964), p. 50.

many called a "chancellor democracy" (*Kanzlerdemokratie*), maintaining the republican institutions but governing without them. During much of this period he held three key posts—as chancellor, foreign minister, and president of the CDU. He ignored his ministers and governed directly through permanent civil servants who reported directly to Adenauer rather than to the cabinet member to whom they were legally responsible. He never allowed any CDU leader to gain prominence or publicity except Ludwig Erhard, who was a technical expert in economic matters and who was indispensable. Of course, his power was increased by the willingness of his ministers and CDU colleagues to accept his dictatorial rule and by the weakness of the SPD, his only real opposition.

Most Germans were quite willing to forgive Adenauer his authoritarian excesses as long as the "German miracle" continued. This was the term applied to the truly remarkable economic recovery the nation enjoyed in the 1950s. From a defeated, occupied state in 1945, Germany had climbed ten years later to third place in industrial production behind the two superpowers. Germany was once again a major exporter of industrial goods, enjoyed a favorable balance of trade, and had one of the world's strongest currencies. Such prosperity was usually credited to Minister of Economics Ludwig Erhard's "social market economy." Erhard argued that the state should interfere in the market as little as possible, intervening only to prevent social abuses such as unemployment, shortages of housing, or monopolization of industries. The goal was increased production, not social equalization or public welfare as in France and England. Therefore, German entrepreneurs were encouraged to take risks and to plow their capital back into investments.

Adenauer's authoritarian democracy also seemed to be remarkably stable. Contrary to events during the Weimar Republic of the 1920s, the passage of time weakened extremist parties until they disappeared altogether. (See Table 19.4.) The two major parties continued to grow, suggesting that Germany might at last evolve a two-party system similar to Great Britain's. These trends were helped along by laws which prohibited antidemocratic parties, enabling the federal court to dissolve the Communist party in 1953, and which denied parliamentary representation to parties obtaining less than 5 percent of the total national vote.

Germany was not, however, being transformed into the model democratic state. Having initially begun along the road to the welfare state, the CDU could not bear to continue. Basing its faith on free enterprise, Adenauer's party "privatized" industries under state control while other west European countries were nationalizing. Shares of ownership in Volkswagen were sold to private citizens. The huge Preussag coal and oil combine was disposed of in the same manner. Certain industrial giants of the Nazi era and before were allowed to once again obtain monopoly powers—the Krupp steel works, once employers at Auschwitz, were permitted to revive. Wealth and power again began to concentrate in a few hands, as an official of the German Federation of Trade Unions pointed out in 1959.

From 1 to 2 percent only of West German businesses dispose of more than a million DM in capital. This 1 or 2 percent control half the country's production and distribution. For the very existence of a democratic state, it is intolerable that such a concentration of economic power be authorized under this form and even encouraged by fiscal legislation and other measures.[3]

Quite aside from such informal, unplanned threats to the German republic, Adenauer followed policies that his opponents denounced as purposeful attacks on democracy. He made major decisions without informing his cabinet—especially concerning foreign affairs and administered the nation directly through the permanent civil service without regard for constitutional channels; he used his two-thirds majority to override the inhibitions on his powers in the Basic Law; and he encouraged former Nazis to resume high posts in government, appointing one, Hans Globke, to head his personal staff and another, Theodor Oberlaender, as federal minister of refugee affairs.[4]

To whatever extent these policies may have scandalized Adenauer's political opponents, they in no way lessened his immense popularity with the German public. The 1957 election campaign was a sounding board for the Social Democrats (SPD) and even the Free Democrats

---

[3] Alfred Grosser, *The Federal Republic of Germany,* trans. Nelson Aldrich (New York: Frederick A. Praeger, Publishers, 1964), pp. 84–85.

[4] Charles Wighton, *Adenauer: A Critical Biography* (New York: Coward-McCann, Inc., 1964), pp. 196–99, 314–15.

(FDP), the second largest party in Adenauer's coalition, to denounce the "Old Man," as papers affectionately called the chancellor; but the electorate endorsed Germany's prosperity and international recovery by increasing the CDU majority. Adenauer's dominance was, if anything, made more secure.

The SPD was stunned by the 1957 results. Certainly they had gained votes, but the CDU had not been weakened. Therefore, the socialists began to question their basic programs. Perhaps their doctrine no longer was applicable to the economic and social conditions of postwar Germany. This was the issue which was debated at the SPD's Bad Godesburg Congress, October 1959. Reformers, who wished to dispense with the orthodox party stand on socialization of the economy in favor of a program of gradual reforms within a capitalistic framework, had been gaining power within the SPD organization during the 1950s. Their increasing influence was strikingly revealed when a reformer, Willy Brandt, was elected chairman of the West Berlin SPD conference in 1958. At Bad Godesburg, then, the reorientation of German socialism was almost a foredrawn conclusion. By a vote of 324 to 16 the conference adopted a new official program that rejected the nationalization of industry, dropped Marxist terminology concerning class conflict, embraced the idea of a property-owning democracy guaranteeing social justice, and accepted the alliance with the West and rearmament, while rejecting the development of nuclear weapons. Each point was a clear and extreme reversal of previous positions, although the majority of the SPD's parliamentary party had adopted such reformism much earlier in day-to-day legislative matters.[5] This "conversion of the opposition" was the strongest evidence of the success of Adenauer's and Erhard's policies.

Yet, at the moment of his greatest prestige, Adenauer was already beginning to lose his political acumen and his control over the governing coalition. Already in 1957 an FDP leader had accused Adenauer of conducting a "one-man government."

Germany has never had a real chance to develop parliamentary skills. Procedure is now being permitted to decay because Adenauer never takes the trouble to tell the Opposition of his legislative programme. He treats ministries as private clubs, parliament as his private secretary, and debate as a farce.[6]

Even the second rank of the CDU was becoming restive, having been denied any influence over national policy. With the term of the federal president to expire in 1959, Adenauer was pushed by his party into announcing that he would stand for election to that figurehead position. Adenauer, however, was not so easy to remove. He requested Hans Globke

[5] David Childs, *From Schumacher to Brandt: The Story of German Socialism 1945–1965* (New York: Pergamon Press, Inc., 1966), pp. 100–05.

[6] Wighton, *Adenauer,* pp. 250–51.

to study the powers of the presidency to see if they could be expanded to supersede those of the chancellorship. The CDU leaders choice for the new chancellor was Ludwig Erhard, probably the most popular man in Germany because of his economic leadership. Adenauer greatly disliked Erhard, and, when he discovered that the presidential powers were small indeed when opposed by a strong man such as Erhard, Adenauer withdrew from the presidential election. He claimed that the international situation had become too dangerous to permit a change of leadership, and, therefore, he must remain the chancellor. This blatant refusal to surrender his personal power, even to the foremost leader of his own party, cost Adenauer and the CDU dearly in terms of public prestige.

The damage that had been done was evident in the 1961 legislative elections. Adenauer campaigned in demagogic manner, warning that the Soviet Union desired the victory of the SPD. The SPD and FDP campaigned against *Kanzlerdemokratie*. The CDU was not helped by a controversy over a supposed revival of nazism, which appeared real not only because of Nazis uncovered in the judiciary system but also because of a wave of anti-Semitic sign-painting in several parts of West Germany. For the first time since 1949, the CDU lost votes and seats in the Bundestag, losing even its majority position. Adenauer was shaken. He gained CDU support for a new cabinet only by promising to retire well before the 1965 election, so the new chancellor, whoever he might be, would have time to prove himself. It was perhaps a small concession for a man of eighty-six years, but it was enough to assure him three more years of power. Unfortunately they were not to be his most glorious years. His greatness had been proved when it was needed—in the first years of the Bonn Republic; nothing, not even his growing authoritarianism, could tarnish that record.

Chapter 20

A NEW SOCIETY

European society from 1919–39 was stagnant. Economic growth was slow; population actually declined in some nations; the transfer of population from the country to the city almost stopped, and in France the process was reversed. Class structure and economic institutions changed little. The dynamism of the nineteenth century seemed to have been destroyed by World War I. Yet, the western European states reversed these trends after 1945. Economic growth was remarkable. New institutions—national and international—emerged to guide this growth and to cope with the problems created by prosperity. The dynamism evident in the economic sphere was only one indication of the new society that emerged from the ruins of the second total war of the century. New styles of life, a new affluence for the majority of Europeans, new ideologies, and new artistic movements were also products of the most profound and fundamental reorientation of European society since the impact of the French and industrial revolutions. While the communist regimes of eastern Europe were irreversibly industrializing the last premodern societies on the Continent, economic planning, the welfare state, and the Common Market were profoundly shaping the culture of the West.

Industrial Growth, Economic Planning, and Individual Mobilization

The really astounding aspect of postwar economic growth was its apparent freedom from the depression-boom cycle that was considered inevitable before 1939. Not only Marxist but also many liberal economists had assumed that capitalist economies would always experience alternating booms and slumps. This had actually been the case during the nineteenth and early twentieth centuries, with the trend culminating in the Great

Depression of 1929. At the time of the depression the index of industrial production of Germany, for example, had decreased by as much as 17.8 percent from the previous year's total, and the decrease had continued for several years. (See Table 7.1.) Since World War II, the European economies (excluding Great Britain) have experienced uninterrupted expansion. Table 20.1 suggests the magnitude of this growth from country to country. The weakness of the British economy should be noted. Table

TABLE 20.1. Compound Rate of Growth of Gross Domestic Product in Selected Countries, 1949–63 (percentages)

Country	1949–54	1954–59	1959–63	1948–63
West Germany	8.4	6.6	5.6	7.6
Italy	4.8	5.6	6.1	6.0
Austria	5.7	5.7	5.2	5.8
France	4.8	4.1	5.1	4.6
Great Britain	2.7	2.3	1.7	2.5
United States	3.6	3.3	. . .	. . .

Sources: Columns 1 and 2 from David S. Landes, *The Unbound Prometheus* (London: Cambridge University Press, 1969), p. 497; columns 3 and 4 from M. M. Postan, *An Economic History of Western Europe, 1945–1964* (London: Metheun and Co., Ltd., 1967), pp. 12 and 56, respectively.

20.2 compares the growth of production per capita of the postwar period with that of the period of most rapid growth before 1945. It is evident that productivity per capita has increased three to four times more rapidly in the recent period.

TABLE 20.2. Rates of Growth of Production Per Capita

Country	1870–1913	1948–62
Germany	1.8	6.8
Italy	0.7	5.6
France	1.4	3.4
Great Britain	1.3	2.4

Source: M. M. Postan, *An Economic History of Western Europe, 1945–1964* (London: Metheun and Co., Ltd., 1967), p. 17.

Many reasons could be given for this rapid and sustained growth. Among the most important factors seem to be the influence of economic planning, the mobilization of labor, and the Common Market. Perhaps more fundamental, however, is the radical change in attitudes and values among politicians, businessmen, and farmers. All three have rejected the liberal laissez faire economics of the interwar period. All have accepted government intervention in the economy, and the debates over the merits of capitalism and socialism have been replaced by debates over how to manage the nationalized industries. This new attitude is a direct result of the depression and the wartime experience. Conservatives who denounced any state intervention in economic matters as "communism" or "bolshevism" were totally discredited by their inability to cope with unemployment, their unpreparedness to resist German agression, and their collaboration with the Nazis. In addition, certain governments—such as the British and the Russian—had shown the usefulness of economic planning and the rational allocation of resources in mounting a war effort. These negative and positive lessons taken together convinced many businessmen as well as resistance fighters that there must be a new order of things after the war, a new society in which the welfare of the national economy would take precedence over the petty greed of individuals, which might actually be contradictory to needs of society. It was also accepted that only if the economy as a whole prospered could individuals within it prosper.

These new attitudes were reflected in a general acceptance of the main tenets of the economic theories of John Maynard Keynes. Keynes published his influential book, *The General Theory of Employment, Interest and Money,* in 1936. No one really acted on his recommendations until after the war; although the British War Cabinet's Labour members were very aware of his precepts. Keynes argues that it is the level of consumption that determines the health of the economy. If consumption of goods is high, then productivity can also be high; if consumption increases, then productivity can expand; but if general mass consumption decreases, the entire economy will begin to slow down. This means that the well-being of industrial capitalists is tied to the well-being (i.e., the level of consumption) of employees. If workers have high salaries, they can purchase more; industry can produce more; profits will be higher; and everyone will prosper. When this theory is accepted by government, management and labor, the element of class conflict inherent in the Marxist dichotomy of employer vs. employee should theoretically be replaced by debates over the proper level of wages to ensure continued economic expansion. In fact, this has been the case in some countries where governments have established wage guidelines and organized labor has accepted them. In others, such as Sweden, labor unions have imposed the wage restraints on their members after three-way negotiations with business and government. The old class conflict had supposedly been reduced to the technical question of how high could wages go without causing inflation and how low could they sink without causing a recession.

The acceptance these ideas received was largely due to their applicability to a mixed economy in which certain key industries were nationalized while the major part of the economic sector could be only indirectly influenced by the government through economic planning. The "planned economies" of western Europe could not be manipulated in the same way as the "controlled economies" of eastern Europe. In the controlled economies, the rate and direction of economic growth could be managed by a centrally directed allocation of real resources (iron ore, coal, manpower); but in the planned economies, more indirect methods had to be employed.

France was the first to adopt economic planning. Her success was so obvious (and such a reversal of past French economic performance) that, by the late 1950s and early 1960s the other states followed the French example. Italy more or less backed into planning in the late 1950s by utilizing nationalized industrial giants that were remnants of the Fascist period. Great Britain and Germany adopted planning in 1962 as a reaction to economic slowdowns in both countries. The governments in the latter three nations were controlled by conservatives when planning was adopted, proving that political issues and attitudes had certainly changed since the 1930s.

The first French Plan was written by Jean Monnet and his staff in 1946. It was to run from 1947–50 and to emphasize industrial recovery, agricultural modernization, and construction of a modern base of heavy industry and energy industries (electricity, gas). The machinery to formulate and execute the plan had been created by de Gaulle by decree in January 1946. A Planning Office (*Commissariat Général au Plan*), headed by Monnet, was the central institution. Under this office, "modernization commissions" were appointed to report on the present state and future prospects of individual industries. This technical bureaucracy was crowned by the Economic and Social Council, a consultative body of 200 members representing various sectors of the economy. The Planning Office formulates a plan by suggesting certain suggested goals of performance to the modernization commissions, which in fact represent both private industry and the planning staff. In these commissions differences between public officials and industrialists, farm groups, and consumer groups are negotiated. The Planning Office then tries to restructure its plan based on the reports of the commissions. The Economic and Social Council reviews the plan before it is sent to the national legislature but rarely asks for modifications. Finally, the plan is submitted to Parliament for approval. The process takes about three years.

The plan consists of projections or forecasts of the desirable rate of growth of each sector of the economy for a set period—in France it is usually four years. The projections are not of a compulsory nature, but are to be used by the government to guide its investments in the public sector, and its policy toward credits and investments in the private sector. Therefore, the French government implements the plan not through coercion but through indirect control of investment, and the French state has several means of guiding investment at its disposal. The state owns directly a large percentage of the nation's industry—the nationalized industries of electricity, gas, railroads, aero-space, etc. Through these, the state controls directly almost half the total annual investment in the economy. Beyond direct ownership, the government can grant or withhold tax concessions and privileges on investments, and the state can give cash subsidies to various industries to encourage private investment. Finally, the state owns the major banking institutions of France, giving it control over the flow of credit to various industries. Using these tools, the French government has transformed the French economy from one of the most backward in western Europe into one of the most dynamic.

There are, of course, factors that have aided the economic growth of Europe that have little to do with government policy. One of these is the remarkable increase in the mobility of the European population. After 1945 more than ever before workers have become willing to go where the jobs are available. This has prevented the anomaly of the nineteenth-century Italian situation in which the land of the South was overcrowded with starving peasants while jobs were vacant in the northern industrial cities. Since 1945 workers are willing to move from country to city, from one region within a country to another, and even to travel to other countries in search of work.[1] Such mobility is necessary for expanding economies since it supplies an abundance of cheap labor rather than forcing employers to compete with one another for an increasingly more expensive, static labor supply. Therefore, they are free to invest their profits in expansion rather than in higher wages without increased productivity.

The events of World War II and the move toward European integration combined to destroy barriers to mobility. During the war approximately 30,000,000 persons were forced to leave their homeland—either in service to the Nazis or fleeing from them. The postwar settlements led to transfers of another 25,000,000. Germans continued to migrate from the communist sector to the Bonn Republic until the construction of the Berlin Wall. Such mass transferals decreased traditional ties to provincial homes and forced individuals to seek out their main chance. Other less tragic sources of migration were from the colonial empires. Not only the European civil servants returned to Great Britain, France, and Holland as the empires declined, but also many Indians, North and West Africans, and Indonesians sought a new life. Economic forces were also at work. The underdeveloped areas on the fringes of the industrial heartland of northern Europe contributed many immigrants. Spaniards, Sicilians, Neopolitans,

---

[1] Alessandro Pizzorno, "The Individualistic Mobilization of Europe," ed. Stephan A. Graubard, *A New Europe?* (Boston: Beacon Press, 1967), pp. 265–90.

This French peasant, working with a hand scythe, might well ponder the effect the "new town" and industrial complex under construction will have on the rural countryside. (Courtesy of UPI)

Greeks, Yugoslavs, and Turks supplied the skilled and unskilled labor needed in northeastern France, Belgium, Luxembourg, the Rhineland, and northern Italy. Unfortunately, these migrants did not achieve social mobility as easily as geographic mobility. They usually were confined to the least desirable jobs, freeing the northern Europeans to take the better paying industrial jobs. In case of a recession they were the first fired. Urban slums appeared in Paris, London, Milan, and in German cities to house the "colored" migrants. Yet, the migration continues for the simple reason that a substandard income in Paris is still a great improvement over Algiers or Sicily.

Another factor that has sustained economic expansion is the transformation of western Europe into a mass consumption society. Automobiles built by Citroën and Renault, Fiat, Volkswagen have become available to approximately half of all families. Television and record player-radios provided cheap at-home entertainment. The proportion of the family budget spent on the necessities of food and drink have decreased leaving much more for leisure expenditures. Workers were able to enjoy annual family vacations for the first time in the late 1950s. All these aspects of an "affluent society" have no doubt made life much easier and more enjoyable for the majority of western Europeans. Yet, it should not be overlooked, as shall be pointed out in the following section, that the benefits of economic prosperity have not been spread evenly throughout the

TABLE 20.3. Progress of Mass Consumption in France, 1954–66 (percentage of households containing item)

	1954: France	1966 France	1966 Great Britain
Refrigerator	7	64	47
Washing machine	8	45	59
Television	1	53	88
Automobile	21	48	44

SOURCE: John Ardagh, *The New French Revolution* (New York: Harper & Row, Publishers, 1969), p. 261.

populace but have tended to improve the living standards of the wealthy more than of the poor. And the prosperity has been selective regionally as well as socially. Inequalities are still great between the average standard of living in England and in Italy, or between northern and southern Italy for that matter; so that an underdeveloped Europe continues to exist along side the new affluence.

Perhaps the most unevenly effected and most diverse sector of the European economy is the agricultural sector. The rush toward industrial modernization presumed the disappearance of the European peasantry, rooted as it was in small, uneconomical parcels of land—too small to support the application of modern farming techniques. The peasantry was also diminished by the funneling of excess population from the countryside into the new factories. Both of these trends have been gathering force in France and Italy. In Great Britain and Germany, where the farmers had already rationalized their holdings and introduced modern methods before 1939, the impact of postwar trends was not as severe, but they still felt the need of a great deal of government support. The agricultural situation in each country differs greatly. For instance, Italy was initiating land reforms to give farmers land, while peasant organizations in France were beginning to demand collective cultivation of the land so that peasants could profit from the advantages of large scale production; but in every country the rural population has benefited least from social welfare measures and mass consumption. Only in the 1960s, when peasant riots shook France, Italy, Belgium, and other countries, did the governments, for so long concerned with urban problems, turn seriously to the plight of the countryside.

Social Structure and Class Conflict in the Welfare State

The mosaic of social reforms that composed the welfare state had been completed in the major west European states by 1950 but were constantly being adjusted in detail. One definition of the welfare state has been offered by Wallace Peterson.

The welfare state has to do with the use of governmental power as an instru-ment for the redistribution of income in society, generally with the dual objec-tives of greater equality in the distribution of money income and a guarantee of some minimum standard of well-being for all citizens.[2]

The means of this redistribution include a matrix of social insurance mea-sures that, in effect, allow the state to purchase certain services for citizens that the citizen could not otherwise afford. Among these ser-vices are medical treatment; insurance against sickness, old age, and dis-ability; education for one's children; and the essentials of a civilized ex-istence if one's income is below a national minimum. Some nations have emphasized one aspect over another. France, for example, has the most far-reaching family support system. So extensive is the French system, in fact, that a working class family with two children might receive one-half of its income from family allowances: "Thirty-five francs for the two chil-dren, another 35 because the wife did not work, and 20 francs rent sub-sidy."[3] Great Britain's Health Service is more complete than that of most other nations. Although minor charges have been added since the service's inception, for all practical purposes medical care is free. The French, on the other hand, have a health insurance system, whereby the patient must pay for his treatment initially but is later reimbursed by the state for 80 percent of his bill.

These services are funded through direct taxes paid by both employers and employees and supplemented by the state. A study of France during the late 1950s revealed, at that time, that the employers' share was paid ultimately by the consuming public in the form of higher prices.[4] In this way, those who benefit from the services provided—the workers, aged, etc.—are also the ones who pay for them. This inevitably raises the ques-tion of to what extent the welfare state has succeeded in redistributing the national wealth and in democratizing west European society. There can be no absolute answer. As Table 20.4 indicates, the amount of money that the state distributes in the form of social services has become a sizable proportion of the income of an average French family. Yet, if

---

[2] Wallace C. Peterson, *The Welfare State in France* (Lincoln, Nebraska: Univer-sity of Nebraska Press, 1960), p. 1.

[3] John Ardagh, *The New French Revolution* (New York: Harper & Row Publish-ers, 1969), pp. 298–99.

[4] Peterson, *Welfare State in France,* p. 105.

TABLE 20.4. Sources of Income of French Households, 1949–63 (%)

	1949	1955	1960	1963
Wages and salaries	37	39.5	40.5	42.5
Privately owned business	37	32	31.5	27.5
Interest, dividends, land rents	4.5	4.5	3.5	3.0
From abroad	2.0	2.0	2.0	1.5
Total	43.5	38.5	37.0	32.0
Transfer income (social services and cash payments from the state)	16.0	18.5	18.5	21.0
Other	3.5	3.5	4.0	4.5

SOURCE: Jean Cuisenier, "Agents et systemes d'action economiques," ed. Jean-Daniel Reynaud, *Tendances et volontés de la société française* (Paris: S.E.D.E.I.S., 1966), p. 183.

those who receive the services, are also those who—through higher prices, direct and, especially, indirect taxes—pay for the services, there is no real redistribution of wealth. Still, the existence of the social services, regardless of who pays for them, does make the working class life more secure, freer from the nagging fear of a crippling illness, or of old age, or of ruinous medical bills. Combining this increased social security with the prosperity of the postwar era, it is difficult to conclude that the lower income groups are not immeasurably more comfortable in the present regime than they were before 1939.

Yet another question must be answered: To what extent has the welfare state democratized west European society and politics? It appears that the increased wealth of the lower classes has indeed changed the class structure, in that a good deal of upward social mobility has been possible at the bottom of the social pyramid. The children of workers and peasants now find it easier to move into the lower-middle class of white-collar workers. Skilled laborers can now live as well or better than some members of the lower-middle class, making the distinction between the two groups purely a psychological one and not an economic one. But this greater social mobility does not exist at the higher rungs of the social ladder. In all west European countries the social and political elite of big business, higher civil service, and parliamentary leadership appear just as exclusive as in the early 1950s, although they may be slightly more open to new members than before 1939. The motor of social mobility is, of course, the educational system. The great expansion of secondary education throughout western Europe has made it possible for lower and middle-class children to obtain the training and the skills necessary for clerical, managerial, and technical occupations. As Table 20.5 indicates, secondary school enrollments, both general and terminal, have expanded by 43 percent from 1950 to 1960.

TABLE 20.5. Expansion of Education in Western Europe, 1950–60

Level	Number of Schools 1950	1960	Number of Pupils 1950	1960	Increase of pupils, %
Primary	285,000	328,000	30,000,000	32,000,000	.06
General secondary	16,500	26,000	5,000,000	6,800,000	.36
Terminal secondary	23,000	24,000	4,700,000	7,100,000	.51
Higher education	194	224	690,000	970,000	.40
Total students			40,390,000	46,870,000	

SOURCE: Frank Bowles, "Education in the New Europe," ed. Stephen R. Graubard, *The New Europe* (Boston: Beacon Press, 1967), p. 445.

Higher education has also expanded rapidly, but West European universities have preserved their character as class institutions. This is not to say that no children of the lower classes enter the universities, nor even that there has not been an increase in lower-class students, but that such students still constitute a very small proportion of the educational elite of various nations. Among the student bodies of the most prestigous universities, such as Cambridge and Oxford in England and *les Grandes Ecoles* in France, one finds an even smaller percentage of students from the lower classes.

TABLE 20.6. Percentage of Manual Workers' Sons in University Student Bodies

	Around 1960	Around 1964
Western Europe		
Great Britain	25.0 (1961)	...
Italy	13.2	15.3
France	5.3	8.3
West Germany	5.2	5.3
Eastern Europe		
Yugoslavia	56.0	53.3
Czechoslovakia	39.3	37.9
Rumania	36.6	31.5
Hungary	33.1	...
Bulgaria	28.0	34.5

SOURCE: Anthony Sampson, *Anatomy of Europe* (New York: Harper and Row Publishers, 1968), p. 406.

This elitist structure of education is maintained by a battery of examinations that are biased, by their literary form and by their very existence, in favor of children from upper class homes where literature and art are commonplaces. In most countries students take one or more examinations between the ages of twelve and fifteen which determine their future academic career. If a student does well, he is put into an academic secondary school that prepares him for a university entrance examination. If he does poorly, he is channeled into a technical and terminal secondary school where he learns a trade. Thus, in early adolescence, the class structure has selected the future leaders of the nation. A university entrance examination completes the process at approximately the age of eighteen. The students are once again divided into two groups. Those who do well on the exam enter the university and prepare to govern their nation, manage its business, and set its social standards. Those who fail the exam enter any number of careers for which their secondary school has prepared them.

Just as greater prosperity has not democratized society, it has not democratized the political or economic leadership of western Europe. To a certain extent this can be explained by the nature and demands of leadership in these areas. Social graces, broad knowledge of national and international affairs, and familiarity with wealth and responsibility are qualities which the upper classes are more likely to possess than are other members of society. This was, however, true before World War II as well. There is a new condition that tends to favor the upper classes because of their educational advantage—the increasingly technical nature of political issues. During the 1940s and 1950s all political parties regardless of ideology desired leaders conversant with economic problems and able to deal with the industrial elite concerning problems of reconstruction and economic planning. Such a technical, trained leadership could only come from the upper classes.

All of the above is not to argue that there has been no change since 1945 in west European social structure. In fact, a very fundamental change has taken place that has essentially changed the manner in which governmental and economic decisions are made. A new social force, perhaps not a class, has appeared in the "technocracy." The technocrats are the economic experts, social experts, military experts who both make and administer government policies. They are more than bureaucrats in that they influence decisions by their "expert advice" which can be ignored by politicians only at the risk of financial calamity, military defeat, or bureaucratic revolt. The technocrats are, of course, the elite of the most rapidly growing sector of modern society, which C. Wright Mills labeled the white-collar class. One author has estimated that the white-collar class amounted to roughly 5 percent of all employed persons in Europe in 1900, but by 1910 had already expanded to 10 percent. The International Labor Organization in 1950 set the figure at 25 percent for Great Britain, 28 percent for West Germany, and as high as 35 percent for Sweden.[5]

Of course, the introduction of economic planning has been the greatest

---

[5] Ralf Dahrendorf, "Recent Changes in Class Structure," ed. Stephen H. Graubard, *A New Europe?*, p. 311.

boost to the technocrats' power. It has increasingly taken decision-making away from the politicians and transferred this power to the technocrats. After the acceptance of planning, politicians cannot make "political" decisions without consulting, for example, economists, because all political decisions in some way effect the use of national resources and, therefore, become economic decisions that might effect the working of the plan. An example of the technocrats' role was the way in which the French Fifth Plan was presented to the Chamber of Deputies in 1965. Three alternative plans were submitted, proposing economic growth rates of 5 percent, 5.5 percent, and 6 percent. Only one plan, however, was developed in detail—the one providing for 5.5 percent growth. Of course, the politicians could not obtain sufficient knowledge of industry and agriculture to contest the technocrats' preference for this plan. This is only one example. The same relationship between the technocracy and parliament holds true for much lesser policy decisions as well.

Not only have the technocrats gained influence in government through their indispensable expertise and inserted themselves into industrial relations because of the inevitable nexus between wages, prices, and economic planning; but they have also become the new masters of private industry as the managers of large corporations. Since World War II the owner-managers of large business firms have practically ceased to exist. This is due basically to the replacement of family or personal ownership of companies by corporate ownership—especially by institutional investors such as insurance companies, banks, and mortgage institutions.[6] As these institutions buy stock in several businesses, ownership and management become truly divorced; for the institutional investors are not interested in direct control but in a reasonable return of their investment. The result is that the management of major firms has passed into the hands of professional executives, the technocrats of the business world. Their goal is corporate expansion, profits, and efficiency—not in assuring the existence of a family firm to pass on to their heirs. They tend to be more adventurous and risk-taking than the owner-managers. Their attitudes have contributed immeasurably to the growth of industry since the war. As a group, these managers are perfectly willing to cooperate with economic planning, not having the same feeling of need to defend private property as the owner-managers. Indeed, there is a high degree of interchange between the high civil service in most nations and the professional managerial class. This naturally leads to an identification of the interests of big business with those of the nation in a different and more fundamental way than when politicians only represented certain interest groups.

Potentially, then, the rise of the technocrats poses a great danger to the west European democratic regimes. Traditional politicians are not

---

[6] M. M. Postan, *An Economic History of Western Europe, 1945–1964* (London: Methuen & Co., Ltd., 1967), chap. 10, "Ownership: Anonymous."

equipped to oppose technical proposals on scientific or economic grounds: nor does there seem to be any practical or desirable way to create barriers between the governmental experts and the industrial managers. It is a dilemma for the industrial state which desires to have a political system free from any single interest. Perhaps the answer is well-educated, technically trained politicians, but there seems to be little chance of that.

The interrelatedness of government, industry and organized labor as it has developed under the planned economies and welfare states of western Europe has led political scientists and sociologists to herald "the end of ideology."[7] These men seem to be saying that class conflict has been ended by the integration of the workers into the Keynesian economy. Both employers and employees agree that economic prosperity will benefit both; so prosperity has become their common goal, making ideas of class conflict archaic. However, these commentators equate ideologies that advocate employer-employee conflict with all ideology and with all conflict. In fact, European governments are just as "ideological" when controlled by the inherent assumptions of the technocrats and liberal-social democratic parliamentary majorities as they would be if the consciously ideological communists were to gain power. The technocrats are not free from ideology; they continually voice their almost utopian faith in a planned, efficient society based on a continually expanding economy.

Nor has social conflict been ended by prosperity, as was amply demonstrated by student revolts in France, Italy, and Germany as well as in Czechoslovakia in the late 1960s. The ideology of consensus, cooperation, and prosperity were dominant during the 1950s, but five million Frenchmen and five million Italians continued to vote for communist, working-class parties. And the very prosperity that has ameliorated the worker's lot has given birth to new social discontent. Demands for participation in decision-making, for controls over one's destiny (threatened by urbanization, anonymous corporations, and class-conscious educational systems), and for increased equality of opportunity cannot be resolved as can questions of wage increases and factory safety. These questions become more fundamental and more urgent in a new society with an educated and literate working class as well as a gargantuan and highly articulate white collar class. These new demands imply a felt need for a restructured institutional framework rather than a redistribution of wealth or products.

Therefore, the welfare state should be seen not as the liberal-democratic state minus class conflict, but as essentially a different form of sociopolitical system from either the liberal democratic state of pre-1939 or the socialist states of Russia and eastern Europe. It is characterized by the preservation of private property and the profit motive as well as by the

---

[7] Chaim Isaac Waxman, ed., *The End of Ideology Debate* (New York: Funk & Wagnalls, 1969).

guarantee of a minimum standard of living to all its members. With the development of mass democracy and the growing political awareness of the laboring classes, a redistribution of national income was all but inevitable. There were several ways this could be done; none of them compatible with laissez faire economics or with liberal democracy. In 1917 the Russian Revolution set the pattern for a redistribution of wealth and property in an undeveloped economy. After World War II western Europe set the example for such a redistribution in a developed industrial society.

Intellectuals Confront the New Society

There have been at least two generations of intellectuals since 1945—those who were mature during World War II and those who matured as artists and thinkers after the war and began producing major works only in the mid 1950s. Perhaps a third group could be added, consisting of men who had matured in the 1920s and who returned to public prominence in 1945. The men and women who were young during World War II, who took part in the resistance movements, became the existentialists and realists of the late 1940s. Sartre, Camus, Jaspers, Silone as well as the filmmakers Rossellini and de Sica wanted to face reality and to force *their* countrymen to join them in a quest for new values. By the middle of the next decade many writers, painters, filmmakers thought they had found their values and were willing to attempt radical experiments with their media—that is, they were relieved of the burden of social despair and chaos that the earlier generation had been forced to confront and were finally free to pursue art for its own sake.

Existential philosophy was one of the most popular and superficial intellectual currents of the postwar years, but it was also one of the most fertile because it required all men of intellect—not only philosophers, but also novelists, poets, painters, theologians—to reconsider their own positions. Jean-Paul Sartre had absorbed the precepts which he later welded into existentialism from German philosophers in the interwar period, especially Martin Heidegger and Edmund Husserl. In 1939 he wrote a novel entitled *Nausea* that dramatized his message that each man must realize the absurdity of his own existence before he could freely assert his individual independence. Sartre's basic position was that since God did not exist and life had no inherent meaning, each man must impose meaning on life by accepting personal responsibility for his actions. Once an individual realized that there were no inhibitions on his behavior except those that he himself imposed, he became a free being, a man in the spiritual sense. Until then, he was merely an object controlled by his environment. The extension of this was that men must assert their existence by making decisions, moral decisions, instead of allowing events to carry them along. Of course, such a position applied very clearly to the occupied France where Sartre lived while he was developing these ideas. They also applied to the immediate postwar period throughout Europe, when old values seemed doomed by the recent destruction. Existentialism seemed to offer the basis for a new ethical standard. Yet it also risked the danger of making every man his own moral policeman; so that he were just as free to make a decision to support concentration camps in the Soviet Union (as Sartre did in the early 1950s) as he was to fight courageously for freedom of expression in France (as Sartre did continuously).

Yet, at first, the need for existentialism was greater than the risks it presented, and it swept through continental intellectual circles as if it were irresistibly contagious. Apart from Sartre, several French authors dealt with the individual and his responsibilities—among them, Albert Camus and Simone de Beauvoir stand out. Also, active and exciting theologians revitalized Christian thought—both Catholic and Protestant— by applying the existentialist critique to man's relationship to God and reemphasizing the need for individual moral anguish rather than simple formalist rules to govern all situations. Men like Karl Jaspers, Paul Tillich, and Pierre Teilhard de Chardin created the theological basis for a new Christian ethics more in tune with contemporary society.

It should not be assumed that all philosophers bowed to existentialism. In fact the logical positivists of Great Britain and Scandinavia (and the United States) rejected existentialism as a metaphysical argument based on assumptions of a consciousness that could not be verified by any scientific test. Indeed, this school, led by Ludwig Wittgenstein (a Viennese expatriate) and Bertrand Russell, rejected any argument that could not be demonstrably proved by rigorous linguistic or mathematical testing. They therefore placed themselves in the role of nihilists, able to destroy arguments but incapable of offering alternative truths. With such diametrically opposed conceptions of the approach to truth as existentialism and logical positivism, there could be no reconciliation. Europe became divided into two general philosophical camps which persist.

In the field of literature deference was paid to the great men of the prefascist period who were still active—Gide and Malraux in France; Thomas Mann in Germany; T. S. Eliot in Great Britain; and Croce in Italy. The war, however, had created a second "lost generation" who wanted to be heard. The existentialists were a part of this generation in France. Italian literature produced the most powerful novels, however—the novelists trying to capture the reality of a nation emerging from fascism and war. The neorealist Italian novels were especially interested in the poverty of southern Italy, a culture some north Italian intellectuals had been forced to share during Mussolini's years when they were exiled there. Carlo Levi's *Christ Stopped at Eboli* is an attempt to arouse northern awareness to the squalid conditions in the south. Ignazio Silone and Alberto Moravia also contributed detailed accounts of the lives of the poor and previously ignored sectors of society. Neither Germany nor Great Britain produced literature to compare with the writings of Sartre, Camus, or Silone. German writers, including the magisterial Thomas Mann, were necessarily preoccupied with the Nazi years and the occupation period. Most forceful were Ernst Wiechert's *The Forest of the Dead,* a personal narrative of his period in Buchenwald, and Ernst von Salomon's *The Questionnaire,* which ridiculed the absurdity of Allied attempts to purge all Nazis from public life and to reeducate the German nation. The British novel was still fascinated by public affairs as it had been before the war. George Orwell published *1984* and *Animal Farm* as warnings against totalitarianism. C. P. Snow and Grahame Greene both wrote a series of novels commenting on public events by analyzing them in fictional situations. The impact of war, therefore, dominated the authors who had lived through it; and the same domination could be seen in other areas—theater, poetry—except where it was transcended by a genius of the stature of Bertolt Brecht, perhaps Europe's greatest playwright, who chose to live in East Berlin because of his own Marxist beliefs, or Dylan Thomas, a Welsh poet, whose robust personality as well as his poetic ability created a cult of admirers.

Nor were literature and philosophy alone in feeling the impact of war. The cinema took a path in 1945, specifically in Italy, that changed the nature of the industry and restored cinematography to the level as an art that it had attained during the 1920s. Roberto Rossellini took his stars and his camera into the streets of Rome in 1945 to make a film on the liberation of Rome from the Germans. In filming *Open City* he allowed his actors to improvise their lines; he rarely used a studio; he used nonprofessional actors to portray themselves on the screen. The result was the birth of the realist film. Rossellini's effort was followed quickly by Vittorio de Sica's *Shoeshine* (1945) concerning the corruption of young Italians by the black market that flourished in liberated Rome. Once again, de Sica went into the streets, employed actual shoeshine boys as his actors, and graphically portrayed the poverty of Rome. Many other films followed in the same vein. By 1950 this heroic period of the Italian cinema had all but ended, but Rossellini and de Sica and others had shown that the cinéist, the director, could be just as creative as the novelist and painter. The lesson traveled throughout Europe and was revived, as we shall see, in the late 1950s by a new generation of film makers.

European painting was still dominated by the "great generation" of early modernism—Picasso, Miro, Matisse. They were lionized by the European public because much of their work had been banned during the fascist years, and now the public wanted to reward them not only for their noncooperation with Hitler but also for having suffered at the hands of antimodernist art critics for so long. Art became big business. Picasso was mass-produced, and the old rebel became a millionaire. The students and disciples of the "great generation" were touted as the new masters. Perhaps it was the presence of the old masters that prevented new departures in European painting. In any case, the first postwar breakthrough occurred in the United States. Jackson Pollock, the American who made "abstract expressionism" the dominant school in both America and Europe, had studied with American traditionalists, Mexican social realists, and European surrealists before he began in 1947 to create paintings of free, informal expression by dripping and smearing paint on canvases that were hanging from the wall or lying on the floor. His paintings have no subject, no specific form, but they are masterfully composed so that rhythm and balance are maintained. Pollock was not the only American to be experimenting—Mark Rothko and William de Kooning were developing abstract styles of their own. These three and other Americans took Europe by storm when an exhibit of their works toured the Continent in 1948. Europeans such as the Frenchman Jean Fautrier and the German Wols had been moving in a similar direction through what they called "informal art." The American show stunned the Europeans; as if the future had suddenly been revealed, and many adopted the new styles.

A hiatus occurred in all fields in the early 1950s. The lessons of the postwar years were being absorbed; the trauma of the war years was gradually being shaken off; and behind the scenes—in artists' studios and in film lots as well as in literary circles—new ideas were fermenting that were to explode between 1955–58 in a dazzling display of creativity. Young men, having matured in the welfare state and in the cold war, amid the affluence of the industrialized society and the insecurity of the nuclear age, were preparing new art forms appropriate for a now stable and frighteningly technological society.

One could begin in almost any of the major states. The French novel is perhaps as representative an example as the British theater or the Italian film. Even Sartre, the perpetual rebel, has described the works of Alain Robbe-Grillet, Michel Butler, and Nathalie Sarraute as "antinovels." Robbe-Grillet won a prestigeous French literary prize in 1955 for *The Voyeur,* the story of a murder, which may or may not have occurred, and the possible murderer. Both Robbe-Grillet and Sarraute had published before, but *The Voyeur* marked the maturation of Robbe-Grillet's theory of *chosisme* (literally "thingism"). He and several other authors of the "new novel" school place far more emphasis on the accurate, meticulous description of objects than on the use of dialogue. In their books *things* have personality, form connections between individuals, influence the character's mental states.[8] Therefore, the general goal of the new novelists

---

[8] Barry T. Moore, *Twentieth-Century French Literature,* vol. 2 (New York: Dell Publishing Co., 1967), chap. 5.

is a heightened reproduction of reality—not for a social cause as in the Italian postwar novel but because this, they argue, is the goal of art.

During the same years that the new novelists were bursting on the scene, French cinema went through a major transformation. It all started in 1956 with a cheaply made film on a realistic subject by an extremely young director. It was Roger Vadim's *And God Created Woman,* which introduced Brigitte Bardot (Vadim's wife at the time). The film, amazingly, was a financial success and encouraged French studios to take a chance on other young directors. Between 1959 and 1963, approximately 170 directors made their first commercial films. Of course, most of the "new wave" were execrable, but a few geniuses appeared who produced classics: Alain Resnais' *Hiroshima Mon Amour,* Jean-Francois Truffaut's *The 400 Blows,* and Jean-Luc Godard's *Breathless* were all released in 1959. These men wrote the scripts, directed the films, and sometimes held the camera themselves. They developed a theory of the *film d'auteur,* the film as an expression of one man's creativity. This concept was in direct conflict with the large studio production of films since the 1920s. It was later to be adopted elsewhere (one example being Dennis Hopper's film *Easy Rider* [American, 1969]).

The French new wave had its parallel in the Italian cinema. Fredrico Fellini created a masterpiece in 1954 when he directed *La Strada (The Road).* With more staying power than the earlier realists, he adapted his style to meet the demands of the commercial theater without sacrificing his creativity (as many of the French directors were unable to do). Always having an air of improvisation (sometimes real, sometimes planned), Fellini's films are psychosocial commentaries such as *La Dolce Vita (The Sweet Life,* 1960), attacking the idle Italian rich, and *8½* (1962), an almost autobiographical study of the psyche of a film director. Fellini's twin at this stage was Michelangelo Antonioni. Like Fellini, Antonioni is basically his own screenwriter, and his films are symbolic of his personal reaction to events. His most notable films are his early features, *The Girl-Friends* (1955), *The Cry* (1957), *L'Avventura (The Adventure,* 1959), *La Notte (The Night,* 1960), and *L'Eclisse (The Eclipse,* 1961). The last three were part of a trilogy in which Antonioni experimented with the use of actual time instead of clipping out the actors' movement, usually considered slow or useless by directors.

The British never developed a cinematic school to rival the French or Italians, but beginning in the mid 1950s the British theater was revived by the angry young men, playwrights who blasted the remnants of class structure in the welfare state as well as denouncing the dehumanization of urban life. Chief among these was John Osborne, whose play *Look Back in Anger* (1956), seemed to sympathize with the rebellious youths it portrayed. In the novel a similar anger at social inequalities was expressed in a satiric way by Kingsley Amis's *Lucky Jim* (1954), which lampooned the pecking order at a provincial university. British films continued to be narrative reproductions of books or plays, but the productions and the subject matter became increasingly realistic—dealing more with lower-middle and lower-class life than with the wealthy. Jack Clayton's *Room at the Top* (1958) indicted the business world by portraying the petty machinations of an ambitious young clerk determined to claw his way to the top. Karl Reisz's *Saturday Night and Sunday Morning* (1960) presented working class life in industrial Nottingham in brutal detail. Similar films followed, raising the standard of British filmmaking substantially in the 1960s.

Germany was effected less than other nations by the new wave phenomenon. One major example of new work was the magisterial novel *The Tin Drum* by Günter Grass. An allegory on the Weimar Republic and the Third Reich, it is a brilliant novel that caused many controversies when it appeared.

European painting was not immune from the new developments. In fact, perhaps painting more than any other creative art came to terms with the vast transformations in technology, science and everyday life. Three movements, developing virtually simultaneously, justify this statement: pop art, op art, and kinetic art. Each of these is, in a specific way, contemporary. Abstract expressionism was still wedded to the canvas and to the use of oils to create a painting. Pop art, the presentation of everyday objects in a structured way, recalled the collage but even went further to present entire objects (such as stylized soap boxes) in a way that bridged the gap between painting, collage, and sculpture. This new art form originated with a 1956 exhibition in the Whitechapel Art Gallery in London. The exhibit's most striking piece was a collage of commercial advertisements in the form of a room. A muscleman holding a popcycle stood in the middle of the room while a woman advertising a vacuum cleaner ascended the stairs behind him. A comic book cover was the family's painting over the fireplace, and the wife was a striptease dancer wearing a straw hat. The artist, Richard Hamilton, made his message clear by entitling his congeries *Just What is it that Make's Today's Homes so Different, so Appealing?* Shocking and disquieting were mild terms for such a radical departure from abstraction. Pop art caught the public imagination immediately. It could be comprehended by laymen. It was *modern*. Hamilton knew what he was doing. In 1957 he gave his criteria for modern art: popular, gimmicky, sexy, transient, low-cost, mass-produced.[9] Perhaps he had gone overboard, but maybe not. Artists on the Continent and especially in the United States were soon painting or reproducing in other ways the most common objects, particularly the symbols of mass consumption—Coca-Cola bottles; photos of Marilyn Mon-

---

[9] Edward Lucie-Smith, *Late Modern: The Visual Arts Since 1945* (New York: Frederick A. Praeger, Publishers, 1969), p. 135.

roe, the Hollywood sex symbol; cigarette packages; comic strips. Op and kinetic art are an accommodation to modern science. The optical tricks reproduced are the result of mathematics as well as of paint brush and canvas. The constantly moving mobiles or sculptures of kinetic art embody the principles of physics and engineering.

The trends noted point to one central conclusion: Artists and intellectuals have finally accepted and some have mastered modern technology. The rejection of form in painting before World War I, the demand for new values by Neitszche, Bergson, Freud, the anti-art of dadaism and surrealism may have been, as Geoffrey Barraclough has suggested, the transition from one culture—the "modern," dating from the industrial revolution—to another, the "contemporary." Barraclough would argue that this transition began around 1890 and ended approximately around 1960. Artists were among the first to perceive the disintegration of old values in the fin de siècle. It appears that they have now ended their revolt against technology, urbanism and mass consumption. Not only the subject matter of pop, op, and kinetic art suggest this, but also the willingness of individuals with creative genius to become film directors rather than novelists, painters, or poets. It is an acceptance of, and a desire to master, technology that is indicated by this choice. And is pop art so different from the *chosisme* of Robbe-Grillet, which emphasizes the effect of the inanimate on man's life? The developments in the arts since 1945 and more particularly since 1955 may prove to be a watershed in cultural history.

PART VII

The de Gaulle Era, 1958–69

Chapter 21

THE de GAULLE ERA

Charles de Gaulle was one of those men who dominated European politics by the force of his mind and personality. There have only been a few: Metternich, Bismarck rank among them. The de Gaulle era began with France in political chaos and ended with France once again being a force in world politics. It began with Europe apparently inescapably divided between East and West; it ended with diversity on both sides of the iron curtain and with ever increasing trade and cooperation between the capitalist and socialist states. It began with conservatives securely in power throughout western Europe; it ended with student revolts verging upon revolutions. Most of these developments were, of course, inherent in European social and political conditions, but the direction they took was usually influenced by de Gaulle.

De Gaulle's Return: The Algerian Tragedy

Both extremes emerged as winners from France's 1956 legislative elections. The Poujadists on the Right and the PCF on the Left refused or were not invited to support any governing coalition. Therefore, all cabinets had to depend on the votes of the center and the traditional conservatives. This might not have been disastrous if the policies of the Right had been in harmony with the needs of the nation. Unfortunately, at the time the national interest demanded an end to French rule in Algeria, while the conservative majority was determined to continue the French presence there.

The Algerian nationalists—the National Liberation Front (FLN)—had begun a campaign of terror in 1954, and the French had increased their military commitment to Algeria by transferring the battle-hardened troops from Indochina to North Africa. By 1958 approximately 500,000 French troops were present. The political situation was similar to that of Indochina in the early 1950s. The French colonists or *colons* were determined to perpetuate their dominance. They were supported by the chief military commanders in Algiers, who were led by Generals Massu and Salan. Together, the military and the *colons* sabotaged every attempt by the Paris government to negotiate with the rebels. Several factors made these men even more adamant about keeping Algeria French than similar groups had been in regard to Indochina. The *colons,* or, more accurately, the European Algerians had been settled in Algeria since the 1830s. This was their ancestral home, and they were more similar to a ruling caste than to conquering imperialists. The army was intensely bitter over the defeat in Indochina. They were determined they could defeat the Algerian rebels—if only Paris would support the effort.

It was just this support that appeared threatened in the spring of 1958 when Pierre Pflimlin, a Socialist who favored negotiations with the nationalist rebels, formed his government. The generals the the *colons* decided that they had to save France from the politicians; even if it meant they must mutiny against the legal government. On the day Pflimlin presented his cabinet to the National Assembly, the *colons* seized the government buildings in Algiers, and established a committee of public safety. The army had supported this coup in hopes of preventing the endorsement of Pflimlin by the legislature. It was only after they discovered the parliament had given Pflimlin a vote of confidence that they called on de Gaulle to take power.

During these events de Gaulle had been a very interested but rarely active observer. He had not initiated he coup in Algeria; but when he saw that it was going to occur, he tried to control it. Although he had retired from politics in 1955, he had said then that he might be called upon to intervene again in France's destiny. The Algerian events constituted just the kind of crisis he had foreseen, and he discreetly informed conservative politicians that he agreed with their condemnation of the weakness of the parliamentary system. He was careful not to mention any disagreement he might have with them on Algeria. In this way, he led the *colons* and generals to believe that he shared their desire to preserve a French Algeria. Still, de Gaulle wanted to take power by legal means; and when he learned that the generals were planning a paratroop invasion of Paris for May 27, de Gaulle hurriedly declared, on the 26th, that he was prepared to form a government. The military called off the invasion at this signal from their supposed chief, and the legislators, terrified at the prospect of a civil war, informed de Gaulle that they were willing to accept him on his own terms.

On June 1, 1958, de Gaulle was named the last premier of the Fourth Republic by vote of the National Assembly. On June 2 the National Assembly passed two bills conferring full dictatorial powers on de Gaulle for six months and empowering him to write a new constitution. De Gaulle's goals were to make the army obedient to the government, to crush the *colon* extremists in Algiers, and to restructure France's governmental system. It took him four years to accomplish these tasks, from 1958 to 1962. Ironically, his chief opponents during that period were not leftists but the very forces that had brought him to power.

During the summer of 1958 he appeased the generals and *colons* without surrendering to them. He flattered them with meaningless gestures, such as appointing Jacques Soustelle, an extremist who had persuaded the army to support de Gaulle, to the post of minister of information and allowing Generals Massu and Salan to lead the Bastille Day parade through the streets of Paris. De Gaulle was buying time, so he could write a new constitution and have a new legislature elected that would support him when he turned on the *colons*. The new constitution was presented to the public in a referendum on September 28, 1958, and was endorsed by 80 percent of the voters.

When, two months later, the first legislature of the Fifth Republic was elected, the Gaullist coalition—Union for the New Republic (UNR)—and the traditional conservatives were the big winners. (See Table 21.1.) The PCF and the Socialists were losers. De Gaulle probably would have desired a more balanced Chamber of Deputies so he would have had more room to maneuver. As it stood, he had to persuade a large part of the conservative majority to follow him. An electoral college, chosen by indirect election, made de Gaulle president of France in December by an overwhelming 62,000 votes out of 79,000. He was inaugurated on January 8, 1959, and would hold the office for ten eventful years.

With a secure grip on power, he began to move cautiously to reassert the control of Paris over Algiers. He replaced Salan, dividing the office he had held between a military man, General Challe, and a civilian, Paul Delouvrier, who was clearly de Gaulle's representative. Other *ultras* were withdrawn from Algeria and reassigned to Germany or to bases in France. All of this was done quietly; so no one would realize the extent of the purge that was occurring. Having consolidated his position, de Gaulle shocked his own supporters in September 1959 by offering to allow the Algerians to decide the colony's future. He had spoken the unspeakable; he had broken with the *colons;* and the result was the second Algerian rebellion.

On Sunday morning, January 24, 1960, the European Algerians staged a mass demonstration. When the civilian governor, Delouvrier, sent the police to dismiss the crowd, the police were fired on from nearby buildings. Fourteen policemen were killed and 123 wounded. De Gaulle did not flinch from the course he had chosen. He ordered Delouvrier to use military force and even to withdraw from Algiers if necessary to plan military action against the city. He then made a television and radio broadcast in which he referred to those who had fired on the police as "liars and

Charles de Gaulle was a master at public relations. Through press conferences (as seen here) he used television to win French support for his policies. (Courtesy of UPI)

conspirators" unworthy of France. The French nation was aroused by the broadcast; even the PCF and the labor unions expressed their solidarity with de Gaulle. A week later the insurgents surrendered.

Throughout 1960 de Gaulle prepared the French nation for Algerian independence. In a referendum on his policy in January 1961, 75 percent of the voters endorsed the concept of independence. Yet, the situation in Algeria itself had been deteriorating. Not only had the FLN continued its campaign of terror, but the *colons* had also formed a terroristic group—the Organization of the Secret Army (OAS). The OAS primarily wanted to frighten Algerians so they would not support the FLN, but they also tried to put pressure on the Paris government and to silence any European living in Algeria who might favor Algerian independence. In early 1961 the OAS extended its terrorism to mainland France, where, in order to save France as they knew it, they assassinated several French politicians, especially communists, who had spoken for Algerian independence.

Yet, it was not from the OAS that the greatest threat to de Gaulle's policy came but from the army. On April 21, 1961, the third (and last) Algerian rebellion—known as the Four Generals Revolt—was attempted. Late in the evening, paratroopers of the foreign legion occupied official buildings in Algiers and arrested civilian officials. The next day they called on all officers and men of the French armed services to join them. Again de Gaulle took firm action. He instituted a financial and trade blockade of Algeria and assumed dictatorial powers under Article 16 of the new constitution. He made a radio broadcast appealing to the military person-nel in Algeria and ordered that every means be used to crush the revolt.

He carefully repeated the phrase "every means." All of France with the exception of the extreme Right, rallied to de Gaulle. The bulk of the army remained loyal, and the four generals were forced to go into hiding and leave French territory.

De Gaulle turned the revolt to his advantage by using it as an excuse to open negotiations with the FLN. These negotiations resulted in the Evian Agreements of March 18, 1962, which set the terms for a peaceful French withdrawal from Algeria. Unfortunately, the European Algerians were not willing to accept an Algerian government. Terror was even increased, with senseless street murders—victims selected at random—occurring daily. The OAS could not, however, prevent 900,000 Europeans from leaving Algeria by the end of 1962. The futile, pointless murders had served no purpose. Algeria was independent.

De Gaulle's Republic

The Algerian crisis had been de Gaulle's excuse for returning to power; it was not his reason for returning. His true purpose was to restructure the French political system to provide for stable government and to restore France to the international stature of a Great Power. His success at Evian had finally freed him to deal with these more important, as it must have seemed to him, problems. He was convinced that France could not have a stable government until she had a strong executive. The 1958 constitution had given the president of the republic extensive powers to dismiss cabinets without consulting parliament, to dissolve parliament and call for new elections, and even, as seen above, to assume dictatorial powers. Yet the constitution had provided that the president be elected by an electoral college, which, as a result of the way it was chosen, was composed of older men and overrepresented rural areas. De Gaulle felt that the only way the president could have true national authority and be free of parliamentary political haggling was to be elected by direct election by all of the voters. He proposed such a reform in September 1962 and called for a referendum on the issue.

The traditional parties were all opposed to the idea, and they put the Gaullist cabinet in the minority on this issue. De Gaulle merely dissolved the legislature and announced that legislative elections would follow the referendum. He won both contests. The direct election of the president was endorsed by 62 percent of the voters; his victory was consummated by a smashing Gaullist victory in the legislative election. Interestingly, in the 1962 election de Gaulle openly identified himself with a political grouping, the UNR, for the first time. He had assured his dominance of the republic at least until the presidential election in 1965 (when his seven-year term would end) and probably until the next legislative election in 1967.

TABLE 21.1. French Legislative Elections, 1956–68

	Seats Won				
	1956	1958	1962	1967	1968
Communists and allies	150	10	41	73	34
Extreme Left	. . .	. . .	. . .	4	. . .
Socialists	94	44	66	116†	57†
Radicals and allies	91	33	39		
MRP	83	56	55*	42*	27*
Gaullists	21	212	268	244	358
Conservatives	95	118	(with MRP)	. . .	ا . .
Extreme Right	52	. . .	. . .	. . .	. . .

* MRP and Conservatives joined in the Democratic Center.
† Socialists and Radicals joined in Federation of the Left.
SOURCE: Philip M. Williams, *French Politicians and Elections, 1951–1969* (Cambridge, England: Cambridge University Press, 1970), pp. 292–93.

De Gaulle tended to entrust the management of domestic affairs to premiers in whom he had absolute confidence—first Michel Debré (1959–62) and then Georges Pompidou (1962–68), and finally, Maurice Couve de Murville (1968–69). It appears the president only intervened to set the general direction of policy or to solve certain specific problems. The Gaullist regime, under this bicephalous leadership, enacted some far-reaching legislation that will have lasting effects on French society. Much of this legislation was the continuation of trends begun in the Fourth Republic; other bills were new and innovative. Most of the major domestic reforms reflected de Gaulle's belief that, to become a power in the world again, France would have to shake off her inhibiting traditionalism without losing her cultural heritage, would have to become more industrialized, modernized, and efficient.

Among the laws encouraging this transformation was the Pisani Law of 1961 dealing with agriculture. Edgard Pisani, minister of agriculture, was being pressured both by Common Market competition and by radical organizations of young farmers to find a solution to the extreme parcelization of farmland. A rural revolution had been underway in France since World War II which had begun to solve the problem. A migration to urban centers had reduced the proportion of the active population in the agricultural sector from 35 to 23 percent, and the failure of many marginal farms decreased the number of farms from 2.5 million to 2.2 million.[1] While this relieved much of the economic pressure on the countryside, the remaining farms were still unproductive because of outmoded methods. The governments of the Fourth Republic, however, under the

[1] Gordon Wright, *Rural Revolution in France* (Stanford: Stanford University Press, 1968), pp. 114–15.

pressure from militant farmer pressure groups, had invested heavily in the production of farm machinery and subsidized the purchase of such machinery. By 1960 the number of tractors had increased from 37,000 in 1945 to 625,000, and the number of harvesters had risen from 250 in 1946 to 42,000. The Fifth Republic continued the policy of modernizing French agriculture. A law was passed in 1960 to allow the state to purchase small farms and resell them in consolidated form. The Pisani Law went beyond this. It provided an attractive pension fund to encourage older farmers to retire. This was meant to clear the way for associations of private farmers, created as legal bodies by the Pisani Law, to buy up the retired land, improve it, and resell it in a way to encourage maximum productivity. The Pisani Law, then, recognized that there were a large number of French farmers willing to cooperate to make agriculture more productive and more competitive. It was evidence of a revolution in attitudes.

Another major reorientation of French life had begun in the Fourth Republic—an attempt to decentralize French state and society through regional development.[2] The goal was to limit the growth and influence of Paris—the intellectual, economic and political center that had drained the rest of France of human talent for centuries—by stimulating the economic and cultural development of other cities and regions. The Fourth Republic had designated regions for purposes of administering the plan. The Fifth Republic put teeth into regionalization in 1964, appointing a regional prefect (governor) with power over the economic development of the several departments within his region. Thereby the ninety departments were consolidated into twenty-one regions each with a capitol city. Beyond this creation of larger units, eight cities have been chosen as future metropolitan areas and the state has dedicated its resources to developing them. Another aspect of decentralization has been the construction of multipurpose art centers in provincial cities. These centers house under one roof concert stage, cinema, art gallery, lecture hall, and library. These were the product of the fertile mind of André Malraux, minister of culture.

The Gaullist state also encouraged industry to modernize by making business mergers attractive by tax incentives and by inviting foreign enterprises to come into France on favorable terms when French businessmen seem unwilling to compete. One example was the partial merger of Renault, a nationalized industry, with Peugeot, a privately owned automobile manufacturer. The new company became the world's third largest car maker outside the United States.

De Gaulle was apparently at the crest of his popularity when his term

---

[2] John Ardagh, *The New French Revolution* (New York: Harper & Row, Publishers, 1969), pp. 115–22.

of office neared its end in 1965. Few commentators expected him to encounter difficulty gaining reelection in France's first direct popular election of a president since 1848. Two major challengers appeared, both supported by impressive coalitions; but neither were considered serious opponents at first. Jean Lecanuet, president of the MRP, led a centrist coalition, the Committee of Democrats, which tried to place itself between Gaullist "reaction" on the Right and "revolution" on the Left. The Socialists, Communists, and most Radicals rallied to François Mitterand, candidate of the Federation of the Left. These two men were young—in their forties—whereas de Gaulle was seventy-five. Lecanuet used American public relations techniques of public opinion surveys, well-planned public appearances and personal salesmanship. It was the first time these had been applied to French politics. Mitterand was much more traditional, hopping about France to make small meetings of the faithful. Neither were given a chance by the pollsters until several weeks before the election.

De Gaulle made the mistake of assuming his own election. He refused to speak on the issues until the very end of the campaign. Lecanuet and Mitterand both attacked his nationalist foreign policy and promised to "build Europe" if elected. Both criticized Gaullist indifference to social problems such as the housing shortage. The government's management of television coverage of the campaign also became an issue. Had they been only one candidate instead of two, they might have defeated the great man; as it turned out, they could only embarrass him. De Gaulle had expected to win an easy majority on the first ballot; instead he received only 44 percent of the votes, while Mitterand obtained 32 percent and Lecanuet 16 percent. Three minor candidates split the remainder. A majority of Frenchmen had voted against de Gaulle. But this was not a referendum; it was only the first ballot. On the second ballot, with just the top two candidates running, de Gaulle received 54.5 percent to Mitterand's 45.5 percent.

Perhaps the most significant effect of the election was the creation of the Federation of the Left. Communists had been accepted as a legitimate party by other parties for the first time since 1947. The campaign had been marked by an absence of anticommunist rhetoric. Still, the major difference between Lecanuet and Mitterand was that the former would not cooperate with the PCF while the latter would. The Federation was not a formal alliance, only a marriage of convenience, but its success encouraged the Left to attempt similar tactics in the legislative election of 1967.

The mandate of the 1962 legislature expired in 1967. Algeria was becoming history, and prosperity combined with governmental stability made French public life almost tranquil. Once again de Gaulle stayed out of the fray, allowing Georges Pompidou to act as the leader of the Gaullist coalition called simply "Fifth Republic." The French voters were obviously being presented a choice between the stable government of 1962–67 and a return to the party system of the Fourth Republic. But the opposition did not want to return to the Fourth Republic either, and both Lecanuet and Mitterand had transformed their coalitions into well-organized, disciplined parties. The Federation made a deal with the PCF to cooperate on the second ballot. Once again the Communists were treated as and proved to be good political partners, fully capable of governing France if the Left should gain a majority. Therefore a polarization seemed to be occurring that was producing two major parties—the Gaullist majority and the Federation-Communist coalition. The election returns proved this to be the case. Although the Gaullists received 38.2 percent of the vote (8.5 million votes), the Federation and the PCF together polled 41.3 percent—the Federation had 18.8 percent (4.2 million votes) and the PCF 22.5 percent (5 million votes), Pompidou still controlled a majority, but the opposition was greatly strengthened.

It was with this majority that de Gaulle and Pompidou had to face the student revolt of May 1968, which is described in Chapter 22. De Gaulle finally restored order by a combination of force, concessions, and masterful political maneuvering. One example of the last was the dissolution of the 1967 National Assembly with its large hostile parties and a call for new elections. De Gaulle made these elections a referendum between himself and chaos. The French begged him to stay, at least until the crisis was resolved, by giving the Gaullists a huge 46 percent of the vote. Once again it appeared that the president had a mandate to govern as he saw fit. His first act was to drop Pompidou, whom many commentators credited with the election victory, in favor of the more submissive Maurice Couve de Murville.

Yet, de Gaulle was not satisfied. He wanted to force the French to prove they not only needed him in a crisis but that they thought him indispensable. In April 1969, he forced a referendum on two unrelated issues: the creation of stronger regional authorities and reform of the Senate. De Gaulle considered the Senate the bastion of the old Fourth Republic party system, since its members were long-time politicians who disliked a strong executive. To destroy the Senate's power he tied its reform to the very popular measure of regionalism. This smacked too much of a political trick—an impression which was reinforced by de Gaulle's insistence that the referendum was actually between "me or chaos." The French had had enough; 53 percent voted "no," and the referendum was defeated. It was de Gaulle's first defeat in eleven years and his only one. He resigned into retirement shortly after the election, leaving the French to chaos.

Not surprisingly, there was no chaos. A rather colorless government steered the country until a new president, Georges Pompidou, could be elected. Gaullism was preserved without de Gaulle.

De Gaulle and Europe

De Gaulle was an extremely complex man, and his foreign policy has bedeviled commentators perhaps more than any other aspect of his politics. This has occurred in spite of the fact that de Gaulle, more than any of his contemporary statesmen, was given to philosophical explanations of his actions. Perhaps it is wisest to accept certain basic points as he presented them time and again, rather than to analyze each individual act. Unquestionably he believed that the nation-state as it had developed in western Europe was the last stage of political evolution. All reasonable diplomatic decisions must, of necessity, be guided by national interest—not by political or social ideologies. Therefore, a stable international system can rest on no other foundation than independent states pursuing their own interest. In 1965, when there was debate on the future of European integration, de Gaulle expressed his view clearly and succinctly.

What are the pillars on which [Europe] can be built? In truth, they are the States, States that are, certainly, very different from one another, each having its soul, its history and its language, its glories and its ambitions, but States that are the only entities with the right to give orders and the power to be obeyed. To fancy one can build something effective in action, and acceptable to the peoples, outside or above the States is a chimera.[3]

France, of course, was a very special state. It stood at the height of Western civilization with an unparalleled cultural heritage to share with the world. Therefore, France above all others must be independent to play her role in international affairs. The clearest symbol and most tangible attribute of national independence is a strong military.

With these beliefs de Gaulle was somewhat isolated in a Europe in which international organizations—NATO, the Common Market, the European Coal and Steel Authority, the Warsaw Pact, Comecon—had become a fact of diplomacy. It was because of his strong belief in the nation-state (not to be confused with the narrow nationalism of the French Right) that de Gaulle's accession to power was not welcomed by the "good Europeans" who favored integration. Especially, the Germans were worried that de Gaulle would cripple the recently formed Common Market. These fears proved to be entirely unjustified. The first general tariff reduction provided by the Rome Treaty was to take place in January 1959, but the weakness of the French franc was so extreme that the other five nations were certain de Gaulle would not participate in a reduction that would surely further weaken France's trading position. He surprised everyone by taking the politically unpopular step of devaluing the franc by 17.55 percent. This made foreign goods more expensive in France

---

[3] F. Roy Willis, *France, Germany, and the New Europe 1945–1967*, rev. and exp. ed. (New York: Oxford University Press, 1968), p. 295.

and French goods cheaper abroad; thereby, French trade was made competitive again, and the tariff reduction could be made on schedule. De Gaulle had risked his popularity at home for the sake of European unity, and his image among the EEC countries changed overnight.

De Gaulle also instituted an exchange of visits with Adenauer—the first being an informal meeting at Colombey-les-deux-Eglises, the General's country estate, in September 1958. Adenauer was greatly reassured and even became one of de Gaulle's admirers. He was convinced that de Gaulle was dedicated to the reconciliation of their nations.

The new friendship was quickly put to the test. Great Britain was still trying, in late 1958, to induce the EEC nations to expand their union into a larger free trade area. The Germans thought that some accommodation was possible and desirable; the French argued that a free trade area—especially if extended, as Britain desired, to the Commonwealth—would destroy any chance for coordinated economic policies. The French position won, and the British created the European Free Trade Association (EFTA) in 1959. A more acrimonious debate developed over establishing a common agricultural policy throughout EEC. The Germans had an extensive system of farmer supports, and farm prices in Germany were among the highest in Europe. Of course, these prices had been protected from foreign competition by high tariffs. Moreover, even with these advantages the German farmers could not produce enough to feed their nation. French agriculture, on the other hand, had undergone a technological revolution during the 1950s and was producing a surplus but had no markets. It was natural that the French would want low tariffs on agricultural products, just as the Germans wanted to preserve their protective tariffs. An added political complication was that the CDU, Adenauer's party, depended on rural votes. De Gaulle, however, was determined that the matter be resolved because it was both an irritant to Franco-German relations, and the lack of a policy placed the Six in a weak bargaining position with Great Britain who had decided by 1961 that she wanted to enter EEC after all. Because of the general desire to settle the question, marathon negotiations were conducted among the Six from January 4 to 14, 1962, and agreement was finally reached. Various products were treated individually. The most important provisions concerned cereals. The EEC Commission was to set target prices for each year which were fair to all nations (in the commission's estimation). If prices in any nation fell far below this target, the commission would pay subsidies to the farmers concerned to prevent hardships. Import quotas were to be increased gradually and tariffs were to be decreased until a common market in cereals would be achieved.

The agricultural agreement had been the result of the Common Market's gravest crisis until that time. In all countries it was heralded as proof-positive that Europe, at least the Six, were on the road to full economic unity and all that implied politically. Indeed, there was much reason for celebration over the performance of EEC. Trade among the members had increased greatly since 1958. Franco-German trade, for example, had almost tripled. German industrial production had swelled by 35 percent, while French production was up 23 percent.[4]

Such economic progress inevitable improved Franco-German relations, and de Gaulle and Adenauer were intent on giving concrete diplomatic form to the sentiment. The way was prepared by Adenauer's tour of France in July 1962, and de Gaulle's German tour the following September. Adenauer was welcomed warmly; de Gaulle was embraced with riotous enthusiasm. The French leader spoke slightly accented German throughout his trip and managed to mention a personal sentiment about each city. The Germans shouted their approval. Having won over the two publics, the leaders announced in November that a treaty providing for close consultations between the two states on foreign affairs would be prepared by the respective foreign offices and signed in January 1963 in Paris. Leaders of other European states and political commentators alike judged that de Gaulle was trying to construct a Paris-Bonn axis to dominate western Europe. They need not have feared. Events intervened to drive the two nations apart once again.

Two crises involving the Common Market occurred between 1962 and 1966, and each caused Franco-German friction. The first was a result of Great Britain's decision to seek entry to EEC. There were many factors that led Harold Macmillan, Britain's Conservative prime minister, to announce on July 31, 1961, that he would like to open negotiations with the Six on Britain's entry. The British economy had been in the doldrums for much of the postwar period. The 1950s had seen an apparent recovery, but Britain's deteriorating trade position was weakening the pound dangerously. In fact, a special budget had to be adopted in the fall of 1960 to prevent a run on the pound. One of Britain's problems was that the end of empire had closed certain markets, since the newly independent states hoped to develop their domestic industry. On the noneconomic side, the growing number of Africans and Asians in the Commonwealth tended to make old imperialists unhappy and willing to seek new international partners. Dependence on the United States for military security also embarrassed many Englishmen, who preferred to be equals in Europe rather than being inferiors in the Atlantic alliance. And, of course, the British could not ignore the economic expansion and prosperity on the Continent when compared to their own sluggish economy.[5]

---

[4] Ibid., pp. 281–82.

[5] Nora Beloff, *The General Says No* (Baltimore: Penguin Books Inc., 1963), pp. 88–96.

Macmillan's announcement was greeted with enthusiasm by the Six, and serious negotiations began in Brussels in November. Instead of removing obstacles to Britain's entry, the talks, which lasted fourteen months, seemed to accentuate them. The real struggle was over British agricultural policy. British food prices were kept low by direct government subsidies to farmers and by the importation of products from Commonwealth countries at very low prices. Macmillan and his cabinet were not willing to sacrifice either of these as would be required by their acceptance of EEC agricultural policy and of the Common Market's tariff on goods from nonmembers. Nor were the Six willing to sacrifice the agreement on a common agricultural system which was achieved with such difficulty in the marathon session of January 1962. So as the talks dragged on through 1962, much of the initial enthusiasm for an enlarged EEC began to dissipate. However, some progress was made. By the end of October the general structure of an agricultural compromise was agreed on, with the Six making major concessions on the status of Commonwealth nations. But then it seemed impossible to achieve a concensus on how to make the transition required by Britain's entry. The British wanted the transition to be made gradually over a period of eight years; the Six argued that Britain would have to adopt the common policy immediately upon entry. The talks stagnated.

During the negotiations, the French seemed resigned to eventual British entry, even though they were certain that any concession to British agriculture would be to the detriment of French agriculture. Toward the end of 1962, however, de Gaulle came to feel that the British demands were exorbitant. Events in December convinced him that, not only were the British not sincere about desiring European unity, they were in fact too closely tied to the United States to ever be truly European. De Gaulle was offended by American nuclear policy that seemed intended to keep the continental nations perpetually dependent on American power. He also resented the American willingness to sell military materials to and share military secrets with the English, while denying them to France. This was the diplomatic situation when de Gaulle hosted Macmillan at Rambouillet on December 15, but neither man mentioned military matters, preferring to devote their time to the Brussels negotiations. De Gaulle was greatly surprised, therefore, when Macmillan met a few days later with the American president John Kennedy at Nassau. Kennedy informed Macmillan that the United States would have to renege on the deliverance of the nuclear Skybolt missile to Britain. This was to have been the basis of a British nuclear defense, but the Pentagon had decided that new technology had made the Skybolt obsolete and, therefore, no more should be produced. Instead, Kennedy offered Macmillan the Polaris missile, launched from a submarine, and all the necessary technical information the British would need to construct the submarines and warheads. Almost simultaneously the young president offered France the new missile but refused to supply the technology required to use it.

De Gaulle was angered by the obvious British dependence on the United States and by the American refusal to share secrets which were being given to the British. It became obvious to him that Britain, if allowed to enter the Common Market, would only be a Trojan horse for America (a phrase used by a Gaullist aide, not by the president). Therefore, just before negotiations were to resume in Brussels, de Gaulle called a carefully staged press conference on January 14, 1963, to veto effectively Britain's bid for entry. He made it clear that he thought the negotiations had reached an impasse and should not be continued.

England is insular, maritime, linked by trade, markets and food supply to very different and often very distant lands. . . . In short, the nature, the structure, the very situation that are England's differ profoundly from those of the continentals. . . . The question arises as to how far it is possible for Great Britain at the present time to accept a truly common tariff, as the Continent does, for this would involve giving up all Commonwealth preferences, renouncing all claims for privileges for her agriculture. . . . Can she do this? That is the question.[6]

De Gaulle further argued that Britain had too many special relationships outside EEC for her to become a full member: the Commonwealth, EFTA, and the United States. These entanglements would destroy the independence of Europe.

The cohesion of all these numerous and very different states would not last long, and what would emerge in the end would be a colossal Atlantic Community dependent on America and directed by America, which would not take long to absorb this European Community.[7]

The door to Europe was closed with Britain on the outside. De Gaulle had spoken. Such unilateral action was deplored by the other five EEC nations, but forced to choose, they preferred France to Great Britain.

This defeat for expansion of the Common Market had come at a very inopportune time for Franco-German relations. Adenauer arrived in Paris one week after the fatal press conference to sign the Franco-German treaty of friendship. What should have been the old chancellor's greatest hour was being denounced by all three major German parties and by most newspapers. The Germans had fought hardest to bring England in, only to be frustrated by the will of one man. They seemed to forget that there had been real obstacles to the negotiations. Adenauer was virtually alone in continuing to consider a reconciliation with France impor-

---

[6] Alfred F. Havighurst, *Twentieth-Century Britain,* 2d ed. (New York: Harper & Row, Publishers, 1966), p. 465.

[7] Alexander Werth, *De Gaulle* (New York: Simon and Schuster, Inc., 1965), p. 329.

tant. The treaty, which provided for regular consultation between French and German officials at several levels, including their chief executives, was signed, but relations between the two nations had begun a deterioration that was to last until de Gaulle resigned in 1969. When the treaty was presented to the Bundestag for ratification, the German legislators attached a preamble that stated that the treaty would in no way change prior commitments of Germany to NATO, the Common Market, or her allies including the United States. This defeated the purpose of the treaty as far as de Gaulle was concerned, but it was ratified by the French parliament without the preamble. At least, there would be official talks between the two nations.

Shortly after the treaty was ratified, Adenauer finally resigned. His successor, Ludwig Erhard, was a confirmed Atlanticist, preferring to base German foreign policy on a strong German-American alliance rather than a Franco-German alliance. Erhard also differed with de Gaulle on the nature of the EEC. The German chancellor wanted both a larger market if possible, which meant inclusion of Britain, and more rapid progress toward political unity. It was inevitable that the two men and the two nations would conflict.

The Six were faced, in 1964, with the need to arrive at uniform agricultural prices, especially for cereals, which would make it possible for them to negotiate a general tariff reduction with the United States. The German desire for a high price for cereals and the French hope for a low price put the two at odds. However, after complex and grueling talks several agreements were reached in November and December which provided for a rather low common price for cereals in all EEC countries by July 1, 1967. The transition to the single market price was to begin on July 1, 1965, and to be cushioned by funds paid by the EEC Commission to farmers who suffered from the reduction in price (the Germans).

The commission recommended measures for administering the agricultural single market in March 1965. The measures shocked everyone by their daring. The commission not only proposed the necessary regulations for dispersal of funds but also recommended that the commission be given its own financial resources and that the European Parliament alone be able to govern the use of those resources. Since under the Rome Treaty majority voting was to replace unanimous voting in the Council of Ministers on January 1, 1966, these proposals amounted to a request for absolute autonomy for the EEC. Individual members would no longer be able to veto the actions of the commission, which would have its own sources of revenue as well. Ignoring the questions of increased EEC autonomy, the French insisted that agreement be reached on administering the single market by July 1, 1965, the day the transition to a single market was to begin. When agreement could not be reached—some said because of French obstructionism, the French foreign minister, Maurice

Couve de Murville, broke off negotiations; and France ended all cooperation in EEC bodies. It appeared that the Common Market was about
to collapse.

During the fall, however, de Gaulle made it clear that he would be
willing to return to the market after certain conditions were met. First,
there must be agreement on the financial regulations concerning agriculture. Second, the commission must abandon its pretensions to becoming
"a major financial power" by collecting and regulating tariffs as well as
dispersing support payments. And finally, the provisions concerning majority voting would have to be stricken from the Rome Treaty. The Five
were shocked that de Gaulle would openly repudiate the ultimate ideal
of political unity, and they were not willing to enter negotiations with
him before the outcome of the French presidential election of December
1965. Both of his major opponents—Mitterand and Lecanuet—were devoted "Europeans," but they were defeated. De Gaulle, then, held the
balance. Either the proponents of integration could accept his conditions
or face a rebellious France.

Negotiations held from January 17 to 30, 1966, focused on the problem
of EEC's supernational authority. Compromises were made on both sides.
It was admitted that majority voting could not be forced on the member
states, but the provisions of the Rome Treaty providing for eventual transition to majority voting were not altered. Therefore, France's partners
seemed willing to allow de Gaulle to have his way, if they could preserve
the principle of political unity to be implemented, perhaps, after he had
left the scene. Agreements on agricultural financing and pricing as well
as measures intended to establish a single market in industrial goods followed. By mid 1966 the Common Market was functioning again. Economic integration could continue; but political integration had suffered
a blow which might still prove to have been fatal.

Having found Franco-German cooperation impossible, de Gaulle increasingly turned his interests, after Adenauer's resignation, to global
diplomacy. His wooing of eastern Europe and Russia became another
sort of friction between France and her West European neighbors, but
that belongs to the following discussion of the cold war. De Gaulle had
achieved some of his goals in Europe. He had prevented the dilution
of the Common Market by the entry of Great Britain and had prevented
the EEC Commission from usurping France's sovereignty. Whether or
not these successes would ultimately effect the processes of European
integration could not be ascertained when de Gaulle resigned in 1969.

De Gaulle in the Cold War

De Gaulle's European policy was dominated by his concept of a
"Europe of States," a grouping of fully independent nation-states that

cooperated for their common good. His broader policy in the world-wide competition between the United States and Russia was the preservation of a "European Europe" and the creation of a "Europe from the Atlantic to the Urals." By calling for a European Europe de Gaulle was appealing to his continental neighbors to assert their independence from the super-powers and to follow policies dictated only by their nation's interests. Only after the European states—both East and West—had achieved such independence could true European unity and peace be achieved. The Europe from the Atlantic to the Urals, however, would not be politically united; rather the various independent states would be tied together by economic and cultural ties. De Gaulle did not always pursue policies that were compatible with this master plan. Usually he would emphasize one of his Europes to the detriment of the other two.

When he returned to power in 1958, he was faced with an international scene that was being fundamentally changed by several concurrent developments. In October 1957, Russia seemed to take the international military and technological lead from the Americans by launching *Sputnik,* the world's first man-made satellite. The entire diplomatic world was astounded; no one more than the Americans, for this meant that Russia possessed rockets capable of carrying nuclear warheads to the North American continent in a matter of minutes. Although the Russian lead later turned out to be far less than at first assumed, the American panic was so great that the United States' allies soon found missile launching pads being installed within their territory. Great Britain, Italy, and Turkey particularly received large numbers of intermediate-range ballistic missiles (IRBMs) capable of striking at Russia. By 1963 these missiles were already obsolete because of the greater power and precision of intercontinental ballistic missiles (ICBMs) that could be launched from underground concrete silos in North America or from submarines. It was an amazing revolution in weaponry that seemed to make traditional military forces only subsidiary factors in international politics. The new missiles were actually too horrible to use, except as a last resort; but few realized this from the launching of *Sputnik* until the Cuban Missile Crisis of October 1962.

A second major new factor in the cold war was the Sino-Soviet split and the freedom this allowed the eastern European regimes. The mainland Chinese were obviously not content to play second fiddle to the Russians, and the split between the two states had reached a potentially explosive point by 1960. This dispute among the communist giants allowed the Russian satellites to play one great power against another and to gain room to maneuver diplomatically. This was indicated most clearly perhaps by increased trade between eastern and western Europe.

Increasingly, non-European events were replacing European problems as the chief concern of the superpowers. The United States had become involved in Southeast Asia even before the French had withdrawn. In 1960 a revolution in Cuba led to the first communist regime in the western hemisphere. Khrushchev had greatly increased Russian aid to newly emergent Asian and African countries such as India, Indonesia, and the Arab states of the Middle East, where the Arab-Israeli conflict seemed to be a magnet for cold war competition between East and West.

Finally, western Europe was no longer dependent on American economic aid, although most Europeans welcomed the security of the Atlantic Alliance that seemed to commit the United States to protect western Europe from a Russian invasion. Prosperity had gone so far that the deutsch mark became, in the early 1960s, a stronger currency than the dollar. Most west European states could raise and support a modern army, but all except Great Britain still lacked the technology to produce nuclear weapons. Many Europeans were beginning to resent their former dependence on the United States and especially the Americanization of their culture. Coca-Cola had been a European commonplace for some time, but the invasion of IBM computers, Libby canned foods, and American business investors was a new and, to some Europeans, frightening development.

Throughout his years in office, de Gaulle fought guerilla warfare against American domination. He began his battle by proposing, shortly after returning to power, that the Atlantic Alliance be restructured so that major decisions would be made by a directorate of three—the United States, Great Britain, and France. He made this proposal because he was certain that the United States had been extending special favors to Great Britain that were denied to the other NATO nations. He also resented the American refusal to share the control over NATO's nuclear arms. Although NATO had a joint command, only the Americans could approve the use of nuclear weapons. President Dwight Eisenhower replied that de Gaulle should not risk weakening the western alliance by unnecessary demands. Therefore, when the United States was encircling Russia with rockets during 1959–60, de Gaulle refused to allow any on French soil.

The apparent need for the continuance of the Atlantic Alliance was demonstrated during the Berlin Crisis of 1958 and 1961. The Russians were still basking in the glow of the Sputnik successes when, in November 1958, Khrushchev demanded the Western occupying powers withdraw their troops from Berlin and negotiate terms of access to Berlin with the East German regime. If these demands were not met within six months, he warned, Russia would unilaterally turn over the access routes to East Germany. When the United States threatened military force, Khrushchev removed his time limit and agreed to negotiate. Eisenhower invited him to the United States for an unprecedented tour. The visit during the early fall of 1959 was a public relations success, with the Russian premier at his most jovial while visiting farms in the Midwest and California. The trip was capped by an inconclusive meeting of the two heads of state at Camp David, Maryland, where they agreed to hold a summit conference in Geneva the following spring.

The summit conference never met. Pressures were mounting that led Khrushchev to reject his policy of detente over Berlin. Not only was he receiving criticism from the Chinese, who desired a confrontation while Russia had a lead in rocketry, but also from the more bellicose sections of Russia's leadership, which had a vested interest in international tension since it necessitated military spending. Finally, it was a presidential election year in the United States, and Eisenhower would only be in office for a few more months. The Russian leader was given the excuse he needed for refusing to meet with Eisenhower when the Russians shot down an American U-2 spy plane. The Americans at first tried to deny the existence of such spying missions until the Russians publicly displayed the pilot of the craft, who had parachuted to safety, and film taken from the plane. Eisenhower then accepted full responsibility for the mission and stated that there would be no more. But Khrushchev had a perfect issue, and he refused to enter into negotiations on Berlin.

Eisenhower was replaced in January 1961 by the charismatic young John F. Kennedy, who was no less a cold warrior than John Foster Dulles but who was infinitely more polished and sophisticated. He met with Khrushchev in Vienna in June 1961 to discuss Berlin, Southeast Asia, and a number of other subjects. Both men were determined to be firm; so, even though an important agreement on the neutralization of Laos was reached, the Berlin question was further from settlement than when the conference began. Khrushchev reinstituted his six-month deadline. Kennedy activated the American army reserve. On August 13 the Berlin Wall was built by the Soviets—a brick, mortar, and barbed wire monument to the cold war.

Throughout all of the various phases of the Berlin Crisis, de Gaulle had been a staunch supporter of the Americans. He did not believe that the German question could be solved by force by either side; he was later to offer his solution.

Another Soviet-American confrontation—the Cuban Missile Crisis—occurred in late 1962. Fidel Castro's rebels had gained power on January 1, 1959, by ousting Fulgencio Batista's conservative dictatorship. Castro looked for foreign aid wherever he could find it. Rebuffed by the Americans, whose property he was nationalizing, he signed a trade agreement with Russia in February 1960. An American sponsored invasion of the island at the Bay of Pigs in April failed miserably. The Russians bragged about the end of the Monroe Doctrine and began secretly to place missiles on Cuba. Kennedy made a dramatic television appearance on October 22, 1962, to announce the discovery of Russian missile launching pads under construction and the imposition of an American blockade of Cuba to prevent the arrival of more material from Russia. After several tense days, while the world watched Russian ships approach the American blockade, Khrushchev agreed to withdraw the missiles. Both nations and the rest of the world as well had realized that they had been living on the brink of nuclear warfare. Both the Americans and the Russians have tried to prevent such a situation from recurring.

Kennedy had taken his action in the missile crisis without consulting America's NATO allies. No clearer example could have been given of de Gaulle's contention that the Atlantic Alliance was no alliance at all, but rather that the west European states were actually at the mercy of American policy. It was this belief that led to the French development of an independent nuclear force and to France's withdrawal from NATO. De Gaulle's *force de frappe* was never intended to be as powerful as that of the superpowers. The Frenchman reasoned that overwhelming nuclear power could not be used as long as there existed the possibility that a nuclear retaliation, no matter how small, might ensue. Therefore, France could be independent from the United States as long as the *force de frappe* was capable of destroying only New York or Moscow. In September 1960 France exploded a nuclear device more powerful than the bomb dropped on Hiroshima. In 1963 the French refused to sign a nuclear test ban treaty agreed on by the superpowers, charging that it was an attempt to keep the weaker states in an inferior position. Finally, a French hydrogen bomb was detonated in 1966. But by then most states had realized that such weapons were for display, not for use.

Perhaps Kennedy's Grand Design and the Multilateral Force (MLF) pushed on Europe by his successor Lyndon Johnson were instrumental in de Gaulle's withdrawal from NATO; but then again, perhaps it was the inevitable logic of de Gaulle's abhorrence of American dominance. The Grand Design that Kennedy proposed was an Atlantic Alliance built on two pillars—the United States and a united Europe. JFK insisted that only when Europe was united politically could the Europeans share in America's nuclear technology. Individual European states—France, Germany, Italy—were not to be trusted. De Gaulle considered this not only insulting but further proof that the United States would never consider the Europeans their equals. His answer to Kennedy was his veto of British entrance to EEC and his attempts to create a second center of power in the West through a Franco-German alliance. The MLF also originated with Kennedy's administration, but it became a special mission with LBJ, who became president when Kennedy was assassinated in November 1963. The MLF was to be a fleet of nuclear submarines assigned to NATO that would be financed, manned, and commanded jointly by all NATO members—that is, it would be a fully integrated military force with no national components. It was an attempt to give the Germans a hand in nuclear decisions and strategy without directly arming them. De Gaulle noted that the MLF would be ultimately dependent on the United States, the only nation that could supply the submarines and the scientific data necessary. This time he received support from the British. The Labour government, elected in October 1964, also rejected the idea. Johnson, becoming preoccupied with Vietnam, accepted this defeat and dropped the idea.

But de Gaulle's disengagement from the Atlantic Alliance could not be halted. His first moves had been to end French participation in NATO naval exercises, because French ships were being ordered to maneuver without prior permission from the French government. In September 1965, he announced that France would not renew its membership in NATO when the original treaty expired in 1969. But he soon decided he could not wait four years. Faced with the unpleasant fact that the further he moved France away from the United States, the closer the Germans moved toward the Americans, de Gaulle concluded that a final break was needed. In March 1966, he sent notes to Johnson and the other NATO heads of state informing them that

France intends to once again exercise complete sovereignty over her own territory, at present infringed upon by the permanent presence of allied military forces and by the use which is being made of her air-space, to end her participation in the integrated command, and to no longer place her forces at the disposition of NATO.[8]

It was an historic statement, signaling the first break in the Western alliance system established in 1949–50. Yet, the break was not complete; for while de Gaulle objected to the *present form* of the Atlantic Alliance—that is, the stationing of American troops on French soil and an integrated command—he specifically vowed his continued support of that alliance as the defender of the "Free World." On July 1, 1966, he further announced that French troops would cease to be under NATO command and that American troops must evacuate France by April 1, 1967. Both timetables were met.

Reactions from de Gaulle's allies varied. He had clearly violated several treaties, and the Americans complained bitterly. The Germans merely negotiated bilateral treaties whereby French troops remained in Germany just as they had under NATO. The fact that de Gaulle could take such action and make it stick is the best evidence to support his argument that the nation-state is still the primary actor in international politics.

While de Gaulle was asserting France's freedom from NATO, he was also attempting to find new roles for France to play. He portrayed France as the architect of a Europe reunified from the Atlantic to the Urals

---

[8] Guy de Carmoy, *Les Politiques étrangères de la France, 1944–1966* (Paris: Editions de la Table Ronde, 1967), p. 373.

Tours of other countries were one of de Gaulle's most effective diplomatic tools. Here he visits Poland. (Courtesy of UPI)

and as the European ally of the undeveloped nations of Asia, Africa, and Latin America. Once again, his twin diplomatic offensives may have been the result of the failure of his German policy, or they may have been inherent in his concept of French grandeur and mission. His approaches to the Third World were publicly symbolized by dramatic and elaborate tours of the nations he was seeking to influence. The manner in which he had disengaged France from Algeria had given him much prestige in Africa and elsewhere, and French aid to her former colonies was extremely generous. In 1964 de Gaulle made a tour of the capitols of the ten South American states, explicitly promising them trade and implicitly promising to end the American economic dominance over them. He curried favor in the Arab world by denouncing Israel in 1967 and was applauded in Asia when he condemned American intervention in Vietnam and referred to the North Vietnamese as true nationalists. French diplomatic recognition of Red China on January 27, 1964, was the first such action by a NATO state. De Gaulle frequently contrasted his policy toward Algeria and other Third World revolutionary governments to that of the United States. He was obviously putting France forward as an alternative to both Washington and Moscow, a wealthy neutralist friend for the newly emerging states. And he had great success in doing so.

De Gaulle was a peculiarly pleasant phenomenon for the eastern European regimes. He was asserting European independence and refused to be anticommunist. He was rewarded in 1964 when the Soviet Union and several satellite states, especially Rumania, signed trade and cultural exchange agreements with France. His intention to go further down this path was made clear in a press conference of February 4, 1965. De Gaulle made several proposals which were in conflict with American policy, such as suggesting that mainland China replace Taiwan on the United Nations Security Council. He also specifically indicated that the United States could not play a role in the resolution of the German problem; rather he stated that this was a European problem to be settled among Germany's neighbors—that is, France and Russia. The Germans were scandalized and announced again that de Gaulle had violated the Franco-German treaty of 1963. But de Gaulle could not be detered from his new course. In April 1965, Andrei Gromyko, the Soviet foreign minister, visited Paris, where he and de Gaulle denounced the American involvement in Southeast Asia, spoke glowingly of Franco-Soviet friendship, and expressed differing but not conflicting opinions on the German question. It was assumed that these were only preliminary talks, and indeed, Gromyko's visit was completely eclipsed by de Gaulle's state tour of the Soviet Union in June 1966. The French president seemed more a visiting monarch than leader of a capitalist state as his airplane leaped from city to city where large and usually enthusiastic crowds greeted him. But de Gaulle remained de Gaulle. While in Russia, he said many things about traditional Franco-

Russian relations, which seemed a reference to alliances against Germany; but he also scolded the Russians by calling East Germany an "artificial Russian invention."[9]

By 1966 de Gaulle had achieved the national independence he desired for France. However, he had also achieved a splendid isolation. He had, in turn, alienated the United States, Great Britain, and Germany. He could hope for only friendship and consultation with Russia. Therefore, the themes of his speeches seemed to turn more and more to the greatness of France, to the French mission of leading the Third World, and to the French policy of sanity toward communism and revolution as compared to the insanity of American military interventions in Vietnam and the Dominican Republic. Oddly, his nationalism made him the spokesman for Europeans and Third World leaders who wished to escape from the cold war polarization into a less ideological diplomatic arena. De Gaulle was at the height of his prestige.

The last year of his presidency was unfortunate for his reputation. His increasingly critical comments about the Israeli state were not approved by the majority of Frenchmen. An attempt to increase French influence in Canada by encouraging Quebec separatists was considered petty even by his admirers. The booming French economy, which had made possible his international independence, began to falter in 1967 and the strikes that accompanied the student revolt of 1968 placed France in a truly critical financial situation. France remained independent, but she could not, in 1969 when de Gaulle retired, afford the grandeur that was the essence of Gaullist policy.

De Gaulle's achievements, as his failures, had been many. His insistence on a common agricultural policy and his defense of EEC against the British desire to change the nature of the Common Market had resulted in a stronger, more integrated Six. His systematic refusal to bow to American policy demands made it possible for other European states to gain their independence. After 1966, Germany under Chancellor Kiesinger began independent explorations of the possibility of improved West German relations with Poland, Czechoslovakia, and other East European states. Italian companies began to build factories in Russia. Italy, Canada, and others followed the French example and opened diplomatic relations with mainland China. In eastern Europe, Rumanian leaders were encouraged by French receptiveness and used it as a lever to gain more concessions from Russia. De Gaulle's overfertile genius had pointed out many new diplomatic paths, some of them dead ends, which made it easier for other diplomats to conduct their own experiments.

---

[9] Alexander Werth, *De Gaulle,* 2d ed. (Baltimore: Penguin Books, Inc., 1967), p. 407.

Chapter 22

1968

Political leaders, technocrats, businessmen, and trade union officials in both western and eastern Europe were quite pleased with the "new Europe" they had created in the two decades following World War II. On both sides of the ideological divide, living standards were constantly improving; economic expansion was constant; and governmental stability appeared to be assured. But they had not spoken with their children. The young felt themselves oppressed by the same prosperous stability—be it communist or capitalist—that the old so applauded. The new society had created its own critics and even its enemies. Sometimes these young critics could find adult allies—as in Czechoslovakia where Alexander Dubcek tried to create a humanitarian communism. More often they were isolated in their opposition to "the Establishment" and turned their universities into fortresses from which they did battle with all forces of authority—as in France, Italy, Yugoslavia, Germany, Spain. Whether because of force of example of because of accumulated frustrations, youthful rebels in virtually every European state engaged in violent protest on a massive scale in the same year, 1968.

This chapter is an attempt to describe and analyze the twin revolutions of that year—the western European student revolt and the Czechoslovak revolt against Russia. Obviously, the two revolts were more dissimilar than they were similar, but there was a significance to their simultaneity that should not be ignored. New social conditions had been created by the affluent society in the West and by the industrialization and democratization of the East which would inevitably cause stresses and strains to political systems created to meet the problems of the 1940s or 1950s. Students rebelling against de Gaulle and Czechoslovaks rebelling against Moscow were demanding that political and social institutions be responsive to change. Both students and Czechoslovaks were challenging authorities which no longer seemed to have legitimacy.

A Cultural Lag in Education

West European universities differed from nation to nation, but they shared one characteristic which was at the root of many difficulties. The expansion of higher education in all countries had been phenomenal since 1950. The university student population had tripled or quadrupled everywhere. Although the proportion of young people enrolled in colleges or universities still fell far short of the proportion receiving higher education in the United States, the student body clearly extended beyond the narrow confines of the upper classes that had dominated university life for so long. Also, the students realized they were no longer being trained to be the elite of the nation in government service, the diplomatic corps, or the clergy; instead they were being trained to be industrial engineers, research chemists, middle-level business executives, insurance salesmen, low-ranking technocrats. They were being trained for functions demanded by modern industry.

TABLE 22.1. Proportion of Age Group 20–24 Enrolled in Higher Education, %

Country	1950	1965
Italy	3.7	7.7
Norway	3.3	7.8
Great Britain	4.0	8.5
Denmark	4.5	8.9
West Germany	3.4	8.9
Sweden	3.7	11.1
Finland	4.2	11.4
Belgium	3.7	14.1
France	4.1	14.1
Netherlands	7.4	14.3
United States	22.0	45.0

SOURCE: Anthony Sampson, *Anatomy of Europe* (New York: Harper and Row, Publishers, 1968), p. 402.

The educational explosion created as many problems as it offered opportunities. The old universities of Paris, Cologne, and Bologna could not be rebuilt to handle the increased number of students. At the Sorbonne, lecture halls were impossibly small. Not infrequently 300 students were enrolled for a course in which the classroon could hold only one hundred. To overcome this, copies of a professor's lectures were sold in university book stores, with the professor getting a royalty from sales; but the cheaply reproduced copies often were still too expensive for one student, so several students would have to study from the same one. All types of research facilities were in short supply. Libraries and laboratories were just as inadequate as classrooms. The curriculum also resisted change, because professors were not willing to rewrite outdated lectures or offer new courses relevant to the students' professional or personal needs.

Problems were perpetuated by the structure of universities. Each national educational system was rigid and inflexible, though in different ways. In France and Italy the state controlled higher education. The French system was overcentralized. Any curriculum change anywhere in France had to be approved by the University of Paris and the minister of education. In Italy, the professoriat was riddled with corruption. A leading politician could have a friend appointed to an academic chair with no requirement that he ever teach a course. German professors were active academics but were also dictators within their disciplines, accountable to no one, holding their chairs for life. The results in all three countries was the same—absolute resistance to change. New courses could not be introduced; young academics were prevented from teaching and could not hope for advancement unless they yielded to the biases of the full professors; and the older men even prevented the expansion of teaching staffs to keep pace with greater enrollments. The ratio of students to professors was, by American standards, too high to permit effective teaching even if the necessary facilities had existed. Where the ratio of students to professors in all American universities in 1967 was 13:1, the French ratio was 23:1, and the Italian was 105:1.

The social bias of the west European educational system was a chief target of student activists and was not caused by expansion but was inherent in the structure of education. Although elementary school education is universal in western Europe, a battery of examinations at ages 11, 15, and 18 (varying slightly from country to country) effectively bar children from working-class families from obtaining a university education. The literary nature of the exams favor children from upper-class and upper-middle class homes who have been exposed to cultural activities. Attempts have been made to escape from this bias, but it persists nevertheless. Also the curriculum at all levels has tended to emphasize traditional subject matter—philosophy, classical literature, composition—rather than practical subjects that would prepare all students for general employment or would train university graduates for careers in a modern economic setting.

The Student Revolt

There were national student organizations, usually calling themselves unions, in every west European state from the early twentieth century. The dictatorships and World War II had caused interruptions of continuity,

FIGURE 22.1.   The Educational Division of Frenchmen

Percentage of Age Group

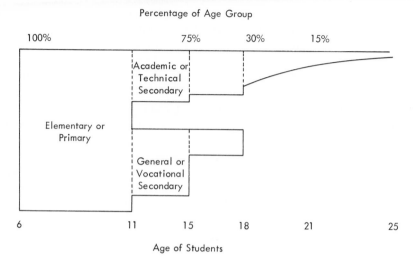

Age of Students

but in general, these organizations saw their role, on the local level, as one of improving students' living conditions, and on the national level, as a lobby for favorable legislation—especially legislation to lessen the cost of education. In short, student groups before the mid 1960s were devoted to improving the system that existed. During the 1960s groups appeared that wanted to restructure not only education institutions but all of society, using the universities as their base. These were the groups that led the massive disruptions of 1968.

The new militancy appeared first in Italy. In 1963 students at the Faculty of Architecture of the University of Milan occupied the Faculty's building demanding a reform of the curriculum to make it more relevant to the problems of society. The fact that architecture students were involved in the occupation is significant. At the time Italy had only one Faculty of Sociology in the nation at a new Catholic university at Trento. Elsewhere, the architecture curriculum dealt with social problems, urban planning, and other issues that might fall under sociology. The demands of the protesting students escalated rapidly and were transformed under the pressure of events. Having occupied the Faculty and facing the hostility of professors, administration, and police, the students began not only to question their curriculum but to question the very structure of the university itself, its role in society, and the function of the profession for which they were being trained. This same dynamic was to be repeated innumerable times throughout western Europe and the United States in the following years. The Milan confrontation ended when the Faculty agreed to make some of the reforms the students demanded, including student representation on administrative committees.

The next major incident was at the University of Trento, a Catholic school opened in 1962, and was led by students of Italy's only Faculty of Sociology. The occasion for the student action was the Chamber of Deputies' consideration of a bill giving full recognition to degrees granted at Trento. The students demonstrated their support for the bill by occupying the university buildings for eighteen days. The evolution of thinking that had occurred at Milan was repeated. Discussions of curriculum reforms broadened into matters of university governance and the relationship of the university to society. Trento's students made two major intellectual contributions to the student movement. One was the demand for *cogestione* (comanagement) or participation in decision-making on all levels. This idea was to become a central theme of the French student revolt. The second contribution was a theoretical conception of the university in modern society:

The university is one of the productive institutions of this social system, which is a mercantile system (i.e., a system of dealing in commodities). As such it produces *man* as a commodity, that is, as skilled [graduate] or semi-skilled [non-graduate] members of the labor force. The goal of this productive institution—the university—is to supply the labor market with such a commodity. There it will be sold and thereafter consumed in the cycle of social reproduction.[1]

This idea of the university as a producer of skilled workers for capitalist economies was widely accepted by student activists.

That Milan and Trento were not just isolated incidents became clear when the 1967–68 academic year began. Disruptions occurred on virtually every campus in Italy. After the Christmas holidays the confrontations between students and administrators led to permanent student occupations of university buildings. One impetus to action may have been the legislative election in May 1968, as the disruptions declined afterwards. By then, however, all universities were closed. The most militant students came from the architecture faculties (and once again sociology at Trento), with their most ardent supporters being students in philosophy and letters, political science, and physics. Law, engineering, and medicine were far less active, and the law faculties were the source of the strongest opposition to the occupations.

Structurally, the organization, goals, and allies of the students were very similar to those of students in other countries. Decisions were made by general assemblies, not by elected representatives. This displayed the absolute distrust of authority (even their own) that marked the student revolt. The goal was to prevent the appearance of "student leaders" who might establish a bureaucracy. "Countercourses" were organized in which

---

[1] Guido Martinotti, "The Positive Marginality: Notes on Italian Students in Periods of Political Mobilization," eds. Seymour Martin Lipset and Philip G. Altbach, *Students in Revolt* (Boston: Houghton, Miflin Co., 1969), p. 191.

students taught themselves or were led by sympathetic faculty in discussions of Vietnam (a burning issue with all European student leaders), homosexuality, neocolonialism, and other topics banned from the regular curriculum. The goals espoused by the students were either very specific and limited (introduction of new courses) or very abstract (how to organize a *permanent* resistance to authority or how to redefine the student's role in society). The students did not greatly stress their need for allies outside the academic community but they did make overtures to trade unions and leftist parties. The PCI was cautiously sympathetic without becoming involved with the students. Their only real ally was the Socialist Party of Proletarian Unity (PSIUP), which represented the extreme left of Italian socialism and had broken from the PSU in protest against its reformism. Interestingly, the only French party to sympathize with student rebels occupied a similar place on the political spectrum—to the left of the Federation of the Left but still noncommunist. It could be that both the students and the PSIUP were protesting against Moro's center-left coalition which seemed to them to have become a part of "the Establishment."

German student radicalism was most definitely a rebellion against similar developments in Germany. When the Grand Coalition was formed in December 1966, there was no effective parliamentary opposition in Germany, and many leftist students felt betrayed by the SPD. The best organized student group was the Student Socialist Federation (SDS). During a visit of the shah of Iran to West Berlin in the summer of 1967, the SDS organized mass protests against the shah's authoritarian regime, the German foreign policy that supported him, and the extension of that foreign policy to support for the United States in Vietnam. The demonstrations became violent and spread to other university towns in West Germany.

On Easter Sunday 1968, the leader of the SDS, Rudi Dutschke, was leaving SDS headquarters on his bicycle when he was shot three times. Dutschke survived after weeks in the hospital, but the shooting set off massive demonstrations. These were directed primarily at the offices of the publishing tycoon Axel Springer, who owned more than half of all newspapers and magazines in West Germany. His papers had continually vilified Dutschke and the SDS, and the students blamed him for the hatred that had led to the shooting. Throughout West Germany students violently and successfully prevented the distribution of Springer's publications. Bombings, sit-ins, theft of newspapers, blockage of streets were all tactics which were used. Police had to erect barbed wire barriers around Springer's offices and printing plants. Springer was not, however, the only focus of student action. For several years they had been trying to democratize German universities by weakening the powers of the dictatorial full professors. Even though the Bundestag had passed several bills to achieve such a reform, each bill could only go into effect when accepted by the professors; so no change was implemented. The student rioters had some success in obtaining student representation on faculty committees, but it was not a significant blow to the citadel of professorial privilege. The weakness of the students was largely due to the lack of support from any party or trade union. They found themselves isolated before a hostile public and political system.

The French students' success in achieving reforms owed much to the fact that they were able to gain considerable support outside of the academic community. The French uprising, by far the largest and most violent student rebellion, began at Nanterre, a new university complex on the western edge of Paris. As if wishing to create young revolutionaries, the French government had built this sterile glass and steel campus, devoted to the social sciences, in the midst of a slum where Arab, Spanish, and Italian immigrants lived in squalor. The contrast was too great for the students to ignore, and many became involved in leftist politics under the influence of the setting. But the demonstrations which led to confrontations were primarily on academic or university matters. Demonstrations in 1967 protested in loco parentis rules barring men from visiting women's dorms. The 1967–68 academic year began with protests over curriculum and free speech on campus. On March 22, 1968, a total of 142 students, led by red-headed Daniel Cohn-Bendit, occupied Nanterre's administration building. They were ousted, but they became the nucleus of the March 22 movement from which all subsequent events grew. They continued to disrupt classes to hold political discussions and demonstrations until May 2, when the dean of Nanterre closed the university. On May 3 the members of the March 22 movement went to the Sorbonne in Paris to meet with the leaders of other student groups, especially with the officers of the National Union of French Students.

It was from this meeting that the mass movement sprang. While Cohn-Bendit and other student leaders conferred in the courtyard of the Sorbonne, the rector of the University of Paris, Jean Roche, called on the police to clear the courtyard, supposedly to prevent a conflict between leftist and rightist students. It was the first time police had entered the academic sanctuary since 1791. Approximately 600 students were herded into police vans, while thousands of other students watched in shock and anger. That Friday evening thousands of students battled police for control of the streets of the Latin Quarter for six hours, shouting "Free our comrades!" The following Monday 20,000 students and young faculty members demonstrated against the police action. Once again the police tried to disband the crowd by force. Several hundred demonstrators and 345 policemen were injured.

For a brief moment in May 1968 French students felt the exhilaration of being part of France's revolutionary tradition. (Courtesy of UPI)

The May Revolution was clearly underway. Both Pompidou, the premier, and de Gaulle were out of Paris, not desiring to rush back as if in a panic. In their absence, Roche, along with the minister of the interior and the minister of education, did not attempt to meet student demands but tried to crush the revolt with force. This only escalated the crisis. Barricades blocked streets in the Latin Quarter; cars and buses were burned; trees were chopped down and laid across the streets to prevent the dreaded charges by helmeted and baton-swinging police. The brutality of the police after arrests were made was generally condemned by the press as were the provocative acts of the students. These tactics by the government had to be abandoned after May 12; on that day workers in a Sud-Aviation airplane factory staged a sit-down strike, holding their manager prisoner in his own office. Students marched to the factory to announce their solidarity, although the workers were not overly enthusiastic about an alliance. The first strike had been called against the wishes of the union leadership. Other spontaneous strikes began to occur throughout France. Huge student-worker solidarity marches were held, but union officials—especially the leaders of the communist union the General Confederation of Labor, the largest union in France—took special pains to keep the workers and students separated, for fear that the revolutionary virus might infect too many rank-and-file union members. The unions concentrated on concrete goals, such as shorter working hours and a general wage increase for all workers. When the cabinet negotiated such an increase on May 27, however, the workers rejected it with cries of "A popular government! Down with de Gaulle!"

The French president had been on a state visit to Rumania when the turmoil began. On his return to Paris, he tried to give an appearance of calm. Yet, when he left Paris for his country home on May 29, speculation was rife that he was writing a resignation speech. Francois Mitterand, head of the Federation of the Left, announced he would stand as a presidential candidate and asked Pierre Mendès-France, the only politician of note who unequivocally backed the students, to be his premier. It was all wishful thinking. De Gaulle secretly flew to Germany to assure himself the support of the army. Evidently he made a deal with General Massu, once as OAS leader, that he would pardon the military men and civilians who had led the Algerian revolt in return for the army's support in the present crisis. Returning to Paris, de Gaulle addressed the nation on live television on the evening of May 30. He announced that army maneuvers were taking place on the outskirts of Paris and that law and order would be restored. He also called new parliamentary elections for June and said that a choice must be made between Gaullism and "totalitarian communism." It was a purely demagogic device, since the PCF had refused to aid the students and had even denounced them as adventurist. Many Frenchmen were quite willing to believe that de Gaulle's analysis was correct, and one million well-dressed Parisians and Gaullists from the provinces (the latter brought to Paris for the occasion) marched down the Champs-Élysées in support of their president. De Gaulle launched the electoral campaign by banning eleven leftist student groups, arresting their leaders, or driving them into exile—as was the case with Daniel Cohn-Bendit. At the end of June the French electorate endorsed these firm measures by increasing the Gaullist representation in the chamber from 200 to 299 while the number of deputies of the Federation and the PCF fell from 194 to 100.

The election and the repression did not signify the complete defeat of the students. They had gained too many sympathizers to be ignored. The main goal of the students had been a restructuring of the university system to allow *cogestion,* (the French version of the Italian word), *contestation,* flexibility, and autonomy for each campus. *Cogestion* or "participation in decision-making" was intended to give students control over their living conditions and academic environment. It would entail a fundamental change in the authoritarian and hierarchical administration of the universities. *Contestation* referred to the right of controversy—over political matters on the university grounds and over academic matters in the classroom. The students wanted to end the system of pontifical lectures by gaining the right to question their professors in class and to debate among themselves. Flexibility and autonomy were inseparable. Since the entire French education system was controlled from the Ministry of Education, innovations were stifled. The students and many professors wanted each faculty and each university to have the freedom to introduce new courses, change requirements, and modify procedures without reference to Paris.

Of these demands, the one that fired the imagination of nonacademic individuals and won the most public support was *cogestion.* Throughout France a sort of generation gap appeared in respect to the question of authority structures. Young workers rebelled against their union leaders and demanded a voice in the management of factories. Young doctors occupied the offices of the National Medical Association and held it for several hours. Architects and lawyers rebelled against the national officers of their professional organizations. Even the dancers of the Folies Bergeres demanded that they be represented in decisions concerning their hours, wages, and working conditions. Frenchmen in all walks of life were demanding control over the places where they worked or studied. And they did this spontaneously, spurred by the imagination of students who had challenged traditions first.

De Gaulle was aware that, though he may repress the students, ideas that had inspired millions of Frenchmen must be reflected in legislation. To free his hands to follow new policies, he removed Pompidou and appointed Maurice Couve de Murville premier. Couve's first speech to the National Assembly promised both educational reforms and "participation," the Gaullist form of *cogestion.* The new minister of education Edgar Faure presented the details of the former in the fall. His proposals provided for the autonomy of France's provincial universities; established student-faculty councils at each campus to advise the administration; allowed more freedom for interdepartmental courses; provided for the training of more faculty; and created eight new university centers in the Paris region. Faure did not grant student demands for influence over financing, personnel, curriculum, the content of national exams, or the requirements necessary to acquire various degrees. Moderates and conservatives of de Gaulle's own party thought he had gone too far, but the reforms passed.

Couve's commitment to "participation" was a reflection of de Gaulle's desire to find a solution to industrial strife. The President had never considered class conflict inevitable and thought employers and employees would both profit from their cooperation. He therefore advertised "participation" as an alternative to both capitalism and communism. A bill was introduced to the Chamber of Deputies on December 5, 1968, that was very advantageous to organized labor. First, it entitled trade unions to organize in all firms with more than fifty employees and made obstruction to such organizing illegal. Firms employing more than 200 were to be required to supply offices to labor union officials. In firms with between 150 and 300 employees, union officials were to be given ten hours per month with pay for union activities. The time was to increase to fifteen hours when employees exceeded 300. Businessmen were being required to subsidize the unions that they had fought for so long.

There can be no doubt that these reforms were direct results of the student revolt, but the ultimate effects of that revolt cannot be measured or analyzed for some time. The revolt in France and elsewhere was the result of changes in European society brought about by the prosperity of the 1950s and early 1960s, by the arrival of the affluent society; by the changing demographic structure which was caused by the baby-boom of the postwar period. These were profound changes that were certain to strain institutions that were too rigid or ossified to adjust. Affluence had changed attitudes toward authority, just as the population explosion and decline of the extended family had changed child-rearing practices, and just as the rise of mass universities dispensing mass education had developed a feeling akin to class consciousness among students. None of these developments could be extricated from the others as the sole cause of the student revolt, but taken together, they indicated that a new European society had matured since 1945, one greatly unlike that which had existed before 1939. Whatever the answers to the many questions raised by the students, they were not to be found in old ideologies of right, left, or center, but in a bold acceptance that new solutions must be devised in keeping with the new society.

A Revolt in the East

At the same time as the students' noisy revolt in western Europe, a quiet revolution was taking place in Czechoslovakia. The leaders of the Communist party there were trying to transform an authoritarian regime into a regime responsive to the sentiments of its citizens without surrendering or endangering the party's dominant role in society. It was a task demanding high statesmanship, delicate diplomacy with other socialist states, and utmost courage. The experiment was crushed by the armies of the Warsaw Pact nations but not before it had given a glimpse, a vision of the framework of a humane socialist society.

When 1968 began, Antonin Novotny was on the verge of being ousted as the leader of Czechoslovakian communism. Novotny had emerged as leader in 1957 when he wrested control of the party machinery from Stalinists and launched a form of authoritarian national communism. The next few years were prosperous ones, and Novotny governed an apparently contented populace. His problems began with the economic crisis of 1962–63 that caused unemployment and even a food shortage. To compound the discontent, Khrushchev's continued de-Stalinization in Russia— especially the events of the Twenty-Second Party Congress of 1961—gave encouragement to those demanding domestic reforms. The demands originated principally among Slovak intellectuals. The cultural division of the nation into Czechs and Slovaks had not been lessened but aggravated by communist rule. There are even two communist parties—one for Czechs and one for Slovaks. The Slovaks had continuously demanded special consideration for their cultural heritage. The Czechs, who dominated the national government and the national party, had followed a centralizing policy, applying laws uniformly to all parts of the state and denying Slovak differences. When economic discontent was added to cultural discontent, the Slovaks became more insistent in their demands for decentralization. Soon they were joined by Czech intellectuals—academics, writers, who argued for freedom of expression. These groups were supported by some party officials who wanted economic reforms. In September 1963, an ardent reformer, Alexander Dubcek, became the secretary of the Slovak Communist party, replacing a Stalinist, Karol Bacilek, who had opposed decentralization. Bowing under mounting pressure, Novotny made concessions—especially in the cultural field—allowing antiregime books to be published, allowing Western literature and films to be sold, and permitting increased travel to Western countries. He also rid himself of his more conservative, hard-line supporters one by one. Gradually, these concessions undermined his control of the party bureaucracy.

During 1966 reformers in the party gained enough power to challenge Novotny's leadership. The issue on which he was most vulnerable was economic policy. The leading force for a change of policy was Dr. Ota Sik, a noted economist and high-ranking Communist as well. Sik offered both the diagnosis and the treatment for the economy's ills: "Rigid centralized planning and management have become the main impediments to greater efficiency."[2] In particular he charged that the state had squandered money on new factories instead of modernizing old ones. This had increased productivity for a time merely because there were more workers, but individual productivity had not increased because technological advances had been ignored. To continue the expansion of industry, then, workers were attracted from other sectors of the economy where they

---

[2] Colin Chapman, *August 21st: The Rape of Czechoslovakia* (New York: J. B. Lippincott Co., 1968), p. 89.

were needed—agriculture, for example—thereby creating a shortage of labor in the deserted sectors for the sake of the inefficient factories. Finally, the economy did not produce enough consumer goods to support light industry. Sik's solution was a radical decentralization of the economy along the lines of Tito's Yugoslavia. At the Thirteenth Czechoslovak Party Congress in June 1966, a coalition of economic reformers and Slovaks forced this policy upon Novotny.

The key feature in the reform was that each factory would have to compete with every other factory. No longer would the state absorb the profit or loss, but the factory managers and workers would share profits or losses according to their competitive ability. Therefore, a profit incentive was introduced along with decentralization. Such competition implied the closure of noneconomic enterprises, and approximately 2,000 factories were closed by the end of 1967. Novotny and his supporters resisted the reforms for they realized that the success of decentralization implied a weakening of the party's control over the economy, as well as the strengthening of Novotny's political opponents.

Actually, Novotny had already lost the battle. On December 19, 1967, at a meeting of the Czechoslovak Central Committee, Ota Sik rose to denounce Novotny and the old guard of the party. He not only blamed them for the nation's economic problems but went further and called for a democratization of the regime. He argued that his economic reforms could not work in an atmosphere of repression. The heated debate lasted for three days before the Central Committee adjourned. When it reconvened on January 5, 1968, Novotny was voted out of office, and the Slovak Dubcek replaced him as first secretary of the party. Novotny remained president of Czechoslovakia until March, when he was replaced at that post by General Svoboda, a military hero not at first identified with reforms but who later became a symbol of resistance to Russian pressure.

From early February to August 20, Czechoslovakia experienced a rebirth of political, cultural and religious freedom. The security police was disbanded as an autonomous agency. Policemen were required to wear badges for the first time, so citizens could report them by their badge number if they acted arbitrarily. Precensorship of the press and literature was ended; students demanding reforms were listened to rather than being punished; and the ultimate heresy was committed in April when noncommunist political organizations were allowed to form. Dubcek was careful to stress, for the benefit of the Russians and his Communist neighbors, that these organizations would be subordinate to the communist-controlled National Front, the bogus coalition of several parties that had supposedly governed Czechoslovakia since 1948. There could be no doubt that the "leadership of the party" in society and government was to be maintained. In fact, the essence of the Czechoslovak experiment was a careful, delicate balance between encouraging spontaneity and maintaining control. The success of the experiment was dependent on moderation, so as not to alarm the Soviet Union or provoke an intervention.[3] But, having tasted the heady brew of free speech, certain groups demanded that Dubcek go faster. The most extreme statement of freedom from Russia was the *Two Thousand Words* manifesto issued by intellectuals and printed by most newspapers on June 27, while Warsaw Pact troops were in Czechoslovakia for practice maneuvers. Expressing support for Dubcek, the manifesto defiantly spoke of showing "our Government we will stand by it, with weapons if need be . . ."[4] The manifesto also attacked the record of the Czechoslovak Communist party and referred to the "errors of socialism." Because Dubcek did not suppress this statement, having ended censorship, the other communist governments assumed he must have approved it.

Still, it would be erroneous to conclude that the threat of further reforms in Czechoslovakia was the only factor determining a Warsaw Pact intervention. It was only one of a complex of circumstances. The diplomacy of the Soviet bloc nations and the political struggles within those nations were equally important. Dubcek had been extremely insistent in repeating his loyalty to the Warsaw Pact and the commitment of his government to abide by all treaties with Russia and the other satellites. He did, however, follow Rumania's example in establishing contacts with West Germany. The Soviets seemed content with the Czechoslovak assurance until April, but then both domestic Russian developments and pressure from East Germany and Poland led to Soviet consideration of intervention. Within the Soviet Union, conservative hard-liners were arguing that Russia had suffered too many foreign policy defeats to allow Czechoslovakia to become another one. They rejected the policy of detente with the United States and liberalization in eastern Europe that had been followed since Khrushchev came to power in 1955. They pointed to the Sino-Soviet split, the humiliation during the Cuban Missile Crisis, the independence of Rumania, and the defeat of the Arabs in 1967 as the fruit of detente. Therefore, they argued, Dubcek must be disciplined.

They were supported by the conservative dictators of East Germany, Poland, and Hungary. Walter Ulbricht feared that Czech willingness to trade with the Bonn Republic might inspire other states to do likewise. He was the most ardent advocate of intervention to crush the reformers. Wladislaw Gomulka was concerned about the domestic stability of his Polish regime (which also was a consideration by Kadar of Hungary) because Gomulka was being challenged both by reformers and extreme

---

[3] Philip Windsor and Adam Roberts, *Czechoslovakia, 1968: Reform, Repression, Resistance* (New York: Columbia University Press, 1969), pp. 10, 33–50.

[4] Journalist M, *A Year is Eight Months: Czechoslovakia 1968* (New York: Doubleday and Company, Inc., Anchor Books, 1971), p. 152.

nationalists who wished more freedom from Russia. In March Polish students at the universities of Warsaw and Cracow demonstrated in favor of democratization on the Czech model. It was indicative, then, of trends in domestic politics as well as of new relations among the Soviet bloc nations that East Germany and Poland, important strategically and as trading partners to the Soviet Union, tried to pressure Russia into a firmer stand. The first public indication of their success was the Warsaw Letter, which issued from a meeting of Soviet leaders with all the satellite leaders, except Dubcek and Ceaucescu of Rumania, in Warsaw on July 14–16. The letter virtually ordered Dubcek to reestablish the dictatorship of the Communist party or suffer an invasion. Dubcek refuted the charges made in the letter and refused to change his course.

To emphasize the seriousness of the situation, the Russians announced a massive military exercise of Warsaw Pact armies from the Baltic to the Black Sea. Some of these maneuvers took place on Czech soil, and an intervention seemed imminent. The Czechs were forced to attempt a compromise and agreed to meet with the Russians at Cierna, a resort town in Slovakia. The leaders of both governments attended. Dubcek repeatedly assured Brezhnev and Kosygin of his support of the Warsaw Pact but just as persistently refused to alter his domestic program. He argued that the Communist party was still in command in Czechoslovakia but that it was merely responding to public needs. The Russians demanded that their troops be stationed permanently on Czech soil as a defensive measure against NATO troops. Dubcek refused. During the conference, Brezhnev received identical letters from the leaders of the French and Italian parties and from Tito stating that Moscow could not depend on any support from parties outside the Soviet satellites if an invasion took place. This concerted effort may have had some influence on the Russian leaders as an indication of world opinion, but Brezhnev's decision not to force a showdown was probably a result of his belief that Dubcek did not intend to allow the reforms to go too far. The two men agreed that their alliance was still intact, and Brezhnev assured Dubcek that Russia would not interfere in Czechoslovakian domestic affairs. The Warsaw Pact troops were then slowly withdrawn from Czech soil.

This development did not please Ulbricht and Gomulka. They demanded a conference of all East European heads of government. The meeting took place in the Slovak town of Bratislava on August 3. Once again it appeared that Dubcek had negotiated skillfully and won a pledge of nonintervention. The Bratislava Declaration recorded Dubcek's promise to follow a Gomulkist policy of domesticism, granting limited freedoms but maintaining the dominant role of the Communist party in Czechoslovak society. Perhaps neither side in the negotiations understood the interpretation placed upon the declaration by the other. It seems that the Warsaw Pact allies expected Dubcek to curb reforms and freedoms, while the Czechoslovaks thought they had been promised more room to experiment without fear of an invasion.

Yet the Soviet Union and the other satellite nations did invade Czechoslovakia on the night of August 20–21. The precise reason for this apparent reversal of Russian policy is still only a matter of speculation. Several events occurred in early August that made it appear that Dubcek's regime was being attracted to neutralism, and this could have been influential in the Russian decision. Both Tito and Ceaucescu, president of rebellious Rumania, visited Prague and were given warm welcomes by both citizens and officials. On August 10 Dubcek made public a draft of new party statutes that contained provisions for the existence of dissident minorities within the CP. This was, of course, strictly contrary to Soviet theory if not Soviet practice. It is probable, however, that developments in Moscow and not in Prague determined the timing and nature of the invasion.[5] There is evidence that the Czech rebellion exacerbated divisions within the Soviet Presidium and Central Committee, and the invasion was the result of a victory of the hard-liners who were disillusioned with detente and with the increasing independence of the satellites. There seems no other reasonable explanation for the rejection of the cautious diplomacy Brezhnev and Kosygin had practiced until August or for the vacillation in the treatment of Dubcek and President Svoboda after the invasion.

When the invasion began, in the late evening of August 20, Dubcek and the Czechoslovak Presidium were arrested, bound hand and foot, and taken to a Polish town as prisoners. Early the next morning, three Czech conservatives who had opposed Dubcek's reforms visited President Svoboda and demanded that he appoint one of them, Alois Indra, as the new premier. Indra had been in contact with the Russians for several weeks. Svoboda's answer was simply to order them out of his home. This decision to resist the invasion by noncooperation was ratified by a secret congress of the CCP Central Committee held in a factory on August 22. The Russians had counted on their quislings taking power easily. The resistance of the CCP and the Czech people greatly surprised and embarrassed them.

The resistance was as heroic as it was futile. The Czechs realized there was no chance of armed resistance, and so they obstructed the progress of Russian troops by changing road markers, side-tracking entire trains, building roadblocks. When the troops reached Prague, they discovered that they were subjects of ridicule rather than saviors as they had been led to believe. Students painted swastikas on tanks, disrupted discipline by holding pornographic pictures in front of soldiers on guard duty, and at several points, engaged in pitched battles with the advancing tanks by bombarding them with Molotov cocktails. The most effective resistance was the continuation of radio and television broadcasts from improvised studios. These broadcasts not only maintained the spirit of the resisters

---

[5] Windsor and Roberts, *Czechoslovakia 1968*, pp. 66–76.

At Bratislava, Kosygin (center) and Brezhnev (right) promised Alexander Dubcek (left) that Russia would not interfere in Czechoslovakia's peaceful revolution. (Courtesy of UPI)

but kept Czechoslovakia's neighbors informed of progress of the occupation. It was through secret radio stations that the West learned of the resistance.

Having refused to appoint a premier of Russia's choosing, President Svoboda was flown to Moscow on August 23. He refused to negotiate until Dubcek, the Czech Presidium and legal cabinet ministers were freed. Although this may have saved Dubcek's life, it could not save the Czechoslovak experiment. Faced with a determined Soviet occupation, Dubcek agreed to withdraw most of the freedoms he had granted and "requested" the permanent presence of Russian troops on Czech soil for defense against West Germany. Five days after the invasion, Dubcek and Svoboda returned to Prague to preserve as much as they could of Czech independence. Eventually Dubcek and his supporters were replaced by Moscow's puppets, and Czechoslovakia lapsed back into authoritarianism.

Comparisons, East and West

French students rebelled against outdated curricula and a dehumanizing, socially biased educational process. Czechoslovak students confronted the cannons of Russian tanks and the bayonets of Russian rifles. Yet both revolts were indicative of the maturation of postwar European society. Looking broadly at the Continent's social, economic, and political evolution since 1945, the observer can see the contours of a new society emerging in the parallel developments of the welfare state and communist states.[6]

Social tension in the 1960s was not at all in the same form as the

---

[6] John Kenneth Galbraith, *The New Industrial State* (Boston: Houghton Mifflin Co., 1967); and Alain Touraine, *Le Mouvement de Mai* (Paris: Editions du Seuil, 1968).

class conflict of the pre-World War I, or even the interwar, period. The laboring classes no longer supplied the mass support for opposition to established institutions. Through the provision of social services in both East and West, through economic planning, and through two decades of economic prosperity, government, management, and labor had become integrated in such a manner as to make their interests similar rather than antagonistic. Workers had gained prosperity while losing alienation. Although communinist parties retained working class support, those parties had developed conservative goals in place of revolutionary goals. This does not mean that, as the social scientists of the late 1950s and early 1960s argued, there were no longer any groups still in conflict with established institutions. In a dialectical manner, the new society was creating new problems, new social stresses, new political movements.

The rapid expansion of education, the economic growth of the 1950s and 1960s, and especially, the affluence enjoyed by the younger generation of Europeans are all evidence of the success of the technocratic society. But these same factors have created the most highly educated, the most economically secure, and the youngest population in European history since the beginning of industrialization. The best educated members of the younger generation—the university students—have rebelled against the conformity, the commercialization, and the social controls which their parents, who still remember the 1930s and the war years, were very willing to accept, even to welcome, in exchange for food, clothing, and medical care. But the students are not alone in their rebellion. As seen in the French student revolt, the same desire to participate in decisions that determine one's life is shared by other sectors of society—especially by highly trained, well-educated technical workers.[7] It is not shared by those who are still relatively deprived and who still hope to gain from the technocratic prescriptions.

The rebellion is not a political revolt in terms of national politics. It takes the form of a protest against the impersonal and dehumanizing institutions of technocratic rationalism. Whether in France or Czechoslovakia the demand of the revolutionaries was not for a new political regime, nor a new economic system, but for new authority relations within schools, factories, and the *existing* political institutions. This demand is not a descendant of the class conflict of earlier times and has no relevance to the cold war debate between capitalists and communists. The new revolutionaries see little difference in the two economic systems, since, they charge, both are based on social controls which stifle the individual. The opposition between technocratic rationalism and demands for personal self-determination will undoubtedly lead to more social conflict rather than less and to more challenges to the imagination of man rather than to intellectual complacency.

[7] Touraine, *Le Mouvement de Mai*, p. 21.

Chapter 23

THE END OF CONSERVATIVE CONSENSUS

In both halves of the Europe divided by cold war, from 1947 to 1960 there had been certain assumptions generally shared by the majority of politicians and ordinary citizens. In the West these assumptions included the belief that government's first duty was to guarantee prosperity and further economic well-being, that anticommunism was the only safe foundation of foreign policy, and that conservative parties could achieve prosperity and fight communism best. In eastern Europe, the communist leadership agreed that safety dictated suppression at home and subordination of national interest to Russian interests in foreign affairs. As we have seen, de Gaulle began to change west European ideas on foreign policy in 1958. During the 1960s domestic politics in western Europe were marked by a revival of leftist parties everywhere and an increasing acceptance of communists as respectable political allies in France and Italy. The Polish and Hungarian revolts of 1956 had begun a loosening of the Soviet bloc that allowed a great deal of variety to emerge in the 1960s.

More fundamental, perhaps, than these political trends were the new social forces that had been created by a decade of affluence in western Europe and by the industrialization of eastern Europe. The Western workers were becoming a part of comfortable, leisure society by purchasing refrigerators and televisions and by taking annual vacations. Three times as many young people were attending universities in both East and West. And the level of education and literacy among the general public in eastern Europe made it more difficult for the socialist regimes to manage public opinion. The results of all of these changes are still difficult to judge, but it was evident by 1968, when students revolted in Italy, Paris, and Prague, that the new European society created from 1945 to

1958 had, in true dialectical form, given birth to new sources of social conflict.

Labour Returns Riding Harold Wilson

Soon after their victory in the 1959 election, the British Conservatives were faced with an economic crisis of major proportions. By October 1960, the economy had ceased expanding and the balance of international trade was going heavily against Great Britain. The accumulated weaknesses—outmoded equipment, shrinking markets for British goods, failure to control inflation—were finally taking their toll, and the deflationary 1959 budget had not helped matters by slowing investment but not checking inflation. Britain became known as the "sick man of Europe." Harold Macmillan, who had been in 1959 the most popular prime minister of the postwar era, rapidly lost support from 1961 until he resigned in 1963.

Spurred by the economic situation, Macmillan rejected the laissez faire attitude the Conservative party had adopted toward the economy in 1957. First, he took several measures to slow inflation. Business was asked to enact a "pay pause" by refusing to raise salaries or wages from July 1961 until mid 1962. The idea was that salaries had risen faster than production and the pause would allow production to catch up. Second, interest rates were increased and indirect taxes were raised. Third, Macmillan adopted economic planning—a violation of Conservative doctrine—by establishing the National Economic Development Council (NED) and the National Incomes Commission (NICKY). NED was to set goals for economic growth and recommend ways to achieve that growth. NICKY had the job of policing industrial salary and wage scales to prevent excessive wage increases that might feed inflation. The two commissions agreed on a growth rate of 4 percent annually, but they had few tools with which to coerce private industry (in contrast to the French Planning Office). Therefore, it became necessary for Reginald Maulding, chancellor of the exchequer, to follow alternately inflationary and deflationary fiscal policies. This "stop-go, stop-go" approach was strongly attacked by the Labour party.

Nineteen sixty-three was a bad year for the Conservatives. It began with de Gaulle's veto of British entrance to the Common Market. Macmillan's cabinet had hoped entry would solve some of their economic problems and had overpublicized the benefits of membership in EEC. As a result, the defeat was more embarrassing than it need have been. Next came the implementation of the Beeching report on the railroads. Dr. Richard Beeching had been hired away from private industry in 1961 to put the British Railroads on a paying basis. His report recommended closing down one-third of all track mileage and one-half of all stations. These were minor passenger stations, servicing only 2 percent of all passengers, but local sensibilities were injured greatly; Macmillan's popularity took another dip.

Then there was the Profumo scandal. On March 21, 1963, several Labour MPs mentioned in Commons rumors in the press associating an unnamed cabinet member with a "call girl," Christine Keeler. Most politicians and members of high society knew that the man in question was John Profumo, a secretary of state for war (a junior member of the cabinet with access to military secrets). On March 22 Profumo appeared in Commons with Macmillan at his side and stated, "There was no impropriety whatsoever in my acquaintance with Miss Keeler." It was soon discovered, however, that Miss Keeler had also been associating with Captain Ivanov, a naval attaché of the Russian Embassy, and that he had requested her to gain information from Profumo relating to Britain's nuclear deterrent. Macmillan hurriedly initiated an investigation and forced Profumo to resign. It seems there had been no breach of security, but this was not general knowledge for some time. The most damaging criticism of the government came from Harold Wilson, who said he would not charge Macmillan with duplicity but with inefficiency, gullibility, and poor judgment. Even some of the Conservative backbenchers accused the prime minister of incompetence. For the time being, however, Macmillan managed to retain his power.

His position had been badly shaken and he did not seem to be the man to lead the party in the election due in 1964. So, when an operation confined him to a hospital just prior to the Conservative party conference in the fall, Macmillan announced he was resigning and appointed as his successor Alec Douglas Lord Home. Lord Home was a compromise candidate whom all factions of the party could accept, but he was not the man to restore public confidence in the Conservative party. He had a frail appearance and was a weak public speaker. The recently chosen Labour party leader, Harold Wilson, contrasted with Home in every way. Wilson was an economist trained at Oxford, short and plump like British workers, and brilliant in debate. He wanted to move Labour away from doctrinaire economics and toward a planned, rather than a socialized, economy. Instead of further nationalizations, he emphasized the creation of new jobs, the need for government support for scientific research, the democratization of secondary education, and modernizing the British economy. Lord Home and the Conservatives concentrated on foreign affairs, an area where they were considered to be more experienced.

The election took place in October. Pundits predicted a Labour victory by a wide margin. The prominent issues as indicated by public opinion polls were all domestic: inflation, education, housing, pensions. On these Labour was strongest. The campaign was notable for the candidate's use of television and modern public relations techniques. Each party tried to sell the party leader much as presidential candidates are sold in the

The British Labour Party owed its electoral success in 1964 largely to the persuasive manner of Harold Wilson. (Courtesy of UPI)

United States.* Wilson easily won the battle of personalities. He appeared warm, affable, and strong-willed, whereas Home seemed weak and indecisive. The vote was surprisingly close. Labour emerged with the remarkably small majority of five votes. A by-election defeat soon reduced this to only four.

Wilson, Britain's youngest prime minister in the twentieth century, could

TABLE 23.1. British Elections in the 1960s

Party	1964	1966
Labour	317	363
Liberal	9	12
Conservative	303	253

SOURCE: T. O. Lloyd, *Empire to Welfare State* (New York: Oxford University Press, 1970), pp. 393, 409.

---

* This emulation of American political techniques was also occurring in other European countries. The French presidential election of 1965 was one example.

either temporize until he could hold another election, compromise with the Liberals to get their support, or enforce strict party discipline and govern as if he had a larger majority than just four votes. He chose the third alternative, convinced that Labour would gain more support by being defeated on important issues than by being overcautious. His first decision was a negative one. He announced that he would not resort to a devaluation of the pound to solve the balance-of-trade problem. Instead, he tried to check inflation and solve the trade problem by the conventional (and Conservative) expedients of cutting government spending—specifically in the military budget—and increasing taxes. An experimental military plane, the TSR-2, which would have given Britain an independent nuclear striking force, was scrapped, and planes were purchased instead from the United States. Taxes were increased for the wealthy in the form of new taxes on capital gains and dividends. For the first time, business entertaining was not allowed as a tax deduction.

Some Labour actions were not so conventional. Wilson attempted to strengthen the economic planning powers of the government by increasing the power of the Department of Economic Affairs to induce or hinder investment in various sectors. A Prices and Incomes Board was created to intervene in salary and wage negotiations to prevent inflationary wage increases or wage increases that were not matched by an equivalent increase in labor productivity. The Labour cabinet made a half-hearted attempt to renationalize the steel industry but dropped the idea when the Liberals expressed their opposition. Wilson had more success, however, in an attempt to democratize the school system by eliminating the "eleven-plus exam," which channeled students into either academic or technical secondary schools, and to force the merger of public schools, general secondary schools, and technical schools into comprehensive secondary schools in which students would be able to change from one curriculum to another easily. These two reforms were largely accomplished, decreasing the chance of a child's future being determined by his or her performance on one examination.

Wilson and the Labour party gained prestige during the Rhodesian crisis of 1965. Rhodesia was an African colonly that was approaching self-government. In May the white supremacists of the Rhodesian Front won a sweeping victory in Rhodesian legislative elections. The front's extremists had hoped a Conservative government in London would grant them independence under a white supremacist constitution. The Labour victory in 1964 led to demands that Ian Smith, prime minister and the Front's leader, unilaterally declare Rhodesia independent. Wilson was faced with a dilemma. He did not wish to allow the establishment of apartheid in Rhodesia because of the effect this would have on Britain's relations with African and Asian members of the Commonwealth. On the other hand, many Britishers had relatives living in Rhodesia; so Wilson did not want to use military force to prevent independence. There was even a rumor that the army might not fire on the white Rhodesians. Consequently, Wilson found a middle course. He refused to recognize Smith's declaration of independence when it was made in November and imposed economic sanctions in hopes of starving the Rhodesians into submission. This policy was strongly approved by British public opinion, and by the end of 1966, the sanctions had been increased so as to prohibit all trade with the rebel government. However, Rhodesia found that South Africa was a ready substitute for Great Britain as a market and as a source of trade. The policy of blockade was popular, but it had failed.

The Rhodesian question had badly split the Conservative party, and Wilson took advantage of the situation by calling an election for March 31, 1966. The Conservatives were not only weakened by their division over Rhodesia; they were also at the disadvantage of having just chosen a new party leader, Edward Heath, who had not yet established himself as a national figure. Like Wilson, Heath was a young man—at 49, Heath was one year younger—and a trained economist. But Wilson was a master at using television, while Heath was colorless and unexciting. The issues as revealed by public opinion polls also favored the Labourites, since domestic affairs such as housing and inflation dominated the public psyche. Wilson's strategy and timing of the election were vindicated by an increase in the number of Labour seats from 316 to 363. The Labour majority was increased from four votes to ninety-seven.

It appeared that Labour might be in power for an extended stay, but Wilson's popularity began to decline almost immediately. Having obtained a strong majority, Wilson was determined to take stern and unpopular measures to curb inflation, to end the budgetary deficit, and to create a favorable balance of trade. This meant severe budget reductions in both military and welfare programs. Military expenditures were cut by beginning a rapid withdrawal of British troops from "east of Suez"—the Persian Gulf and the Far East (except from Hong Kong), by refusing to build aircraft carriers previously promised to the Royal Navy, and by cancelling an order of fifty F-111 jet fighters built in the United States. The Labour cabinet also felt the need for limiting its domestic social program. The price for National Health Service perscriptions was increased, while required contributions to National Insurance (social security) of both employers and employees were raised. The government stopped supplying free milk to school children and delayed the rise in the school leaving age from fifteen to sixteen years, which would require many more teachers, for three years. The housing and road building programs were both revised downward.

The significance of these individual reforms was great. They formed a trend toward a reinterpretation of Britain's international role and of the nature of the welfare state in Britain. No longer would Great Britain even pretend to be a world power, but would concentrate on the defense of Europe rather than of excolonial possessions. The welfare state, which had been applied universally, to all citizens, during the prosperity of the 1950s, was being redefined so that its benefits would go selectively to those most in need.[1] These were fundamental policy changes justified by necessity rather than by doctrine.

The Labour government was behaving in a very Conservative manner, emphasizing austerity instead of expansion and innovation. Wilson took further steps in this direction in reaction to the financial crisis of 1966 and 1967. An international financial panic appeared in the making as foreign speculators sold their holdings of sterling for stronger currencies such as the deutsch mark. To counter this trend Wilson attempted deflationary policies, hoping to avoid a devaluation. Interest rates were steeply increased and the Prices and Income Board made price and wage increases illegal for the next six months. These measures succeeded only in infuriating organized labor, which was already greatly disenchanted with the reductions in social welfare. The trade balance worsened until, contrary to his promise of 1964, Wilson was required to announce a 14 percent devaluation of the pound (from £1 = $2.80 to £1 = $2.40) on November 18, 1967. The public was enraged, especially the working classes who could least afford the increase of prices on imports that devaluation entailed.

Events went from unfortunate to disastrous for the Labour party. The devaluation, although later effective, did not at first arrest the economic crisis, and by August 1968 Britain's unemployment was higher than at any time since 1945. Inflation also continued to climb, and new tax increases were needed. An attempt by Wilson to negotiate with Smith of Rhodesia ended in farce when the ship on which they met rocked so much that everyone aboard became ill. A government white paper on industrial relations, "In Place of Strife," which advocated government intervention to delay strikes for twenty eight days, was denounced by the trade unions. In mid 1969, public opinion polls indicated that, if an election were held, 28 percent more of the electorate would vote Conservative than would vote Labour.

An economic surge in the fall of 1969, however, contributed to a radical shift in public opinion. Labour candidates even won several by-elections in the spring of 1970. Wilson felt that this would be the most propitious moment to risk an election and announced that polling would be on June 18, 1970. A major factor in the economic recovery had been a sharp improvement in the trade balance. Compared with a $1.9 billion deficit in 1964, the British economy had achieved a $1.5 billion surplus in 1969, and the Labour party claimed full credit for the turnaround. Wilson's

[1] *The Annual Register of World Events in 1968* (London: Longmans, Green and Co., Ltd., 1969), p. 2.

cabinet approved a round of sizable salary increases in early 1970, and Edward Heath, the Conservative leader, accused Wilson of trying to purchase votes. The campaign was unusually bitter and unruly, with many public rallies disrupted by fist-fights and heckling that was rougher than usual.

Partially, the overheated tempers were due to the persistence of unemployment and trade union resentment of Wilson's tough stand on wage increases. More of an irritant, however, was the race question. Since 1945 (and especially since the mid 1950s), a large number of Indians, Pakistanis, and inhabitants of the former African colonies had immigrated to Great Britain. These were predominantly professionals—doctors, accountants; but they found discrimination in hiring prevented them from obtaining good jobs and discrimination in housing forced them into undesirable apartments. Clashes between white British youths and the immigrants began in the early 1960s. Against some heated Conservative opposition, the Labourites enacted a Race Relations Bill on April 9, 1968. It made it unlawful to discriminate by refusing to hire, rent to, or sell to a person because of national origin. During the debate on this issue, Enoch Powell created a national scandal by stating, "As I look ahead I am filled with foreboding. Like the Roman I seem to see the River Tiber foaming with much blood."[2] Powell was immediately ousted from the Conservative party's shadow cabinet because of this inflammatory statement, but he had made his mark as a politician of national recognition.

Wilson's campaign was low-keyed and relaxed. He did not speak forcefully on issues such as immigration or unemployment. He seemed to believe the political pundits who predicted Labour would easily maintain its majority. Heath worked very hard. He still was rather stiff on television, but he spoke on the domestic issues of housing, inflation, and unemployment. In general, he promised to reverse the trends toward more government intervention in the economy of the Price and Incomes Board type. The turnout, despite the physical violence of the campaign, was light, and the Conservatives won a thirty-seat majority. Heath had offered stability, and after the years of economic crisis, the public had responded.

From Adenauer to Willy Brandt

The German government, like the British, had been dominated by conservatives during the 1950s, and the German Social Democratic party, like the British Labour party, became strong enough to gain power in the 1960s. The Christian Democratic Union (CDU) had held the chancellorship since 1949, and until 1963, Konrad Adenauer dominated the CDU. After the 1961 elections Adenauer had promised the officials of his party

---

[2] *Annual Register of World Events in 1968* (London: Longmans, Green and Co., Ltd., 1969), p. 13.

that he would soon step down for a younger man. Unfortunately for him and his party, he was beginning to lose his political acuity more rapidly than he would admit. There is no other way to explain some of the political mistakes of his last years. The worst of these was probably the *Spiegel* affair.

Der Spiegel is a German news magazine similar to the American *Time*. It had long been critical of Adenauer's minister of defense, Franz Joseph Strauss, head of the Bavarian branch of the CDU. In October 1962, *Spiegel* printed an exposé of the weakness of the German infantry as revealed by the fall maneuvers. Strauss seized this opportunity for revenge. Although the article was little more than a compilation of articles previously published elsewhere, Strauss accused the magazine's editors of printing military secrets, had them arrested, and charged them with high treason. The case was eventually dismissed by the courts for lack of evidence, but not before the police had occupied *Spiegel's* offices and uncovered all the magazine's informants, hoping evidently to dry up its sources of information. Attacked in the Bundestag, Strauss denied his role in the police action. Adenauer not only defended Strauss but also accused the editor of *Spiegel*, Rudolf Augstein, of being a man "dominated by the desire to make money out of treason." This charge was made before the case had even come to court. Adenauer furthermore called on all advertisers to boycott *Spiegel*.

These highly arbitrary and authoritarian actions brought almost unanimous condemnation for Adenauer from the press, university circles, and other politicians—even some within the CDU. It was perhaps a healthy sign that so many Germans were willing to criticize their government on a matter of civil liberties. The Free Democratic party (FDP) threatened to withdraw from their coalition with the CDU if Strauss remained in office. Strauss resigned, and Adenauer reshuffled his cabinet but was still able to purchase only a few more months of political life.

His prestige, undermined by the *Spiegel* affair, was all but destroyed by the cavalier manner in which de Gaulle vetoed British entry to the Common Market only days before the signing of the Franco-German treaty. The Germans had been deeply committed to British entry, and they were highly insulted by the French action. Adenauer's own party was divided into the "Gaullists," who put a Franco-German friendship above other foreign policy goals, and the "Atlanticists," who felt the Atlantic Alliance system was more important. Adenauer and Strauss led the Gaullists, while Ludwig Erhard was the foremost Atlanticist. As the debate over ratifying the Franco-German treaty progressed, the Atlanticist wing of the CDU became clearly dominant. Adenauer resigned in October 1963, after fourteen years as chancellor.

Ludwig Erhard became the new chancellor. His first job was to reunite the CDU in anticipation of the legislative elections due in 1965. He continued Adenauer's domestic policies, which he had personally helped create, but he made clear his disenchantment with the Franco-German entente and remained faithful to NATO. These cautious policies were rewarded by the outcome of the 1965 election, which guaranteed continued CDU dominance.

TABLE 23.2.   German Elections in the 1960s

Party	1961	1965	1969
SPD	190	202	224
CDU/CSU	242	245	242
FDP	67	49	30

The 1965 election, however, marked the beginning of a political decline for the CDU. Signs of the end of Germany's economic miracle were multiplying. Demand for coal and steel was decreasing; the production of heavy machinery and the construction of housing were also in a slump. Until 1966 Germany had a shortage of labor, but by the end of 1966, there were 320,000 unemployed. Although they were only 1.6 percent of the total work force, the unemployed were a troubling phenomenon in a country that had experienced full employment since 1950. One year later the unemployment had doubled to 674,000, or 3 percent, of the workers. Erhard was a victim of the uncontrolled economy he had developed. His only resort was to enact unpopular tax increases while cutting social welfare expenditures. He tried to reduce military expenditures by canceling orders for equipment made in the United States, but the Americans argued that these purchases were to defray the cost of stationing American troops in Germany and a cancellation would force the United States to reconsider its commitment to Germany. Whether it was an empty threat or not, Erhard backed down and made plans for another tax increase. The FDP rebelled against the tax proposal and withdrew their support from the cabinet. Unable to gain a majority without FDP votes, Erhard was forced to resign in November 1966.

The CDU turned to Kurt Georg Kiesinger for their new chancellor. Kiesinger had a controversial past. He had been a ranking government administrator during the Nazi years, although he had never been an active Nazi supporter or party member. As many other Germans, he had remained at his post, finding nothing immoral in the Nazi regime before 1939. Yet, with the questionable past, which might have led one to expect conservative policies, Kiesinger initiated bold innovations in several areas. His first break with CDU tradition was to turn away from the FDP and to form a "grand coalition" with the SPD. He evidently did this because he felt the FDP too cautious in its approach to the economic crisis. A coalition with the Socialists would give him an overwhelming majority and make strong action possible. The power and positions of the new cabinet were balanced delicately. While Kiesinger was chancellor, Willy Brandt, the SPD leader, was foreign minister. Control over economic matters was shared by the parties by the appointments of Strauss as minister of finance and Karl Schiller (SPD) as minister of economics. It was a tenuous but also formidable coalition.

Kiesinger proved to be a strong chancellor, acting firmly to meet the economic crisis. Taxes were raised to curb inflation by taking money out of circulation, but in a break with convention, interest rates were lowered (usually considered an inflationary move) to encourage capital investment that would create jobs. Unproductive coal mines were closed and production from other mines was limited, resulting in 80,000 unemployed miners. Simultaneously, industrialists were given incentives to locate in the Rhineland, creating new jobs for the miners. Kiesinger did not shrink from cutting military expenditures against the wishes of his own minister of defense, the German military, and the Americans. Because of these energetic measures, the German economy began to recover rapidly by mid 1967. And Kiesinger had remained true to his pledge to the SPD that he would not sacrifice social welfare programs.

Germany's foreign policy was not immune from Kiesinger's innovations. In his first speech to the Bundestag, Kiesinger had announced a new *Ostpolitik,* a new Eastern policy, that rejected the Hallstein Doctrine. Guided by the Hallstein Doctrine, Adenauer and Erhard had refused to establish diplomatic relations with any state that recognized the East German regime. Kiesinger indicated that he was ready to have full relations with the satellite states except East Germany. The first fruits of this policy was an exchange of ambassadors with Rumania in January 1967. Russia and East Germany protested loudly and denounced the resurgent Germany. A trade agreement with Czechoslovakia followed in August 1967. The opening of relations with Yugoslavia in January 1968 was the last major accomplishment of the *Ostpolitik* before the Russian invasion of Czechoslovakia, which delayed any further progress. The Russians charged that the West Germans had been the prime instigators of counterrevolution among the Czechs, and the Kiesinger cabinet refused to sign a nuclear nonproliferation pact as long as the crisis in eastern Europe continued.

Kiesinger gained great prestige both demestically and internationally because of his bold initiatives, but there were troubling signals of new dangers for German society. The most worrisome was the increase in political extremism outside of parliament. A visit by the shah of Iran in 1967 was the occasion of violent student demonstrations in West Berlin against German support for American foreign policy. During the mélée, one student was shot by a policeman and died. Demonstrations then spread to other German universities, in a dress rehearsal for the much larger student riots of 1968. The most militant student group was the Socialist Student League (SDS), which adhered to an anticapitalist ideology.

Far more ominous, if less noisy, than the student demonstrations was the growing popularity of the neo-Nazi National Democratic party (NPD), which claimed an active membership of 60,000 in 1968. The NPD was largely a product of the economic crisis of 1963–68, but it had several precursors in the postwar period. The German Party of the Right had been active from 1946 until 1949. Composed of ex-Nazis, it succeeded in winning several seats in the first Bundestag election. It was immediately replaced by the Reich Social party (SRP), headed by ex-General Otto Ernst Remer. It achieved its greatest popularity in 1951 when it polled 11 percent of the vote in an election for the *Land* parliament of Lower Saxony. Its membership was approximately 20,000 when the Constitutional Court ruled that the party was unconstitutional because of its anti-republican program and ordered it be banned in 1952. The neo-Nazi movement died away after the court's action until it was revived in the form of the NPD in 1964.

The National Democratic party quickly became a political force of considerable strength in certain regions. It scored its most notable successes in 1967 when it won forty-eight seats in six *Land* parliaments and had party organizations in 466 of the 496 Bundestag constituencies. Although the membership was at first limited to the lower-middle class, the NPD began to gain working class support during 1967, when unemployment was at its worst. Right-wing extremism fed on left-wing extremism during 1968 as the neo-Nazis, playing on the fears generated by student riots, won twelve more seats in *Land* elections. The CDU/SPD coalition discussed the possibility of asking the court to ban the NPD as antidemocratic, but it was decided that it would be preferable to defeat the neo-Nazis at the ballot box. It was also felt that the NPD could be denied working class support if left-extremist parties were allowed to form. Following this reasoning, the German Communist party was allowed to reform in September 1968, on the condition that it would not advocate the overthrow of the Basic Law. The test of these libertarian policies was to be the 1969 Bundestag election.

In preparation for the legislative election, the SPD had been negotiating with the FDP. The first evidence that an anti-CDU alliance had been formed was the election of a Socialist, Gustav Heinemann, president of the republic in March 1969. He was the first Social Democratic president since 1925. It appeared that Kiesinger's effective leadership had not been sufficient to reverse the steady growth of the SPD. This was confirmed in the Bundestag election in September. (See Table 23.2.) While the CDU suffered only marginal losses, the SPD gained twenty-two seats. An SPD/FDP cabinet was formed with Willy Brandt as the new chancellor, and the twenty-year rule of the Christian Democrats had come to an end.

Italy's Opening to the Left

The central event in Italian politics during the 1960s was the formation and collapse of a center-left coalition based on a reconciliation of the Christian Democrats (DC) and the Socialist party (PSI). The coalition was comparable to the German "grand coalition" between the CDU and the SPD. Although the necessary conditions for this "opening to the left" seemed to have been created by the parliamentary elections of 1958, the formation of the coalition was not completed until 1963, when the PSI entered a cabinet for the first time since 1947. This event was the tangible expression of the shift of political opinion among the Italian electorate from the center-right to the center-left. The DC leadership justified its political dominance by understanding this shift and following it. There was, however, no true consensus among the leftist parties; and after five years of fruitful cooperation, the center-left coalition dissolved once again into its constituent parts and plunged Italy into a new period of immobilism and crisis more severe than that of the 1950s.

Just before the 1958 election Amintore Fanfani, then premier and secretary-general of the DC, and Pietro Nenni, the PSI leader, had both espoused a policy of collaboration of the noncommunist left. The PSI developed a campaign program that was to serve as a basis for coalition action. The program emphasized the need to weaken the great industrial corporations by either nationalization or more restrictive regulations, to strengthen the state's control of the economy through economic planning, and to insure more public participation in and control over government by creating regional elected governments. These goals were complimentary. It was felt that the extreme centralization of power in Rome made the government more susceptible to pressures from big business. One example was the success of the electrical industry in preventing state regulation of its prices. The PSI specifically desired the nationalization of this industry, which would give the state a monopoly of sources of industrial power since it already owned the petroleum industry. The 1958 election results seemed to be an endorsement of the opening to the left. The parties that would enter such a government made gains at the expense of the PCI and the extreme right.

The conservative wing of the Christian Democratic party was strong enough, however, to prevent Fanfani from forming a center-left cabinet. Only weeks after the election Fanfani was defeated in parliament, and he resigned not only as premier but also from his post as secretary-general. Aldo Moro, a moderate whom the conservatives trusted, replaced Fanfani as head of the DC. Fanfani's ouster was indicative of deep divisions within

TABLE 23.3.　Italian Elections to the Chamber of Deputies, 1958–68

Party	1958		1963		1968	
	Seats	Change	Seats	Change	Seats	Change
Communist	140	− 3	166	+26	171	+ 5
PSIUP*	...	...	...	...	23	...
Socialists	84	+ 9	87	+ 3	91	−29
Social Democrats	22	+ 3	33	+11		
Republicans	6	+ 1	6	0	9	+ 3
Christian Democrats	273	+57	260	−13	265	+ 5
Liberals	17	+ 3	39	+22	31	− 8
Monarchists	25	−15	8	−17	6	−11
MSI (neofascist)	24	− 5	27	+ 3	24	− 3
Others	5	...	4	...		

* Socialist Party of Proletarian Unity.

the Christian Democrats. The party was not an autonomous organization, but it depended on the support of conservative groups in Italian society for its financial and organizational existence. For example, the Confindustria, the national lobby for big business, had been the DC's chief source of funds since the 1940s, and the party had counted on the Catholic Action Society, a lay group that reflected the interests of the Catholic hierarchy, for getting out the voters at election time. The Catholic church itself had taken an active role in politics since World War II, and many priests and bishops issued threats of excommunication at each election for anyone who voted for a socialist or communist candidate. Fanfani had been trying to end these dependencies by creating an autonomous party organization in each constituency, and it was for this as much as for his leftist policies that he was attacked in 1958.

The governments that followed were conservative and weak. One of them, led by Ferdinando Tambroni, almost touched off a civil war by its open support of the neofascist Italian Socialist Movement (MSI). But the party organization was still moving leftward. Moro was convinced by PSI and PGI gains in local elections that the DC would have to accommodate itself to the leftward trend among the electorate or it would lose its place as Italy's leading party. Slowly and skillfully, Moro built a majority within the party organization in favor of an opening to the left. He encouraged branches of the DC to experiment with center-left coalitions on the local level. In January 1961, the DC and PSI formed a municipal council coalition in Milan. The same thing was done in Genoa in February and in Florence in March. By the end of the spring there were forty such local coalitions.[3] At the DC party congress in January 1962, Moro and Fanfani won a victory on a vote favoring an alliance

---

[3] Norman Kogan, *A Political History of Postwar Italy* (New York: Frederick Praeger, Publishers, 1966), pp. 176–77.

with the PSI. Shortly afterwards, in March, Fanfani formed the first cabinet based on a center-left coalition. Three parties held cabinet posts—the DC, the Republicans (PRI), and the Social Democrats—and the PSI pledged its support without taking a ministry. Fanfani's long battle had been won.

The program of Fanfani's government was almost identical with that of the PSI in the 1958 election, and most of the program was enacted in the year before the next legislative elections in April 1963. The electrical industry was nationalized and a state corporation, the Electrical Undertakings Trust, was created to manage it. A National Commission for Economic Planning was formed to unify the state's various means of influencing the economy's growth. Various other reforms were enacted that were not central features of the orginal PSI program, such as the imposition of a capital tax on investments in stocks and real estate, a notable increase in social welfare benefits, a reorganization of the school system to make it more democratic, and the establishment of fourteen years as the lowest age a child could leave school. One major bill could not be passed: the regional autonomy bill. Christian Democrats opposed this bill because they were convinced that the popularity of the PCI in central Italy would result in the election of Communist regional governments in a "red belt" across the peninsula just north of Rome. Socialists insisted that decentralization was necessary to make democracy work in Italy by creating state governments between the municipal governments and Rome. Since the issue was not resolved, it was an issue in the 1963 elections, as was the very existence of the center-left coalition.

The parties of the left were aided in that election by a change in the Vatican. Until 1958, under Pope Pius XII, the Catholic church had stood squarely behind the right wing of the DC. The new Pope chosen in 1958 was more liberal John XXIII. For several years John XXIII played no role in domestic politics as he settled into office, allowing the bishops and lower clergy to continue their conservative politics. In 1961, however, he began a transformation of the Vatican's position. His encyclical *Mater et magistra* (*Mother and Teacher*) endorsed the concept of a mixed economy and economic planning, while condemning the abuses of the uncontrolled free markets and making a plea for social justice. In March 1963, John welcomed Khrushchev's daughter and son-in-law to Rome in a private audience. This was a remarkable gesture with great impact on Italian politics. A second major encyclical the following month, *Pacem in terris* (*Peace on Earth*), emphasized the need for tolerance of freedom of conscience and once again stressed the church's commitment to social justice. This was broadly interpreted as a repudiation of the practice of threatening to excommunicate communist voters. It would be difficult to overestimate the importance of John's leadership in aiding Moro's and Fanfani's efforts to move the DC towards social reforms.

The 1963 election took place only weeks after the publication of *Pacem in terris*. The results were interpreted by Fanfani's supporters as a confirmation of the center-left coalition. But, while the PSI and the PSDI had gained seats, the DC had lost several seats and the PCI had gained twenty-six. (See Table 23.3.) The DC leadership interpreted the election as an indication that Fanfani had been too far to the left, and they replaced him as premier with the more moderate Moro. After some initial difficulty, Moro formed a cabinet with representatives from the conservative faction of the DC as well as from the PSI and with a program only slightly less reformist than Fanfani's. It was the first cabinet in which the PSI had participated in sixteen years. The similarity with the formation of the grand coalition in Germany in 1966 is striking. Although he had to shuffle his cabinet several times, Moro presided over this coalition as premier until 1968.

Moro had the misfortune of taking office just as Italy was entering its first major economic crisis since the 1940s. Of course, this was a period of general economic slowdown throughout Europe as seen in the discussions of British and German politics above, and the crisis was not an indication of basic weaknesses in Italian industry. Moro (as Wilson and Kiesinger) moved decisively to reduce domestic consumption by increasing taxes and restraining wage increases. This slowed the flow of imports and controlled inflation. Moro then subsidized exports to create a favorable trade balance and obtained loans from the United States and from the International Monetary Fund to support the value of the lira. These emergency measures were remarkably successful and within a matter of months the economy had begun a rapid recovery. In order to gain the confidence of the business community for his financial measures, however, Moro had to postpone social, administrative, and economic reforms. Therefore, the very reason for the existence of the center-left coalition came into question.

Although Italian foreign policy remained primarily based on the Atlantic Alliance and antagonistic to de Gaulle's attacks upon the Alliance, Moro did initiate a more independent policy than his predecessors had followed, especially in the realm of Italo-Russian relations. Gromyko, the Soviet foreign minister, visited Italy in April 1966. One week after his visit an agreement was signed for the construction of a Fiat industrial complex in Russia. Not only would the complex make cars with the latest technology, but it would also perform all the preliminary industrial functions—such as smelting the steel. The Russians considered this an excellent way to learn Western technology, while the Italians saw it as aid for their balance of payments problem. Within the month a similar agreement was reached between Fiat and Poland. The following January another high-ranking Russian, president of the Soviet Union Podgorny, paid an official visit to Rome, and he was granted an audience with the Pope.

Aldo Moro, architect of the opening to the left, bows to newly elected Italian President Saragat, December 1964. (Courtesy of UPI)

The success of the center-left coalition had initiated a series of realignments among the parties of left. The acceptance of parliamentary responsibility by the PSI made possible negotiations for the reunification of PSI and PSDI. The last real obstacle to this was removed when Giuseppi Saragat, the PSDI leader, was elected president of the republic in 1964. This made Nenni the unchallenged head of Italian socialism. After very arduous discussions, the Unified Socialist party (PSU) was founded on October 30, 1966. The PCI was as a result isolated, and in addition, it was plagued by internal divisions, weak leadership, and lack of program. Palmiro Togliatii, leader of the party since the liberation, had been gradually making the party increasingly more independent of Moscow since the Hungarian Revolt of 1956. When he died in 1964, he was replaced by Luigi Longo, who was more submissive to Moscow than many PCI voters would have liked. To compound the problems, several extremist factions broke with the PCI because it was becoming too conservative. These minor groups usually pledged their support to Mao Tse-tung in the Sino-Soviet dispute.

The apparent disorder among the communists and the steady decline of the extreme right pointed to the continued dominance of the center-left as the legislative election of 1968 approached. During 1967 the coalition parties passed several reforms meant to win votes and to fulfill its original program. The first fully integrated five-year plan was adopted with provisions for an annual growth rate of 5 percent. The regional administration bill finally passed the Chamber of Deputies, the lower house, but it was delayed in the Senate. A school construction bill provided for tangible proof that the voters could see in their communities of the advantages of center-left government. The message evidently did not reach the voters. (See Table 23.3.) While the Christian Democrats did gain five seats over 1963, they were still below their 1958 total. The PSU lost to the PCI, which gained five seats, and to the Socialist Party of Proletarian Unity (PSIUP), a dissident faction of the old PSI which preferred to cooperate with Communists rather than bourgeois parties. Of the twenty-nine seats the PSU lost, at least twenty-three were won by the PSIUP. The two extreme-left parties accounted for one-third of the entire electorate. It was obvious that the leftward trend that Fanfani and Moro had seen in the early 1960s was continuing.

After the election, the center-left coalition began to disintegrate. The Socialists blamed their losses on the conservative policies of the DC and refused to enter another cabinet until the end of the year. Trade union and student demonstrations and occasional violence made it even more difficult for the left wing of the PSU to support DC-led cabinets. In 1969 the PSU split into its constituent elements again. A minority reclaimed their freedom from the center-left coalition and renamed their group the PSI. The PSU majority remained faithful to the DC premier, Mariano Rumor, but they demanded concessions that were difficult for Rumor to meet. The result was that Italy gradually slipped into a political quagmire. Parliament was paralyzed for lack of a clear, coherent majority, and demands from newly militant groups—students, trade unionists, farmers—were constantly creating new crises.

Was There a Pattern?

The similarities in evolution of domestic politics and foreign policy in Germany, Great Britain, and Italy during the 1960s may be an illusion. Not enough time has passed to allow one to know whether the revival of the left in all three countries is leading to similar future developments or whether the peculiar circumstances in each national setting are so different that the Labour government of Wilson, the grand coalition of Kiesinger, and Fanfani's opening to the left are only surface similarities. It does seem that the left became more respectable in the voters' eyes. This may be due to the fact that the West European socialists were becoming more conservative, and not that the electorate was more eager for reforms. Certainly, in office, the leftist parties dealt with the economic crisis in much the same way conservatives would have. It should be noted that France should not be excluded from the comparison. In 1965 the French Socialists and Communists cooperated in the presidential election and continued that collaboration in the legislative election of 1967.

It is very probable that the decline of the cold war tensions of the 1950s was a major reason for the revival of the left. Each of the four major West European states began independent probes of eastern Europe for purposes of trade. They usually did this unilaterally, often without American approval—diplomatic postures that were not even considered during the most frigid years of the cold war. Europe was asserting herself again.

BIBLIOGRAPHY

The following bibliography is intended as a modest guide for students and teachers who wish to know more about the events of European history in the twentieth century. Most of the books included contain more detailed bibliographies concerning specific topics.

GENERAL WORKS

Arendt, H. *The Origins of Totalitarianism* (rev. ed., 1966).
Aron, R. *The Century of Total War* (1954).
Barraclough, G. *An Introduction to Contemporary History* (1964).
Carr, E. H. *The New Society* (1951).
Hale, O. J. *The Great Illusion, 1900–1914* (1971).
Holborn, H. *The Political Collapse of Europe* (1951).
Landes, David S. *The Unbound Prometheus: Technological Change and Industrial Development in Western Europe from 1750 to the Present* (1969).
Mayer, A. J. *Dynamics of Counterrevolution in Europe, 1870–1956* (1971).
Mowat, C. L., ed. *New Cambridge Modern History, vol. XII: The Shifting Balance of Power* (rev. ed., 1968).
Sontag, R. *A Broken World, 1919–1939* (1971).
Stearns, P. *European Society in Upheaval* (1967).
Tuchman, B. *The Proud Tower* (1962).
Wright, Gordon. *The Ordeal of Total War, 1939–1945* (1968).

PART I. EUROPE, 1900–39

A. Economic and Social

Alpert, P. *Twentieth Century Economic History of Europe* (1951).
Bruck, W. F. *Social and Economic History of Germany, 1888–1938* (1938).
Cole, G. D. H. and R. Postgate. *The British Common People* (1961).
Dobb, Maurice. *Soviet Economic Policy since 1917* (1948).
Dovring, F. *Land and Labor in Europe, 1900–1950* (1956).
Feis, H. *Europe, the World's Banker, 1870–1914* (1930).
Galbraith, J. K. *The Great Crash, 1929* (1955).
Gerschenkron, A. *Bread and Democracy in Germany* (1943).

Hodson, Henry V. *Slump and Recovery, 1929–1937* (1938).
Kindleberger, C. *Economic Growth in France and Britain, 1851–1950* (1964).
Klein, L. *The Keynesian Revolution* (2d. ed., 1966).
Kulischer, E. M. *Europe on the Move: War and Population Changes, 1917–1947* (1948).
Laursen, K. and J. Pedersen. *The German Inflation, 1918–1923* (1964).
Lewis, W. A. *Economic Survey, 1919–1939* (1949).
Marwick, A. *The Deluge: British Society and the First World War* (1964).
Nove, A. *The Soviet Economy* (1965).
Pollard, S. *The Development of the British Economy, 1914–1950* (1962).
Stolper, G. *The German Economy, 1870 to Present* (1940).
Sturmthal, A. *The Tragedy of European Labor, 1918–1939* (1951).
Svennilson, I. *Growth and Stagnation in the European Economy, 1913–1945* (1954).
Tracy, M. *Agriculture in Western Europe: Crisis and Adaptation since 1880* (1964).
Volpe, P. *The International Financial and Banking Crisis, 1913–1933* (1945).
Wright, G. *Rural Revolution in France: The Peasantry in the Twentieth Century* (1964).
Wunderlich, F. *Farm Labour in Germany, 1810–1945* (1961).

B. Intellectual and Cultural Developments

1. Philosophy, Psychology and Social Thought

Barnett, L. *The Universe and Dr. Einstein* (1952).
Benda, J. *The Treason of the Intellectuals* (1955).
Bendix, R. *Max Weber: An Intellectual Portrait* (1960).
Bentley, E. *A Century of Hero-Worship* (2d ed., 1957).
Crossman, R. *The God That Failed* (1950).
Curtis, M. *Three Against the Republic: Sorel, Barrès and Maurras* (1959).
Déak, I. *Weimar Germany's Left-Wing Intellectuals* (1968).
Freud, S. *A General Introduction to Psychoanalysis* (1938).
Gay, P. *Weimar Culture: The Outsider as Insider* (1968).
Graves, R. *Goodbye to All That* (2d rev. ed., 1957).
Graves, R. and A. Hodge. *The Long Week-End: A Social History of Great Britain, 1918–1939* (1941).
Hall, C. S. *A Primer on Freudian Psychology* (1954).
Horowitz, I. L. *Radicalism and the Revolt Against Reason: the Social Theories of George Sorel* (1968).
Joll, J. *Three Intellectuals in Politics: Blum, Rathau, Marinetti* (1960).
Klemperer, K. *Germany's New Conservatism, Its History and Dilemma in the Twentieth Century* (1957).
Laqueur, W. and G. Mosse, eds. *Journal of Contemporary History, I, 2: Left-Wing Intellectuals Between the Wars, 1919–1939* (1966).
Laqueur, W. and G. Mosse, eds. *Journal of Contemporary History, II, 2: Literature and Society* (1967).
McElwee, W. *Britain's Locust Years, 1918–1940* (1962).
Masur, G. *Prophets of Yesterday: Studies of European Culture 1890–1914* (1961).
Mitzman, A. *The Iron Cage: An Historical Interpretation of Max Weber* (1969).
Rieff, P. *Freud: The Mind of a Moralist* (1959).
Stuart-Hughes, H. *Consciousness and Society: The Reorientation of European Social Thought* (1958).
Stuart-Hughes, H. *The Obstructed Path: French Social Thought in the Years of Desperation, 1930–1960* (1968).
Wood, N. *Communism and British Intellectuals* (1959).

2. Literature

Brée, G. and M. Guiton. *An Age of Fiction: The French Novel from Gide to Camus* (1962).

Carmody, F. J. and C. MacInytre. *Surrealist Poetry in France: a Bilingual Anthology* (1953).

Ellman, R. and C. Feidelson, eds. *The Modern Tradition: Backgrounds of Modern Literature* (1965).

Gray, R. D. *The German Tradition in Literature 1871–1945* (1961).

Guicharnaud, Jacques and June Beckelman. *Modern French Theatre* (1961).

Henning, Edward B. *Fifty Years of Modern Art, 1916–1966* (1966).

Hunter, Sam. *Modern French Painting, 1855–1956* (1957).

Karl, Frederick R. *The Contemporary English Novel* (1962).

Lemaitre, Georges. *From Cubism to Surrealism in French Literature* (1941).

March, Harold. *The Two Worlds of Marcel Proust* (1948).

Peyre, Henri. *The Contemporary French Novel* (1955).

Peyre, Henri. *French Novelists of Today* (1967).

Shattuck, Roger. *The Banquet Years: The Arts in France, 1885–1918* (1958).

Wilson, Edmund. *Axel's Castle: A Study in the Imaginative Literature of 1870–1930* (1931).

3. Fine Arts

Bauer, Marian. *Twentieth Century Music* (new ed., 1947).

Clough, Rosa. *Futurism: The Story of a Modern Art Movement* (1961).

Haftmann, Werner. *Painting in the Twentieth Century* (rev. ed., 1965).

Hunter, Sam. *Modern French Painting: Fifty Artists from Monet to Picasso* (1956).

Jaffé, H. L. C. *Twentieth-Century Painting* (1963).

Joedicke, Jurgen. *A History of Modern Architecture* (1962).

Langui, Emile. *Fifty Years of Modern Art* (1959).

Martin, Marianne W. *Futurist Art and Theory, 1909–15* (1968).

Read, Herbert. *A Concise History of Modern Sculpture* (1964).

Seuphor, Michel. *Abstract Painting: Fifty Years of Accomplishment from Kandinsky to Jackson Pollock* (trans. Hauben Chevalier) (1964).

Stearns, Marshall W. *The Story of Jazz* (1956).

4. Cinema

Balázs, Bela. *Theory of the Film* (Eng. trans., 1953).

Kracauer, Siegfried. *From Caligari to Hitler: A Psychological History of the German Film* (1947).

Leda, Jay. *Kino, A History of the Russian and the Soviet Film* (1962).

O'Leary, Liam. *The Silent Cinema* (1970).

Rotha, Paul. *The Film Till Now* (rev. ed., 1967).

C. Diplomacy

1. 1900–1918

Albertini, L. *The Origins of the War of 1914* (3 vols.) (1952–57).

Anderson, E. M. *The First Moroccan Crisis, 1904–1906* (1930).

Askew, W. C. *Europe and Italy's Acquisition of Libya, 1911–1912* (1942).

Barlow, J. C. *The Agadir Crisis* (1940).

Brunschwig, Henri. *French Colonialism, 1871–1914: Myths and Realities* (1966).

Carroll, E. M. *French Public Opinion and Foreign Affairs, 1870–1914* (1931).

Carroll, E. M. *Germany and the Great Powers, 1866–1914: A Study in Public Opinion and Foreign Policy* (1938).

Fay, S. B. *The Origins of the World War* (1928, 1930).

Fischer, Fritz. *Germany's Aims in the First World War* (1967).

Fraser, Peter. *Joseph Chamberlain, Radicalism and Empire, 1868–1914* (1966).
Helmreich, E. C.   *The Diplomacy of the Balkan Wars, 1912–1913* (1938).
Lafore, Laurence. *The Long Fuse* (1965).
Langer, W. *The Diplomacy of Imperialism, 1890–1902* (1925).
Mayer, A. J. *Wilson vs. Lenin: Political Origins of the New Diplomacy* (1964).
Michon, G. *The Franco-Russian Alliance 1870–1914* (1931).
Remak, J. *Sarajevo: The Story of a Political Murder* (1959).
Robinson, Ronald and John Gallagher, with Alice Denny. *Africa and the Victorians: The Climax of Imperialism* (1961).
Schmitt, B. E.   *The Coming of the War: 1914* (1930).
Semmel, Bernard. *Imperialism and Social Reform* (1960).
Thanden, E. C. *Russia and the Balkan Alliance of 1912* (1965).
Townsend, M. E. *European Colonial Expansion since 1871* (1941).
Tuchman, Barbara. *The Guns of August* (1962).
Winslow, E. M. *The Pattern of Imperialism, A Study: The Theories of Power* (1948).
Woodward, E. L.   *Great Britain and the German Navy* (1935).

2. Versailles to 1939
Baerd, George W. *The Coming of the Italo-Ethiopian War* (1967).
Birdsell, P. *Versailles Twenty Years After* (1941).
Craig, G. and F. Gilbert (eds.). *The Diplomats, 1919–1939* (1965).
Eubank, K. *Munich* (1963).
Fontaine, André. *History of the Cold War, 1917–1950* (1968).
Freund, G. *Unholy Alliance: Russian-German Relations from the Treaty of Brest-Litovsk to the Treaty of Berlin* (1957).
Furnia, A. H. *Diplomacy of Appeasement: Anglo-French Relations and the Prelude to World War II, 1931–1938* (1960).
George, Margaret. *The Warped Vision: Britain's Foreign Policy, 1933–39* (1965).
Gilbert, Martin. *The Roots of Appeasement* (1966).
Hall, M. Margaret. *Post-War German-Austrian Relations: The Anschluss Movement, 1918–1936* (1937).
Hilger, G. and A. G. Meyer. *The Incompatible Allies: A Memoir-History of German-Soviet Relations, 1918–1941* (1953).
Jordan, Wm. Mark. *Great Britain, France and the German Problem, 1918–39* (1943).
Lafore, Laurence. *The End of Glory* (1970).
Mayer, A. J. *Politics and Diplomacy of Peacemaking, 1918–1919* (1967).
Micaud, Ch. *The French Right and Nazi German* (1942).
Taylor, A. J. P. *The Origins of the Second World War* (1961).
Thompson, J. M. *Russia, Bolshevism and the Versailles Peace* (1966).
Thompson, Neville. *The Anti-Appeasers* (1971).
Ulam, Adam B. *Expansion and Coexistence: The History of Soviet Foreign Policy, 1917–1967* (1968).
Wheeler-Bennett, J. W. *Munich: Prologue to Tragedy* (1948).
Wiskeman, Elizabeth. *The Rome-Berlin Axis* (1949).
Wolfers, Arnold. *Britain and France Between the Wars* (1940).

D. Socialism, Communism and Labor Movements

Borkenau, Franz. *European Communism* (1954).
Borkenau, Franz. *World Communism, a History of the Communist International* (1962).
Braunthal, Julius. *History of the International* (1967).
Brower, Daniel R. *The New Jacobins: The French Communist Party and the Popular Front* (1968).

Bullock, Alan. *The Life and Times of Ernest Bevin, Vol. I, Trade Union Leader, 1881–1940* (1960).
Cole, G. D. H. *Communism and Social-Democracy, 1914–31* (1958).
Cole, G. D. H. *Socialism and Fascism, 1931–1939* (1960).
Colton, Joel. *Leon Blum: Humanist in Politics* (1966).
Drackovitch, M. M. and B. Lazitch. *The Comintern: Historical Highlights* (1966).
Fainsod, M. *International Socialism and the World War* (1935).
Joll, James. *The Second International, 1889–1914* (1955).
Lichtheim, G. *Marxism: An Historical and Critical Study* (1961).
McKenzie, Kermit E. *Comintern and World Revolution, 1928–1943* (1964).
Marcus, John T. *French Socialism in the Crisis Years, 1933–1936. Fascism and the French Left.* (1958).
Mitchell, Harvey and Peter N. Stearns. *Workers and Protest (The European Labor Movement, the Working Classes and the Origins of Social Democracy), 1890–1914* (1971).
Schorske, Carl E. *German Social Democracy 1905–1917* (1955).
Stearns, Peter N. *Revolutionary Syndicalism and French Labor: a Cause Without Rebels* (1971).
Wohl, Robert. *French Communism in the Making, 1914–1924* (1966).

E. Fascism

Carsten, F. L. *The Rise of Fascism* (1967).
Cross, Colin. *The Fascists in Britain* (1963).
Derrick, Michael. *The Portugal of Salazar* (1939).
Drennan, James. *BUF: Oswald Mosley and British Fascism* (1934).
Dutt, R. Palme. *Fascism and Social Revolution* (1934).
Eisenberg, Dennis. *The Re-Emergence of Fascism* (1967).
Laqueur, Walter (ed.) and George L. Mosse. *Journal of Contemporary History: I, 1, International Fascism* (1966).
Mayer, Arno J. *Dynamics of Counterrevolution in Europe, 1870–1956* (1971).
Moore, Barrington. *The Social Origins of Dictatorship and Democracy: Lord and Peasant: The Making of the Modern World* (1966).
Nolte, Ernst. *Three Faces of Fascism: Action française, Italian Fascism, National Socialism* (1966).
Payne, Stanley. *Falange* (1961).
Rintala, M. *Three Generations: The Extreme Right-Wing in Finnish Politics, 1917–1939* (1962).
Weber, Eugen. *Varieties of Fascism: Doctrines of Revolution in the Twentieth Century* (1964).
Weber, Eugen and Hans Rogger. *The European Right: A Historical Profile* (1965).

F. World War I

Albrecht-Carrié, R. *The Meaning of the First World War* (1965).
Falls, Cyril. *The Great War, 1914–18* (1959).
Guinn, Paul. *British Strategy and Politics, 1914–1918* (1965).
King, Jere C. *Generals and Politicians; Conflict Between France's High Command, Parliament and Government, 1914–1918* (1951).
Marshall, S. L. A. *The American Heritage History of World War I* (1964).

G. Great Britain

Arnstein, Walter. *Britain Yesterday and Today* (1966).
Cole, G. D. H. *British Working Class Politics 1832–1914* (1941).
Cross, Colin. *The Liberals in Power, 1905–1914* (1962).

Dangerfield, George. *The Strange Death of Liberal England* (1935).
Ensor, R. C. K. *England, 1870–1914* (1949).
Feiling, Keith. *The Life of Neville Chamberlain* (1946).
Halévy, Elie. *A History of the English People in the Nineteenth Century,*
    Vol. 5, Imperialism and the Rise of Labour (1929).
Havighurst, Alfred F. *Twentieth Century Britain* (1966).
Jenkins, Roy. *Asquith: Portrait of a Man and an Era* (1965).
Jones, Thomas. *Lloyd George* (1951).
Kamm, Josephine. *Rapiers and Battleaxes: The Women's Movement and*
    Its Aftermath (1966).
Lyman, R. W. *The First Labour Government, 1924* (1957).
McCormick, Donald. *The Mask of Merlin: A Critical Study of David Lloyd*
    George (1963).
McKenzie, R. T. *British Political Parties: The Distribution of Power within*
    the Conservative and Labour Parties (2d ed., 1963).
Marwick, Arthur. *The Deluge: British Society and the First World War*
    (1965).
Mowat, C. L. *Britain between the Wars, 1918–1940* (1955).
Pelling, Henry. *A Short History of the Labour Party* (1961).
Phelps Brown, E. H. *The Growth of British Industrial Relations: A Study*
    from the Standpoint of 1906–14 (1959).
Pigou, A. C. *Aspects of British Economic History, 1918–25* (1947).
Pollard, Sidney. *The Development of the British Economy, 1914–1950*
    (1962).
Raymond, John. *The Baldwin Age* (1960).
Rayner, Robert Macey. *The Story of Trade Unionism from the Combination*
    Acts to the General Strike (1929).
Rock, William R. *Neville Chamberlain* (1969).
Symons, Julian. *The General Strike: A Historical Portrait* (1957).
Taylor, A. J. P. *English History, 1914–45* (1965).
Watkins, K. W. *Britain Divided: The Effect of the Spanish Civil War on*
    British Political Opinion (1963).
Wilson, Trevor. *The Downfall of the Liberal Party, 1914–1935* (1966).
Young, George Malcolm. *Stanley Baldwin* (1952).

H. France

Binion, Rudolf. *Defeated Leaders: The Political Fate of Caillaux, Jouvenel,*
    and Tardieu (1960).
Brogan, D. W. *France under the Republic, Vol. 2* (1940).
Buthman, Wm. *The Rise of Integral Nationalism in France* (1939).
Cameron, R. E. *France and the Industrial Development of Europe,*
    1800–1914 (1961).
Cobban, A. G. *A History of Modern France, Vol. 3* (1965).
Colton, Joel. *Leon Blum: Humanist in Politics* (1966).
Ehrmann, Henry W. *Organized Business in France* (1957).
Goldberg, H. *The Life of Jean Jaurès* (1962).
Joll, James, ed. *The Decline of the Third Republic* (1959).
King, Jere. *Foch vs. Clemenceau; France and German Dismemberment,*
    1918–1919 (1960).
King, Jere. *Generals and Politicians (1914–18)* (1951).
Larmour, Peter. *The French Radical Party in the 1930s* (1964).
Levine, Louis. *Syndicalism in France* (1912).
Osgood, Samuel. *French Royalism and the Third and Fourth Republics*
    (1960).
Partin, Malcolm O. *Waldeck-Rousseau, Combes and the Church 1899–1905*
    (1969).
Remond, René. *The Right Wing in France: From 1815 to DeGaulle.* (Tr.
    by James M. Laux) (1966).

Tint, Herbert. *The Decline of French Patriotism, 1870–1940* (1964).
Weber, Eugen. *Action Française: Royalism and Reaction in Twentieth Century France* (1963).
Weber, Eugen. *The Nationalist Revival: France, 1906–1914* (1959).
Werth, Alexander. *The Destiny of France* (1937).
Werth, Alexander. *France in Ferment* (1935).
Werth, Alexander. *France and Munich* (1939).
Werth, Alexander. *The Twilight of France* (1942).
Wohl, R. *French Communism in the Making 1914–1924* (1966).
Wright, Gordon. *Raymond Poincaré and the Presidency* (1942).

I. Germany

1. Germany to 1933

Angress, Werner T. *Stillborn Revolution, The Communist Bid for Power in Germany, 1921–1923* (1963).
Becker, H. *German Youth* (1946).
Bruck, Warner Frederick. *Social and Economic History of Germany from William II to Hitler, 1888–1938* (1938).
Demeter, Karl. *The German Officer Corps in Society and in the State, 1650–1945* (Rev. ed., 1962).
Dorpalen, Andreas. *Hindenburg and the Weimar Republic* (1964).
Eschenburg, Theodor et al. *The Path of Dictatorship, 1918–1933: Ten Essays.* (Trans. John Conway) (1966).
Eyck, Erich. *A History of the Weimar Republic, 2 vols. Vol. 1—1918–1924; Vol. 2—1924–33* (1962).
Gatzke, Hans W. *Streseman and the Rearmament of Germany* (1954).
Gordon, Harold J. *The Reichswehr and the German Republic, 1919–1926* (1957).
Halperin, William. *Germany Tried Democracy: A Political History of the Reich from 1918 to 1933* (1946).
Hunt, Richard N. *German Social Democracy, 1918–1933* (1964).
Massing, P. W. *Rehearsal for Destruction: A Study of Political Anti-Semitism in Imperial Germany* (1949).
Mosse, George. *The Crisis of German Ideology* (1964).
Pinson, K. S. *Modern Germany* (Rev. ed., 1966).
Pulzer, Peter G. J. *The Rise of Political Anti-Semitism in Germany and Austria: 1867–1918* (1964).
Rosenberg, A. *The Birth of the German Republic, 1871–1918* (1931).
Schorske, C. E. *German Social Democracy 1905–17* (1955).
Stern, Fritz. *The Politics of Cultural Despair* (1961).
Stolper, G. *German Economy, 1870–1940* (1940).
Turner, Henry. *Streseman and the Politics of the Weimar Republic* (1963).
Von Klemperer, Klemens. *Germany's New Conservation; Its History and Dilemma in the Twentieth Century* (1957).
Waite, G. L. *Vanguard of Nazism: The Free Corps Movement in Postwar Germany, 1918–23* (1952).
Wertheimer, Mildred Salz. *The Pan-German League, 1890–1914* (1924).
Wheeler-Bennett, J. W. *The Nemesis of Power: The German Army in Politics, 1918–45* (1964).
Wheeler-Bennett, J. W. *Wooden Titan: Hindenburg in Twenty Years of German History* (1936).

2. The Third Reich

Allen, William Sheridan. *The Nazi Seizure of Power: The Experience of a Single German Town* (1965).
Arendt, Hannah. *Eichmann in Jerusalem* (1963).
Bracher, Karl Dietrich. *The German Dictatorship* (1970).
Bullock, Alan. *Hitler: A Study in Tyranny* (Rev. ed., 1962).

Delarue, Jacques. *Gestapo, a History of Horror* (1964).
Donohue, James. *Hitler's Conservative Opponents in Bavaria, 1930–1945: A Study of Catholic, Monarchists and Separatist Anti-Nazi Activities* (1961).
Dulles, Allen W. *Germany's Underground* (1947).
Harris, W. R. *Tyranny on Trial: The Evidence at Nuremberg* (1954).
Heberle, Rudolf. *From Democracy to Nazism: A Regional Case Study on Political Parties in Germany* (1945).
Hilberg, Raul. *The Destruction of the European Jews* (1961).
Kogon, Eugen. *The Theory and Practice of Hell* (1950).
Lewy, Guenther. *The Catholic Church and Nazi Germany* (1965).
Mayer, Milton. *They Thought They Were Free: The Germans, 1933–45* (1955).
Mommsen, H. et al. *The German Resistance to Hitler* (1970).
Mosse, George L. *Nazi Culture* (1966).
Poliakov, Leon. *Harvest of Hate* (1954).
Prittie, Terence. *Germans Against Hitler* (1964).
Reed, Douglas. *Nemesis: The Story of Otto Strasser* (1940).
Robertson, E. M. *Hitler's Prewar Policy and Military Plans, 1933–39* (1963).
Schoenbaum, David. *Hitler's Social Revolution: Class and Status in Nazi Germany, 1933–39* (1966).
Schweitzer, Arthur. *Big Business in the Third Reich* (1964).
Smith, Bradley L. *Adolf Hitler: His Family, Childhood and Youth* (1967).
Stern, Fritz. *The Politics of Cultural Despair* (1961).
Strasser, Otto. *Hitler and I* (1938).
Taylor, Telford. *Sword and Swastika: Generals and Nazis in the Third Reich* (1952).
Thyssen, Fritz. *I Paid Hitler* (1941).
Zeman, Z. A. B. *Nazi Propaganda* (1964).

J. Italy

Cammett, John M. *Antonio Gramsci and the Origins of Italian Communism (1900–1922)* (1967).
Chabod, Frederico. *A History of Italian Fascism* (1963).
Clough, Shepard B. *The Economic History of Modern Italy* (1964).
Delzell, C. F. *Mussolini's Enemies: The Italian Anti-Fascist Resistance* (1961).
Fermi, Laura. *Mussolini* (1961).
Finer, Herman. *Mussolini's Italy* (1935).
Germino, Dante L. *The Italian Fascist Party in Power* (1959).
Halperin, Samuel William. *Mussolini and Italian Fascism* (1964)
Kirkpatrick, Ivone. *Mussolini, a Study in Power* (1964).
MacGregor-Hastie, Roy. *The Day of the Lion* (1964).
Rossi, A. (pseud. for Tasca, Angelo). *The Rise of Italian Fascism, 1918–22* (1938).
Salomone, A. William. *Italy in the Giolittian Era, 1900–14* (1960).
Smith, Dennis Mack. *Italy: A Modern History* (1959).
Villari, L. *Italian Foreign Policy Under Mussolini* (1956).
Webster, Richard A. *The Cross and the Fasces* (1960).

K. Russia

1. Russia to 1917

Black, Cyril E. *The Transformation of Russian Society* (1960).
Florinsky, M. T. *The End of the Russian Empire* (1931).
Miller, Margaret. *The Economic Development of Russia, 1905–1914* (2nd ed., 1967).
Pares, Bernard. *The Fall of the Russian Monarchy* (1939).

Seton-Watson, H.   *The Decline of Imperial Russia* (1952).
Shub, D.   *Lenin* (Rev. ed., 1966).
Wolfe, Bertram D.   *Three Who Made a Revolution* (Rev. ed., 1964).
Yarmolinsky, Avrahm.   *Road to Revolution: A Century of Russian Radicalism* (1957).

2. Soviet Russia, 1917–39

Bauer, R. A.   *The New Man in Soviet Psychology* (1952).
Carr, E. H.   *The Bolshevik Revolution, 1917–1923* (1950).
Conquest, Robert.   *The Great Terror: Stalin's Purge of the Thirties* (1968).
Deutscher, Isaac.   *The Prophet Unarmed: Trotsky, 1921–1929* (1959).
Deutscher, Isaac.   *Stalin: A Political Biography* (1949).
Dobb, Maurice.   *Soviet Economic Development Since 1917* (1948).
Erickson, J.   *The Soviet High Command, a Military-Political History, 1918–41* (1962).
Erlich, Alexandre.   *The Soviet Industrialization Debate, 1924–28* (1960).
Fischer, Louis.   *The Soviets in World Affairs* (1930).
Inkeles, Alex.   *Social Change in Soviet Russia* (1968).
Kennan, George F.   *Soviet-American Relations, 1917–1920. I. Russia Leaves the War. II. The Decision to Intervene* (1956, 1958).
Lewin, M.   *Russian Peasants and Soviet Power; a Study of Collectivization* (1968).
Randall, Francis B.   *Stalin's Russia; an Historical Reconsideration* (1965).
Schapiro, Leonard.   *Origins of Communist Autocracy: Political Opposition in the Soviet State, First Phase, 1917–22* (1955).
Seton-Watson, Hugh.   *From Lenin to Kruschev: A History of World Communism* (1960).
Sorlin, Pierre.   *The Soviet People and Their Society, from 1917 to Present* (trans. Daniel Weissbort) (1969).
Treadgold, Donald W.   *Twentieth Century Russia* (2d ed., 1964).
Von Laue, Theodore H.   *Why Lenin? Why Stalin? A Reappraisal of the Russian Revolution, 1900–1930* (1964).
Wheeler-Bennett, J. W.   *Brest-Litovsk: The Forgotten Peace, March, 1918* (1939).

L. Austria and Eastern Europe

1. Austria-Hungary

Dedijer, Vladimir.   *The Road to Sarajevo* (1966).
Glaise von Horsteman, Edmund.   *The Collapse of the Austro-Hungarian Empire* (1930).
Jaszi, P.   *The Dissolution of the Hapsburg Monarchy* (1929).
Kann, Robert R.   *The Multinational Empire: Nationalism and National Reform in the Hapsburg Monarchy, 1848–1918* (1950).
May, Arthur J.   *The Hapsburg Monarchy 1867–1914* (1951).
Strong, David Fales.   *Austria (Oct. 1918–March 1919) Transition from Empire to Republic* (1939).
Zeman, Z. A. B.   *The Breakup of the Hapsburg Empire, 1914–18* (1961).

2. Austria, 1918–1939

Buttinger, J.   *In the Twilight of Socialism: A History of the Revolutionary Socialists of Austria* (1953).
Diamant, Alfred.   *Austrian Catholics and the First Republic: Democracy, Capitalism, and the Social Order, 1918–1934* (1960).
Gulick, Charles A.   *Austria from Hapsburg to Hitler. Vol. 1—Hapsburg to Hitler. Vol. 2—Fascism's Subversion of Democracy* (1948).
MacDonald, M.   *The Republic of Austria, 1918–1934: A Study in the Failure of Democratic Government* (1946).
Strong, D. F.   *Austria, October 1918–March 1919* (1939).

3. *Eastern Europe, 1918–1939*
Seton-Watson, Hugh. *Eastern Europe Between the Wars, 1918–1941* (1962).
Tokis, Rudolf L. *Bela Kun and the Hungarian Soviet Republic* (1967).
Zurcher, A. J. *The Experiment with Democracy in Central Europe* (1933).

M. Spain and the Spanish Civil War

Brenan, Gerald. *The Spanish Labyrinth: An Account of the Social and Political Background of the Civil War* (1962).
Cattell, David. *Communism and the Spanish Civil War* (1955).
Cattell, David. *Soviet Diplomacy and the Spanish Civil War* (1957).
Jackson, Gabriel. *The Spanish Republic and the Civil War, 1931–1939* (1965).
Payne, Stanley. *Falange: A History of Spanish Fascism* (1961).
Payne, Stanley. *France's Spain* (1967).
Peers, E. Allison. *Spain in Eclipse, 1937–1943* (1943).
Sedwick, Frank. *The Tragedy of Manuel Azana and the Fate of the Spanish Republic* (1963).
Thomas, Hugh. *The Spanish Civil War* (1961).
Weintraub, Stanley. *The Last Great Cause; the Intellectuals and the Spanish Civil War* (1968).

PART II. EUROPE SINCE 1939

A. World War II (Political and Diplomatic)

1. *Military*
Collier, Basil. *The Second World War. A Military History.* (1967).
Falls, Cyril B. *The Second World War* (1948).
Feis, Herbert H. *The Atomic Bomb and the End of World War II* (rev. ed., 1966).
Fuller, John F. C. *The Second World War, 1939–1945: A Strategical and Tactical History* (1962).
Greenfield, Kent R. *American Strategy in World War II: A Reconsideration* (1963).
Hinsley, Francis H. *Hitler's Strategy* (1951).
Irving, David. *The Destruction of Dresden* (1964).
Snyder, Louis L. *The War: A Concise History* (1960).
Werth, Alexander. *Russia at War, 1941–1945* (1964).

2. *Diplomatic and Political*
Churchill, Winston. *The Second World War*, 6 vols. (1948).
Deakin, Frederick. *The Brutal Friendship: Mussolini, Hitler, and the Fall of Italian Fascism* (1962).
Ehrlich, Blake. *Resistance: France 1940–45* (1965).
Feis, Herbert H. *Between War and Peace: The Potsdam Conference* (1960).
Feis, Herbert H. *Churchill, Roosevelt, Stalin: The War They Waged and the Peace They Sought* (1957).
Funk, Arthur Layton. *Charles de Gaulle: The Crucial Years, 1943–44* (1st ed., 1959).
Howell, Edgar M. *The Soviet Partisan Movement, 1941–44* (1956).
Hytier, Adrienne. *Two Years of French Foreign Policy: Vichy, 1940–42* (1958).
International Conference on the History of Resistance Movements. *European Resistance Movements, 1939–45: Proceedings, 1 and 2 (1958, 1961)*.
Jabach, Wenzel. *Europe's Road to Potsdam* (Eng. trans.) (1963).
Kogan, Norman. *Italy and the Allies* (1956).
Langer, William L. *Our Vichy Gamble* (1947).

Langer, William L. and S. Everett Gleason. *The Undeclared War* (1953).
McNeill, William H. *America, Britain and Russia: Their Cooperation and Conflict, 1941–1946* (1953).
Morse, Arthur. *While Six Million Died* (1968).
Neumann, William L. *After Victory: Churchill, Roosevelt, Stalin and the Making of the Peace* (1967).
Neumann, William L. *Making the Peace 1941–1945* (1950).
Snell, John L. *The Meaning of Yalta: Big Three Diplomacy and the New Balance of Power* (1956).
Snell, John L. *Wartime Origins of the East-West Dilemma over Germany* (1959).
Toynbee, Arnold and Veronica Toynbee. *Hitler's Europe* (1955).
Viorst, Milton. *Hostile Allies: FDR and Charles de Gaulle* (1965).
Weinberg, Gerhardt L. *German-Soviet Relations, 1939–1941* (1954).
White, D. S. *Seeds of Discord: DeGaulle, Free France, and the Allies* (1964).
Wright, Gordon. *The Ordeal of Total War, 1939–1945* (1968).

B. Society and Economics

1. Economic History

Ardagh, John. *The New French Revolution* (1968).
Bain, George Sayers. *The Growth of White-Collar Unionism* (1970).
Dijilas, M. *The New Class: An Analysis of the Communist System* (1957).
Dow, J. C. R. *The Management of the British Economy, 1945–60* (1964).
Ellul, Jacques. *The Technological Society* (1964).
Graubard, Stephen R., ed. *A New Europe?* (1963).
Gregg, Pauline. *The Welfare State: An Economic and Social History of Great Britain from 1945 to the Present Day* (1969).
Halls, W. D. *Society, Schools and Progress in France* (1965).
Halpern, Joel M. *A Serbian Village* (1958).
Kassalow, Everett M. (ed.). *National Labor Movements in the Postwar World* (1963).
Klein, Lawrence. *The Keynesian Revolution* (2d ed., 1966).
Marcuse, Herbert. *One-Dimensional Man* (1964).
Montgomery, John. *The Fifties* (1965).
Morin, Edgar (trans. A. M. Sheridan-Smith). *The Red and the White: Report from a French Village* (1970).
Oxenfeldt, Alfred R. and Vsevolod Holubnychy. *Economic Systems in Action: The United States, the Soviet Union and Great Britain and France* (1965).
Postan, M. M. *An Economic History of Western Europe, 1945–1964* (1967).
Sampson, Anthony. *Anatomy of Europe* (1968).
Schichtman, J. B. *Postwar Population Transfers in Europe, 1945–1955* (1962).
Schuchman, A. *Codetermination: Labor's Middle Way in Germany* (1959).
Wylie, Laurence. *Village in the Vaucluse* (1957).

2. Welfare State and Planning

Bauchet, Pierre. *Economic Planning, the French Experience* (1964).
Bruce, Maurice. *The Coming of the Welfare State* (1966).
Dow, J. C. R. *The Management of the British Economy, 1945–60* (1970).
Eckstein, Harry. *The English Health Service: The Origins, Structure, and Achievements* (1958).
Einaudi, Mario et al. *Nationalization in France and Italy* (1955).
Farndale, William A. J. *Trends in the National Health Service* (1964).
Gregg, Pauline. *The Welfare State: An Economic and Social History of Great Britain from 1945 to the Present Day* (1969).
Hackett, John and Anne-Marie Hackett. *Economic Planning in France* (1963).
Halls, W. D. *Society, Schools and Progress in France* (1965).

Lewis, B. W. *British Planning and Nationalization* (1950).
Lindsey, Almont. *Socialized Medicine in England and Wales* (1962).
Myrdal, Gunnar. *Beyond the Welfare State* (1964).
Peterson, Wallace. *The Welare State in France* (1960).
Robson, William. *Nationalized Industry and Public Ownership* (1960).
Soltow, Lee. *Toward Income Equality in Norway* (1965).
Titmuss, Richard Morris. *Essays on the Welfare State* (1958).
Titmuss, Richard Morris. *Income Distribution and Social Change* (1962).

C. Intellectual and Cultural

Allsop, Kenneth. *The Angry Decade: A Survey of the Culture Revolt of the 1950s* (1958).
Armes, Roy. *French Cinema since 1946,* 2 vols (1966).
Beauvoir, Simone de. *The Mandarins* (1954).
Bochenski, Innocentius M. *Contemporary European Philosophy* (1956).
Caute, David. *Communism and the French Intellectuals* (1964).
Choay, François. *Le Corbusier* (1960).
Cruickshank, John. *Albert Camus and the Literature of Revolt* (1959).
Daiches, David. *The Present Age in British Literature* (1958).
Ellul, Jacques. *The Technological Society* (1965).
Herberg, Will. *Four Existentialist Theologians* (1958).
Hughes, H. Stuart. *The Obstructed Path: French Intellectual History, 1930–1960* (1968).
Kaufmann, Stanley. *Existentialism from Dostoevsky to Sartre* (1956).
Lucie-Smith, Edward. *Late Modern: The Visual Arts Since 1945* (1969).
McMullen, Roy. *Art, Affluence and Alienation* (1968).
Manvell, Roger. *New Cinema in Europe* (1970).
Nadeau, Maurice. *The French Novel Since the War* (1967).
Smith, George E. K. *The New Architecture of Europe* (1961).
Taylor, John R. *The Angry Theatre* (1962).
Waxman, Chaim Isaac (ed.). *The End of Ideology Debate* (1969).
Wolfenstein, Martha and Nathan Leites. *Movies: A Psychological Study* (rev. ed., 1970).

D. Diplomacy

Alperovitz, Gar. *Atomic Diplomacy: Hiroshima and Potsdam* (1965).
Amme, Carl H. *NATO Without France* (1968).
Calvocoressi, Peter. *Suez: Ten Years After* (1966).
Capelle, Russell Becket. *The MRP and French Foreign Policy* (1963).
Davison, W. Phillips. *The Berlin Blockade: A Study in Cold War Politics* (1958).
Druks, Herbert. *Harry S. Truman and the Russians, 1945–1953* (1966).
Fitzsimmons, Matthew A. *The French Policy of the British Labour Government 1945–51* (1953).
Fleming, Denna Frank. *The Cold War and Its Origins, 1917–1960,* 2 vols. (1961).
Fontaine, André. *History of the Cold War, 1917–50* (1968).
Freund, Gerald. *Germany Between Two Worlds* (1961).
Hartmann, Frederick H. *Germany between East and West: The Reunification Problem* (1965).
Horowitz, David. *Containment and Revolution* (1967).
Horowitz, David. *The Free World Colossus* (1965).
Kaiser, Karl. *German Foreign Policy in Transition: Bonn Between East and West* (1968).
Kaplan, Lawrence S. *NATO and the Policy of Containment* (1968).
Kolke, Gabriel. *The Politics of War: The World and United States Foreign Policy, 1943–1945* (1968).

Kolko, Joyce and Gabriel Kolko. *The Limits of Power* (1972).
Kulski, W. W. *De Gaulle and the World: The Foreign Policy of the Fifth French Republic* (1966).
LaFeber, Walter. *America, Russia, and the Cold War, 1945–1966* (1967).
Northedge, F. S. *British Foreign Policy: The Process of Readjustment, 1945–1961* (1962).
Richardson, James L. *Germany and the Atlantic Alliance: The Interaction of Strategy and Politics* (1966).
Serfaty, Simon. *France, de Gaulle and Europe: the Policy of the Fourth and Fifth Republics Toward the Continent* (1968).
Thomas, Hugh. *Suez* (1967).
Ulam, Adam B. *Expansion and Coexistence: The History of Soviet Foreign Policy, 1917–1967* (1968).
Ulam, Adam B. *The Rivals: America and Russia Since World War II* (1971).
Willis, F. Roy. *France, Germany and the New Europe, 1945–1967* (1968).
Windsor, Philip. *City on Leave: A History of Berlin, 1945–1962* (1963).
Woodhouse, C. M. *British Foreign Policy since the Second World War* (1962).

E. European Integration

Benoit, Emile. *Europe at Sixes and Sevens: The Common Market, the Free Trade Organization, and the United States* (1961).
Camps, Miriam. *Britain and the European Community* (1964).
Camps, Miriam. *European Unification and the Six: From the Veto to the Crisis* (1966).
Cleveland, Harold B. *The Atlantic Idea and Its European Rivals* (1966).
Coppock, John O. *Atlantic Agricultural Unity: Is It Possible?* (1966).
Cottrell, Alvin J. and James E. Dougherty. *The Politics of the Atlantic Alliance* (1964).
Diebold, W. *The Schuman Plan* (1959).
Freymond, Jacques. *Western Europe since the War* (1964).
Kitzinger, U. W. *The Politics and Economics of European Integration* (1963).
Lamfulassy, A. *The United Kingdom and the Six* (1963).
Lister, Louis. *Europe's Coal and Steel Community: An Experiment in Economic Union* (1960).
Newhouse, John. *Collision in Brussels: The Common Market Crisis of 30 June 1965* (1967).
Ritsch, Frederick F. *The French Left and the European Idea, 1947–1949* (1966).
Spinelli, Altiera. *The Eurocrats: Conflict and Crisis in the European Community* (1966).

F. Great Britain since 1939

Beer, Samuel H. *British Politics in the Collectivist Age* (1965).
Bonham, John. *The Middle Class Vote* (1954).
Broad, Lewis. *Winston Churchill, 1874–1951* (1952).
Butler, David E. *The British General Election of 1951* (1952).
Butler, David E. *The British General Election of 1955* (1955).
Butler, David E. and Richard Rose. *The British General Election of 1959* (1960).
Butler, David E. and Anthony King. *The British General Election of 1964* (1965).
Butler, David E. *The British General Election of 1966* (1966).
Calder, Angus. *The People's War: Britain 1939–45* (1969).
Crosland, C. A. R. *The Future of Socialism* (1963).
Davis, William. *Three Year's Hard Labour: The Road to Devaluation* (1968).

Dow, J. C. R. *The Management of the British Economy 1945–1960* (1964).
Foot, Paul. *The Politics of Harold Wilson* (1968).
Gregg, Pauline. *The Welfare State: An Economic and Social History of Great Britain from 1945 to the Present Day* (1969).
Knaplund, Paul. *Britain: Commonwealth and Empire, 1901–1955* (1956).
Krug, Mark M. *Aneurin Bevan: Cautious Rebel* (1961).
Mansergh, Nicholas. *Survey of British Commonwealth Affairs: Problems of War Time, Cooperation and Post-War Change, 1939–1952* (1958).
Nicholas, Herbert G. *British General Election of 1950* (1951).
Rogow, A. A. *The Labour Government and British Industry, 1945–1951* (1955).
Shrimsley, Anthony. *The First Hundred Days of Harold Wilson* (1965).
Watkins, Ernest. *The Cautious Revolution* (1950).

G. France

Ambler, John S. *The French Army in Politics, 1945–1962* (1966).
Aron, Raymond. *France: Steadfast and Changing* (1960).
Aron, Robert. *France Reborn: The History of the Liberation, June 1944–May 1945* (1959).
Aron, Robert. *The Vichy Regime, 1940–44* (1954).
Caute, David. *Communism and the French Intellectuals, 1914–1960* (1964).
Clark, Michael K. *Algeria in Turmoil* (1960).
Cohn-Bendit, Daniel and Gabriel Cohn-Bendit. *Obsolete Communism: The Left-Wing Alternative* (1969).
Domenach, Jean-Marie, and Robert de Mintvalon. *The Catholic Avant-Garde: French Catholicism Since World War II* (1967).
Duroselle, J-B; Fr. Goguel; Stanley Hoffman; Charles Kindleberger; Jesse Pitts; Laurence Wylie. *France: Change and Tradition* (1963).
Ehrmann, Henry W. *French Labor from Popular Front to Liberation* (1947).
Ehrmann, Henry W. *Organized Business in France* (1957).
Einaudi, Mario. *Communism in Western Europe* (1951).
Einaudi, Mario and François Goguel. *Christian Democracy in Italy and France* (1952).
Fejto, François. *The French Communist Party and the Crisis of International Communism* (1967).
Funk, Arthur L. *Charles de Gaulle: The Crucial Years, 1943–1944* (1959).
Gaulle, Charles de. *The Complete War Memoirs of Charles de Gaulle, 1940–1946*, 3 vols. (1955–1960).
Gladwyn, H. J. G. J. *DeGaulle's Europe; or, Why the General Says No* (1969).
Goguel, F. *France Under the Fourth Republic* (1952).
Graham, Bruce Desmond. *The French Socialists and Tripartism 1944–47* (1965).
Gretton, John. *Students and Workers: An Analytical Account of Dissent in France, May–June 1968* (1969).
Halls, W. D. *Society, Schools, and Progress in France* (1965).
Kulski, W. W. *De Gaulle and the World: The Foreign Policy of the Fifth French Republic* (1966).
MacRae, Duncan. *Parliament, Parties and Society in France, 1946–1958* (1967).
Meisel, James H. *The Fall of the Republic: Military Revolt in France* (1962).
Newhouse, John. *De Gaulle and the Anglo-Saxons* (1970).
O'Ballance, Edgar. *The Algerian Insurrection, 1954–1962* (1967).
Paxton, Robert O. *Parades and Politics at Vichy: The French Officer Corps Under Marshal Petain* (1966).
Rieber, Alfred J. *Stalin and the French Communist Party, 1941–1947* (1962).
Ritsch, Frederick F. *The French Left and the European Idea 1947–49* (1966).

Rossi, A. *The Communist Party in Action: An Account of Its Organization and Operation in France* (1949).
Singer, David. *Prelude to Revolution, France in May 1968* (1970).
Werth, Alexander. *De Gaulle: A Political Biography* (1966).
Werth, Alexander. *France: 1940–1955* (1956).
White, Daniel and Charles S. Maier (eds.). *The Thirteenth of May: The Advent of De Gaulle's Republic* (1968).
Williams, Philip M. *The French Parliament (1958–1967)* (1968).
Williams, Philip M. *French Politicians and Elections, 1951–1969* (1970).
Williams, Philip M. *Politics in Post-War France* (2d ed., 1958).
Wilson, Frank L. *The French Democratic Left: 1963–1969: Toward a Modern Party System* (1971).
Wright, Gordon. *Rural Revolution in France* (1964).

H. Germany since 1945

Bolling, Klaus. *Republic in Suspense: Politics, Parties and Personalities in Postwar Germany* (1964).
Braunthal, Gerard. *The Federation of German Industry in Politics* (1965).
Bunn, Ronald F. *German Politics and the Spiegel Affair; a Case Study of the Bonn System* (1968).
Childs, David. *From Schumacher to Brandt: The Story of German Socialism, 1945–65* (1968).
Dahrendorf, Ralf. *Society and Democracy in Germany* (1967).
Davidson, Eugene. *The Death and Life of Germany: An Account of the American Occupation* (1959).
Dornberg, John. *The Other Germany* (1968).
Drzewieniecki, W. M. *The German-Polish Frontier* (1959).
Ebsworth, Raymond. *Restoring Democracy in Germany: The British Contribution* (1960).
Edinger, Lewis J. *Kurt Schumacher* (1965).
Gimbel, John. *A German Community under American Occupation: Marburg, 1945–52* (1961).
Golay, John. *The Founding of the Federal Republic of Germany (1945–49)* (1957).
Grosser, Alfred. *The Federal Republic of Germany: A Concise History* (1964).
Hangen, Welles. *The Muted Revolution: East Germany's Challenge to Russia and the West* (1966).
Hanhardt, Arthur. *The German Democratic Republic* (1968).
Hartmann, Frederick H. *Germany Between East and West: The Reunification Problem* (1965).
Haurieder, Wolfram F. *West German Foreign Policy, 1949–1963: International Pressure and Domestic Response* (1967).
Hiscocks, Richard. *The Adenauer Era* (1967).
Kitzinger, U. W. *German Electoral Politics: A Study of the 1957 Campaign* (1960).
Landauer, Carl. *Germany: Illusion and Dilemma* (1969).
Montgomery, John D. *Forced to be Free: The Artificial Revolution in Germany and Japan* (1957).
Nettle, J. P. *The Eastern Zone and Soviet Policy in Germany, 1945–1950* (1951).
Prittie, T. *Germany Divided* (1960).
Stolper, Wolfgang F. *The Structure of the East German Economy* (1960).
Szaz, Zaltan Michael. *Germany's Eastern Frontiers: The Problem of the Oder-Niesse Line* (1960).
Tauber, Kurt P. *Beyond Eagle and Swastika: German Nationalism since 1945*, 2 vols. (1967).
Vali, Ferenc A. *The Quest for a United Germany* (1967).
Wighton, Charles. *Adenauer, A Critical Bibliography* (1964).

Willis, F. Roy.   *The French in Germany, 1945–49* (1962).
Zink, Harold.   *United States in Germany, 1944–1955* (1957).

I. Italy since 1943

Blackmer, Donald L. M.   *Unity in Diversity: Italian Communism and the Communist World* (1968).
Deakin, F. W.   *The Brutal Friendship: Mussolini, Hitler and the Fall of Italian Fascism* (1962).
Einaudi, M. and F. Goguel.   *Christian Democracy in Italy and France* (1952).
Grinrod, Muril.   *The Rebuilding of Italy: Politics and Economics, 1945–1955* (1955).
Horowitz, Daniel.   *The Italian Labor Movement* (1963).
Hughes, H. Stuart.   *The United States and Italy* (1965).
Kogan, Norman.   *A Political History of Postwar Italy* (1966).
Kogan, Norman.   *The Politics of Italian Foreign Policy* (1963).
LaPalombara, J.   *The Italian Labor Movement: Problems and Prospects* (1957).
LaPalombara, J.   *Italy: The Politics of Planning* (1966).
Mammarella, Giuseppe.   *Italy after Fascism: A Political History, 1943–1965* (1966).
Posner, M. V. and S. J. Woolf.   *Italian Public Enterprise (1945–1963)* (1967).
Pryce, Roy.   *The Italian Local Elections of 1956; a Nuffield College Election Study* (1957).
Webb, L. C.   *Church and State in Italy, 1947–1957* (1958).
Webster, Richard A.   *Christian Democracy in Italy, 1860–1960* (1961).

J. Smaller States of Western Europe since 1945

Ander, O. Fritof.   *The Building of Modern Sweden: The Reign of Gustav V, 1907–1950* (1958).
Bader, W. B.   *Austria Between East and West, 1945–1955* (1966).
Bourneuf, Alice.   *Norway: The Planned Revival* (1958).
Eckstein, Harry.   *Division and Cohesion in Democracy: A Study of Norway* (1966).
Fleischer, Frederic.   *Sweden: The Welfare State* (1956).
Lijphart, Arend.   *The Politics of Accommodation: Pluralism and Democracy in the Netherlands* (1968).
O'Ballance, Edgar.   *The Greek Civil War, 1944–49* (1966).
Payne, Stanley G.   *Politics and the Military in Modern Spain* (1967).
Rustow, D. A.   *The Politics of Compromise: A Study of Parties and Cabinet Government* (1955).
Stearman, W. L.   *The Soviet Union and the Occupation of Austria: An Analysis of Soviet Policy in Austria, 1945–1955* (1961).

K. Russia since 1939

Brown, Emily Clark.   *Soviet Trade Unions and Labour Relations* (1966).
Crankshaw, Edward.   *Khrushchev* (1966).
Dallin, David J.   *From Purge to Coexistence* (1964).
Dallin, David J.   *Soviet Foreign Policy After Stalin* (1961).
Deutscher, Isaac.   *The Unfinished Revolution: Russia, 1917–1967* (1967).
Fainsod, Merle.   *How Russia Is Ruled* (2d ed., 1963).
Floyd, D.   *Mao against Khrushchev* (1966).
Frankland, Mark.   *Khrushchev* (1967).
Laird, Roy D., D. E. Sharp and R. Sturtevant.   *The Rise and Fall of the MTS as an Instrument of Soviet Rule* (1960).
Leonhard, Wolfgang.   *The Kremlin Since Stalin* (1962).
Linden, Carl A.   *Khrushchev and the Soviet* (1966).

Mazour, Anatole G. *Soviet Economic Development: Operation Outstrip: 1921–1965* (1967).
Mosely, Philip. *The Soviet Union Since Khrushchev* (1966).
Parry, Albert. *The New Class Divided: Science and Technology Versus Communism* (1966).
Schwartz, Harry. *The Soviet Economy Since Stalin* (1965).
Shulman, Marshall. *Stalin's Foreign Policy Reappraised* (1966).
Tatu, Michel. *Power in the Kremlin From Khrushchev to Kosygin* (1970).
Werth, A. *Russia at War, 1941–1945* (1964).
Zagoria, Donald S. *The Sino-Soviet Conflict, 1956–61* (1962).

L. Eastern Europe since 1939

Auty, Phyllis. *Tito: A Biography* (1970).
Bombelles, J. T. *Planning and Economic Growth in Yugoslavia 1947–1964* (1968).
Borkenau, Frederich. *European Communism* (1953).
Brant, Stefan. *The East German Rising* (1957).
Brown, J. F. *The New Eastern Europe: The Khrushchev Era and After* (1966).
Brzezinski, Zbigniew K. *The Soviet Bloc: Unity and Conflict* (Rev. ed., 1967).
Burks, R. V. *The Dynamics of Communism in Eastern Europe* (1961).
Ceczel, Tamas. *Ten Years After: The Hungarian Revolution in the Perspective of History* (1967).
Chapman, Colin. *August 21st: The Rape of Czechoslovakia* (1968).
Fischer-Galati, Stephen. *The New Rumania: From People's Democracy to Socialist Republic* (1967).
Floyd, David. *Rumania: Russia's Dissident Ally* (1965).
Griffiths, William E. *Albania and the Sino-Soviet Rift* (1963).
Hamm, Harry. *Albania: China's Beachhead in Europe* (1963).
Hoffman, George W. and F. W. Neal. *Yugoslavia and the New Communism* (1962).
Ionescu, Ghita. *The Break-up of the Soviet Empire in Eastern Europe* (1965).
Ionescu, Ghita. *The Politics of the European Communist States* (1967).
Journalist, M. *A Year is 8 Months: Czechoslovakia 1968* (1971).
Kaser, Michael. *Comecon: Integration Problems of the Planned Economies* (1965).
Kecskemeti, Paul. *The Unexpected Revolution: Social Forces in the Hungarian Uprising* (1961).
Korbel, Josef. *The Communist Subversion of Czechoslovakia, 1938–1948* (1959).
Laqueur, W. and Leopold Labedz (eds.). *Polycentrism: The New Factor in International Communism* (1962).
London, Kurt (ed.). *Eastern Europe in Transition* (1966).
Neal, Frederick. *Titoism in Action: The Reform in Yugoslavia After 1948* (1958).
Popovic, Nenod D. *Yugosavia: The New Class in Crisis* (1968).
Seton-Watson, Hugh. *The East European Revolution* (1951).
Skilling, H. G. *Communism National and International: Eastern Europe After Stalin* (1964).
Stehle, Hansjakob. *The Independent Satellite: Society and Politics in Poland Since 1945* (1965).
Taborsky, Edward. *Communism in Czechoslovakia, 1948–1960* (1961).
Voli, Ferenc A. *Rift and Revolt in Hungary: Nationalism Versus Communism* (1961).
Windsor, P. and A. Roberts. *Czechoslovakia, 1968* (1969).
Zeman, Z. A. B. *Prague Spring* (1969).
Zinner, Paul E. *Revolution in Hungary* (1962).

INDEX